W9-CFR-010

Municipal Management Series

Managing Fire Services

**International
City
Management
Association**

The International City Management Association is the professional and educational organization for chief appointed management executives in local government. The purposes of ICMA are to strengthen the quality of urban government through professional management and to develop and disseminate new approaches to management through training programs, information services, and publications.

Managers, carrying a wide range of titles, serve cities, towns, counties, and councils of governments in all parts of the United States and Canada. These managers serve at the direction of elected councils and governing boards. ICMA serves these managers and local governments through many programs that aim at improving the manager's professional competence and strengthening the quality of all local governments.

The International City Management Association was founded in 1914; adopted its City Management Code of Ethics in 1924; and established its Institute for Training in Municipal Administration in 1934. The Institute, in turn, provided the basis for the Municipal Management Series, generally termed the "ICMA Green Books." ICMA's interests and activities include public management education; standards of ethics for members; *The Municipal Year Book* and other data services; urban research; and newsletters, a monthly magazine, *Public Management,* and other publications. ICMA's efforts for the improvement of local government management—as represented by this book—are offered for all local governments and educational institutions.

Editorial review board

(affiliation at time of review)

Franklin D. Aleshire
City Manager
Scottsdale, Arizona

Louis J. Amabili
Director
Delaware State Fire School

Joseph N. Baker
Vice President
Public Technology, Inc.

John J. DeBolske
Executive Director
League of Arizona Cities and
Towns

William V. Donaldson
City Manager
Cincinnati, Ohio

Martin E. Grimes
Assistant Vice President
Governmental Affairs
National Fire Protection
Association

Porter W. Homer
President
Public Technology, Inc.

Robert A. Kipp
City Manager
Kansas City, Missouri

Walter Lambert
Director of Research
International Association of
Fire Fighters

David A. Lucht
Deputy Administrator
U.S. Fire Administration

Sherman Pickard
Director of Services
North Carolina League of
Municipalities

Myrle K. Wise
Fire Chief
Denver, Colorado

Municipal Management Series

Managing Fire Services

Editors

Published for the
Institute for Training in
Municipal Administration

By the
International
City
Management
Association

John L. Bryan
Professor and Chairman
Fire Protection Engineering
University of Maryland

Raymond C. Picard
Fire Chief
Huntington Beach, California

Municipal Management Series

David S. Arnold Editor

Managing Fire Services

Community Health Services

Developing the Municipal Organization

Effective Supervisory Practices

Local Government Personnel Administration

Local Government Police Management

Management Policies in Local Government Finance

Managing Human Services

Managing the Modern City

Managing Municipal Leisure Services

Policy Analysis in Local Government

Principles and Practice of Urban Planning

Public Relations in Local Government

Small Cities Management Training Program

Urban Public Works Administration

Library of Congress Cataloging in Publication Data

Main entry under title:
Managing fire services.

  (Municipal management series)
  Intended as a successor to Municipal fire
administration.
  Bibliography: p.
  Includes index.
  1. Fire-departments—Management. I. Bryan,
John L., 1926–   II. Picard, Raymond C.
III. Institute for Training in Municipal Administration.
IV. Municipal fire administration.
TH9145.M26   352'.3   79-10067
ISBN 0-87326-018-X

Copyright © 1979 by the International City
Management Association, 1140 Connecticut Avenue,
N.W., Washington, D.C. 20036. All rights reserved,
including rights of reproduction and use in any form
or by any means, including the making of copies by
any photographic process, or by any electronic or
mechanical device, printed or written or oral, or
recording for sound or visual reproduction, or for
use in any knowledge or retrieval system or device,
unless permission in writing is obtained from the
copyright proprietor.

Printed in the United States of America.

Foreword

Over a decade ago the International City Managers' Association, as we were then known, published *Muncipal Fire Administration*. This book became one of the most popular of the Green Books in our Municipal Management Series. The seventh edition (1967) of a work that first appeared in 1935, *Municipal Fire Administration* served literally tens of thousands of fire service professionals, other local government managers, and students and teachers in colleges and universities.

The International City Management Association, as we are now known, is publishing *Managing Fire Services* as a successor to *Municipal Fire Administration* in order to better serve the needs of today's local government manager (whether inside or outside the fire department) and today's aspiring local government professional in colleges and universities who seeks an understanding of the fire service function. We are confident that *Managing Fire Services* will speak to the needs of such readers in an authoritative, up-to-date, and comprehensive fashion, thus continuing in the tradition of its predecessors. Much has changed in the provision of local government fire services over the last decade, in areas as diverse as technology, labor relations, emergency medical services, fire prevention, an emergent federal role, data collection and analysis, and arson investigation. *Managing Fire Services* reflects these and other changes.

Three points may be made about this book, with application to the Municipal Management Series in general. First, every effort has been made in planning, writing, and editing *Managing Fire Services* to emphasize the managerial perspective, whether it be that of the fire chief or other departmental managers or of those outside the fire department— city managers, elected officials, department heads, involved citizens, and students and teachers in fire science and related disciplines. We have striven to illuminate the latest theories and research by linking them to specific managerial examples, and also to widen the horizons of local government practitioners by showing how day-to-day decision making fits into wider theoretical perspectives. The book is neither a theoretical treatise nor a detailed administrative manual: instead, it primarily attempts to identify and discuss the key managerial issues and techniques in this complex and fast-changing area of local government.

Second, the authors of individual chapters, or portions of chapters, have been selected on the basis of their expertise in a particular subject area, and their ability to communicate the managerial aspects of that expertise to specialist and non-specialist alike. They have also been given appropriate latitude to discuss their subjects and to express their own policy preferences in terms, and by examples, that they feel appropriate. A lively blend of individual perspectives has emerged; the result is a text that offers a range of authoritative managerial coverage not available elsewhere.

Third, this book, like others in the Municipal Management Series, has been published for the Institute for Training in Municipal Administration. The Institute offers in-service training specifically designed for local government officials whose jobs are to plan, direct, and coordinate the work of others. The Institute, sponsored by ICMA since 1934, has prepared a training course to accompany this book.

We have spent several years in planning *Managing Fire Services* and in bringing the project to fruition. This time has been spent in a comprehensive effort to involve a representative spectrum of practitioners and others in the fire protection community in the planning, writing, and editing stages of the book. The results of this process have indeed been broad based, and it is a pleasure to acknowledge the roles of those involved.

The Editors of the book, John L. Bryan, Professor and Chairman of the Fire Protection Engineering Department at the University of Maryland, and Raymond C. Picard, Fire Chief of Huntington Beach, California, both distinguished in fire protection, are owed a particular debt of thanks for their work during the planning and manuscript review stages of the project with the authors, the Editorial Review Board members, and the ICMA staff. The text owes much to their insight and many hours of careful review. The members of the Editorial Review Board, too, have played an important role in drawing up the outline for the book and assessing first drafts of manuscript. The individuals involved, and their organizational affiliations at the time of the assignment, are as follows: Franklin D. Aleshire, City Manager, Scottsdale, Arizona; Louis J. Amabili, Director, Delaware State Fire School; Joseph N. Baker, Vice President, Public Technology, Inc.; John J. DeBolske, Executive Director, League of

Arizona Cities and Towns; William V. Donaldson, City Manager, Cincinnati, Ohio; Martin E. Grimes, Assistant Vice President for Government Affairs, National Fire Protection Association; Porter W. Homer, President, Public Technology, Inc.; Robert A. Kipp, City Manager, Kansas City, Missouri; Walter Lambert, Director of Research, International Association of Fire Fighters; David A. Lucht, Deputy Administrator, U.S. Fire Administration; Sherman Pickard, Director of Services, North Carolina League of Municipalities; and Myrle K. Wise, Fire Chief, Denver, Colorado.

It is a pleasure to acknowledge the continued cooperation of the National Fire Protection Association, whose former staff members Horatio Bond and Warren Y. Kimball made extensive contributions to every earlier edition of *Municipal Fire Administration*. The NFPA staff provided information and illustrations suggestions which were most helpful in the development of *Managing Fire Services*.

In addition to the formal review board, a number of other reviewers and experts have assisted in an informal review of the successive outlines and chapter drafts, or otherwise helped during the editorial development of the book. We are particularly indebted to Wayne F. Anderson, Executive Director, Advisory Commission on Intergovernmental Relations; Howard Boyd, President, Fire Marshals Association of North America; Alan Brunacini, Fire Chief, Phoenix, Arizona; Derek Jackson, Fire Chief, Calgary, Alberta; James Kolb, Battalion Chief, Los Angeles City Fire Department; Donald L. Loeb, Fire Fighting Analysts, Dunkirk, New York; Lisa Stevenson and her staff in the Management Research Center at ICMA; and Louis Witzeman, President, Rural/ Metro Fire Department, Scottsdale, Arizona. Finally, a special word of thanks is owed to Albert G.

Kirchner, then a District of Columbia firefighter and subsequently Acting Associate Superintendent for Assistance Programs, National Fire Academy, U.S. Fire Administration, who provided able assistance during the early stages of the project. The Municipal Management Series is the responsibility of David S. Arnold Director, Publications Center, ICMA. Richard R. Herbert, Senior Editor, had primary responsibility for working with the Editors in bringing this project to fruition. Ellen W. Faran, Editorial Associate, also worked closely with the Editors and authors and coordinated editorial and production schedules. Emily Evershed was responsible for the final editing of the manuscript and for the preparation of the Index. Paul M. Dunbar, of Design Associates in Washington, D.C., planned the presentation of illustration material for the book and prepared the line art.

Mark E. Keane
Executive Director

International City
Management Association

Washington, D.C.

Preface

In the dozen years since the predecessor to this book was published under the title *Municipal Fire Administration,* profound changes in the personnel, organization, and management of the delivery of fire and rescue services by local governments have occurred within the United States and Canada. For example, the men and women in the fire service, because of extensive development of fire science training in community and four year colleges, are better educated and psychologically prepared to accept the challenges and the innovations needed in today's fire service. Another change can be seen in that the fire service is currently moving away from the evaluative techniques and procedures of the insurance industry. For the first time since the initial publication of *Municipal Fire Administration* in 1935, the text does not reproduce the Insurance Services Office *Grading Schedule.*

The title of this book, *Managing Fire Services,* is intended to help demonstrate that fire departments can be managed to provide effective emergency fire and medical services on an immediate need basis. Of equal importance, the fire service profoundly affects the long-term goals for control of the built environment to prevent fire problems and to educate citizens in life saving and fire prevention procedures that are deemed effective.

The emphasis in this book differs from that of the previous volumes, with greater emphasis on the functional, evaluative, and management aspects of the fire service, with a reduction in emphasis on the technical aspects of community fire protection. Thus, the technical coverage relative to water supply requirements, apparatus and equipment design, and the operational and tactical aspects of fire suppression have been dropped. The authors have emphasized the practical, effective, economical, and innovative concepts that have been and are being introduced into the fire service to increase total operational efficiency.

The structure and content of *Managing Fire Services* are the result of a careful planning process. The book is divided into five parts. The first, "The Context of Fire Management" (Chapters 1 through 5), explores such basic areas as the evolution of fire services, management options in fire protection, and the roles of the fire department and other organizations in fire service areas; it also contains a preview of the role of productivity, technology, and data collection.

Part Two, "Managing Fire Protection" (Chapters 6 through 11), begins with an examination of management and planning for fire protection, then takes a closer look at the management cycle involved in such specialized areas as fire prevention, inspection services, fire control, emergency medical and rescue services, and fire and arson investigation.

Part Three has four chapters on the more general themes of the budgetary process, personnel management and labor relations, measurement and evaluation of productivity, and training and education.

Part Four explores, in Chapters 16 through 20, various areas in which technology is of critical importance: management of innovation; communications systems; data collection, processing, and analysis; facilities location and management; and equipment and apparatus management.

Part Five (Chapter 21), under the heading "The Outlook," provides a short but important survey drawing together the main themes of the book and taking a look at what the future may hold for the fire service.

Every effort has been made to minimize overlapping between chapters and to provide coordinated cross references between sections of the book, while allowing individual authors appropriate latitude to discuss their subject areas.

The Editors believe many of the concepts and techniques developed and discussed by the individual authors in *Managing Fire Services* will prove to be of significant value to fire service personnel, city and county managers, and other local government officials who continually accept responsibility for the effec-

tiveness and efficiency of the fire service in their communities.

This book like its predecessors was the result of persistence, fortitude, and many hours of effort on the part of the chapter authors. The National Fire Protection Association, the United States Fire Administration, and Public Technology, Inc., have generously contributed to this effort with the services of personnel, and by providing information, data, and illustrations. The editors wish to thank the members of the Editorial Review Board for their diligent accomplishments; the many other knowledgeable persons who reviewed portions of the texts; the individual authors; Emily Evershed, Editor, Publications Center, ICMA, who handled final editing and preparation of the index; Ellen W. Faran, ICMA Editorial Associate, who helped in a variety of tasks on text and illustrations; and, most importantly, Richard R. Herbert, Senior Editor in the ICMA Publications Center, who piloted the entire publication to its completion.

John L. Bryan
College Park, Maryland

Raymond C. Picard
Huntington Beach, California

Contents

**Part four:
Technology,
communications,
and data**

417

Figures

Tables

Part one:
The context
of fire
management

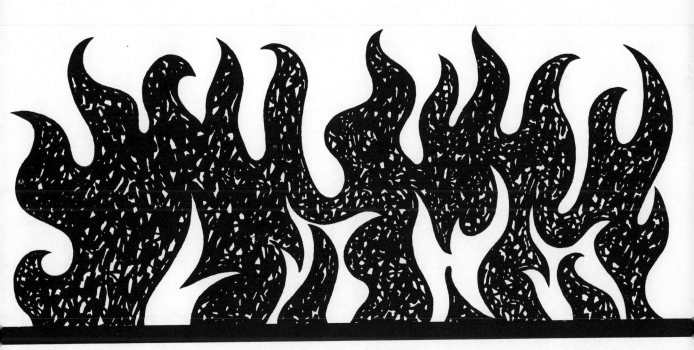

The evolution of fire services

Throughout the history and prehistory of the human race fire has served as a protector and an agent of progress—and has also unleashed forces of destruction that have been one of humankind's greatest curses. Learning to bring fire under control and thus to modify our terrestrial environment has presented us with one of our greatest challenges, for in learning to control fire we have had to learn to control ourselves. Had we not been successful in meeting that challenge, we would not have been able to inhabit most of the earth's surface, let alone develop a technology to take us above and beyond it. Nor would we have been able to enjoy those conveniences of an urban, industrial society that a good proportion of the world's population now considers necessities and to which many of the remainder aspire.

Yet, although great progress has been made in accumulating knowledge and developing skills necessary to harness fire as a servant, all too frequently fire breaks out of control and assumes its destructive role. Nowhere is this dreadful toll of death, injury, and property destruction more prevalent than in the industrialized nations, with the United States itself possessing the worst record. (And this is quite apart from the threat posed by the awesome firepower assembled in the nuclear arsenals of the world.)

Most frequently destruction of life or property by fire results from ignorance or lack of attention: in short, human factor. It is now recognized that contemporary efforts to control fire must include education to reduce ignorance and indifference as well as research to determine new ways of controlling the complex physical and chemical processes of fire itself. This chapter therefore addresses that educational need by presenting an overview of the uses and abuses of fire by humankind and of the evolution of contemporary fire services. It thereby sets the scene for the more specialized discussions of fire management principles and practices found in subsequent chapters of this book. It is true that such topics as the discovery of the uses of fire and the myths and hazards associated with its control comprise some of the most interesting pages in the human story. But it is also true that these topics remind us that the problems we face today in taming fire have their roots deep in the past, and that knowledge of this background can serve to illuminate and deepen our day-to-day work as we review or implement fire service operations.

The discussion in this chapter is divided into seven sections. First, there is an overview of the origins of controlled fire and the challenge it presented to our remote ancestors. Second, the early steps in fire protection are recorded. In the third section a closer look is taken at the experience of the seventeenth and eighteenth centuries, while in the fourth the deepening experience of the nineteenth century—the century of industrialization—is assessed. The discussion in the fifth section focuses on the experience of America burning in the twentieth century. The sixth section examines the evolution of firefighting equipment, and the seventh outlines the main features of the organizational development of the American fire services. The chapter ends with a brief concluding note.

The main focus of the chapter as it proceeds is on the evolving experience of the United States. Space alone precludes coverage of the equally fascinating story of fire and its control in other countries: in the centrally planned economies of the Soviet Union, Eastern Europe, and China; in the other industrialized nations from Britain to Japan, Australia to Canada; and in the developing nations that are home to the majority of the world's population. Even within the United States the emphasis is similarly on the mainstream of our tradition, even though the Napoleonic codes of New Orleans or of the areas of Spanish heritage in the Southwest provide interesting contrasts to fire protection experience based on English common law. Fire knows no national boundaries and is found at all times and in all cultures: readers are encouraged to use this chapter as a basis for further explorations of their own in the literature.

The origins

Humankind discovers a benefactor

At some point before recorded history began human beings observed that fire set by such natural forces as lightning, meteorite impact, or volcanic eruption provided certain benefits. Fire drove game over cliffs or into natural corrals, cleared forest of undergrowth so that game could be better seen and hunted, and cleared other land so that it could be used for agricultural purposes. In time our ancestors learned that they could control fire to produce desired benefits. They learned that burning the brush produced better grasslands, which in turn attracted and supported more game. They found that they could use fire to destroy (or afford protection against) their enemies—insects, beasts, or even other people. They also learned that fire could alter the characteristics of materials and elements to better provide for their needs: for example, they learned to fire pottery and bricks and—a giant step forward—to smelt metals. Heat for warmth was, however, probably the first benefit of fire to be discovered. It was closely associated with the heating of food, a use that naturally led to the discovery that food warmed over a period of time changed its characteristics and became more palatable.[1] The uses and benefits of fire were legion—and they are still being explored today, hundreds of thousands of years later. But as great as many of these discoveries have been, none was more significant than the art of firemaking itself.

The discovery of ignition sources

The method first used to ignite fire is, of course, unknown. However, it is logical to conclude that the knowledge was gained slowly over hundreds of thousands of years by observing such physical and natural phenomena as the spark produced when striking flint against pyrites, or the fire produced by lightning, molten lava, the "spontaneous ignition" of plant matter, or the friction of dry branches being rubbed together by the wind.

A lesson from the trees? The last possibility was suggested in 1859 by Adelbert Kuhn, an early expert on primitive languages and mythology. Most of his contemporaries did not believe Kuhn's explanation. However, Leo Frobenius, a German explorer of the East Indies, was told by the natives of the island of Buru that they knew forest fires were often started by the rubbing of dry branches against one other. As a young man Frobenius had read about Kuhn's theory and had considered it erroneous. He asked the natives if this happened often and, if so, with what kind of tree. The natives claimed that fires occurred this way quite often, but not every year, and usually involved only one kind of tree. Frobenius was shown this type of tree, from which he took a branch to a botanist for identification. A Dutch botanist at the botanical garden at Buitenzorg (now Bogor) on Java immediately identified the branch as coming from the

Kinas tree (*Kleinhovia hospita*), a tree familiar on Java. There, too, it was said to start forest fires in very dry years.[2]

Whether the discovery of the method of starting fire by friction was the result of observing tree branches rubbing together is not known—but, nevertheless, the friction method of ignition was common among early peoples throughout the world.

The archaeological record   What does archaeology tell us? Studies in this field have concluded that we have possessed the knowledge of methods to make fire for hundreds of thousands of years. The earliest evidence was found in a site in France, near Nice, which may have been occupied as early as a million years ago.[3] However, the antiquity of this site is exceptional. It is not until the Middle Pleistocene (approximately 500,000 years ago) in Chinese and (later) in European sites that an abundance of evidence indicating our ability to control fire is found. Indeed, the movement of peoples into these cold northern areas during interglacial periods would not have been possible without this ability.

Peking Man (*Sinanthropus pekinensis*), who inhabited the famous Choukoutien Cave some forty miles from Peking about half a million years ago, is unquestionably the earliest clearly identified user of fire. "The unwholesome cannibal of this chilly, fire-heated den," Joseph Campbell describes him; he also notes that "the remarkable thing about the Chinese find [of the cave] was the evidence of fire in the cave. For although a number of proto-human remains of this general period have been found elsewhere in the world, Choukoutien is unique in the evidence of fire."[4] It was not until the time that Campbell calls "the period of the far more highly developed races of the temple caves, *c*. 30,000–10,000 B.C.," however, that the "art of roasting" was invented.[5] In other words, both Peking Man and—200,000 years later—Neanderthal Man were eaters of raw food, although they possessed fire. Campbell suggests the following possibility:

The earliest hearths . . . could have been shrines, where fire was cherished in and for itself in the way of a holy image or primitive fetish. The practical value of such a living presence, then, would have been discovered in due time. The suggestion is rendered the more likely when it is considered that throughout the world the hearth remains to this day a sacred as well as secular institution. In many lands, at the time of a marriage, the kindling of the hearth in the new home is a crucial rite, and the domestic cult comes to focus in the presentation of its flame.[6]

Be this as it may, the archaeological records provide no explanation as to *how* fires were ignited. The natural sources already described were of course available. All that would have then been necessary was a way to *store* fire—in the form of slow burning roots, logs, coals or "slow matches" made from twisted bark in which a spark was buried. Undoubtedly the ability to start fire at will was not acquired until the passage of thousands of years of our development.

Friction, compression, and percussion   The most universal ancient method of firemaking was by the conversion of muscular energy into heat through friction. A commonly used instrument was a fire drill, consisting of a wooden rod or stick resting in the hollow of a fire board adjacent to tinder. The stick was rapidly rotated between the palms of the hands or with the assistance of a thong with a loop around the stick. A variation of the fire drill was an up and down action of a pump drill. After a few minutes of these operations enough heat was generated at the point of contact between the stick and the fire board for tinder to be ignited. This ancient method of firemaking can be found among contemporary preliterate people and survived until recent years in peasant Europe.

Mechanical fire drills were developed by the Eskimos, the ancient Egyptians, the Asians, and a few American Indians. Other related forms of friction methods include the fire saw and fire plough. Both of these instruments were used in Indonesia, Southeast Asia, and Australia. The fire saw in Southeast Asia consisted of a piece of bamboo with a nick cut into the side. A thick, sharp-edged splinter was drawn back and forth in the nick until sufficient heat was generated to ignite the tinder. The fire plough consisted of a grooved board and a stick that was rubbed back and forth in the groove until the collecting wood dust ignited. The fire plough was common in Polynesia and was used in some parts of Africa.[7]

A most innovative device used sporadically in areas from Southeast Asia to the Philippines was the fire piston. This device operated on the principle that heat is produced when gases are subjected to pressure. The fire piston consisted of a cylinder (such as a bamboo tube) with a plunger that, when sharply struck, was driven downward, thus compressing the air within the cylinder. Tinder placed at the base of the cylinder would be ignited from the heat generated from the compressed gases.[8]

Percussion methods such as striking pyrite (a compound of iron and sulfur) were probably also invented in the early years of our development. This method is known to have been used by the Eskimos. In the Old World the striking of iron on flint to produce sparks for firemaking was widespread from the beginning of the age of ironworking, about 3,500 years ago. Much later, during the Industrial Revolution, after steel was invented, it was discovered that a very hot spark was easily produced by striking this metal with flint. This ignition method became very popular, and the principle was adapted for use in the development of relatively lightweight firearms. The metal "strike-a-light" was an item most desired by the American Indians in their trading with the Europeans.[9]

Preservation, borrowing, and perpetuation Whatever the early method of ignition, our ancestors had to carefully preserve fire, and, through trial and error, learn to perpetuate it. As families, clans, and tribes moved away from their original habitats, they no doubt moved their fire with them. If the fire went out, members of the family or tribe were at the mercy of the cold until a new fire was found. The easiest method of re-igniting fire was probably a trip to a neighboring community where embers could be borrowed.

If a neighboring fire was not available, the wait for nature to reprovide may have been long indeed. Considering the importance of fire in the primal society, an extremely high level of responsibility would have been placed upon those assigned to maintain the tribal fire.

Evidence of reliance upon fire borrowing was found by Karl Weule, director of the Ethnological Museum in Leipzig, during a 1906 expedition to East Africa. One of Weule's areas of inquiry was the methodology of firemaking. However, in his early investigations he was unsuccessful in finding any type of firemaking devices. Each time he asked natives if he could see their firemaking devices, he was told they did not have any. After some observation it was realized that the Africans simply did not start a new fire if they could help it. A dead tree trunk would be dragged to a convenient site and some fire from elsewhere would be used to ignite the log which would burn slowly and leave embers that would glow for many days. These embers were then used to light other fires. When an African went on a journey he would carry a glowing marrow or smouldering reed with him. Weule discovered that, although these Africans knew how to start fire through the use of a fire drill, they found it more convenient to "borrow fire."[10]

All of these early methods of firemaking were tedious and cumbersome. The invention of the wooden match with a chemical head was thus of great significance. The earliest matches of this type were ignited by contact with burning tinder or by being immersed in sulfuric acid. The first friction match has been attributed to an English inventor, John Walker, in 1827.[11] The head of this match contained phosphorous sulphate, essentially the same as is used today, and was ignited by drawing the match between layers of sandpaper. In 1855 safety matches were invented in Sweden and their use spread rapidly because they were relatively cheap, were easy to use, and were very dependable.

The modern technique of producing fire by introducing an electrical spark into a combustible gas–air mixture has been of even greater significance. This ignition method has made possible the internal combustion engine, which in turn is used to power most of our modes of transportation and to provide the drive for a vast array of tools and equipment.

Myths and rituals

Long before archaeologists and others identified through actual findings the early methods of making fire, a fascinating web of myths was woven to satisfy the mystery and doubt in human minds as to the origin and potency of fire—striking testimony to fire's psychological and social importance.

Figure 1–1 The Hindu deity
Siva dancing in a
circle of flames.

It is impossible in this brief space to give anything but a sampling of this rich area of study. The reader is referred to a number of basic works for further inquiry. These include *The Golden Bough,* the twelve volume study of folklore by J. G. Frazer; the Index to this work contains several pages of references to the myths and rituals associated with fire.[12] Other works range from those on the psychoanalysis of fire to an elaborate study in French on the symbolism of fire.[13] A brief sampling of myths and rituals follows.

Myths concerning the origin of fire generally refer back to the times when humanity suffered in subjection to the elements without fire for protection against the cold or for use in cooking.

Some myths center on the sun as the giver of fire.[14] Men were supposed to have climbed to the sun with the assistance of a rope anchored to a cloud and there retrieved the gift of fire. In the Western world the hero of mythology was

Prometheus, the Greek fire giver who recognized the suffering and plight of man without fire. In his pity he stole fire from the sun's chariot so that he might bestow this gift upon mankind. For this transgression, according to Greek mythology, Zeus ordered Prometheus chained to a mountain.[15]

Folktales, too, contain explanations for the origin of fire. Many such tales identify animals as the first possessors or donors of fire. In the folktales of certain American Indians fire was transmitted through a chain of animals until, after encountering and overcoming many obstacles, humans ultimately received it. It is not unusual in these fables for mammals, reptiles, birds, and fish to participate in the chain of fire bearers. The last carrier in the chain of fire bearers was often venerated and protected from being killed.[16]

In many cultures personified deities were believed to have held special powers and associations with fire. The Vedic god Agni was a protector against the mystery of darkness. The Phoenician god Baal received human sacrifices by fire. It was Baal whom Isaiah challenged on Mount Carmel when he called upon the God of Abraham, Isaac, and Jacob to send down fire to consume his sacrifice. The Roman god of fire was Vulcan, whose name survives today in the English verb vulcanize. To the Aztecs of Mexico the fire deity was Xuihtecutl and to the Polynesians it was Maui. Throughout time, fire has been so essential to all cultures that the ability to summon and control this phenomenon has been the object of fear, worship, and the greatest respect.

Freud gives two striking examples of the symbolic power of fire, both of them from studies of New Zealand Maoris. The first example is from Frazer and involves a taboo on the contact of a Maori chief with fire.

A Maori chief would not blow on a fire with his mouth; for his sacred breath would communicate its sanctity to the fire, which would pass it on to the meat in the pot, which would pass it on to the man who ate the meat which was in the pot, which stood on the fire, which was breathed on by the chief; so that the eater, infected by the chief's breath conveyed through these intermediaries, would surely die.[17]

The second example is of the dire effects of breaking a taboo associated with a chief's use of fire:

The tinder box of a Maori chief once cost several persons their lives. The chief had lost it, and those who found it used it to light their pipes. When they learned whose property the tinder box was they all died of fright.[18]

Fire has also held a place in more developed religious ceremony and in philosophy. In ancient Vedic scriptures, Agni is the personification of the sacrificial fire and is the messenger between humanity and its gods. Brahman households are still supposed to maintain a sacred fire for the worship of Agni, much as the virgin priestesses of ancient Rome cared for the perpetual holy fire at the temple of Vesta, the goddess of the hearth. The Greeks called the same goddess Hestia and tended her sacred fire in a public hearth in every city, and transported this fire with the greatest care to kindle the fire on the hearth of any new colony.[19] For the Zoroastrians of Iran, fire was the very center of religion and the greatest and most sacred power. In the Zoroastrian belief, fire was presented to humanity directly from heaven and was kindled by the Deity Himself.

The Koryak and Chuckchi peoples of Siberia and their Buryat neighbors kept all filth and impurities away from their fires and hearths in honor of their fire god. The need to keep fire from being contaminated was also a belief of peoples in North and South America, Africa, and elsewhere. The Bemba of Northern Rhodesia believe that a child who eats food cooked on flames contaminated by an unpurified person—such as an adulterer—may die.[20] Sacred flames were used to worship gods of fire by the Aztecs of Mexico and the Incas of Peru. Even the Greek scientists and philosophers found fire to be of greatest significance. Aristotle postulated that fire, along with earth, water, and air, was among the four general and essential elements of life and of all things. Plato believed that the four elements were used by God in the creation of the world, while Heraclitus declared fire to be the essential force for creation.

The need for protection from fire

Fire was indeed a potent force in myth and ritual—and an even more potent one in real life when its power for destruction was unleashed. For with the ever increasing ability to ignite fire at will came a familiarity and lack of respect. As it became unnecessary to establish a watch to make certain a fire did not extinguish, fire was left without concern. Over the millennia many disastrous and tragic lessons have taught humanity the folly of this lack of attention. Yet modern men and women seem almost as vulnerable to this carelessness as were their ancestors. Indeed, modern society affords greater opportunity as the invention of products and chemicals to produce fire and to utilize the energy of fire have all brought with them hazards. These hazards have often not been recognized until the price of ignorance has been paid through much suffering and sorrow.

Precautions, safety measures, and regulations to reduce the hazards of fires began to be generated as the characteristics of fire and various materials were discovered. People also found that they had to develop ways to protect themselves and their possessions when fire broke out of control or when fire ignited accidentally.

The first organized firefighting force that can be traced in history was established in Rome by Caesar Augustus around 23 B.C. Moved to action by a bad fire, Augustus gave to the city magistrates a body of some 600 men belonging to the *familia publica*, "servants of the commonwealth," who were stationed near the city gates for the specific purpose of fighting fires.[21] The shortcoming of these firefighters was the fact that as slaves they had little or no stake in the society in which they were forced to live. They were accused of being slow in responding to fires and of being reluctant to endure physical risk to save the lives or property of their Roman masters. Eventually, their work was supplemented by companies of volunteers, but these companies never enjoyed the favor of the government.[22]

After another bad fire in 6 A.D., Augustus set up a corps of professional firefighters known as the *vigiles* or watchmen. These were freedmen, divided into seven battalions or *cohortes* of 1,000 men each, and commanded by the *praefectus vigilium* (a prefect of the equestrian rank who was directly responsible to the emperor: the predecessor of the fire chief in today's modern fire department). The *vigiles* were distributed throughout the city, each battalion being responsible for two of the fourteen wards into which Augustus had divided the city. The cost of maintaining the corps was paid by the public treasury, and each fire prompted an official inquiry which, in the case of fires judged to be caused by negligence, resulted in the punishment of the careless citizen.[23]

Protection through codes

Throughout history, holocaust and structural collapse have resulted in tragedies that have taught the world's inhabitants—particularly its city dwellers—how vulnerable they are to destruction. On some occasions, when lessons have been learned and understanding gained, corrective measures have been taken to prevent reoccurrence of a tragedy. On other occasions corrective measures have not been taken until the tragedy has been repeated and the concerned public has demanded greater protection. Most improvements in construction design, public fire protection, and built-in safety and fire protection features have resulted from experience gained through loss of life and property.

Efforts to reduce vulnerability to fire and structural collapse date back thousands of years. Many of these efforts were in the form of improved structural design and organization to suppress fires, but building and fire codes and regulations were also involved. Since the history of code regulation is neither dramatic nor romantic, it is difficult to find. Nevertheless, some references are available.[24]

Early building codes

The earliest known code of law regulating building construction is that of Hammurabi, founder of the Babylonian empire. A translation of the table containing the code is as follows:

228: If a builder build a house for a man and complete it, that man shall pay him two shekels of silver per sar (approximately 12 square feet) of house as his wage. 229: If a builder has built a house for a man and his work is not strong, and if the house he has built falls in and kills the householder, that builder shall be slain. 230: If the child of the householder be killed, the child of that builder shall be slain. 231: If the slave of the householder be killed, he shall give slave for slave to the householder. 232: If goods have been destroyed, he shall replace all that has been destroyed; and because the house was not made strong, and it has fallen in, he shall restore the fallen house out of his own material. 233: If a builder has built a house for a man, and his work is not done properly and a wall shifts, then that builder shall make that wall good with his own silver.[25]

The burning and rebuilding of Rome

Through the centuries the story has been told of the cruel, obese, and truculent Emperor Nero who "fiddled as Rome burned." However true this description, Nero was apparently a man of vision and intelligence who fully recognized the dangers of unregulated construction. Prior to his rule, Rome had expended its wealth and resources on the construction of public edifices. Unfortunately, the construction characteristics of almost all other buildings were ignored. Tenements were built without any type of control and many of these structures collapsed before they were completed, resulting in the maiming and killing of workers by the scores. Rome was in fact in a chaotic state of affairs prior to its burning in 64 A.D.

It is interesting to note that Nero had a master plan for the development of a new Rome prepared prior to the great conflagration, and immediately after the fire reconstruction was commenced. Nero's attitude toward the conditions that had existed in Rome before the fire were well known, and the accusations that he ordered the incineration have seemed well founded to some historians. Nevertheless, Nero must be credited with reconstructing Rome in accordance with sound principles of construction, sanitation, and utility. From this time until the fall of Rome, both public and private building was closely regulated.[26]

Early English fire regulations

Information regarding early efforts at combating and preventing fire after the collapse of classical Mediterranean civilization is incomplete. There is fragmentary evidence from areas as diverse as the great urban centers of medieval Islamic culture and the black cities of sub-Saharan Africa, the ancient cities of India and of China, and the emergent urban strongholds of Europe that grew with feudal society. In view of the roots of American culture, however, it is of interest to take a quick look at some of the regulations found in medieval England.

It is known, for example, that a curfew requiring fires to be extinguished at a fixed hour in the evening was adopted in Oxford in 872 A.D. After 1066 a general curfew was established in England by William the Conqueror, who directed that a bell be rung in every community, sometime between seven and nine o'clock each night. At this signal a metal fire cover was placed over the open hearth fires in each home to prevent sparks from igniting the rushes on which the people slept. (Of course, William had this law enforced not so much as a fire prevention measure but rather as a means of preventing revolt against his rule.)

An interesting instance of community action for fire prevention occurred in Canterbury in 1177, when shops that were considered a fire hazard to Canterbury Cathedral were purchased by the cathedral authorities and relocated a safe distance away. An ordinance requiring that new buildings have stone walls and slate or tile roofs was issued in 1189 by the first lord mayor of London. This legislation demonstrates that government officials were becoming concerned about rapid fire spread in their growing communities.

Richard I, who reigned during the last decade of the twelfth century, decreed that walls sixteen feet high and three feet thick be erected between neighbors to prevent the spread of fire. The enforcement of this requirement for fire walls evidently was not successful, since fires continued to spread and destroy large sections of London.

Possibly the first two enactments undertaken in England to prevent fires in which the subject was not related to the buildings themselves were a 1566 ordinance in Manchester requiring safe storage of fuel for bakers' ovens and a 1583 parliamentary act forbidding tallow chandlers to melt tallow in dwellings.

Seventeenth and eighteenth century fire experience

Colonial America's fire experience[27]

Hope for a new life, for freedom, and for property had a magnetic draw for courageous immigrants from England, France, Spain, the Netherlands, and the Scandinavian lands. In spite of the dangers presented by crossing the treacherous ocean, the spread of disease, hostile Indians, and the threat of famine, early colonists set sail for the New World by the hundreds. As they landed in the New World they were forced to hastily construct shelter and, consequently, they chose the most expedient means available. Some carved caves in the sides of hills, others collected brush, tree limbs, clay, and grasses to build small cottages with thatched roofs. To protect themselves from the bitter northeastern winters, the colonists in this area built central fireplaces in their dwellings. These fireplaces were constructed of bricks and mud or clay, and the chimneys were made of brush and stalks or wooden planks covered by a thick mixture of mud or clay. These combustible chimneys, in conjunction with the thatched roofs, presented a hazard even greater than the natural elements or hostile Indians. Many commodities common in the homes of the colonists—notably beer, whiskey, brandy, and gunpowder—were also major contributors to the rapid spread of, and destruction by, fire. To make matters worse, the colonists followed the European tradition of building their structures up rather than out and clustered them side by side. These closely built settlements offered the colonists protection against Indian raids but greatly increased vulnerability to rapid fire spread.

Early conflagrations The first permanent colony was founded in Jamestown, Virginia, in 1607. On 7 January 1608 the young colony was devastated by fire. As a result of this first American conflagration, most of the colonists' lodgings and provisions were destroyed. Many died that winter from exposure and hunger.

Five years later Dutch sailing vessels, the *Tiger* and the *Fortune,* landed near the mouth of the Hudson River to trade with the Indians. A few wooden huts were soon erected, and this was the beginning of the first settlement on what is now Manhattan Island. The *Fortune* returned to Holland leaving its companion ship, the *Tiger,* anchored near the settlement. Fire again struck in the New World, but this time it was aboard ship. The *Tiger* burned completely and sank, leaving a small crew isolated from the rest of the world for a year until they were able to construct a new ship. The Indians inhabiting the island were quite friendly and helped to provide shelter for the settlers. Because of this friendly reception and the interest of the Indians in trading, the settlement of Nieuw Amsterdam was later established by the Dutch.

In 1620 the colony at Plymouth, Massachusetts, was settled. Three years later a fire spread out of control and destroyed seven buildings and almost all of the settlement's meager provisions. This fire nearly ended the existence of the colony. Governor William Bradford blamed roistering sailors as the cause. Whatever the source of ignition, the rapid spread of fire could be attributed to the combustible nature of the dwellings.

Boston had the dubious distinction of having had the most numerous and most destructive fires of any of the other colonial towns. One authority states that "before the Revolution, it experienced nine conflagrations, while America's two larger cities—Philadelphia (second in size only to London in the British Empire) and New York—had yet to have one."[28]

Perhaps luck played a great role because fire was no less a threat in Philadelphia and New York. However, excellent building stone and material for making bricks were available in Nieuw Amsterdam (later to become New York City), while Boston's building stone was inferior. Consequently more wooden buildings were erected in Boston. Flammable construction was undoubtedly a major contributing factor to Boston's poor fire record, but also contributing was the lax enforcement of fire prevention and building laws. After numerous fires, Massachusetts passed a law in 1638 prohibiting smoking outdoors. It was the first no smoking law in America. A number of the other colonial settlements followed this lead.[29]

Peter Stuyvesant and fire prevention[30]   It is quite possible that Nieuw Amsterdam would have experienced the same fire destruction as Boston had it not been for the strong personal leadership of Governor Peter Stuyvesant. Recognizing the hazard of combustible chimneys, Governor Stuyvesant succeeded in having a law passed in 1648 which prohibited construction of wooden or plaster chimneys. This was the first of many fire laws that were to be passed by the American colonists in their efforts to prevent fire disasters. Peter Stuyvesant's next step was to appoint four volunteer fire wardens to enforce the law and inspect the chimneys to see that they were properly swept.

These fire wardens were required to levy fines of three guilders to owners of faulty chimneys. Such fines had become common in other colonies, and it became evident that measures had to be taken if the colonies were to survive. Much greater fines of thirty-five guilders were assessed the residents of Nieuw Amsterdam who were found guilty of negligently causing a fire. Assessing fines for such negligence was in keeping with the European tradition. Monies collected from the fines were used to purchase firefighting equipment such as ladders, three gallon water buckets, hooks, and swabs.

The greatest threat of major fire spread was presented by fires that occurred at night when people were sleeping. These fires would gain considerable headway before detection, and consequently became extremely difficult to control and extinguish. Partially for this reason Boston, Nieuw Amsterdam, and other towns adopted a curfew. A ringing of a bell at 9:00 P.M. would order the extinguishment or covering of all fires until 4:30 A.M. An additional step was taken in 1658 by Peter Stuyvesant when he appointed eight young men to roam the streets of Nieuw Amsterdam at night to watch for fires. These men were clad in long capes and carried a wooden rattle that was twirled to sound an alarm. The Rattle Watch soon grew from eight to fifty members and began to arouse opposition among the townspeople. Soon there were many who considered the Rattle Watch more as prowlers than protectors. Resentment to the ironfisted rule of Peter Stuyvesant and to such impositions as the fire wardens and the Rattle Watch helped lead to the takeover by the British in 1664.

The British renamed the colony New York and took over where Peter Stuyvesant had left off. An ordinance was soon adopted regulating the burning out of chimneys at regular intervals and forcing the use of chimney sweeps. The ordinance carried a forty shilling fine with the stipulation that the money collected would be used to provide ladders and leather buckets.

Other early laws adopted to protect the citizens from fire were those enacted to make possible strict prosecution of arsonists. The first law relating to arson was passed in Maryland, in 1638, and carried the death penalty.[31]

The Great Fire of London:
the hazard of combustible construction

In 1666 the Great Fire of London destroyed almost two-thirds of that city. Some historians have stated that the destruction of the city was more of a blessing than it was a tragedy, for London was a filthy, crowded city consisting of low wood frame houses and warehouses. Most thoroughfares had open drains which carried raw sewage, and housewives threw their garbage into the streets. The dwelling units were overcrowded, sanitation was unknown, and epidemics were common. Plague had ravaged London for about a year prior to the fire with hundreds dying per week at its worst period.

Whether it was a blessing or not, the London fire raged for five days and nights destroying 13,200 homes, eighty-seven churches, St. Paul's Cathedral, the law courts, twenty warehouses, and about 100,000 boats and barges, and leaving 200,000 people homeless. Trade and industry collapsed. Miraculously, only six lives were lost.

As a result of the tremendous loss experienced in the London fire, measures were taken in many countries to prevent the recurrence of such a catastrophe. The English Parliament passed regulations called the London Building Act. However, it required two years for them to enact this legislation and then it applied only to the City of London boundaries. Sir Christopher Wren, architect of St. Paul's Cathedral, implored Parliament to enact laws which would require wider streets, greenspaces, building setback, and the use of noncombustible materials in construction. Unfortunately, his pleas were ignored and London was rebuilt in much the same style as before the fire. Wren is reported to have remarked, "The citizens of London have proved themselves unworthy of so great a fire."[32]

The German Empire's fire prevention ordinance

Probably the most advanced and progressive ideas and organization in fire protection anywhere in seventeenth century Europe were embodied in the fire ordinance of the German Empire passed in the 1670s. This ordinance required that fireplaces and chimneys be rebuilt with, or enclosed by, tile or stone. Chimneys had specifications requiring sufficient size to enable the passage of a person whose responsibilities included annual cleaning and maintenance. Preventive measures adopted in regard to the storage and handling of materials ranged from relocating grain storage barns to points outside the city, to measures requiring housewives to store fats and grease in subcellars.

Special equipment such as fire axes, water tubs on sledges, squirt guns, leather buckets, and long ladders had been developed and provided in German communities. Regulations in the fire ordinance specified the location and availability of this equipment so as to maximize the effectiveness of its use.

Further fire prevention efforts in America

As a result of the experiences gained from the London fire and several devastating fires that swept through a number of the American settlements, some colonies attempted to legislate against the use of combustible construction. For example, after a series of fires in the summer of 1679, the Boston general court established legislation which required that all dwellings erected in Boston be built of stone or brick and be covered with slate or tile roofs. Obviously, this law was not enforced since Boston later experienced several conflagrations in which combustible construction was a contributing factor.[33]

In a burst of fire consciousness, the Pennsylvania legislature established a law in 1696 prohibiting the smoking of tobacco on the streets of Philadelphia. A fine of twelve pence was established for violation of this law, and no record can be found that the law was ever repealed.

Benjamin Franklin was an early champion of fire prevention. Franklin's writings in his *Pennsylvania Gazette* had much to do with increasing public awareness of fire safety and forming opinion regarding the importance of fire prevention. He also succeeded in influencing city officials to buy fire suppression equipment and pass fire safety regulations. Franklin coined one of his most familiar epigrams, "An ounce of prevention is worth a pound of cure," in a letter warning the citizens of Philadelphia about the hazards of carrying burning firebrands or coals in a full shovel from one room to another and recommended the use of a closed warming pan for this purpose. Franklin warned that scraps of fire might fall from the shovel into a crevice and smolder undetected until midnight, "when your stairs, being in flames, you may be forced (as I once was)," he wrote, "to leap out of your windows and hazard your necks to avoid being over-roasted."[34] Franklin also campaigned for clean chimneys and for officially appointed chimney sweeps.[35]

Insurance to reduce the impact of loss

Prior to the Great Fire of London, victims of fire depended on a traditional system of collecting donations from neighbors, friends, and sympathetic countrymen in other communities to restore their losses. Such practice was satisfactory in most cases. Collections for victims of the London fire were, however, insignificant compared to the loss experienced. The system was totally inadequate, and from this experience the first fire insurance companies were formed. The idea of forming a company to insure against fire loss soon spread to the colonies, but apparently most, if not all, of the American companies soon failed.

In addition to his other contributions to fire prevention (including the founding of a volunteer fire company in 1736),[36] Benjamin Franklin is also credited with founding the first successful American fire insurance company on 13 April 1752. In the beginning the company was named the Contributorship for the Insurance of Houses from Loss by Fire. Later the name was changed to the Hand-in-Hand Insurance Company. The company remains in business today.

Within a short time thereafter, several insurance companies were formed. Since those early beginnings, fire insurance companies have fought a continued battle for fire prevention. Of course they have had a vested interest, but that interest has caused the promulgation of fire prevention regulations, improvements in structural conditions, increased safety in industrial processes, improvements in public fire protection, and the installation of built-in fire protection features and systems.

Into the nineteenth century: the fires continue[37]

The nineteenth century was an exciting era for the United States, as it expanded westward and thousands of immigrants swelled the population. American industry was expanding and the merchant fleet and navy vessels were gaining recognition. Along the Eastern Seaboard cities and harbors were developing and older cities were expanding outward and upward. Also of considerable significance was the development of greatly improved fire apparatus and equipment and the establishment of organized and paid fire departments. The century was filled with growth, enterprise, discovery, and innovation.

Since people first learned to ignite and control fire, they have recognized its potential as a weapon. In every century of recorded history, skill and ability to use fire as an instrument of destruction have increased many times over. And throughout the history of America, military use of fire has been cruel and

Figure 1–2 The great fire of 1835 in New York City. (Source: National Fire Protection Association.)

effective. There has never been a war fought in this nation without ruthless burning and destruction of property. A similar willful and malicious devastation by fire is exhibited by the arsonists who, since the founding of the colonies, have continuously plagued the American public with misery, suffering, and destruction of property. Even more ominous is the power to destroy that has been developed incrementally over the past 200 years. No structure—no city—is safe from destruction by fire used by the unscrupulous and the unmerciful, whether it be in the form of a match, a bullet, an explosive device, or a nuclear weapon.

Numerous major fires and conflagrations occurred in America during the nineteenth century, but the greatest happened after the Civil War (noted for the conflagration that burned part of Atlanta in 1864). The first of these post-war conflagrations occurred on 4 July 1866 in Portland, Maine, when a firecracker went off in flammable material and ignited a wind driven blaze that swept quickly through the heart of that city. The fire destroyed a triangular section of the city nearly a half mile long and left 10,000 homeless. Sympathetic citizens in many parts of the country organized public subscriptions to raise funds for those who had suffered such severe loss.

Rumors quickly spread that many of the Portland insurance claims would not be paid because several of the insurance companies were driven to bankruptcy. To quell these rumors, representatives from a number of insurance companies in New England and New York held an emergency meeting on 7 July in New York City and passed a resolution declaring that all Portland claims would be paid. The information was made public in the newspapers at once. Of interest is the fact that a resolution was also passed in this critical meeting which led to the founding of the National Board of Fire Underwriters on 18 July 1866.[38] This organization provided outstanding leadership in promoting fire prevention and fire protection until 1965, when this oldest national business association merged with two other organizations to become the American Insurance Association.

The great Chicago fire

Perhaps one of the most prophetic fire insurance advertisements in history appeared on the front page of the *Chicago Tribune,* 8 October 1871. It read: ''Fire-Fire, Prepare for Fall and Wintery Fires.'' That night a fire broke out in the vicinity of the barn owned by Mr. and Mrs. Patrick O'Leary at 137 DeKoven Street (now the site of the Chicago Fire Department Training Academy). Tradition lays the blame for the start of the conflagration on Mrs. O'Leary's cow who supposedly kicked over a kerosene lantern and kindled the fire. Whether the cow was to blame is not known, but most other circumstances surrounding the fire, including the extent of the losses, are well known. The fire burned for twenty-seven hours, destroying 17,500 buildings, killing 250 to 300 people, and leaving approximately 100,000 homeless. The fire loss was estimated at $200 million, but only $88 million was insured. Because of multiple bankruptcies of insurance companies, only $45 million was actually paid.

Fire storm in a forest

On the same day that Chicago was being devastated by fire, the small lumbering community of Peshtigo, Wisconsin, suffered one of the most severe fires in terms of loss of life experienced in the history of the United States. On 8 October 1871 a forest fire in the area surrounding Peshtigo accelerated into a fire storm and swept through the town destroying every building except for one home under construction. Of much greater tragedy than loss of property was the loss of nearly 800 lives.

Being a lumbering town, Peshtigo was built of wood. Not only were the buildings and sidewalks constructed of wood, but sawdust was used on the roads to reduce the dust. The fire moved so fast the people could not flee. Some sought refuge in buildings, where they soon perished. Others rushed to the river, where many drowned. Still others found protection in a marshy area on the east side of the river where the combustible vegetation had burned in a previous fire. It was miraculous that over 950 members of the community survived the holocaust that destroyed timber in an area sixty miles north and south and twenty miles east and west.

The Boston conflagration

Several other major fires occurred before the end of the nineteenth century, but the last conflagration was the great Boston fire of 1872. This conflagration destroyed 776 buildings in an area of the business district approximately one mile square. The fire claimed the lives of thirteen victims, including two firefighters, a foreman, and an assistant foreman. The losses were estimated to be about $75 million.

Boston's fire protection was pitifully poor at the time of the conflagration. Although the fire department had 472 members, only 89 were permanent. The water supply was totally inadequate, being provided mainly through four-inch mains while the hydrants were fed by three-inch branch lines. Witnesses testified that hose streams did not go above the third floor. Many of the buildings were five and six story structures, but the longest ladder only reached forty feet. There were few building regulations and combustible construction was common.

To make matters worse, most of the horses were sick with a type of equine influenza. Consequently, the heavy steam engines, ladder trucks, and hose wagons had to be dragged to the fire by volunteers. Help came from thirty outside fire departments including those of New Haven, Connecticut; Portsmouth, New Hampshire; Biddeford, Maine; and Providence, Rhode Island.

Nineteenth century fire lessons

Two obvious lessons were learned from the nineteenth century conflagrations. First, combustible types of construction, particularly wood siding and wood shingles, are conflagration breeders. Secondly, the nineteenth century fire protection methods were totally incapable of coping with the magnitude of the fire potential. As Americans moved into the twentieth century they greatly reduced their vulnerability to conflagration through improved building construction with fire resistive materials; increased water distribution capacity; the development of powerful motorized fire apparatus with high capacity pumps, aerial ladders, and elevated streams; and installation of built-in fire protection systems and warning devices.

America burning in the twentieth century

Technological and scientific advancement have proliferated so rapidly in the twentieth century that the phenomenon exceeds the grasp of the human mind. Even so, the greatest and most destructive fires in this nation, in terms of both life and property loss, have occurred during this era of achievement. From the disastrous Hoboken waterfront fire of 30 June 1900, with over 300 deaths, and the Jacksonville, Florida, conflagration of 3 May 1901, with a loss of 1,700 buildings, fires have roared through the century destroying billions of dollars worth of property and killing and maiming people by the thousands.[39]

In the following discussion an overview will be given of the sweeping conflagrations in the first quarter of this century. Space does not permit a detailed examination of the holocausts in confined places that have plagued us throughout the century up to the present day, although Figure 1–3, which covers the period from 1900 to the later 1970s, demonstrates that there have been many tragic fires in schools, institutions, nightclubs, hotels, and various factory and industrial facilities (see Figures 1–4 to 1–7).

An era of sweeping conflagrations[40]

The conflagration which struck the city of Baltimore on 7 February 1904 may be regarded as the first of the great fires of the twentieth century. The fire broke out in the basement of the six story Hurst Building on Liberty Street, in a storage area containing highly combustible celluloid novelties. Within a few minutes the fire spread through an unenclosed shaft and burst from the top floor. Nearby buildings with unprotected openings were soon ablaze and the fire swept out of

Location	Date	Deaths
Rhoades Opera House, Boyertown, Pennsylvania	12 January 1903	170
Iroquois Theatre, Chicago, Illinois	30 December 1903	602
S.S. *General Slocum,* New York, New York	15 June 1904	1,030
Lakeview School, Collinwood, Ohio	4 March 1908	175
Triangle Shirtwaist Company, New York, New York	25 March 1911	145
Cleveland School, Beulah, South Carolina	17 May 1923	77
Schoolhouse, Babb's Switch, Oklahoma	24 December 1924	32
Cleveland Clinic Hospital, Cleveland, Ohio	15 May 1929	125
State Penitentiary, Columbus, Ohio	21 April 1930	320
Home for the aged, Pittsburgh, Pennsylvania	24 July 1931	48
S.S. *Morro Castle,* off New Jersey coast	8 September 1934	134
Consolidated School, New London, Texas	18 March 1937	294
Rhythm Club Dance Hall, Natchez, Mississippi	23 April 1940	207
Cocoanut Grove nightclub, Boston, Massachusetts	28 November 1942	492
Circus tent, Hartford, Connecticut	6 July 1944	168
East Ohio Gas Company, Cleveland, Ohio	20 October 1944	130
LaSalle Hotel, Chicago, Illinois	5 June 1946	61
Winecoff Hotel, Atlanta, Georgia	7 December 1946	119
Centralia Coal Company, Centralia, Illinois	25 March 1947	111
St. Anthony's Hospital, Effingham, Illinois	4 April 1949	74
C. W. & F. Coal Company, West Frankfort, Illinois	21 December 1951	119
Our Lady of the Angels School, Chicago, Illinois	1 December 1958	95
State Fairgrounds Coliseum, Indianapolis, Indiana	10 October 1963	74
Golden Age Nursing Home, Fitchville, Ohio	23 November 1963	63
Dale's Penthouse (restaurant), Montgomery, Alabama	7 February 1967	25
Convalescent home, Marietta, Ohio	1 January 1970	31
Silver mine, Kellogg, Idaho	2 May 1972	91
Discotheque, Port Chester, New York	30 June 1974	24
Social club, Bronx, New York	24 October 1976	25
College dormitory, Providence, Rhode Island	13 December 1977	10
Beverly Hills Supper Club, Southgate, Kentucky	28 May 1977	165
Maury County Jail, Columbia, Tennessee	26 June 1977	42

Figure 1–3   Selected major fires in confined places, 1900–1977.
(Source: Information from various sources; methods of recording vary.)

control. As the conflagration gained in intensity the mayor placed urgent calls requesting help from several major cities, including Washington, D.C., Chester, Pennsylvania, Wilmington, Philadelphia, and New York. These cities responded by sending fire apparatus and firefighters on flatcars to the stricken city. When the out-of-city fire companies arrived at the scene of the conflagration, they laid out their hose and learned to their dismay that their hose couplings did not fit the Baltimore fire hydrants. The firefighters were able to overcome the problem by digging up the cobblestone streets, building dams around the hydrants, and with their pumpers drafting water from the artificial ponds that were formed when the hydrants were opened. By the time the conflagration finally died down at Jones Falls (a fifty foot wide canal), 155 acres of mercantile property valued at $50 million had been destroyed and 50,000 people had been put out of work.

The great lesson learned from the Baltimore conflagration, in addition to the hazard of unprotected vertical shafts and unprotected openings, was the need to standardize threads on hydrants, hose, and fittings. Virtually all cities and towns throughout the nation have now adopted standard uniform couplings and threads.

The Municipal Inspection and Grading System of the National Board of Fire Underwriters was established as a result of the Baltimore conflagration. Insurance men were convinced that it was possible to contain fires more effectively and reduce the threat of conflagrations. In the early part of 1904 a team of engineers was retained by the National Board of Fire Underwriters to survey the congested centers of urban communities in all parts of the country. The engineers moved very quickly from city to city evaluating the potential for conflagration. As early as 5 October 1905 an article in *World's Work* reported that thirty-two cities had been inspected. The report noted that several improvements had already been made in the fire defense in a number of evaluated cities, and that there had been a reorganization of the fire service in every one of the thirty-two cities.[41] From this beginning in 1904, the grading of cities' fire defense by the insurance industry has become the single most important influence on improvements in public fire protection. In response to the underwriters' evaluation and grading of the municipal fire defense, cities have made long lists of improvements. The threat of higher insurance premiums or the reward of insurance savings has provided a large measure of the needed motivation.

In the fall of 1905 a committee of twenty fire prevention engineers from the National Board of Fire Underwriters conducted surveys of San Francisco to make a preliminary evaluation of the conflagration potential. Following the inspection a report was written which demonstrated that the engineers were well aware of the potential for disaster. An excerpt from the report read:

Not only is the hazard extreme within the congested value district, but it is augmented by the presence of a surrounding compact, great-height, large-area, frame-residence district itself unmanageable from a fire-fighting standpoint by reason of adverse conditions introduced by topography.

In fact, San Francisco has violated all underwriting traditions and precedents by not burning up; that it has not done so is largely due to the vigilance of the fire department, which cannot be relied upon indefinitely to stave off the inevitable.[42]

On 18 April 1906, only six months after the insurance inspection team report, an earthquake lasting only one and a half minutes devastated the city and resulted in the greatest conflagration in American history. The fire burned uncontrollably for two days and consumed 4.7 square miles, destroyed more than 25,000 buildings, and took the lives of approximately 450 victims. The amount of loss resulting from this conflagration has been estimated at from $350 million to $1 billion.[43]

In fact, the loss experienced in the San Francisco conflagration was so great the sum was equal to the aggregate of all of the large conflagrations in the United States during the preceding fifty years. It is interesting to observe that over 22,000 of the more than 25,000 buildings destroyed were of wood frame construction. And what was the lesson from this greatest of all American conflagrations? It was the hazard of combustible construction. But the lesson was not yet learned.

Chelsea, Massachusetts, was devastated by a conflagration just two years after the great San Francisco earthquake. On Sunday, 12 April 1908, a fire starting in rags, in a district of the city with numerous rag shops, was quickly driven to adjacent property by high winds. Within a few minutes the fire was whipped into a conflagration of a magnitude that ultimately destroyed about one-half of the improved area of the city. In the course of the fire some 3,500 buildings were destroyed in an area of nearly 275 acres. The monetary loss from the fire was estimated at $12 million, the insurance loss at over $9 million. The hazard of combustible roofs and the vulnerability of ordinary buildings to sparks and embers was again emphasized. That the lesson was still not learned is evident in the fact that on 14 October 1973 once again Chelsea on a Sunday experienced a conflagration almost identical in fire origin, fire spread, and fire control problems.

Conflagrations hit the citizens of the United States frequently during the first quarter of the twentieth century. In 1913 a major fire in Hot Springs, Arkansas,

Figure 1–4   On 25 March 1911 a fire in the Asch Building in New York
City took the lives of 145 factory workers, many of whom jumped
to their deaths from upper story windows rather than face the flames.
This tragedy, called the Triangle Shirtwaist fire (after the company on
the eighth floor where the fire started), drew national attention to the
need for laws requiring adequate fire escapes, fire drills, and sprinklers
in factories. This view of the Asch Building during the fire illustrates
the ineffectiveness of the hose streams directed from the street, which
were inadequate to fight the fire inside the upper floors of the building.
(Source: National Fire Protection Association.)

destroyed over 500 buildings. On 25 June 1914 fire swept through Salem, Massachusetts, destroying some 1,600 buildings in its path. While a conflagration on
21 March 1924 was destroying some 1,440 buildings in Paris, Texas, Nashville,
Tennessee, was fighting a fire that destroyed approximately 650 buildings. The
following day a conflagration in Augusta, Georgia, burned over 680 buildings in

Figure 1–5   The much publicized fire in the Cocoanut Grove nightclub in Boston on 28 November 1942 claimed the lives of 492 persons. Overcrowding, a revolving door which was soon blocked, together with other doors which were locked, and also flammable decorations in the club, contributed to the disaster. The fire prompted the strengthening of fire codes and increased enforcement of fire prevention regulations in many cities. (Source: Wide World Photos.)

the center of town. Atlanta experienced simultaneous fires on 21 May 1917 which resulted in the destruction of over 1,900 structures. Then, on 12 October 1918, the most disastrous life loss conflagration of the second decade struck as forest fires in Minnesota swept through fifteen townships and claimed the lives of 559 victims, a sad reminiscence of the 1871 Peshtigo forest fire.[44]

Completing the list of conflagrations during the first quarter of the twentieth century were: the Astoria, Oregon, fire on 8 December 1922, which destroyed thirty blocks in the center of town during a rain storm; and a brush fire which destroyed 640 dwellings in Berkeley, California, on 17 September 1923.

Conflagrations dwindled during the second quarter of the twentieth century as fire resistive construction became more prevalent, fire suppression capabilities improved, and fire and building codes became more stringent and were more strictly enforced. Nevertheless, potential for conflagration in the United States still exists, particularly in those parts of the country with large areas of combustible brush and forests. An example of the potential devastation that can result from brush fires was demonstrated in Los Angeles, California, on 6 November 1961. Losses totaling an estimated $35 million were experienced as high velocity ''Santa Ana'' winds drove roaring flames into the Bel Air and Brentwood residential sections of the city and destroyed more than 450 expensive homes. As was common with other North American conflagrations, wood shingle roofs were a major contributing factor. Southern California has since suffered similar conflagrations. One thing is certain: until the tremendous hazard of combustible roof exposure to explosively combustible brush is abated, more conflagrations can be anticipated.

Figure 1–6   Over ninety students and three teachers died in the fire in
Our Lady of the Angels school in Chicago on 1 December 1958.
Immediately after the fire the public demanded additional safeguards
for children confined in classrooms and in multistory buildings. Fire
prevention regulations including fire drills have since been more
strictly enforced in schools throughout the country. (Source: National
Fire Protection Association, Chicago Tribune photograph.)

Holocaust in confined areas

As the threat of large, sweeping fires diminished in the United States, the large
loss of life and property in individual occupancies became a great concern. Fires
that have trapped victims in confined areas have cost the lives of thousands and
taught Americans many tragic lessons.[45] (See list in Figure 1–3.)

Large loss of life from fire and panic in confined areas has plagued the American public throughout the twentieth century. The list is long and the lessons are
often repeated. The first of the grim lessons began with the staggering loss of 602
lives in the Iroquois Theatre fire on 30 December 1903. It was learned that the
absolutely "fireproof" building is far from safe when combustible contents are
added and when exits and fire protection systems are not designed or provided
to protect the occupants. Soon after the tragedy scores of regulations were
passed from coast to coast requiring better exiting provisions. Exit doors were

Figure 1–7 A fire on 28 May 1977 took the lives of 165 patrons and employees of the Beverly Hills Supper Club in Southgate, Kentucky. This disaster reaffirmed the need for stringent requirements for adequate exits and noncombustible decorations and building materials in places of public assemblage. Most importantly, the club had no automatic sprinkler system; such equipment would no doubt have greatly reduced the loss from the fire. (Source: National Fire Protection Association.)

required that open in the direction of exit travel when pressure is applied to a releasing device. The required width for aisles was increased, scenery and curtains were required to be made of fire resistive materials, lights were required to be placed in caged-in compartments, and automatic sprinkler systems were ordered installed in certain locations. It is tragic that we must pay so dearly before learning good fire safety practices.

The numerous disastrous fires that were occurring with alarming frequency during the early part of the twentieth century bit deeply into the public consciousness. Editions of magazines and newspapers began to feature articles on fire safety in places of public assembly, factories, offices, and homes. Finally, the average person was being taught the basic principles of fire safety and was becoming familiar with precautions that could be taken to prevent fires in the home or the place of business. But in spite of efforts in fire prevention education, a great loss of life in confined areas and a large property loss from major fires are written indelibly on the pages of twentieth century history.

As the nation entered the latter half of the twentieth century, the fire service faced an ever increasing range and magnitude of fire problems. High rise structures, modes of transportation, industrial process, highly combustible and toxic materials, all demonstrated the urgent need for better fire protection training, organization, and equipment.

America burning today

What are the dimensions of today's challenge? As stated by the National Commission on Fire Prevention and Control in their 1973 report, *America Burning,* it is appalling that the richest and most technologically advanced nation in the world leads all the major industrialized countries in per capita deaths and property loss from fire.

Annually, fire claims nearly 12,000 lives in the United States. Among causes of accidental death, only motor vehicle accidents and falls rank higher. Most of fire's victims die by inhaling smoke or toxic gases well before the flames have reached them.

The scars and terrifying memories live on with the 300,000 Americans who are injured by fire every year. Of these, nearly 50,000 lie in hospitals for a period ranging from 6 weeks to 2 years. Many of them must return, over and over again, for plastic and reconstructive surgery. Many never resume normal lives.

The price of destructive fire in the United States amounts, by conservative estimate, to at least $11.4 billion a year. . . .Beyond calculation are the losses from businesses that must close and from jobs that are interrupted or destroyed.[46]

The causes of the American fire problem are numerous. But the roots are fed by ignorance and indifference.

But indifference exists where it is least excusable. For example, there are those in the fire services who are unaware of the technological state-of-the-art in their field. There are fire department administrators who pay lip service to fire prevention and then do little to promote it. . . .

Designers of buildings generally give minimal attention to fire safety in the buildings they design. They are content, as are their clients, to meet the minimal safety standards of the local building code. . . .

The Federal Government also has been largely indifferent to the fire problem. The Federal programs that exist (some of which are excellent) touch only small portions of the total fire problem.

Lastly, the American public is indifferent to and ignorant of the heavy toll of destructive fire.[47]

The nation's firefighters are among those paying the most heavily for the poor fire record in this nation.

In 1971, the injury rate for firefighters was 39.6 per 100 men—far higher than that of any other profession. That same year, 175 firefighters died in the line of duty; an additional 89 died of heart attacks and 26 are known to have died of lung disease contributed to by the routine smoke hazard of their occupation.[48]

This indictment retains its validity today. This is the challenge facing our nation at the start of its third century. The management of contemporary methods of preventing, controlling, and suppressing outbreaks of fire will, of course, be the subject of the chapters that comprise the remainder of this book. To place those efforts in perspective, however, we must again look to our roots and consider two additional important themes in the evolution of our struggles against fire: the development of firefighting equipment, and, most significant of all from the managerial viewpoint, the growth and organization of the firefighting services themselves.

The evolution of firefighting equipment[49]

The development and use of firefighting equipment in the American colonies was greatly influenced by fire control practices and inventions in Europe and England. Devastating European conflagrations during the sixteenth and seventeenth centuries had led to practical fire control methods, but attention to means of distributing water for firefighting was lacking. Pumps and water systems had been used during the Egyptian dynasties and during the time of the Roman Empire, but these measures seem to have been forgotten until the early years of the seventeenth century.[50]

An illustration of a fire pump described by Heinrich Zeising in 1612 depicted a two-cylinder force pump with a swivel nozzle mounted in a tank on wheels. An air tank was later added to maintain pressure in the delivery side of the pump so that a continuous stream could be delivered. This invention was not adopted by the English pumps for another fifty years. Meanwhile, hand operated pumps in the form of a syringe, a fire squirt, or a small stirrup pump with attached hose, were used for extinguishing small fires.[51]

Fire engines and ingenuity

Firefighting tactics in the early days of the American colonies required the turn-out of all available citizens, who would gather the town's supply of leather buckets and form two lines from a source of water, such as a cistern or pump, to the fire scene. One line, usually women and children, would pass the empty buckets to the water supply, where they were filled and then returned by the supply line.

These bucket brigades required fifty or more people for every 100 feet of distance from the water supply to the fire. Obviously, such tactics were ineffective, and once a building became involved in fire, the best defense was to drop the structure so as to prevent the fire from spreading to neighboring buildings. To accomplish this demolition, the colonists fashioned circular iron hooks which were attached to ropes approximately thirty feet long. These hooks were thrown over the roofs involved in fire and then dragged back so as to peel off the roof. The hooks were then used to haul down the walls. Later the hooks became part of the standard equipment for the companies carrying ladders, and these rigs became known as hook and ladder companies. When the structures were more substantial in construction and the hooks inadequate to haul down the walls, gunpowder was used for the demolition. Often the result of this fire strategy was additional fires to combat.

In some communities the colonists were reimbursed if their houses were hooked down or blown up in the course of firefighting. As has been noted, one of the greatest contributors to fire spread was the highly combustible nature of the roofs. Sparks from chimneys or burning buildings would drop on the roofs and start spot fires. If these small fires were not quickly extinguished, the entire roof was soon ablaze, emitting flying embers to ignite the neighboring roofs. Boston required each household to have a swab attached to a twelve foot wooden pole readily available to extinguish roof fires. When dipped in water and applied directly to a small fire the swabs were quite effective.

The first recorded reference to a fire engine in America was contained in a 1653 agreement between the selectmen of Boston and Joseph Jynks (or Jenks). Jynks, an ironworker in nearby Saugas, was to build "ingines [*sic*] to convey water in case of fire."[52] The reference may have been to hand held water syringes, rather than pumpers, but in any case the Jynks engines did not prove satisfactory. An early morning conflagration in Boston on 27 November 1676 (which destroyed about fifty homes and warehouses) resulted in the selectmen voting to buy the best fire engine London had to offer. The best London had to offer did not amount to much by today's standards, but this action resulted in placing the first practical fire engine in America in service on 27 January 1678. The device consisted of a wooden box approximately three feet long and eighteen inches wide. It stood on four legs and had handles at the front and rear to facilitate its being carried to the fire. A hand operated pump mounted inside the box fed a flexible snakelike nozzle, while a bucket brigade provided the supply of water.

Manually operated fire engines were to improve considerably during the eighteenth century. An English manufacturer, Richard Newsham, built a fire engine superior to any other engine in the early 1700s. Newsham produced engines in six sizes, the largest of which, he claimed, could squeeze through a three foot passageway, a feat which no other fire engine could perform. The engine consisted of a wooden box with a pump mounted inside and a swivel nozzle affixed to the top of the pump housing; the pump handles—called brakes—extended on each side. The four largest pumps were mounted on wheels; the two smaller models had handles for carrying. Operation of the pump required three men on each side and, depending on the size, could deliver from 30 to 170 gallons (of water) per minute (GPM) at distances ranging from 78 to 120 feet. One of the major disadvantages of the Newsham was that the pulling handle did not pivot. Consequently, to turn the rig from one street into another the firefighter had to pick up the engine and swing it around.

The ingenuity of American craftsmen soon resulted in greatly improved machines. In 1768 Richard Mason of Philadelphia devised a successful pumper that had the brakes extending from each end rather than the sides. This end-stroking

Figure 1–8   Firefighting
in New York
in the 1770s.
(Source: National Fire
Protection Association.)

made it easier for bucket brigade men to feed the pump's cistern. With a faster entry of water, the pumping capabilities were improved. Mason's engines came in four sizes and compared favorably with the Newsham. The end-strokers were dubbed "Philadelphia-style" and won a large following, particularly because of resentment that was building up toward British-made products.

Efforts to build rotary types of fire pumps were less successful. For example, the coffee mill type of engine had a side-mounted crank which turned an axle that rotated a gear with teeth that scooped water from the box and forced it through a mounted nozzle. A variation of the coffee mill type pump was the cider mill, or windlass, engine. This engine had long poles extending horizontally from the rotary pump which were pushed by men on horses running in circles around the engine. Neither of these styles of pumps enjoyed great success and a rotary fire engine was not to become practical until steam and gasoline engines provided the power needed for effectiveness.

The rotary engine was used with some degree of success by a group of New York volunteers who in 1800 formed a new type of fire company. They built America's first fireboat by placing a coffee mill pump mounted amidships in a scow which had a sharp bow and square stern. The floating engine was rowed to fires by the company's twelve volunteers. Winter weather and rough water made rowing of the scow very difficult and the firefighters were often exhausted before arriving at the fire. But in spite of such difficulties the fireboat remained in service for twenty-four years.

The demise of the bucket brigade

Around the beginning of the nineteenth century, the following three innovations marked a great change in the methods and effectiveness of fire attack and in the number of volunteers required to apply water to a fire: (1) the water mains system, (2) the fire hydrant, and (3) copper-riveted leather hose.

Before 1800, water for firefighting was drawn from wells, cisterns, and natural bodies. But a major advance was made in 1801 when Philadelphia opened its water mains system. The system, consisting of hollowed logs beveled on the ends to fit together, was supplied by the Schuylkill River. Frederick Graff, chief engineer of the Philadelphia Water Works, designed the first post type fire hydrant the same year. The hydrant was of a T shape with a faucet for drinking water on one side and a fire hose connection on the other. New York installed a similar water system a little later, but hydrants were not installed. New York firefighters had to dig down to the wooden water main and drill a hole in the pipe to fill their engines. When the fire was extinguished, a wooden plug was inserted in the hole that had been drilled in the pipe and the main was covered over. (The word *fireplug* stems from this practice.)

Leather hose was first made in Amsterdam around 1672. However, this hose had stitched seams (the way shoemakers made boots) and leaked badly. In 1807 two Philadelphia volunteer firefighters devised a method of improving leather hose through using metal rivets to bind the seams. This method of construction greatly reduced leaking and made the hose strong enough to withstand the pressures produced by the large hand pumpers. The hose itself was made from the thickest and best cowhides. The hides were cut into pieces three feet in length, formed into a tube, and the ends and joints riveted together. The hose lengths ran from forty to fifty feet and, including the couplings, weighed in excess of eighty pounds. In spite of the weight, the hose became immediately popular and was sold throughout the United States. Leather hose was highly successful but was not the best answer. Not only was it expensive but it required care to prevent rot and cracking. Still, it served well for over a quarter of a century until the development of rubber hose.

A new type of fire apparatus

With the availability of good water supply and fire hose, the hose wagon became an important new type of fire apparatus for the fire service. The companies using it could carry three times as much hose as the engine companies, whose hose capacity was limited by the weight of the pump.

A Philadelphia firefighter, Reuben Haines, conceived the idea of the hose wagon and formed the first hose company in 1803. Their rig was a four wheeled box about seven feet in length with a twenty-four-inch deep hose bed. It carried 600 feet of folded hose (in short lengths) and cost $98. In addition to getting the money together for their rig, this first hose company also had to raise money for the hose (spelled variously in advertisements of the day as *Hoose, Hoase,* and *House*).

The first response of Philadelphia Hose No. 1 was to a fire on 3 March 1804. The hose company caught the interest of other Philadelphians and several more companies were formed. By 1823 there were nineteen hose companies in the city of Philadelphia.

Hose companies did not catch on as quickly in such cities as New York because of poor water supply systems. However, with the innovation of riveted hose, which made possible the pumping of water under pressure and the suctioning of water from draft, it became more practical for pumpers to relay water from the source to a fire some distance away. The engine company at the source would suction water into the apparatus and the volunteers at the brakes pumped water through their hose to the tub of the next engine. That engine in turn relayed the water on until the engine nearest the fire pumped the water at a strong pressure through the nozzle and onto the fire.

With riveted hose and relay pumping the capability of a strong fire attack was improved many times over. Mayor Josiah Quincy of Boston remarked in 1825 that 100 feet of hose could do the work of sixty men with buckets. On one fire in New York, Chief Harry Howard counted thirty engines pumping in a line a mile and a half long from the water supply to the fire. The era of bucket brigades was drawing to a close and the great reduction in manpower needed to apply water to the fire provided a step toward the possibility of a fully paid fire department.

The greatly increased demand for hose caused by the introduction of relay pumping had to be satisfied. This demand provided opportunities for the organization of many new volunteer hose companies. These new companies, caught up in the spirit and competition of the day, immediately began devising ways to arrive, lay their hose, and begin fighting a fire ahead of their competitors. Soon four wheel hose reels that rolled out precoupled hose were designed. This gave a definite edge to the companies using the system. In 1819 David J. Hubbs built a two wheel hose cart. This rig carried a large reel which revolved on the axle. These Hubbs' Babies, as they were called, were very fast and could be pulled by two volunteers or hauled behind an engine.

Reaching upward

A third type of volunteer company to evolve was the hook and ladder. The ladder companies did not proliferate as rapidly as the engine companies and the hose companies. These rigs carried ladders of varying length along with hooks for stripping roofs and hauling down structures. Axes, leather buckets, and other firefighting tools were also carried. As the ladder company evolved through the years this rig was to become a toolbox on wheels. All of the various salvage, rescue, and overhaul equipment began to be loaded on the "truck."

Developing the capability for reaching upper floors of multistory buildings has always presented a problem for the fire service. The length of ladders was limited by weight and size factors. Both the ladders and the wagon carrying them had to be fairly short in order to turn corners in the narrow streets. This problem was partially solved by rigs built with pivoting wheels in the front and rear. The rear tongue, or tiller, was later replaced by a steering wheel above the rear axle with a seat for the tillerman. The problem of ladder length was a more difficult one to solve. Extension ladders were built that could reach just over seventy feet, but these ladders were heavy and awkward to handle, requiring nine men to put them into place. With the increasing heights of structures, it became evident that manually operated portable ladders could not provide the answer.

The genesis of a solution to the problem came with the invention of the apparatus-mounted aerial ladder. The first practical example was George Skinner's patented aerial which consisted of three telescoping wooden sections which reached up to 101 feet when a portable extension was placed at the top. The Skinners, as they were called, were flimsy and few firefighters liked them. Another early aerial was the Scott-Uda, which had eight separate sections stacked in the wagon bed. The base section was attached to the wagon's frame. Several of these rigs were sold to American cities; however, New York turned against these and other aerial ladders after a Scott-Uda broke during a demonstration on 14 September 1875, killing three firefighters.

The first successful aerial ladder truck was built by Daniel D. Hayes, a machinist in the San Francisco fire department. Hayes patented his aerial on 23 February 1868. The wooden aerial ladder extended eighty-five feet and was raised by a single horizontal worm gear turned manually by a long handle. The aerial was operated by four to six men. Recognition for Hayes's invention came slowly and he sold his patents to the LaFrance Fire Engine Company in 1882. The name of LaFrance was well known and identified with quality, consequently the LaFrance-built Hayes aerials were placed in service as fast as they could be built. Because of its early tragic experience with the Scott-Uda, New York did not get its first Hayes until June 1886. But shortly thereafter New York had eight aerials in service and Brooklyn had fourteen. Other manufacturers quickly joined the race to build better aerials and improvements soon followed, which increased the usefulness of the aerial ladder.

The advent of the steamer

Another important advance in fire suppression capability came with the invention of the steam-driven fire engine. This powerful pumper could discharge as much water as six or more hand operated pumpers, each requiring upward of twenty men on the brakes. Furthermore, while the steamer could pump as long as coal was fed to the firebox, the volunteers on the hand operated pumpers had

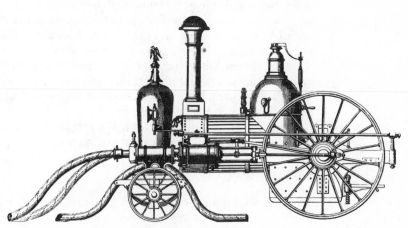

Figure 1–9   This steam engine built by P. R. Hodge in 1840 began the era of self-propelled fire engines. (Source: National Fire Protection Association.)

to change crews every twenty to thirty minutes. It was the advent of the steam pumper, with the reduced manpower requirement, that made the organization of paid fire departments feasible. But that was not to happen until citizens became disenchanted with the volunteers.

The steam fire engines had a number of problems, the first of which was weight. The first successful steam fire pumper, built by Latta and Shaw under contract to the city of Cincinnati, weighed 22,000 pounds and required four horses to draw it to its maiden public demonstration on New Year's Day, 1853. As it rumbled down the street shaking buildings on both sides and belching smoke and sparks, it ground the street's cobblestones to powder.

Other problems with the steam fire engine included time delay in building up steam pressure to get the pump in operation, the threat of additional fires caused by sparks flying from the boiler stack, and the hazard of explosion. These engineering problems were soon resolved by improved design and innovations, but the major problem encountered by the steamers was the resistance of the firefighters. Wherever and whenever city officials considered purchasing a steamer, the volunteers rose in opposition. They recognized only too well that the steam-driven fire pumper posed a threat to their ascendancy and were quick to emphasize the disadvantages and hazards of the "sham squirt."

Over the decades firefighters themselves have been the inventors and the innovators in improving firefighting apparatus, equipment, and tactics. Nevertheless, they have at times also been obstructionists to improved methods and organization. No better example of this is evident than the resistance organized against the steam engine.

The chemical engine: an answer for small fires

A presentation by French scientists in 1864 demonstrating the reaction of a soda, acid, and water mixture had a marked impact upon the fire service. It was shown that the addition of sulphuric acid to a mixture of bicarbonate of soda and water resulted in the liberation of carbon dioxide gas. When the chemicals were combined in a closed container, sufficient gas pressure was generated to expel the water in a strong stream through an attached nozzle. This principle was quickly adopted and within five years the chemical engine company became a part of the American fire service. These engines, carrying one or two 35 to 100 gallon tanks and at least one hose reel, offered a wide range of uses. They could respond to a fire and immediately start attack while the steamers and hose companies were hooking up and getting into operation. The chemical engine was also valuable in suburban and rural areas where water supplies were limited.

Before the advent of the chemical engine, firefighters had relied on the two-and-one-half-inch hose, but for minor fires this was an extreme case of overkill. The small one-inch hose on the chemical engine was adequate for the majority of small fires, and water damage was held to a minimum. These rigs were not the ultimate answer, but for over half a century they were used to extinguish at least 80 percent of all fires in most communities.

Elevated streams

With the development of the aerial ladder truck, firefighters soon devised ways of placing a nozzle at the top rung so as to have the advantage of an elevated stream. Streams from the ground were, in fact, ineffective for the upper floors of taller buildings.

Another partial solution to the need for an elevated stream was provided by the invention of the water tower. A patent for such a device was acquired by Abner and Albert Greenleaf and John B. Logan on 21 November 1876. The tower, consisting of a base pipe mounted on a wagon deck with two extension pipes, could reach fifty feet. The stream from the nozzle located at the top could be directed and controlled by a rope held by firefighters on the ground.

As with other innovations and inventions in fire apparatus and equipment, improvements to the design of the hose tower quickly followed. A telescoping tower raised by hydraulic pressure was designed by Fire Chief George C. Hale of Kansas City. These towers were soon preferred to the Greenleaf tower by most major eastern cities. With several improvements, hose towers were produced by American fire equipment manufacturers until the last one was sold to Los Angeles by American LaFrance in 1937.

The era of the fire horse

Early models of the steam pumper included self-propulsion capability; however, this apparatus was far too cumbersome and heavy to be practical. The answer to the problem of moving the steamers to the fire ground lay in reduced weight through engineering so that the rigs could be drawn by volunteers, or, as that became impractical, by a team of horses. It was the weight of the steamers, chemical engines, and ladder trucks that inaugurated the next era of the American fire service.

From the end of the Civil War until about 1923, American firefighters shared their stations with the fire horse. While at first firefighters did not want to live in the same building with a horse, these animals soon became department pets.

Figure 1–10   The Boston fire department's five horse hitch responds to an alarm. (Source: National Fire Protection Association, Boston Fire Department photograph.)

The fire horses were bred, selected, trained, and matched to produce superb teams of strength and stamina. Some cities had training stables, but only Detroit claimed a horse college. The grounds of the college had the appearance of a small whitewashed farm in the Bluegrass Country. Included on the grounds was a fire station with apparatus, training stalls, a feed room, a 700 foot racetrack, and a horse hospital. Report cards on progress were carefully maintained and graduate horses went on to their life's career in the fire service.

Some fire horses were so intelligent and well trained that they could recognize the number of bells signaling their company and, when released from their stalls, could without direction take their place in front of their rig. The status of the horse in the American fire service of the day is evident in the fact that Philadelphia horses received annual vacations many years before the firefighters did.

As has been mentioned, in the great Boston fire of 1872 that city suffered severe losses, partly because of the inadequacy of its fire department at that time, but also because the horses were ill with a kind of epidemic equine influenza.

The resistance expressed by firefighters to the introduction of horses into the fire station was mild compared to that exhibited toward their replacement with motorized apparatus. But progress was inevitable, and on 20 December 1922 the final run for fire horses in New York ended in a ceremony wherein the last team of horses was exchanged for a shiny new gasoline powered pumper. Less than two months later, on 5 February 1923, Chicago's last pair of fire horses answered their final call. The requiem for the fire horses of Philadelphia came on New Year's Eve, 1927, when a pair of white stallions hauled a chemical engine on their final run. Citizens of Rochester, New York, eulogized their fire horses in a Fire Horse Day parade on 15 July 1927, and later mounted a bronze memorial plaque on the city hall annex.

Motorized apparatus

Motorized fire apparatus began appearing on the fire scene shortly after the beginning of the twentieth century. One of the earliest motorized rigs was a hose and chemical apparatus built in 1903 by American LaFrance for the volunteer Niagara Engine Company No. 1 of New London, Connecticut. Around 1907, Alameda, California, received a Waterous-built pumper with a single four-cylinder engine that powered the apparatus to fires and also pumped about 600 GPM.

During the 1908 annual fire chiefs' convention in Columbus, Ohio, a motorized Seagrave hook and ladder, starting from a point three miles away, raced up to them and raised its seventy-five foot aerial ladder in a total time of seven minutes and forty-five seconds. Within a few minutes a Webb combination engine and hose rig covered the same distance and discharged a stream in only six minutes and eleven seconds. These demonstrations did much to convince the chiefs that the future firefighters would be riding on gasoline powered apparatus.

In 1911 the Savannah, Georgia, fire department became the nation's first completely motorized department. Chief Thomas Ballantyne explained that he did it by purchasing seven American LaFrance pumpers, one chemical engine, and four combination chemical and hose wagons on an installment plan. Such a commitment required a lot of courage on the part of the chief and demonstrated the faith of the city fathers in the chief's judgment and in the future of the horseless engine.

Within a decade, more than 200 makers of motorized fire apparatus entered the market to compete with the established manufacturers. Many of these companies remain in business today because of the high quality of their product and their commitment to research and development. A number of automobile manufacturers such as Ford, Chevrolet, and Pierce-Arrow built fire apparatus. But since the construction of fire apparatus did not lend itself to mass production methods, there were no automobile manufacturers that approached the success of American LaFrance, Mack, and Seagrave. It was Seagrave that revolutionized fire engines with the development of the centrifugal pump for firefighting in 1912.

Although motorized fire apparatus rapidly received acceptance, engineering and mechanical problems postponed its replacement of the steamers and horses for several years. New York placed an order for twenty-eight steamers as late as 1912, but this was the last big order placed in the United States. American LaFrance, the largest manufacturer of fire apparatus, made its last steamers in 1914 and at that time was booked to capacity for motorized rigs.

Firefighting apparatus has improved rapidly since the demise of the horse drawn steam engine. These improvements include large capacity diesel powered pumpers capable of discharging 1,500 to 2,000 GPM; a super pumper with a discharge volume as high as 8,800 GPM; smooth operating and stable aerial ladders, typically elevating 85 to 100 feet; elevating platforms such as the "snorkel" invented by Chicago Fire Commissioner Robert Quinn, or Calavar's Fire Bird, reaching 150 feet; and telescoping booms 50 to 75 feet in length with remote control nozzles. There have also been great improvements and innovations in fire equipment. Perhaps the most important for the safety of the firefighter has been the self-contained breathing apparatus. But also of great significance have been the mobile and portable radios; the spray nozzle; lightweight and large diameter hose; remote and radio control valves and engines; improved safety clothing; lightweight ladders; effective portable fire extinguishers; and water additives that reduce friction, penetrate deep-seated fires, and produce foam. The list goes on and on. The items listed above give only a brief idea of the scope and the technological sophistication involved. (Further details on today's apparatus and equipment can be found in Chapter 20.)

The evolution of the American fire service

Though colonial Boston had the poorest fire record in America, the selectmen were very aggressive in attacking their fire problem. Having acquired from London in 1678 the first fire engine to be placed in service in America, the selectmen then established the first American firehouse (the rough shed where the engine was kept) and hired Thomas Atkins to captain the rig. In so doing, Boston became the first American city to have a paid firefighting officer. Atkins was a carpenter by trade, a skill he would need to keep the engine in working order. Atkins appointed twelve assistants and together they formed the first American paid fire department. However, it is likely that they were only paid by the fire and for training, a practice that is still common in many areas of the United States. It is interesting to note that the tradition of excusing firefighters from certain civic duties, such as military service and jury duty, was also begun by the selectmen of Boston.[53]

In addition to having the distinction of purchasing the first fire engine, housing it in the first firehouse, and manning it with paid firefighters, Boston was also the first to form "mutual aid societies." The first society was established on 30 September 1717. The primary purposes of these societies were firefighting and saving the property of their members.[54]

Apart from colonial Boston, there is no record of a paid fire department in an American city until Cincinnati established an all-paid fire department in 1853. This action was demanded by the citizens as a protection against the rowdyism and indiscretions of the volunteers. Until then, practically every firefighter in America was a volunteer, and the fire departments and fire companies were private organizations, though most often semiofficial by virtue of a charter.[55]

Volunteer firefighters: American heroes

The idea of forming volunteer fire companies soon spread to other cities. In Philadelphia, Benjamin Franklin formed the Union Fire Company on 7 December 1736.[56] Savannah, Georgia, purchased its first hand engine in 1759 and fifteen townsmen organized a fire company, agreeing "to keep the engine in good repair and attend upon any accident of fire."[57] George Washington became an active volunteer in Alexandria, Virginia, and later bought a fire engine for the city's Friendship Fire Association. A number of settlers in Baltimore met and formed the Mechanical Company on 22 September 1763. In Wilmington, Delaware, the citizens organized Friendship Fire Company No. 1 on 22 December 1775. Volunteer fire companies were also organized in Newark, New Jersey, in 1797; Louisville, Kentucky, in 1798; and Georgetown, Maryland, in 1789.

In the earliest years the volunteer fire companies were formed and led by distinguished civic leaders. Men such as George Washington, Benjamin Franklin, John Hancock, Samuel Adams, Paul Revere, Alexander Hamilton, and Aaron Burr were among those whose names were associated with early fire prevention and firefighting organizations.

The rivalries begin

Beginning around 1800 and continuing for over a century, the volunteer fire companies became a very tightly knit social group in their communities. Even today volunteer fire companies constitute major social groups in certain parts of the United States. Many of the early companies were very proud, exclusive, influential, and competitive. They engaged in intense rivalries, which began with seeing which company could decorate its equipment most impressively.

The most expensively decorated hose rig was purchased by a group of New York businessmen who formed the Amity Hose Company No. 38. The rig cost $8,000 and they spent another $1,500 to paint its finest hardwood snow-white. They decked it out with silver fittings and pineapple-shaped red lamps.

New York's Engine Company No. 44 was composed of shipyard workers who acquired hand-carved figurines of two sabre-carrying Turks during a trip to Constantinople. They mounted the figurines on the engine in a way to suggest they were guarding a painting behind them of oriental beauties floating on clouds. On the backside of their engine, "Old Turk," beneath the painting of a refined American Lady, was the company motto emblazoned in gold leaf: "Extinguish One Flame and Cherish Another."[58]

The rivalries between the volunteers extended to interference with each other in responding to the fire scene and finally resulted in fights and riots, whether at a fire scene or off duty. Competition between volunteer fire companies became so intense that they would actually race to the fire scene and use all kinds of trickery to keep rival companies from beating them. It was considered a disgrace for a company to be passed by another company while pulling its rig to a fire. To prevent such disgrace, a slower company might run a zigzag path down the narrow streets, or, when the streets were rough or muddy, the volunteers would take to the sidewalk to gain speed. In so doing they would knock down pedestrians or anything else that got in their way.

An even greater disgrace than being passed en route to a fire was to be "washed." As engine companies lined up to relay water to a fire, each company would pump to the tub of the next engine in line. The faster the water came into the tub, the faster the volunteers would have to pump to keep their tub from overflowing. Tremendous competition resulted in engine companies endeavoring to overflow, or wash, the engine ahead of them while desperately trying to keep the company below from washing their engine. When a company was washed, it was not unusual for a black drape to be placed over the engine until the score was evened.[59]

Fistfights would often break out as companies battled for hydrants. History records that many buildings burned to the ground during these brawls, some of which turned into riots. In some cities the rivalry became so intense that thugs were hired to guard the hydrants. These "plug-uglies" would run ahead of their companies, and upon locating the best available hydrant, fend off all comers until their engine arrived.[60] Making matters even worse were rewards and bonuses offered by insurance companies to the first fire company to get water on the fire of an insured building. It is reported that in five years the "Old Honey Bee" of New York won $600.[61] Such winnings naturally increased the competition and rivalry. (In order to identify insured buildings, insurance companies placed their "mark" visibly on the structure. These marks, made of metal and wood, were very distinctive. For example, the Fire Association of Philadelphia used the outline of a wooden fire hydrant; and the Philadelphia Contributorship for the Insurance of Houses from Loss by Fire issued a mark showing clasped hands. As noted earlier, the Contributorship was founded in 1752 by Benjamin Franklin and became the first successful fire insurance company in America. Because of its distinctive fire mark it became known as the Hand-in-Hand Insurance Company.)

Rivalry, indiscretions, riots, and total disrespect for law resulted in citizen disenchantment with and even animosity toward the volunteers. Nevertheless, American cities were vulnerable to fire, and organized fire protection was essential. Until some means of reducing the number of firefighters required to combat a fire was developed, it was economically impossible to change over to a paid department.

The steam fire engine was to provide the answer to the citizens' dilemma. One steamer and a crew of three men—the driver, the stoker, and the engineer—were capable of producing as much water as six or more hand operated engines with 120 to 200 men on the brakes.

The Cincinnati experience[62]

A fire in a Cincinnati wood planing mill on a fall night in 1851 set into motion the events that were to lead to the eventual downfall of the volunteer fire service in large American cities. On that night Western Fire and Hose Company No. 3 and Washington Company No. 1 began fighting; soon ten more companies joined in. These companies were soon joined by friends from across the river in Covington, Kentucky, who sighted the flames and came to lend their aid. The mill burned to the ground as the thirteen companies rioted. The citizens were outraged. There had been 123 fires and several riots during the past year. Losses had doubled in one year and insurance companies had raised their rates. The citizens demanded that the city officials take corrective action. Though the 1,800 volunteers felt confident that the whole incident would be forgotten, such was not to be the case.

For quite some time leading citizens of Cincinnati had been intrigued with the possibilities of designing a steam-powered fire engine. If such a pumper could be developed, the number of firefighters required to apply water to a fire could be greatly reduced; a paid department could become a reality, and the major problems presented by the volunteers could be eliminated. The incident at the wood planing mill was the last straw. The city council would stand for no further destruction or outrages by the volunteers. Within a short time they signed a contract for the construction of a steam pumper with Latta and Shaw. The pumper was demonstrated on New Year's Day, 1853. This steamer became the first to enter the American fire service. It had many shortcomings. Even so, it impressed the city council so much that they decided it was now possible to eliminate the volunteers. A resolution to establish a salaried department was quickly passed. The volunteers mustered their members to fight the resolution, but the council was determined, and on 10 March 1853 they voted for a paid department. Thus, the Cincinnati volunteers destroyed their own organization by their irresponsible actions and became the first major volunteer department to be disbanded.

The practicality of the steam fire engine was soon recognized, and the volunteers in all major cities were on shaky ground. However, their disbandment and the establishment of salaried departments were to be delayed. On 12 April 1861 Fort Sumter was bombarded and this nation entered into a Civil War. Volunteer firefighters in every city dropped their battles against fire, rival companies, steamers, and paid departments to join in the battle between the North and the South. The war was to see the death of thousands of volunteers as well as the destruction of large portions of American cities and many pieces of fire apparatus. As the war ended, volunteers began returning home to rebuild their cities, reorganize their companies, and restore their equipment. It was disappointing to see the destruction that had occurred during the months of their service, but burned out areas were soon rebuilt and new apparatus acquired. But the days of the volunteers in the major cities were numbered.

The end of an era[63]

Although the process was slow at first, within a decade of the advent of the first steamer in Cincinnati steam fire pumpers were rapidly being acquired by major American cities. With the addition of these mighty pumpers, great numbers of volunteers were no longer required. Relieved from complete dependency on volunteers and tired of their abuses, one by one the major cities disbanded their volunteers and organized salaried departments.

It can be said that the burning of Phineas T. Barnum's American Museum on 13 July 1865 sent the New York volunteers out in a blaze of glory. For some years the officials in New York had been trying to eliminate the volunteers. But these companies had very strong political influence and all efforts to disband them met with defeat. Barnum's American Museum fire was a circus indeed: roaring flames, wild animals freed from their cages, screaming crowds, heroic rescues, and hundreds of spectators. But above all else on center stage were the volunteers on their hand pumpers pitted against the steamers. So obvious was the supremacy of the steam fire pumper that political influence could no longer save the volunteers. All their misdeeds, rivalries, and indiscretions had come home to roost. On 31 July 1865, just eighteen days after the Barnum fire, New York established a fully paid department, thus bringing to a close a colorful era of American history.

The new paid departments were organized on paramilitary lines, a system that continues today. Titles for officers took on military connotations after the Civil War. The title of company foreman became lieutenant or captain; over several companies was a battalion commander or chief. A division commander was over the battalion chiefs and above the division commander was the deputy chief. The highest position in the department was given the title of fire commissioner, fire chief, or chief engineer.

Within a short period after organization, the New York fire department had a paid membership of 500 firefighters manning eighty-nine steamers, eleven hook and ladders, and fifty-four hose companies. The firefighters worked a twenty-four hour shift for seven days a week, except for one twenty-four hour day off each month. The organizational framework was set for what was to become the prevailing mode of paid fire departments.

It should be emphasized, however, that 1 million dedicated volunteer firefighters are still providing fire protection for two-thirds of the nation's communities. They are quite different from their late nineteenth century predecessors. The typical volunteers of today are dedicated to the protection of life and property from fire and are well trained in suppression tactics, and their spirit of competition is directed toward improvement of self and of community.

Meeting today's challenge

Traditionally, the provision of fire protection in the United States has been a local responsibility. Officials in each of the hundreds of individual jurisdictions throughout the country have established the form, organization, and level of public fire protection determined to be adequate. This local responsibility has resulted in the establishment of approximately 21,000 call and volunteer fire companies supported by over 1 million personnel, and in the organization of approximately 1,600 fully paid fire departments with 185,000 members. The decision as to the form of organization (whether volunteer, part-paid or fully paid) has been influenced by the extent of the local fire problem and the availability of personnel—and by financial constraints.

Also central to the determination of alternative forms of fire protection is the consideration of the scope of activities to be designated as responsibilities of the fire department. Such functions as fire suppression, life safety and paramedical services, fire prevention, fire safety education, deteriorated building hazards, regional coordination, data development, and community relations can all be included in a fire department's responsibilities today (these activities are discussed elsewhere in this book).

Through the years of evolution, personnel in the American fire service have struggled to develop a fire defense capable of coping with the magnitude of the ever increasing fire potential. Vastly improved fire apparatus and equipment, along with improved organization and training, have greatly strengthened the fire attack, and the adoption of building and fire codes has succeeded in limiting the threat of fire spread. Furthermore, the fire service has received support for strengthening the public fire defense from the insurance industry, as the threat of increased premiums or potential for insurance savings has motivated public officials to make improvements.

But in spite of the advancements toward meeting the challenge of the American fire problem, the cost for public fire protection (particularly for firefighters' salaries and benefits) has escalated so rapidly that communities throughout the nation are being forced to reassess the costs and consider alternatives. For many communities the alternative selected has been to reduce manning levels of fire companies, usually below what fire officials believe is safe or adequate. Some communities with paid departments are considering the possibility of reducing the number of paid employees and replacing them with auxiliary or volunteer personnel. Other communities are strengthening mutual aid agreements or considering contracting for fire protection with neighboring cities or counties. Still other localities are exploring the possibility of forming larger fire protection districts or areas so as to take advantage of economies of scale and better distribution of fire companies.

Central to these various alternatives for furnishing fire protection are two fundamental questions that each community needs to answer: What is an adequate level of fire protection? And what is a reasonable community cost? These questions will be considered throughout this book, along with the potential of many management techniques and innovations that are useful to the fire manager.

Regardless of the approach taken, fire protection is a major consideration in every American city. The phenomenal growth of this nation, both in population and structural development, has presented American fire service agencies with fire protection problems of such magnitude that their capabilities to prevent large loss of life and property have often been overtaxed. The challenges that lie ahead in reducing the American fire problem are legion. But the most critical include: (1) educating the public in fire safety so as to remove the ignorance and indifference that presently exists; (2) establishing laws that will encourage built-in fire protection and will limit the fire potential to the protection capability of the fire service agency; (3) designing and building structures that are fire safe for occupants of all ages and physical conditions; (4) developing apparatus and equipment that will provide firefighters with adequate protection in hostile environments; (5) reducing the potential for fire and explosion in vehicles, ships, and planes that transport people and commodities; (6) developing means to better protect grasslands and forests through more effective laws, management, and fire control methods; and (7) reducing the flammability of products such as clothing, furnishings, interior finishes of buildings, and personal commodities with which the American public is in constant contact.

In addition to the above challenges, the fire service is also faced with many internal challenges including the need to: develop improved training techniques and delivery systems; improve fire attack methods and capabilities; increase fire prevention activities; improve management skills in the areas of planning, budgeting, organizing, leading, and evaluating; develop successful affirmative action programs; develop close cooperation between labor and management; and increase skills in labor relations. Suggestions for meeting the future challenges facing the American fire service managers are unfolded in the chapters that follow.

1   The resulting division into raw and cooked food was of fundamental importance in the development of human categories and systems of thought. See: Claude Levi-Strauss, *The Raw and the Cooked,* tr. John and Doreen Weightman (New York: Harper & Row, Publishers, 1969).

2   Science Service, *Fire* (New York/London: Nelson–Doubleday, Inc., and Odhams Books, Ltd., 1969), pp. 14–15.

3   *Encyclopedia Americana,* 1975, vol. 2, p. 241.

4   Joseph Campbell, *The Masks of God: Primitive Mythology* (New York: Penguin Books, 1976), p. 361.

5   Ibid., p. 395.

6   Ibid.

7   *Encyclopedia Americana,* vol. 2, p. 242.

8   Ibid.

9   Ibid.

10 Science Service, *Fire,* pp. 32–34.

11 *Encyclopedia Americana,* vol. 2, p. 242.

12 J. G. Frazer, *The Golden Bough,* 3rd ed. rev., 12 vols. (London: Macmillan and Co., Ltd., 1925). The Index references are found in vol. 12, pp. 270–72.

13 Gaston Bachelard, *The Psychoanalysis of Fire,* tr. Alan C. M. Ross (Boston: Beacon Press, 1964); Jean-Pierre Bayard, *Le Feu* (Paris: Ernest Flammarion, 1958).

14 For a broad survey of mythology, including references to fire, see: Campbell, *The Masks of God: Primitive Mythology;* Joseph Campbell, *The Masks of God: Occidental Mythology* (New York: Viking Press, 1964); and Joseph Campbell, *The Masks of God: Oriental Mythology* (New York: Viking Press, 1962). For sun myths, see: William Tyler Olcott, *Myths of the Sun* (New York: Capricorn Books, 1967); and Bayard, *Le Feu,* especially Chapter 17, "Les Feux dans la Religion et dans L'Inde," pp. 213–24.

15 Robert Graves, *The Greek Myths,* vol. 1, rev. ed. (Baltimore: Penguin Books, 1969), pp. 144–45. For a discussion of fire theft in mythology generally, see: Campbell, *The Masks of God: Primitive Mythology,* pp. 277–81.

16 *Encyclopedia Americana,* vol. 2, p. 242. For general studies of totemic associations with animals, including fire-related aspects, see: Sigmund Freud, *Totem and Taboo,* tr. A. A. Brill (New York: Vintage Books, 1946); and Claude Levi-Strauss, *Totemism,* tr. Rodney Needham (Boston: Beacon Press, 1963).

17 Freud, *Totem and Taboo,* p. 39.

18 Ibid., p. 58.

19 Edith Hamilton, *Mythology* (New York: New American Library, 1971), p. 35.

20 Mary Douglas, *Purity and Danger* (New York: Frederick Praeger and Sons, 1966), pp. 154–55.

21 Henry Thompson Rowell, *Rome in the Augustan Age* (Norman, Okla.: University of Oklahoma Press, 1962), p. 116; Rodolfo Lanciani, *Ancient Rome* (New York: Houghton Mifflin, 1888), p. 221.

22 Lanciani, *Ancient Rome,* p. 221.

23 Ibid., p. 222; Rowell, *Rome in the Augustan Age,* p. 116.

24 Robert E. O'Bannon, *Building Department Administration* (Whittier, Calif.: International Conference of Building Officials, 1973), p. 1/8.

25 Ibid., pp. 1/8–9.

26 Ibid., p. 1/2.

27 Except where otherwise indicated, the text under this heading draws on the following book: Paul Robert Lyons, *Fire in America!* (Boston: National Fire Protection Association, 1976), pp. 1–9. This material is used with the permission of the publisher: the National Fire Protection Association, Boston.

28 Paul C. Ditzel, *Fire Engines, Firefighters* (New York: Crown Publishers, Inc., 1976), p. 16.

29 Ibid., p. 18.

30 Unless otherwise indicated, the material under this heading draws on the following book: Ditzel, *Fire Engines, Firefighters,* pp. 18–19. This material is used with the permission of the publisher: Crown Publishers, Inc., New York.

31 Lyons, *Fire in America!* p. 6.

32 O'Bannon, *Building Department Administration,* p. 1/3.

33 Lyons, *Fire in America!* p. 7.

34 Ditzel, *Fire Engines, Firefighters,* p. 29.

35 Ibid.

36 Ibid.

37 Much of this section is excerpted, with some editorial changes, from: Lyons, *Fire in America!* Chapters 2–4. This material is excerpted with the permission of the publisher: the National Fire Protection Association, Boston.

38 A. L. Todd, *A Spark Lighted in Portland: The Record of the National Board of Fire Underwriters* (New York: McGraw-Hill Book Company, 1966), p. 12.

39 Lyons, *Fire in America!* passim.

40 Much of this section is excerpted, with some editorial changes, from: Lyons, *Fire in America!* Chap-

ter 5. This material is excerpted with the permission of the publisher: the National Fire Protection Association, Boston.

41 Todd, *A Spark Lighted in Portland,* p. 44.

42 Ibid., p. 45.

43 Ibid., p. 46.

44 John V. Morris, *Fires and Firefighters* (Boston: Little, Brown and Company, 1955), p. 383.

45 For background on two of the most serious of such twentieth century fires, see: Leon Stein, *The Triangle Fire* (New York: Lippincott, 1962); Corinne J. Naden, *The Triangle Shirtwaist Fire* (New York: Franklin Watts, 1971); Paul Benzaquin, *Fire in Boston's Cocoanut Grove* (Boston: Branden Press, 1967); National Fire Protection Association, *The Cocoanut Grove Night Club Fire* (Boston: National Fire Protection Association, 1943).

46 National Commission on Fire Prevention and Control, *America Burning* (Washington, D.C.: Government Printing Office, 1973), p. 1.

47 Ibid., pp. 3–4.

48 Ibid., p. 2.

49 The major part of this section is excerpted, with some editorial changes, from: Ditzel, *Fire Engines, Firefighters,* Chapters 3, 4, 7, 12, 15, and 17. This material is used with the permission of the publisher: Crown Publishers, Inc., New York.

50 Lyons, *Fire in America!* p. 12.

51 Ibid.

52 Ditzel, *Fire Engines, Firefighters,* p. 21.

53 Ibid., pp. 22, 23.

54 Ibid., pp. 29, 31.

55 Paul C. Ditzel, "The Rowdy Early Days of the Volunteer Fire Departments," *The American Legion Magazine,* April 1971, p. 12.

56 Ditzel, *Fire Engines, Firefighters,* p. 29.

57 Lyons, *Fire in America!* p. 99.

58 Ditzel, *Fire Engines, Firefighters,* pp. 53, 60.

59 Ibid., p. 68.

60 Ibid., p. 66.

61 Ibid., p. 62.

62 A major part of this section is excerpted, with some editorial changes, from: Ditzel, *Fire Engines, Firefighters,* Chapter 12. This material is used with permission of the publisher: Crown Publishers, Inc., New York.

63 A major part of this section is excerpted, with some editorial changes, from: Ditzel, *Fire Engines, Firefighters,* Chapter 14. This material is used with permission of the publisher: Crown Publishers, Inc., New York.

Management options in fire protection

The preceding chapter has outlined the main features of the background to and basis of contemporary fire protection. The present chapter examines some of the strategic roles or management options open to decision makers (both inside and outside of the fire department) concerned with fire protection. (These roles will be further examined in Chapter 3 with respect to the management of the fire department itself and in Chapter 4 with regard to the roles of other organizations involved in fire protection, from the private sector to state and federal government.)

The present chapter begins with an introductory overview which discusses relevant aspects of the fiscal and political climate of contemporary fire protection and poses some basic questions that local government decision makers need to answer. A framework for examining management options is then presented. The remainder of the chapter discusses such options in detail. First to be assessed are options based on demonstrated organizational performance. This is followed by an analysis (central to the chapter) of management options in ways of organizing fire protection services. Next, there is a preview of the management options regarding fire insurance, fire prevention, and master planning—three subjects that are treated in greater detail in later chapters. A brief summary concludes the chapter.

Three general points should be made at the outset. First, the options described are illustrative rather than prescriptive. For example, a possible systems approach to organizational structure is introduced and developed: it is *not* suggested that such an approach is the one right way for managers; it *is* suggested that the problems addressed by such an approach are common to all fire protection decision makers and it is hoped that the discussion presented will serve as a point of departure.

The second point is that it is realized that fire protection in the United States today involves a vast range of small, medium-sized, and large communities; a mosaic of climatic and environmental backgrounds; a multiplicity of organizational forms (in which the widespread role of the volunteer department should not be overlooked); and a great variety of socioeconomic, legal, and political contexts. While any discussion of management options needs to be broad enough to cover the complexities of operation in larger jurisdictions, it is hoped that selective versions of the options introduced will be found equally workable in the managerial environment of smaller communities.[1]

The third point is that, as has already been noted, the following discussion of management options is not intended to preempt the detailed discussions found in later chapters but rather to point to the basic principles common to a number of separate functional areas.

The key questions

In the late 1970s Americans were learning that public problems could not be effectively solved simply by pouring dollars into new programs. In fact, a wave of opposition was rising against increased spending at all levels of government.[2]

The governmental climate

The growing opposition to increased spending for public service delivery systems is of deep concern to local officials. Fire chiefs in particular find themselves in a paradoxical situation. The fire service is under pressure to upgrade the level of service while at the same time the fire chief is told to hold the line on the taxes needed to pay for improved or expanded services.

City administrators and fire officials are recognizing increasingly that traditional methods of service delivery are no longer affordable. The same officials also know that fire protection services cannot be abandoned. Fire safety is a primary function of local government and fires and fire losses are a continuing problem.

The managers of public fire safety need to examine carefully fresh approaches to the service delivery function. A fundamental question then emerges: How can the fire protection delivery system meet the standards of efficiency and effectiveness demanded by service conscious, fiscally aware citizens? This question prompts another, which is this chapter's theme: What are the options available to local governments in the area of fire prevention, fire protection, and emergency service delivery as we enter the 1980s? This matter is taken up in the discussion that follows.

The public administration perspective

Service delivery options should be viewed today within the broad context of public administration. The relevance of sets of options needs to be examined with regard to public acceptance and public opinion. This is not new. James Madison, in *The Federalist Papers*, wrote that valued occurrences which may be good for some can be detrimental to others.[3] Therefore, beyond considering the mixed bag of advantages and disadvantages or benefits and costs of any public fire service option, decision makers should ask themselves the following four pertinent questions (and should then ensure that the options adequately satisfy the answers):

1. What is the level of risk that a municipality is willing to accept? This issue should be addressed from both a life safety and a property safety perspective. The answer represents a formulated policy based on both citizen and professional expectations.
2. Who benefits and who is deprived under each option set? It is important to determine how a given fire service delivery system will affect property owners, various socioeconomic levels, specific sectors of the community, and potential life safety problems. In other words, the degree of social equity provided by any option is an important concern to the decision maker.
3. What are the scope, objectives, and methods of providing a fire safety delivery system? The scope and level of fire services exert a wide-ranging influence over the functions of fire protection, fire prevention, fire suppression, rescue services, emergency medical care, life support services, and large-scale disaster services.
4. On the basis of the political climate, the economic constraints, and the legal restrictions, what are the realistic sets of options that could be implemented in a given community? Evaluations under this framework should identify both limitations and opportunities for program achievement. Also of signal importance are possible future courses of action intended to change or modify decisions that might limit the achievement of structured objectives.

A wider mission

Management options in fire protection might also be framed in the context of an emerging theory best described as a movement towards a "new public administration." H. George Frederickson stresses that this new public administration is nothing more than a reweaving of the fabric of administration so that a new design becomes more readily apparent.[4] According to Frederickson, the "new" emphasis is not only concerned with the efficient and effective management of administrative resources but is committed also to developing the means of achieving social equity and a better quality of life.[5] Functional service managers in municipalities are directed to be more publicly perceptive, client-oriented, and normative in their awareness of and actions toward the administration of urban affairs. Fire service options in the future will need to address the issues of improving the quality of life and reducing the risk for those being served. But again, it should be stressed that such a mission will take place in a difficult political and fiscal climate.

A framework for examining management options

Experience has shown that, to be effective, management options in fire protection should be set in the context of an evaluation framework of one kind or another. The framework can be prepared by breaking down the vague concept of fire protection into elements that can be more easily dealt with and analyzed. Management options can then be appraised with respect to the known or perceived impact of each of the defined elements or structured groups of elements. Issues of efficiency and effectiveness—the classical management yardsticks— can be related to these elements as well.

Time intervals as a measure

Swersey and Ignall indicate that a logical evaluation framework can be obtained by considering the time between the start of a fire and its extinguishment. They establish the following sequence pattern:

At some point in time a fire starts. After some time the fire is detected and reported. The alarm is processed and fire-fighting units are directed to respond to the alarm. Some time later these units arrive. Finally, the fire is extinguished and the units become available to serve other alarms.[6]

These authors further establish the following six evaluation intervals between the time junctures, or time lines, given above:

[These intervals are:] (1) the time before the fire, (2) the time from occurrence to detection, (3) the time from detection to dispatch of units, (4) the time from dispatch to arrival of units, (5) the time from arrival to extinguishment, and (6) the time after the fire. Some policy-related research areas can be identified with a particular interval; others cut across several intervals.[7]

Figure 2–1 shows the time factors, time intervals, and policy issues raised by Swersey and Ignall. This figure may be examined in terms of management options in fire protection. For example, the basic question in this chapter may be rephrased as: What options are available to local government that will have a positive effect on the interval structure?

The options open to decision makers may be structured and evaluated through use of the framework in Figure 2–1. For example managers can ask: What options have the highest payoffs in terms of reducing the time line while remaining economically feasible? Related questions might be: What options contain the greatest leverage for reducing fire losses? Do these options derive from improved fire prevention, early detection of fires, sprinklers, or fire department operations? The balance of this chapter will consider some of the potential options that are usually available to fire service managers within the interval framework structure. However, to avoid extensive duplication of material and concepts appearing in later chapters, the primary focus will be on fire service management options in Interval 1: before the fire starts.

Operational definitions

An examination of our evaluation framework requires the use of terms that need to be further defined. The definitions given immediately below were prepared

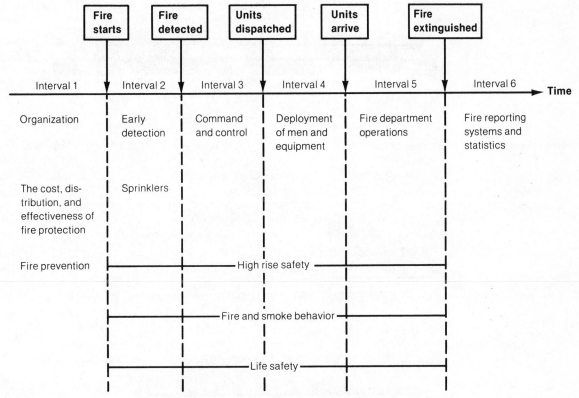

Figure 2–1 Evaluation framework for management options. (Source: Arthur J. Swersey, Edward J. Ignall et al., *Fire Protection and Local Government: An Evaluation of Policy-Related Research,* New York City–Rand Institute Report R–1813–NSF, Santa Monica, Calif.: Rand Corporation, 1975, p. 4.)

by the Research Triangle Institute (RTI), the International City Management Association (ICMA), and the National Fire Protection Association (NFPA) for the *Municipal Fire Service Workbook*.[8]

The *organization of fire service delivery* refers to "the set of patterned, public activities performed within a designated area to prevent unwanted ignition and to control and extinguish fires when they occur." This definition "assumes that the first division of activities in public fire protection is between *fire prevention* and *fire suppression*."[9] On the basis of this definition, the term *fire protection*, as used in the chapter title, connotes the incorporation of activities concerned with fire prevention and fire suppression.

Prevention is the attempt "to decrease the chances of unwanted ignition and, to some extent, to limit the spread of fire by methods which are independent of actions taken after ignition occurs."[10] The workbook goes on to state:

Fire prevention activities involve those services of the fire department such as public education, control of flammable liquids, in-service inspections, fire cause investigations, and many others. In support of the fire department prevention activities, building department prevention activities include:

(a) the required review of building plans,
(b) construction inspections,
(c) building code maintenance inspections, and
(d) other regulatory functions and incentives to private investment to provide a fire-safe environment, regardless of which level of government or which governmental agency is responsible for providing them.

Thus, fire prevention is taken to be a community-based activity rather than the service of a specific department or agency.[11]

Suppression is the set or array of actions begun after ignition and designed to limit loss of life and of property. It covers the process from detection and spread or reporting of uncontrolled fire through extinguishment of the fire. "Fire suppression constitutes those activities which are traditionally understood as fire protection service delivery," the workbook states, "whether they be carried out by a municipal or county fire department, or an incorporated volunteer or private, profit-making company providing service under contract." The workbook defines suppression-related activities as "recruitment, training, and dispatch functions."[12]

Another term that merits definition is *emergency services delivery system,* which includes in its meaning organizational operations, duties, and activities concerned with direct public emergency services which emphasize one or more of the following functions: fire suppression, emergency rescue, emergency medical services, life support services (paramedics), and disaster control. In the broad sense, functions of the emergency service delivery system are not limited to emergency services. Depending upon municipal or county objectives and the level of service implemented, members of the emergency services delivery system may be assigned duties associated with the total fire protection operations.

Variables that can be analyzed and evaluated

To be effective, management options in fire protection should be related to a select group of "city" variables. As a point of departure, three main variables can be used to facilitate the effective outcomes of adopted options. These three variables also provide consistency with the organizational evaluation controls used in the *Municipal Fire Service Workbook.* The controlled variables used in the workbook are: (1) size of population protected by the fire service, as community size is directly related to defined levels of fire service activity; (2) personnel composition of a fire department, as the proportion of paid to volunteer staff has an obvious effect on department expenditures; and (3) city type of which there are the following three: *center, ring,* and *fringe,* which indicate the degree of urbanization and the location in the metropolitan region of the community.[13] The workbook presents the following definitions of the city types:

1. *Center* cities are defined as urban areas with populations greater than 50,000; generally they have greater population density, high-rise structures, and fully paid fire departments.
2. *Ring* cities are communities in an urbanized area that border center cities.
3. *Fringe* cities are communities located in a metropolitan county but outside an urbanized area. [Figure 2–2] illustrates the relative size of these three city types and their general location in the metropolitan region.[14]

In the remainder of this chapter these variables are used for purposes of comparative and contrasting analysis.

Management options based on demonstrated organizational performance

How can the categories and variables just discussed be used as tools in planning and implementing management options, particularly in the area of organization? The evidence seems to indicate that the type of fire service organization that

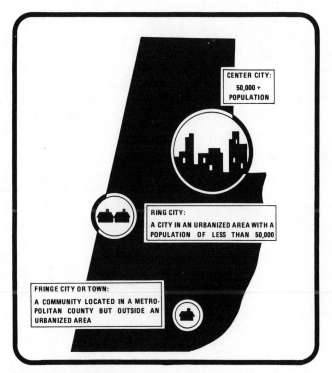

Figure 2–2   Three types of cities and their general location in a metropolitan area. (Source: Research Triangle Institute, International City Management Association, and National Fire Protection Association, *Municipal Fire Service Workbook*, Washington, D.C.: Government Printing Office, 1977, p. 6.)

exists and the population categories serviced by the respective department types appear to be important considerations in defining management options for fire protection. The *Municipal Fire Service Workbook* points to great differences among jurisdictions in total organizational performance (TOP).[15] The discussion in this section details the research findings and analyses reported in the workbook.[16] The findings are divided into three population groups: (1) towns of less than 5,000 population; (2) cities of 5,000 to 25,000 population; and (3) cities with over 25,000 population. These categories exhibit marked differences in performance characteristics and provide benchmarks for illustrating fire service performance delivery capability.

Towns of less than 5,000 population

Towns with populations of less than 5,000 persons constituted almost 50 percent of the fire service delivery organizations included in the study sample. The following observations that were made from the array of data present an interesting insight into service delivery conditions. These insights will be used to identify certain management options that are available to fire service managers who are responsible for the protection of similar areas. The following two parallel conditions are in evidence in these small communities:

1. The incidence of fire is disproportionately high in this category of communities
2. The property loss per capita is also relatively higher than that sustained by larger towns and cities.

The factors affecting these conditions appear to be the following:

1. In general, the small town grouping has less land area to protect, less housing density per square mile, and more housing which is in relatively good condition. However, as low population density and good housing quality are characteristically associated with a low hazard profile, the general physical characteristics of these small localities do not seem to be determining factors for either the high incident rate or the severity rate they experience.
2. There appears to be nothing in the social character of small towns to explain the high incidence and severity rates. Many of the small towns sampled are inhabited by relatively homogeneous, preponderantly middle-class populations.
3. The time intervals from alarm to arrival on the scene are longer for fire departments in small towns, partly because of the overwhelming proportion of communities served solely by volunteer personnel.
4. Fewer basic resources in terms of staff, time, and money per capita are allocated by small communities to deal with unwanted fire. However, a key study finding is that a greater level of effort, in terms of training, staffing, and departmental expenditures as these activities are presently constituted, does not appear to reduce either the incident rate or the severity rate (amount of property loss) experienced by small towns as a result of uncontrolled fires.
5. The small town group provides few fire prevention services, and 60 percent of the surveyed towns have no building or fire prevention code in effect. The rate of fire incidence is lower for those towns that have at least *one code* in effect. Also, at the community population level, the total number of fire prevention activities is *strongly* associated with lower fire incidence.
6. Of special note is the fact that if at least some of the fire department staff are paid personnel the likelihood is increased that some prevention functions are performed.
7. On the training side, only 36 percent of the small towns under 2,000 population and 45 percent of those between 2,000 and 5,000 require firefighter recruit training. For those that do have training programs, whether provided by the town itself or by another level of government, the average number of hours spent in training is less than half of that in the larger jurisdictions.
8. Furthermore, while less revenue is required to maintain a predominantly volunteer force, these smaller towns do not typically invest the resultant savings in personnel costs to provide prevention services (prevention is used here in its broadest sense).

9. The savings in operational expenses which result from a volunteer fire service delivery system for fire protection at the "village" level do not offset the higher loss from fire which is suffered by incident and severity levels of fire reported in these small towns. Overall, the total cost of the fire problem borne by the residents of the smaller communities is considerably higher than in the other population categories studied.
10. Finally, small towns which invest proportionately more for fire prevention activities have a lower rate of fire incidence and sustain a smaller loss from the incidents that are reported.

Cities of 5,000 to 25,000 population

This is an important population grouping which fire service managers should study carefully in terms of performance characteristics, as cities of 5,000 to 25,000 population, taken as a whole, tend to have fewer fires than other city size category and also tend to have the lowest median total loss per capita. The reasons for this observation are important to the effective selection and implementation of management options. The total organizational performance characteristics for this population grouping are the following:

1. Those fire protection jurisdictions that deliver more prevention services have fewer fires.
2. Those jurisdictions that provide their own fire investigation service are more likely to have fewer fires than those that depend on other levels of government for all or part of this service.
3. Fire protection jurisdictions located in states that have adopted one of the recognized model building codes have fewer fires than those in states without such a code.
4. The range of prevention services provided by the fire department (i.e., public education, inspection, and enforcement) does *not* have the expected beneficial effect of reducing fires. A closer examination of this condition reveals that fire departments in cities of this size category are less likely to provide firefighter training in fire prevention functions, and those that do so devote fewer hours to training in this area than do larger jurisdictions. This may explain part of this puzzling relationship.
5. Jurisdictions with a larger number of firefighters, regardless of type of department, have fewer fires.
6. Cities that are stable and relatively homogeneous, with few very rich or very poor, have fewer fires.
7. Cold or windy weather is not associated with higher frequency of fires in this population range, although these factors may influence the severity of fires. However, the greater the amount of precipitation (rain or snow) is, the higher the average losses are likely to be.
8. While the length of the total training program seems to have no direct beneficial effect on reducing losses in jurisdictions in this population range, the number of hours spent in training in the nature of fire and firefighting tactics is associated with lower average fire losses.
9. The greater the market value of the property in cities of this size is, the higher the losses are likely to be.
10. The higher the proportion of full-time paid firefighters is in cities of this size, the lower the average dollars of property loss are.

Cities with over 25,000 population

The total organizational performance characteristics revealed by the workbook authors would seem to indicate that specific factors influence the various performance scores in municipalities with over 25,000 population. The level and functional involvement of the fire service delivery system in cities of this size appear to have a different impact on the fire problem from that found in the smaller towns and cities. The identification of these differences and their potential impacts are given below.

1. A 10 percent increase in fire prevention activities is associated with almost a 10 percent decrease in the incidence of fire in the larger cities in the sample. Prevention activities are noted to include building inspections, code enforcement, and building plan review.

2. With respect to building inspection activities, three observations are pertinent. First, the greater the population is, the higher is the cost of building inspection activities. Second, the larger the area covered by the fire protection delivery system is, the higher the total inspection costs are. Third, when the fire department and the building department both perform building inspection functions, the community's costs for building inspection salaries increase. Therefore, the population size, the service delivery area, and the duplication of inspection services all have an escalating effect on additional costs to the local building inspection program.

3. High levels of demand are associated with high expenditures for suppression activities regardless of the type of fire department protecting the area. In other words, the number of fires experienced by a community dictates the level of demand, which in turn produces a need for more suppression services and increased expenditures for these services.

4. Expenditures for fire suppression activities are directly related to the level of fire loss. As the fire loss increases in a community, the level of expenditures for suppression tends to increase in response.

5. The effect of tall buildings has a directly related impact on suppression costs. This appears to be due to the costs of specialized equipment.

6. The existence of unions in departments with fully paid personnel increases personnel expenditures by about 9 to 10 percent. An increase in expenditures for personnel, however, increases the overall cost of suppression activities by only 5 to 7 percent.

7. Fully paid fire departments seem to operate under conditions of increasing returns to scale. That is, while the total number of fires rises in communities with fully paid departments, the cost per fire in the community tends to decline. A 10 percent increase in the number of fires in communities with paid fire departments is associated with only a 3 to 4 percent increase in suppression expenditures.

It should be noted that all of the above statements concern activities or actions within the control of local fire service managers and community administrators. These conditions can be used to identify potential program options for fire service managers. These options are reviewed below following a brief discussion of the relationship of organization to population in the larger jurisdictions (over 25,000).

Some community characteristics exist which contribute to a community's fire problem but which are beyond the control of decision makers. These characteristics must also be taken into account in planning and executing optional fire protection programs. The study analysis on which the workbook is based has revealed the following major influences on a community's fire experience in the larger jurisdictions:

1. Population: the demand for fire protection services parallels the rate of population growth of a community. A municipality which anticipates a 10

percent increase in its population over the next decade could anticipate an 8 to 10 percent increase in the number of calls for emergency fire service.

2. Climate: the number of days during which a community experiences high winds and temperatures below zero degrees Fahrenheit has a directly related impact on the increase of fire incidence.

3. Type of construction: cities which have a large number of structures built before 1939 register a higher rate of loss from fire.

4. Density: housing density has an influence on fire incidence, but it is relatively small.

5. Socioeconomic factors: fire incident rates increase in proportion to the number of residents on welfare rolls.

6. Residential stability: residential instability appears to be the community characteristic most consistently associated with whether a town has one type of fire department organization or another. If there is a great deal of residential stability in a municipality, its residents are likely to maintain a volunteer fire department. As residential turnover increases, residents tend to add some call or paid personnel to their largely volunteer departments. Finally, in towns with considerable residential turnover, residents appear to prefer a fully paid department to a partly paid or a volunteer department.

A *summary of the research conclusions*

The above information from the *Municipal Fire Service Workbook* might cause managers to conclude that this research points out some important considerations for improving both the loss experience and the overall social conditions in towns, municipalities, and cities, regardless of size. The stress is on what is important in assuring a safer community.

The following points summarize the principal factors that should be considered in reorganizing a fire service delivery system. These considerations can serve as a basis for future options.

1. Increased investments in fire prevention activities related to building plan review, inspections, and code enforcement have a positive payoff in reducing the number of incidents and lessening the severity of those incidents that do occur.

2. Cities that have adopted strong building codes have significantly lower per capita losses.

3. The training of fire personnel in fire prevention, in inspection work, and in fire suppression management (strategy and tactics) results in lower losses for the protection area.

4. High value areas experience high losses. Possibly the shift to internal protection (i.e., sprinklers) will reverse this trend.

5. High levels of fire suppression demand are accompanied by high levels of expenditures. This is counterproductive to the aims introduced at the beginning of this chapter. High demand levels may require a shift of responsibility for those losses to the private sector through early warning detection and built-in fire suppression capability.

6. The more stable the neighborhood environment is, the smaller the fire problem is and the lower the cost requirements are for the fire service delivery system. The fire service manager may find it advantageous to work with other community service delivery systems (education and police) and community neighborhood groups to improve social stability and cohesiveness around the fire station.

The organization of fire protection services and management options

This topic involves two important considerations. One revolves around the type of organization providing the emergency service delivery system; the other focuses on the structure of the organization. Each consideration is reviewed below.

Type of organization

Swersey and Ignall note that large cities are usually protected by fully paid "professional" fire departments.[17] The cities under 10,000 in population are usually protected by a volunteer type fire service, although there are some exceptions to this general observation. Between the small volunteer fire departments and the large paid fire departments there is a growing number of combination type fire departments, usually about 75 percent volunteer and 25 percent paid. In addition, a few cities have arranged for private companies to supply fire protection services. Some political jurisdictions have merged their police and fire departments into a consolidated arrangement of public service, and some jurisdictions are using regional consolidations.

Combination type fire departments Organizational options that are most readily available to fire protection managers appear to focus on the combination paid and volunteer services. Arthur Bennett examined the fire protection benefits (if any) offered by sixteen independent fire departments in Montgomery County, Maryland, that included volunteer departments, paid departments, and combination departments. Using several performance measures, Bennett concluded that in general the paid and combination departments perform equally well and both perform significantly better than volunteer departments. Most important was the finding that combination fire departments provide generally equivalent fire protection services at a lower cost than the fully paid departments.[18]

This research suggests that the high performance of the combination departments results from the quick response of the paid firefighters and the large manpower resource provided by the volunteer members.

There is one interesting optional consideration with combination type fire departments that is not identified in the research findings. Some combination fire departments, especially in the suburbs and dormitory communities, are essentially manned by paid personnel during the day and rely on volunteers at night. A properly organized and dedicated volunteer service at night can provide both a quick turnout time and an adequate complement of personnel. This can be provided by personnel who are assigned to the stations for the night period. It should be noted that the Insurance Services Office (ISO) grading schedule evaluates volunteers on an equal basis with paid personnel on the night shift where the attendance is regular and adequate records are kept of this activity. (Options concerning fire insurance are discussed later in this chapter.)

Public versus private fire departments In a doctoral dissertation, R. S. Ahlbrandt takes the view that it is not necessary for the public sector of local government to produce the fire service delivery system. Ahlbrandt contends that the benefits from competing business interests will inherently produce a service more responsive to customer desires and also more efficient. To test his hypothesis, Ahlbrandt compared several publicly supported fire departments with one privately operated fire department. Using data from the states of Arizona and Washington, this investigator found that the per capita costs of a given level of fire protection were about the same in both states. He then examined the cost for Scottsdale, Arizona, where Louis A. Witzeman (president, Rural/Metro

Fire Protection Company) was operating a private firm to supply fire suppression services. The cost for the service delivery in Scottsdale was found to be significantly lower.[19]

Swersey and Ignall reviewed this research and made the following observation:

One case is not conclusive, but Ahlbrandt's approach is reasonable for judging the efficiency of different means of supplying fire protection. The Scottsdale firm serves several adjacent communities, which highlights another possible advantage of private suppliers: They may be able to change the scale of their operations to meet changing demand and to find the most efficient level of production more easily than can publicly operated fire departments.[20]

Consolidation of emergency services   One of the major goals of public administration is the attainment of the desired service level at the least cost. The efficiency doctrine has led a number of cities to explore and adopt fire and police department consolidation.[21] Consolidation efforts appear to have followed one of two patterns. One is the merging of the fire and police administrations into a single public safety unit. The other involves the dual training of line personnel to perform some or all of the respective service delivery functions. It is also claimed that the potential economies of a larger organization and the minimization of fire suppression personnel on standby time lead to greater efficiency.

The question of consolidation of fire and police functions as a viable option for fire protection management rests with the need or pressure to reorganize the service delivery system. Reorganization of a fire department consists essentially of changing the management responsibilities and the functional task assignments. Accounting, purchasing, and maintenance are fairly independent of the type of service, so consolidation would eliminate duplication of these tasks. However, tasks specialized by the type of service (i.e., fire suppression) are not so easily integrated into an alternative specialized service whether it be on an individual or a group basis.

The *Municipal Fire Service Workbook* refers to a consolidated organization as a *public safety organization,* or PSO. With respect to overall characteristics, fire prevention and suppression activities, and involvement in emergency medical services, the following observations are noted in the workbook:

Overall, on the average, the 20 PSO's:

- protect smaller places than non-consolidated, mostly paid departments,
- do not protect central cities or heavily industrialized areas,
- experience fewer fire incidents but record slightly higher property losses per fire than comparable non-PSO's. . .
- experience fewer civilian injuries and deaths per fire but more firefighter injuries and deaths, and
- have a lower departmental budget both per capita and per dollar value of the property protected.

With respect to *prevention activities,* compared with non-PSO departments, the PSO's examined generally:

- provide more prevention services,
- have prevention services consolidated within various city departments, not within the fire department,
- demonstrate more building inspection department responsibility,
- are more likely to be involved in home-safety inspection activity,
- spend less on fire prevention presentations,
- give fewer fire prevention presentations,
- spend less on average total building inspector salaries, and
- have a lower incidence of arson, as well as more authority to prosecute arson cases.

As to *suppression activities,* on the average, the PSO's examined:

- have smaller scale mutual aid agreements,
- have fewer hours devoted to firefighting skills,
- spend more in training salaries, and
- spend more in communications salaries. . . .

With respect to emergency medical [and rescue] services [EMRS], on the average, the PSO's:

- have fewer personnel trained in EMRS techniques,
- handle all emergency calls,
- spend less on EMRS.[22]

While the pros and cons of police–fire consolidation will continue to be debated, as of the later 1970s only a small percentage of communities were serviced by these combined units.

Regional consolidation The political boundaries between established fire districts present a management problem to many fire districts. The issue of the nearest fire company responding to an incident even though it is in a different political jurisdiction has generated considerable interest. The issues of mutual aid and automatic aid arrangements appear to be growing between contiguous fire districts and are critical for meeting the resource requirements of large-scale disasters. Political boundaries may also fade away under the conditions of fire service delivery consolidation where individual towns, communities, and cities join together in different arrangements to provide unified fire service delivery. This consolidation approach to fire protection organization has the effect of reducing many of the problems associated with spillovers.

Regional consolidation is both an important and a viable option for fire protection management. Swersey and Ignall indicate that the regional consolidation of two or more fire departments has the potential advantages of: (1) trimming the duplication of administration; (2) centralizing the dispatching and communications network; (3) significantly improving response times, because units would be dispatched from the stations closest to the incident even if they are not in the same city; and (4) improving the capacity to respond to a crisis of fixed proportions, as the consolidated fire department would have more resources and specialized equipment than any individual fire department.[23] Related to the last mentioned advantage is the notion that supplemental field units for additional alarms can be supplied to a given focal point rapidly, as required, avoiding the time lags that have occurred in the past. Furthermore, it may become possible to eliminate one or more fire companies without reducing overall effectiveness. It should also be noted that consolidation, properly accomplished, may have a positive impact on ISO grading in the consolidated district by changing and improving the factors that are used to determine the insurance rate.[24] (It should be noted, as well, that advantages can be identified for consolidating some functions without necessarily fusing fire and police departments completely.)

Regional consolidation raises a basic organizational question. Can the objectives and interests of public fire safety be served better by introducing a broader organizational base? The fire service literature gives many examples of the shortcomings of attempts to retain public fire safety as an entity within an incorporated city, town, or municipality. A number of authorities have pointed to the advantages of elimination of overlapping, unification of fire prevention codes and fire prevention practices, economies of scale, more and better qualified manpower, and a broader tax base.

When analyzing management options for public fire safety it is important to consider specific problems associated with continued operation of public fire protection at the lowest level of local government. The restrictive nature of local autonomy can be summarized as follows:

1. The financial resources for public fire safety simply may not be sufficient to achieve the desired levels of public fire safety.
2. Manpower and equipment resources may be totally inadequate for a serious fire situation.
3. The manpower talent may not be available to provide the associated technical services needed to carry out the established fire service objectives.
4. Tied indirectly to the financial problem is the possible inability to provide a viable fire prevention program, a maintenance program, a command–control–communications system, research facilities, organized public relations, and data processing needs.
5. The talent required for the efficient and effective administration, management, and operations of public fire safety may simply not be available.[25]

The concept of providing public fire safety on a multijurisdictional base needs to be carefully examined as a management option. The fire protection manager must be aware of the two requisites for providing desired levels of public fire safety: adequate resources and responsiveness to local interests. One approach to the satisfaction of these requisites is to enlarge the local geographical base to a county administrative and service level. A few county fire departments already exist in the United States. One of the largest and best recognized of these is in Los Angeles County, California. Other examples of countywide departments, either in administration or line operations, or in both, include: Baltimore, Anne Arundel, Montgomery, and Prince George's Counties in Maryland; Prince William, Chesterfield, Henrico, Fairfax, and Arlington Counties in Virginia; and Wyoming County (Rural) in New York.

The advantages that may be realized with regional or county forms of organization include, according to William E. Clark, the aforementioned broader tax base and elimination or reduction of overlapping and duplication of services, as well as centralized purchasing and maintenance, centralized communications systems, and centralized fire prevention and service training programs.[26]

Despite these management pluses for more efficient fire protection, Swersey and Ignall point out that any form of regional consolidation entails a difficult transition period. Cost saving may involve some loss in local autonomy and possibly elimination of some jobs. Substantial political problems can be associated with consolidation efforts. Historically, voters have not been receptive to the consolidation reform movement. Acceptance of home rule charters, county incorporations, and county "tax reform" are the exception rather than the rule.[27]

Organizational structure forms

The type of organization has just been discussed. What are the available organizational structures? The fire service delivery system in most municipalities is based on a traditional form of organization that neatly fits the theoretical classical hierarchical pyramid. But some inherent difficulties are experienced with the traditional organizational structure in the fire service. Certain basic problems tend to restrict fire service management rather than to offer it potential options.

Basic problems The following conditions are prevalent in varying degrees in paid fire department organizations, but they are considerably more prevalent in the combination type fire departments and are most prevalent in the volunteer type of organizations.

Constitutions, bylaws, rules, and regulations are promulgated to establish working relationships, authority, and responsibilities. The reason for such formal organizational documentation is that without it there appear to be more opportunities for the informal organization to operate, more opportunities for split

54 Managing Fire Services

authority relationships, more fragmentation of loyalties, and more opportunities for social objectives to outweigh fire safety objectives. These problems are real and should be given due consideration by fire protection managers in developing proposed structural–functional relationships in public fire safety organizations.

The evolutionary stage of a traditional type of fire service organization depends largely on the size of its city. When a municipality expands beyond the capabilities of a single engine company, a layering process is initiated as more companies are added to the organizational framework. The evolutionary process continues, primarily on the basis of the size of the city, until eight or more companies are organized. At this level of growth the concept of span of control is introduced into the traditional structure and the pyramid gains a new level. Battalions are formed for every eight companies or fraction thereof. Also, a deputy chief is now recommended so that a chief fire officer is on duty at all times.

When or before a department reaches the size of eight individual companies, another organizational development takes place. The administrative load is becoming sufficiently heavy to require staff support. Therefore, one finds an organizational division taking place that separates the total structure into what are normally called line functions and staff functions. This divisional process begins to impose some additional management restrictions.

The normal organizational intention of staff function is to spread the administrative and management staff load. In a typical traditional fire department organization several staff functions are generated. One of the first areas to be created as the organization expands is the training staff, then a maintenance staff, followed by a fire prevention staff, and, on the basis of work load, a communications staff, a personnel staff, a finance staff, a public relations staff, and other special designations. A typical end point of this evolutionary process is presented in Figure 2–3. The basic function of a staff group in any organization is to support the administrative effort and the line functions. In the specific case of fire department organizations, management should be concerned that the staff functions complement and reinforce the suppression function. In practice, the basic blocks that are found on the organization chart reflect reality in the actual operation of some departments. The staff groups are involved with their own activities and the fire companies go about their duties without coordinating and without communicating with each other. Typically, the communication process is downward from the chief to the individual segments of the organization. The management dynamics of communication and coordination across organizational lines are lacking.

Thus, one of the major management problems of existing fire department organizations is compartmentalization. Each unit on the organization chart seems to develop its own internal objectives. The unit objectives predominate to the detriment of the total organization. This makes organizational coordination extremely difficult for the top level manager to achieve.

The subject of top level management focuses on another existing problem. The top management administrative responsibilities and the operational responsibilities are both the province of the fire chief. It should be recognized that as the organization becomes more complex so does the list of management tasks. An unfortunate corollary, however, is the fact that the fire chief remains the commander of the emergency fire service functions. The fire chief invariably is ultimately responsible for fire control—legally, morally, and/or by personal conviction. This division of duty requires the fire chief to be a specialist in many functions. But few fire chiefs can serve multiple masters well, and these responsibilities severely limit top management in the range of functional options.

A systems option?　　In light of the above discussion, many managers might agree that the organization, administration, and management of public fire safety will need to be significantly altered if public fire safety is to become truly responsive

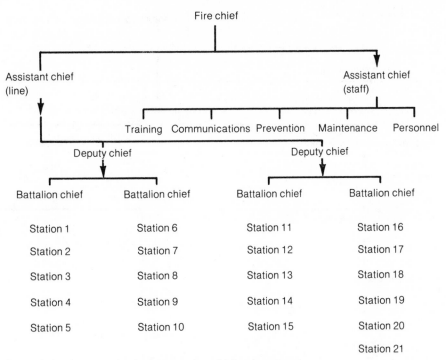

Figure 2–3 An example of a large-scale paid fire department
organization. (Source: Harry E. Hickey, *Public Fire Safety Organization:
A Systems Approach,* Boston: National Fire Protection Association,
1973, p. 47.)

to fire prevention and control objectives formulated from professional and citizen expectations. What forms, then, can fire reorganization take? One solution might be a systems organization concept for public fire safety—suitably modified for local conditions, especially for smaller communities.

One of the attractive features of an organization based on the systems approach is that the organization has the characteristic ability to remain dynamic, to grow, and to adapt to change. This feature in itself should be an important option in the administrative management of the fire service delivery system. A well-planned systems organization permits management to solve those problems associated with growth and adaptation.

The systems approach provides top managers with a structural–functional relationship for properly locating decision points within the organization. This means that the management decision-making process takes place at more than one level in the organization. Under the systems concept there may be several decision nodes within the upper and middle management levels. Common decision points are found at the administrative management level, the resource level, and the operations level. When decisions occur at these points care must be taken to ensure that they are communicated to all other interacting elements of the total system.

The conversion of a fire department organization from a traditional line and staff type of operation to an integrated systems operation involves several significant management options and considerations. These include: the structural framework of the organization, the identification of the structural components, the man–machine support complex, and also the function of the components and the integrated activity of the components. Some aspects of such a systems structure are examined below. It should be emphasized that the discussion is illustrative rather than prescriptive.

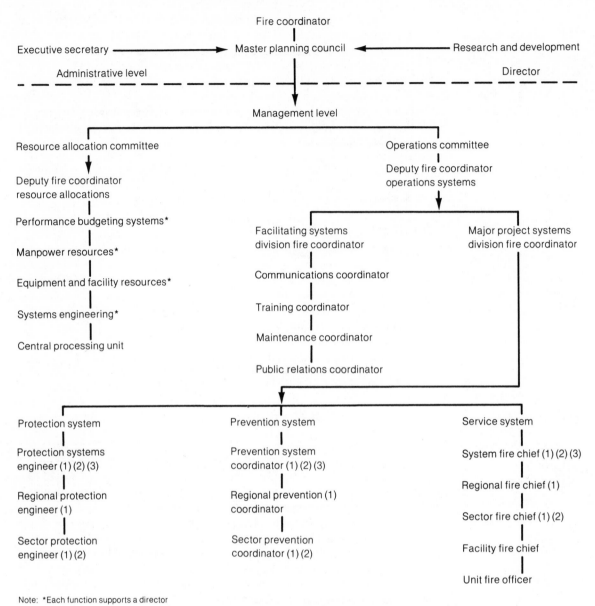

Note: *Each function supports a director

Figure 2–4   A public fire safety systems organization. (Source: Hickey, *Public Fire Safety Organization*, p. 55.)

The specialized systems organization structure   Figure 2–4 depicts the transition that takes place from the traditional line and staff type of fire department organization to the public fire safety systems organization. To provide an understanding of the figure, and hence the structure of the public fire safety organization, certain key concepts are explained as follows:

1. The organization chart shows the pattern of hierarchical arrangements. However, the traditional pyramid has been flattened out. Vertical lines remain to demonstrate the evolution of the organization and to portray subsystem unity.
2. Two major levels are evident in the systems structure. The top structure is designated as the administrative level. The second level is designated as the management level. The essential difference between the two levels relates to policymaking functions, total systems planning, and total

systems coordination. At this stage of development it is sufficient to note that the administrative level is concerned with the total system while the management level is concerned with the subsystems of the organization. The differentiation between administration and management will be clarified below.

3. A major departure from traditional organization is the introduction of the master planning council at the administrative level and the resource allocation committee and the operations committee at the management level. In keeping with the systems concept of integrating the components of the system, the committee structure is introduced to improve channels of communication, to improve the decision-making process, and to enhance the coordinating mechanism within the organization.

4. Vertical lines connecting designated elements of the system actually detract from the systems concept. The interconnections are of the step-down design, demonstrating a quasi-chain-of-command type of structure. The total system subdivides into subsystems which further divide into sub-subsystems, etc. The chart is presented in a conventional hierarchical form simply to illustrate the individual functional elements. It should be understood that for simplicity several horizontal and vertical connectors between elements have not been introduced into the framework at this time.

5. There is a significant difference in descriptive titles and subsystem headings from those on the traditional chart. Most notable is the fact that the fire chief is not positioned at the apex of the organization. The fire chief by title remains as the director of the fire suppression and rescue service subsystem. Some might view this new structure as nothing more than a sophisticated administrative overlap to the normal structural – functional arrangement of a public fire department. This would be a superficial conclusion. The whole conceptual framework of the organization has been changed, not just the administrative structure. Titles are intended to be descriptive of the unit functions. The functions have been grouped into subsystem areas that would most closely act together in accomplishing the objectives of the system.

6. Subunits under the major project systems display the numerical categories of 1, 2, and/or 3. The numbers indicate potential levels of service. In other words, the system is structured to adapt readily to variable service needs. The organization arrangement provides for a basic subsystem service (level 3), a subsystem service with geographical sectors (level 2), and a subsystem service with both sector arrangements and geographical regions (level 1) within the broad public fire safety system.

The administrative level The administrative level of the proposed public fire safety system organization represents the highest level of decision making and policy formulation. Decisions made at this level should be reviewed only by an individual or group outside of the public fire safety system. This point alone distinguishes the administrative level from the management level. Management level personnel may be capable of making decisions and developing policy for a subsystem within the fire safety system, but such decisions and policies have the effect of recommendations, since they are subject to review by the master planning committee or the fire coordinator. The administrative level is also distinguished by its ultimate level of responsibility. The fire coordinator as an individual and the master planning committee as a group retain ultimate responsibility for the performance and maintenance of the total system. Decision making at this level of responsibility cannot be delegated to the management level.

A further differentiation exists between the administrative level and the management level. The management level is charged with the implementation of administrative decisions and policies. No direct or indirect service is performed by the administrative level beyond the preparation of policy criteria, directives, and rules and regulations for the organization, and the transmittal of prepared documentation to the designated management level functions.

The administrative stress is on policy development and implementation. The policy process closely coordinates the relationship of the public fire safety system with the larger urban environment (system).

The fire coordinator   The fire coordinator is established as the central administrator for the public fire safety system. The role of the fire coordinator in the organization differs considerably from that of the fire chief under most existing forms of local government. It is intended that the fire coordinator accomplish exactly what the title implies—the coordination of the allocation of resources, activities, and output services associated with the handling of the overall fire problem within the geographical jurisdiction. The position is a very broad one: it is not restricted to the internal arrangement of the public fire safety system. Rather, it implies an encompassing view of fire safety within a total environmental context.

The coordination function is necessarily restricted to organizational administration. Under this concept the fire coordinator does not assume the role of directing fire suppression forces. The suppression element is delegated to the system fire chief under the operating subsystem. On the basis of the systems theory, it is hardly feasible or practical for the top administrator in the organization to fulfill the responsible and diverse roles of both administrator and fire chief. The scope and responsibility of this position should be more evident as the description of the complete public fire safety system develops.

Following are some of the broad areas of responsibility and functional duties ascribed to the fire coordinator.

In the area of policy formulation, the fire coordinator is responsible for the following:

1. The preparation of policy statements concerning organization performance levels to be provided by the responsible public fire safety systems organization in a defined geographical jurisdiction
2. The preparation of policy statements concerning the implementation of the public fire safety systems organization and the projected level of service at projected future time periods
3. The establishment of policy relations statements with external urban subsystems (this would involve defining mutual support areas, joint funding areas, mutual aid agreements, and personnel representation on committees with mutual interest problems)
4. Policy formulation in accordance with state and local legal requirements
5. The structuring of organization policy through the establishment of procedural–operational rules and regulations.

As regards administrative planning, the fire coordinator is responsible for the following:

1. The establishment of a formal plan of organization for the level of service to be provided
2. The establishment of short-range plans (one year or less) and long-range plans (five, ten, and twenty years) on the basis of projected growth or recession patterns in resources, services, and jurisdictional areas
3. The coordination of planning development with external planning groups
4. Program planning and evaluation on the basis of problem identification.

In the area of administrative coordination, the fire coordinator is responsible for the following:

1. The coordination of the study areas, the investigation areas, the report areas, and the agenda areas of the three administrative and management organization committees
2. The coordination of the mission and objectives of the public fire safety system through the chairmanship of the master planning committee
3. The coordination of internal and external subsystems through membership on external committees, commissions, and study groups
4. The coordination of research and development areas through direct liaison with the director of systems research and development.

Administrative control is another area of responsibility for the fire coordinator. Administrative control of the organization is established essentially through techniques of management by exception. Each exception is reported to the fire coordinator within a specified time period. The identified exceptions can then be corrected to maintain control of the system within the established limits. Deviations from the standard might signify the need to revaluate existing criteria.

The fire coordinator has a number of responsibilities in the area of administrative communications.

First, it is vitally important that the fire coordinator establish lines of communication with elements of the external urban system. The systems concept is intended to facilitate avenues of communication.

Second, the position of executive secretary is one line of communication between the fire coordinator and each planning level. The executive secretary serves as both the recording and the corresponding secretary for each organizational committee. In this manner the secretary is in a position to influence the formal and informal nature of each group.

Third, the fire coordinator serves as editor for special study reports by the respective organizational committees. This function provides both continuity and authority to all system level documents.

Fourth, in accordance with administrative control, the fire coordinator receives a report of "conditions by exception" from several functional areas of the system.

Fifth, the fire coordinator communicates to the internal system through two basic published items. One is the published *Directives of the Fire Coordinator*. Sequential directives represent updates of the official policy document that governs the day-to-day operations of the organization. The second document is less formal. It is a periodic administrative letter to all personnel. Such a letter might include news items, new programs, personnel changes, equipment purchases, comments on outside meetings, and research areas. The intent of this document is to keep the organization correctly informed of current events.

Finally, the fire coordinator communicates with the internal organization, the external organization, and the public through a monthly and annual administrative report. Such a report might identify statistical trends, problem areas, and significant accomplishments.

Implementation of the public fire safety systems organization Adaptation to specific requirements is a basic concept associated with the systems approach to organization. If the system is well designed it should be adaptable to the variety of conditions encountered in providing public fire safety for a selected jurisdictional area. One might question how this is to be accomplished with such an extensive organizational framework supporting close to two dozen separate elements. A reader familiar with a small community volunteer fire department type of public fire safety organization might feel that the organization described would possibly fit a large metropolitan complex but certainly not the average size American community. Again, if the system has been properly tailored the organizational framework presented should adapt to all situations that accept a defined set of objectives for public fire safety. The established systems approach *may not adapt to localities that do not subscribe to specific and prioritized objectives* which take account of the fact that demands for kinds of services can change over time. (Aspects of the implementation of a systems concept are discussed briefly at the end of this chapter, and are also explored in Chapter 6.)

Management options concerning fire insurance

As is noted in Chapter 4, the fire insurance industry and the public fire safety delivery systems have been closely related for nearly a hundred years. It should be remembered that the earliest fire departments in the United States were formed and supported by the fire insurance industry. Therefore, it is not surprising that many, if not most, city fire departments are organized and operated according to standards established by the fire insurance industry.

At the turn of this century the capital stock fire insurance interests became concerned over the growing number of conflagration-scale fires and the potential for even more conflagrations. The former National Board of Fire Underwriters made an extensive engineering study of the fire defenses needed to cope with the conflagration problem. On the basis of this study a *Standard Schedule for Grading Cities and Towns with Reference to Their Fire Defenses and Physical Conditions* was developed and adopted in 1916. Several revisions have been made over the years.[28]

In recent years the traditional and perhaps rather unquestioning reliance on the ISO grading schedule has come to be questioned, and the whole concept of grading and of the powerful private sector involvement that it has been held to represent has come under frontal attack from some quarters.[29] In the following discussion a few concepts are presented to illustrate viable options that may be open to those municipal fire protection managers who still wish to favorably affect the municipal insurance rate structure. It should not be forgotten that, while the grading concept may be under attack, it is still a fact of managerial life in many communities.

Over-reliance on the grading schedule

In the ISO grading schedule, the city classification on a scale of 1 to 10 is the basis for a "key rate" to cover the individual classes of property in the city. This basic rate is affected by improvements or deteriorations in the fire defense of the city and may result in a change in classification. Theoretically, the closer that fire protection conforms to the criteria enumerated in the grading schedule the lower the fire insurance rates should be. Many fire protection managers over the years have chosen to comply with the criteria of the grading schedule as closely as possible so as to lower the town class and thereby minimize the community's insurance cost. Conversely, municipal fire protection managers have been reluctant to deviate from the insurance grading schedule criteria for fear the insurance rates would increase. This general concept has led fire service managers to press for more personnel and more equipment to hold the line or to reduce insurance premiums.

Can the schedule still be used?

The thesis of this chapter asserts that over-reliance on the grading schedule is no longer a sound approach. Yet the grading schedule must be considered to some degree in planning for fire safety. The following five points identify some of the options that would appear to be involved.

A management document   The grading schedule may be examined from the perspective of a management document. The municipal evaluation process is based on a thorough and complete inventory of equipment and the documentation of activities. The lack of documentary support (i.e., training records, pump tests) is grounds for charging deficiency points. It should be remembered the grading schedule features are concerned with two basic considerations: adequacy and reliability. Good supporting documentation in these areas can help effectively to reduce the number of deficiency points charged against a city.

Codes as the key   The implementation of model fire prevention and building codes can have only a positive effect on the town grade. Effective enforcement of codes and ordinances is one of the keys to preventing fires and limiting the damage from fires that do occur. The grading schedule recognizes that adequate fire protection is reflected just as much in building codes as in shiny fire apparatus.

Water supply   Fire service delivery managers should remember that as much attention is paid to the water supply as to the fire department. Improvements in the adequacy and reliability of the water distribution system may be as important to the town grade (if not more so) as the addition of equipment and personnel to the fire service. A properly engineered water supply system for fire protection is also of key importance to adequate fire protection.

Sprinklers   With regard to water supplies, the 1974 edition of the grading schedule provides fire service managers with an option not previously accountable in the grading process. On the basis of suggestions from Public Technology, Inc., the 1974 edition of the ISO *Guide for the Determination of Required Fire Flow* included a proportional reduction in fire flow requirements where sprinklered buildings exist. The guide indicated that the value obtained for the estimate of fire flow required can be reduced by up to 50 percent for complete automatic sprinkler protection. Where buildings are either of fire-resistive or noncombustible construction and have low fire hazard, the reduction may be up to 75 percent.

Consolidation   Considerable attention has been given in this chapter to the concept of regional consolidation of fire services. The ISO grading schedule specifies the ways in which a regional approach to fire protection can be used to offset the deficiency charges assigned to a municipality.

A case study of the grading schedule's effectiveness

In 1977 the author completed a study to determine whether the ISO grading schedule criteria are the most effective and efficient guide for allocating fire suppression forces for fire protection in Alexandria, Virginia.[30] The study thesis was that the grading schedule was not the most efficient and effective method for controlling the actual and potential fire problems in the selected test city. The study objective was fulfilled and the thesis tested by the comparison of a fire protection resource allocation plan that meets the grading schedule criteria with six alternative resource allocation plans.

Each of these allocation plans incorporates a set of concepts, operational techniques, and resource components to provide a definable level of service to a given municipality. A number of quantitative measures were defined and used in this study to evaluate each response allocation plan. A principal measure related to potential fire department response time distribution profiles for each plan with respect to given study parameters. These service delivery indicators were established and evaluated to identify who benefits and who is deprived under any given allocation plan.

The comparative analysis of resource allocation plans also considered several cost-effectiveness parameters. This method accounted for economic variables not previously treated in fire protection studies (e.g., an accounting of insurance premiums, predicted annual fire loss, and the fire protection allocation cost estimates).

Principal study results   This study led the author to a number of significant conclusions. The criteria of the grading schedule do not provide for the most effective and efficient fire suppression delivery system in the city of Alexandria, Virginia. Other conclusions were as follows:

1.   Alternative allocation methods can provide approximately the same response time capability at reduced costs
2.   Alternative allocation methods require fewer resources and cost less, yet do not adversely affect the ISO town class
3.   The cost differences between town class basis insurance rates in Alexandria are not a major factor in the consideration of resource allocation plans
4.   Surprisingly, alternative allocation methods differ markedly in the number of fire stations required to meet the fire company distribution criteria specified in the grading schedule and still receive few deficiency points.

The case study approach to individual working fires appears to be the most powerful indicator for studying the potential impact of alternative resource allocation plans for urban fire safety. The time spectrum for a developing structural fire illustrates the functions that have the greatest effect on damage levels. Data analyzed for the Alexandria study indicate that the response time of fire apparatus is not the key variable; the preburn time, or time before the alarm is given, appears to be the most significant factor in estimating the potential damage to structures.

Furthermore, this study extends the concept initiated in Mountain View, California, that increased community fire problems cannot be successfully met by continually adding more fire stations, equipment, and manpower. There is a threshold at which the adequacy of public fire protection in the urban environment has to be shifted to the private sector. It may be important to recognize that even if a fire company is placed at the front door of a high rise building it may not be capable of containing a fire to the compartment of origin. The time needed to ascend twenty floors with appropriate tools and equipment may be too long. The answer to this type of problem has to come from internal fire protection systems. Therefore, an important consideration in urban fire protection planning is the level of service that should be provided by the public sector and the amount of internal protection that should be provided by the private sector.

Study conclusions   Although the conclusions developed in this study cannot be transferred as a whole to any other community, city administrators and senior level fire service managers should feel more comfortable in evaluating and implementing fire protection plans that may deviate considerably from the grading schedule criteria. However, the grading schedule can be used as an important base line for evaluating alternative resource allocation schemes, and should be carefully considered in any study of management options for municipal fire protection. Furthermore, it should be recognized that conclusions reached in the Alexandria study may not apply to other communities. The principal impact of this study is to motivate fire administrators and the research community to apply this methodology to other cities. Therefore, an option for fire service managers might be to conduct a similar study. The results should have an important bearing on the future planning process in any given municipality or region.

The management option switch to fire prevention

In the 1980s fire prevention will become the primary focus of the urban fire safety delivery system. Fire prevention is the management option of the future. The concepts revolving around fire prevention will replace the more conventional form of urban fire safety delivery system that focuses on a service after the fact: a fire suppression force that is committed to doing its best often after a building has become an inferno.

An overview

Fire prevention is a broad and inclusive term. The range and intensity of activities involved in fire prevention varies considerably among fire service delivery systems. Fire prevention has the objective of reducing the risk from unwanted fires through incident reduction and control, and through the limitation of fire severity. Traditionally, the primary attention in fire prevention has been given to the life safety of building occupants and residents. Documented fire prevention activities include fire prevention education in the community, in-service type inspections, fire cause investigation, and fire prevention bureau inspections. Most fire prevention activities are carried out in conjunction with adopted codes and ordinances relating to fire prevention and buildings. (Prevention and inspections are dealt with in Chapters 7 and 8, respectively.)

The *Municipal Fire Service Workbook* states that a municipal building department traditionally supports fire prevention through three major procedures: ''(1) the issuance of building permits; (2) the review and sign-off of new construction; and (3) code-related inspections during construction or after major renovations.''[31] The workbook also evaluates community fire prevention activity in the area of code enforcement.[32]

A municipal code may be an important indicator of the risk a community is willing to assume. The code clearly defines either by specific action or performance criteria the potential modular loss a community is willing to accept in terms of building heights and areas for a given class of occupancy. In other words, the limits placed on heights and areas by a corresponding level of fire resistance represents one measure for defining the modular loss level that a community is willing to accept.

To lower the risk to both life and property the building code may add such features as alarm systems and automatic sprinkler protection. Problems that are beyond the capability of the fire department may be addressed through provisions in the building code. Existing problems in buildings may also be controlled through retroactive features in the building code—although the time factor and the legal constraints may severely reduce the potential of this approach.

Basic management options

Fire service managers may wish to carefully consider meeting objective fire safety criteria through the adoption or revision of building codes. Emphasis in this area is related to the confinement of fires to modular levels in which the fire department can control and extinguish the fire. Even more important is the concept of life safety. Building codes provide for means of egress in the event of emergency and for the notification of the fire department.

Although this is not a popular option, building code criteria can also be used to correct existing problems that present a serious threat to the welfare and safety of the community. Many times the case can be made that it is both cheaper and more reliable to control a potential problem internally than it is to provide for control externally, because the latter usually involves spending more money at the municipal level to muster a reasonable capability to cope with the fire problem.

The concept of internal protection is emerging as one of the most effective ways of reducing life-threatening situations and conserving property. As of the late 1970s early warning detection was being endorsed by the fire protection community and accepted by the public in some areas of the country. The impact that fire detectors will have on reducing life loss from fires is very promising.

Another area of internal protection is receiving renewed interest from the research community. Automatic sprinklers have demonstrated a high level of effectiveness and efficiency in controlling unwanted fires in commercial and industrial properties for the past hundred years. Because of the inherent specification criteria associated with conventional sprinkler protection, the installation of sprinkler systems in residential properties has been minimal; the costs appear to outweigh the benefits.

However, several research projects and feasibility studies are currently being conducted on performance-oriented sprinklers for essentially single family and multiple family residences. Preliminary indications are that a residential sprinkler system designed to control incipient fires can be developed for attachment to the domestic water system. The cost for a single family dwelling sprinkler system is in the range of $500 to $800. The cost–benefit ratio for such a system appears attractive, especially when some of the trade-offs between private protection and public protection are considered.

Master planning as a management option to incremental decision making

A high priority program of the U.S. Fire Administration is to assist states, regions, and municipalities to develop fire prevention and control master plans. Fire master planning, properly introduced, appears to be a valuable tool in identifying management options for providing desired fire service levels to a community. The final plan should define the needed community service level and should fix the price which the public can afford. (The subject of fire master planning is treated at length in Chapter 6, with appropriate references.)

An illustration

A Tale of Two Cities is a report that compares two fictitious cities to show the merits and payoffs in conducting master planning.[33] The cities, Sampleton and Exville, portray the contrast between a city that is committed to master planning and a city that continues to follow a crisis response to physical and budget problems. The two cities are identical for all practical purposes, except that Sampleton uses the fire prevention and control master planning concept, while Exville does not. The two cities are followed over a ten year period during which they experience the same fire history, but with differing effects on the community.

In Exville the only extended or long-range planning relates to a future land use map which is both out of date and insensitive to community growth and development. Functional planning tends to be an annual response to the budget cycle—a year-to-year activity. Any other planning is only in response to some external prompting (e.g., state and federal mandates, the need for external funding, pressure from special interest groups, or in the case of fire protection the response to a disaster). Exville is a reactionary community.

In Sampleton the motivation and drive for fire safety master planning comes from both the fire chief and the city manager. A planning team is organized under the overall guidance of a steering committee made up of representatives of community interest groups. The key to the success of the master planning effort is a functional process that revolves around a number of structured steps. In particular, the planning team's purpose is to (1) identify the community and its boundaries to provide a defined level of fire safety; (2) define the fire problem and the fire situation in total; (3) establish fire safety goals and objectives for the community; (4) define selection criteria; (5) define, investigate, and analyze the total fire safety system alternatives; (6) select from among alternatives the best combination of fire prevention and emergency service delivery components that will meet the established objectives, including an in-depth cost analysis; and (7) prepare a plan.

The importance of defining alternatives

One specific element in the master planning process focuses on the entire theme of management options in fire protection: the definition, investigation, and analysis of total fire safety system alternatives. Underlying this concept is the notion that alternative means of providing adequate community fire protection do exist —alternatives to the conventional mode of simply asking for or providing for more fire suppression equipment and manpower. Even more basic to the concept of adequate fire safety is the recognition that fire protection is both a public and a private concern. Adequate fire protection therefore is a unique combination of private property protection reinforced by an emergency service delivery system. Furthermore, and possibly most important, there is the realization from careful investigation that private property may be carrying an unrecognized high risk if the concept of adequate fire protection relates solely to the level of fire suppression forces, to the response time of these forces to a given emergency, and to the capability of these forces to conserve property after they arrive. The analysis may reveal that the private sector has expectations from the suppression forces that are not realistic. In other words, there are limits to the capability of fire suppression forces to save lives and property. This capability needs to be defined in each community. An examination of the alternative fire protection aspects encourages the fire protection manager to evaluate not only a public sector but also a private sector approach to fire safety.

The final plan should reflect a quality of community or regional fire safety based on both professional and citizen expectations; it should clearly define the level of risk the community or region is willing to bear; it should clearly document the costs associated with the planned level of service; and it should plot a future course of action to either achieve or maintain prescribed levels of community or regional safety over at least a ten year period. Above all, the master planning process should identify both the capabilities and the limitations of the public fire service delivery system. On this basis the option is presented of reliance on public fire service delivery or the possible transfer to the private sector to maintain the acceptable risk level. Finally, the potential impact of the plan on the jurisdiction's knowledge of its capabilities and limitations in the area of fire services has implications for planning in such other areas as police protection, highway construction and maintenance, zoning and land use policies, water supply for both private consumption and fire protection, parks and recreation, and public personnel policies.

At present, master planning provides the best management option for fire protection. This is so because in the master planning process the fire protection system is carefully defined, risk levels are identified, and alternative courses of action are structured to cope with the problem. From this perspective the fire protection manager is now in a position to select and support the most desirable option. Whether managers will rise to the challenge is another matter.[34]

Summary

A framework for examining management options in the field of fire protection has been presented in this chapter. Not all of the areas necessary for examining the fire service delivery system have been covered here; some topics are taken up later. What appears to be important is the realization that management is not locked into conventional or traditional ways of providing fire safety to communities. The discussion has focused primarily on (1) aspects of the service delivery system that can be managed before the actual occurrence of an incident and (2) conditions that affect the organization of the fire service delivery system. It is hoped that this subject will alert fire protection managers to the alternatives that are available for providing defined levels of public service to meet fire safety objectives. The succeeding chapters should be studied carefully as aids in assessing the specific nature of these alternatives.

1 See: "Public Safety: The Firefighting Function," booklet 7 in *Small Cities Management Training Program* (Washington, D.C.: International City Management Association, 1975).

2 John C. Houlihan, "Six Bold New Public Safety Ideas in Search of a City," *Nation's Cities,* September 1977, p. 20.

3 Vincent Ostrom, *The Political Theory of a Compound Republic: A Reconstruction of the Logical Foundations of American Democracy as Presented in* The Federalist (Blacksburg, Va.: Virginia Polytechnic Institute and State University, 1971), p. 23.

4 H. George Frederickson, "Toward a New Public Administration," in *The Dimensions of Public Administration,* ed. Joseph A. Uvegas (Boston: Holbrook Press, Inc., 1975), p. 54.

5 Ibid., p. 55.

6 Arthur J. Swersey, Edward J. Ignall et al., *Fire Protection and Local Government: An Evaluation of Policy-Related Research,* New York City–Rand Institute Report R–1813–NSF (Santa Monica, Calif.: Rand Corporation, 1975), p. 4.

7 Ibid.

8 Research Triangle Institute (RTI), International City Management Association (ICMA), and National Fire Protection Association (NFPA), *Municipal Fire Service Workbook,* prepared for the National Science Foundation, Research Applied to National Needs (Washington, D.C.: Government Printing Office, 1977).

9 Ibid., p. 4.

10 Ibid.

11 Ibid., pp. 4–5.

12 Ibid., p. 5.

13 Ibid.

14 Ibid.

15 Ibid., p. 53.

16 The discussion in this section is excerpted, with some editorial changes and excisions, from ibid., pp. 53–58.

17 Swersey, Ignall et al., *Fire Protection and Local Government,* p. 14.

18 Arthur M. Bennett, "Applying Operations Research to County Fire Protection," *Firemen,* July 1968, pp. 34–37.

19 R. S. Ahlbrandt, Jr., "Efficient Output of a Quasi-Public Good—Fire Services" (Ph.D. dissertation, University of Washington, Seattle, 1972).

20 Swersey, Ignall et al., *Fire Protection and Local Government,* p. 16.

21 Swersey and Ignall (ibid., p. 17) have thoroughly reviewed the literature and point to three major authors. Charles S. James, a proponent of such consolidations, produced two studies in the 1950s. The first, *Police and Fire Integration in the Small City* (Chicago: Public Administration Service, 1955), is an application of emergency service consolidation to small cities; the second, *A Frontier of Municipal Safety* (Chicago: Public Administration Service, 1955), extends the concept to larger cities. In the 1960s Cunningham examined both the British and the American experiences with police–fire consolidation and concluded that some consolidation of the administrative functions of police and fire services may prove cost-effective in small cities but is not recommended for large cities. In 1970 Henry W. More, Jr., reviewed five variations on the theme of consolidated services and formulated a basic plan for its implementation in a community (see his *The New Era of Public Safety* [Springfield, Ill.: Charles C Thomas, 1970]). This model is more of a staff functional management option than an integrated line function activity. For additional information on such consolidation, see: Marie Hayman, *Public Safety Departments: Combining the Police and Fire Functions,* Management Information Service Reports, vol. 8 no. 7 (Washington, D.C.: International City Management Association, July 1976); and Laurie S. Frankel, *Police/Fire Consolidation in Municipalities 10,000 and Over,* Urban Data Service Reports, vol. 9 no. 9 (Washington, D.C.: International City Management Association, September 1977).

22 RTI, ICMA, and NFPA, *Municipal Fire Service Workbook,* p. 74.

23 Swersey, Ignall et al., *Fire Protection and Local Government*, p. 16.

24 Ibid., p. 17.

25 Harry E. Hickey, *Public Fire Safety Organization: A Systems Approach* (Boston: National Fire Protection Association, 1973), p. 41.

26 William E. Clark, "Advantages of a County Fire Service," *Fire Engineering* 121 (December 1968): 38.

27 Swersey, Ignall et al., *Fire Protection and Local Government*, p. 17.

28 Insurance Services Office, *Grading Schedule for Municipal Fire Protection* (New York: Insurance Services Office, 1974).

29 See: Porter W. Homer, John W. Lawton, and Costis Toregas, "Challenging the ISO Fire Rating System," *Public Management,* July 1977, pp. 2–6. Available from Public Technology, Inc., 1140 Connecticut Avenue, N.W., Washington, D.C. 20036.

30 Harry E. Hickey, *A Comparative Analysis of Resource Allocation Plans for Urban Fire Safety* (Laurel, Md.: The Johns Hopkins University Applied Physics Laboratory, 1977).

31 RTI, ICMA, and NFPA, *Municipal Fire Service Workbook,* p. 6.

32 Ibid., pp. 7–9.

33 Institute for Local Self Government, *A Tale of Two Cities: Master Planning—An Alternative to the Common Practice of Incremental Decision-Making,* Alternatives to Traditional Public Safety Delivery Systems, no. 4 (Berkeley, Calif.: Institute for Local Self Government, 1977).

34 For further reference, see: National Fire Prevention and Control Administration, National Fire Safety and Research Office, *Urban Guide for Fire Prevention and Control Master Planning,* and *A Basic Guide for Fire Prevention and Control Master Planning* (both Washington, D.C.: National Fire Prevention and Control Administration, [1977]). Available from the U.S. Fire Administration, Attn.: FSRO, P.O. Box 19518, Washington, D.C. 20036.

3 The fire department: management approaches

The traditional objectives of the fire department were summed up in the opening paragraph of this book's predecessor, *Municipal Fire Administration,* as follows: "To prevent fires from starting, to prevent loss of life and property when a fire starts, to confine a fire to the place where it started, and to put out the fire."[1]

Over the past decade there has been considerable dissatisfaction with the delivery of public fire protection. As part of a consequent process of reformulation, attempts have been made to lay a sounder philosophical foundation by the development of what have been perceived as better, or at least more articulate, objectives. Two examples of such objectives are listed below. In the first list the six objectives are:

1. To provide a fire frequency performance level that is acceptable to the citizens of a jurisdiction
2. To provide a life safety level that is acceptable to the citizens of a jurisdiction
3. To confine initiated fires to the modular level that is acceptable to the property occupants in a jurisdiction
4. To suppress initiated fires with the least amount of property damage and interruption of occupancy possible
5. To provide selected emergency services as related to life safety and property damage for a defined jurisdiction
6. To meet performance levels that have been established under a favorable ratio of cost-to-performance effectiveness.[2]

The second example offers the following three goals for what is termed the *fire defense program:*

1. The first and foremost objective of the fire defense program is to serve, without prejudice or favoritism, all of the community's citizens by safeguarding collectively and individually, their lives against the death-dealing and injurious effects of fires and explosions.
2. The second most important objective of the fire defense program is the safeguarding of the general economy and welfare of the community by preventing major conflagrations and the destruction by fire of large payroll, economically essential industries and businesses.
3. The third objective of the fire defense program is to serve all of the community's citizens and property owners by protecting their individual material wealth and economic wellbeing against the destructive effects of fire and explosions. In meeting this objective, all property deserves to have an equivalent degree of protection, commensurate with the actual property hazard involved and not with geographical location or monetary value.[3]

While there are many examples of such listings as those given above, it is not an understatement to say that, unfortunately, for many of those who staff and lead our fire departments such goals are nearly irrelevant. As one scholar has noted, "The administrative level of public fire safety requires an expertise and temperament that may not be compatible with achievement levels of suppression forces of existing fire departments."[4] Management practitioners, speaking more informally to their peers, might express the same sentiments even more succinctly. To take one example from the author's experience, in the 1970s a city manager who came up out of the fire service made the following statement to a University of Illinois fire department management seminar: "I expect two things of my fire department . . . one, to take care of the fires, and, two, to give me trouble!"

The aim of the present chapter is thus to complement the discussion of management options set out in the preceding chapter by focusing on management approaches to the fire department itself. The chapter is divided into three sections. The first presents certain features of the fire department in order to set the background for the contradiction between goals and realities already mentioned as presenting a major management challenge. The second section introduces the basic problems encountered in mobilizing for management. (This process, which involves the manager in taking actual departments through the familiar management cycle of planning, organizing, staffing, directing, controlling, and monitoring, is treated here as a general introduction. It is discussed in greater depth in Chapter 6 and other subsequent chapters.) Finally, since a crucial aspect of contemporary management is to adequately guide and control (as much as is possible) the future as it rapidly becomes the present, there is a discussion of the technocratic, managerial, and political aspects of a fire department's futures (and the plural is used advisedly). The text ends with a brief concluding note and summary.

Two further points should be made to better place this chapter in its context. First, as is emphasized throughout this book, the discussion presented is illustrative, not prescriptive. There is no single best way of managing a fire department, and there is no simple checklist that can be followed in such a variety of community environments. Second, it is recognized that there is wide variation between small, medium-sized, and large fire departments in terms of the constraints (or opportunities) within which the decision maker's managerial philosophies can function. Nevertheless, there are broad managerial themes that can be discussed and assessed with profit to all those concerned with fire department decision making. To do so is the aim of the following analysis.

Basic features

How did the contradiction between the goals and the managerial realities of today's fire departments arise? What are the areas of concern that need to be addressed by a fire department manager if even a minimum level of effective service is to be provided? Through what delivery systems (or nonsystems) and what jurisdictional variations are such services provided? This section will set the scene for discussion of the above, and for the rest of the chapter, by briefly noting the basic features of the fire department and by answering some of these questions.

The suppression function

The historical development of the American fire service has been explored in the first chapter of this book. From the realistic perspective demanded of today's fire department manager, however, it is worth repeating the fact that most fire departments did not spring full-blown into existence rationally dedicated to establishing a fire protection system based on primary fire prevention activities with a suppression subsystem designed only to be activated upon the breakdown of the prevention subsystem. The record demonstrates that most fire departments organized themselves for the purpose of fighting fires. Fire prevention, important as it is, was usually added later to the suppression organization.

This suppression organization generally fits within a rather standard organizational structure. This structure has a fire chief at the head and various subordinate chief levels below that rank. These share a frequently bewildering conglomeration of titles—deputy chief, assistant chief, division chief, battalion chief—with the superiority or inferiority of one to another being largely a matter of local preference.

Delivering firefighting capacity is usually the task of teams of firefighters grouped together in fire companies (though, in some jurisdictions, the word *company* designates what elsewhere would be termed an entire *fire department*), serving one or more major pieces of motorized mobile fire apparatus. Some fire departments operate a single piece of such fire apparatus, out of a single fire station. Larger fire departments, operating many pieces of apparatus out of many fire stations, may group clusters of such companies and stations under the supervision of one of the subordinate chiefs mentioned above. At times these clusters are grouped to provide the supervising subordinate chief officer with a manageable span of control. At other times fire departments (often those covering extensive land areas) may be more concerned with grouping companies geographically. Each individual fire company or station may be under the command of an officer called captain, lieutenant, sergeant, foreman, or even leading firefighter.

Fire companies are often further designated by the major function of the piece or pieces of apparatus assigned. The National Fire Protection Association (NFPA) sets out minimum consensus standards for such fire apparatus.[5] The broad area of fire equipment management is treated extensively in Chapter 20, but a few brief words are appropriate here.

The piece which mounts a pump with a rated capacity of at least 500 gallons per minute (GPM) at a pressure of 150 pounds per square inch (psi), a water tank of a few hundred gallons capacity for initial fire attack, one or more hose beds for attack and supply fire hose, miscellaneous nozzles and other tools and equipment, plus two or three ladders capable of reaching dwelling roofs and the roofs and lower stories of other buildings, is called a *pumper* or an *engine*—depending on local traditions.

The piece of apparatus mounting a power operated aerial ladder or elevating platform and equipped with approximately 200 feet of various length ground ladders and miscellaneous tools and equipment for effecting forcible entry into buildings, for opening walls, floors, ceilings, and roofs, for preventing excessive water damage, etc., is called a *ladder* or *truck*—again depending on local traditions.

A piece of apparatus specially equipped not for pumping water or handling truck work functions but for light and heavy duty rescue operations, for extricating victims from auto accidents, and for performing emergency medical services short of patient transportation is usually termed a *rescue squad,* though, of course, all firefighters are concerned with rescuing human beings (or animals) threatened by fire.

Finally, vehicles equipped for providing emergency medical services (discussed in detail in Chapter 10), including patient transportation, are, of course, termed *ambulances.*

Three key concerns

There are three main areas of concern which should be attended to by a fire department if it is to provide even a minimum level of effective service: fire prevention, emergency operations, and support services.

Fire prevention   The fire prevention area of concern may include: provision of inspection services for code enforcement and for noncode enforcement fire and life safety related community needs; provision of public education services aimed at improving fire and life safety in the community; provision of plan review services related to proposed construction projects in the community; and provision of fire and life safety related consulting services to individual citizens and commercial/industrial/institutional enterprises within the community.

Emergency operations The emergency operations area of concern includes: provision of fire suppression, rescue, and emergency medical services (when these last are provided by the community through its fire department); provision of services for controlling significant accidental releases of hazardous or otherwise troublesome materials which could threaten public safety; and provision of less-than-emergency-level services which are still very important to the community and its individual citizens (releasing trapped animals, assisting individuals accidentally locked out of their homes, etc.).

Support services The support services area of concern includes: provision of the comprehensive personnel recruitment, development, and training program necessary to improve performance at every level and in every area of concern; provision of performance evaluation services; provision of the record keeping and reporting systems necessary not only to evaluation but also to nuts and bolts fire protection; provision of a service system to assure proper maintenance and repair of fire department buildings, facilities, apparatus, and equipment; provision of a supply service appropriate to departmental needs; and provision of liaison with other fire-related departments and agencies.

This area points up the contradiction between goals and realities, for if there is an area of concern in the American fire service which receives more lip service and less delivered attention than fire prevention, it is the general area of support services. These areas of management are dealt with elsewhere in this volume, but it is worth noting here that experience has demonstrated that fire administrators would be wise to pay close attention to the reality behind the support services paperwork generated within their departments.

Delivery systems

Fire departments deliver whatever services they deliver, at whatever level they deliver them, through a bewildering variety of systems or nonsystems, to a bewildering variety of jurisdictions.

Local pride, and perhaps an ignorance of other alternatives open to them, may lead a volunteer group of concerned enthusiasts in a tiny, unincorporated suburban housing tract to acquire a used gasoline tanker, fill it with water, and respond to highly informal requests for help, squirting water in the general direction of the flames, using the fuel delivery pump and hose, without the protection of fire helmets, coats, and boots, and without such legal shields as incorporation and workmen's compensation.

At the other extreme one might find sophisticated, bureaucratized, professional organizations which may, indeed, have grown too large to effectively deliver fire protection services at reasonable costs. The British, having nationalized the diverse conglomerate of community fire brigades which proved unable to deal with the fire bomb conflagrations of early World War II, decentralized this huge bureaucracy after the war into regional brigades which today, in terms of standardization and economies of scale, still provide useful models for America's fragmented and fiercely independent fire jurisdictions.

In between lie a variety of fire departments, or agencies providing fire department type services. Some of these are staffed by members who are essentially unpaid, or are paid a token sum either on an annual or per call basis; some are staffed by both the latter type of members and members who are paid a salary for services regarded as full-time, while some are staffed solely by full-time members. In addition, some jurisdictions receive fire protection from organizations whose full-time members are paid to perform dual functions, usually police patrol and fire suppression. In these last organizations, specialization in either field usually occurs above the basic rank or level. For our purposes these organizations will be termed public safety departments or public safety organizations (PSOs).

It would be possible to take up several pages of description setting out the various types of fire departments and indicating their relative rankings in terms of size, personnel, and similar features. Such a level of detail is beyond the scope of this chapter and, of course, the statistics of a given year are subject to frequent updating.[6] (The National Fire Protection Association has been building an inventory of fire departments in the United States. This effort has attempted to identify all fire departments in the country and to capture some basic information about those fire departments. As of early 1979, 28,500 fire departments had been identified. Figure 3–1 shows how these departments break down by size of jurisdiction protected, and thus helps to give a broad framework within which the discussion in this chapter may be set in context.)

Number of residents	Number of fire departments
1,000,000 or more	7
500,000 to 999,999	26
250,000 to 499,999	41
100,000 to 249,999	131
50,000 to 99,999	306
25,000 to 49,999	729
Under 25,000	27,260

Figure 3–1   Estimated number of fire departments in the United States, by population protected. (Source: National Fire Protection Association.)

For our present purposes, the data set out in a leading fire service study of the late 1970s can serve as a point of departure for giving an organizational overview of contemporary American fire departments. The study involved an intensive and comprehensive survey of some 1,400 fire jurisdictions in fifty standard metropolitan statistical areas (SMSAs) across the United States—jurisdictions protecting a population of over 43 million people. The authors of this study, in the workbook which grew out of it, group fire departments (or fire jurisdictions) into the following four categories (public safety organizations were not included):

1. Volunteer (including jurisdictions which pay members some token amounts but which employ no full-time fire protection personnel)
2. Mostly volunteer (full-time personnel make up less than half the membership)
3. Mostly paid (full-time personnel make up more than half but less than 100 percent of the membership)
4. Fully paid.[7]

These fire departments may be tax supported by a municipality, a township, a county, or a special tax district. Illinois has perhaps more special tax districts than any other state, and a great many of these are fire protection districts, often gerrymandered across the landscape without apparent regard for other jurisdictional boundaries. Before a mid-1970s court decision severely restricted the right of fire protection districts to enforce fire prevention codes within their boundaries (*Glenview Rural Fire Protection District* v. *Raymond,* 19 Ill. App. 3d 272, 311 N.E. 2d 302), this patchwork "system" made for a less than systematic delivery of fire protection beyond mere suppression.

A fire department may also be an independent not-for-profit corporation, funded either by donations (and some are funded quite well by this means) or by the contracting of fire services to other governmental jurisdictions which raise the contract fees through taxation. One successful example of this arrangement is the mostly volunteer fire department protecting three Twin City suburbs in Minnesota: Blaine, Spring Lake Park, and Mound View. Before Minnesota enacted statewide building and fire prevention codes, this fire department's chief had negotiated terms with each city and had enforced a uniform set of building and fire regulations, passed separately into ordinance by each city council.

A very few fire departments are independent, profit-oriented corporations. Perhaps the most successful and well known is the Rural/Metropolitan Fire Protection Company, with headquarters in Scottsdale, Arizona, for some twenty-five years.[8] With stations located in several large Arizona counties, Rural/Metro provides primarily fire suppression services by contracts to municipalities and to individual property owners, although fire prevention activities are included in the Scottsdale contract.

Its full-time employees as private sector workers come under the regulations of the Occupational Safety and Health Act, the Social Security Act, the Fair Labor Standards Act, and similar legislation. In addition to providing fire suppression and, if part of the contract, fire prevention and emergency medical services, these full-time employees may also be involved in building pumper and pumper/tanker fire apparatus for the corporation. Rural/Metro would be classified as a mostly volunteer fire department, even though in Scottsdale other municipal employees are expected, as part of their municipal duties, to function as volunteer firefighters.

Within the four categories listed above, 35 percent of fire departments in the study were fully volunteer, and they protected approximately 13 percent of the protected population. Mostly volunteer fire departments accounted for 24 percent of all departments and protected 14 percent of the population. Twelve percent were of the mostly paid variety, protecting 9 percent of the population. Fully paid fire departments made up 29 percent of the sample but protected a whopping 64 percent of the protected population. These data may be set in perspective if we note that almost two-thirds of all United States cities and towns with populations greater than 5,000 were protected by fully paid fire departments.[9]

The same study indicates that in a very general sense a different type of fire department predominates in each major geographical area of the country, with fully volunteer departments more common in the Northeast, mostly volunteer departments in the North Central region, mostly paid departments in the West, and fully paid departments in the South.[10]

Mobilizing for management

How are fire departments put together? What do representative departments actually deliver at the scene of a fire? What is the role of water flow? How effective can a public safety organization be? How does an effective manager set up and maintain links with other departments? These are questions that will be examined again in detail, and from differing perspectives, throughout this book. The process of answering these questions together can be described as mobilizing the resources both inside and outside of a fire department for good management.

Organization and manning

Some of the management options for putting together a fire department and relating it to its neighbors or to other departments within the local government
have been explored in the preceding chapter. To provide a framework for the
following discussion, some specimen types and levels of fire department organization appear in Figures 3–2 to 3–6. The text in this section discusses fire departments (and one public safety department) familiar to the author. These are

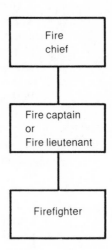

Figure 3–2 A typical three level organizational
structure used by small volunteer or paid
fire departments. This is a basic line
organization with all personnel performing line
or staff duties as required. The basic composition
would work in departments of one to
three fire companies.

examined not necessarily from the standpoint of their representative nature but
as an indication of some of the ways in which fire protection organizations can
be put together and managed. For example, how can a volunteer fire department—the backbone of fire protection in many smaller communities—be effectively managed?

One of the most effective fully volunteer departments in this country protects
the 85,000 people and thirty-eight square miles of Bloomington, Minnesota.
This six station fire department is staffed by some 140 paid-on-call members
and has no full-time firefighters. Civilian secretarial staff is provided by the city.
Two civilian employees of the building department devote their full time to fire
prevention and fire investigation pursuits. Fire alarm receipt and dispatch are
police communications center functions.

The volunteers are recruited, accepted, and trained on the basis of when they
are available for emergency service. An applicant who works from 9:00 A.M. to
5:00 P.M. many miles away, or who is otherwise unable to respond to alarms
during normal daytime working hours, is assigned to a group expected to respond during evenings or deep night hours. As is the case with many other volunteer fire departments, recruiting volunteers who are available to respond to
alarms during the daylight hours, Monday through Friday, is a problem for
Bloomington. In addition to night workers, real estate agents and on-duty city
employees are two occupational groups that have provided a number of daytime
volunteers.

The Bloomington fire department asks a great deal of its volunteer members.
Until recently, members were required to live within a block and a half of the
fire station to which they were assigned; however, there were ways of helping
these volunteers secure low interest loans to buy such housing. Bloomington
volunteers must respond to 30 percent of all alarms, must back their automobiles into their driveways or garages to facilitate rapid response, and can be fired
for missing three scheduled training sessions. (Every Monday is training day,

with drills held at noon, 4:30 P.M., and 6:30 P.M. to accommodate the several working schedules of the volunteers.)

A logical question might be: What can a volunteer be fired from? In Bloomington, from a great deal. Bloomington volunteers are rewarded by a pension equivalent to one-third of a police officer's salary upon the successful completion of twenty years of service and upon reaching fifty years of age. In addition, the volunteers conduct a variety of fund raising projects during any given year, and volunteers who retire during that year get a severance pay split of the pot (which is *not* city money) which may amount to several thousand dollars.

So proud and fiercely independent are these volunteers that when the Insurance Services Office (ISO) surveyed Bloomington in 1977 and awarded it a coveted class 4 (just eighty-four points off from class 3), the volunteers formally protested that they fully deserved class 3. (See Chapter 4 for a discussion of the ISO grading system.)

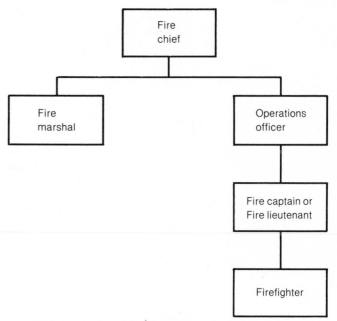

Figure 3–3   A typical four level organization that could be either volunteer or paid. Probably the fire marshal will be full-time and paid. The total structure is still all line functions, as fire prevention is a direct service line activity. Staff duties would be performed by all personnel as required. This organization would apply to a department of two to five fire companies.

Bloomington has managed to achieve by persuasion the installation of automatic sprinklers in more buildings than the state building code requires in this city. The business person or builder may be encouraged to believe that even though the state code may not require a particular structure to have automatic sprinklers, it would be best to do so to contribute to the continued ability of the volunteers to cope with fire risks.[11]

However a fire department is staffed, part of its fire suppression viability depends on what size teams of firefighters arrive in an organized manner with fire apparatus to fight fire. In Bloomington a detached or semidetached dwelling fire draws a three station response including three engine companies and two truck companies. An alarm for any larger building draws a four station response including four engines and three trucks. Companies are allowed to respond with only four firefighters aboard but are encouraged to wait a few moments for the fifth to arrive at the station from home or work.

The size of the force

Bloomington's effort to balance day and night manning levels is an example of concern with delivering adequately manned firefighting crews, day or night, capable of effecting an appropriate fire attack and/or fire rescue operation. But

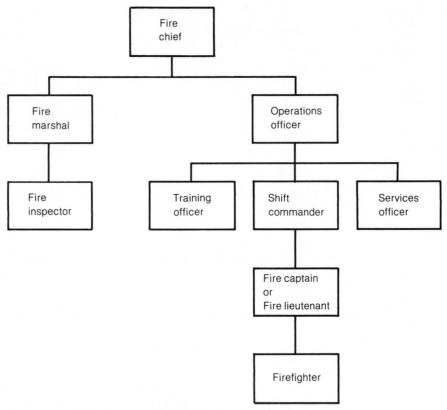

Figure 3–4   A typical five level organization for a department deploying four or more fire companies. The size of the organization dictates staff positions, possibly with some subordinates and sufficient line officers to provide an adequate span of control for multicompany fire operations.

how many people are enough? There has been little hard research on the politically controversial matter of what is an appropriate manning level. Perhaps this is also so because of the complex nature of the tasks required at a major (as opposed to a routine) fire scene.

Between 62 and 85 percent of day-to-day fire alarms in Alexandria, Virginia, can be handled by a two person crew on a smaller-than-standard pumping capacity unit called a *mini pumper*[12] (an innovative piece of apparatus about which more will be said in Chapter 20).

Illustrative cases   To further explore the question of how much manpower is enough (an important question for fire managers), we should look at some illustrative cases.   The National Fire Protection Association reports that some

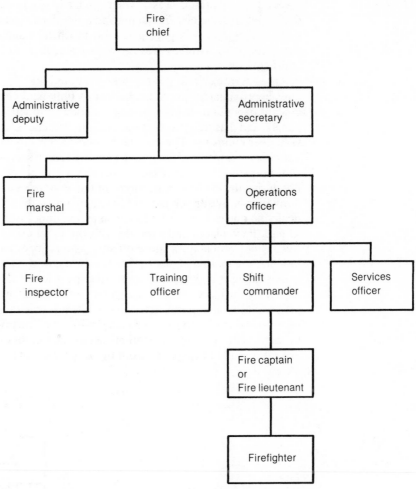

Figure 3–5   A typical structure for a department of nine or more operating fire companies. This is also a five level structure (as in Figure 3–4). The intent is to provide lower level staff officers before upper level officers are employed.

0.2 percent of reported fires cause 14 percent of our fire losses.[13] For example, DeKalb, Illinois, a university community of perhaps 35,000 population, nine square miles in area, was protected in 1975 by a forty-two person fully paid fire department. This department also provided full emergency medical services (EMS) and contracted fire, rescue, and EMS services to a fifty-one square mile fire protection district. A 1975 study done locally indicated that the department was responding to slightly more than one fire alarm per day and yet had only twelve fires in that year which amounted to $2,000 or more loss each. (Anyone who has painted, redecorated, or furnished a home or even a room in a home knows how little real damage in terms of replacement cost is accounted for by $2,000.) One fire that year exceeded a $100,000 loss, and it was set by the same arsonist who the previous year had set a fire of similar magnitude. DeKalb moved from a class 6 city to a class 5 city on the ISO scale that year. The basic on-duty attack force amounted to two four man engine companies under the command of a shift commander. Two firefighter/emergency medical technicians would usually be left behind during fire calls to cover ambulance calls, but the shift commander could order them to bring the department's elevating platform to the fire scene if he thought it necessary. Off-duty firefighters were expected to respond to "working fires" when recalled, via home radio receivers. Some critics felt that the city, in supporting a fire department budget of just under $1 million annually, was paying far too much in maintaining a fire suppression force for only twelve fires a year exceeding $2,000 damage. Are there alternatives?

An eastern city that is very similar in area and population to DeKalb maintains approximately the same number of fully paid people on duty—with a significant exception. It has a strong tradition of independent volunteer fire companies and has six fire stations within its nine square miles, one for each volunteer company. The paid firefighters in this city are drivers for the various volunteer companies. One paid battalion chief serves each on-duty group as shift commander. According to interviews conducted by the author a working fire during the daytime, when most of the volunteers are unable to respond, may draw four or five driven pieces of fire apparatus, the shift commander, and practically no one else. In order to get an attack under way most of the drivers have to park their pieces and form up with the others until sufficient volunteers arrive. Quite probably, a more effective attack operation could be consistently mounted by closing all but one or two of the best distributed stations and companies (at least with regard to covering them with paid personnel) and grouping the eleven or more on-duty firefighters into two or three companies capable of organized fire and rescue activities. While it is true that little fire prevention can be accomplished by individual paid drivers, a company of firefighters in contact by radio with the communications center can go out on in-service inspections and be capable of response from the inspection site.

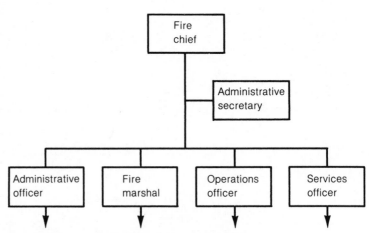

Figure 3–6   A typical upper hierarchy for a very large department of twenty fire companies or more. The general design is to keep the span of control at, preferably, five (or no more than seven) positions. The same is true of the number of levels (preferably five, or no more than seven).

When one midwestern city with a population of 120,000 in thirty-five square miles abandoned a difficult nine year attempt to make various forms of fire and police combinations work, it eliminated the police/public safety officers who had supplemented the essentially two person crews on more than twenty first-line engine and truck "companies." It also hired approximately fifteen additional firefighters, and it never seriously examined the overall effectiveness of its manning practices, the number and distribution of companies and stations, and similar factors. When these two person companies encounter the working fires which are beyond the capacity of such crews to handle, this city is in difficulty.[14] Fewer, better located, manned, and innovatively equipped stations and companies might deliver more effective protection according to one authority, but the political realities of strong, conservative union leadership opposed to innovation, coupled with the political realities involved in closing even poorly placed neighborhood fire stations, militate against such corrective measures.

Useful measures   One approach to determining the adequate amount of manpower may be to look at what actually has been provided by fire departments that have excellent reputations on the scene of multiple alarm or serious fires. Working with the Los Angeles fire department, a team from the National Fire Protection Association analyzed forty-five multiple alarm fires in that city from the standpoint of gallons per minute of water applied to achieve control and of the sheer numbers of firefighters on the scene at the peak of the operation. Simple division yielded a figure on the average GPM per firefighter which, in the Los Angeles fires with a range of 3 to 106 GPM, was 35 GPM per firefighter.[15] (Water flow as a measure is discussed in the section immediately following.)

On the scene of a working fire—a fire that is continuing to grow and is threatening lives and property not yet involved or destroyed—there are several critical tasks which must be accomplished almost simultaneously (a priority is not suggested by the listing order, because of the coordinated simultaneity of a complex fireground operation). Enough firefighters should be on the fireground, and should be there in organized teams with appropriate apparatus sufficient to accomplish the following:

1.   To advance initial attack lines to the most critical positions necessary to confine the fire or protect exit ways being used by fleeing occupants
2.   To advance backup lines and place heavy stream appliances, supply sprinkler systems, etc.
3.   To operate pumping apparatus to supply water to the initial attack lines, to sprinkler systems, to later advanced backup lines, to heavy stream appliances, etc.
4.   To provide forcible entry to the fire building and/or to immediately threatened buildings; to accomplish initial ventilation to enable the initial attack and rescue operations to proceed; to open ceilings, floors, and walls to search for hidden fire
5.   To raise ladders for rescue, attack, and ventilation crews
6.   To accomplish the rescue of occupants unable to escape on their own
7.   To handle the miscellaneous tasks of first aid for injured rescuees and firefighters; to perform salvage operations to prevent needless water and smoke damage; to provide emergency lighting service, etc.

While three or four firefighers can successfully advance a large hose line, get water pumped to it, and get 200 or 300 GPM flowing, it is the multitude of additional tasks necessary at the same time that whittle away at the GPM per firefighter figure.

In 1969 the Dallas, Texas, fire department ran a comprehensive series of exercises designed to determine the relative effectiveness of various size fire crews doing engine and truck work.[16]

Though perhaps the great number of variables considered makes the validity of overall averaging open to question, the averaged results are still interesting. Dallas decided to use the completion time and physical abilities of six person crews to accomplish a standard fire ground evolution and be prepared to accomplish further work as 100 percent. A five person crew was determined to be approximately 80 percent as effective as the six person crew, even though the manpower reduction was less than 17 percent. A four person crew was approximately 52 percent as effective as the six person crew, even though the reduction in personnel was 33.33 percent. A three person crew was approximately 32 percent as effective as the six person crew, even though it was just half the size.

Only two fire ground evolutions showed little difference in performance between six person crews and three person crews. These evolutions were the following:

1. Advancing a single one inch or one-and-one-half-inch attack hose line where ladder work or rescue or ventilation activities are unnecessary
2. Setting up and supplying water to a heavy stream appliance such as a deck gun or deluge set (large diameter nozzles capable of supplying upward of 500 GPM from a relatively fixed position).

Interestingly enough, these two evolutions are at nearly opposite ends of the fire suppression spectrum. The single line room and contents fire on the first or second stories of a detached or semidetached dwelling which does not penetrate walls or ceilings does not present a major fire attack problem for most fire departments. The heavy stream appliance may well come into play when it is necessary to stop the sweep of a budding conflagration or perhaps to knock down a fire completely involving one or more floors of a major building.

Water flow as a measure

If there is a relationship between a crew's size and that crew's ability to perform work, it is perhaps easier to relate crew size to the ability of an engine company to deliver some amount of water on a fire than to the varied tasks of a truck company. In 1966 the National Fire Protection Association issued its *Training Standard on Initial Fire Attack*.[17] The training guideline proposed in this pamphlet indicated that the firefighters arriving aboard the first two pieces of fire apparatus on a fire scene should be able to get two attack one-and-one-half-inch hose lines, flowing at least 150 GPM total, into operation within 60 seconds of arrival, followed by a two-and-one-half-inch backup line flowing at least 250 GPM within 180 seconds of arrival.

In "requiring" an initial 400 GPM within 180 seconds, the pamphlet was silent on the number of firefighters necessary to accomplish this delivery and, of course, was silent on the matter of crew strength required for the several other immediately necessary fire ground tasks discussed earlier.

Research has indicated that a rate of flow of water, properly delivered, of one GPM is sufficient to absorb the heat normally generated within 100 cubic feet of fire involved space.[18] In planning minimum requirements for controlling a fire in an unsprinklered building, a fire department should calculate the number of cubic feet in the largest potential fire area within the building, then divide it by 100 to get the rate of flow necessary for control.

Then the planner should use a factor of approximately 50 GPM per firefighter and a figure of 500 GPM flow per pumper on the scene (regardless of its rated capacity) to determine the minimum number of persons and pumpers required for control.[19]

For example, a building with an undivided, unsprinklered storage area on the fourth floor measuring 60 feet by 100 feet with a 15 foot ceiling would, theoretically, require a minimum of eighteen firefighters, two engine companies, and appropriate aerial ladder/elevating platform apparatus, rescue apparatus, etc., working with a minimum 900 GPM attack fire flow. (Of course, a fire department lacking these resources will still do the best it can in the circumstances.)

How the military organizes

Further examples of ways to mobilize the people and other resources of a fire department from the managerial perspective may be taken from the military.

The U.S. Department of Defense operates a large number of fire departments, both structural and aviation crash/rescue. Aviation crash/rescue fire departments are rather different and specialized operations, with apparatus designed with a different orientation from that of structural vehicles, and with different protective clothing, different attack methodologies, etc. Crash/rescue crews tend to concentrate their efforts on laying down a protective foam blanket rescue path to a crashed vehicle, down which a team of rescue specialists quickly moves to extricate the living and dead victims of an aircraft crash.

Turret nozzles atop the completely enclosed vehicles keep the path open and free from the encroaching spilled flammable liquid flames, although other firefighters may also work the path with handlines. These vehicles do not lay supply hoses as a rule, for they are self-contained and highly mobile, dealing as they do with fire situations which do not yield themselves to operations from fixed positions.

Structural fire departments operated by the U.S. Navy are staffed and equipped as follows. The required fire flow for the largest potential loss on the base is calculated. This is an engineering calculation and not the GPM = volume/100 mentioned above. Then two-thirds of that flow is divided by 750 GPM, yielding the number of pumpers which will be assigned. Four person on-duty crews are standard for most installations, though crews assigned to crash/rescue stations or to potentially high fire hazard areas such as shipyards may be assigned five person crews.[20]

The U.S. Army, several years ago, determined that some 80 percent of its structural fire losses resulted from just 1 to 2 percent of all on-base fires, and decided further that the provision of automatic sprinkler systems was the most cost-effective way of dealing with major loss potentials. The management conclusion was that on Army bases the size of the fire department had very little relation to the end result of such large loss fires. While there are a few Army installations with more than two engine companies, management's feeling seems to be that if the fire is beyond the control of the first arriving company, it is going to be lost. So, because the typical Army post lacks serious conflagration potential, the typical post operates but one or two companies. Aerial ladders are quite scarce, existing only at West Point and at one or two other installations. A standard civilian Army fire crew consists of a crew chief, a driver/pump operator and two firefighters, supervised by a fire chief.[21]

In U.S. Air Force fire stations, cross-manned and cross-equipped to provide both structural and crash/rescue services, usually the first two structural rigs will be fully manned with four person crews each, as will the first two crash/rescue units. Secondary structural and crash/rescue units tend to be half-manned by cross-trained firefighters capable of moving back and forth between structural or crash apparatus, depending on the nature of the alarm. An Air Force chief warrant officer noted (only half joking) that it was against military regulations to have a major structural fire at the same time that one had a major crash.[22]

Organizing a public safety department: the Durham example

Compared to the total number of fire departments in the United States, the number of police–fire combined departments, or public safety organizations (PSOs), is quite small. The principles involved in setting up such departments are nevertheless of interest to all concerned with the effective management of fire departments. An example helps demonstrate this point.

Perhaps the largest and most carefully trained and organized public safety department in the United States is that protecting Durham, North Carolina. Instituted without national fanfare in the early 1970s, the Durham operation was designed to overcome the weaknesses observed by city researchers in other public safety organizations across the United States.[23]

In the early 1970s Durham operated eight stations, three of which were staffed by traditional fire forces: eighteen firefighters and officers in station 1 manning two engines, a truck, and a two piece pumper/tanker unit which responded to assist Durham County volunteer fire departments; eleven firefighters and officers in station 2 manning two engines and a truck; four firefighters including the company officer manning a single engine at station 3 (before the completion of station 8, a public safety company also responded out of station 3). The other five stations were public safety officer companies.

The success of the Durham operation rests on the detailed analysis of the PSO systems around the United States which failed or which delivered less effective fire and police protection at greater cost than that provided by traditionally separate departments. It was discovered that one reason for failure was the failure of a city to sell the system politically to the traditional fire and police forces, or, if that proved impossible, the failure of the city to coerce compliance effectively. Another reason for failure was the failure of a city to devote enough serious attention to adequate and ongoing fire training for public safety officers. A third reason for failure was the failure of a city to organize and staff effectively for simultaneous police and fire incidents which would drain a bare bones PSO organization in two directions at once. Durham designed its plan to cover these areas.

After laying the political groundwork, Durham sought volunteers from both traditional departments. No one was to be forced in. Only 7 of Durham's nearly 150 firefighters volunteered, although most police officers did. All volunteers then went through a mandatory sixteen week training program, split half and half between fire and police training, with an emphasis on cooperation. Out of the first class, the persons who showed strong leadership were selected as public safety supervisors, a position combining the duties of a fire company officer and a police sergeant. All fire department volunteers were appointed supervisors.

To make up the difference between volunteering PSOs and the number of positions which needed to be filled, an intense recruiting effort was mounted locally, with emphasis on bright young college students. These recruits similarly went through sixteen weeks of combined training.

The typical PSO patrol/fire response district has a five person crew on duty. All PSOs work an eight hour day forty hour week (traditional firefighters work a fifty-six hour week on twenty-four hour shifts). Two PSOs are assigned to each engine. The PSO supervisor and two other PSOs patrol the district in one person patrol cars equipped with fire protective clothing, self-contained breathing apparatus, fire extinguishers, forcible entry tools, and police weapons and paraphernalia. Except for the supervisor, who always patrols, PSOs rotate duty—one month on the fire engine, one month on street patrol.

The supervisor is required to keep at least three PSO trained persons free for fire response—himself or herself and the two persons assigned to the station. The downtown area, which is fire protected by the two well-manned traditional stations, does not require PSO services but is the base area for a pool of more than a dozen PSO trained people who can be detailed out to any PSO district which finds its own officers tied up and potentially unable to respond either to police or fire incidents.

Above the level of PSO supervisor, PSOs are expected to specialize in police pursuits. Durham officials feel that, for several years to come, a sufficient pool of able firefighters exists in the traditional departments to provide future company officers, assistant chiefs, and fire prevention persons. The fire department training officer during this period had the unique experience of having been a fire captain, a PSO, a PSO supervisor, and then a fire department assistant chief. He will probably remain the only exception to the police specialty rule.

But the training function makes the Durham public safety department work from a fire suppression standpoint. Twenty to thirty standardized basic firefighting and rescue evolutions exist and are rigidly calendarized and scheduled for PSO personnel who must, as a team, complete the scheduled two hours of fire training during every eight hour on-duty shift. A slightly different set of standardized evolutions exists for traditional fire forces, who must train for two hours during each twenty-four hour on-duty shift. An annual computerized review of training completed by each PSO and traditional firefighter indicates just which persons have not completed required training. These persons are required to make up the drills on their own time to qualify for merit pay increases.

In addition to the two hours per eight hour shift, PSO crews are subject two days each week to unannounced "hot" or "cold" fire drills. A hot drill is an actual fire, set for training purposes, under the supervision of the fire training officer and the public safety director. A cold drill is usually a simulated fire in an abandoned building. Only after PSO cars and engine companies have received the alarm are they notified that the call is a drill and they are to obey traffic regulations.

A knowledgeable source in the traditional fire department has remarked that a great deal more training took place in the fire department after the installation of the PSO program than before.

The successful initiation of the PSO operation in Durham allowed the city to reduce the traditional fire department workweek from seventy-two hours (two platoon) to fifty-six hours (three platoon) at the same time that it was able to nearly double the number of patrolling squad cars on the street. Durham, North Carolina, was rated by the Insurance Services Office after installing its public safety operation and was awarded a class 3.

Establishing links with other departments

The consolidation process just described provides an interesting example of a successful response to a managerial challenge. But there are other, more significant aspects of fire protection which demand the attention of fire department managers attempting to mobilize their resources. A significant report of the early 1970s, *America Burning,* makes the following statement:

While consolidation [of fire and police] plans make valuable use of firefighters' non-emergency time, there are functions related to fire protection that deserve higher priority: fire prevention inspections, fire safety education, rescue and paramedic services among them. Moreover, no community can say with full assurance that its fire problem is small.[24]

Unfortunately, even some of those fire departments that have made strong, if traditional, fire prevention efforts have failed to establish working linkages with other municipal government agencies with fire-related missions. (Such linkages are discussed in Chapters 7 and 8.) The reasons for this failure and the roots of this unfortunate separateness are often obscure.

The building department and code enforcement Much of the content of model building codes used in the United States today is concerned with the safety from fire of building occupants, the structural resistance to fire of the buildings, and the need to install and maintain built-in fire detection and suppression systems in certain of these buildings.

An unfortunate situation stems from the fact that in many jurisdictions fire officials do not have a strong position in approving or denying building permits on fire safety grounds, or in forcing compliance with fire safety requirements when this need for compliance is not seen by the building code enforcement officials as having the same urgency.

Firefighters who have been trained in the basics of fire behavior in buildings, and who have experienced the results of uncontrolled fire in buildings, are sometimes understandably more sensitive to enforcing fire safety concepts than building officials may be who have not enjoyed or endured such experience. Some agencies have moved to alleviate this problem in the following ways: (1) by structuring cooperation, (2) by improving fire department and building department communication, and, at times (3), by bringing the building department functions under the aegis of the fire department.

A former executive director of the Building Officials and Code Administrators International has written that there is a desperate need for thousands of professional code enforcement officials in the United States today.[25] It seems myopic indeed to many progressive fire officials to overlook the potential source of first level code officials represented by fire company teams already in existence.[26] Looking at the points raised in the previous paragraph in reverse order, we see that here and there American fire departments have taken building code enforcement responsibilities in their home communities.

Fairborn, Ohio, and DeKalb, Illinois, did bring building department responsibilities under the fire department, although in the latter community those responsibilities were transferred back out with the departure of the city manager and fire chief who had instigated the move. Fire departments which move to an active code enforcement mode sometimes feel that they lose the "good guy" image which has so long been theirs.

Thoroughgoing fire prevention code enforcement demands a degree of preparation and work which may not be compatible with the rank and file suppression-oriented firefighters' views of themselves. In fire departments with very busy fire/rescue services there may also be real time constraints on training for and running company level code enforcement operations. But general building code administration and enforcement demands even greater intensification/specialization, and if qualified code enforcement specialists, fire protection engineers, etc., cannot be hired in laterally, the fire department may face significant internal training and development problems. Human beings of "ordinary capabilities" are nearly infinitely trainable at the levels required of basic code enforcement, but if the firefighters we expect to train and utilize for these duties do not want to be so trained and utilized—and if they cannot be replaced by those more amenable to such change—making a combined inspection program work will be difficult to impossible, which was, in part, the problem in DeKalb.

Firefighters not amenable to change objected to public safety officer programs in many communities with the argument that fire and police duties were too dissimilar to be performed by one normally intelligent human being. Though many traditional Durham firefighters took eagerly to rescue and emergency medical technician training, some raised the same sort of objections when PSOs pushed to receive such training so that the rescue squad could also be a PSO operation.

However true or untrue such assertions may be, firefighters will have a more difficult time rejecting building inspection duties on the grounds of dissimilar tasks than they have in rejecting police/public safety officer activities. After all, firefighters in many communities already do pre-fire planning inspections of many occupancies, and some of these inspections are rather sophisticated in terms of data collection, processing, and retrieval.

It seems a small step from inspecting buildings to learn how to more effectively fight fire in them, to inspecting them for purposes of code enforcement to prevent or limit the extension of fire therein. And it seems a step less fraught with negative political implications and potentials.

Oak Ridge, Tennessee, and Phoenix, Arizona, both did outstanding jobs in the middle 1970s in training company level firefighters and officers as basic fire prevention code enforcement people and are now delivering far more effective prevention services than when such services were exclusively the province of fire prevention bureaus.

In Oak Ridge, territorial battles erupted between the fire department and the traditional code enforcement departments, which slowed the takeover of more generalized inspection duties beyond fire prevention. By the mid-1970s, the Oak Ridge fire department was enforcing the locally adopted model housing code in addition to the fire prevention code and was still actively planning to move to enforcement of the Standard Building Code.

Baltimore County, Maryland, has developed an improved coordination among fire, public works, and building department people in county government through its Building Engineering Emergency Response Team (BEERT) program instituted in the late 1970s. This program seems to be related more to the suppression and rescue operations side of fire protection, however, and is activated for major fires, building collapses, etc., where such a coordinated, interdepartmental combination of abilities can be crucial.

The fire prevention bureau in Baltimore County, like the fire prevention bureaus in St. Paul, Minnesota, and some other communities, also actively participates in business licensing inspections. In St. Paul, when the *See v. City of Seattle* (387 U.S. 541 [1967]) U.S. Supreme Court decision seemed to indicate that fire inspectors would be forced to get warrants for inspections, the city council transferred business licensing responsibilities to the fire department on the theory that a business that did not want a fire inspection and insisted on a warrant before allowing the inspector on the premises should not do any further business in a city that requires municipal licensing. While *See v. Seattle* did not have the expected negative impact, the fire department did not return licensing inspections to the building department.

In Baltimore County one full-time, seven nights a week, mission position of the fire prevention bureau is "pleasure licensing" inspections for special events in county places of public assembly, to assure fire and life safety. The county fire prevention bureau also maintains a fire protection engineer on staff, and two field engineering specialists devote full time to new construction inspection for code enforcement and to assure that the construction going up actually conforms to the plans approved by the fire protection engineer.

Other departments For a number of years the fire chief in Elk Grove Village, Illinois, sat with the village planning commission on such matters as assuring that no confusing street name similarities or duplications occurred in plotted subdivisions which might lead the fire department to respond to wrong locations.

Even today many fire prevention people do not communicate effectively with their colleagues in planning and zoning, building, housing, electrical, and other related code enforcement departments. Administrators would do well to encourage even informal interractions between such agencies. If cooperation can be instigated as a result of a few cups of coffee, fire safety may benefit. It would seem far better to build these bridges *before* they are needed to deal with some complex issue.

Similarly, if fire prevention people, fire department water supply officers, and fire chiefs actually know their counterparts in public works, water and sewers, and similar departments, the whole city can benefit. In the same way, although in some jurisdictions fire departments are severely restricted in the amount of code enforcement they can accomplish with independent jurisdictions such as school boards or state operated institutions, it is far better to build good bridges before problems develop.

Police–fire rivalries often build up over many years of doing battle over scarce tax dollar resources at budget time, and perhaps also as a result of often more effective public relations/political homework jobs done by police administrators and other police officials. Fire chiefs may take offense because paid firefighters have been stereotyped as nonproductive except during the small percentage of time when they are combating emergencies, while police officers are "productively" driving around on "preventive" patrol. The fact that many thoughtful police administrators admit that preventive patrols probably prevent very little seems to make little difference. Patrolling officers look busy!

Where police–fire relations are especially poor, some fire chiefs have forbidden police response to fire scenes for traffic control and security unless the fire chief specifically calls for their assistance. However, if the fire is a "worker" these police may arrive too late to prevent spectators from choking the scene with their automobiles.

Examples of difficulties between police and fire departments, or of other interdepartmental rivalries afflicting local governments, could be multiplied. Recognizing a problem is the first step toward bringing it under control through the stages of the management cycle. Many managers with fire department responsibilities would agree that recognition of such problems involving linkages between departments is an important practical aspect in the mobilization of resources for fire department management.

Fire department futures

A completely different—but equally significant—perspective on the management approach to the contemporary fire department is to pose the question: What is the future of the American fire department? More pertinently, one might ask: What are the *futures* of the American fire department? We might look at these futures as if they fall into three parts: the technological future, the managerial future, and the political future.

The technological future

In many ways it is difficult to consider technology and management separately, but this chapter will try to consider technology separately in the sense of innovative uses or modifications of existing information, equipment, or ideas. Public Technology, Inc. (PTI), is a not-for-profit organization in Washington, D.C., dedicated to applying existing technologies to problems of the cities. Several PTI projects have related directly to fire department problems. These have included: (1) breathing apparatus; (2) protective clothing; (3) the Probeye device, for scanning a smoke-obscured room; and (4) a hose nozzle device which enables the operator to increase or decrease water flow or pressure by means of a radio transmitter. These are discussed in detail in Chapter 20. PTI is continuing to refine its computer-based fire station location package. (See Chapter 19 for a discussion of fire station location.)

Other innovations that are being used successfully by fire departments include: (1) the radio controlled hydrant valve employed by Syracuse, New York; (2) Rapid Water, also used in Syracuse; and (3) the mini pumper, again, in use in Syracuse. These innovations are discussed in detail in Chapter 20.

The increasing sophistication possible in data gathering, processing, and retrieving as it concerns building inspections for pre-fire planning is perhaps best reflected in the mobile command units developed by two of the Montgomery County, Maryland, independent volunteer fire departments: Silver Spring and Hillandale. Silver Spring's mobile unit is the older of the two, though Hillandale's was a product of a research project of the National Bureau of Standards on grant money from the National Fire Prevention and Control Administration (NFPCA), now the U.S. Fire Administration.

Although each of these two mobile units represents different philosophical concepts, they represent a technological breakthrough for fire suppression and disaster planning.

Very detailed pre-fire plans, including print as well as graphic information, are committed to microfiche or other compact data storage media capable of rapid retrieval. Tactical planning is facilitated by aerial photos and isometric projections, keyed to the microfiche compilations. The units are equipped with radio and telephone facilities suitable to sophisticated command post operations, complete with cramped but adequate room for key staff persons.

The managerial future

Changes in working tours Perhaps no specific management change offers the opportunity for increasing the productivity of paid firefighters more than a change from the traditional working tours, which include sleeping time, standby time, etc. The twenty-four hour tour of duty builds in substantial amounts of nonproductive nonemergency time, even if eight hours of productive nonemergency are programmed into every on-duty shift. The split ten hour day fourteen hour night is an improvement over the twenty-four hour shift in that perhaps sixteen hours each day can be devoted to productive nonemergency work: the day shift works and then goes off duty, then the night shift comes on, works, and goes to bed.[27]

Following the strike of its firefighters in the mid-1970s, Kansas City, Missouri, went to a forty hour week with eight hour duty tours for its firefighters. In addition, the city began a slow conversion to a Syracuse style mini–maxi fire company with an important exception. According to the plan, separate engine and truck companies would be a thing of the past, the maxi pumper being a quintuple combination of pump, water tank, hose bed, and ladder complement, plus a 100 foot aerial.

Because a forty hour week requires nearly five firefighters on the payroll for each one on duty, whereas the fifty-six hour week requires something less than four, a change to forty hours can mean increasing the number of firefighters in the department. Both Syracuse and Kansas City largely met this problem by analyzing their fire departments and determining that, through the combining of companies and relocating of stations, adequate coverage could be maintained with fewer stations, companies, and firefighters. While in both cases a few additional firefighters still had to be added, the additions were far fewer than would have been necessary if more people had merely been added on to traditional organizations. Kansas City believes that the increased productivity possible with eight hour shifts and no sleeping on duty more than compensates for the additional personnel costs.

However, when a forty and eight is imposed on firefighters against their will, they are not going to be inclined to make the arrangement particularly productive or the transition to it particularly smooth.

Master planning Perhaps the most significant long-range management impact has been made by the U.S. Fire Administration (formerly the National Fire Prevention and Control Administration) in developing a model guideline for community fire defense master planning (covered in detail in Chapter 6). By stressing that fire protection is a local problem which must be dealt with by local citizens and officials (*local* may be interpreted as municipal, county, or regional), the U.S. Fire Administration may have taken a most significant step in helping to assure that master planning for fire protection in the last quarter of the twentieth century will not merely produce books of federal recommendations fit only to gather dust on the shelves of the people who made them and the politicians who paid for them.

By stressing the necessity of involving the total community—fire department labor and management, builders and other business persons, municipal administrators and other agency people, multi-partisan political representatives, and diverse community interest groups—the U.S. Fire Administration has provided the careful, perceptive public official with a methodology for learning what the community really expects and how it perceives the fire problem and the fire department. The careful fire chief will not only learn through using this process but will be able to do an educational job, will be able to establish working linkages with community interest groups access to which was not previously available, may be able to protect the department from ill-conceived panaceas for fire department problems, and may be able to further improve community understanding during negotiations with firefighter organizations.

Resource allocation Harry Hickey's model for analyzing resource allocation for urban fire safety may—if it is simplified—also provide fire chiefs or fire safety planning groups with some genuine alternatives to "the way we've always done it."[28]

The political future

Labor–management relations Recent years would seem to indicate that organized firefighters have done better jobs of political homework than have fire administrators, and if the union perceives a management program as detrimental to its own interests, that management program is in difficulty.

Managerial improvements such as uniform fire incident reporting should not meet with much organized opposition, but managerial improvements perceived by the firefighters as interfering with traditional perquisites of their trade will be resisted.

Public employee unrest, which increased in the 1970s, is of course, nothing new. Neither is such unrest among firefighters, who are generally held to be among the most difficult public employee groups with which to bargain collectively. This is true in part because of the potency of a threat to withhold such an essential service. It is also true in part because of the built-in social club atmosphere of the firefighter's job. While firefighter unrest will probably increase in the future, as part of the general trend, there are indications that cities need not automatically capitulate to the walkout threat. (Management–labor relations that maximize the professionalism required on both sides are explored in detail in Chapter 13.)

It should be noted, however, that labor–management problems are not limited to paid fire departments. In fire departments with strong volunteer firefighter traditions any management moves by public administrators to gain more effective control over the volunteers is certain to generate problems. And, since the volunteers may be much more effectively linked up with the community than a public administrator is, such problems can provide the administrator with a set of walking papers.

The Montgomery County experience There are examples, however, where an uncertain political future has been successfully turned into a manageable present. Montgomery County, Maryland, has tried to develop an effective combination fire operation using modern techniques while attempting to retain the community-based virtues of the volunteer system. In that county, sixteen independent volunteer fire departments and two rescue departments provide suppression and EMS services to 590,000 people from approximately thirty-five stations across the county's 506 square miles. Career personnel account for some 630 positions supplementing approximately 1,000 volunteers. Approximately 60 persons work for the Department of Fire and Rescue Services itself, providing countywide communications, training, fire prevention, and fire investigation services.[29] The balance of the career personnel are actually employed by most of the independent volunteer fire departments and work a variety of duty arrangements, from regular, round-the-clock company manning to straight days during the normal working hours when few volunteers are available. Only a very few chief officers are career personnel, the vast majority being volunteers elected to their positions from within the individual departments.

Budget requests come up out of the individual fire departments to the "fire board," made up of one chief and one delegate from each fire or rescue department (and, therefore, essentially controlled by the volunteers), and from that board to the elected county executive and legislature.

Thus, by dint of political compromise, Montgomery County has worked out an arrangement that reaps the benefits of a competent career civil service while sustaining the benefits of local roots, political support, and sense of community service which accrue to a volunteer system. There are, of course, problems between some career personnel, who may have a tendency to regard themselves as the "real" firefighters, and some volunteers. The potential for difficulty is somewhat ameliorated by the fact that many of the career personnel are also volunteers in departments other than the one in which they are employed.

The management–politics mix The mix of management and politics is a purposeful one. Traditionally, public management groups from the International City Management Association to the International Association of Fire Chiefs have taken the philosophical position that elected officials set policy while appointed officials carry it out. While this is a neatly tied package, the reality in many communities is that public management is a very political business. Whenever there is a conflict for scarce tax dollars, whenever a government policy decrees that one interest group is going to advance at the cost of another, that is politics.

Furthermore, because the appointed managers often control the information available to the elected officials, the former can to a certain degree control the formation of the policies they will be expected to enforce. Alvin Toffler, writing in *Future Shock,* makes the following statement:

The introduction of [planning-programming-budgeting system] and the systems approach is a major governmental achievement. It is of paramount importance in managing large organizational efforts. But it leaves entirely untouched the profoundly political question of how the overall goals of a government or a society are to be chosen in the first place.[30]

Toffler also states the following:

The politician's time horizon usually extends no further than the next election. Congresses, diets, parliaments, city councils—legislative bodies in general—lack the time, the resources, or the organization forms needed to think seriously about the long-term future. As for the citizen, the last thing he is ever consulted about are the larger, more distant, goals of his community, state or nation.[31]

Toffler, of course, was not speaking to the national fire problem, but his words are well worth heeding, should a fire department choose, for example, to launch into the master planning process.

A concluding note

To conclude on a practical note, the Institute for Local Self Government in Berkeley, California, addressed futures for fire departments with the six books published in September 1977 under the collective title Alternatives to Traditional Public Safety Delivery Systems.

The first book, *A Public Safety Employees Contractual System,* explores an alternative to the lifetime tenure nature of present day employment practices in fire and police departments. The next volume, *Municipal Fire Insurance,* explores the possibility of a municipality's being the insuring agent for its citizens. *Public Safety Inspection Consolidation* discusses the effective use of the on-duty nonemergency time of company firefighters and officers for code enforcement activities. *A Tale of Two Cities* is a careful, honest hypothetical story about identical communities, one of which adopts a master planning approach, while the other maintains its traditional approach. *Civilians in Public Safety Services* explores a range of approaches, from the total contracting of a Rural/Metro type of service to the now fairly common use of civilians as communications operators and dispatchers. It makes the point that careful planning and training can make the difference between success and a failure which may defeat further innovative attempts—as the discussion earlier in this chapter of Durham, North Carolina, illustrated. *Alarm Systems Management* explores alternatives for dealing with the false alarm problems plaguing many cities.[32]

Master planning for community fire protection seems to be the key to success in any innovative area, both inside and outside of the purview of the six volumes described above. If the fire chief and the chief's superiors do not fully understand the community's fire protection goals, what risks are acceptable to the people, what degree of regulation/taxation the citizens are willing to impose on themselves, then their every innovation has the potential for failure. If the *process* of master planning is thoroughly embedded in the political psyche of the community, then the chief and the chief's superiors may spare themselves a scar or two while leading their community toward a safer collective future.

This chapter has moved from a discussion of certain basic features of the fire department, to a detailed review of the chief factors in mobilizing for fire department management, to an examination of several aspects of fire department futures. Throughout, the emphasis has been on the managerial role and on placing departmental management approaches in the proper context. The next chapter marks a shift from the fire department's internal concerns to its interaction with certain other, external, organizations.

1 International City Management Association, *Municipal Fire Administration,* 7th ed. (Washington, D.C.: International City Management Association, 1967), p. 1.
2 Harry E. Hickey, *Public Fire Safety Organization: A Systems Approach* (Boston: National Fire Protection Association, 1973), p. 7.
3 National League of Cities, *The Grading of Municipal Fire Protection Facilities* (Washington, D.C.: National League of Cities, 1967), p. 8. Quoted in David B. Gratz, *Fire Department Management: Scope and Methods* (Beverly Hills, Calif.: Glencoe Press, 1972), p. 17.
4 Hickey, *Public Fire Safety Organization,* p. viii.
5 National Fire Protection Association, *Automotive Fire Apparatus,* NFPA no. 1901 (formerly no. 19) (Boston: National Fire Protection Association, 1975).
6 Data on fire departments, particularly regarding personnel, salaries, and expenditures, can be found in the various editions of *The Municipal Year Book,* published annually by the International City Management Association in Washington, D.C., and also in the Urban Data Service Reports of that association.
7 Research Triangle Institute (RTI), International City Management Association (ICMA), and National Fire Protection Association (NFPA), *Municipal Fire Service Workbook,* prepared for the National Science Foundation, Research Applied to National Needs (Washington, D.C.: Government Printing Office, 1977), p. 9.
8 See: Fred S. Knight, *Fire Service Productivity: The Scottsdale Approach,* Municipal Management Innovation Series no. 16 (Washington, D.C.: Inter-

national City Management Association, March 1977).
9 RTI, ICMA, and NFPA, *Municipal Fire Service Workbook,* p. 72.
10 Ibid.
11 Fresno, California, a fully paid fire department, so reduced the incidence of downtown business district fires after forcing the automatic sprinklering of all commercial buildings that at least one entire engine company was able to be closed out and relocated in a residential neighborhood.
12 Harry E. Hickey, *A Comparative Analysis of Resource Allocation Plans for Urban Fire Safety* (Laurel, Md.: The Johns Hopkins University Applied Physics Laboratory, 1977), p. 123. For detailed information on the mini pumper, see: Fred S. Knight, *The Mini-Pumper: New Applications and New Potential,* Municipal Management Innovation Series no. 1 (Washington, D.C.: International City Management Association, Jauary 1975).
13 National Fire Protection Association, *Fire Protection Handbook,* 14th ed. (Boston: National Fire Protection Association, 1976), p. 1:14.
14 Richard L. Ulrich, "Partial Combination of Fire and Police Services in Peoria, Illinois" (unpublished paper for Master of Arts in Public Administration, University of Illinois at Urbana–Champaign, 1973).
15 Warren Y. Kimball, "Fire Department Manpower and Applied Fire Flow," *Fire Journal,* September 1966, pp. 26–27.
16 City of Dallas Fire Department, "Manpower Analysis-1969" (unpublished study, Dallas, Texas, 1969). Summarized by E. E. Spillman in *Proceed-*

ings, *Fire Department Instructors Forty-second Annual Conference* (Kansas City, Mo.: City of Dallas Fire Department, 1970), pp. 95–100.

17 National Fire Prevention Association, *Training Standard on Initial Fire Attack,* NFPA no. 197 (Boston: National Fire Protection Association, 1966).

18 Iowa State University, Fire Service Extension, *Water for Fire Fighting: Rate-of-Flow Formula* (Ames: Iowa State University Press, 1967), p. 18.

19 William E. Clark, *Fire Fighting: Principles and Practices* (New York: Dun·Donnelley Publishing Corporation, 1974), p. 55.

20 U.S., Department of the Navy, OPNAVINST 11320.26 Op–44F, 1 July 1976.

21 Richard L. Ulrich, "On-Duty Fire Company Manning: A Survey" (unpublished graduate study, University of Illinois at Urbana–Champaign, 1968).

22 Ibid.

23 The material on the Durham, North Carolina, public safety department is based on: Richard L. Ulrich, "Public Safety in Durham," parts 1, 2, and 3, *Fire Chief,* March, April, and May 1974, pp. 28–29, 46–48, and 45–51, respectively.

24 National Commission on Fire Prevention and Con-

trol, *America Burning* (Washington, D.C.: Government Printing Office, 1973), p. 23.

25 Richard L. Sanderson, *Perspectives for Code Administrators* (Chicago: Building Officials and Code Administrators International, Inc., 1974), p. 88.

26 Richard L. Ulrich, "Some Alternatives to Police/Fire Consolidation," part 2, *Fire Chief,* September 1972, p. 6.

27 For a discussion of changed working tours, see: Stephen R. Harrell and Jewell D. Scott, *Alternative Work Schedules for Firefighters: The 8-Hour Day,* Management Information Service Reports, vol. 10 no. 10 (Washington, D.C.: International City Management Association, October 1978).

28 Hickey, *A Comparative Analysis of Resource Allocation Plans for Urban Fire Safety.*

29 Montgomery County, Maryland, Department of Fire and Rescue Services, *Annual Report, 1976* (Rockville: Montgomery County, Maryland, Department of Fire and Rescue Services, 1976).

30 Alvin Toffler, *Future Shock* (New York: Random House, Inc., Bantam Books, 1970), p. 472.

31 Ibid., p. 483.

32 These reports are available from the Institute for Local Self Government, Hotel Claremont Building, Berkeley, Calif. 94705.

Other organizations and the fire service

What are the various organizations, agencies, and other groups that the fire administrator will need to, or will wish to, work with to achieve greater efficiency and a broader scope in managing the fire department? This chapter provides an introduction and background information for fire administrators, and others in local government fire service, on the many organizations, institutions, and agencies that may be connected with their work.

The chapter opens with a discussion of the insurance industry, and gives major attention to the Insurance Services Office and the development and application of fire rating and grading schedules. The next major section, on the membership and professional community, provides a summary of a variety of professional and informational organizations in the fire service field. This is followed by a section devoted to the academic and research interests in fire service, including the many kinds of fire-related educational programs offered in community colleges, four year institutions, and graduate schools, and some of the major research programs and agencies that have had significant impact. The next major section deals with federal programs in fire service that are important for local government, especially the work of the U.S. Fire Administration. This is followed by a section reviewing the role of state governments in fire prevention and control. The chapter concludes with an overview of the significance of these many types of organizations to the local fire service.

A: The insurance industry

Fire insurance is a method of insuring property against loss from fire in consideration of a payment generally proportionate to the risk involved. It is coverage by contract in which one party agrees to indemnify or reimburse another for loss that occurs under the terms of the contract. An entity (person, premises, corporation) may elect to be self-insured or partially or totally insured by others.

Self-insurance may be a savings or accrual program in preparation for unanticipated losses, supported without outside assistance. For those risks and probable losses to which a premises may logically be exposed and may not avoid, the normal course is to arrange for the more critical risks to be underwritten by others. The arrangement is usually a contract with an insurance carrier, which spells out the extent of risk protection and the conditions under which the carrier agrees to assume the liability set out in the contract. The contract may also cover property management responsibilities as part of the agreement. A contract providing total coverage without any local management responsibility is questionable when one considers the real world and all the conceivable direct and indirect losses that could occur.

The development of fire insurance

Insurance philosophy in one form or another existed as far back as ancient Babylonia and Assyria, where officials were empowered to levy contributions for a common fund to pay damages from calamities. Marine insurance (ships and cargo) was probably the earliest form of actual insurance. During the period 1635–60 England tried to organize institutions to insure individuals against fire. Because of the number of wars during the period these attempts failed. The advent of modern fire insurance is considered an outgrowth of the 1666 Great Fire of London when a major portion of that city was destroyed, including more than 13,000 buildings and over 500 acres (see Chapter 1).

The first actual fire insurance company was formed in London in 1680 with a second following about 1687. It was not until 1752 that the first actual American fire insurance company was established in Philadelphia. A century later two companies began fire insurance sales in the San Francisco area.

The various bases for determining fire insurance premiums did not directly use property value until the early 1700s. With insured values based on property values, magnitude of potential loss from fire became more clearly defined and firefighting organizations supported by fire insurance companies came into being. The fire mark attached to buildings identified those who had an insurable interest in the welfare of the structure as well as a fire suppression responsibility.

During the 1790s the first state legislative act providing for incorporation of an insurance company paved the way for many insurers to be incorporated under special charters. Many of these charters introduced the first form of state regulation of fire insurance company operation, particularly for required funding and operational reports. Special chartering of individual companies was gradually discontinued in favor of general state laws governing a wider range of insurers with regulation still related mainly to required capital and the handling thereof. By the mid-1800s insurance boards or commissions had been created in a few states, but the individual state statutes provided very little detail by which evaluations could be effected. Many state enactments were primarily concerned with obtaining income from taxes levied on the business of insurance.

Up to and through the early 1900s questions about the legality and propriety of federal versus state regulation of insurance were raised. One of the major issues was whether insurance was commerce as anticipated by the federal Constitution. Provisions for regulation varied from state to state and were often considered inadequate to assure reasonably effective and competent performance on behalf of the public. During the period 1942–44, federal litigation resulted in an indictment of insurance company interests as being in violation of the Sherman Antitrust Act. In 1944 the U.S. Supreme Court held that interstate commerce was affected and the federal government could regulate insurance.[1]

The current regulatory framework

In 1945 Congress passed the McCarran–Ferguson Act, which in effect clarified the federal position on insurance regulation, particularly as such regulation might be interpreted under the Sherman Antitrust Act. The McCarran–Ferguson Act provided for a moratorium during which states without adequate regulatory laws could pass legislation. In other words, states were told that if federal antitrust provisions do not apply to insurance there must be significant and meaningful state regulatory provisions. With state regulation, then, considered to be in the public interest, most states with inadequate laws adopted new regulations by 1948.

Regulatory changes have continued to receive the attention of state governing bodies, and states now have state insurance departments and insurance commissioners (or their equivalents) responsible for the administration of regulatory criteria, particularly for insurer solvency and fair rate-making practices. Although state insurance commissioners had engaged in active cooperation since the late 1800s, the current National Association of Insurance Commissioners provides a functional medium through which various issues may be clarified.

Insurance rating organizations, which function on a state or regional basis and are often referred to or titled as *rating bureaus,* are regulated along with insurers. These organizations furnish service to insurance companies which may be members of the organization or may subscribe to its services. (For example, a property rating organization may relate with a state insurance department concerning regulatory matters on behalf of an insuring company affiliated with the rating organization.)

State regulations are not uniform from state to state. Although many states could be grouped as having, for practical purposes, the same type of rate regulatory law, numerous variations in details and applications may exist. This makes it difficult to list states by a defined category (without oversimplification) as a basis for tabulation. In addition, different procedures may be used within a given state for one type of insurance as compared with another (the same may be said for an insurer's rates and rules as compared with its insurance policy forms).

Where does your insurance dollar go? Premiums for property and liability insurance totaled $72.4 billion in 1977, a 20 percent increase in dollar volume over 1976 ($60.8 billion) which, in turn, was a 20 percent increase over 1975 ($50 billion). Of the total premiums written in 1977 for property and liability insurance, $30.5 billion was for auto insurance, broken down between $19.9 billion for liability insurance and $11.5 billion for auto physical damage insurance. Other forms of liability insurance, including medical malpractice, totaled $7.1 billion.

Other major forms of insurance, as measured by premiums paid in 1977, were for workers' compensation ($9.4 billion); homeowners' multiple peril, which includes fire insurance ($6.8 billion); commercial multiple peril, which includes fire insurance ($5 billion); and fire insurance and allied lines ($4.5 billion).

The largest single type of insurance, as measured by premium, was all forms of liability, totaling $26 billion or 36 percent of the total.

Source: Insurance Information Institute, *Insurance Facts* (New York: Insurance Information Institute, 1978), p. 10.

The prevalent types of state regulatory laws are *prior approval, file and use,* and *use and file.* For prior approval, proposed actions anticipate a filing of pertinent information with the state and a delay in implementation pending state approval in accordance with that state's prescribed procedures. For file and use, pertinent information is filed and the proposed actions may then be effected in accordance with prescribed procedures. Use and file is the reverse, with filing usually contemplated within a set time period.

Variations in state regulatory procedures include time elements, mechanics of approval or disapproval, mandatory use of a rating organization, adherence to bureau rates, provisions for deviation from otherwise mandatory rates, bureau rates that are advisory only, and specific affirmative approval versus tacit approval (filings not disapproved within a specified time period may be deemed approved).

In a limited number of states no filing of rates is required nor is there affirmative approval action by the commissioner. Advisory information as to insurer activity is provided to the commissioner. The insurance department of the state of Texas determines and promulgates rates for that state.

Basic state regulation, irrespective of type, contemplates an insurance company or a rating organization that can demonstrate compliance with the laws of the state.

The structure of the industry

There are several types of insurers; the two most frequently encountered are stock companies and mutual companies. A stock company is capitalized by public purchase of shares; through additions of collected premiums a financial foundation is established for loss payments. The stock company is in business for a profit and, when experience permits, dividends are paid to stockholders as an investment return. A stockholder need not be a policyholder.

In the case of a mutual company, a policyholder is considered a member of the company and there are no shareholders. Favorable operational experience may result in dividends to the policyholder to reduce premiums. The more common mutual company does not assess members as necessary to meeting operational obligations. Premiums are determined on a basis sufficient to provide for expense of operation and loss payments.

Some basic service organizations   Thousands of insurance agents and brokers representing hundreds of insurance companies make up the marketing segment of the insurance industry throughout the United States. The average citizen usually gains his or her impressions of fire insurance by personal contact with an agent or broker on personal or commercial property insurance protection and loss adjustment. Not always readily evident are the over fifty national and state insurance service organizations usually supported by the insurance companies. These organizations, entirely or closely related to insurance, provide varied services in support of marketing operations. Many of these service organizations have been in existence for decades. Organizational realignment occurs from time to time to meet changing needs and to respond to innovations in the marketing and servicing of insurance protection.[2]

Many organizations are maintained to serve a specific purpose such as highly specialized underwriting (nuclear energy, for example), and others may provide insurance industry educational mechanisms or technical and administrative services. Some are rating organizations providing member and subscriber companies with selected services only, such as rate filing and statistical reporting. There are also organizations relating to types of insurers or made up of several insurers of one type. Two significant examples of the latter are the Factory Mutual System and the American Insurance Association.

The Factory Mutual System is an outgrowth of the philosophy that the financial risk of underwriting can be reduced by sharing the benefits of positive protection instead of just sharing the risk. In other words, recognition of the good risk through rate (premium) reduction is considered preferable to merely allowing the good risk to help pay for the bad. Today, the core of the system comprises four of the world's largest mutual property insurance companies, all established between 1835 and 1887. These four companies also jointly support the Factory Mutual Engineering and Research (FMER) complex. FMER has as its main objective the provision of aid to policyholders through programs that help make properties and production facilities safe from damage by fire, explosion, and wind, and from boiler, pressure vessel, and machinery accidents. FMER resources include consulting services, property inspection, water supply and sprinkler system evaluation, safe operation of industrial processes, research, and numerous other property-related factors relating to insurance. Hazard reduction and control is not confined to the Factory Mutual System (see the discussion of the highly protected risk [HPR] concept later in this section). For further information on the Factory Mutual System, see under Factory Mutual Laboratories in Section B of this chapter.

The American Insurance Association (AIA) was organized in the 1860s as the National Board of Fire Underwriters (NBFU). Comprised of interested stock companies, the organization developed into a means of assessing and promoting sound practices and underwriting for factors other than insurance rates (the latter being considered a function of state rating boards and bureaus). Effective methods of building construction, fire protection, and fire prevention were specific objectives. The title American Insurance Association was adopted in 1965 when other organizations, including one called the AIA, were consolidated with the NBFU. Basic services of the AIA today encompass, among others, insurance industry engineering, building and fire prevention codes, industrial safety, and special reports on significant matters affecting insurance underwriting. For further information on the AIA, see under Code Developing Organizations in Section B of this chapter.

The Insurance Services Office   One of the most significant organizational modifications took place in 1971 when the Insurance Services Office (ISO) was created. ISO consolidated five of the national insurance industry service groups into an organizational format also conducive to incorporation of state and regional fire rating boards and bureaus. The diverse needs of the insuring public, state insurance regulatory bodies, producers, and companies are met through a wide range of advisory, rating, actuarial, statistical, and other services provided by ISO. Many of these services would otherwise have to be performed by each insurance company to meet regulatory requirements and remain competitive. ISO operates for fire insurance in forty-four states. Five states—Hawaii, Idaho, Louisiana, Mississippi, and Washington—and the District of Columbia have independent fire insurance rating bureaus. In Texas insurance rating is handled by a state operated commission.

Because ISO is a nonprofit, unincorporated association, its range of services is available to property and liability insuring companies to the degree each company desires. Information used in developing individual commercial property insurance rate relativities is gathered by ISO's inspection staff, located throughout the country, who perform individual property and public protection evaluations. To perform the services and meet individual state requirements, ISO is licensed in all fifty states, Washington, D.C., and Puerto Rico; it acts as a fire rating organization in most of the jurisdictions and as an advisory organization to independent state fire bureaus in the jurisdictions noted in the preceding paragraph.

Setting fire insurance rates

A licensed rating organization has the legal requirement to develop rates that are "adequate, not unfairly discriminatory, and not excessive" as required by state insurance law. A rate that is "not unfairly discriminatory" is a rate that produces equity. In most states, depending on the insurance law for that state, a rating organization is required to file with the state insurance department any rate level or rating procedure change that is made. Statistics are furnished in support of the filing. After submission, this information is available for public review at the insurance department.

A rate that is adequate is one that will provide insurance companies with sufficient capital, on an overall state basis, to pay all losses and company expenses and include a small profit. A reasonable profit has been defined by most state insurance departments as 5 percent.

The simplest approach to generate sufficient capital to pay all losses and cover company operating expenses would be to charge everyone buying insurance the same rate. However, one of the basic principles used in the insurance mechanism is that individual policyholders contribute their fair share. If there were no equity built into the rating structure, low hazard properties which have infrequent losses would essentially be subsidizing the cost of the insurance for those properties with high hazard and frequent losses.

So that equitable rates may be achieved for commercial fire insurance, the rate-making process takes into consideration aspects of numerous disciplines—especially those that are statistical, actuarial, legal, and engineering—because of the varying nature and degree of hazards encountered.

Two common methods are used for rate making: specific rating and class rating. Specific rating involves use of a rating schedule by individual assessment of those properties with a frequency or variety of features and hazards affecting the fire exposure of the premises. As a rule such premises are the larger commercial and industrial occupancies or buildings. There are, however, similar occupancies of small size requiring individual treatment because of their very nature (for example, plastics manufacturing or restaurants). A class rating procedure may be used for habitational properties and buildings (apartment buildings, rooming houses, motels, institutional housing, etc.) housing commercial and service occupancies that do not have the frequency or variety of features and hazards associated with larger structures.

Several schedule systems had been used throughout the United States to establish fire insurance rates. Following the consolidation of rating bureaus into the Insurance Services Office, the decision was made to develop a new rating schedule for nonsprinklered property, with a parallel development of a simplified class rating method for smaller buildings. This decision was made in order to increase rate-making efficiency and also to provide insurers and property owners with businesses in many different states with a uniform fire rating system. All principal rating schedules in use were analyzed, and the results of various special studies made since 1945 were researched. A large volume of fire tests by Underwriters Laboratories, Inc., were also analyzed in order to review the damageability of various building assemblies and materials. Several thousand fire reports were analyzed, including all the reports made by fire rating bureaus in the United States since 1945, in order to obtain additional data on the principal factors in fire loss.

A new *Commercial Fire Rating Schedule* for use in specific rating of properties was published in 1975. Intended for eventual use in all states, it provides uniform risk analysis across the country. For commercial buildings of limited size, habitational properties, and certain special properties, a companion document, the *Fire Class Rate Manual,* also became available.[3]

The current commercial fire rating system will not (nor was it ever intended to) give a dollar-for-dollar insurance cost saving for each dollar spent on reducing hazards. The current system does provide an inducement for loss prevention that should be considered a supplementary benefit of improving fire protection. However, the potential for loss of life, jobs, and other nonproperty insurance related considerations should be the primary reason for improvements.

ISO procedures ISO's rate-making procedure begins with an evaluation of the overall premium (rate times each $100 insured) required in a state. This is accomplished by analyzing the loss experience reported to ISO by its affiliated companies. Once the overall premium required has been determined, a further review of the existing statistical information is made to determine the proper occupancy group relativity. Properties are grouped by their general occupancy, with the loss experience of each group evaluated separately. The amount of premium increase or decrease required for each group is then related to the overall state experience; this process results in an adjustment that reflects the relative experience of a particular group to the overall state experience.

Within an individual statistical group of occupancies, there are many variables in construction, occupancy hazards, private protection from hazards, fire spread potential from adjacent buildings, and public protection which must be considered to provide equity in the rate-making process. These aspects of a commercial property are evaluated by the use of a structured rating analysis which places buildings in their proper hazard relatively to each other. Each of these basic elements is compared to nationally recognized standards and practices for all subjects on which they are available. Standards developed by the National Fire Protection Association (NFPA) and the American Water Works Association (AWWA), as well as the four model building codes which are in use in the United States, are used extensively.

The interrelationship of the various components is demonstrated by the structured analysis of the *Commercial Fire Rating Schedule*. The schedule develops scaled relativities of risk analysis from building to building. The actual monetary insurance rate is developed from the overall state insurance experience which is then correlated to the individual relativities.

Of the principal individual property components, building construction is considered first. Buildings of combustible construction have higher potential than those of fire resistive construction. Protection of floor openings, individual floor areas, roof covering, and interior finish receive specific analysis. A building occupancy and the control of its operational facilities are most important. Attention is directed to such factors as how flammable liquids are handled and stored, spray painting methods, condition and type of heat producing appliances, control of cooking hazards, housekeeping, and electrical equipment defects.

Growth of insurance Liability (other than automobile) and workers' compensation are the fastest growing forms of insurance in terms of premium dollars. Over the period from 1953 to 1977, liability insurance, other than auto, increased from $0.5 billion to $7.1 billion, a seventeenfold increase. The major reasons for increased coverage are the increased number of lawsuits and the average size of claims, particularly against doctors and other professional people and manufacturers of consumer products.

Workers' compensation premiums have increased from $1 billion in 1953 to $9.4 billion in 1977, an eightfold increase. One of the major reasons is expanded coverage because of changes in state laws. The expanded coverage applies not only to benefits but also to groups of employees not previously covered.

Source: Insurance Information Institute, *Insurance Facts* (New York: Insurance Information Institute, 1978), pp. 16–17.

An analysis of the available fire protection establishes the relativity of special (individual) and public facilities available for detection and control. Properly installed and maintained built-in sprinkler, fire alarm, and special protection systems receive recognition. As an adjunct to the rating schedule, the application of a municipal fire grading schedule reflects what can be expected from public fire forces once a fire becomes reality. This schedule is discussed later.

To further expand the principle of equity in the rate structure, ISO has selected large cities to receive individual adjustment of premium. In accordance with the applicable state insurance law, ISO implements changes in fire insurance rate levels for these major cities to reflect the credible loss experience which has been accumulated. This more equitably spreads the cost of insurance.

The loss experience in each state is reviewed on an annual basis; this results in an upward, downward, or no-change adjustment of rate levels. When a city creates enough premium volume to generate sufficient statistical credibility, it is treated essentially as a separate state. The rate level adjustment derived for these cities is separate from the normally generated state rate level adjustment and reflects only the loss experience of the municipality. The loss experience of such cities is omitted from the statewide rate level adjustment.

Commercial fire data collection and rate making   Detailed commercial fire insurance statistics are gathered by ISO to the level of detail necessary for ISO to review and revise commercial fire insurance rate levels. In general, statistical plans require the reporting of certain information on both premiums and losses. Evaluation of this premium and loss information then permits the determination of rate levels.

Since 1 January 1979 all ISO commercial statistical reporting companies report to ISO using the Commercial Statistical Plan (CSP). This plan requires the reporting of unique records to ISO for each policy which a company writes and for each loss which it incurs. The following is a listing of some of the coding required by the CSP for commercial fire insurance:

1. Transaction effective and expiration dates: identify the period for which coverage is provided
2. State and territory codes: identify the place where coverage is provided, or where a loss occurs
3. Type of policy code: identifies whether coverage is provided under a straight fire (called a monoline) policy, or under a package policy which also provides other coverages, such as third party liability
4. Classification code: identifies the type of business (e.g., apartment building, mercantile building, office, bank)
5. Coverage code: identifies the type of coverage provided (i.e., buildings, contents, time element)
6. Rating identification code: identifies whether a risk is schedule rated, class rated, or sprinklered schedule rated
7. Construction code: identifies type of construction
8. Protection code: identifies the protection class of the municipality in which the risk is located
9. Deductible code: identifies the amount of deductible, if any, which is applicable to any losses
10. Exposure field: identifies the amount of coverage provided
11. Rating modification and rate departure factors: identify the amount of overall departure from ISO manual rates.

The data reported under a statistical plan are then used in evaluating rate levels so that they meet the standards which are generally prescribed by law (i.e., rates must be adequate, not excessive, and not unfairly discriminatory). In reviewing commercial fire rates, ISO uses five years of data. However, before being used to adjust rates, the data must be adjusted to reflect future expected loss and premium levels, since rate making has as its goal the establishment of future equitable rates and not the recoupment of past losses. Briefly, the adjustments made are as follows:

1. Losses are adjusted to reflect past and anticipated future inflationary increases in the cost of replacement materials. Such increases in loss costs are offset by increasing amounts of insurance.
2. Premiums are adjusted to reflect past rate changes.
3. Coverage changes, such as the introduction of mandatory deductibles which reduce losses, are reflected.
4. A "large loss adjustment" is made wherein some actual large losses (defined as that portion of any loss over $100,000) are replaced by expected large losses. This adjustment is made in recognition of the fact that large losses tend to be random by nature; hence, whether a large loss has occurred does not necessarily give credible information concerning anticipated future losses.

After these adjustments have been made, five years of data are used to obtain an adjusted actual loss and loss adjustment expense ratio (defined as the ratio of adjusted losses and loss adjustment expenses to adjusted premiums). The actual ratio is compared to an expected loss ratio to determine a state's overall rate adjustment, where the expected loss ratio is that portion of the premium dollar which is left after paying for expenses and profit (i.e., the portion of the premium dollar which is available to pay for losses and loss adjustment expenses). If the actual ratio is greater than the expected loss ratio, then a rate increase is needed; if the actual is less than the expected, then a decrease is in order. The next step in the procedure is to determine which classes and territories are better or worse than average. Their rates are then adjusted accordingly.

Rate making for private dwellings The rating of commercial property has been discussed thus far. This section will turn to the subject of private dwellings. From an insurance standpoint, individual risk analysis is minimal since most private dwellings are similar in nature, and inspection for such dwellings would be economically prohibitive. Dwellings are class rated on the basis of their basic construction and available public protection. However, ISO has introduced some incentives for loss prevention measures in private dwellings. There are certain premium credits which can be made available to private dwellings insured under the homeowners' program for the installation of fire alarm or automatic sprinkler systems. These types of protection credits for homeowners are introduced state by state as individual conditions permit.

Certain public protection classifications are being grouped for private dwelling properties so that the same rate is used for different public protection classes. The actual loss experience of private dwellings does not vary significantly with varying degrees of public protection.

In addition to statistical justification, there are other general observations which explain why such a grouping is logical for private dwellings. First, private dwellings are fairly similar in their construction and occupancy hazards. Therefore the fire department's response to residential fires is fairly uniform in most communities. Second, the availability of water for extinguishment is generally not a problem in any community with a public water supply, since great quantities of water are not required to extinguish a dwelling fire as compared to a large commercial establishment.

A class rate approach based on construction, occupancy, and protection is used for rating many small commercial properties with common characteristics. There are a number of important reasons for class rating smaller commercial buildings. Basically, when the occupancy and area are limited in these mercantile and service occupancies, the smaller buildings do not have the frequency or variety of hazards found in the larger size buildings. The rate variations among the great majority of these smaller buildings will be relatively limited, and the average class rate approach is then a feasible and efficient rate-making technique. Another important factor is that class rating is a more economical method in favor of insurance policyholders.

Where habitational occupancies are not covered by the dwelling program, class rating provisions are incorporated in the *Fire Class Rate Manual* for apartment houses, rooming houses, motels, and similar occupancies. The number of units within these occupancies will govern the rating technique.

With insurance rates based on premiums collected and losses incurred, and with premiums collected based on values insured, the relationship between loss and fire protection must consider the values at risk. It is the values at risk which determine the premium and, to a great extent, the losses. If losses are compared to values, the worth of protection and the differences in protection can be shown. There is a relationship between public protection classes and percent of loss to value. As the level of fire protection increases, the percent of loss to value at risk decreases.

Classifying municipal fire protection service

The ISO *Grading Schedule for Municipal Fire Protection*[4] classifies public fire protection service and is an outgrowth of the *Standard Schedule for Grading Cities and Towns of the United States with Reference to Their Fire Defenses and Physical Conditions,* which was first issued in 1916 by the National Board of Fire Underwriters. The original schedule was developed as an underwriting tool for insurance companies and, because of the concentration of values, it and subsequent editions placed a great deal of emphasis on the downtown business district. The trend toward decentralization of values justified greater recognition for areas outside the downtown district, and later editions issued by ISO analyze the municipality as a whole. The downtown business district is treated on the same basis as other commercial districts. This change of emphasis makes the grading schedule a more realistic tool for establishing relative classifications used in fire insurance rating.

The *Grading Schedule for Municipal Fire Protection* provides the insurance industry with a means of identifying, for insurance purposes only, a relative analysis of what may be expected from public fire services. It is an engineering evaluation portraying a logical distinction among areas with no public protection, those with minimum basic protection, and those with reasonably good protection. The grading of public protection does not affect the overall rate level for a state or for large cities receiving individual assessment, but it does provide a relativity for recognizing the quality of public fire protection for the reduction of property loss.

In retrospect, grading schedule criteria too often were used as the sole or predominant basis for a community decision affecting a change or an improvement in protection. However, as there was no other procedure readily available for translating a community's character and protection facilities into the equivalent of a cost-effective analysis, the reliance upon the grading schedule was understandable. The boards and bureaus of the insurance industry applying the schedule were at that time more than ready to promote schedule criteria on the theory that improved municipal fire protection meant fewer losses. While this idea had some merit, it did not include, nor was it intended to include, factors to facilitate overall cost-effective analysis. These were left to community officials—as they should be.

As early as the 1950s, segments of the insurance industry began to modify public relations activity, particularly with respect to the role of the grading schedule. This trend became general, and accelerated during the 1960s and into the 1970s. It has become very evident that while the schedule served a need within the rate-making process, it was not necessarily the answer to the needs of a political subdivision. Changing times and the availability of professional consultants in fire protection opened up more appropriate avenues for public officials to use in reviewing fire protection.

ISO has an obligation to its affiliated companies to continue analyzing public fire protection so that the relative degree of available protection can be determined and used in the rating and underwriting process. The grading schedule provides the means of meeting the obligation. Although the provisions of the schedule may be of assistance to public officials when used in conjunction with analysis of their local situations, the schedule is not intended to serve as a planning guide. Improvements in municipal services that are made to upgrade fire protection should be undertaken for the purposes of conserving life and property, keeping in mind the serious adverse economic losses to the community that can be caused by severe fire damage to local business and industry. Reductions in insurance rates *alone* are generally not sufficient to justify the municipal expense involved in making the necessary improvements to advance from one public protection class to the next better class. Any such reduction should be considered a supplementary benefit to the improved safety of life and property. In other words, the insurance cost–benefit ratio should be considered by public service managers as only one element of the public service package.

Defining the ISO grading schedule   What is the *Grading Schedule for Municipal Fire Protection?* What does it contain? How is it used? As in the case of specific ratings, the schedule is a tool for insurance industry representatives to use in comparing existing conditions with relative criteria for those public protection components that have significant influence upon a community's fire protection system. The established basic criteria used for comparison will vary depending on the characteristics of the individual community. The schedule provides ways to make such variations in the use of basic criteria. The principal features (components) are water supply, fire department, fire service communications, and fire safety control. Each comprises items addressing an element used for comparative purposes. Within predetermined maximums and minimums, the sum of the items of a feature provides the grading of the feature and, in turn, the sum of the features creates the grading and resultant fire protection classification.

The protection classes range from 1 to 10, equally weighted as to spread, class to class. The classification spread of 1 to 10 is a scale of relative values whereby a municipal fire protection system may be compared with others. It is also indicative of a system's ability to defend against the major fire which may be expected in any given community. Where class 10 is assigned, there is usually no protection. However, very minimal protection in a community of extensive development may grade class 10. Protection class 1 represents a fire protection system of extreme capability. Such a system, however, may be neither cost-effective nor a realistic objective for any given community. In general, for classes 2 through 8, each community must decide to what degree protection facilities will satisfy local need and be practical and reasonably cost-effective. The fire defense system of one community grading at a certain protection class does not mean that another having a similar characteristic, such as population, should have the same grade. As an example, a mountain town at a high elevation, with a population of 5,000, may have characteristics resulting in much greater annual costs to provide protection equivalent to that of a town of similar population located on flat land.

The evaluation of items may be by either a debit or a credit system, by assigning deficiencies for divergence from schedule criteria or by assigning credits for the degree to which conditions relate to the criteria. Historically, the grading schedule assigned deficiency points for each item in which conditions did not meet item criteria, with a maximum of 5,000 grading points. This is divided into 500 points per class. Under this method, the fewer the points the better the protection class. Class 1 equates with 0 to 500 points and class 10 with 4,501 to 5,000 points.

Each schedule component, usually referred to as a feature, has a maximum number of points that can be assigned. These maximums have been adjusted with schedule revisions as features and provisions have been updated or revised to reflect changes in public fire protection. Because the schedule is subject to change, the exact mechanics and details of each item are not presented here. Schedule concepts are discussed, however, since these are not expected to experience significant change.

To be eligible for full schedule application, certain minimum facilities are expected under the water supply and fire department features. Without these minimums, a community protection class may be established by definition: for example, not better than class 9 if there is no minimum recognized water supply. A minimum recognized water supply is 250 GPM (gallons per minute) maintained for two hours. With such a system, but without a minimum recognized fire department, the fire department feature may be assigned its maximum allowable deficiency under a debit system while the other features may be graded in the usual manner. If there is no fire department at all, it can be seen that a class 10 would automatically exist because there is no public protection. Should the water supply and fire department features vary widely in grading results, the one that is considerably poorer can be expected to detract from the capabilities of the better one, and a ceiling may apply to the overall community protection class.

Water supply For firefighting purposes, the three most important factors of water supply are the amount of water available for the system, the degree to which the system is capable of moving the available water throughout the community, and how readily the fire department has access to the water wherever and whenever it is needed.

Pumping capabilities and static sources feeding via gravity usually comprise, singularly or in combination, the water available for distribution. The arrangement and size of distribution facilities—normally water mains—will basically control the water quantities that may be moved throughout the community. The design and frequency of fire hydrant installations usually have a direct bearing upon fire department access to water as necessary for fire control and extinguishment. The quantities of water and the rate at which these quantities are available will obviously have a direct effect upon otherwise adequate distribution and hydrant arrangements. An ample supply of readily available water and frequent hydrant installations are of reduced value if the distribution facilities are inadequate.

Where do fires occur? Two-thirds of all structural fires in the United States in 1977 occurred in residential occupancies, mostly one and two family dwellings. Residential occupancy fires totaled 797,000 out of 1,179,000 structural fires. No other type of structural fires totaled even 10 percent of the total. The next largest group, storage facilities, totaled 96,000 fires, or 8.1 percent.

Source: Insurance Information Institute, *Insurance Facts* (New York: Insurance Information Institute, 1978), p. 38.

What is adequate? During the 1970s, ISO began using a guide for determining the desired quantity of water (fire flow) at representative locations throughout the community. The grading schedule is applied on the basis of fire flow commensurate with what there is to burn rather than on a factor such as population, which is no longer indicative of the character of the community. Since it is recognized that any political subdivision, regardless of size, may experience an emergency well beyond its practical level of preparedness, the major portion of the grading of the water supply feature is predicated on the usual large fire to be expected and not on the worst case possible. Worst case potential is, however, assessed, but not to the extent that it controls the grading. For example, a community with several large properties generating needed fire flows on the order of 4,000 to 5,000 GPM and one or two at 7,000 GPM may be graded primarily on considerations stemming from a 5,000 GPM rate. The 7,000 GPM would be reflected in only two or three items.

Fire department The fire department feature centers around four important factors: equipment, personnel, their distribution, and the expertise with which existing protection facilities are used (training and operations). The numbers and types of equipment, together with assigned firefighters, will, in general, depend on needed fire flow and response distances throughout the community. As a rule of thumb, one can say that the greater the necessary fire flow the greater the need for available facilities at lesser distances. There are different arrangements by which on-duty or equivalent firefighters may be provided. Effective response, irrespective of methodology or procedure, is the "proof of the pudding."

Firefighters are usually thought of as personnel with a principal occupation dedicated to prevention and suppression of the unfriendly fire. The desirable arrangement is to have these well-trained personnel on duty with firefighting equipment, ready for immediate response in sufficient numbers to effectively handle the emergency. Where local economics or other constraints preclude such a force, a lesser number of on-duty personnel may be augmented by the response of off-shift personnel, auxiliary personnel paid by the call, other municipal employees with a collateral fire service assignment, or volunteers from the ranks of other occupations. The on-duty firefighter is considered, for grading purposes, as being more readily available for immediate response. Since a fire does not know the difference between the on-duty personnel and those responding under other arrangements, all personnel assigned to firefighting duty are judged to need equivalent training for the fire conditions which may be expected.

Many communities are satisfactorily served by a department entirely made up of volunteers. Others may elect to contract for protection provided by the fire department of an adjoining local government. Two or more communities may arrange for mutual assistance, called automatic aid, where the fire departments operate as one agency, which usually reduces the facilities otherwise necessary for each. Several political entities may arrange for a separate agency, such as a fire protection district, to supply fire department protection for all. There are other variations to meet personnel and operational objectives for effective fire protection. Each is graded on its own merits.

Fire service communications   The three paramount factors in support of the fire service communications feature are: Does the fire alarm dispatching center have the necessary means to receive fire notification from the citizen? Do the central and the field forces have the needed facilities for immediate dispatch of apparatus? Do the field forces have the facility for fire ground operations and control?

Fire safety control   Under the fire safety control feature, the grading approach centers around the hazards the community permits to exist and the regulation and control it exercises in order to maintain occupancy hazards within acceptable limits. The locally adopted codes and regulations, together with effectiveness of enforcement and actual conditions, are the core of this feature. At best, the evaluation of an effective fire prevention program is a difficult process. Although the grading is concerned with potential, a long period of accurate records may suggest how many fires are prevented by local effort should there be a reduction in numbers and losses.

The insurance grading representatives will use community records as far as possible to take advantage of locally recorded data and to minimize inconvenience to community officials. Some information may be obtained by witnessing local procedures and operations. Examples are actual flow testing of hydrants, watching condition tests of fire department pumpers and department training evolutions, and accompanying fire prevention inspectors as they visit various premises.

A municipal fire protection grading is not a finite process. Since the visit to the community is short and usually does not provide the opportunity to witness first hand a fire control operation, the assessment of community fire defenses is an indication of potential capability and not a definitive measurement—as some would prefer. Further evidence that the procedure is an indication rather than a precise measurement are the hydrant flow tests. On any given day the water system flow characteristics may vary depending on consumer consumption demands at the moment of testing a given hydrant or group of hydrants. In addition, no two firefighters may use available water in the same manner on the same fire. The grading schedule application technique provides for "representative" usages and applications in recognition of the variables that do exist from day to day. The point spread per protection class, for example, accommodates this concept for the overall grading.

Sources of guidance When using the grading schedule, guidance can be obtained from nationally recognized standards, predominantly those of the National Fire Protection Association (see Section B of this chapter) and the American Water Works Association (6666 West Quincy Avenue, Denver, Colorado 80235). Examples are the fire department equipment and fire communications standards, together with related guiding material, of the NFPA generated by way of voluntary consensus procedure. The fire hydrant and water pipe standards and system operational manuals of the AWWA are also used and are recommended for consideration by the municipal official.

Opposition to the ISO grading schedule There has been opposition to the use of the ISO grading schedule, which has sometimes been attributed to "schedule overdesign" or "unrealistic requirements." From the viewpoint of the municipal official who uses the schedule as *the* development guide, the opposition point of view may have merit.

To develop a protection classification methodology that will provide a meaningful class spread for insurance purposes, schedule criteria must reflect relative conditions that most communities would be hard pressed to meet. Should the schedule criteria be of a stature easily met by most political subdivisions, it stands to reason there would be difficulty in providing a scale of classes that would hold any significance for rating purposes. In lieu of recognizing public protection as a factor in rate making, the insurance industry could grade protection on a standard common to all and then adjust the rates on the basis of other contributing factors. As yet the insurance industry feels public protection relativity is important, particularly for commercial and industrial properties.

Some opposition to the schedule is predicated on the premise that the schedule is inflexible and that its application cannot recognize municipal innovations. The following quote from the grading schedule provides a basis for recognition of performance and innovation:

Where conditions differ widely from those usually found in the average municipality, certain portions of the Schedule may have to be interpreted in a manner consistent with the unusual conditions encountered and the extent to which they affect the fire protection problem.[5]

ISO encourages consultation about a community innovation and its estimated effect upon a grading. For example, a community may elect to install fire hydrants at a less-than-usual frequency because the fire department uses four or five inch pumper suction hose, with each engine company laying its own water main, so to speak. In conjunction with manifolds, or equivalent, the department has a performance capability that provides what might be called a portable hydrant that can be used in a location near every potential fire ground. The grading schedule does not preclude this operation as at least partially offsetting an otherwise deficient distribution of hydrants.

ISO regradings The frequency with which ISO regrades a community's fire defenses may vary. The regrading may be initiated by a request from the community, reporting changes and improvements favorably affecting fire protection.

Installations of new or larger water mains, additional fire hydrants, additional fire stations, the placing of additional fire apparatus in service, and the hiring of additional firefighters are examples of changes which may be improvements.

Occasionally, significant changes are made that do not bring about a protection class improvement when a regrading is made. An example might be a community in which conditions had changed as a result of the development of previously unimproved land and the annexation of large land areas that had had little prior protection. Providing additional protection facilities was necessary to retain the previously established protection class.

An ISO-affiliated insurance company may ask for updated information for underwriting purposes because of reported changes within a community, and a grading review of protection facilities will then be scheduled. ISO will also initiate a regrading when the previous grading becomes over age (usually ten years) or when local circumstances have caused an obvious curtailment in local fire protection.

Should a regrading reveal a retrogression in protection class, ISO consults with community officials to determine if an improvement program may be conducted to regain the previous class. If a program is deemed feasible by the community, no rerating of properties is effected and a one or two year period is established for program completion.

For ISO-initiated gradings, the community is notified several weeks in advance of the starting date for field work. If major changes with a bearing on fire protection are under way, the field inspection may be delayed pending their completion.

Following grading completion, the community is provided with copies of hydrant flow test information for its water and fire department files. ISO offers no recommendations related to grading schedule application unless officially requested to do so by community management. Although there may be some inconvenience to local officials at the time of grading field inspection, favorable insurance effects may be available to the citizens if a better protection class results from the grading.

It is the ISO policy to make available to the public the grading schedule, its companion *Commentary,* and the *Fire Flow Guide,* prepared for and intended for the use of the ISO public protection representatives. In view of this intent, ISO can make no warranty for any use by others.

Other insurance organizations and carriers

Emphasis has been directed toward the principal fire rate-making agency as it relates to analysis of community efforts. There are numerous other fire insurance industry related organizations which have a direct or indirect bearing upon a community's fire safety profile. Some insurance brokers, fire insurance companies, and specialty underwriting organizations provide diverse services to clients and insureds, each having some effect upon a community's future. Professional hazard control, loss prevention, loss reduction, risk management, and management consulting services all can help reduce fire potential through individual premises improvement.

For example, certain insurance carriers specialize in what is called the *highly protected risk* (HPR). The HPR concept of reducing the frequency and severity of fire loss is a result of cooperation between the insurance industry and property owners to prevent losses rather than to simply depend on insurance indemnification. No insurance program can fully compensate for all real financial losses incurred when a manufacturing plant burns or the inventories within a huge modern warehouse are destroyed.

This HPR program anticipates that larger premises have certain characteristics in order to profit from specialized fire protection engineering. HPR provides preferential rates and premiums. For premises to benefit from the program, there must be such activities as premises management to reduce loss probability; periodic and thorough inspection with results minimizing loss; maintenance of a high level of detection and suppression facilities; and preservation of construction in a good condition. The cooperation between private premises and specialty underwriting insurance interests should be of mutual benefit to the community within which the property is situated. Job security for employees may be increased as a result of hazard and loss reduction efforts.

Other types of organizations play an integral part in the property insurance relationship with the community. Everyday losses are adjusted by an insurance company's staff or an adjusting company retained by the insurer. What about the catastrophe or the large loss exceeding the capacities of the local adjusters? Examples are the wide destruction of the rampaging wildfire experienced in California, the many fires that can follow a major earthquake, and the windstorm losses from several tornadoes or a single hurricane. There are industry supported organizations which mobilize catastrophe teams, such as those fielded by the Property Claims Service of the American Insurance Association. These industry efforts accelerate relief to the individual and to the community by assembling a number of experienced adjusters to expedite claim service and available financing for reconstruction.

Various segments of the insurance industry provide public relations and general information on behalf of the industry and the public. One of the roles of the Insurance Information Institute (III) is to compile and provide basic facts relating to the property insurance business. Although it does not have a statistical research staff, III cooperates with other insurance organizations and with commercial publishers of insurance data to make detailed information available about the property insurance business. As a part of this effort, III annually publishes a yearbook, *Insurance Facts,* which reviews current insurance information, statistics, and loss facts, and provides background reference material.

With *Insurance Facts* (1978) reporting approximately $145 billion total premiums written by insurance companies in 1977 in the United States for all types of insurance, of which $72 billion was for property and liability insurance, the important role played by insurance in our country's economy becomes most evident.

Summary

The fire insurance industry is concerned with marketing its product predicated upon rates that are adequate, are not excessive, and are not unfairly discriminatory. In most states a rating organization develops advisory rates on behalf of insurance companies.

There are two principal methods of determining a building rate: the assessment of individual properties and the grouping of properties by class of occupancy. Each method takes into consideration building construction, private and public protection, and hazards of occupancy. Loss experience and rate relativities in geographic areas such as an entire state and large cities are periodically assessed and adjusted as appropriate.

Public protection available throughout a community is usually evaluated at intervals, normally not exceeding every ten years, to classify the protection based on relative values. A community's fire protection system is judged by existing conditions compared with criteria relating to the character of the community. This procedure is accomplished by applying the grading schedule of the Insurance Services Office and thus providing a relativity for recognizing the quality of the public protection.

Individual properties—usually the larger ones in the commercial and industrial categories—can use special fire insurance programs providing for beneficial rating when high levels of property preservation are maintained.

The future

The insurance industry, and in particular ISO, continually reviews and evaluates rate-making schedules and procedures. Changing times, including sociological modifications and amended insurance rate regulatory laws, require recognition in the marketplace. Advanced technology, including electronic data processing, opens doors to both simplified and more comprehensive systems of data collection and analysis.

Factors currently considered significant in rate making may be deemphasized. Or these factors may be replaced, depending on changing conditions. New factors may be introduced to satisfy new conditions and to meet different needs of the public and the industry.

For example, the current procedure for evaluating and classifying public fire protection is expected to receive rather extensive modification in keeping with the purpose and use of protection classes by the industry. Although significant and extensive changes may take place in protection evaluation procedures, their application would be expected over an extended period of years before a great number of community classes were based on revised methods. At such time as ISO may effect significant procedural changes, appropriate means would be employed to apprise the public of the event.

B: The membership and professional community

Personnel in local government fire service belong to a variety of professional and informational organizations covering both specific and general situations in building construction, fire or smoke propagation, hazard recognition and control, and regulation of operations and functions within occupancies which may threaten lives and property.

In general, the informational and professional organizations in fire protection have developed out of a recognized need for organization of the knowledge, procedures, and methods applicable to the developing technology of fire protection. The organizations engaged in developing standards provide technical guides with recommended procedures and knowledge relative to fire protection.

Consensus standards organizations

The consensus standards organizations in fire protection develop standards or technical guides of procedures, information, and knowledge. These organizations use voluntary committee members with a consensus approach, which essentially means the approval and agreement of all the interested parties in the development of the standard. Standards for public fire protection are highly influential in the purchase of fire apparatus and equipment, in choice of personnel protective clothing and appliances, in the training of personnel, and in the adoption of legal codes and ordinances—primarily fire prevention and building codes.

Participation by fire service personnel on the technical committees of the consensus standards organizations may provide important financial benefits to the local government through the control or elimination of cost-increasing items in a standard.

The consensus process which is involved in all of the committees of the National Fire Protection Association and the American Society for Testing and Materials has been described by Robert Dixon in the following manner:

The "consensus" feature that dominates private standards-making also suggests that the process is more qualitative than quantitative. Although there may be variations, the goal seems to be to work toward near-unanimity of agreement. . . . In terms of speed of standards-making, and number of standards, this cuts two ways. A stress on achieving consensus allows strong or vocal members to block action, or at least to slow it down considerably. At the same time, for those standards that are approved there is a correspondingly strong assurance that they have high "quality" in the sense of being workable, acceptable, useful, and reasonable in their economic implications.[6]

National Fire Protection Association   The National Fire Protection Association (NFPA) (470 Atlantic Avenue, Boston, Massachusetts 02210) was organized in 1896 with membership from the capital stock insurance companies to develop automatic sprinkler installation rules and to establish insurance rates for buildings with automatic sprinklers.[7] The first annual meeting of the association in 1897 received reports from three technical committees in the areas of: automatic sprinklers; fire doors, shutters, and wire glass; and hose and hydrants.

The National Fire Protection Association in the late 1970s had approximately 2,400 persons serving on 150 technical committees which develop more than 220 technical standards.[8] NFPA is a private, voluntary, nonprofit association whose activities, in addition to production of technical and professional standards, include information exchange, fire safety technical standards development, technical advisory services, public education, fire safety research, and services to public protection agencies.[9]

Total NFPA membership was approximately 32,000 persons as of the late 1970s. Seven professional sections serve members with specialized interests: industrial; railroad; electrical; health care; fire marshal; fire science and technology educators; and fire service. Membership is available in a number of categories and is not a prerequisite for service on the technical committees.

American Society for Testing and Materials   The American Society for Testing and Materials (ASTM) (1916 Race Street, Philadelphia, Pennsylvania 19103) is a scientific and technical organization for the production of voluntary consensus standards. The organization was founded in 1898 for "the development of standards on characteristics and performance of materials, products, systems, and services, and the promotion of related knowledge."[10]

Members with technical expertise volunteer their services to develop standards for both private and governmental organizations. The activities of concern to public fire service management personnel are the standards developed by Committee E–5, Fire Tests.[11] These standards include the procedures for conducting fire endurance tests on wall, floor, and ceiling or roof, door, and window assemblies which result in fire resistance ratings, expressed in time durations, which are incorporated into building codes throughout the United States. The committee also develops the procedures for measuring flame spread along the surface of interior finish materials, including floor coverings and carpets.

The Fire Tests Committee of ASTM has a balanced membership of producers and manufacturers of materials, users of materials, and general interest members from areas of professional concern. Fire prevention personnel, fire service officers, and fire marshals, who are constantly involved with the effects of building components, furnishings, and interior finishes in fire situations, should provide their valuable empirical experience to the development of the research and fire test standards produced by Committee E–5. Membership in ASTM is not necessary for appointment to the standards producing committees or subcommittees.

Code developing organizations

The standards developed by ASTM and NFPA are utilized in both building and fire prevention codes to establish requirements for the construction of and the operations and processes within the building. Four regional professional organizations develop building codes for adoption by local governments. These organizations are the American Insurance Association (AIA) (85 John Street, New York, New York 10038), the Building Officials and Code Administrators International (BOCA) (17926 South Halsted Street, Homewood, Illinois 60430), the International Conference of Building Officials (5360 South Workman Mill Road, Whittier, California 90601), and the Southern Building Code Congress (900 Montclair Road, Birmingham, Alabama 35213). The AIA, the International Conference of Building Officials, and BOCA all produce a fire prevention code as well as a building code. It should also be mentioned that the National Fire Protection Association produces a life safety code, a fire prevention code, a national electric code, and a flammable liquids code.

The American Insurance Association produces the National Building Code and the National Fire Prevention Code. The International Conference of Building Officials produces the Uniform Building Code and the Uniform Fire Code. The Building Officials and Code Administrators International produces the Basic Building Code and the Basic Fire Prevention Code. The Southern Building Code Congress produces the Southern Standard Building Code. These building codes are often referred to as regional or "model building" codes,[12] since they are adopted by agencies and organizations including units of both state and local government.

Other organizations are involved in the development of pertinent ancillary codes for fire protection and prevention. These organizations include the American Society of Mechanical Engineers (345 East 47th Street, New York, New York 10017); the American Society of Heating, Refrigeration and Air-Conditioning Engineers (345 East 47th Street, New York, New York 10017); the American Public Health Association (1015 18th Street, N.W., Washington, D.C. 20036); and the American National Standards Institute (1430 Broadway, New York, New York 10018).

Fire protection testing laboratories

The fire protection testing laboratories test and evaluate fire protection and construction assemblies, devices, and equipment in accordance with standards developed by the technical committees of the National Fire Protection Association and the American Society for Testing and Materials. The equipment or devices evaluated that are of the most concern to municipal officials and fire department officers are fire department pumping apparatus, fire hose, fire extinguishers, fire alarm signaling equipment, fire and smoke detectors, stationary fire pumps, automatic sprinkler heads, and foam producing nozzles and foam liquid additives.

Underwriters Laboratories, Inc.   The Underwriters Laboratories, Inc. (ULI) (207 East Ohio Street, Chicago, Illinois 60611), founded in 1894, is an independent nonprofit corporation engaged in testing for public safety. The objectives of Underwriters Laboratories are stated in their certificate of incorporation in the following manner:

By scientific investigation, study, experiments and tests, to determine the relation of various materials, devices, products, equipment, constructions, methods, and systems to hazards appurtenant thereto or to the use thereof affecting life and property and to ascertain, define and publish standards, classifications and specifications for materials, devices, products, equipment, constructions, methods, and systems affecting such hazards . . .[13]

ULI was created by the National Board of Fire Underwriters with fiscal support from both the Chicago and a midwestern group of fire underwriters. The purpose of this original electrical testing laboratory was to test and evaluate the electrical installations being designed and installed at the Columbian Exposition of 1893. The Columbian Exposition was the first extensive place of public assembly to be illuminated by electricity, and the underwriters were concerned over the fire hazard.

Following the establishment of the American Insurance Association in 1965 and the cessation of the National Board of Fire Underwriters, the ULI began testing fire department pumping apparatus at the manufacturer's plant to ensure that the apparatus would perform to the requirements of NFPA standard no. 1901.[14] The testing of fire detection devices, primarily smoke detectors, has assumed greater importance since many local governments now require a greater amount of installed fire protection as part of building construction.

Factory Mutual Laboratories   The Factory Mutual Laboratories (FML) (1151 Boston–Providence Turnpike, Norwood, Massachusetts 02062) were developed for evaluating fire protection devices and equipment primarily in industrial fire protection. FML was organized as an extension of the Factory Mutual Associated Insurance Companies (now the Factory Mutual System, discussed earlier in this chapter). The laboratories are thus involved with the evaluation of fire protection equipment utilized by fire service personnel, including the installed systems in buildings, such as sprinkler systems, detection and alarm systems, and portable equipment, including extinguishers.

Private laboratories   A number of private laboratories perform fire testing and evaluation on a contract basis, primarily for producers of building materials. Many manufacturers need detailed technical evaluation data on the performance of their materials before submitting the materials to an approvals testing laboratory for evaluation. Examples of these private testing laboratories are the Southwest Research Institute, Ambric Testing and Engineering Associates, Associated Dallas Laboratories, and Approved Engineering Test Laboratory. The U.S. Department of Commerce has developed a voluntary accreditation system for the evaluation of fire testing laboratories.

In addition, some manufacturers and trade associations provide testing and research facilities. The manufacturers' laboratories and their association laboratories provide fire testing and evaluation as a continuing technical service for their sponsors on products which require evaluation by standard fire tests as a prerequisite for building or fire prevention code acceptance. Examples of these laboratories would be the Portland Cement Association Laboratories, Armstrong Cork Company, Monsanto Corporation, Jim Walter Research Laboratories, the Hardwood Plywood Manufacturers Association, the Gypsum Association, and the United States Steel Corporation Research Laboratories.

Federal laboratories   It may be in order at this juncture to discuss several laboratories that are a part of the federal government. The United States government has been engaged in fire research for many years, and some of the most significant developments in fire protection technology and equipment have been products of government laboratories. The National Bureau of Standards has probably been involved in fire research, with the evaluation of equipment systems and building materials, for a greater period of time than any other federal agency. However, other government laboratories which have made significant contributions are located, organizationally, within the Forest Service, the Bureau of Mines, the Federal Aviation Administration, and the Navy.

Center for Fire Research, National Bureau of Standards   The Center for Fire Research at the National Bureau of Standards is pursuing a multidisciplinary program involving contract research to colleges and universities and internal research. The internal program involves basic research on fire development and propagation with the inhibition of fire development through chemical and physical mechanisms. The fire equipment and applications sections of the center is involved with the development and improvement of the fire detection and suppression systems. The Center for Fire Research also has been involved in studying the behavior of the occupants of structures in fire incident situations, including their interaction with the physical environment of the structure, and the fire protection systems, facilities, and equipment provided in the building.

Forest Products Laboratory, U.S. Forest Service   The Forest Products Laboratory at the University of Wisconsin in Madison has been involved in research for the development and improvement of wood and wood-related products. ASTM standard E–286 concerning the eight foot flame spread tunnel test procedure was developed by the research personnel at the Forest Products Laboratory. As might be expected, much of the laboratory's effort has been concerned with evaluation of fire-retardant surface and impregnation treatments for the development of fire-retardant characteristics in wood products.

Bureau of Mines Research Laboratory   The U.S. Bureau of Mines, at the coal mining research laboratory and test mine facility near Pittsburgh, Pennsylvania, has been active for many years in the determination of the factors and variables affecting coal mine fires and explosions. The bureau has introduced unusual procedures for suppressing and extinguishing mine fires which have been adapted to urban fire situations.

Federal Aviation Administration   The Federal Aviation Administration (FAA) operates a number of research laboratories and facilities concerned with aviation-related research programs. The FAA Atlantic City Test Facility has been involved for over ten years in the study of the propagation of aviation fuel spill fires, the extinguishment of these fires, and the possible procedures that may be incorporated into the design of aircraft to reduce the occurrence of fire under crash landing procedures.

Naval Research Laboratory   The U.S. Naval Research Laboratory (NRL), in Washington, D.C., has developed a very effective fire research group to study fire problems which occur aboard naval vessels. The most severe fire hazard situations generally involve flammable liquid fuels, armaments, or the ammunition. Thus, NRL has been intensively involved in the development of procedures, techniques, and extinguishing agents for the control and extinguishment of flammable liquid fires. Two of the most significant developments of NRL for municipal fire departments are potassium bicarbonate dry chemical and an aqueous, film-forming foam agent. They are used in combination by fire departments for controlling and extinguishing flammable liquid fires of the spill type involving large area, shallow depth fuel configurations.

Professional organizations

The professional organizations developed for fire service members have been typically classified according either to rank or to functional responsibilities. Thus an organization such as the International Association of Fire Chiefs is based on the rank of the individual (in this case fire chiefs), while such an organization as the International Society of Fire Service Instructors covers function (in this case instructional and educational personnel). These organizations have been developed to meet the needs of professional advancement, educational opportunity, and improved social and/or economic status.

International Association of Fire Chiefs   The International Association of Fire Chiefs (IAFC) (1329 18th Street, N.W., Washington, D.C. 20036) evolved from the National Association of Fire Engineers, which held its initial meeting in 1873. In 1894 the name was changed to the International Association of Fire Engineers. The final name change, to the International Association of Fire Chiefs, was made in 1926. IAFC membership approximated 5,800 in the late 1970s, primarily chief officers of paid and volunteer fire departments. IAFC is active in applied research for improving local government fire departments in the United States, for example, developing apprenticeship training programs for firefighters and for emergency medical technicians.

International Association of Fire Fighters   The International Association of Fire Fighters (IAFF) (1750 New York Avenue, N.W., Washington, D.C. 20006) was organized in 1918 with an initial membership of 36 delegates from 24 locals in the United States and Canada. IAFF in 1978 consisted of approximately 916 locals with 175,000 dues paying members. IAFF has been most active in seeking improvements in the working conditions of members and in reducing hazards to firefighters through the development of personnel protective equipment. Firefighter safety has been dominant in union activities since 1971 when the first Symposium on the Occupational Health and Hazards of the Fire Service was held at Notre Dame University.

Fire Marshals Association of North America   The Fire Marshals Association of North America (470 Atlantic Avenue, Boston, Massachusetts 02210) was organized in 1906. Membership is limited to governmental and public fire marshals and directors of fire prevention bureaus. State, county, and provincial fire marshals and fire investigators are also eligible for membership. The association, an affiliate of the National Fire Protection Association since 1947, is active as a forum in which state and local fire marshals may exchange ideas, concepts, and solutions to national problems, which currently include arson and incendiary fires.

The Society of Fire Protection Engineers   The Society of Fire Protection Engineers (60 Batterymarch Street, Boston, Massachusetts 02110), organized in 1950 as an affiliate of the National Fire Protection Association, is a professional engineering society that has been autonomous since 1971. The membership as of the late 1970s numbered approximately 2,400, with twenty-six chapters in the United States. The society has been active in establishing requirements for registration as professional engineers in the discipline of fire protection engineering.

Fire protection engineers are being utilized by some cities and other governmental units for fire protection and prevention in either building departments or fire departments. Fire protection engineers in fire departments have been engaged in a variety of tasks, primarily of a research, data analysis, or design nature.[15] Fire protection engineers in fire departments are primarily involved in developing equipment and apparatus purchase specifications, assisting in design of fire stations and selection of fire station locations, evaluating water distribution and supply systems, studying the factors aspect of fire department prevention and suppression activities, and developing changes in fire prevention codes and regulations. Fire protection engineers have been used in the fire departments of Philadelphia, Los Angeles, San Francisco, and San Jose, and also in Alexandria, Virginia, and Dayton, Ohio.

International Society of Fire Service Instructors   The International Society of Fire Service Instructors (P.O. Box 88, Hopkinton, Massachusetts 01748) is concerned with fire service education and training, including the professionalization of instructors. The membership, which in the late 1970s included approximately 1,000 persons, is organized into four sections: state instructors, industrial instructors, college instructors, and municipal and volunteer instructors.

International Fire Service Training Association   The International Fire Service Training Association (Fire Protection Publications, Oklahoma State University, Stillwater, Oklahoma 74074) includes training personnel at both state and local levels involved with fire service and fire department training. The association provides a forum for the development of educational and training materials to be included in the fire service training manuals developed by the Department of Fire Protection and Safety Engineering Technology at Oklahoma State University. The concept of the original four states represented at the organizing conference in 1934 was to facilitate the cooperative development of fire service training materials. The adoption list for these fire service training manuals in the late 1970s consisted of forty states, six Canadian provinces, Bermuda, Queensland, Australia, and various United States government agencies including the National Aeronautics and Space Administration, the Navy, the Air Force, and the Army. The association meets once a year at Oklahoma State University in Stillwater to review proposals and develop additional material for the training manuals.

International Association of Arson Investigators   The membership of the International Association of Arson Investigators (97 Paquin Drive, Marlboro, Massachusetts 01752) includes, in addition to fire service personnel, private investigators, consultants, insurance company investigators, and police officers. Membership is available to fire department personnel who are engaged in incendiary and arson fire investigation duties. Thus, fire marshals or fire inspectors in most fire departments or fire prevention bureaus would be eligible for membership.

International Municipal Signal Association   The International Municipal Signal Association (IMSA) is a professional and educational organization for signal and communications officials in local and state governments. The association includes personnel from fire and police communications systems and from traffic control systems. The supervising officer of the fire department communications center in most fire departments would be concerned with membership in this organization. (See Chapter 17 for more information on the programs and services of IMSA.)

Associated Public-Safety Communications Officers   Membership in the Associated Public-Safety Communications Officers (APCO) includes communications personnel with fire, police, highway maintenance, civil defense, emergency medical, and other services at all levels of government. Radio frequency coordination and other phases of public safety communications are the major interest of APCO. (See Chapter 17 for further details on APCO.)

International Association of Black Professional Fire Fighters   The International Association of Black Professional Fire Fighters (230 West 113th Street, New York, New York 10026) is a union affiliated with the AFL–CIO through the International Association of Fire Fighters. The organization, founded in 1970 to encourage the selection of black minority personnel for fire department positions, had twenty-four affiliated locals or chapters in the late 1970s.

National Association of Fire Science and Administration   The National Association of Fire Science and Administration (103 Park Avenue, New York, New York 10017) is an outgrowth of the fire science programs established in the Brooklyn Community College, and the John Jay College of Criminal Justice in New York City in the late 1960s and early 1970s. The objectives of the association are presented from its periodical as follows:

The purpose of NAFSA shall be: to promote and encourage the education and professionalization of the fire service; to upgrade the sciences of fire prevention, fire protection, fire suppression and fire administration; and to promote and encourage close cooperation between fire protection engineers, fire fighters and industry. In furtherance of such activities, the Association shall encourage research and the preparation of papers, documents and reports on fire service topics and the development of standards, codes and recommended practices in the fire service field.[16]

Joint Council of National Fire Service Organizations The Joint Council of National Fire Service Organizations was formed in 1970 to study fire service problems. The affiliated organizational members of the council are: National Fire Protection Association, International Association of Fire Fighters, International Association of Fire Chiefs, Fire Marshals Association of North America, International Association of Arson Investigators, International Association of Black Professional Fire Fighters, International Fire Service Training Association, International Society of Fire Service Instructors, International Municipal Signal Association, and National Association of Fire Science and Administration.

As an example of collective action, the Professional Qualifications Board for the Fire Service was appointed by the Joint Council. The Joint Council has also sponsored the formation of technical committees under NFPA auspices, with the Professional Qualifications Board, for the development of the NFPA standards concerning recommended minimum performance qualifications for firefighters (NFPA no. 1001); fire inspectors, fire investigators, and fire prevention education officers (NFPA no. 1031); fire service instructors (NFPA no. 1041); fire service officers (NFPA no. 1021); and fire apparatus driver/operators (NFPA no. 1002). In this way the process of peer development and evaluation was used to develop the minimum standards for professional qualification.

The Professional Qualifications Board is working with various states to establish a certification procedure for the evaluation of fire department personnel in relation to minimum performance standards.

C: The academic and research community

Public fire service personnel have valid reasons to be intensely interested in the developments in fire protection and fire science taking place in academic and research institutions. Most of the progress in the initiation of fire-related education programs in academic institutions over the past decade has involved members of public fire departments. The significant accomplishments in fire research have primarily been a result of increased federal government funding accompanied by interest in fire research from the National Fire Prevention and Control Administration (now the U.S. Fire Administration) and contract and grant procedures of the Office of Extramural Research, Center for Fire Research, National Bureau of Standards.

***Fire-related education programs
in the academic community***

Fire-related education programs in the academic community can be classified by duration and purpose. The spectrum of these programs includes fire protection engineering programs, two year fire science and fire technology programs, four year baccalaureate degree programs, and graduate programs.

Fire science and fire technology programs The first program specifically developed to meet a demand for "academic" education for the fire service was a two year certificate program in fire protection that was started at Oklahoma A&M College in 1937. The program progressed to an associate degree program about 1952, as the expected educational progression from the two year certificate program. In 1972 this program was reorganized and expanded into a four year program offering a bachelor's degree in fire protection and safety technology.

Following World War II, with the increased educational benefits available to veterans, two year fire related education programs were established on a limited scale in California, starting in 1949 at Contra Costa Community College and East Los Angeles Community College. The community and junior college development in the United States was, however, primarily limited to California and the West Coast; the fire service of that time was not extensively interested in academic development through two year, fire-related education programs. Extensive development of two year programs for the fire service began in the 1960s. The first two year associate degree program in fire protection technology was established in 1964 at the Rowan Technical Institute in Salisbury, North Carolina.

Two year fire science and technology training programs spread when fire department personnel, with assistance from the International Association of Fire Fighters, began urging the establishment of these programs upon the community and junior colleges. Favreau, in his original survey of the fire science programs in 1966, reported a total of eleven states with twenty-one two year programs. Upon examination of this report, it is interesting to note that ten of these programs were established in California.[17]

Favreau conducted a follow-up survey on the fire science programs in 1968, which indicated a total of sixty-one two year programs in eighteen states. California again reported the greatest amount of activity, with thirty-two programs, a logical consequence of extensive development of community and junior colleges throughout the state.[18]

Favreau's final study in 1971 indicated a total of 135 two year fire-related education programs in thirty-one states. As in previous studies, the state of California had the greatest number of programs, totaling 51. Of the remaining programs reported by Favreau in 1971, only four states had 5 or more programs: Massachusetts (10); New York (9); Illinois (6); and Michigan (5).[19]

The consortium study conducted for the National Fire Prevention and Control Administration in 1975 showed 223 two year fire-related educational programs offering associate degrees. These programs were reported in forty-four states (all but Idaho, Montana, North Dakota, South Dakota, Vermont, and Wyoming). The largest numbers of programs were reported for: California (44); Illinois (18); Florida (17); Arizona and Texas (14 each); and Massachusetts and North Carolina (11 each).[20]

Studies of various reports indicate that enrollment in such programs more than quadrupled between the late 1960s and the mid-1970s. Thus, it would appear that two year programs in fire science, fire technology, and fire administration have been widely accepted by fire department personnel. The primary institutions of higher education concerned with these educational programs are the community colleges.

Four year fire-related education programs   One of the earliest four year, fire-related education programs was offered at the University of Southern California in 1948; it offered a bachelor's degree in public administration with concentration in fire administration. This program was very successful for a number of years, since the program also offered master's and doctor's degrees in public administration, with the fire administration concentration. The program was discontinued in 1969–70 for the bachelor's and master's degrees, while the doctorate program continued a few years longer.

New York City fire department personnel can enroll in a two year program in fire science technology at the New York City College in Brooklyn. Organized in

1965, the program offers an associate in applied science degree. This program has been most popular. It is the initial component of a fire-related education program that enables a student to go into a four year college of the New York City college system and, if desired, go on for a master's in public administration in the city college system.

The University of New Haven in 1970 initiated two baccalaureate programs, one with a major in fire science administration and the other with a major in fire science technology. These four year programs have provided a popular option for graduates of two year fire programs to obtain a bachelor's degree in either the technical or administrative aspects of fire science.

The consortium study mentioned earlier located nineteen baccalaureate programs in colleges and universities in 1975.[21] The complete list of program titles and institutions is shown in Figure 4–1.

Apparently the four year fire-related education programs, with the exception of programs in forestry, fire protection engineering, and, to some extent, fire protection technology, have been articulated for the graduate of the two year fire-related program in the community college.

Graduate programs   The only existing graduate program in fire protection engineering for a master's degree was initiated in 1975 at the University of Edinburgh in Scotland under Professor David Rasbash. This program involves a full calendar year of study. The program appears to be well established and has graduated four classes.

The University of California at Berkeley has awarded one Ph.D. in fire protection engineering under the Civil Engineering Department in 1976. This program appears to be an option in the doctorate program and provides the student with an opportunity to conduct dissertation research in the fire research program at the University.

The consortium study identified two graduate programs leading to a master's degree in a fire-related educational program. Both of these programs were related to the forest fire problem with two master's degrees and one doctorate being offered through the forestry programs of education, research, and study at both Humboldt State University, California, and the University of Washington, Seattle.[22]

A cooperative education program at both master's and doctorate levels has been offered between the College of Forest Resources, University of Washington, Seattle, and the United States Forest Service since 1967. This graduate education program at the University of Washington is designed for two master's degrees as well as the Ph.D. One master's is a professional degree for the forest fire manager (master of forest resources). These M.S. and Ph.D. programs are highly specialized with flexible entrance requirements and are designed for the forest fire researcher. Interdisciplinary study is encouraged, and study areas have involved sociology of fire prevention, chemistry and physics of fire behavior, and cost-effectiveness of fire control systems.

The type of graduate education established at the University of Washington, with economic and personnel support from the United States Forest Service, would appear to be an effective model for graduate education in fire protection engineering.

One of the newest programs was initiated in 1977 at Pepperdine University in the School of Education. The program offers a master's degree in fire service administration.[23]

The research community and the fire service

Fire research has traditionally been supported, financed, and directed by segments of the fire protection community. The mutual insurance industry supports the fire research of the Factory Mutual Laboratories. Research on fire protec-

Institution	Title of program
California State University Los Angeles	Fire Protection Administration
Humboldt State University Arcata, California	Forest Fire Science
University of New Haven New Haven, Connecticut	Fire Science Administration Fire Science Technology
University of South Florida Tampa	Industrial and Technical Education for Fire Administrators
Illinois Institute of Technology Chicago	Fire Protection and Safety Engineering
Eastern Kentucky University Richmond	Fire Prevention and Control
University of Maryland College Park	Fire Protection Engineering Urban Studies—Fire Science
Boston State College Boston	Public Service—Fire Science
Madonna College Livonia, Michigan	Fire Protection and Occupational Safety
University of Minnesota Minneapolis	Independent Study
Central Missouri State University Warrensburg	Public Services—Fire Science
Jersey City State College Jersey City, New Jersey	Administration of Safety and Security Services
John Jay College of Criminal Justice New York	Fire Science Fire Service Administration
University of Cincinnati Cincinnati	Fire and Safety Engineering Technology Fire and Industrial Safety Technology
Oklahoma State University Stillwater	Fire Protection and Safety Engineering Technology

Figure 4–1   Fire-related baccalaureate degree programs. (Source: International Association of Fire Chiefs, International Association of Fire Fighters, International Society of Fire Service Instructors, and National Fire Protection Association, *Report on a Survey of the Fire Education and Training Programs,* Washington, D.C.: National Fire Prevention and Control Administration, 1975.)

tion is also pursued at the Underwriters Laboratories (both laboratories are discussed earlier in this chapter). Fire departments have for a number of years conducted research through their fire prevention or training divisions, and some departments—Los Angeles, for example—maintain research offices within the department. The New York City fire department established its planning and operations research office with both fire officers and civilian analysts in the early 1970s.

The federal government, since passage of the Fire Research and Safety Act in 1968, has increased its efforts in fire research. Federal fire research has increasingly relied on the funding of private research organizations and colleges or universities.

In addition to governmental efforts, several private organizations are in the forefront of fire research. The following discussion summarizes the work of four of these organizations and adds a concluding summary of research in colleges and universities.

New York City–Rand Institute The New York City–Rand Institute initiated research projects in New York City in 1969 on all types of problems confronting the city government. Work with the fire department has involved systems and operations research in delays in dispatching, excessive false alarms, and excessive response rates. Some engine companies in 1968 were responding to approximately 9,000 alarms per year.

Many innovative ideas were initiated as a result of the efforts of the fire department and Rand research staff.[24] Tactical control units were utilized, which involved fire companies placed in service only during the period of peak demand, between 3:00 P.M. and midnight. Adaptive response patterns have cut the number of fire responses by over 100,000 per year. Allocation models were developed to determine where and when to deploy firefighting resources, and a computer-aided command and control system was designed to provide flexible and responsive deployment of firefighting units.

The Rand-developed models for allocation of fire companies and location of fire stations have been adapted to other localities, with Rand conducting similar studies in Yonkers, New York, and Wilmington, Delaware. The development and introduction of Rapid Water as a friction-reducing agent to the pump on an engine resulted in the use of smaller, lighter-weight hoses. As a result of this development, by 1976 eighty-one engine companies were so equipped, allowing a reduction in manning of from five to four firefighters per shift, thus saving approximately $10 million per year. (Rapid Water is further discussed in Chapter 20). When the New York City–Rand Institute was phased out in 1976, it was estimated that the research programs in fire protection had enabled the city to save over $20 million a year, with a total cost to the city of approximately $3 million.

Institute for Local Self Government The Institute for Local Self Government, established in 1955, is involved in research and education to promote and strengthen local self-government. Since early 1975 the institute has been studying public safety services, with special attention to the systems for service delivery. Funding for these studies has been provided by the Lilly Foundation. The Institute for Local Self Government has completed six innovative reports relative to management and operational problems in the public fire service. This work is further discussed in Chapter 3.

Research Triangle Institute The Research Triangle Institute, in cooperation with the International City Management Association and the National Fire Protection Association, in a study funded by the National Science Foundation, attempted to develop a data base for comparison of the effectiveness of fire protection in governmental units of similar characteristics. This study, the results of which are available in the *Municipal Fire Service Workbook,* was designed to answer the question: "How do you measure the performance of a fire service delivery system?"[25] This primary question is related to one of the objectives of the research effort: "How well are the organizations of fire protection service delivery within the study universe minimizing human casualties and property losses by helping to prevent unwanted fires and to suppress uncontrolled fires in a way that losses are held to a minimum?"[26]

Extensive fire service information was collected and analyzed for fifty standard metropolitan statistical areas (SMSAs). Within these fifty SMSAs, fire and building department managers and city executives were interviewed. In addition, information was collected first hand from these areas and from U.S. Bureau of the Census and other statistical publications. This study, and the resultant *Municipal Fire Service Workbook,* are discussed in later chapters of this book, particularly Chapters 7 and 14.

Public Technology, Inc.   Public Technology, Inc. (PTI), studies problems which affect the management effectiveness and efficiency of governments. A fire station location model was developed by PTI for selection of fire station sites by computer analysis and other evaluation of relevant variables. In addition, PTI has developed a complete analysis of the latest edition of the Insurance Services Office grading schedule.[27]

The National Aeronautics and Space Administration has been working with PTI to adapt the results of the extensive space research programs to the solution of public fire protection problems. Under this program the Nomex fabrics have been adapted for protective clothing for firefighters, and light-weight, self-contained breathing apparatus has been designed. These and other innovative studies by PTI are discussed elsewhere in this book, particularly in Chapters 19 and 20.

Colleges and universities   The Center for Fire Research has identified twenty-nine colleges and universities involved in fire research activities supported by the center. Their studies include topics ranging from understanding fire propagation rates within a single department to the behavior of individuals in fire situations.

D: The federal government

Fire suppression and prevention are responsibilities of many agencies of the federal government, especially the armed forces, but also the Forest Service, the National Park Service, and other agencies that are working with and are concerned with the physical environment. From the local government point of view, however, the most significant federal program in fire service undoubtedly is the range of activities carried out by the U.S. Fire Administration (USFA) (until 1978 the National Fire Prevention and Control Administration). In this section, major attention will be given to the origin, development, and programs of the U.S. Fire Administration. This will be followed by brief coverage of the Consumer Product Safety Commission, the U.S. Department of Health, Education, and Welfare, and other agencies whose work is of direct concern to local government.

U.S. Fire Administration

When Congress passed Public Law 93–498, the Fire Prevention and Control Act of 1974, it set forth major purposes of reducing fire loss through better fire prevention and control, supplementing existing programs of research and training, stepping up research into the treatment of burns and smoke injuries, and establishing the National Fire Prevention and Control Administration (NFPCA). In the preamble to the act, Congress recognized the fire service field in stating the legislative intent to set up a "coordinated program to support and reinforce the fire prevention and control activities of State and local governments." (In late 1978 the NFPCA became the U.S. Fire Administration [USFA].)

Organization and program   The act establishing the National Fire Prevention and Control Administration placed it within the Department of Commerce, and called for four agencies within NFPCA:

1. Public Education Office: "to educate the public and to overcome public indifference as to fire and fire prevention." By awarding grants for statewide fire education resource systems, this office hopes to reduce fire-related deaths and injuries.
2. National Academy for Fire Prevention and Control: "to advance the professional development of fire service personnel and of other persons engaged in fire prevention and control activities." The academy provides training for technical experts, the fire service, and the public. Courses cover a range of topics from fire/arson investigation to labor–management relations and emphasizes "training the trainers."
3. National Fire Data Center: "for the selection, analysis, publication, and dissemination of information related to the prevention, occurrence, control, and results of fires of all types." This office gathers and analyzes nationwide data on fire causes, injuries and deaths, occupational hazards, firefighting activities, fire prevention and control laws, and other major aspects of fire protection.
4. National Fire Safety and Research Office: to make available "improved suppression, protective, auxiliary, and warning devices incorporating the latest technology." This office handles the planning, research, and technology programs affecting fire-caused deaths and injuries and the cost-effectiveness of fire protection. Programs such as firefighter safety, residential fire safety, and master planning are administered by this office.

In addition, the act provided that the research program of the Fire Research Center "shall be determined in consultation with the Administrator of the National Fire Prevention and Control Administration." The Fire Research Center is part of the National Bureau of Standards which, in turn, is part of the U.S. Department of Commerce. The Fire Research Center conducts research, heavily based on the physical and biological sciences, into such subjects as fire processes, questions of combustion, fire behavior, design concepts for fire safety, effects of toxic substances, the psychology of the arsonist, cardiac conditions and other hazards that occur from fire exposure, and stress as it affects firefighters.

An important function of the NFPCA, according to its enabling legislation, was to "encourage and assist . . . States and political subdivisions" in establishing master plans for fire prevention and control. The act defines a master plan as "one which will result in the planning and implementation in the area involved of a general program of action for fire prevention and control." Broadly stated, fire master planning involves the entire community deciding what it wants in terms of an adequate level of fire protection, what it is willing to spend for fire protection, and what level of risk it is willing to accept. Emphasis is placed on aiding local governments to determine what fire protection strategies would work best for them.

The method ultimately chosen to foster the establishment of master plans at all levels of government was a modeling approach of sorts—the development of model planning tools. These planning tools, the *Urban Guide for Fire Prevention and Control Master Planning* and the *Basic Guide for Fire Prevention and Control Master Planning*,[28] enable communities of all types and sizes to follow a step-by-step process for a total community fire protection plan. Using these planning guides, communities can examine fire protection alternatives, analyze potential costs and benefits of fire prevention and control programs, and develop a plan of action to carry out what the community needs and is willing to pay for.

The report *Fire Prevention and Control Master Planning: The First Four Years* chronicles the accomplishments of the USFA and describes the following nine programs which support the development of fire master planning:

1. *Urban Guide* Project provides step-by-step guidelines for municipalities to prepare total community master plans for fire prevention and control. Clearly stated procedures include techniques for implementing and regularly updating the plan.
2. *Basic Guide for Fire Prevention and Control Master Planning* is designed for the unique fire protection problems of small communities and rural areas, but it can also be used by larger cities, as well as by multijurisdictional regions and even state governments with relatively uncomplicated planning environments.
3. Multijurisdictional County and Regional Project is intended for comprehensive community fire protection planning in multijurisdictional environments.
4. State Fire Master Planning Project assists the states in identifying their problems through developing a master planning document.
5. Federal Fire Master Planning incorporates comprehensive fire protection planning into the existing fire protection systems of federal agencies.
6. Program Promotion—Media presentations involves national conferences and national public interest groups in promoting fire master planning.
7. Program Monitoring and Evaluation includes independent assessment of the transferability of the fire master planning process, a utilization study of the *Urban Guide for Fire Prevention and Control Master Planning,* and an on-site evaluation of master planning in forty-two jurisdictions.
8. On-Going Procedural and Planning Guidance Support. A variety of (USFA's) ongoing programs support the master planning activities. These include the master planning library, which contains procedural and technical documents; the National Fire Incident Reporting System, which supports the development of standard, statewide, fire incident reporting systems; the National Fire Academy's Planning Assistance Program, which provides the master planning outreach program; and the Public Education Assistance Program, which is intended to build state capacity to support public fire education at the local level.
9. Outreach Programs. Through a variety of means, including conferences and seminars, USFA actively seeks to produce a greater understanding of fire master planning.[29]

From the results of three surveys conducted for the U.S. Fire Administration in 1977, it was estimated that approximately 1,200 local communities were engaged in master planning for fire prevention and control.[30] The majority of this activity was occurring in towns and cities in the 10,000 to 100,000 population range and in communities where a high percentage of fire service personnel is employed on a full-time, paid basis. Almost all of the planning communities are incorporated jurisdictions, and about one-third are council-manager cities.

Transfer to Federal Emergency Management Agency   In 1978 the President sent a reorganization plan to Congress for consolidating five major disaster agencies into a single new Federal Emergency Management Agency (FEMA). The reorganization was an attempt to make a single agency, and a single official, accountable for all federal emergency preparedness, mitigation, and response activities; to create a single point of contact for state and local governments that have strongly urged consolidation of federal emergency programs; to enhance the dual use of emergency preparedness and response resources at all levels of government; and to provide a better basis for determining the relative benefits and cost-effectiveness of spending for hazard mitigation, preparedness planning, relief operations, and recovery assistance. In addition to the Defense Civil Preparedness Agency, the Federal Disaster Assistance Administration, the Federal Preparedness Agency, and the Federal Insurance Administration, the plan affects the U.S. Fire Administration.

The reorganization, which placed the U.S. Fire Administration within FEMA, was controversial. Critics pointed out that 80 percent of all fires affect only single family homes; therefore an agency concerned with fires does not belong in a larger organization concerned with major disasters. In testimony before the Senate, Mayor Charles F. Horn of Kettering, Ohio, representing the National League of Cities, stated:

The reorganization plan shows a serious misunderstanding of the nature of the fire problem, the congressionally mandated mission of the NFPCA, the way institutions operate and the needs of the cities. . . .

In a disaster agency, the concern with daily fires of single homes would not fare well when compared to the glamour of holocaust, disasters, earthquakes, floods, tornadoes, collapsed dams, hurricanes, killer snowfalls, nuclear accidents and/or enemy attack. Fire no more belongs in the new agency than does the National Highway Traffic Safety Administration.[31]

Firefighting groups for the most part supported the transfer. Before the Senate panel, John L. Swindle, president of the IAFC, stated, "We feel it will benefit the fire services . . . by assuring that the national focus on fires will be strengthened and not diffused or subordinated to disaster-related activities."[32]

Six smaller programs also are included in the reorganization: the National Weather Service's community preparedness program for weather emergencies, earthquake hazard reduction, dam safety coordination, and the federal emergency broadcast system of the White House Office of Science and Technology, and two independent programs—coordination of emergency warning, and federal response to terrorist incidents.

Programs of other federal agencies

Several other federal government agencies are engaged in programs and activities in the fire service area that impinge on local governments. The pertinent activities of the Consumer Product Safety Commission and other agencies are described in the paragraphs that follow.

The Consumer Product Safety Commission, an independent regulatory agency, regulates the distribution of products which may endanger the consumer. Fire safety is a major consideration in this undertaking. The Consumer Product Safety Commission has issued regulations on household insulation, primarily covering fire safety characteristics of cellulose insulation. The Commission also regulates the safety, from a fire standpoint, of certain items of clothing, mattresses, and other consumer items.

Fire safety in health care facilities is a major interest of the U.S. Department of Health, Education, and Welfare (HEW). This department, in funding patient care under the Medicaid and Medicare programs, requires facilities housing patients to meet minimum fire safety standards. This program has had considerable effect, especially in states in which retroactive sprinkler requirements had not been imposed for health facilities. Surveys to assure compliance with fire safety standards of Medicaid and Medicare are normally carried out by state fire safety agencies. There is usually an opportunity for the local fire marshal to cooperate with the state inspector in surveying these facilities. Sanctions are available. Although HEW cannot close a federal facility, payments for patients can be cut off.

The U.S. Department of Labor through the Occupational Safety and Health Administration (OSHA) has had some impact on fire safety. Fire safety is not one of the primary objectives of OSHA, but its regulations include a number of fire safety requirements for employee safety. Portions of several National Fire Protection Association standards are included in these regulations. OSHA inspectors concentrate on safety in places of employment, and industries with high accident rates are targeted for intensive inspection.

The OSHA program has improved fire safety, primarily flammable liquid and gas safety and portable fire extinguishing equipment.

Under federal law states may carry out OSHA inspections with their own forces under a matching fund program. Under this arrangement, state inspectors must comply fully with federal guidelines and are, in fact, agents of the U.S. Department of Labor. In those states not electing to carry out enforcement, the Department of Labor directly provides inspection and enforcement.

Unfortunately, opportunities for joint inspection and enforcement by OSHA and local fire prevention personnel have been few. The plant operator is faced with the possibility of an OSHA inspector visiting the facility and imposing many requirements related to fire protection, while the next day the local fire prevention inspector visits and also imposes requirements. There is no opportunity for resolution of any differences that may arise. This condition has probably lessened the effectiveness of local fire prevention efforts in industry, although the Department of Labor has administratively declared that OSHA regulations do not supersede state or local fire prevention codes. They do, however, supersede state and local safety regulations.

Communities on navigable waterways must consider the effects of Coast Guard enforcement of fire prevention regulations in facilities contiguous to waterways. Federal law provides for such jurisdiction and enforcement. Coast Guard personnel have been cooperative in conducting joint inspections with local fire prevention personnel. These inspections occur at bulk petroleum terminals, piers, wharves, and other facilities over which dangerous cargoes may be handled. A strong feature of the Coast Guard regulations is the vigorous control of cutting and welding operations on waterfront facilities.

Many grain elevators are subject to inspection by representatives of the U.S. Department of Agriculture. These inspections encompass certain safety requirements.

The Federal Highway Administration and the Federal Railroad Administration of the Department of Transportation conduct safety inspections in the transportation of hazardous materials. The local fire prevention manager needs to know how to contact appropriate federal personnel to bring about cooperative action against recalcitrant truck and railroad operators. Local fire regulations generally apply to vehicles in interstate transportation as long as the regulations are not in conflict with federal regulations.

Pipeline safety is also regulated by the U.S. Department of Transportation. Local regulations have been preempted by federal regulations. Therefore, it is essential that the local fire prevention manager know where to get in touch with appropriate federal personnel for assistance.

E: State governments

The late 1970s witnessed a growing awareness of state participation in fire prevention and control. This was dramatically illustrated when the two principal nationwide organizations which represent state level fire authorities convened for the specific purpose of addressing the question of where the state fits into the total fire service delivery system.

The State Directors of Training Section of the International Society of Fire

Service Instructors, and NFPA's Fire Marshals Association of North America, met in the late 1970s to define the fire protection roles of state governments and how those roles interrelate at local and national levels.

The results of these separately conducted intensive work sessions—involving the nation's leading state level fire authorities—provided remarkably compatible conclusions and recommendations. The two summary reports, *Recommendations on the Relationship between the National Fire Prevention and Control Administration and the State-Level Fire Community*[33] and *State Fire Marshals' Conference Report: Recommendations on Federal and State Roles in the Fight against Fire,*[34] are destined to profoundly influence the evolution of the state role in fire protection.

These two reports highlight the fragmentation, lack of coordination, and parochial attitudes prevalent in state level, fire-related programs. They document the necessity for establishing a single "fire focus" at the state level, and identify and emphasize the importance of creating a complementary working relationship among federal, state, and local governments which will encourage a coordinated effort to achieve the common goal of effectively reducing the nation's loss to fire.

In analyzing the role of the states, a basic question becomes obvious: With the exception of protecting state wildlands, fire protection is a local responsibility—why should the state be involved in the first place?

For those living in metropolitan areas, local fire protection seems quite self-sufficient, with little or no outside assistance required. And in most cases this is true. Often overlooked, however, are the demographics. The majority of Americans do not live in big cities. Fifty-four percent of our population lives in communities under 25,000. Almost half (about 45 percent) live in communities of less than 10,000, with extremely limited fire protection resources.

We can now better visualize the state level perspective. On the one hand, large, well-equipped, adequately staffed, and professionally trained modern fire departments provide a wide range of prevention, suppression, emergency medical, and related services. At the other extreme, totally volunteer fire companies depend on cake sales to buy fuel for one piece of apparatus.

State government roles by fire service function

How does a state administration address this great diversity of need? Are there identified needs which are common to all and yet are beyond the resources of most? Yes, and that is where we find the pieces marked "state role" which complete the framework of fire protection and control.

The degree of state level involvement in fire protection systems varies dramatically. This is certainly understandable if one considers the variations in the fire problem (what there is to burn), availability of resources, statutory obligations, and political policies and interests.

Diversity among states is to be expected; therefore, no single set of rules can be proposed as a model plan. However, there is general recognition that certain fire protection system functions can only be provided effectively either directly by state government or by state assistance, direct or indirect, to local governments. These functions are: water supply and distribution; communications; regulatory functions; training and education; state-owned property; public fire education; fire cause investigation and reporting; arson processing and prosecution; data collection and dissemination; research and development; planning; personnel administration; interjurisdictional coordination; emergency/disaster services administration; and fire insurance administration.[35]

In spite of the differing organizational relationships and functional details of state government involvement in fire protection related activities, many similarities can be found which suggest broad agreement as to division of authority.

The state role in the direct services of *fire suppression, fire prevention,* and *fire-related rescue* is essentially the same. By their very nature these must be provided by local forces (with the general exception of state and federally owned land). The state role is generally restricted to providing the statutory authority for the establishment and operation of local fire protection services.

Water supply and distribution   Water supply and distribution for fire protection is typically a local responsibility; however, states do provide some minimum standards such as hydrant characteristics and hose thread specifications. California law, for example, requires that all hose couplings and hydrant fittings meet the standard adopted by the National Fire Protection Association.[36]

Communications   Providing communications equipment and service for fire protection is mainly a local responsibility, but the states have typically adopted an active role when multijurisdictional (often statewide) communications networks are needed for large-scale emergency and disaster needs.

The coordination of radio frequencies may be assumed by the state. This may be expanded to actually setting and regulating communication standards and codes such as the adoption of the 911 telephone number for reporting emergencies. (See Chapter 17 for a detailed discussion of communications.)

Regulatory functions   Regulatory functions is one of the largest areas in which states have a fire protection role. Any state regulation which has a fire safety interpretation affects the overall fire protection provided to citizens. The very nature of a state, with its inherent powers, indicates that regulatory functions are primarily a state responsibility. The state may of course delegate to local jurisdictions the authority to exercise these responsibilities, and this is often the case. However, because of the lack of uniformity among the states it is difficult to summarize these except in a very general sense.

A Research Triangle Institute research project analyzed some 344 specific provisions in state legislative codes and grouped them into six categories. The report indicated that even when these 344 provisions are organized into their six categories, the number and variety of specific laws make it difficult to locate a general pattern of state fire laws. The report concluded that although a great diversity exists in state laws across the country, most states have been fairly consistent in adopting statutes regulating the structure and operations of local prevention and suppression services. However, it is clear that the substance of the vast majority of state statutes does not, of itself, bring about the intent of the legislation. The enormous body of state law intended to encourage and regulate effective fire safety seems to have little influence on local fire safety delivery except in large-fire experience and fire department professionalism.[37]

The state role with regard to regulatory functions, then, can be summarized as follows. On a nationwide aggregate basis, states regulate in all subject areas of interest. Even though there are similarities, the set of regulations adopted in each state, and the organization to administer them, is unique to that state.

Training and education   Continuing training and education of fire service personnel gained increasing attention in the 1970s as administrators recognized the cost-effective benefits to be gained from a well-trained, professional, and physically fit fire force.

Large municipalities generally have sufficient resources to provide adequate levels of training internally, or to pay for specialized training by using an outside source. On the other hand, smaller jurisdictions are limited (in varying degrees) in the scope of training they can provide, and volunteer departments generally must rely completely on outside help.

Some states, such as Illinois, Texas, Oregon, and California, have adopted minimum performance standards for various ranks within the fire service career ladder. The state can: provide training directly through centralized, regional, and local academies; coordinate delivery through existing educational institutions, such as community colleges and vocational training centers; and provide resource materials (training manuals, instructors' guides, lesson plans, audiovisual aids, etc.) to facilitate local training. The state also can assist by supporting the adoption of fire protection related educational programs in its university systems.

States can provide incentives for persons who seek career development opportunities. State certification of persons at levels of job skills has stimulated great interest within the fire community. These incentive systems are frequently administered by state level boards or commissions.

State-owned property　The high percentage of land that is owned by the government generally comes as a surprise to most people. For example, of the 160,000 square miles that make up the state of California, only 87,000 square miles (or 54 percent) are privately owned; the balance is divided among local, state, and federal governments.

The protection of these commonly owned resources is government's responsibility. The role is not so clear, however, for buildings and other physical properties which are owned and occupied by the state but are located within the boundaries of a political subdivision (i.e., city, county, township, town, or borough). Publicly owned property is commonly exempt from local property taxes, yet the local jurisdiction is required to provide fire protection service for this property.

Another controversy is the preemption of local fire ordinances by the state in state-owned or state occupied buildings. In other words, the local government—which has fire control responsibilities—often cannot enforce its own ordinances in state-owned or occupied buildings.

The many arguments pro and con concerning these issues will not be discussed here, but the local government administrator should be aware of potential conflicts and therefore should be familiar with state government authority.

Public fire education　The one component of the fire protection delivery system that has probably garnered more attention in recent years than any other is public fire education. The fire community now recognizes that if the number and severity of fires are to be reduced, people must be convinced that it is worthwhile to modify those aspects of their personal behavior which contribute to fire hazards.

The most effective means of providing public fire education is at the community level. The state, however, has three important roles: (1) assisting communities in identifying and analyzing their fire problems through a statewide fire data system; (2) providing a means for exchanging and pooling fire education experience and resources; and (3) directly providing public information by issuing fire prevention information for print and electronic media and by other means.

The Public Education Office of the U.S. Fire Administration took the lead in 1977 in encouraging innovative approaches to the development of state level public education information systems by awarding assistance grants to four pilot states: California, Delaware, Illinois, and Oregon. Later programs were begun in Georgia, North Carolina, Connecticut, Oklahoma, and Missouri. The results of these three year development projects are being thoroughly documented by the U.S. Fire Administration as model programs for use by other states.

Fire cause investigation: arson　Property loss from the crime of arson consistently exceeded the combined losses from auto theft and robbery (the next two highest property loss crimes) in the United States during the decade of the 1970s.

Arson can have a devastating effect at every level of government. Major arson usually involves business and commercial properties, therefore tax revenue, jobs, social benefits, and insurance costs, plus prospects for future community development, are all adversely affected. There is an even more direct cost to government when schools and other publicly owned properties are the target.

Fire cause investigation begins as a local matter. Larger municipalities generally have specialists on their staff who can carry investigations through to completion entirely at the local level. Most local governments, however, are assisted by either the state or the county in arson investigation. A Research Triangle Institute study of 1,248 departments showed that intergovernmental arrangements existed in 62 percent of the cities—with the most common arrangement being combined local–state effort, which occurred in 38 percent of the cases.[38]

A few states take the primary responsibility for investigation of incendiary fires, typically in the office of the state fire marshal or the state police agency. An important role which was emerging in the 1970s is state provision of training to local fire personnel in basic arson detection and fire scene investigation. (See Chapter 11 for a detailed discussion of arson.)

Data collection, dissemination, and analysis How many fires are occurring? What do they burn? Where, when, and why do they start? The answers to these and a multitude of related questions depend almost entirely upon the collection and analysis of fire incident data.

The state has three roles to perform: (1) to provide a centralized system with the technical capacity to collect, compute, organize, and disseminate local fire data for use by the individual reporting agencies; (2) to analyze the reported data for use in the decision-making processes associated with the state's interests (i.e., evaluation of building codes and fire-related regulations, information for the legislature, establishment of fire prevention education priorities, etc.); and (3) to contribute the state's fire experience to the National Fire Data Center for analysis on a nationwide basis. (Data collection and analysis are discussed in detail in Chapter 18.)

Research and development With impetus from the U.S. Fire Administration, states are more active in research and development. The U.S. Fire Administration has provided impetus, direction, and funds so that the states can pursue innovative solutions to fire protection problems. Most of the early U.S. Fire Administration projects have involved some form of sophisticated planning such as development of rural, city, and state master planning for fire protection, statewide master plans for fire education and training, and fire information and education resource system designs.

The process works on a technology transfer basis. Federal grants are made to pilot states. Documentation of resulting model programs is then distributed to other states with an interest in the particular subject concerned.

Planning The state's planning role emanates from its inherent responsibility to achieve maximum effectiveness for each fire protection dollar invested. This implies a coordinated, joint effort among all state level, fire-related agencies, which is virtually impossible without some form of agreement—or plan.

States can also provide planning assistance to local governments. Examples in the late 1970s included technical assistance for local communities in systematic planning for public fire education by the states of California, Delaware, Illinois, and Oregon. (Planning is discussed in detail in Chapter 6.)

Personnel administration In addition to personnel administration for state employees, the states provide varying degrees of local personnel administration through the promulgation of laws and regulations. Typical areas of involvement include pay, benefits, working hours, and on-the-job safety. Some state legislatures establish minimum salaries, work schedules, disability pay, and pensions for firefighters and other public safety employees. Some states provide state-developed personnel testing for the selection of entry level firefighters. (Personnel management is discussed in detail in Chapter 13.)

Interjurisdictional coordination   In its most basic sense interjurisdictional coordination is mutual aid, which can be simply defined as "one neighbor helping another." Because of the "neighborly" relationship, mutual aid is generally achieved on a local basis with or without written agreements. The state's role is evident when the need for mutual aid extends to large areas encompassing a multitude of jurisdictions where a more formalized agreement—or plan—is necessary. The state can then act as the catalyst to bring the involved interests together.

Emergency/disaster services administration   The scope and level of service required to handle a large-scale emergency or disaster is beyond local capabilities. Of necessity the state must be involved. State government services range from providing administrative support to supplying firefighting, rescue, and medical aid personnel, along with supporting resources, in time of need. Typical functions include inventorying and cataloguing fire and rescue resources within the state; developing uniform emergency mobilization, dispatch, and coordination procedures; administering mutual aid; providing technical and resource assistance to local departments in emergencies; providing emergency advanced planning assistance to local departments; and operating emergency communications networks.

Fire insurance administration   Regulation of the insurance industry is generally reserved as a state function. All states have a department of insurance (or the equivalent) whose primary function is regulating the insurance industry according to state and federal laws. States tend to be in one of three groups, depending on the general character of these laws:

1. Nonfiling (open competition): no requirement to file rates with the state insurance commissioner
2. File and use: rates must be filed but the insurance carrier may use them immediately; rates are subject to later override by the state
3. Prior approval: rates must be filed and approved by the state prior to use.

The actual rates are determined initially by the insurance carriers on the basis of information and recommendations supplied by their service organizations.

Organization and coordination by the states

Now that the major areas of state involvement in fire protection have been identified, it would be helpful to review how these functions are organized and coordinated on a statewide basis.

Some generalizations are virtually impossible because of the great diversity among states. For example, forty-eight of the fifty states have a state fire marshal, but the scope and level of functions, responsibilities, and authority vary dramatically from one state to another. Even though the title is the same, it has little meaning in understanding the role that it represents. A similar situation exists for state training directors and their related programs.

Typical state government structures seem to favor separate and relatively independent functions scattered among various departments and agencies. This approach fails to recognize the interdependence of the components in the fire protection system. This traditional approach inhibits progress because it lacks central direction; it defeats the cost-effective efficiency that can be gained through integrated, coordinated, and goal-oriented administration.

Training and education are an example. It is not unusual to find three, four, or even more different state agencies—plus organizations outside of the state government—providing fire-related training: recruit academies, volunteer training, fire/arson investigation, instructor training, mutual aid and disaster control, wildland and forest fire fighting, etc. Duplication, overlapping, and wasted resources are the result.

These deficiencies can be overcome, and a much higher degree of unified. systems effectiveness achieved, with the integration of all state level, fire-related responsibilities under a single fire administrator. This requires a departure from the traditional approach by identifying functions with roles rather than with titles. Divisions can be established for each major functional responsibility (i.e., fire control, emergency services, fire prevention and investigation, training and education, research and development, data collection and analysis, promulgation of laws and regulations, etc.)—all responsible to one head, the fire administrator, who should be conversant with the state fire protection system but should also be sensitive to the myriad of competing priorities existing outside the system.

F: Overview

The local government fire service had the luxury of relative isolation, as compared to many other local government services, until the late 1960s and early 1970s when the forces of change began to be felt. Established practices of many kinds were called into question, including organizational arrangements, personnel assignments, costs, equipment and apparatus standards, and other subjects that were considered almost within the exclusive province of fire service professionals. Several reasons can be offered for these currents of change. Probably the most important are population location and relocation; rising expectations for local government service; rising educational standards and levels of achievement for many members of the fire service; increasing emphasis on efficiency and effectiveness in all government services; new problems and issues, such as arson, that have come to the fore; and the pervasive effects of developments in engineering, manufacturing, and technology.

Most fire departments probably have been, in bureaucratic jargon, both proactive and reactive in adapting to these and other changes.

One of the major purposes of this chapter is to give the reader both an appreciation and a better understanding of the many organizations, institutions, and agencies that impinge on the local government fire service. Most of these organizations are a direct and significant resource for fire department employees with respect to standards, personnel guidance, research, evaluation, and educational development. The value of many of these organizations lies in the areas of the pooling of information and experience, the provision and encouragement of educational development, the setting of standards by consensus, and the provision of professional and technical assistance.

Not all of these organizations, of course, are necessarily organized for the primary benefit of the fire service. The International Association of Fire Fighters is a labor union; its interests are its members. The Insurance Services Office is serving property and casualty insurance companies.

The chapter opened with a description of the insurance industry, including its development and its current regulatory framework under state laws. The structure of the industry is such that it needs some formal way of pooling information on potential hazards in property to be insured and on fire losses. The most significant organization for this purpose is the Insurance Services Office. Organized in 1971 through the consolidation of five national insurance industry service groups, ISO is licensed in all fifty states and serves as the fire rating organization in forty-four of those states. Engineering inspections and evaluations, fire loss experience, and rating and grading schedules are the primary tools used by ISO in its work.

One of the contributions of the first major section of this chapter, which describes the insurance industry and the Insurance Services Office, is to review the insurance rate-making process—who, why, how, where, and when. In addition to describing rating and grading schedules, this review shows the relative importance of loss experience for states and major cities and the significance of commercial and industrial properties, ratios of losses and loss adjustment expenses to premiums, and kinds of insurance carriers. This review helps show that improving local government fire service personnel and facilities by no means guarantees a move to a better fire insurance class; that fire hazards in relation to potential loss through large loss fires is a major concern of insurance carriers no matter what the ratings may be; that fire loss experience for one and two family dwellings does not correlate with the extent of public protection; that the grading schedule should not be the sole or predominant basis for a local government decision to improve fire service; that many other resources are available for fire service measurement; that simplistic application of the ISO grading schedule, and insurance industry insistence on unquestioning adherence to the schedule, have been questioned increasingly since the early 1950s; that any organization for the local fire service is satisfactory (from an insurance industry point of view) so long as it meets objectives for fire protection; and that "public protection relativity"—that is, fire service protection provided by local government—still counts significantly for commercial and industrial properties. Particularly helpful is the way in which this discussion shows that the protection class in which a city is placed is only one of several elements involved in setting insurance rates. And the fire protection class is not necessarily the most important element, because so much depends on the type of property and fire loss experience.

All is not well with the industry, however. It has been charged that ISO acts as a kind of unofficial local policy maker in that it forces basic local fire protection decisions. The ISO *Grading Schedule for Municipal Fire Protection* is especially criticized for discouraging innovation, setting unrealistic standards, working from tradition rather than research, and inhibiting or constraining the application of local government fire resources where they should be placed. The charge also has been made that the ISO grade does not reflect efficiency and effectiveness of the local fire service and that the grades do not correlate with fire loss experience.[39]

The changes that are occurring in the fire service, described elsewhere in this book, provide the information base, approach, and point of view needed to plan and evaluate the fire service in relation to insurance gradings, insurance rates, loss experience, and the insurance industry itself.

The section on professional and service organizations in this chapter shows the wide range of outside organizational resources available to the fire service. Two of these organizations, the National Fire Protection Association and the American Society for Testing and Materials, are of particular importance because of their wide range of interests, the opportunities they provide for service on many kinds of committees—including committees that develop standards and technical guides—and their range of publications and other information media. When combined with the educational opportunities described in the following section of the chapter, they provide a practical expression of career development and lifetime learning.

The next two sections of the chapter, reviewing federal and state government activities, give some indication of the developing interest and commitment on the part of these governments. The U.S. Fire Administration symbolizes the first national recognition of the fire service. USFA is particularly important in providing a central, consolidated point for professional development, data gathering and analysis, and fire suppression and protection research.

The discussion of the role of state governments helps provide perspective on fire service needs in smaller communities. This section shows that state governments can take a significant part in developing standards, facilitating multijurisdictional communications networks, encouraging career development through state sponsored training, and adopting regulations that back up local fire service needs. In summary, state governments seem to have their best opportunities in coordination, education and training, and data compilation and analysis.

No attempt will be made at this point to pull all of these forces, influences, and resources into an overall framework. This chapter does provide background and ways to gain understanding from several perspectives. The chapter provides more than a roster: it helps show the many forces and interests, both complementary and competing, that fire administrators belong to and work with.

1   *U.S.* v. *South-Eastern Underwriters Assn. et al.,* 322 U.S. 533 (1944).

2   Names, addresses, phone numbers, and capsule descriptions of insurance and service organizations in the property–liability field, which covers fire among other losses, are shown in each edition of *Insurance Facts,* issued annually by the Insurance Information Institute, 110 William Street, New York, New York 10038. This annual also presents extensive insurance industry information and data on major fires, fire trends, fire causes, earthquakes, windstorms, and other disasters.

3   Both the *Commercial Fire Rating Schedule* and *Fire Class Rate Manual* are available from the Insurance Services Office, 160 Water Street, New York, New York 10038. Those interested should write to the Product Distribution Division.

4   Insurance Services Office, *Grading Schedule for Municipal Fire Protection* (New York: Insurance Services Office, 1974).

5   Ibid., p. 2.

6   Robert G. Dixon, Jr., *Standards Development in the Private Sector: Thoughts on Interest Representation and Procedural Fairness* (Boston: National Fire Protection Association, 1978), p. 54.

7   See: Percy Bugbee, *Men against Fires: The Study of the National Fire Protection Association, 1896–1971* (Boston: National Fire Protection Association, 1971).

8   See: National Fire Protection Association, *Yearbook and Committee List* (Boston: National Fire Protection Association, 1978), pp. 1–3.

9   Ibid., p. 1.

10 American Society for Testing and Materials, *1977 Annual Book of Standards* (Philadelphia: American Society for Testing and Materials, 1977), p. iii.

11 Ibid., Part 18, "Thermal and Cryogenic Insulating Materials; Building Seals and Sealants; Fire Tests; Building Constructions; Environmental Accoustics."

12 Richard L. Sanderson, *Codes and Code Administration: An Introduction to Building Regulations in the United States* (Chicago: Building Officials Conference of America, Inc., 1969), p. 38.

13 Underwriters Laboratories, Inc., *Annual Report,* 1977 (Northbrook, Ill.: Underwriters Laboratories, Inc., 1978), p. 3.

14 National Fire Protection Association, *Automotive Fire Apparatus,* NFPA no. 1901 (Boston: National Fire Protection Association, 1975).

15 See: William H. Everard, "F.P.E. Offers Broader Viewpoint to Fire Services as a Staff Aide," *Fire Engineering* 123 (August 1976): 37–38.

16 National Association of Fire Science and Administration, *NAFSA News,* August 1978, p. 23.

17 See: Donald F. Favreau, *Fire Science Technology Curricula Survey* (Albany: State University of New York at Albany, International Fire Administration Institute, 1966.)

18 See: Donald F. Favreau, *Higher Education in the Nation's Fire Service* (Albany: State University of New York at Albany, International Fire Administration Institute, 1968.)

19 Donald F. Favreau, *Fire Service Education, 1971: A Survey and Historical Developments of Fire Service in the United States* (Albany: State University of New York at Albany, International Fire Administration Institute, 1971), p. 35.

20 International Association of Fire Chiefs, International Association of Fire Fighters, International Society of Fire Service Instructors, and National Fire Protection Association, *Report on a Survey of the Fire Education and Training Programs* (Washington, D.C.: National Fire Prevention and Control Administration, 1975), p. 8–1.

21 Ibid., passim.

22 Ibid.

23 Clyde A. Bragdon, Jr., "L.A. Develops Master's Degree Program," *Fire Command,* September 1978, p. 11.

24 See: New York City–Rand Institute, *Final Report: 1969–1976* (Santa Monica, Calif.: Rand Corporation, 1977).

25 Research Triangle Institute, International City Management Association, and National Fire Protection Association, *Municipal Fire Service Workbook,* prepared for the National Science Foundation, Research Applied to National Needs (Washington, D.C.: Government Printing Office, 1977), p. 3.

26 Ibid., p. 4.

27 See: Public Technology, Inc., *New Provisions of the I.S.O. Grading Schedule* (Washington, D.C.: Public Technology, Inc., 1974).

28 National Fire Prevention and Control Administration, National Fire Safety and Research Office, *Urban Guide for Fire Prevention and Control Master Planning,* and *A Basic Guide for Fire Prevention and Control Master Planning* (both Washington, D.C.: National Fire Prevention and Control Administration, [1977]).

29 International City Management Association, *Fire Prevention and Control Master Planning: The First Four Years,* prepared for the U.S. Fire Administration (Washington, D.C.: International City Management Association, 1978).

30 The Mission Research Corporation, Santa Barbara, California, conducted, for NFPCA in 1977, two surveys of recipients of the *Urban Guide for Fire Prevention and Control Master Planning* and one survey of recipients of the *Basic Guide for Fire Prevention and Control Master Planning.*

31 S. Scott Rohrer, "The Disaster Reorganization Plan Takes on an Organizational Disaster," *National Journal,* 8 July 1978, pp. 1088–89.

32 Ibid., p. 1089.

33 International Society of Fire Service Instructors, State Directors of Fire Training Section, *Recommendations on the Relationship between the National Fire Prevention and Control Administration and the State-Level Fire Community,* Final Report NFPCA Contract 7X003 (College Park, Md.: International Society of Fire Service Instructors, 1977).

34 Fire Marshals Association of North America, *State Fire Marshals' Conference Report: Recommendations on Federal and State Roles in the Fight against Fire,* Conference Report NFPCA Grant 77006 (Boston: Fire Marshals Association of North America, 1977).

35 Mission Research Corporation, *A Conceptual Description of Statewide Fire Protection Master Planning,* abstract of MRC Report No. 7602–1–276, "Development of a Methodology and Process for Statewide Fire Protection Master Planning and Programming," prepared for the State of Illinois and the National Fire Prevention and Control Administration (Santa Barbara, Calif.: Mission Research Corporation, 1976), pp. 20–32. This reference provides the basic framework for the discussion of the listed functions.

36 State of California, *California Health and Safety Code,* Chapter 2, Section 13025.

37 Research Triangle Institute, International City Management Association, and National Fire Protection Association, *Evaluating the Organization of Service Delivery: Fire,* prepared for the National Science Foundation, Research Applied to National Needs (Research Triangle Park, N.C.: Research Triangle Institute, Center for Population and Urban–Rural Studies [1977; no longer available]).

38 Ibid.

39 For a critical discussion of the fire rating system and the Insurance Services Office, see: *Public Management,* July 1977, entire issue. This issue, which carries the pejorative title of "The Ratings Game," also reviews fire master planning in relation to the grading schedule and new approaches to provision of fire service.

Productivity, technology, and data collection

The present chapter is the last in the series of five that make up Part One of this book under the general title "The Context of Fire Management." The previous chapters have, respectively, begun to fill in that context by describing the evolution of fire services, the management options in fire protection, the fire department and its management approaches, and the role of other organizations, ranging from the private sector insurance industry to the activities of the federal government. Until a few years ago those descriptions, taken together, would have been quite sufficient to fill in the context of fire management. Changes in scientific knowledge, and in the attitudes to the use of that knowledge in fire protection management, now make such an approach insufficient. The changes associated with what is variously termed an "explosion" or a "revolution" in scientific and technological knowledge mean that these areas are now an integral, rather than a peripheral (if they ever were), concern of fire protection managers. They are an essential part of the context of Part One of this book.

The purpose of this chapter is therefore to present a brief overview of three critical areas—productivity, technology, and data collection—as they relate to the overall context of fire management. This chapter provides a bridge between that general context and the detailed coverage to be found later in the book (in Chapter 14, which investigates the measurement and evaluation of productivity; in Chapter 18, which analyzes data collection, processing, and analysis; and, indeed, throughout Part Four, which has the general theme of managing technology, communications, and data). It is not the purpose of this short chapter to supplant those later portions of the book, or even to coordinate with the coverage to be found there in any detailed fashion. It is its purpose, however, to round off the coverage in Part One in the manner described by reminding readers of the increasing importance of these areas.

The chapter is divided into five sections. The first outlines some of the general considerations involved. The second, third, and fourth focus on the changing roles of the resource triangle—productivity, technology, and data; and the fifth provides a brief summary.

General considerations

The 1970s mark a significant turnabout in the awareness of the fire problem in the United States and of the identification of new strategies to meet that problem. The work of the National Commission on Fire Prevention and Control, which issued the report *America Burning* in 1973,[1] was a landmark accomplishment which brought into focus the extremely high burden of fire—in terms of injury, death, disfigurement, psychological trauma, and property loss—borne annually by the American public.

This document brought about the realization that the fire suppression strategies of the last sixty years, although admirable in themselves, had not brought about a low level of fire losses per capita. As a consequence of *America Burning,* two major events occurred. The first was the creation of a federal fire focus on fire problems, with the organization of the National Fire Prevention and Control Administration (NFPCA), now the U.S. Fire Administration, to coordinate and concentrate federal resources on the fire problem. The second event was an understanding that if inroads were to be made into the problem of fire losses, they would have to be made through a far more concentrated effort on fire prevention strategies rather than through a continued aggregation of fire suppression resources and activities.

However, local government and fire service administrators were becoming hard pressed to provide an ever *increasing* array of essential services to the public, while at the same time they were fighting more furiously for a share of the ever *decreasing* local resources.

To complete the challenge, the Insurance Services Office (ISO), which for a long time had dominated the local government fire protection evaluation procedure through its use of its *Grading Schedule for Municipal Fire Protection* (see Chapter 4), announced strategies in the late 1970s which would lead to a gradual diminishing of the impact of this grading schedule. A rapidly increasing responsibility was shifted onto the already hard pressed local government administrators: namely, that of defining appropriate levels of fire protection service and methods of performing fire service evaluation and risk management.

This combined pressure on local administrators and fire service officials produced a timely opportunity for action on the three issues of productivity, technology, and data collection, which are discussed in this chapter. Although each issue is slightly different, all three of these variables combine to define and circumscribe the activities of effective fire service management. Data are the essential cornerstone of any independent and objective analysis of the manner in which fire department services are delivered. Technology is the process by which modern ideas are translated into action through the availability of machines, new apparatus, or new information or procedures. Productivity defines the manner in which a balance is struck between the achievement of goals and the efficiency through which those goals are attained. What, of course, is missing from this triangle of resources is the personal leadership and management ability of the individual manager, which are absolutely necessary to bring one or more of these elements into play in a local government context. Without a strong personal commitment to improve fire department service delivery, and without a deep understanding of the issues which relate to data, technology, and productivity, data run the risk of remaining on the bookshelf or on someone's desk; technology runs the risk of being left on the shop floor unused and unrequested; and productivity remains a fancy term to use in academic lectures.

Productivity

Productivity is a term that is very easy to define, and yet causes the greatest amount of consternation, confusion, and in some cases outright belligerence in a local government context. A textbook will define productivity as the ratio between inputs into a process and outputs derived from that process. In other words, productivity can be viewed as a means through which resources provided for the fulfillment of a particular task are *converted* into deliverable and/or observable and/or measurable programs or services. The difficulty in applying concepts of productivity to fire services begins not with the definition of the inputs to the system, but with the definition of the outputs or the attained measurable service levels.

The inputs are usually apparent: manpower, equipment, physical plant, communications, and other support services are all factors in what is traditionally known as the fire service delivery system. The researcher might also want to include the fire insurance business, since insurance provides part of the risk management system to the individual. In addition, many indirect costs (such as construction costs mandated by fire codes) can also be considered as an outlay toward fire service delivery.

A measurable and objective way of defining the outputs of the fire department service delivery system, however, has as yet eluded all researchers in terms of a consensus agreement. Early efforts to measure the outputs of the fire service delivery system included the various elements which were to be found in traditional fire department annual reports of the 1950s and 1960s. Items such as the amount of hose laid, the number of ladders raised, and the number of responses were all assumed to be important indicators of output measures of the delivery system. In the 1970s efforts were made to identify additional indicators which might be a more tangible and defensible way of measuring and monitoring fire service delivery. In a 1974 report,[2] Schaenman and Swartz suggested outputs

---

Productivity improvement case study
In 1973 the city of San Bernardino, California, with a population of 130,000 and a fire department operating out of ten fire stations to cover an area of forty-five square miles, decided to investigate the potential for the relocation of some of its fire stations. Many of these fire stations had been built in areas of the city where the demand for fire protection had been significantly reduced, at the same time that new service demands had arisen in areas which were not effectively covered by the existing locations of fire stations.

Through the use of a computer-based technique for fire station locations provided by Public Technology, Inc. (PTI), a project team of fire department and city planning officials developed an analytical profile of the city's fire protection needs. This profile indicated the current capability of the ten existing fire stations to provide adequate coverage, and presented several alternative strategies for consideration. After a nine month study of the alternatives, the decision makers chose to move to a configuration

of stations which would provide an improvement in service delivery as measured by the response time to each potential hazard location in the city. This improvement was measured to be a reduction in the average response time of from 4 minutes to 3.25 minutes. This reduction in average response time was achieved through the closing of four of the ten fire stations and the building of three new ones, for a net reduction of one station. This was the equivalent of increasing service levels while reducing costs—a significant achievement which has allowed the city to provide a more efficient fire service delivery system at less cost.

The implications of this case study are significant. Although a city that attempts to duplicate San Bernardino's study cannot expect necessarily to achieve the same results, it can be seen that it is essential that an investigation of more productive uses of local government resources be undertaken by every city. A detailed analysis may identify possible productivity gains which otherwise might go unnoticed.

---

such as fire loss per capita, fire suppression expenses per capita, and other measures which pointed toward the more refined studies which appeared in the 1977 report of Hatry and others.[3] In this later work elements such as fire spread, inspection effectiveness, and other measures were included to provide a more detailed and comprehensive picture of outcome measures. A lengthy study was undertaken in the mid-1970s which addressed the measurement of fire service productivity according to econometric models developed to analyze an extensive data base which was initially collected concerning fire service delivery systems and their costs and impact in hundreds of jurisdictions across the country.[4]

In addition, individual researchers attempted to utilize regional or national data bases and draw valuable conclusions that might fit a theoretical model of productivity and economic behavior. In one of the more important of these efforts the researcher attempted to develop a rational economic model of productivity for the fire department which considered both labor and capital expenditures.[5]

These extensive efforts to develop theoretical and empirical models of fire service output measurement were at times criticized by members of the fire departments as not being truly comprehensive, descriptive, and inclusive of the total scope of the activities of the fire service in the 1970s. It was felt by many that the multiplicity of variables which determine the effectiveness of the delivery system for fire protection services from one local government to another raises barriers to the development of common standardized and transferable productivity measurement techniques. The positive impact of this thrust of research studies of fire service productivity caused the level of attention traditionally given to measurement issues in the fire service to escalate. This produced a growing sense of awareness of the necessity to define and measure not only the input parameters of the fire protection system (as traditionally carried out by the grading schedule of the Insurance Services Office), but also the effect which these resources were having, in some measurable and definable manner.

Productivity has also had a tendency to be much maligned and misunderstood by many fire departments. It has been easy to associate and equate productivity with budget cutbacks, labor force reductions, and in general, a "meat axe" approach to managing fire department resources. Although a general reduction of fire department resources may have provided the impetus in a limited number of implementations, it would seem inappropriate to attach such a definition to the general concept of productivity. The most aggressive and positive way to look at productivity and the possibilities for productivity improvement is suggested in Figure 5–1.

Figure 5–1
Management
strategies for
productivity
improvement.

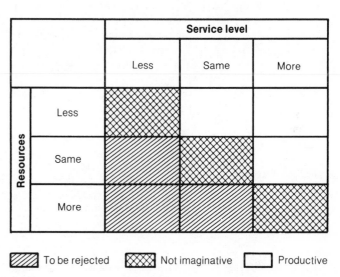

In this figure, the inputs to the fire service system which are assumed to be inputs of a resource nature are matched against the outputs of the system. The outputs are not defined but could be a variety of parameters such as response time to fires, fires prevented, saves effected, inspections conducted, or other measurable criteria of fire department effectiveness. A quick review of the matrix in Figure 5–1 indicates that some strategies can be rejected immediately. For example, a program that would require additional resources and yet would provide a lesser level of service would not be supported. The second option, which is also not challenging, is the mid-rank, which includes the do nothing or status quo option of spending the same money and getting the same level of service—or of spending less money and getting less service, or spending more money and getting more service. These options do not involve much imagination from a management perspective and might be viewed as a traditional recourse for fire service management.

It is the third classification of the matrix in the upper right-hand corner that appears to be a truly good definition of a productive approach to fire service management and also offers a challenge to the fire service manager. Providing the same level of service with fewer resources, providing a better level of service with the same resources, or providing a higher level of service with a lower level of resources are three potential opportunities for fire service management. These options would fulfill the identification of a productive service delivery system and would also ensure that scarce resources were being used in the most effective and efficient way possible.

Technology

Fire service management has long lamented the fact that, although many other municipal fields have seen massive changes in the last sixty years, fire service technology (the theme of Part Four of this book) basically remains at the same level: fires are still being fought with the application of water streams and that application is basically accomplished through the use of traditional techniques. Several studies have attempted to explore the reasons why technological innovations are slow to penetrate the fire service market[6] without producing conclusive evidence as to a possible explanation. However, it would appear that the strict paramilitary organizational structure of the fire department, coupled with the lack of incentives for innovation within the fire service, may be viewed as the primary barriers to technology development in this key sector.

Technology in the fire services When more than eighty local government officials were asked by the International City Management Association about the potential for technology in municipal operations, the majority of suggestions which were received by that association in early 1970 were concerned with issues of fire department management. Specifically, one of the top priorities noted was a need for a method of using innovative technology to free the pump operator who traditionally would stand by the side of the fire apparatus and control the pressure and water flow for the various hoses in use at the fire scene. After long and careful study by a user requirements committee made up of fire service personnel, city managers, budget directors, and aerospace technology experts, a new concept of the nozzle pump operator (NPO) was developed and was introduced into the local government market in 1976.

The NPO, a device consisting of a radio transmitter on the end of the nozzle, allows the person operating the hose nozzle to automatically relay to the engine the exact amount of water flow that is needed at the fire scene; the NPO automatically adjusts the water flowing through the hose to the requested flow and pressure. The NPO has met with increasing attention and interest on the part of local government managers and is expected to play a major role in the productive use of personnel in the 1980s.

In the years when the ISO grading schedule reigned supreme it was difficult for a fire chief or a city manager to argue for the purchase of a new piece of technologically innovative apparatus which would not relieve deficiency points under the grading schedule and might in fact increase deficiency points in the rating of that particular city.

On the other hand, the fire service manager who attempted to use a particular technological innovation in a fire department also bore the brunt of the potential failure of that innovation. With the total lack of mechanisms which might diffuse the responsibility if a particular technology was found deficient, it is easy to understand why technological innovations were not accepted easily in fire department service delivery—where these innovations might affect not only budgetary outlays but human life itself.

However, the 1970s brought an increasing awareness of the potential for technology in the fire service and a growing belief in the possible value and utility of technology in the fire service from two different sectors. One of these was the private sector, which was able to dedicate research and development dollars toward new technologies in the fire service area in a variety of contexts.

Figure 5–2 The nozzle pump operator (NPO), a device consisting of a radio transmitter on the end of the hose nozzle, allows the person operating the nozzle to automatically relay to the engine the exact amount of water flow that is needed at the fire scene. The NPO automatically adjusts the water flowing through the hose nozzle to the requested flow and pressure.

The major factor in the private sector's involvement with new technologies in the fire services was the acceptance of local governments as an equal partner in the development, testing, and eventual marketing of new technologies. It had traditionally been assumed that the people best qualified to define and specify the requirements for a new technology were people other than local government administrators and fire department officials. It had also been implied that the needs of fire department personnel in one city differed significantly from those in another city. This unique and specific needs concept created a customized approach to the development, manufacture, and sale of fire apparatus. This specific needs concept was abandoned in the early 1970s with the development of fire department apparatus under the auspices of "user requirement committees" made up of administrators, representatives of local governments, and fire service officials. These user requirement committees were able to define performance and cost requirements for new technologies which have found their way into the commercial marketplace.

The second contributor to the upsurge of new technology development and dissemination in the 1970s was the federal government. The National Aeronautics and Space Administration (NASA) became convinced that the expertise which it had developed in responding to the protection requirements for astronauts in hostile space environments could be transferred to the hostile fire environment.

The development of the U.S. Fire Administration as a focus of concern of fire safety issues at the national level also facilitated the federal role in technology development. However, this federal thrust could not have been possible without the direct involvement of local officials and their commitment to a program of research, development, demonstration, and testing of new technologies. This involvement was supported by the development of a unique organizational entity—Public Technology, Inc. (PTI)—in the early 1970s, which developed a strong fire program in response to these technology opportunities and pioneered the use of user requirement committees in technology development efforts. This aspect of new technology utilization—the direct involvement and support of the local officials—is crucial to an understanding of the role technology can play in the local government context.

Data collection

A city manager or fire department manager can do very little in terms of planning or designing a fire service delivery program without first determining what the fire problem is in the community and what kinds of resources are currently being used to alleviate the problem. In a way, a fire service manager is totally dependent on the existence of good, reliable, and objective data which not only provide the definition and delineation of the fire problem but also attempt to measure the way in which the individual local government is currently allocating and using resources to meet the needs and demands of the fire problem. (This topic is explored in detail in Chapter 18.) This aspect of data collection defines and sets the stage for the important role that data play in the overall context of fire service management. Data are *essential*. However, unless special care is

---

Data use at the local level In the mid-1970s the city of Wichita, Kansas, altered its traditional way of presenting the fire department annual budget. Previously, the fire department annual report had included a confusing array of lengthy tables detailing the number of incidents, type of apparatus dispatched, losses, etc. It was decided that computer technology and information processing technology could be used to develop a more efficient method of presentation. As a consequence, a visual presentation approach was initiated in which a computer generated map provided the same information. This new approach resulted in a drastic reduction in the number of pages of information provided to the public and a significant improve-

ment in the transfer of information to the reader. A picture is indeed worth a thousand words, and an annual report which includes such a presentation is indeed making appropriate use of the data elements that a particular city may have at its disposal.

This type of presentation also allows individuals, elected officials, administrators, and other department heads to rapidly gain an understanding of the extent and nature of a fire-related problem as well as its geographic implications for the city. This supports the development of rational resource targeting strategies which can diminish, or perhaps ultimately solve, the identified existing fire problem.

---

taken to define the rationale, appropriateness, accuracy, and ease of comprehension of the data elements, the data will simply remain unused, in the form of large stacks of paper or computer printouts which contribute nothing to an understanding of the fire problem or to the resolution of that problem.

There are three major sources of data that can be useful to a fire department manager. These are the following: the dispatch or communication office, the field officer in the fire department, and the administrative staff. The dispatch data will usually include information on how many alarms are received in a given period of time, the nature of those alarms, the nature of the response, and

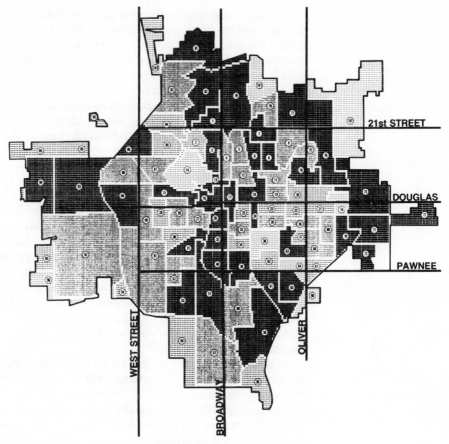

Figure 5–3   This computer generated map replaces the confusing
lengthy tables formerly used in the annual budget presentation
in Wichita, Kansas. The various areas indicate
the alarm pattern for one year
according to census tract.

possibly the disposition of the alarm. Such data elements are important because
they help to establish a profile of the need, as well as an understanding of the
initial response to that emergency need.

The second major source of data is represented by the field officers of the fire
department, who are concerned with the issues of fire protection, fire suppression, and fire prevention on a day-to-day basis. These field and fire officers are
expected to complete specific reporting forms when an unusual event occurs
and also to report on periodic and expected events, such as inspections or training exercises of their personnel. These information elements contribute a significant insight into how the fire problem, and also the provision of services to meet
that problem, are perceived by those who perform the service and response
function.

The third major source of data is the administration office, which can provide
budgetary figures on the costs, funds, and revenues which might be generated
through a variety of means. This office can often provide graphical and other
techniques for the illustration and presentation of the various data elements.

Although traditionally these data elements have been used in an extremely
limited sense, the opportunities for future use are unlimited. Data can be useful
in managing fire department operations more effectively, in planning for future
resource allocation decisions for the fire department delivery system, and in
providing the fire department with an equivalency to those services which have

traditionally been able to use data analysis techniques to evaluate their service delivery system. With the development of inexpensive data processing equipment, including small mini- or micro-processing equipment which can store and retrieve information as needed for a very low cost, the data analysis and data storage problem for most fire departments becomes a very tangible and tractable one. The true challenge, however, is to ensure that the most relevant items are identified and used in a periodic management review.

A real responsibility exists to identify those information elements which are important at the local level, and to eliminate from a data collection system those elements which appear only because of historical expediency or tradition.

Summary

This chapter has addressed the triangle of productivity, technology, and data collection as three significant tools that a city manager or fire service manager can use to improve the fire service delivery system. However, the thesis has also been put forward that these three elements of an improvement program cannot be utilized without the management aptitude, attitude, and ability within the fire department to implement studies, to utilize new technology, and to explore more productive uses of resources and more productive delivery of services. This concept emphasizes the importance of the individual, especially the mid-level fire department manager, who is going to be challenged increasingly in the immediate future.

Traditionally, the mid-level manager in the fire department represented an individual with firefighting experience who had progressed through the ranks to a mid-level management position primarily on the basis of firefighting expertise. However, it is anticipated that the mid-level fire manager of the late 1970s and early 1980s will require an understanding of and capabilities in data analysis, productivity evaluation, and technology utilization, in addition to the expertise in firefighting and fire prevention. To produce such individuals, innovative programs need to be developed which will ensure the existence and availability of trained mid-level fire managers who can understand the needed improvements and can implement the innovative programs of the future.

In the final analysis, the real evolving challenge of the fire services is one of diminishing resources and increasing requirements for service in a changing environment of fire service delivery. Thus, to understand the options available to the fire service, and to develop an effective fire department service delivery system in this confusing and complex environment, it is necessary to accept and use the opportunity which data, technology, and productivity offer to the fire service professional. As has been noted, a more detailed discussion of these issues can be found in Part Four of this book.

1   National Commission on Fire Prevention and Control, *America Burning* (Washington, D.C.: Government Printing Office, 1973).

2   Philip Schaenman and Joe Swartz, *Measuring Fire Protection Productivity in Local Government* (Boston: National Fire Protection Association, 1974).

3   Harry P. Hatry et al., *How Effective Are Your Community Services? Procedures for Monitoring the Effectiveness of Municipal Services* (Washington, D.C.: The Urban Institute and International City Management Association, 1977).

4   Out of this study came the following book: Research Triangle Institute, International City Management Association, and National Fire Protection Association, *Municipal Fire Service Workbook*, prepared for the National Science Foundation, Research Applied to National Needs (Washington, D.C.: Government Printing Office, 1977).

5   Malcolm Getz, "Production in the Public Sector: A Case Study of the Urban Fire Service" (unpublished paper, 1977).

6   See: Alan Frohman and Edward Roberts, *Factors Affecting Innovation in the Fire Services* (Cambridge, Mass.: Pugh-Roberts Associates, Inc., 1972); and John W. Lawton, *A National Agenda for Programs To Increase the Introduction of Innovations in the Fire Services* (Washington, D.C.: Public Technology, Inc., 1973).

Part two:
Managing
fire protection

6 Management and planning for fire protection

The planning for and management of fire protection in the local community are themes addressed by this book as a whole and (from varying functional and technical perspectives) by its individual chapters. Before discussing them in detail in this chapter, it will be helpful to do the following: first, to set this chapter within the overall framework of this book; second, to define the terms *fire protection, management,* and *planning* as they are used here; and third, to outline the discussion that is the main theme of this chapter.

The framework

Part Two of this book, of which this is the opening chapter, is designed to build on the general framework of Part One (which addressed the context of fire management) by concentrating on the management of key functional areas ranging from prevention and inspection services to fire and arson investigation. The present chapter provides a general overview of management and planning that puts the subsequent, more detailed, treatment of the key functional areas into perspective. It thus addresses questions of overall and often systematic concern: questions which can extend beyond the organizational boundaries of a fire department or, for that matter, of a local government into that complex but fundamental process whereby a community, its elected representatives, and the local government employees determine the kinds of risks they are prepared to confront and contain where fire is concerned.

A definition of terms

How are the terms *fire protection, management,* and *planning* to be defined for the purposes of the following discussion?

Fire protection

Fire protection refers to all of the public and private services which are provided to protect people and property from fire. Fire protection can include fire prevention, inspection, fire control or suppression, rescue and emergency medical services, and fire cause determination and arson investigation and prosecution services. As has been noted, management of each of these services is discussed in detail in subsequent chapters.

The services mentioned above are (or should be) provided by the fire department—the notable exceptions in practice being building inspections (particularly during construction) and hospital emergency room care. There are many other services, however, which can and should be considered part of fire protection but which are provided by public and private entities. These include fire safety education in schools; fire insurance premium rate setting; formulating and applying building and fire codes or governmental and quasi-governmental standards; design, installation, operation, and maintenance of built-in protective devices such as smoke and fire detectors, sprinkler systems, alarm systems, and automatic elevators and roof vents; and design, operation, and maintenance of "utilities" such as water systems, communications systems (including telephones), and highway and other transport systems. (Land use planning can also be a critical variable.) As can be seen, then, fire protection is a *system* of interrelated and interdependent services, many of which are not provided by the fire department but all of which directly or indirectly may affect the protection of people and property from fire.

Management and planning

To manage is "to control the movement or behavior of; to have charge of; direct."[1] Fire protection management is the act of controlling, directing, or otherwise being in charge of the fire protection system.

To plan is "to devise a scheme for making, doing, or arranging something; to have in mind as a project or purpose."[2] Planning for fire protection is a tool used in managing the system—and a plan is a prerequisite for successful management. Responsibility and accountability are the key links between management and planning; they are also the criteria by which effective administration is measured.

Planning—the creation of plans—is carried out on several levels. For fire protection three levels might be identified (these are apart from other mechanisms, such as organization development): long-range or master planning, operational planning, and tactical planning. Tactical planning is pointed toward achieving a particular objective, as is done in pre-fire planning. Operational planning is the planning done to make the system work and is basically administrative in nature; it is exemplified by organizational planning, response planning, and the like. Long-range or master planning is concerned with devising, constructing, and changing the fire protection system. It is by nature policy-oriented, long range in time, and wide in scope. It is the level of planning with which we are concerned in this chapter.

Long-range planning is not a new concept. It has been used by industry for many years for the development and marketing of products. Government, particularly the federal government, uses long-range planning, especially in technology-intensive areas such as space exploration. Long-range planning has been used by the military, especially since World War II, to define the military threat and to define, develop, and acquire systems to protect against that threat.

In the past, long-range planning has not generally been applied to service-oriented organizations, perhaps because the end product lacks the visibility of, for example, a transit system. Because of this, long-range planning, to be useful to the decision maker, must contain the following key elements: definition of the problem(s), identification of the solution(s), and a scheme or plan to implement the solution(s). Since fire protection is a system of interacting elements, as noted above, the planning for and management of fire protection can use this concept of system analysis to advantage.

An overview

The discussion which follows is divided into three main sections: a review of the systems concept in planning; a look at contemporary management and planning practices (from risk management to zero-based budgeting), and a detailed examination of the planning process. There is a brief concluding summary and outlook.

For purposes of this discussion, it is important to emphasize that there is a need for good management and planning from the point of view of professional administrators and other policy level decision makers. It is also the elected representatives, the mayors and the council members, who make the decisions as to how safe our communities will be. But good policy decisions cannot be made without objective and thorough planning. And once those decisions are made their intended impact may not be realized in an effective way without good, on-going, professional management. This connection between policy level decision making and planning and management cannot be emphasized too strongly.

It should also be emphasized that, although this chapter concentrates on systematic aspects of fire protection planning and management, it is fully recognized that existing fire protection schemes (some of which will not have been developed by the master planning process described later in this chapter) will be subject to continued refinement as they are tested in practice in actual communities, large and small, over the years ahead.[3]

The systems concept in planning

System analysis is a much used, much abused, and often misunderstood term. It has its genesis in the notion that large systems must be viewed as a whole, rather than as a number of component parts put together, because these parts interact with a resultant effect on each other and on the system, and also because the system has an effect on the outside world (and vice versa). While system analysis has come to mean, variously: the body of analytical methods used to analyze a system, the act of doing an analysis, and even more restrictively the analysis of computer systems, we shall use the term in its original meaning—that is, as the analysis of a system viewed as a whole, taking into account the component parts and their effect on each other and on the system, as well as the interaction between the system and the environment in which it operates.

System analysis, in a general form, can be thought of as a closed-loop feedback process, as illustrated in Figure 6–1. The process gets started with recog-

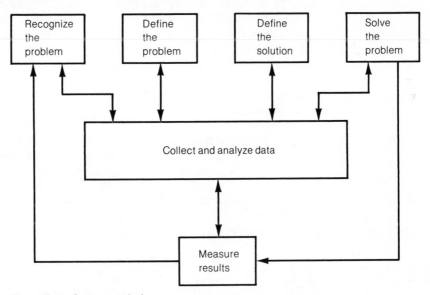

Figure 6–1   System analysis.

nizing the problem, usually by a vague statement such as, "We have a problem." The next thing to do is to define what the problem is and what it is not. This may mean collecting some data and analyzing that data. Once the problem has been defined, an appropriate level of solution can be established, and a method of solving the problem consistent with the desired level of solution is chosen, perhaps from among many methods. The method of solution is put to work and the results are measured by analyzing data. If the problem is not solved satisfactorily the process is repeated, with changes in the level and/or method of solution until the desired result is obtained.

A fire protection system is composed of many elements: these consist of material things, such as apparatus, equipment, and structures, and also of people. These elements are bound together by an organizational structure and operate under rules and regulations which prescribe what the system can and cannot do and where the system can and cannot operate. All of these elements, and the organizational structure, have an effect on each other, either directly or indirectly. For example, the building and fire codes (regulations) determine the state of a structure (a thing) to the extent that the codes are enforced (a rule or policy), which in turn determines the size and caliber of the fire prevention organization and the suppression force (organizational structure and people). All of these basic elements are affected by, and in many cases affect, the number of dollars spent for fire protection. The resulting system is thus a trade-off of cost versus accepted risk in an attempt to balance resources and services.

Master planning, or long-range planning, in the fire department uses the techniques of system analysis to determine the level of performance provided by the community fire protection system and uses the concept of goal setting to establish the level of performance desired in the future. (It should be noted that there are no absolute requirements, in the legal sense, which determine or establish the *level* of fire protection to be provided by a community.) The techniques of system synthesis are then used to formulate various ways and means of providing the desired level of fire protection, and these systems are then analyzed and compared, and the best system is selected. Then and only then is a plan for acquiring and operating the selected system put together.

These systems concepts are augmented by the use of such management concepts as management by objectives (MBO) and zero-based budgeting (ZBB). Together, the systems approach and the management techniques and skills can combine to give a better understanding of the fire protection needs of a community and of the best means of meeting them. This approach also indicates how to obtain and effectively use the people, the organization, the rules and regulations, and the equipment that comprise the fire protection system.

Contemporary management and planning concepts

There are several management and planning concepts or techniques which can be used to aid in preparing and managing a long-range fire protection plan. Those to be discussed here are: risk management, management by objectives, scenarios, forecasting, program planning and budgeting, and zero-based (or zero-base) budgeting. Many of these are used today by forward-looking managers, and some are just beginning to receive attention; all can be of value when properly applied.

Risk management

Risk is the possibility of loss or injury. Because risk is a *possibility* it has an element of uncertainty, which can be estimated and, to a certain extent, can be controlled or managed. (Technically, risk is in fact a certainty; it is the reality of its occurrence in a particular place at a particular time that is a possibility—and the rate of that occurrence is a probability.) This is a basic concept in the insurance industry, where the risks of death or injury or property loss from fire or other causes can be estimated through actuarial means and can be controlled through various mechanisms. In the case of fire, the insurance industry provides incentives to communities to decrease the risk level, through reduced insurance premium rates and through periodic grading of the local fire service protection elements consisting primarily of the water supply system, the fire department suppression capability, and the communications and fire prevention organization. (This is just one example of several interesting private/public sector relationships, others being water supply, electric power, telephones, and similar quasi-public utilities.)

Those involved in risk management need to have information on the nature and extent of the risk, a determination of the level of risk it is prudent to assume, and means of controlling the risk to the level desired. This information is obtained by collecting and analyzing data to estimate the extent and causes of the risk: for example, the number of deaths from fire for various age and socioeconomic groups, the causes of the deaths, and the causes of the fires. The prudent level of risk is obtained by setting goals and objectives on the one hand and limitation criteria on the other: for example, a goal to eliminate all deaths due to fire would clearly be technically, economically, and socially infeasible because we would not be able to pay for all the protection (a cost limitation), and would not be willing to live in unheated concrete houses or sleep on rocks (life-style limitations). The means of controlling the risk to the desired level can be singular, such as providing only fire suppression, but are more likely to be multi-faceted, such as combining suppression, legislation, education, inspection, and rescue services into an organized and long-term system intended to control fire deaths.

Risk management, in summary, identifies the problem and sets a level of service which is affordable; in so doing, it sets a level of risk which is acceptable, devises means to control the losses to the acceptable level, and continually monitors the results and changes the means as necessary. Risk management is thus a closed-loop self-correcting process, which may well be of value in determining the level of fire protection—provided its use becomes widespread. A critical factor in its success, of course, is the skill of the manager concerned (and the level of attention given to the system).

Management by objectives

Management by objectives (MBO) is a method of motivating managers to achieve greater efficiency and effectiveness. The term was first used by the organization theorist Peter Drucker in 1954, who stated the following:

What the business enterprise needs is a principle of management that will give full scope to individual strength and responsibility and at the same time give common direction of vision and effort, establish teamwork, and harmonize the goals of the individual with the common weal. The only principle that can do this is Management by Objectives and self-control.[4]

The method requires that managers set quantitative objectives, within a set of overall guidelines, for the work for which they and their organizations are responsible. The objectives should reflect, insofar as possible, the personal work goals of the manager and should be measurable and attainable but not trivial. The theory is that more effective management results when the organizational objectives and the manager's personal goals are integrated. This concept is diagramed in Figure 6–2. When the objectives of the organization and the personal goals are not in conflict, and when the organizational objectives have not been imposed from outside, theoretically the manager should be a more effective and a happier manager. In properly run MBO programs this is generally true.

MBO, as noted above, was originally devised for business, in which measurement of performance is fairly easy because of the profit orientation. However, it has been used in governmental agencies with some success, although not without difficulty. The chief problem is finding measures which can be used to gauge results. In the long-range planning process described later in this chapter, MBO precepts are used primarily through the setting of fire protection goals and objectives on a community-wide basis by representatives of the community, and then by using the objectives as measures of performance or success. (MBO is also discussed in Chapter 12, where it is applied to the budgetary process.)

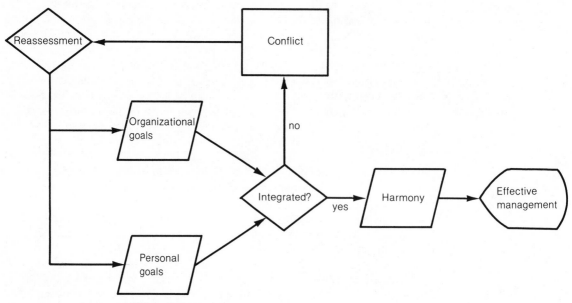

Figure 6–2   The basic proposition of management by objectives.

Scenarios

Losses from fire result directly from a sequence of events embedded in a set of circumstances. If the chain of events should be broken or the circumstances altered, the end result—a loss—could be averted. Greater knowledge of the events and circumstances and of their causal relationships could lead to increased loss avoidance through intervention in the chain of events or modification of the circumstances. This increased knowledge can be gained by means of an analytical tool known as a scenario. A fire scenario is a sequential listing of the events and circumstances resulting in a loss.

The losses, events, and circumstances of fires can be grouped into six categories: type of loss, type of occupancy, time of day, ignition source, item ignited, and direct cause of loss. Major constituent elements of each category can then be defined. (Figure 6–3 is an example of such a grouping.) A scenario can then be formed by linking the elements, using one from each category (for example: death—residence—night—smoking—furnishings—smoke and gas).

This scenario indicates that death occurs directly from smoke and gas emitted from burning furnishings, such as a mattress or a blanket, which were ignited by smoking materials, perhaps a cigarette which was carelessly handled, at night in a residence. It might be pointed out that this sequence of events, or scenario, is a very common one, perhaps the most common cause of fire-related death.

The generation of a scenario is not arbitrary; it is the result of ranking the

Type of loss	Type of occupancy	Time of day	Ignition source	Item ignited	Direct cause of loss
1. Death 2. Injury 3. Property	1. Industrial 2. Commercial 3. Public assembly 4. Institutional 5. Transportation 6. Residential 7. Independent of occupancy	1. Day 2. Night	1. Friction 2. Flame 3. Matches/lighters 4. Smoking material 5. Electrical equipment 6. Electrical wiring 7. Heating/cooking surface 8. Spontaneous 9. Arson 10. Other	1. Flammable fluids/gases 2. Furnishings 3. Structure 4. Interior finish 5. Apparel 6. Other	1. Smoke/gas 2. Heat/flame

Figure 6–3   Fire scenario elements.

elements using fire incident data. The process of rank ordering of scenarios is as follows:

1. Ranking losses in order of frequency
2. Ranking occupancies in order of frequency of each of the losses (death, injury, property)
3. Ranking time of day in order of frequency for each occupancy
4. Ranking ignition source in order of frequency for each time of day
5. Ranking item ignited in order of frequency for each ignition source
6. Ranking direct cause of loss in order of frequency for each item ignited.

In general, the data needed to perform fire scenario analysis are obtained from fire incidence reports which should contain the following information for each fire incident:

1. The occupancy identification
2. The time of day of the fire occurrence
3. The source of ignition
4. The spreading agent (item ignited)
5. The direct cause of loss
6. The loss(es).

The scenarios give a good picture of the causes of fire losses and the relative importance of these causes. This information can be used to devise intervention strategies such as educational programs, automatic suppression devices, and early warning devices, which would break the scenario chain of events and would thus prevent or reduce the loss.[5]

Forecasting

Long-range planning by its very nature depends on data which describe the future. Such data are obtained from forecasts. There are many methods by which forecasts can be made; some of the more common and usable methods are discussed below.

A very useful method that can be used by anyone is called Delphi, after the ancient Greek oracle. It is a consensus method which avoids the problems that arise from groups and which uses feedback to get a consensus opinion. In this method, a topic for which a forecast is to be made is chosen and a panel of experts in the field is identified. The director of the forecast then asks each panel member to make a forecast. The topic might be, for example, ''What is the best level of manning for engines?'' The panel might consist of fire chiefs, captains of engine companies, insurance representatives, pumper manufacturers, and union officials. Each is to give an answer and the rationale for that answer. No partici- pant knows what answer is given by another participant. The director then sum- marizes the answers statistically, feeds them back with the rationales to the par- ticipants, and asks for another estimate. The process is repeated until little or no change occurs in the answers. The process works very quickly and is usually surprisingly accurate.[6]

Another method commonly used is known as trend projection or extrapola- tion. Here, past data are projected into the future to give an idea of what might happen. This method is commonly used for forecasting such subjects as popula- tion growth, number of fires, and the value of the dollar. Trend projection is useful only if little or no change in surrounding circumstances occurs over the period of the forecast.

A third method is called genius forecasting. The process is to ask an expert to give a forecast on a topic of interest. This method can be extremely accurate but is dependent on the capabilities of a single individual and is therefore not as practical as some other methods.

There is also a set of analytical methods—or causal models. These models depend on a knowledge of relationships between cause and effect, and so are mathematical in nature. (An example would be the personnel cost of an organi- zation, which can be computed for any size group if the average cost per person is known.) These methods include regression models, econometric models, input–output models, and simulations of all kinds; descriptions of them may be found in any basic text on statistics.

The selection of a forecasting method depends on the following factors: the context of the forecast, the availability of data, the accuracy desired, the time span of the forecast, and the time and funds available for the forecast. Forecast- ing is an art, not a science, and any results should be interpreted with an appre- ciation of this fact.

Program planning and budgeting

Program planning and budgeting, or PPB (also known as planning–program- ming–budgeting system, or PPBS), is a systematic process used to identify cross-impacts and trade-offs among programs pointed toward the same end, to analyze performance of the programs, and to connect the program objectives to the budget. PPB provides a systematic approach to identifying and evaluating the costs and consequences of objectives (the planning), obtaining the time- phased resources needed to carry out the objectives (the programming), and de- termining the time-phased finances to get the resources (the budgeting).

The PPB concept is used in many forms by many levels of government with varying degrees of success. Its advantages are that both overlapping and gaps across all programs that are leading toward the same objective can be seen (in this way duplication can be avoided, gaps can be filled), and in addition, total resources needed or expended to gain the objective are known. The major dis- advantages are that cost estimates are likely to be in error because of the lengthy time lag between the estimate and actual implementation; that sensitivity of the end result to changes in funding levels for each program cannot easily be deter- mined; and that PPB does not focus on continual evaluation of ongoing pro- grams. Nevertheless, PPB is used very successfully at times; its concepts are used in the master planning process described later. (PPB is also discussed in Chapter 12.)

Zero-based budgeting

Unlike PPB, which is a process of budgeting from the top downward, zero-based budgeting (ZBB) is a budgeting process that goes from the bottom upward. It establishes goals and objectives and measures results as part of the budgeting cycle. In ZBB, each year at budget time an organization is required to justify its ongoing as well as its new and proposed programs and its funding levels from scratch. (This is different from the way most agencies budget now, when the greatest justification is usually required for increases over the previous year's budget only.) ZBB is intended to weed out programs which are unnecessary or are no longer useful. It is a painful task for most managers to have to justify the empire so carefully built, but the exigencies of public funding demand that this be done.

There are two basic steps in the ZBB process: development of decision packages, and ranking or giving priority order to these decision packages. A decision package describes a single function or activity in such a manner that it can be evaluated and compared with other activities. The description includes goals and objectives of the activity, what would happen if the function were not performed (the impact of not performing it), performance indices (measures of effectiveness), alternative activities or functions, and goals and benefits of the original function and the alternatives. The ranking of the decision packages is based on the benefits derived from performing the function or activity. The packages are ranked in decreasing level of benefits; then each level of management (in an upward direction) reranks the decision packages and eliminates programs and/or combines them, until the *final* ranking values reach top management level.

Zero-based budgeting is really common sense put into a systematic method. In the late 1970s it was being instituted in the federal government. It can also be useful at the local level. (ZBB is also discussed in Chapter 12.)

The planning process

Long-range or master planning is a systematic process that has been in use in various forms for at least three decades in industry, in the military, and in the federal government. It is a proven process and is used in many communities throughout the country, not only for fire protection but also for law enforcement, parks and recreation, and other community services. It is applicable to any type of community—rural, suburban, urban, a county, a region (council of governments), or a state.

The U.S. Fire Administration (USFA: formerly the National Fire Prevention and Control Administration) has prepared (and is continuing to prepare) a series of guides which are available to aid communities in their master planning.[7] The procedure and process presented in these guides have been tested and validated in a number of communities.

Underlying philosophies

Before describing in some detail the master planning process, this chapter will give some consideration to the underlying philosophies. The most important ingredient of master planning is that of *commitment*. Long-range planning by its very nature requires commitment over a long period of time. Commitment is obtained by cooperative involvement of the many community agencies which participate directly or indirectly in fire protection, through formal organizations and through approvals of the planning products.

Cooperation is the key to commitment. To be successful, a plan must be understood and accepted by all who are to participate—and in fire prevention and control that is more or less everybody in the community. A plan frequently fails because some person or group was not committed to it, perhaps through a misunderstanding. When people are involved in a plan, they will identify with it, support it, and make it work. (This is also a fundamental precept of MBO.)

It follows that commitment can best be achieved through *community* cooperation. This includes not only the fire department but all agencies involved in fire protection. These would include the obvious agencies, such as the planning department, building department, and water department, and others less obvious, such as the public works department and the police, and, in the private sector, merchants' associations, builders' associations, homeowners' groups and industry representatives.

Phases and activities

With these philosophies—community, commitment, and cooperation—in mind, it is time to look at the planning process itself and at the methodologies or techniques used in the process. Master planning can be thought of as being carried out in three phases or stages (Figure 6–4): preparation, planning, and implementation. The latter two phases are iterative or repetitive, reflecting the fact that planning never stops, and that implementation contains planning and planning is part of implementation.

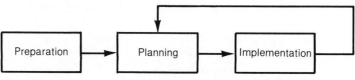

Figure 6–4   The three phases of master planning.

A more detailed picture of the planning process is shown in Figure 6–5, where the major activities and their relations to each other can be seen. Here the iterative nature of the process is more apparent. Briefly, the primary planning activities are the following:

1. Deciding whether to undertake master planning
2. If deciding to go ahead with master planning, getting organized for it
3. Collecting and analyzing data to find out what the problems are
4. Setting goals and objectives, and establishing system selection criteria, on the basis of the data
5. Defining various alternative fire protection systems and determining their functions and resources
6. Comparing and selecting the best system, using the selection criteria
7. Preparing a master plan to obtain and maintain the selected system
8. Implementing the plan
9. Updating and modifying the master plan.

At several points in the process approvals are needed (indicated by the symbol Ⓐ in Figure 6–5). Approvals of interim products of planning are necessary to maintain community awareness and participation and to provide a record of commitments made during the planning. Approvals are made by elected officials, appointed groups, and high ranking employees, depending on what is appropriate.

Deciding whether to undertake master planning

The preparation phase is just what its name indicates—getting ready to undertake planning. First, a conscious decision by the fire protection leadership in the community must be made to embark on master planning. This is not to be made lightly: master planning to be successful requires a great deal of time and resources. It also requires that the right climate for planning exist in the community, since long-range planning is not necessarily acceptable to everyone. The decision to plan or not to plan should be made as a result of stating and examining reasons for and against it. Some reasons for planning might be an unacceptable level of fire deaths or property loss, the desire to stabilize or reduce public fire protection costs, the need to better justify the fire protection budget, or rapid growth in the community. Some reasons against planning might be the existence of a satisfactory master plan, satisfaction with the status quo, or lack of legal authority to prepare a plan.

Getting organized

If the decision to go ahead with planning has been made, the next step is to get organized. There are many things that need to be done: selecting a planning leader and team, forming an advisory group, and estimating the cost and schedule for doing the planning. All of this can be formalized in a planning proposal—a "plan for planning"—which is approved by the authorities involved. This approval constitutes the authorization to proceed with the planning. The proposal might contain the following:

1. A discussion of the need for a fire protection master plan, such as high fire loss or anticipated rapid growth
2. The benefits potentially available from a master plan, such as increased citizen awareness of fire risks and fire protection, increased private sector participation with resulting reduced public sector costs, reduced fire insurance premiums, and improved fire and building codes
3. Identification of the planning organization, including planning team membership and functions, advisory committee membership and functions, and the authorities and responsibilities of these groups
4. The budget and the schedule, with milestones, for the planning work.

The advisory group or committee, mentioned in item 3, is an ad hoc organization convened especially for the planning effort. It is comprised of community leaders who as a group provide guidance to the planning team so that the community is represented in the process. Typical membership includes representatives of the following bodies: the city administrative office, the fire department, the planning department, the building department, the water utility (public or private), the fire commission, citizen groups, industry groups, educational institutions, labor organizations, and many similar groups.

The planning team does the planning work. It is composed of a permanent cadre of a few planning- and management-oriented professionals, augmented by resource persons as needed. Typical membership includes persons from the fire department, the planning department, the finance department, the building department, the water department, and school administrations. The team is headed by a planning team leader whose functions are to assign tasks and provide guidance to the team members, to coordinate the work, and to report progress. The team members should be able to make decisions—to commit the group they represent—without having to obtain authorization. In other words, they have responsibility backed up by the requisite authority; this is very important—if it can be obtained.

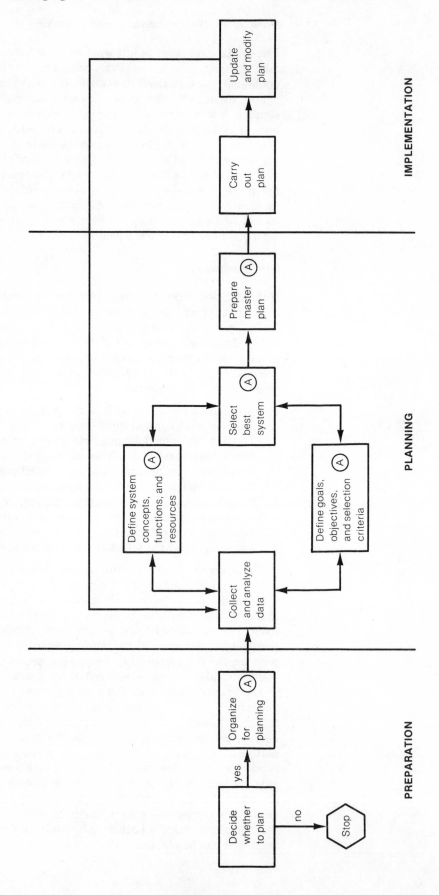

Collecting data

Upon approval of the "plan for planning" and authorization to proceed (which might be a resolution by the governing body), the team starts the planning phase. The initial step is to collect and analyze data to determine the fire problem. (For a more detailed discussion of data collection and analysis, see Chapter 18.)

Data collection and analysis can take a long time and can involve considerable effort, but it is an extremely important step. A community cannot develop a master plan for fire protection without knowing what the fire problem is. Good data may not produce a good system and plan, but poor data never will.

To avoid collecting unnecessary data it is important to understand what the data are used for. It can be seen from Figure 6–5 that the data are used in all steps subsequent to and including collection. Also, the data base is continually updated and used to measure the progress of implementation and the success or failure of the fire protection system, and to update and modify the plan.

Categories of data The data required will probably fall into eight generalized categories: demographic, geographic and physical, building and occupancy, fire incidence and loss, organizational and functional, financial, legislative and legal, and resource. Within each of these categories specific data items can be identified. To support the subsequent analysis and planning, data are needed that describe what has happened, what is happening, and what will probably happen. The historical and current data can be projected for insights into the future.

Demographic data Demographic data can be related to fire incidence. For example, U.S. Fire Administration studies[8] indicate that age, sex, income level, ethnic background, educational level, and neighborhood can be correlated to fire incidence and loss.

Geographic and physical data The geography and physical characteristics of a community are important to fire protection. For example, terrain and weather have an impact on station locations and response times, as do transportation networks such as highways, roads, rivers, and railroads; terrain and weather also affect water supply. Natural disasters such as tornadoes and floods influence emergency and rescue services; also, climate and weather affect the burnable environment and fire ground operations.

Building and occupancy data For most communities the major fire problem results from and occurs in the "built" environment (that is, existing structural conditions). For this reason building and occupancy data regarding type and location of occupancies, number of occupancies protected by alarm systems and sprinklers, age of buildings, heights and areas of buildings, and required fire flows are very important.

Fire incidence and loss data Fire incidence and loss data indicate where, when, and what kinds of fires have been and are occurring, and, therefore, are likely to occur in the future. These data can be manually stored, retrieved, and analyzed, or an automated data system can be used. There are several auto-

Figure 6–5 The planning process. (Source: Adapted from National Fire Prevention and Control Administration, National Fire Safety and Research Office, *Urban Guide for Fire Prevention and Control Master Planning*, Washington, D.C.: National Fire Prevention and Control Administration, [1977], Figure 3–1, pp. 3–4.)

mated systems which can be used directly or modified for local use,[9] all closely related through the use of National Fire Protection Association (NFPA) Standard No. 901—*Uniform Coding for Fire Protection*—as the basis. Most of these systems use two or three forms for recording the data: usually a fire incident form, a casualty form, and sometimes a form for nonfire emergency service.

The main advantage of these systems is that they employ a common language for reporting, which makes it reasonably certain that similar incidents in different jurisidictions are similarly reported. This similarity permits aggregation to regional, state, and national levels for comparison purposes. The major disadvantage is that the forms are somewhat detailed, which generates some resistance to their use. Another disadvantage is that loss data are generally estimated at the scene, with no follow-up to check on the validity of the estimate. In addition, deaths may occur later as a result of injuries received in a fire but these deaths are not attributed to the fire. These latter disadvantages are not a fault of the reporting system but are, rather, problems of recording which will occur within any system if follow-up measures are not provided.

Organizational and functional data   Fire protection is seldom performed solely by the fire department; other agencies, public and private, also perform fire protection functions in most communities, for example: water departments provide and service water systems used for fire protection; landlords install smoke detectors; businesses install and maintain sprinklers; public works departments maintain roads and conduct weed abatement programs; police control traffic; planning departments collect and analyze data; and building departments inspect buildings. These functions, and the departments or agencies performing them, should be identified. One way to do this is to draw up a matrix, as in Figure 6–6 (which is a partial example, showing only some of the functions and some of the agencies).

Financial data   The determination of the *total cost* of providing fire protection services requires the inclusion of all cost elements, some of which may not be traditionally recognized. For example, certain expenditures by the water department (such as expenditures for water storage tank capacity and water pumps) directly or indirectly support fire protection, and certain expenditures by the police department (such as expenditures for traffice control and riot control) also support fire protection. The following are some examples of cost elements:

1. Operating budgets of community departments, with expenditures related to fire protection identified as such
2. Capital departmental budgets, similarly identified
3. Annual insurance premiums, by occupancy classification
4. Private expenditures for fire protection (such as annual fire detector sales; sprinkler installation and maintenance; alarm systems installation, maintenance, and operation; industrial fire brigades; rescue and ambulance services; and hospital emergency care and burn centers)
5. School fire safey education curricula, materials, and staff time.

Cost data can be most easily obtained *after* identification of the fire protection *functions* of the various public and private agencies contributing to and involved in fire prevention and control. Financial data other than costs are also of interest; such data would include, for example, the following:

1. Assessed (or market) value by land use categories (such as residential, industrial, commercial, farmland, grassland, and wildland); these data indicate the total property value at risk

Function	Organization							
	Fire	Data processing	Planning	Building	Water	Public works	Industry	Homeowner
Suppression								
Suppressant application	X						X	X
Planning	X	X	X	X	X	X	X	X
Training	X	X	X	X	X	X	X	
Sprinkler design, installation, maintenance	X						X	
Data collection, analysis	X	X	X	X	X	X	X	
Prevention								
Inspection	X						X	X
Plan check	X			X				
Planning	X	X	X	X	X	X	X	X
Investigation	X			X			X	X
Data collection, analysis	X	X	X	X	X	X	X	
Support								
Dispatch	X				X		X	
Planning	X	X	X	X	X	X	X	X
Training	X	X	X	X	X	X	X	
Education	X						X	
Rescue	X						X	
Emergency medical service	X						X	

Figure 6–6   Function/organization matrix.

2. Total public revenues available by category (such as taxes, revenue sharing funds, grants, and fees); such data can be used to give an idea of how much of the total revenue "pie" is taken by public fire protection expenditures
3. Bond indebtedness—both current level and legal limitation
4. Taxation limitation.

Legislative and legal data   There are many legislative acts and legal decisions which affect the provision of fire protection. An informed planner needs to keep in touch with these developments at the local, state, and federal levels. The data should include current legal decisions and legislation, and projected future actions. Examples of such data are: Occupational Safety and Health Act provisions and their enforcement, hazardous material transport regulations, affirmative action plans, NFPA codes and standards, state fire marshal regulations, state emergency medical and rescue service regulations, and building or fire code provisions.

Resource data   Finally, data describing the resources available for fire protection are needed. Resources from the public and private sectors should be catalogued and identified with the functions obtained earlier. In general, the resources are personnel, facilities, apparatus, and equipment.

Sources of data   When the required data are identified, the possible sources should be identified as well. Data may be obtained from many sources within the community and from outside sources as well. Local sources include city departments (fire, planning, building, water, finance, public works, the administrative office, school administration, the attorney's office, the clerk's office); commercial establishments and organizations (insurance companies, merchants' associations); and industry. Other sources include county agencies, regional agencies (such as councils of governments and regional planning organizations), state agencies, and federal agencies. A matrix of data required together with their sources can be constructed. Figure 6–7 is an example of this (although it is not as detailed as it would be for a particular community).

Collection methods When the data required and data sources are known, the data collection assignments should be made. As good a match as possible should be made between the collector and the source: for example, someone who is credible and known to the insurance industry will have a much better chance of obtaining insurance premium data than someone who is not.

In some localities there may be resistance to supplying data. In such instances some selling will need to be done—particularly to the private sector which may be reluctant to supply data if they feel it might be misused. (It should be remembered that confidentiality of data is all important.) Each data collector should be prepared to explain why the data are needed and how they will and will not be used; the desired format should also be explained, and assurance of confidentiality should be given.

Data source	Geographic	Demographic	Building and occupancy	Fire loss and incidence	Organizational and functional	Financial	Legislative	Resource
Fire department			X	X	X	X	X	X
Planning department	X	X	X		X	X	X	X
Building department			X		X	X	X	X
Water department					X	X	X	X
Finance department					X	X	X	
Public works department	X				X	X	X	X
Administrative office	X	X			X	X	X	
School administration		X			X	X	X	X
Attorney's office					X	X	X	
Clerk's office	X	X			X	X	X	
Commerce					X	X		X
Industry					X	X		X
County agencies		X		X	X	X	X	X
Regional agencies		X			X	X	X	X
State agencies		X		X	X	X	X	X
Federal agencies		X		X		X	X	X

Figure 6–7 Data required and sources of data.

In some instances the required data may not be available locally (fire insurance premiums are an example). In such cases, substitute data from other cities, or state and national data, or "best estimates," may be used, provided the limitations of such data are taken into account.

There are many means of collecting the data; those employed will depend on the particular data desired. Building and occupancy data, for example, can be collected from building department records, fire inspection records, planning department zoning maps, and special surveys of the pre-fire plans of the fire department. Fire loss and incidence data may be obtained from fire department reports and insurance records—but these traditional sources will not indicate unreported fires or losses not covered by insurance. To complete the loss/incidence data, a survey of homeowners and businesses might be conducted. The survey could be by mail (in water bills, for example), by telephone, and/or in person. Such a survey could be instituted on an annual basis. Requests for data from potential sources should be formal and should explicitly state what is wanted, why, and by what date.

Analyzing data and identifying problems

When sufficient data are available it is time to organize and analyze the data to find out what the fire situation is within the community. The fire situation can be divided into two major parts: (1) the fire problem, or what there is to burn, which includes all of the structural and nonstructural hazards; and (2) the management problem, which includes all the other aspects of fire protection, such as prevention, public education, rescue and emergency medical services, personnel, labor contracts and agreements, and measures of effectiveness (MOEs).

The fire problem   The fire problem can be analyzed in several ways, one of which is to make a statistical summary of the structures and nonstructures in the planning area, including, for example, the distribution of building age, building height, and fire flow required. Such a summary will give a picture of what there is to burn and how it will change with time in the future.

Another method of analysis would be to summarize the fire history within the community. Such a summary might include, for each year, the numbers of the following: responses, actual fires, fires by type, fires by time of day, fires by occupancy, fires by source, fires by type and form of material, fires by ignition factor, civilian deaths by age and by cause, firefighter deaths by cause, civilian and firefighter injuries by type. Other information that might be included is property loss by occupancy and total property loss. These fire histories can be extrapolated to the end of the planning period to get a projection of the fire experience for the near future.

Another means of displaying the fire incident history is by use of fire scenarios. Fire scenarios, as has been stated, can be used to link the type of loss with the events of a fire. They provide an understanding of the many elements of the fire problem in a concise form that is easy to comprehend.

Once a numerical and historical understanding of the fire incidences and losses in both structural and nonstructural occupancies in the planning area has been obtained, the planning personnel should examine the data and identify those structural and nonstructural areas that could be classified as major, key, or typical risks.

A *major* risk or hazard is one requiring the maximum amount of fire protection resources or one which could result in the greatest life loss or property loss. Probably the easiest measure of the resources required is fire flow (built-in fire protection systems), and the best measure of potential property loss is assessed or replacement value. Potential life loss is difficult to estimate, but demographic data (such as age, sex, income level, educational level), geographic data (such as access), fire history data, and resource data (such as water supply, response time, built-in fire protection systems) can be combined with the occupant data (such as occupant function, evacuation, density) to identify major life loss risk. Examples of major fire loss risks might be hotels, office buildings, nightclubs, and convalescent homes, and major property risks might include chemical plants, lumber yards, warehouses, and petroleum storage tanks.

A *key* risk or hazard is one which would be a significant loss to the community if destroyed. Probably the greatest loss would be economic, but other factors might also be important, for example beauty (a church), prestige (a museum), or historical significance (George Washington slept here). Key risks would also include the major industrial plant in town (employing many local people), a major tourist attraction such as a "fisherman's wharf," or a historical site or area such as a "Boot Hill" or Civil War courthouse.

A *typical* risk or hazard is one which exemplifies the occupancy category. For example, one typical occupancy might be a single story four family dwelling, and another typical occupancy might be a five story apartment house. The typical risk is the one which would normally be anticipated in the community.

These risks, then, define what there is to burn. The next stage in the planning process is to define the management problem (or management challenge).

The management problem The management problems of concern are not the short-range problems such as operational tactics or training, but rather the problems which are long range in nature, such as the effects of hiring practices or of increased arson.

As with fire problems, management problems can be *categorized* and *classified* to achieve a perspective. Some categories might be the following:

1. Functional: a set of problems arising from gaps or overlaps in the fire protection functions of various agencies in the planning area (resulting, for example, in waivers granted by building inspectors which cause or contribute to fire problems, or which cause conflict with the fire code)
2. Organizational: a set of problems resulting from organization (for example, problems of a rapidly developing area without an organized fire protection service)
3. Technical: a set of problems stemming from lack of technology (such as the inability to detect flammable dust concentrations)
4. Legislative or legal: a set of problems which arise because of legislative action by the federal, state, county, or local governments (such as a mini–max state housing code, or because of legal actions such as lawsuits)
5. Labor or personnel: a set of problems which result from differences of opinion between management and labor (for example, regarding equality of entrance standards for men and women firefighters)
6. Financial: a set of problems related to the costs of the service (in a labor-intensive service problems concerning pay and benefits, especially pensions, are critical).

After categories have been established, a set of classes can be employed to identify the problems in each category. One simple way of doing this is to rank them in terms, for example, of difficulty (very difficult, difficult, average, easy, very easy).

These planning procedures should result in a set of management problems and a set of fire problems which together comprise the fire situation through the end of the planning period. The fire situation represents the total risk to the community from fire.

Setting goals and objectives
and defining selection criteria

The next major activity is to define the goals and objectives and establish the system selection criteria (see Figure 6–5).

Goals and objectives Together, goals and objectives establish the level of service to be provided in the community. The goals are statements of *desire;* they represent an end which is striven for. Objectives, on the other hand, are explicit statements of how to achieve goals and levels of service at a given time; in this sense they are milestones. The objectives are related to the goals in a hierarchical manner.

An example might be that one goal is "to reduce life loss due to fire." Corresponding objectives might be "to reduce death rate by 67 percent in nursing home and hospital fires in ten years," "to provide self-exiting for ambulatory patients in nursing homes and hospitals in five years," and "to institute fire safety education for patients and staff of all hospitals and nursing homes in two years." The effect of objectives can be seen in Figure 6–8, which shows the current risk level being reduced through incremental accomplishment of objectives to a planned risk level, in this case to one-third of the current risk level.

The goals and objectives should address the fire situation—the fire and management problems—and should be as independent of the means of accomplishment as possible. In the example above, the methods of self-exiting and education are left open; the goals and objectives state what to do, not how to do them. The latter is addressed later in the formulation of the systems.

Figure 6–8   Reducing risk level through attainment of objectives.

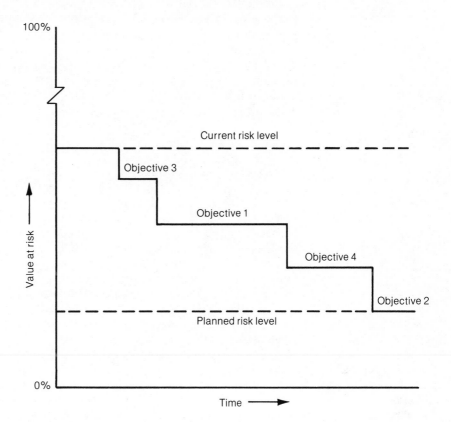

Selection criteria   Selection criteria are the yardsticks by which the systems formulated later are measured to determine which is the best. Selection criteria are chosen *before* the systems are formulated, to prevent biases from creeping in which might favor one system over the others. The criteria measure how well each system satisfies the objectives and relates to the goals. There are five general categories of criteria: cost, benefit, legislative, political, and "other"; there should be at least one criterion in each category for each objective. Some examples of criteria are: least cost, maximum reduction in fire insurance premiums, maximum number of major risks covered by building and fire codes, and least public reaction.

Formulating systems

At this point in the planning process, the preliminaries are completed and the process of formulating different fire protection systems can begin. Each system must meet the objectives but can (and should) meet them in different ways. For example, one system could retain the conventional fire suppression forces while another would depend primarily on built-in suppression devices such as sprinklers or detectors; one system might depend primarily on public sector participation while another might depend primarily on private sector participation and a third on a more or less even mix of public and private sector responsibilities. Each system should be described as completely as possible, with regard to fire protection philosophy, fire suppression means, fire prevention programs, fire protection organization, mutual or automatic aid, fire and building codes, and support functions employed.

Comparing plans and selecting the "best"

Each system is then subjected to a series of analyses which define the *functions* performed by each system and the *resources* required by each system. The purpose of these analyses is to provide information for comparing the systems by use of the selection criteria. This comparison yields the "best" system. At this point the nature of the system, its costs and benefits, and its legislative and political aspects are known and documented. Through use of this information, the system is presented for approval.

Preparing the master plan

When the system has been approved, the master plan for acquiring and maintaining the system throughout the planning period is prepared. The master plan, stripped to its essentials, presents the programs or projects, the costs, and the schedules for developing and maintaining the fire protection system that has been accepted and approved by the community, along with supporting information. The master plan is intended to be directed toward, and used by, the agencies and people responsible for providing fire protection in the community—the fire department, the community chief executive, the fire commission, and the city council, for example. The master plan forms the basis for the fire protection budgets of all community agencies involved in community fire protection, through identification and description of time-phased programs and projects to be implemented throughout the planning period. (Later on, of course, when the plan is being updated and modified, the budgetary process will be a major expression of this phrase.)

The master plan can be written in two volumes. The first would contain: (1) the fire protection goals and objectives of the community; (2) a time-phased description of the programs for achieving the goals and objectives through implementation of the selected fire protection system, and the funding required; and (3) assignment of authority and responsibility, and the procedures for carrying out and updating the plan. The second volume would contain the reference data for the master plan. The data recorded here are the data base that should be continually updated to review, update, and modify the master plan.

Approving and adopting the plan

When it is completed the master plan is presented for approval and adoption. Adoption of the plan is the final step of the planning phase; it is here that the community commits itself to the plan. Commitment means that the level of fire protection service, and therefore the level of risk, is fully understood and accepted. It also means that the costs and the resources needed to provide the protection are understood and accepted. This is especially important where changes in current methods are to be made—for example, increased private sector participation through mandatory installation of smoke detectors or sprinkler systems, or organizational changes in the public sector through consolidation of such similar functions as building and fire inspections or through fire–police consolidation.

Approval of the plan should take into account the fact that the plan will probably operate under more than one governing body, and, therefore, care should be taken that the plan will be acceptable to future government. A typical approval might be by a resolution which accepts a summary of the plan; in this way the governing body accepts the plan in concept. The summary might include: the major elements of the plan such as the goals and objectives, a description of the system, and the estimated costs and schedules; the responsibilities for implementing the plan; and a recommendation that staff prepare, for governing body action, necessary legislative material such as general plan revisions, building or fire code revisions, and capital improvement procedures, to implement the plan. Approval in this manner rather than by ordinance will facilitate changes to the plan, because changes can be handled administratively rather than by legislative action.

The planning phase is now complete; but it is not the end of fire protection master planning. Master planning, as we can see from Figures 6–4 and 6–5, is a continuing activity, carrying on into implementation and being resorted to continually for purposes of updating and modification.

The outlook

What is the outlook for management and planning for fire protection? Perhaps the forecast might be as follows:

1. Fire protection will become less reliant on suppression and will incorporate more prevention activities
2. Fire protection responsibility will be assumed increasingly by the private sector.

With these changes kept in mind, the following might be said:

1. Management of fire services will not be the same as it is today. The fire service will no longer have a place for the person who is just "chief firefighter"; he or she will be not only technician but also politician, salesperson, motivator, educator, supervisor, diplomat, and manager.
2. Planning, organizing, implementing, and measuring will be the main functions of the fire service manager. He or she will be managing a service which no longer includes just uniformed personnel; other community agencies and the private citizens will be part of the fire protection force. The fire service manager of the future will be continually assessing the future fire situation and planning to meet it rather than reacting to it when it suddenly appears. With actors other than the fire department involved, the manager will plan much more systematically than before and will be more concerned with policy planning than with operational planning.

It should also be kept in mind that an important criterion in assessing the effectiveness of the fire department manager will be the ability to manage change and innovation (see Chapter 16).

Systematic long-range master planning for fire protection is in its infancy; it is too early yet to ascertain how well the concept will be received. The need for it is evident, however, and the methodology is available. Whether master planning can help solve some of the problems of providing fire protection will undoubtedly depend on how public sector managers perceive the benefits and costs of initiating and implementing planning.

There are definite costs or disincentives to planning. Perhaps the foremost is the consideration that the planning should be participatory—that is, that the planning is best done by the community, not by an outside consultant or by a small group in the fire department. Only through complete community participation will the commitment and cooperation be forthcoming from the community to support the programs put forth in the plan. In these days of big government, citizens and community officials alike may find it both awesome *and* rewarding to return to a participative democratic process. Many of the cities that have performed fire protection master planning have discovered that the process of planning was as important as the end product. In many instances the planning project provided a unique opportunity for an interdisciplinary effort toward a common goal: the experience of fire department members working with water and building department members and with citizens gave the participants a new perspective, which was just as important as the plan.

A related problem is the historical semiautonomy of the fire department. In many cities the fire department carries out its functions with little public awareness, except perhaps at budget time. Master planning will change this, because public awareness will be greatly increased through participation. Fire departments will cease to be more or less autonomous and fire management will need to adjust to the new circumstances.

Master planning can also be very costly. The creation of a data base alone can take a year or so and considerable personnel time, while the whole process from inception to completion of the plan can take two or more years. It is for this reason that commitment to planning is so important—it is all too easy to be diverted by new problems which need to be solved. (Chances are that some of the new problems would not be problems if a master plan were implemented.)

Another problem—one which is more apparent than real—is a lack of planning expertise and experience. Many communities, especially small ones, feel that they have no personnel with sufficient planning and management abilities to lead or participate in a master planning project. The planning guides available from the U.S. Fire Administration[10] contain easy to follow step-by-step procedures which may be used by any fire department or other government official. Additional help is also available from the U.S. Fire Administration in the form of technical assistance, including training programs and courses. Planning expertise is, of course, helpful but not necessary.

In summary, the outlook for fire protection management and planning indicates that these functions will be practiced not only at the operational level but, increasingly, at the policy level. Fire service management will become more interdisciplinary, gaining professionalism in areas other than the traditional one of suppression. Long-range or master planning will become one of the primary tools of the new manager, and, in fact, will become a way of life for the nation's fire departments.

1 *Webster's New World Dictionary of the American Language,* revised popular library pocket-size edition (New York: World Publishing Company, 1973).

2 Ibid.

3 A valuable reference to this area for the administrator and for policymaking personnel is: International City Management Association, *An Assessment of the Transferability of the Community Fire Master Planning Program* [with *An Executive Summary*], report prepared for the National Fire Prevention and Control Administration [now the U.S. Fire Administration] (Washington, D.C.: International City Management Association, June 1977).

4 Peter Drucker, *The Practice of Management* (New York: Harper & Row, Publishers, 1954). Quoted in John W. Humble, *How To Manage by Objectives* (New York: AMACOM, 1973), p. 4.

5 A discussion of scenarios will be found in the following book in the Municipal Management Series: Kenneth L. Kraemer, *Policy Analysis in Local Government* (Washington, D.C.: International

City Management Association, 1973), pp. 128–32.

6 Discussions of Delphi technique will be found in the following books in the Municipal Management Series: Richard S. Bolan, "Social Planning and Policy Development in Local Government," in *Managing Human Services,* ed. Wayne F. Anderson, Bernard J. Frieden, and Michael J. Murphy (Washington, D.C.: International City Management Association, 1977), p. 109; Edward Schoenberger and John Williamson, "Deciding on Priorities and Specific Programs," in ibid., p. 163; and Kenneth L. Kraemer, *Policy Analysis in Local Government* (Washington, D.C.: International City Management Association, 1973), pp. 127–28.

7 Two of these guides were available as of the end of 1977. These are: National Fire Prevention and Control Administration, National Fire Safety and Research Office, *Urban Guide for Fire Prevention and Control Master Planning,* and *A Basic Guide for Fire Prevention and Control Master Planning* (both Washington, D.C.: National Fire Prevention and Control Administration, [1977]). These guides and other pertinent documents may be obtained

from the U.S. Fire Administration, Attn. FSRO, P.O. Box 19518, Washington, D.C. 20036.

The *Urban Guide* may be used at any level of government but is primarily aimed at large cities with complex problems and sophisticated planning resources. The *Basic Guide,* while suitable for larger cities, multijurisdiction regions, and even low population density state governments, is particularly well suited to small communities and rural areas. Further guides are planned to cover the particular problems of counties and the role of states in fire protection.

The fourteen *official* validation sites for the *Basic Guide* were: Williamsburg, Pennsylvania; Spring Lake, California; Princeton, Massachusetts; South Charleston, Ohio; Longmont, Colorado; Madeira Beach, Florida; Seymour, Tennessee; Devils Lake, North Dakota; Forest Grove, Oregon; Godfrey, Illinois; Flagstaff, Arizona; Clarendon County, South Carolina; Northwest Missouri Region Council of Governments; Benton County, Arkansas. The thirteen validation communities for the *Urban Guide* were: Tulsa, Oklahoma; Virginia Beach, Virginia; Fremont, West Covina, Covina, and Azusa, California; Fayette-ville and Springdale, Arkansas (Northwest Arkansas Regional Planning Commission); Springfield, Illinois; Richardson, Texas; Edmonds, Washington; Ketchum, Idaho; and Washington Township (Gloucester County), New Jersey.

8 See, for example: National Fire Prevention and Control Administration, *The Human Factor in High Fire Risk Neighborhoods: A Pilot Study in New Orleans, Louisiana* (1976); *Highlights of the National Household Fire Survey* (n.d.); and *Fire Education Planning* (May 1977) (all Washington, D.C.: National Fire Prevention and Control Administration).

9 See, for example: National Fire Incident Reporting System (NFIRS), developed by the NFPCA; Uniform Fire Incident Reporting System (UFIRS), developed by the NFPA; California Fire Incident Reporting System (CFIRS); Fire Incident Reporting and Evaluation System (FIRES), developed and used by the cities of Huntington Beach, Seal Beach, Fountain Valley, and Westminster, California; Field Incident Reporting System (FIRS), EDP system developed by the Los Angeles fire department in the early 1960s.

10 See note 7, above.

7 Managing fire prevention

The lives and property of everyone in a community can be threatened by fire, hence everyone should (and can) play a role in fire prevention—the head of a household who decides to buy (or not to buy) a smoke detector; the child who has learned (or has not learned) what steps to take if his or her clothing catches fire; the restaurant patron who makes a point of checking exits in a crowded establishment before enjoying a meal (or who remains oblivious to basic precautions in places of public assembly). Such individual actions, or the lack of them, can be construed as part of fire prevention management (or mismanagement) in the broadest sense. Similarly, individual and managerial responsibility for fire prevention can permeate many agencies (local, state, and federal) far beyond the administrative boundaries of a fire department, as the media coverage of a major fire disaster demonstrates.

Within the fire department the duties normally carried out by a fire prevention bureau are related to fire code enforcement, public fire education, and fire investigation. Each of these functional areas embodies complex and detailed activities and may well involve close ties with other local government agencies. Using a managerial perspective, this chapter concentrates on the role and activities of fire prevention bureaus. To set this discussion in its context, a brief overview, given below, surveys the range of fire prevention activities; indicates how the coverage in this chapter relates to the discussion in certain other chapters; and provides an outline of the main topics covered in the remainder of this chapter.

Overview

As has been noted, the duties normally carried out by a fire prevention bureau are related primarily to fire code enforcement, public fire education, and fire investigation. Code enforcement includes review of plans and specifications to assure compliance with fire safety features of building and fire prevention codes; control of structures through inspection to assure proper exits, interior finishes, fixed fire protection equipment, and other related features; control of occupancy through such measures as enforcement of capacity and smoking regulations; and control of sales and use of materials and equipment. The last function includes control or limitation of sale of explosives and fireworks and control of sale of flammable liquids and gases. In recent years the function has added the control of sales of fire detection and protection devices. This effort is expended to assure that individuals purchasing such equipment are obtaining devices that operate properly.

Practically all fire prevention bureaus have a responsibility in public fire education. While this function has been referred to as *fire prevention education,* it actually encompasses far more than education in fire prevention. Fire reaction training is included; therefore, the term *public fire education* may be more appropriate. Citizens are taught means of summoning the fire department, evacuating homes at the time of a fire, and other post-fire procedures. With the growing emphasis in recent years on fire prevention as well as on fire suppression, public fire education has become increasingly important.

In many communities fire investigation and arson suppression are responsibilities of the fire prevention bureau. The assignment of arson suppression as a fire prevention bureau function is a logical one. Personnel can be employed for inspections during times when fire investigation loads are light. Conversely, personnel can be reassigned from inspection to investigation duties during times of heavy fire activity. Such cross training and dual use are especially desirable in smaller communities. In cities over 200,000 in population there is normally a sufficient work load in the investigation field to warrant assignment of personnel on a full-time basis. There is still an advantage, however, to being able to use all bureau personnel in either area of responsibility.

Condemnation of structures, although a code enforcement function, may be thought of as a separate activity because of its far-reaching legal and social ramifications. This activity may be carried out by the building department or the fire prevention bureau. Normally, structures can be condemned only if they are open for trespass and present a hazard to adjoining structures or property.

Record keeping duties are assigned to some fire prevention bureaus. Firefighting companies are required to submit all reports to the bureau. The communications headquarters also forwards its daily activity reports to the bureau for compilation. This record keeping function may be assigned to the administrative offices within the department; however, there appears to be a growing tendency to place the responsibility in the fire prevention bureau.

In some communities the fire marshal's office is responsible for maintenance of patrols within the business district. These patrols, normally carried out on foot, are for the purpose of detecting fire hazards, especially during nighttime hours. A typical program includes visiting alleys in the business district after closing hours to assure the timely removal of trash. This activity is not now as widespread as it was some years ago.

Another function of the fire prevention bureau is that of issuing permits, certificates of approval, and licenses. Permits are normally utilized in bringing about improved code enforcement. Many municipal fire prevention codes require the obtaining of a permit in order to carry out certain hazardous processes. Paint spraying and flammable liquids storage, for example, normally require a permit from the fire prevention bureau. The lack of a permit constitutes a violation and the process can legally be shut down until conditions are improved to the point at which a permit can be issued. The permit is normally required to be posted on the premises. Since the fire prevention code requires the permit for operation of the process, refusal of entrance for inspection constitutes prima facie evidence for closing down the operation.

Certificates of approval are normally issued for flameproofing compounds, as well as for fire extinguishers, smoke detectors, and other fire detection and extinguishing devices. The sale of such units without proper certificates of approval would usually constitute a violation of the fire prevention code. This control is provided in order to assure the sale of suitable devices and to relieve the public of concern for reliability of equipment purchased.

The fire prevention bureau may issue licenses to individuals or corporations for carrying out certain activities within the community. For example, many cities regulate fire extinguisher recharge and service personnel in this manner. In order to legally recharge or service fire extinguishers, the individual must usually satisfactorily complete a test on recharge and service procedures. In the same way some communities require testing and licensing of automatic sprinkler installers and other trades which relate to fire prevention or protection activities. Individuals responsible for shooting public fireworks displays may also be required to obtain a license from the fire prevention bureau, as may explosives handlers.

As can be appreciated, these licensing and certification activities place fire prevention personnel in a unique relationship with the individuals to be certified or licensed. Because livelihoods are at stake, pressures may be brought to bear to assure prompt issuance of the permit or license. These pressures may be of a political nature or of a more direct nature which may involve questions of impropriety. In some jurisdictions fees are charged for issuance of these documents. Normally revenues collected go into the general fund of the municipality rather than into the fire department's budget. Fee collecting activities do not normally support the fire prevention bureau in the way that they support building department operations.

A great deal of the work of the fire prevention bureau could in fact be classified as consultative in nature. An active bureau will be looked to for advice in

---

Mini–max building codes The minimum–maximum state building code concept, presently in effect in several states, is a barrier to home rule and to an innovative attitude toward combating the fire problem at the local level. This type of code simply provides that a local code cannot be more restrictive than the state code. Therefore, the state code is not only the minimum code, as is common, but is also the maximum code effort allowed.

With this constraint local government does not have the latitude to require additional built-in fire protection to complement the public fire forces in the detection and suppression of fire in its incipient stage. With the increasing cost of fire protection, rampant inflation, declining revenues, and citizen demands for tax relief, the fire problem is likely to multiply. Meanwhile, state governments with mini–max codes are placing a constraint on local government by determining the level of fire protection, by limiting code requirements, and by not providing fiscal resources to supplement local tax monies which support the fire department.

Virginia Beach, Virginia, served as a validation city for the master planning project of the U.S. Fire Administration. The Virginia Beach experience outlined

168 fire protection objectives the city wished to accomplish. Nearly 70 percent of the objectives were discarded because they were in conflict with the provisions of Virginia's mini-max code.

The argument for this code is that it provides uniformity. The code usually results from the lobbying efforts of architects, engineers, developers, and others in the construction and building industry. Support of the mini–max concept is also enhanced where local jurisdictions have no codes or use codes to restrict or prohibit low income housing. A fragmented state fire service is fair game for enactment of the mini–max code and is unable to cope with the lobbying efforts of the pro-code forces.

Should the method of determining fire insurance premiums be changed from the present municipal grading schedule system of the Insurance Services Office, jurisdictions covered by a mini–max code will have the options of increasing municipal fire services or doing nothing and hoping that the fire rate will decrease. Local government managers should be aware that if their state enacts a mini–max code it could be in conflict with the Life Safety Code of the National Fire Protection Association or with the regulatory requirements of numerous federal agencies.

---

fire safety matters by citizens. This is an especially desirable situation because citizens will consult the bureau, for example, prior to making any changes in process or to relocating fire extinguishing equipment, and in other situations where good advice can prevent fires. To increase citizen awareness, representatives need to go out into the community, appear before civic organizations, and generally become well known and respected by the citizens. No citizens' group should be too small for a visit from the fire prevention bureau.

Although not generally enforced by the fire prevention bureau, the mini–max building code is another factor which has had an effect on fire prevention efforts. Mini–max building codes have generally stifled fire safety improvements in communities within the states in which they are enacted. The local jurisdiction cannot, for example, require sprinkler protection, smoke detectors, or other fire protection devices if such requirements would exceed those of the mini–max building code. Any improvements or changes in the codes must be made by a consensus of a statewide group, which generally has few if any fire service representatives. For these reasons the fire services in many states have opposed a concept of mini–max building codes. There may not be as much resistance to a minimum statewide code; however, fire officials generally want to have leeway in imposing specific fire safety requirements in a jurisdiction. Often these requirements are tailored to the unique problems within the community.

As this brief survey indicates, fire prevention, although often focused on the local fire prevention bureau, is a complex and many-sided activity, reaching out to numerous aspects of fire service management and to the general life of a community.

How does the discussion in the present chapter fit into the coverage elsewhere in this book? The management of fire inspection is a topic of sufficient importance to warrant a chapter of its own, and this topic is in fact covered in detail in the chapter immediately following this one. Fire and arson investigation, too, is an important topic, and a detailed treatment of that subject is found in Chapter 11. Finally, public fire education is an activity that permeates all aspects of a fire department's contacts with the general public and is therefore discussed not only in this chapter but also in Chapter 15 (on training and education) and elsewhere throughout this book, as appropriate.

The discussion below is divided into eight parts. The first looks at the managerial principles involved in basic organization for fire prevention. The second discusses organization, and the third discusses training and management concepts. The fourth examines codes and their role in fire prevention, while the fifth emphasizes the role of public education. Relationships with other agencies are the major subject of the sixth section; the seventh takes a look at some of the legal implications involved in fire code enforcement. The eighth section surveys evaluation and record keeping. The chapter closes with a brief summary and outlook.

It should be mentioned that the topics discussed here, like others in this book, should be considered in relation to—and modified to suit the needs of—management priorities in communities that differ widely in terms of size, socioeconomic composition, and political and administrative environment. It should also be kept in mind that the discussion which follows concentrates on bringing out both the managerial principles involved and the key areas of decision making.

Basic principles

Historical perspective

Although most fire departments were formed primarily for suppression purposes (as Chapter 1 has indicated), the incorporation of fire prevention as an adjunct service has slowly developed through the years. In Milwaukee, Wisconsin, for example, a volunteer fire department was formed in 1837. A paid force was established in 1867, and in 1877 company foremen were given responsibility for conducting building inspections in their districts. A full-time bureau of inspection was established in 1915 with the appointment of four full-time inspectors and a captain.[1]

In some cities formal prevention activities began even earlier. The New York fire department's manual of instruction makes the following statement:

Fire prevention has been a function of the New York Fire Department ever since it has been in existence. For more than 200 years members of the Department have been inspecting buildings and the rules have provided the officers must be familiar with all the buildings in their districts, ever since there have been any rules.[2]

In Norfolk, Virginia, the first volunteer fire company was organized in 1731. In 1871 a paid fire department was established; however a fire prevention bureau was not organized until 1920. It is interesting to note that the first recorded reference to fire matters in Norfolk was an act of the assembly in 1730 which prohibited wooden chimneys in the city.[3] A number of other colonial cities had similar ordinances as well as prohibitions against other fire hazards of the era (see Chapter 1).

During the early years of the twentieth century the National Fire Protection Association (NFPA), the National Board of Fire Underwriters, and the International Association of Fire Chiefs were leading influences in the establishment of state fire marshal's offices and of prevention bureaus in fire departments over the United States. This step has largely been completed.

Fire prevention interests and activities should not, however, be confined to the fire prevention bureau. Every member of the modern fire department, whether paid or volunteer, should play a role.

Measuring effectiveness

Until recent years, little had been done to measure the effectiveness of fire prevention efforts. Available fire prevention methods were used without much regard for the possible values of the approaches. The major reasons for this situation were probably lack of research abilities together with a belief that methods being used were effective and therefore research was not necessary.

Beginning in the mid-1970s, with the formation of the National Fire Prevention and Control Administration (NFPCA; now the U.S. Fire Administration) as the federal focal point for fire safety, and with the general increased interest in analysis of all government programs, some excellent research projects were undertaken. An example is the *Municipal Fire Service Workbook,* prepared for the National Science Foundation by the Research Triangle Institute, the International City Management Association (ICMA), and the National Fire Protection Association. This book suggests that the measure of fire prevention effectiveness is the number of fires per 1,000 population protected. This number includes "residential, commercial, and industrial fires, vehicle, outside, and structural fires; it does not include false alarms or emergency medical or rescue runs." This measure is effective because a key object of fire prevention is "to reduce the number of fires that actually occur."[4]

The report goes on to note that fire prevention activities of the building department, as well as private prevention investment in sprinkler systems, would be reflected in this measure. It further notes the following:

The number of fires is not the only "prevention effectiveness" measure that could be used. Additional measures could possibly include the number of building and fire safety inspections per structure, number of citizens reached through prevention education, etc., and any other measure that would affect the number of fires. Similarly, a more ideal "fires" measure would be broken down on the basis of the type of fire (structural, grass, vehicle, etc.) cause, and location, so that fire and other local administrators would better know how to concentrate fire prevention efforts.[5]

The report indicates that "total losses—whether of life, health, or property—are related to both suppression and prevention activities."[6] It also notes that, under the measure property loss per $1,000 market value, prevention efforts are measured as well as suppression efforts, because "prevention efforts can greatly reduce the extent of loss sustained in a fire, for example, with fire walls and similar building code requirements and safety efforts." Civilian injuries and deaths per 100,000 population also give some measure of the effects of prevention as well as suppression activities. "A reduction in the number of deaths and injuries implies a reduction in fires."[7]

One source recommends a program of hazard and loss analysis to better determine the nature of fire problems and detect trends. The types of analysis recommended to assist the fire prevention effort are as follows:

1. Location of fire within a tract versus trends in fire activity
2. Type of occupancy versus fire prevention inspection
3. Industrial processes involved in fire versus fire prevention inspection
4. Location of fire versus changes in zoning and population densities
5. Fire trends by hour, day, or week versus requirements for inspection.[8]

Unfortunately the goals and objectives of the fire prevention manager have often been looked upon as being vague and undefined. This attitude has developed because of the extreme difficulty in equating fire loss experience to fire prevention activities. Many fire service members feel that they should be able to realize a loss reduction in ratio to efforts expended in fire prevention. This is, of course, a difficult objective to obtain. One major loss fire can completely distort fire loss statistics in a community which has had an outstanding fire prevention program.

It is far more rewarding for the fire prevention manager to study effective programs, establish reasonable guidelines for local fire prevention activities, and proceed with such activities after receiving proper authorization and support. The citizens of a given community should not be receiving less service from a fire prevention standpoint than are citizens of other communities in the state. Fire prevention officials should ensure the existence of at least minimal fire prevention safeguards in all facilities within the community.

Guidelines

Guidelines in the code field are readily available, with model fire prevention codes, fire safety standards, and manuals being published by several national organizations.[9] Guidelines on inspection frequency, public education goals, and other features of fire prevention bureau operation are not so readily available. The manager must look to other fire prevention bureau managers for such guidance.

The fire marshal's office

Although the division of the modern fire department that supervises activities relating to fire prevention is commonly referred to as the *fire prevention bureau,* the title *fire marshal's office* perhaps more appropriately describes its duties. The latter term is especially appropriate if duties assigned include arson suppression and public fire education duties, neither of which is strictly related to fire prevention. Another drawback to the fire prevention bureau title is that it implies that the fire suppression forces are not engaged in fire prevention activities, while in a modern fire department they should be as interested in prevention as in suppression.

The term *fire marshal* connotes the marshaling of forces to overcome fire — the exact job performed by an individual who marshals forces to conduct inspections, to educate the public in fire-related matters, to assure the safety of buildings constructed, and to bring to justice those responsible for setting fires. The fire marshal in a fire department might be looked upon as the commanding officer of a military force occupying a territory for peacekeeping purposes during peacetime. However, once war begins additional forces and a higher level of command become directly involved. War might be compared to a major fire outbreak, bringing in suppression forces under the command of the chief deputy.

Organization

Location and facilities

The physical location of the fire prevention bureau should be considered as having a bearing on the bureau's effectiveness. Location is an important consideration for potential "customers" and will also have some effect on the public's attitude toward the bureau.

Members of the public should not have to go through sleeping areas used by firefighters in order to reach the fire prevention bureau's office. Availability of parking space for customers' vehicles should also be considered. There should be provision for receipt of telephone calls during all normal working hours. The person responsible for taking telephone messages should be conversant with the bureau's responsibilities and objectives and should have a positive attitude toward fire prevention.

The physical facilities provided should be suitable for conducting necessary business. A closetlike office in a remote corner of a fire station gives the public the impression that the bureau is of little importance in the overall mission of the fire department. Suitable space should be provided for inspectors to prepare reports and carry out other necessary duties.

There should be a specific mailing address for the fire prevention bureau. Mail designated for the bureau should not have to go through a departmental mail routing system which may delay receipt, as many communications refer to correction notices and similar matters and should be handled without delay.

Some fire prevention bureaus maintain satellite offices in the local building department. This procedure enables architects and engineers to receive plan reviews by fire prevention personnel at the same time that building department officials are reviewing the plans. Larger cities may have satellite offices in several areas of the city in order to provide better services. These may be located in fire stations or in community service centers.

Uniforms

Although most fire prevention bureau personnel wear fire department uniforms during their duty hours, there is a growing tendency to use blazers and dark trousers as inspection attire. This practice has been well accepted by business operators in that the presence of the fire inspector is not so obvious within the establishment. A number of communities have found that the blazer concept is desirable from a community relations standpoint. Some individuals have a resentment toward uniforms of any kind and these persons are placated by inspectors attired in blazers.

General organizational considerations

A 1974 report suggests that fire prevention in the majority of urban fire departments includes some or all of the following activities:

1. Inspection of buildings and premises
2. Public education
3. Some training of industry in self-protection
4. Supervision of the safety of public assembly
5. Participation in preparing and revising laws and fire regulations
6. Licensing of hazardous processes and storage of hazardous materials
7. Enforcement of regulations
8. Fire investigation
9. Disposition of arson cases.[10]

Such a range of activities requires a well planned system of organization.

Concepts for organization of fire prevention bureaus vary more widely than do concepts for fire suppression organizations. While fire suppression forces are organized around the company or task force as a component which may be multiplied as the community grows, fire prevention bureau organization may be based on one of several varied duty assignment arrangements.

The first variable is that of basic assignment of responsibility for the fire prevention function. In many communities the responsibility for fire prevention is divided between the operating fire companies and the fire prevention bureau. In those cities fire company personnel are responsible for the initial routine inspection and reinspection of the average building in their districts. They are trained to conduct such routine inspections and to prepare appropriate reports of their findings. The majority of inspections in these cities are handled entirely by fire company personnel. In order to be effective, company personnel must be convinced of the importance of their mission. They must look upon it as a major part of their responsibility to the community.

In Birmingham, Alabama, for example, fire companies conduct over 65,000 inspections per year. In New Haven, Connecticut, over 20,000 inspections are conducted each year. All commercial properties are inspected each spring by Moline, Illinois, firefighters, and this department also has an active home inspection program.

Fire prevention bureau personnel, under such a procedure, devote their efforts to following through on difficult situations encountered by fire company personnel and to providing initial inspection and reinspection of complicated facilities such as chemical manufacturing plants, hospitals, and other places where special expertise is needed to carry out inspections. Such facilities should, of course, also be visited by fire companies for pre-fire planning purposes.

Close coordination between the two inspection groups is paramount to the effectiveness of the program. The overall departmental organization chart should include fire prevention as a responsibility of firefighting companies. Coordination will need to be provided, perhaps by a district or battalion fire prevention coordinator who is assigned from the fire prevention bureau as a staff position to the district or battalion commander. This individual can assure that conflicts and misunderstandings do not arise. The coordinator should also be responsible for maintaining records on inspection accomplishments of the fire suppression forces so that these may be incorporated into the fire prevention report of the department. Such a program needs the full support of the battalion or district commanders to be successful. Unfortunately, such support is not always easily obtained.

All fire prevention bureau personnel under such a scheme are generally specialists. The total number assigned to the bureau will not be as great as under the plan in which all fire prevention inspection activities are carried out by the fire prevention bureau. (The number assigned will, of course, be determined by the inspection coverage desired by the administration.) When all inspection activities are carried out by the fire prevention bureau, general inspectors will usually be employed in addition to some specialists.

General inspectors are those qualified to conduct routine inspections. Such individuals are able to identify common fire hazards and causes as found in most occupancies. They are capable of handling a full inspection of office buildings, service stations, theaters, schools, apartment houses, dwellings, mercantile establishments, or hotels, however, they may encounter some problems with such facilities as large flammable liquid installations, hospitals, complicated manufacturing plants, and generator stations. In these latter cases, the specialist would be assigned to inspectional responsibilities with specific recognition of the inspector's specialization (i.e., flammable liquids and gases; chemical processes).

Many communities do not use the generalist–specialist concept. Small communities with only one or two individuals assigned to the bureau would not find such a scheme feasible; each person would have to devote maximum effort to mastering all problems encountered, regardless of complexity.

Some larger communities that could make use of the concept do not because of the problems entailed in providing adequate coverage. One inspector may be expected to handle all inspections within an assigned area of the city. This procedure results in less time lost in travel to and from facilities and gives the zone inspector full familiarity with all facilities in the zone. The use of general inspectors to handle all inspections has a possible disadvantage over and above the obvious one of the possibility of an inferior inspection in complex structures. There is also the possibility that inspections of like facilities in different areas of the city will not cover the same features. The hospital on the west side may be inspected with differing emphasis from the one on the east side. If one inspector were assigned to all hospitals this would be less likely to occur.

One feature of general organization that is growing in acceptance is the assignment of fire prevention personnel to night shifts. This is of great value in checking places of assembly during hours of maximum use.

Training and management concepts

Training courses for fire prevention personnel have been limited in number and scope until recent years. The advent of fire training programs in most states and provinces has brought with it an availability of at least minimal training in matters related to fire prevention. A leader has been the Ontario Fire College at Gravenhurst, which has included extensive training, both basic and advanced, for fire prevention bureau personnel for many years. The United States Navy's Structural Fire Fighting School at Norfolk, Virginia, has offered a one week school in fire inspection practices for a number of years. Texas A & M has included a fire prevention school as part of its fire training curriculum for over twenty years. A number of other state fire schools hold seminars for inspectors on a periodic basis.

The University of North Carolina has held a one week fire prevention school at its Institute of Government for a number of years, offered on a three year progressive basis. Two sessions, basic and intermediate, or intermediate and advanced, are offered each year. A student must attend all three courses in order to complete the program. Hundreds of fire inspectors from as far away as Guam have completed this excellent training program.

For the most part, however, formal training courses for personnel assigned to fire prevention bureaus have been quite limited. Training is primarily of the on-the-job type. Occasionally, personnel from smaller communities go to larger cities to obtain this type of training. Most frequently, however, the incumbent trains a newly assigned inspector. Although this procedure may be satisfactory in a medium-sized or larger department, it is not a very satisfactory arrangement in a smaller community, which may have only one individual assigned to fire prevention. Deaths or transfers have caused many individuals to have to learn by the trial and error method.

Professional qualifications system

A major advancement in fire prevention training should come through the advent of the National Professional Qualifications System for fire service personnel as established by the Joint Council of National Fire Service Organizations. This system, established in 1972, includes standards for firefighters, fire service instructors, and fire service officers, as well as fire inspectors, fire investigators, and fire prevention education officers. The system is designed for persons following a career in the fire service and does not include provisions for nonuniformed personnel, such as fire protection engineers, who might be assigned to one of the specialties. Volunteer fire services can also use the system.

Individuals progressing through the ranks in the fire service are required to meet certain qualifications prior to advancement. Each individual is tested on ability to master certain performance objectives related to a field of specialty. A person entering the fire service starts as a Fire Fighter I and may progress to a Fire Fighter II, then to a Fire Fighter III.[11] After reaching Fire Fighter III the person has the option of going into the fire inspector/fire investigator and fire prevention education officer specialty. The beginning level within the specialty is the Fire Inspector I. After completing requirements for this level the individual has the option of progressing to a Fire Inspector II, a Fire Investigator II, or a Fire Prevention Education Officer II. The next step would be progression to level III in one of the three specialties. Progression from I to II entails additional technical competency in the field of specialization while progression from II to III is primarily concerned with the mastering of administrative capabilities such as budget preparation, personnel administration, and preparation of statistical data.[12]

The system is designed for use in medium-sized to large fire departments; however, it can be used in a smaller department with certain modifications. Personnel assigned to a fire prevention bureau in a smaller department may find it necessary to master all of the requirements because of the limited number of billets. A department with one or two persons assigned to the fire prevention bureau will find it necessary to ensure that those individuals are competent in all three specialties, as they will be called upon to perform these duties on a daily basis. The qualifications system is designed to be managed at a state level; therefore, individuals could be in a position to relocate from one department to another as they move up the career ladder within the system. No time constraints are involved; the individual's progression is based on ability to master the performance objectives as administered by an approved evaluator and on the department's billet structure. The system closely parallels the promotional program used within the enlisted ranks of the military services and is based on proven abilities rather than a written test.

It is envisioned that training programs will be developed to prepare individuals for movement in the professional qualifications system. No rank structure is attached to these qualifications; however, each community is free to design rank structure as it desires. The program is not mandatory or obligatory unless it is so designated by the community or state. Increasing use of the professional qualifications system for fire inspectors should increase the capability of all fire prevention bureau personnel.

Assignment of personnel

Assignment of personnel to fire prevention bureaus has been on a random basis through the years. Unfortunately, many individuals have been assigned to bureaus because of physical limitations (for example, from injuries) which have precluded their assignment to active fire suppression duties. Although many of these persons have performed satisfactorily, a sizable number are not adaptable to fire prevention duties and their work reflects this shortcoming. Some are indifferent, knowing that they will be reassigned to suppression duties once they are recovered. Others are unable to perform satisfactorily owing to difficulty in climbing stairs or in bending, or to other physical limitations. In some fire departments the bureau is looked on by other department members as a "resting place" for individuals with physical limitations.

Another problem in assignment of personnel to fire prevention duties is that of "dead end" limitations. Individuals who become proficient in fire prevention may find themselves assigned to such duties throughout their careers with little opportunity to move into command positions within the department. This is especially true of senior captains and even battalion chiefs who have been assigned to fire prevention for a number of years. Department promotional procedures should include a means for such individuals to move back into the line organization if they are otherwise qualified.

Some departments have a policy of assigning all individuals to fire prevention duties upon promotion to the rank of lieutenant or captain. This procedure brings about an understanding of the responsibilities of fire prevention on the part of all persons moving through the rank structure. However, it has a limitation in that individuals assigned know that they will be reassigned within a year or two and may not have a genuine interest in their duties. Such an outlook could cause adverse reaction in dealings with the public.

Training arrangements

Probably the most desirable arrangement is that of providing training in fire prevention at the recruit level for all trainees. This procedure has been used in Dallas for many years. All recruits understand that fire prevention is a major function of the fire department and appreciate its importance even if assigned to a fire suppression company. In many communities fire suppression companies are used for inspection; therefore the training is of direct benefit. It is important that the recruit in any fire department, whether paid or volunteer, understand the vital role of fire prevention in the overall fire department mission. In some communities individuals have been assigned to ranking positions in fire prevention after years of strictly suppression experience. These individuals have been "lost" and have had considerable difficulty in mastering a new field which really should have been part of their original training. Some fire departments include basic indoctrination in fire prevention in their recruit training programs but few match the extensive offerings of Dallas.

Inclusion of fire prevention in recruit training is emphasized in the basic training of forest rangers in which forest fire prevention is emphasized as a major part of the job. Unfortunately, many individuals join fire departments with the impression that the entire job of a firefighter is that of fire suppression.

Several fire departments are using a limited number of nonuniformed civilian personnel in their fire prevention bureaus. These individuals are generally selected from applicants who have completed two year fire science programs. They are looked upon as fire prevention specialists and are not required to complete the basic training school for recruits within the department. These individuals are limited in progression and usually cannot move into positions of command responsibility within the department. Although this practice has the short-term advantage of using individuals trained in fire prevention and fire protection, it has several disadvantages, including the previously mentioned lack of mobility in promotion within the department. It also has a possible disadvantage in that the lack of fire suppression experience on the part of the civilian inspector limits that individual's ability to speak with authority on fire spread possibilities or on reasons for certain suppression activities.

Fire management arrangements

One of the most promising concepts is that of the fire management area program for utilization of fire company personnel for all fire service duties in their areas. This concept as employed in Springfield, Illinois, makes the local fire company responsible for inspections, pre-fire planning, and hazards evaluation within its geographic areas of response. Each shift is, in turn, responsible for one-third of the area. Fire company personnel conduct all fire prevention activities within the area. They contact the fire prevention bureau for assistance when problems are encountered. In addition, fire losses are tabulated by submanagement area. This gives the department a good measure of relative problems within areas of the city and can be useful in determining potential fire station location. Citizens feel that the local fire station is part of the community.

Oklahoma City, Los Angeles, and Cincinnati employ intensive fire inspection tactics as a means of reducing losses in areas which are shown to have major fire problems. The same procedure is followed if death rates increase alarmingly. Accurate records of fire experience make this program possible. This concept incorporates the idea that efforts should be directed toward demonstrated problems rather than being made on a uniform or random basis.

The fire prevention manager should be sufficiently high in the organization chart to facilitate proper functioning in both staff and line capacities. This individual is the principal adviser on fire prevention matters to the fire chief. As a staff position, the bureau chief also serves as adviser to fire suppression chief officers. Of course, the bureau chief serves in a line capacity in supervising fire prevention personnel activities.

Fire departments in which the fire prevention chief is at equal level with the suppression chief in the organization structure include those of Long Beach and Oakland, California; Tucson, Arizona; and Montréal, Québec, and Saint John, New Brunswick, Canada.

Some communities assign the rank of lieutenant to the individual in charge of the fire prevention bureau. Except in a small community with a very low level officer structure, this rank is generally too low for the incumbent to achieve successful results. A number of cities designate the fire prevention manager as a division, district, or battalion chief. It is most desirable, however, that the incumbent have the rank of assistant chief or deputy chief, depending on the rank structure of the department. The position should be equal in importance to the chief officer in charge of suppression activities. In some fire departments the fire prevention bureau is placed under a deputy or assistant chief who is responsible for all service activities other than control of fire suppression companies. In such a scheme an operations chief may be in charge of the fire suppression forces. A more logical approach might be that of dividing the responsibilities into those which involve direct contact with the public and those in which contacts are internal. The assignment of responsibilities in this manner may provide for greater coordination of fire prevention and suppression duties and for increased fire prevention activities on the part of suppression personnel. The Prince George's County, Maryland, fire department was reorganized incorporating this concept and excellent results have been noted.

Fire prevention is a responsibility of the operations division of the District of Columbia fire department. (The placement within the organization of the fire prevention function is also touched on in Chapter 8.)

The role of codes

Code selection

Selection of a fire prevention code for promulgation is an important activity for the fire prevention manager. The effectiveness of enforcement is directly related to the code provisions adopted. A comprehensive, stringent code which cannot be feasibly enforced by available personnel may be detrimental to the cause of improved fire safety. The code should follow nationally recognized practices. It is most desirable, in fact, to promulgate a code based entirely on nationally recognized and adopted standards. Probably the most popular code enacted at the municipal level is the model municipal fire prevention code of the American Insurance Association.[13] This code may be adopted by a community with very few local modifications. In recent years the Building Officials and Code Administrators International, the International Conference of Building Officials, and the Southern Building Code Congress have developed model fire prevention codes.[14] These codes generally assign fire protection equipment supervision and general fire prevention maintenance to the fire official, while the building official continues to have responsibility for basic fire protection design features.

Some communities have adopted the model fire prevention code of the National Fire Protection Association.[15] This code embodies a number of NFPA standards which are included by reference. Other communities have adopted the entire National Fire Codes, a compilation of all NFPA standards. While this arrangement may be desirable from the standpoint of covering all possible conditions which might arise, it has the disadvantage of being so voluminous that the average inspector is incapable of comprehending all features entailed. Members of the public could not be expected to master the code, and municipal officials may be reluctant to advocate such a comprehensive code.

Use of a model fire prevention code as opposed to a locally developed document has the advantage of providing an interpretation procedure under which the local official can contact a committee at the national level to learn their reasoning on any given provision. The local manager may disagree, for example, with an architect on the intent of a section of the code. The committee that has developed the code may be requested to render an interpretation or clarification on the matter.

The nationally developed code also has the advantage of recognition of experiences of communities throughout the country. Input into the development of the nationally recognized code is from individuals with a wide variety of experience and training.

Municipal, county, and volunteer arrangements

Municipal charters normally spell out means by which a fire code may be promulgated. Normally, the code is suggested by the enforcement official followed by public hearings by the city council. The public is given an opportunity to comment on specific portions of the code which might be offensive or otherwise undesirable. It is usually wise for the council to follow the nationally recognized standards; however, local deviations can be made if found necessary. The use of a nationally recognized code is advantageous also from a community development standpoint in that architects, engineers, and builders are generally familiar with the code and can readily adapt their plan to code-required measures.

A number of counties have organized fire prevention bureaus or fire marshal's offices. (These bodies have the code enforcement responsibility.) These bureaus can sometimes be provided more economically on a countywide basis than on a municipal basis. This may be an especially desirable arrangement in a county with a large number of volunteer or partly paid fire departments. Fire marshal's offices in Nassau County, New York, and Montgomery County, Maryland, are pioneer agencies of this type.

In addition, some townships which have several separate fire departments maintain paid fire prevention bureaus. Such an organization is found, for example, in the town of Brookhaven, New York. In some counties the entire fire protection effort is on a countywide basis and, of course, fire prevention activities are incorporated within the department.

Although much of this chapter has dealt with fire prevention bureaus operated by paid personnel, there is no doubt that many effective volunteer fire inspection programs are in existence. Concepts and procedures used by these volunteer departments can be basically the same as those used by career departments. Volunteer fire inspectors do encounter difficulties in arranging for court time and it may be desirable to use such personnel in fire education and preliminary inspection activities, leaving the enforcement aspects to paid personnel from the county or state. County or state fire marshal's offices may well provide enforcement backup for volunteer fire departments.

Enforcement

The *Municipal Fire Service Workbook* notes that "almost 95% of all jurisdictions with populations over 5,000 are covered by some kind of code (building, electrical, fire safety, housing, boiler, or mobile home)."[16] The report notes that in towns with populations under 5,000 the incidence of fire and the fire loss per capita is disproportionately high. It further notes that towns which invest more in prevention activities have a relatively low rate of fire incidence.[17]

Members of the fire prevention bureau have a moral responsibility to bring all hazardous conditions to the attention of individuals responsible for the operation of the premises. Retroactive code enforcement may not be possible; however, the inspector should make a note of conditions which endanger life and property in order to give the property owner the benefit of this vital information. The owner may elect to ignore the suggestions; however, the fire inspector will have at least fulfilled a moral responsibility to the citizens of the community.

Procedures for code enforcement vary considerably. State statutes and municipal charters generally delineate means utilized in giving notices and bringing about enforcement. The fire inspector should have legal means available to force immediate compliance where serious life hazard conditions are found. In some communities the inspector may issue a summons to operators who refuse to move impediments to egress or to abate imminent fire hazards, or who otherwise fail to correct serious deficiencies. It should not be necessary for the inspector to have to return to his or her headquarters when such conditions are encountered, any more than the traffic officer should have to go to the police station prior to writing out a traffic ticket.

The correction of major deficiencies should entail the sending of a letter, followed by a reinspection in a predetermined period of time. Failure to comply at that time would result in the issuance of a formal order, the violation of which would be a misdemeanor.

Fire prevention personnel have often been reluctant to press for code compliance; however, municipal charters normally require such action on the part of enforcement personnel. (At times fire prevention personnel have been reluctant to alienate citizens of the community because of the general feeling of goodwill toward the local fire department.)

Appeals from orders of the fire marshal may be taken to a board of appeals in many jurisdictions. In some jurisdictions there is no appeal procedure other than going directly into court. There is a practice in some states of staying the application of an order when an appeal is filed. However, several legal decisions indicate that the filing of an appeal in a public safety matter does not have the effect of staying the order but that the work must proceed or the condition must be abated.

The next step after an appeal has been lost, or after the order has been found to have been ignored, is that of arrest of the perpetrator (usually on misdemeanor charges). The violator is then required to go to court and may be found guilty or not guilty, or the case may be disposed of in some other manner. In some cases the court may decree that the work must be done to bring about compliance and that, if the violator fails to do the work in a timely fashion, contempt of court is involved.

Review of plans and specifications

A phase of fire prevention related activity which has yet to reach its full potential is that of review of plans and specifications. In this activity persons assigned to fire prevention reach the ultimate in technical responsibility.

All structures and facilities built in the community should be fully in compliance with applicable fire prevention codes and with fire safety features required by applicable building codes. The fire department is the only agency that should be responsible for seeing to it that this is, in fact, the case.

Plan and specification reviews provide the fire department with an opportunity to see that proper safeguards are provided. This responsibility, which is often assigned by charter, should not be abrogated to another agency. Regardless of responsibilities for plan review or construction supervision which may be assigned to the building department, the fire department is ultimately responsible for fire matters and should assert itself to see that it occupies a place of prominence in the review of all plans and specifications for new construction in the community.

Procedures should be developed under which all such plans are funneled through the fire prevention bureau. In many communities simultaneous submissions by architects are made to the building department and the fire prevention bureau. Both sets may be sent to the building department, in which case the fire prevention bureau is responsible for picking up its own set for review. This submission of two sets for simultaneous review lessens the possibility of long delays in the review process. Review delays cause increases in the cost of construction. (A recent analysis of review procedures in one fire prevention agency revealed, for example, that each day of delay of review of plans resulted in an increased cost of over $20,000 per day to construction in the jurisdiction served, in view of inflation.)

Many fire prevention bureaus have not been adequately staffed to carry out this important function. The assignment of unqualified persons to this duty has caused problems for fire services, builders, architects, and engineers alike. Often, the unqualified individuals hesitate to conduct thorough reviews and defer comments to those who may be more knowledgeable. Unfortunately, more knowledgeable persons from a fire safety standpoint may not be included in the plan review process. A new, unsafe building may be the result. On the other hand, an unqualified individual may impose requirements which are expensive but unnecessary, or may unwisely waive important safeguards through lack of knowledge.

Qualified individuals are becoming increasingly more available for those duties, primarily as a result of additional educational opportunities in fire science and fire protection engineering. Fire science programs are now available in community colleges in most population centers. Fire department career personnel may be at least partially prepared for plan review functions through completion of fire science programs. The graduate fire protection engineer, however, provides the ultimate in plan review capability for the fire department.

A fire protection engineer often has an advantage over the fire service career plans examiner because advanced training provides the engineer with credentials and capabilities which are recognized and respected by other professional persons. Normally, a fire protection engineering position within a fire department is a nonuniformed staff position. The individual is not a career member of the department and cannot expect advancement within the ranks. Such a position can probably be more effective as a staff position than as a line position, although the position has line functions in imposing requirements for code enforcement on architects, engineers, and builders.

Whenever possible, plan review personnel, whether career fire service or engineering, should be able to make field inspections of buildings under construction to assure compliance with requirements imposed. This activity may be carried out in concert with the building department.

Smaller communities may find it more feasible to rely on a state or county fire marshal's office for plan review services. The volume of plans reviewed may not warrant the addition of a fire protection engineer to the local fire department's staff. The state or county may provide this service on a more economical basis.

Retroactive application

Retroactive application of codes is a major source of concern in the operation of a fire prevention bureau. Proper handling of this delicate problem can spell success for the entire fire prevention program in the community.

Normally, statutory provision at the state level, or municipal ordinance or charter provisions, delineate retroactive code application possibilities. As a rule, codes cannot be retroactively enforced upon implementation unless conditions in existing buildings or facilities are determined to be inimical to public safety. Of course, a code upon enactment is applicable to all new structures and facilities. This leaves the fire code enforcement official with the responsibility for determining which structures and facilities in the community contain conditions which, from a fire safety standpoint, are inimical to public safety. The official must exercise a great deal of judgment in determining what features and improvements are needed in existing structures in order to bring them up to a condition where reasonable safety is provided. The official should be prepared to go to court to defend any action taken on a retroactive basis to upgrade existing structures. The official should also be prepared to defend lack of action if a fire occurs. This is especially important if there are fatalities in the fire.

As can be appreciated, considerable cost may be entailed in upgrading existing facilities. It is easy for the enforcement officials to sit back and say that the code applies only to new facilities, but this is not really the answer in that the majority of fire and life safety problems in a community are in older structures and facilities. The fire code official must come to grips with conditions in these structures if an effective job is to be done.

Other enforcement activities

Occasionally fire prevention managers have been persuaded to take responsibility for enforcement of regulations which are not strictly related to fire prevention. An example is the enforcement of "no smoking" regulations. There are many locations in which smoking is a fire hazard; however, the fire prevention manager must be in a position to justify any such ban in a court of law. It is not enough to be able to say that smoking at any location might start a fire. The hazard in an ice-skating rink, for example, is rather modest.

The fire official should not use fire prevention measures to enforce bans which contribute primarily to some other field of health or safety. In this case of course improved health is the primary goal. In the same light the code enforcement official must recognize that it is practically impossible to completely eliminate all hazards and provide a fire safe atmosphere. The official is faced with having to recommend codes for adoption which provide as great a degree of safety as can be reasonably enforced.

Recently, fire preventionists have given increased credence to the problem of combustible materials within structures. The advent of foam rubber, plastics, and similar materials has substantially increased rapidity of interior fire spread. Abatement action in the field of control of combustibility of materials is looked upon as an extremely meaningful part of fire prevention. Much of this enforcement activity is at the national level in that most of the material is transported in interstate commerce.

Some communities assign fire prevention personnel to standby duties during public events at which large crowds are expected. Uniformed personnel may be assigned to the city auditorium to see that exits are unobstructed and available for use and that "no smoking" regulations are enforced. The fire inspector would probably also check for combustibility of scenery and would be prepared to take steps to abate overcrowding. While assignment of personnel in this manner provides for direct code enforcement, it places the enforcement officer in a position of possible conflict with members of the audience in that few will welcome comments about aisle blocking or smoking. A confrontation situation is possible under these conditions.

Some fire prevention bureaus are responsible for enforcement of fire lane violations. Fire lanes may be established under provisions of a number of fire prevention codes, including the model code of the American Insurance Association. This places the fire prevention officer in the position of a traffic officer in that parking violations are dealt with by citations. It may be more desirable to have a local ordinance providing for fire lane designation and enforcement, thereby enabling the police department to enforce fire lane requirements.

As a management function, pre-fire planning may be coupled with fire prevention inspection carried out by fire suppression companies. If such a procedure is followed, the business owner should be made aware of the fact that the inspection is going to encompass note of possible violations as well as consideration of firefighting impediments and suppression objectives. Many departments prefer to separate these two functions rather than take a chance of misunderstanding on the part of management. Demands on time and fuel consumption considerations make it desirable that both programs be carried out in the same visit.

Public education

Public education in fire prevention and fire reaction has become a major program in many fire prevention bureaus. The report of the National Commission on Fire Prevention and Control, *America Burning,* gave recognition to the importance of fire safety education, stating the following:

Among the many measures that can be taken to reduce fire losses, perhaps none is more important than educating people about fire. Americans must be made aware of the magnitude of fire's toll and its threat to them personally. They must know how to minimize the risk of fire in their daily surroundings. They must know how to cope with fire, quickly and effectively, once it has started.[18]

The term *public fire education* is used to refer to activities relating to the dissemination of information on fire hazards and causes, and precautions against fire, as well as reaction procedures in the event of fire occurrence. This term, as mentioned earlier, encompasses the same programs that have been referred to as *fire prevention education* for many years. Normally, these duties are assigned to the fire prevention bureau or fire marshal's office.

One of the most successful education programs in fire safety is the home inspection program. This program apparently originated in Cincinnati in 1912. After one year the city experienced a 60 percent reduction in fires. Inspections were made by personnel assigned from the fire companies and 80,000 structures were inspected each year. Cincinnati has continued to conduct home inspections on a continuing basis as part of an outstanding fire prevention program which could well be emulated by other cities.

A number of other cities—including Wilmington, Delaware; Providence, Rhode Island; Portland, Oregon; and High Point, North Carolina—have carried out successful home inspection programs for many years. Results have generally been gratifying. Although the word *inspection* is used there is generally no legal backing for the program in that fire services are usually precluded from conducting mandatory inspections in one and two family dwellings. The program is primarily a public education one and should be approached as such if success is to be realized. The public should be made aware that fire service personnel are giving advice and suggestions in an effort to reduce fire experiences in the community.

Ample training is paramount to a successful home inspection program. It should also be noted that, owing to the public relations aspect of home inspection efforts, individuals who are overbearing or uncooperative cannot be successfully used in contacting home occupants. Advance publicity is necessary in order to prepare occupants for the inspection. It is also desirable to leave a check-off sheet at the time of inspection in order to give the occupant reference material for making necessary corrections. A great deal of thought and planning should go into any department's home inspection program. Normally, fire prevention bureau personnel are assigned as coordinators and as instructors for fire suppression personnel who carry out the actual inspections, using in-service apparatus for transportation.

Civic organizations provide excellent avenues for public fire education. Talks and demonstrations before these groups can have considerable impact within a community. Parent–teacher associations, fraternal organizations, scout groups, and community associations also provide sounding boards for fire prevention messages. Some communities have had success with fire safety clinics and seminars. Community fire prevention parades have been used to advantage in some localities. Fairs, dances, and other organized programs have been used in some communities with varying degrees of success.

One of the more successful approaches is that of the citizen fire safety association. A pioneer program is under way in Montgomery, Alabama. Montgomery's Citizens Fire Safety Association is an incorporated organization designed to increase the awareness of the public to fire danger. The association has membership from each council district in Montgomery and is assisted by the Montgomery fire department.

Many public fire education programs that use the schools are quite effective. There are many opportunities to promote fire prevention and fire reaction within public and private schools. Studies have shown that these efforts are rewarding. In some cases the fire department gives demonstrations before assemblies or to individual classes; in other cases teachers are responsible for implementation of fire education programs. The arrangement used will depend on the limitations of the local fire department and the attitude of the school system. One of the most successful school level fire prevention programs is the Junior Fire Marshal program of the Hartford Insurance Group in Hartford, Connecticut. Periodic assignments are given to students, and the local fire department monitors the activities. The National Smoke, Fire, and Burn Institute, in Boston, has developed a fire drill program entitled Get Low and Get Out, which is sponsored by the Aetna Life and Casualty Company, Hartford, Connecticut.

Fire safety games have been found to be useful adjuncts to educational programs. These games incorporate learning experiences and are well received in some school systems.

One of the most successful citywide programs is that of Santa Ana, California. In addition to reaching the first through the sixth grades in the schools, the Santa Ana program includes annual community cleanup campaigns, fire safety beauty contests, soapbox fire engine derbies, and many other measures designed to bring about total involvement of Santa Ana citizens in fire prevention.

In some communities burn prevention programs have been successfully coordinated with the fire safety programs of the fire department. One of the most successful is that of the Chicago fire department in cooperation with the burn unit of the Cook County Hospital.

Nationwide efforts such as the Learn Not To Burn campaign of the National Fire Protection Association, in Boston, can be effectively used by individual communities. This campaign incorporates some excellent television strips; a number of lives have been saved as a result of local showings. There is an opportunity for the community fire department to be tied in on such television publicity. National Fire Prevention Week can also be used for local mileage in fire prevention.

Public interest in smoke detectors has provided an excellent opportunity to publicize these devices. Promotional material may be designed to include home fire drills as well.

Research projects of the U.S. Fire Administration have been helpful in providing direction for public education programs. Several excellent projects have

IF YOUR CLOTHES EVER CATCH FIRE, DROP DOWN AND ROLL. THE ROLLING WILL SQUASH OUT THE FIRE AND HELP SAVE YOUR SKIN.

Figure 7–1   A cartoon from the Learn Not To Burn campaign, a long-term national public education effort launched in 1975 by the National Fire Protection Association in cooperation with The Public Service Council. The campaign, which avoids both "scare tactics" and statistics, is centered on a series of simple, basic actions that citizens can take to prevent fire or to save their families and themselves if fire should strike. The program has included public service messages on television by actor Dick Van Dyke.

analyzed approaches and procedures which are most desirable in reaching various high risk groups including the elderly, infants and small children, and some inner city residents. Guidance provided by these projects will enable the fire prevention manager to correctly assign forces for the most productive results.

One concept which is gaining support as a bureau activity is the use of the mobile fire safety team. This program uses a van-type vehicle equipped with public education material and a limited amount of fire extinguishing equipment. Personnel take the van to a shopping center, for example, and set up for public fire education purposes. Displays and demonstrations are included. The van can move from one location to another and is available by radio contact to respond to alarms which may be nearby. The personnel are trained to use the fire extinguishers carried in the vehicle to control incipient fires. Display equipment is not elaborate and can be set up in a short time, thereby enabling the crew to cover a number of locations in a day.

Innovative and unique public fire education programs are necessary if positive results are to be obtained, as the fire prevention programs are competing with many other efforts to capture the citizen's eye and time. Examples of innovative programs include New Rochelle, New York's, year-round cleanup, in which over 7,000 tons of discarded furniture and other combustibles have been removed, and Beloit, Wisconsin's, public education program which combines fire prevention with CPR training.

Internal and external coordination

Internal relations

Coordination within a fire prevention bureau involves internal as well as external considerations. Internal conflicts need to be avoided in the interests of a smoothly working machine for external cooperation. An organization with strong internal conflicts cannot work well with outside agencies.

A factor of conflict in fire prevention bureau operation may be that of working hours. Most personnel in fire prevention bureaus work the same hours as fire department administrative personnel—normally, a thirty-seven to forty hour week. In past years, most fire department suppression personnel worked a seventy-two or fifty-six hour week. This made the fire prevention bureau a desirable location from the standpoint of working hours. The advent of the forty and forty-eight hour workweek for suppression personnel has made the bureau a less desirable assignment from this standpoint. Personnel assigned to fire suppression on either a ten and fourteen hour or twenty-four and forty-eight hour basis have days off during the week in which they can work at other jobs. One day of leave may result in as much as a week off on the twenty-four and forty-eight hour shift, which makes it possible to take extended hunting and fishing trips, for example. This condition has made it difficult for some communities to obtain personnel for fire prevention duties in that bureau hours are normally the same as the Monday through Friday administrative workweek.

Other sources of conflict arise from time to time between personnel assigned to the fire prevention bureau and those assigned to suppression duties. Included are problems resulting from the practice of assignment of department vehicles to some bureau personnel on a twenty-four hour a day basis so that an inspector may respond to certain calls during normal off-duty hours. (In some cities the inspector starts conducting inspections in the morning without going into the office.) The automobile may be looked on as a status symbol, which can cause resentment on the part of department personnel.

Some suppression personnel may resent the fact that bureau personnel are in the public eye on a daily basis through their contacts with members of the business community in the city, and resentment may also arise because bureau personnel are not normally subjected to the dangers inherent in firefighting duties. In addition, injuries are less common among bureau personnel.

Another possible problem in fire prevention bureau operation is the relationship between the fire marshal or chief of the bureau and the fire chief. Although the fire chief is technically responsible for all fire prevention activities, the fire marshal or bureau chief is usually much more conversant with prevention problems which are of a technical nature. The fire chief must depend on the bureau chief for guidance and, unless the fire chief has a prevention background, great dependence must by placed upon the bureau chief's recommendation. If there is conflict between these two individuals, unfortunate circumstances may arise.

The chief is often faced with having to comment on fire prevention activities without having the bureau chief available for technical advice. In one case, for example, a fire chief made statements before the governing council of the community heralding battery operated smoke detectors as being far more desirable than electrically connected detectors. The chief did not consider that local codes as well as technical considerations dictated that electrical systems be installed. The press gave wide coverage to the chief's remarks, which caused embarrassment to the bureau chief and brought about a forced change in policy which was not really in the best interest of fire safety in the community.

A number of major cities have promoted fire prevention chiefs to the department chief's position. (In fact, the two assignments that seem to lead to the chief's position in a number of cities are the fire prevention chief's and training division chief's billets.) While this practice has advantages in that the chief has a background in the field and will normally continue to support fire prevention, it may be detrimental if the chief continues to attempt to operate the fire prevention bureau on a day-to-day basis.

Relations with other agencies

The fire prevention bureau must maintain a close relationship with other municipal agencies in order to bring about effective fire safety activities within the community. A number of other municipal agencies have responsibilities which relate to fire prevention in some way. The Las Vegas, Nevada, fire department, for example, has an officer assigned to liaison duties with other city agencies.

The zoning commission or board has regulations which necessitate clearances between structures. These clearances may effectively limit the spread of fire from one structure to another. Zoning regulations also include prohibitions against bulk storage of flammable liquids in specified areas of the city. Storage of explosives and liquefied petroleum gases are likewise limited by zoning regulations.

The building department, of course, has a major responsibility in fire prevention through control of new construction in the city. This control should be in cooperation with the fire department. In addition to inspection of buildings for structural integrity, the building department usually has responsibilities for ensuring that construction classifications are met and that proper materials are used in a building. Provision of adequate means of egress, proper interior finishes, fire extinguishing and alarm systems, and other fire-related features may also be a responsibility of the building department.

Normally, electrical inspection is carried out as a subfunction of the building department. A primary purpose for electrical inspection is that of provision of proper electrical installation from a fire safety standpoint. An improper or poorly designed installation can easily result in a fire. Electrical inspection is a procedure which requires a great deal of specialized training and expertise.

The local police department may be of assistance to the fire prevention bureau in carrying out code enforcement. Police officers can, for example, notify fire department personnel of facilities in which overcrowded conditions occur. They can also be helpful in fireworks and explosives regulation enforcement. And, of course, many communities depend upon police department support in suppression of arson.

Managers of municipal fire prevention bureaus will have to consider the impact of federal and state fire prevention regulatory activities. These activities have an effect on the operation of the bureau and especially on the attitude of operators of facilities undergoing inspection.

Federal agencies   Federal activities in the fire prevention field have increased considerably in recent years. Although federal involvement in fire prevention has traditionally been associated with interstate commerce types of operations such as transportation of hazardous materials, recently these interests have expanded to include such matters as product safety and health facility safety. (For a more detailed discussion of the federal role, see Chapter 4.)

State agencies   The fire prevention manager also needs to consider the impact of state fire prevention activity in planning a local program. State fire marshals' offices exist in forty-seven states, although responsibilities vary considerably from state to state. Such offices exist in all provinces in Canada. In the average state the fire marshal has some statewide enforcement responsibilities. Enforcement of explosives regulations, health facility fire safety standards, and general fire prevention regulations may be included. In a number of states a legally designated local fire marshal is an ex officio deputy state fire marshal for the purpose of carrying out state enforcement activities in the local jurisdiction.

In some states, state inspectors are required to handle all occupancies of certain classifications throughout the state. In such a state the local fire prevention manager should attempt to arrange for joint inspections of the facilities within the local jurisdiction in order to avoid conflict and misunderstanding. An example would be the health facility, which is usually inspected by state level personnel.

In some states personnel of the health department, department of labor and industry, department of welfare, bureau of mines, racing commission, and other state regulatory agencies conduct inspections which include some fire safety considerations. As a rule these inspections are not coordinated with local fire prevention activities. (For additional discussion of the state role, see Chapter 4.)

Other relationships   One of the most effective means of achieving fire prevention enforcement is through the use of licensing and permit requirements of other agencies, at the city, county, or state level. If other regulatory agencies add fire prevention code compliance requirements to their regulations, lack of compliance with fire regulations can be used as a reason for withholding licenses to operate. A number of communities, for example, have effective cooperative arrangements with the liquor board which entails an assurance by the fire marshal as to the fire safety of a restaurant, cabaret, or nightclub prior to the issuance of a liquor license. A similar arrangement may exist with the departments of health and education, racing commissions, and other regulatory agencies. The economic sanction of denial of a license may bring about much more rapid compliance with fire requirements than would direct enforcement by the fire prevention bureau.

Membership in fire marshals' organizations is a necessity for a progressive fire prevention manager. The Fire Marshals Association of North America is the principal national organization for fire marshals, with membership from the United States and Canada. A number of regional and state level fire marshals' groups provide an opportunity for interchange of information and development of statewide programs. Among the more active are those in Texas, Illinois, New Jersey, California, and North Carolina.

Several communities have discontinued full-time fire prevention bureaus in favor of amalgamated municipal inspections services. Individuals assigned to these agencies perform all types of city inspections pertaining to structures, including electrical, sanitation, plumbing, building, zoning, and fire safety. This approach is designed to bring about reduced expenditures; however, the value of inspections conducted by generalists in specialized fields is questionable. The city of Milwaukee has pioneered this method, but few other cities have followed suit. The fire department has an advantage over any other municipal inspection agency in carrying out inspections: the fire department member is generally recognized as an experienced practitioner in his or her field of specialization. Most citizens are of the opinion that the fire department inspector is competent and is less subject to political pressures than are other municipal inspectors; for this reason the fire department inspector is generally more successful in obtaining compliance.

In communities operating public safety departments in which the same individuals function as both police and fire personnel, a distinction is generally made between the police routine law enforcement function and the public safety officer's fire prevention function. The latter duty cannot, it is generally felt, be carried out in the same manner as traffic or penal code enforcement. Fire code enforcement in such a community is generally carried out in the traditional fire department manner.

Problems alluded to in the use of other municipal employees for fire safety inspections should not discourage the establishment of a cooperative program for interchange of violation information among city agencies. Fire inspectors should advise health department sanitarians of possible sanitation violations they observe in restaurants, for example. Conversely, sanitarians should report immediately to the fire department any possible fire prevention violations they might observe. In either case the receiving agency—the one with primary responsibility—should take immediate steps to check the validity of the report and, if it is found valid, to bring about prompt compliance. Such arrangements should exist with the building department, the zoning department, the weights and measures division, and any other city or state agency that might be able to assist. The inspection forces available to the city government are too limited in number to operate on any basis other than that of total cooperation. Cleveland, Ohio, fire prevention personnel, for example, regularly report problems to building, electrical, housing, air pollution, heating, plumbing, and health agencies, as well as to the police department.

Certain precautions, however, should be taken in connection with possible cooperation with police departments. Although full cooperation is desirable, fire prevention bureau personnel cannot place themselves in the position of using the right of entry for fire inspection purposes as a means of entering to look for the results of crimes. On several occasions fire inspectors have unwittingly involved themselves in an untenable legal situation by entering a structure for the primary purpose of looking for narcotics, disposed weapons, or other fruits of crime; this route was used in order to avoid the complications of obtaining a search warrant. Generally, the courts have not upheld the submission of evidence obtained under such conditions. However, several seizures have been upheld when the fruits of crime were found during a search subsequent to a fire.

Legal implications of enforcement

The fire prevention manager needs to consider legal implications of fire code enforcement. Several court decisions have provided direction to the enforcement official, although prudent managers will be well aware of the need to obtain expert legal advice (for which the following discussion is no substitute) in areas of difficulty.

The U.S. Supreme Court decisions in *See* v. *City of Seattle*[19] and *Camera* v. *Municipal Court*[20] require the obtaining of a warrant by the fire inspector if permission to enter has not been given.

A decision of the Minnesota Supreme Court, *City of Minneapolis* v. *William Krebas,*[21] affirmed the fire department's power to require an enclosed stairway under provisions of the fire prevention code. Minneapolis adopts the fire prevention code published by the American Insurance Association. The code contains a general provision under which the correction of hazardous conditions, including lack of adequate exits, may be ordered. The appellant argued that the fire prevention code was unconstitutional because of vagueness and alleged that it was based on improperly delegated legislative power. The court disagreed and thus upheld the fire department's authority to require exit upgrading under the fire prevention code.

Three decisions of the Alaska Supreme Court also have a bearing on fire prevention enforcement. These decisions, handed down in the 1970s, involved fires in hotels. *Adams* v. *State of Alaska*[22] came as a result of an Anchorage hotel fire in which five persons were killed and several injured. Representatives of the deceased and injured entered suit for damages naming, among others, the state of Alaska as a defendant. The state fire marshal's office, with proper legal authority, had made an inspection of the hotel more than eight months prior to the fire and had found an inoperative fire alarm system and several other fire safety violations. The fire marshal's office had not taken positive steps to notify the owner of the violation.

The court held that the state, by inspecting the hotel, assumed the duty of protecting the occupants. The court upheld the right of suit in this case. The possible adverse affect of the decision on fire prevention enforcement was noted by the court through the following statement:

We think it unlikely that limited liability for negligence in an inspection will force the state from the field of fire inspection. Fire prevention is a recognized government function, not an experimental program. The cost of fire prevention, including the risk of liability is still less than the cost to the state of disastrous fires, in terms of fire fighting effort, lost taxes and the impact on the economy.[23]

In the second Alaska decision, *State of Alaska* v. *Jennings*,[24] a fire had taken eleven lives. The survivors sued the state, the city of Fairbanks, and the hotel management. In this case the state fire marshal had turned over inspection responsibility in Fairbanks to the city fire prevention bureau in accordance with policy permitted by statute. The court held that the state had no responsibility in this case, but the city fire prevention bureau was found to be responsible for inspection. This bureau had made a number of inspections over the years and had sent many letters to the owners requiring correction of deficiencies. These inspections and letters were ignored by the owners. The court held that the city was negligent in allowing continued operation of the hotel and further noted that the city had an obligation to obtain compliance once inspections were commenced.

The third case, *Northern Lights Motel, Inc.,* v. *Sweaney*,[25] pertains to an Anchorage motel fire in which there was only one victim. The victim's representative successfully sued the motel and the motel operators appealed the decision. The fatal fire had apparently started in a room which had been occupied by another guest and spread into the room in which the victim was asleep. Testimony indicated that the motel was constructed of three-eighths to one-half inch plasterboard while the prevailing fire code required a fire rating which would necessitate the use of at least five-eighths inch plasterboard.

Local fire department inspections had found certain defects in ceiling construction; however, there had been no determined effort to obtain compliance. The court held that the owner had an obligation to build the structure in accordance with codes and found the suit to be in order. An expert witness testified that the fire had been able to spread because of the construction deficiency.

Evaluation and record keeping

Evaluation

The fire prevention manager unfortunately has few sources of help in evaluating performance of bureau personnel. Although the grading schedule of the Insurance Services Office includes some consideration of fire prevention activity, it is not designed to provide criteria for full measurement of organizational effectiveness. In the United Kingdom evaluation of performance is carried out by the Inspector of Fire Services in the Home Office for England, Wales, and Northern Ireland. Personnel of this office visit communities for the purpose of evaluating fire prevention effectiveness. They inspect facilities, for example, and then check the fire brigade report to see if the deficiencies were noted in the most recent inspection. A similar program function is carried out by the Inspector of Fire Services for Scotland.

While no such agency exists in the United States, some evaluations of local fire prevention bureau effectiveness are conducted in Canada by the Ontario fire marshal's office. Some fire marshals have proposed that teams be organized to visit fire prevention bureaus and evaluate effectiveness. These teams might be formed in the manner employed by academic accreditation organizations, using personnel from several cities who would meet to inspect a given bureau. This arrangement would offer the opportunity of bringing in new ideas in addition to generally evaluating the effectiveness of fire prevention efforts.

Budget percentage allocations to fire prevention have been used by some evaluators in determining the degree of emphasis on fire prevention in a department. It may be noted, for example, that 5 percent of Haywood, California's, fire department budget is devoted to fire prevention, while in Oakland 4 percent is devoted to this activity. Calgary, Alberta, devotes 3 percent of its fire department budget to fire prevention. All three cities have excellent programs; however, the way in which activities were categorized in the compilation vary, and comparisons are almost meaningless.

A 1974 report suggests the following needs in research pertaining to fire prevention:

1. Effectiveness of various prevention activities in terms of loss reduction, as well as cost/effectiveness
2. Analysis of fire losses and the implications for prevention activities
3. Public education needs: media effectiveness; type of education most needed; population strata to which education should be directed
4. Effectiveness of codes and regulations
5. Penalties as a deterrent to carelessly started fires
6. Use of hazard analysis as a basis for prevention effort allocation.[26]

Record keeping

The fire prevention manager should ensure that accurate records are kept of all activities within the bureau. This should include records and reports of all inspections, consultations, plans and specifications reviews, public fire education activities, complaints received and handled, assignments to crowd control, and other services performed by the bureau. It is easy to forget to keep accurate records of activities during the day. Often, fire prevention personnel carry out a number of varied duties during a given day and it may be difficult to record each. The manager needs such information in order to accurately assess the performance of personnel. This information is also necessary in an evaluation of the bureau's performance by the chief of the department.

The advent of the National Fire Incident Reporting System of the U.S. Fire Administration has given impetus to record keeping activities within the fire service. It is envisioned that the system will some day include data from all fifty states and fire prevention bureau personnel will be major contributors. In a number of communities bureau personnel are responsible for reviewing and analyzing incidence reports as prepared by fire suppression companies. This seems to be a logical adjunct to the bureau's duties in that personnel are able to glean valuable information from the reports. This information on fire causes and specific problems encountered can be of great assistance in public fire education activities, as well as in proposing alterations and additions to the fire prevention code in order to reflect new hazards.

In Canada the Dominion Fire Commissioner maintains a nationwide fire reporting system in concert with provincial fire marshals.

Annual reports

The annual report of the fire department provides a good platform for publicity on activities of the fire prevention bureau. Detailed information on activities should be included. The means by which violations are dealt with should be outlined in the report. The Columbus, Ohio, fire department's annual report, for example, notes that careless fire violations received sentences totaling a stated number of days and a stated amount of fines in a given year. The Lee's Summit, Missouri, report includes a breakdown of violations found. Such information is helpful in determining priorities.

Losses in inspected versus uninspected buildings are noted in the Arlington County, Virginia, fire department's annual report. In Detroit a separate annual report is prepared each year by the city fire marshal's office; this report gives detailed information on all bureau activity and includes trends and projections in the field. In Oregon the annual report of the state fire marshal includes information from each department as to budget expenditures in fire protection, numbers of inspections, permits issued, and fire safety talks given.

The Boise, Idaho, fire department's annual report lists the following types of activities for its well-operated fire prevention bureau: routine inspections; routine night inspections; federal and state inspections; home inspections; plan checks; plan check field inspections; plan check field inspections completed; tank inspections; notices served; notices completed; total violations; corrections; burning permits issued; meetings; fire drills; code classes; public appearances; office work (reports); arson investigations; fire investigations; interviews; dark room.

A review of activities of fire prevention bureaus in cities of comparable size can give the fire prevention manager a basis for comparison. Such a review can also be useful for obtaining ideas on new methods of reducing losses.

It is useful for the manager to review total time devoted to each activity, as well. In one city a detailed study of fire prevention bureau time allocations revealed that 80 percent of personnel time was devoted to the servicing of complaints. Many of these were of a neighborhood feud type and few really pertained to actual fire prevention; therefore, a reallocation was made.

The Cincinnati Fire Division's annual report for 1976 contains a statement regarding fire prevention activities that could well summarize the goals and objectives of fire prevention managers throughout North America:

The statistics that accompany this report indicate that the past programs instituted in Fire Prevention are having a decided effect in curtailing loss of life, property, injuries, and loss to the economy caused by fire. The major factors contributing to this continuing effect are the company inspection program, the Cincinnati Fire Prevention Code, the Fire Prevention Specialists, the voluntary, as well as on duty, education programs of the entire Fire Division and the on-going, updating of the Fire Prevention Bureau operations. The deficiency in manpower (uniformed and civilian) precludes a faster or more positive approach, particularly in education and to a lesser degree in inspection and investigation. Some of the more noticeable statistics are fronted with the fact that 21,646 fire hazards were remedied in 1976 side by side with 2,343 building fires. This ratio of fires prevented to fires extinguished in buildings is *9* to *1*. It can be stated that for every fire fought, the Division prevents *9*.[27]

Summary and outlook

The discussion in this chapter has indicated that fire prevention activities can extend outward from the fire prevention bureau, however it is organized, to involve the entire fire department, other local government agencies, and citizens of the community. Good management of the fire prevention bureau and other related activities, and good planning and coordination, are, however, prerequisites for a successful fire prevention program. This chapter has touched on the key areas that local government managers have found important in conceiving and implementing such programs. It has provided a basic overview of the subject and the managerial principles involved and then has considered organization, training, and management concepts. The role of codes, public education, internal and external relationships, legal implications, and evaluation and record keeping have been discussed in turn.

What of the future? Many people involved in this field would agree that in the future greater emphasis will be placed on measured performance of duties carried out by fire prevention bureau personnel. Increased standards for entry into the fire prevention field will give the manager a more clearly defined means of measuring performance.

Fire prevention will become a greater part of all fire department activities. Cost considerations will dictate this approach. Spotlights will be focused on fire prevention activities with such intensity that hopefully another Beverly Hills Supper Club type disaster cannot occur in any area having a bona fide fire code enforcement program. Increased emphasis will be placed on public fire education, and homeowners and citizens generally will play a greater role in fire prevention.

Greater use will also be made of the computer for scheduling of inspections, reviewing hazards and causes, and carrying out other fire prevention related tasks. There will be more federal involvement in fire prevention matters. The chief responsibility, however, as now, will rest on the shoulders of competent local government managers both inside and outside of the fire department.

1 R. L. Nailen and James S. Haight, *Beertown Blazes: A Century of Milwaukee Fire Fighting* (Milwaukee, Wis.: NAPCOGraphic Arts, Inc., 1971), pp. 21–22.

2 Lowell E. Limpus, *The New York Fire Department: Manual of Instruction* (New York: E. P. Dutton & Co., Inc., 1940), p. 179.

3 Norfolk Firefighters' Association, *History of the Fire Department, Norfolk, Virginia* (Norfolk, Va.: Norfolk Firefighters' Association, 1975), pp. 8, 23.

4 Research Triangle Institute (RTI), International City Management Association (ICMA), and National Fire Protection Association (NFPA), *Municipal Fire Service Workbook*, prepared for the National Science Foundation, Research Applied to National Needs (Washington, D.C.: Government Printing Office, 1977), pp. 25–26.

5 Ibid., p. 28.

6 Ibid.

7 Ibid., pp. 28–29.

8 David E. Fyffe and Ronald L. Rardin, *Fire Pro-Protection Service Management,* prepared for the National Science Foundation, Research Applied to National Needs (Atlanta: Georgia Institute of Technology, 1974), p. 270.

9 Of particular help are the published standards of the National Fire Protection Association (NFPA), Boston, Massachusetts.

10 Fyffe and Rardin, *Fire Protection Service Management,* p. 269.

11 National Fire Protection Association, *Fire Fighter Professional Qualifications,* NFPA no. 1001 (Boston: National Fire Protection Association, 1974).

12 National Fire Protection Association, *Professional Qualifications for Fire Inspector, Fire Investigator, and Fire Prevention Education Officer,* NFPA

no. 1031 (Boston: National Fire Protection Association, 1977).

13 American Insurance Association, *Fire Prevention Code* (New York: American Insurance Association, 1975).

14 Fire prevention codes of: Building Officials and Code Administrators International, Chicago; International Conference of Building Officials, Whittier, California; and Southern Building Code Congress, Birmingham, Alabama.

15 National Fire Protection Association, *Fire Prevention Code,* NFPA no. 1 (Boston: National Fire Protection Association, 1975).

16 RTI, ICMA, and NFPA, *Municipal Fire Service Workbook,* p. 77.

17 Ibid., p. 55.

18 National Commission on Fire Prevention and Control, *America Burning* (Washington, D.C.: Government Printing Office, 1973), p. 105.

19 *See* v. *City of Seattle,* 387 U.S. 541 (1967).

20 *Camera* v. *Municipal Court,* 387 U.S. 523 (1967).

21 *City of Minneapolis* v. *William Krebas,* No. 44880, Minnesota Supreme Court (1975).

22 *Adams* v. *State of Alaska,* Opin. No. 1318, Alaska Supreme Court (1976).

23 Ibid.

24 *State of Alaska* v. *Jennings,* Opin. No. 1119, Alaska Supreme Court (1976).

25 *Northern Lights Motel, Inc.,* v. *Sweaney,* Opin. No. 1386, Alaska Supreme Court (1977).

26 Fyffe and Rardin, *Fire Protection Service Management,* pp. 280–81.

27 City of Cincinnati Fire Division, *Annual Report, 1976* (Cincinnati, Ohio: City of Cincinnati Fire Division, 1977), p. 32.

Managing inspection services

Effective inspection practices and their management are key areas of successful overall administration of the fire services in a community. The management of inspection services may not have been in the forefront of fire management in the past, but this is no longer the case today. Competing demands on the tax dollar and a shift in emphasis to fire prevention as well as fire suppression mean that inspections, as a segment of a broader prevention program, have become an important factor in managerial decision making.

The discussion in this chapter focuses on the management of inspection services as a vital component of an overall fire prevention program. The dimensions of that program have been set out in Chapter 7 and, as the introduction to that chapter states, the coverage in these two chapters should be regarded as complementary.

The present chapter is organized as follows. There is an introductory overview which sets the management of inspection services in context and provides a framework for the remainder of the chapter. The central portion of the chapter covers the full management cycle related to inspection services. It begins by outlining the various components of the process with reference to the basic steps in a flowchart which illustrates the discussion. (The components discussed are: goals and objectives; current process analysis; decision; preparation; documentation; decision; implementation of the revised process; and process evaluation.) Planning, organizing and staffing, the strengths and weaknesses of organizational arrangements, and questions of coordination and control are then discussed. The chapter ends with a brief conclusion and outlook.

Overview

The applications of fire prevention in relation to the inspection function vary widely across the nation and in communities of differing sizes. Three key areas or subfunctions of inspection may be identifed for purposes of discussion—(1) the basic core of routine inspections and the two ancillary areas of (2) fire prevention education and (3) public relations generally. Each of these categories might be worthy of a lengthy discussion, and the last two named would take us into the realm of the behavioral scientist. Indeed, it is important to emphasize at the outset that, in some form or another, even the most routine inspection of an occupancy has some educational or public relations implication.

The concept of routine inspections may well have different meanings in different fire departments. In those areas using statewide minimum–maximum (popularly *mini–max*) building codes, routine inspections might be strictly defined as a subfunction only after the building in question is constructed and released for occupancy. In other cases routine inspections might consist of practices initiated in the design stage of a structure and carried through to its occupancy and subsequent use within the community. It would be in the nature of these inspections to include an educational and public relations component, as day-to-day contact with special interest groups within the community, as well as with the general public, would be involved.

Historical perspective

To some degree the historical development (or lack of it) of these three areas—routine inspections, education, and public relations—reflects one or more of three other factors: (1) the resources available to a given fire manager; (2) that manager's own understanding (or lack of it) of fire prevention needs; and/or (3) the results of external activities dictated by the political and socioeconomic environment (and the pressure groups reflecting that environment) in the given community.

The management of inspection services in the United States can be traced to two key factors: (1) the insurance companies' loss control management practices; and (2) repeated or catastrophic losses in a municipality. One of the earliest examples of the latter can be found in the activities of several New England cities which (as noted in Chapter 1) developed ordinances limiting the use of combustible material in roof and chimney construction. For example, in the seventeenth century Boston passed ordinances prohibiting the use of such combustible material after several disastrous fires.

Indeed, one of the most influential factors in the historical development of inspection services is unquestionably what can be called (for lack of a better term) the *catastrophe theory,* or *design by disaster.* This occurs in the following way. Prior to a catastrophe the concerns of firefighters or, for that matter, of citizen groups, have been discussed or tabled. Then disaster strikes. As a result of subsequent publicity and outcry, stringent fire regulations and ordinances are developed.

Time, however, seems to have a diluting effect on the historical significance of these catastrophes. Today, for example, we have building codes which allow use of the same materials that contributed significantly to past disasters. Specifically, wooden shingle roofs have been identified as a major contributing factor in serious fire incidents. Today, more and more use of this material is allowed in building construction.

The pressures to relax stringent fire prevention measures are in fact extreme. In most cases these pressures are related to the economic impact of providing fire protection. Therefore, it is not surprising to examine the historical circumstances of major catastrophes, superimpose those conditions on current activities, and find similar contributing conditions. To some extent typical fire prevention efforts contribute to this by their lack of understanding of the total managerial environment in a given municipality. Obviously, many complex issues are involved, but if fire protection personnel are to assume the leadership role in reducing and preventing damaging fires, it is critically important for them to approach and present the problem with a clinical detailed analysis. Rhetoric alone will not accomplish this end.

If inspection services are to eliminate, or at least control, the conditions contributing to major incidents, these services need to put their concerns forward and to defend them in a professional way. For example, defenses without analytical data, cost considerations, and other significant factors will not suffice on either a local or a national basis.

Managerial perspective

In light of the above discussion, from a managerial standpoint modern fire service administrators need to examine inspection services, and fire prevention in general, clearly and with all aspects of fire service delivery in mind. In many cases the assessment of the impact of inspections on administrative as well as on suppression practices has not been an ongoing process. But with the tremendous dollar drain caused by manpower, apparatus, and station costs, and many other items, the average municipality cannot afford to provide all of the equipment that the fire manager may deem appropriate. This is not to say that anyone should underplay the seriousness of current risk management in a given community, but risk management includes not only suppression but also those prevention practices which will inhibit or limit fire development. As an integral part of the overall fire service delivery system, inspections can have a direct minimizing effect on fire suppression activities and, thus, their costs. For some fire officers this rationale can be a totally new experience, but it is one that successful future managers must incorporate. The luxury of considering inspection services as a separate, more or less nonrelated element of a typical fire service delivery system is a thing of the past.

In larger municipalities, or in those using paid personnel, inspections are handled in several different ways. One of the methods least frequently used is the delivery of inspection services by the volunteer firefighting community. Historically, volunteers have viewed fire suppression as their primary role. To some degree this is useful in view of the extreme liabilities involved in providing and maintaining inspection services. However, there is a growing and distinct new role for the volunteer community in fire prevention, a role which includes public relations, public education, and public awareness. The pros and cons of volunteer inspection services should be weighed carefully. In any event, the modern volunteer community cannot afford the luxury of nonparticipation in fire protection practices.

The management cycle and inspection services

Components of the cycle

In the following discussion eight components of the management cycle (or process) as it relates to inspection services are introduced and analyzed. These components are set out in the form of a flowchart in Figure 8–1. The organizational schematic set out in Figure 8–1 is not all-inclusive. It merely reflects, in very simple format, a thinking process that has proved itself useful in the light of managerial responsibilities for and to inspection services.

Goals and objectives   The administrative tools of management by objectives (MBO), risk management, performance programs, cost–benefit analysis, and other analytical tools (discussed in Chapters 6 and 12) are vital to inspection service goals and objectives. Performance measures are a primary need.

Performance measurement   Until recently, there was little in the way of literature defining measurable and manageable units within inspection services. Since the middle and later 1970s, however, a greater body of literature has become available to the modern fire service manager. These works enable the manager to approach specific elements of fire protection and prevention practices in a professional manner. Several comprehensive works give detailed coverage to performance measurement, not only in inspection services but in fire prevention and protection in general.[1] Certain other publications which deal with productivity in municipal services as a whole are also of use to the fire manager.[2] These works and other related research underscore the need for specific performance measurement. (Productivity is discussed in detail in Chapter 14.)

In some cases the transfer of industrial or business measurement tools to fire service measurement is acceptable and efficient. In other cases, however, specific performance measurements must be developed by the fire service for subsequent adoption and presentation to local government. For example, the impact of inspection services in materially reducing fire severity in specific occupancies may never be measured fully. Nevertheless, some rationale to

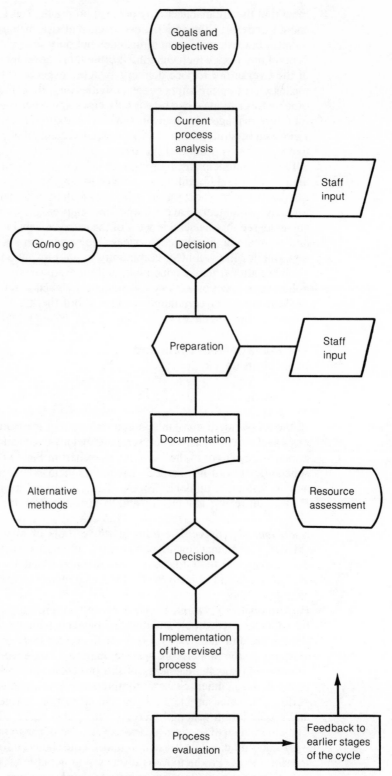

Figure 8-1   The management cycle in fire inspection.

show the basic application and productivity of the inspector's time in relation to subsequent fire development is important. Obviously, many variables will affect a performance yardstick of this nature. This is another example of the extremely complex cause and effect relationship of inspection services to fire origin, spread, and suppression. Without definable measurements, fire inspection cannot expect to be effective in the eyes of the municipality and cannot expect to compete successfully for the dollar resources available to the fire department.

Goal and objective determination Typically, certain basic considerations need to be developed by the fire service manager in the inspection area. An example would be: defining the current role of inspection services in the community; defining the resources available to perform the inspection function; defining the alternative methods that are available or that can be developed; and defining what the manager wants the inspection services to perform in relation to overall managerial responsibility and to the provision of fire service. Perhaps the bottom line to the development of goals and objectives is the question: What is the problem? From this basic question an enormously complex structure emerges. Identification of the strengths and weaknesses of any typical inspection service is the basis from which logical and objective performance standards are developed. In this sense the words *performance standards* and *goals and objectives* are somewhat interchangeable. To establish your goal and subsequent objectives is in itself to isolate in a step-by-step process what those requirements and results should be. And it is also to define the problem.

One of the first areas that fire service managers can establish, in terms of performance measurements, is the current expenditure of time and resources given to inspection services. For this purpose, a close examination of the community in terms of all occupancies, of frequency of inspection, and of manpower available to perform inspection duties can be developed graphically. From this data base fire service managers may develop reasonably objective statements in terms of the ability of inspection services to provide basic programs. They should be able also to address specific deficiencies (that is, those considerations which they cannot develop physically or initiate with existing resources).

Once a definition concerning existing capabilities has been structured, fire service managers should develop the rationale and project specific goals and objectives (see Figure 8–2 for an example of such objectives). If their resources are not adequate to maintain basic inspection services, fire managers will have to isolate clearly what they can or need to do. In other words, they should state the priorities of those functions that are absolute essentials in relation to available resources.

Once priorities are defined and supported with objective data, managers should prepare the arguments for increased support of inspection services and, simultaneously, should prepare a list of alternative means or methods of accomplishing these goals and objectives. If the basic resource—manpower—will allow service only to critical occupancies (institutions, schools, commercial districts, for example), and if other areas must also be provided with the inspection service, then fire service managers need to support this contention to the budget process and, at the same time, examine resources in other divisions of the fire department that might be tapped to alleviate immediate and long-term needs.

In summary, fire service managers should have some idea of what they want inspection services to encompass. To this extent, traditional goal setting with subsequent objectives is the first and foremost activity to be undertaken.

Current process analysis Once fire service managers have formulated the direction they want inspection services to follow, they should undertake a thor-

To obtain better life safety conditions
1 Secure proper maintenance of fire escapes and exits and keep aisles, halls, stairs, and exits unobstructed

To keep fires from starting
1 Eliminate or control fire hazards

To check maintenance of fire protection equipment
1 Obtain proper maintenance of private fire extinguishing equipment and secure adequate water supply
2 Secure proper maintenance of devices designed to limit the spread of fire
3 Secure proper maintenance of fire detection and alarm equipment
4 Determine adequacy of public hydrants and water supply

To assemble facts concerning building and contents
1 Obtain detailed information concerning building construction and occupancy
2 Note all exposures
3 Assemble facts useful in fighting fires in the building
4 Gather information useful in fire investigation after a fire

To help owner or occupant to obtain better life and fire safety conditions
1 Inform owner or occupant of existing conditions and help improve hazards by advice and suggestions
2 Encourage a year-round fire prevention and protection program
3 Reduce area and property likely to be involved in a fire
4 Examine watchman service

Figure 8–2   Principal objectives of fire inspection.
(Source: Greenfield, Wisconsin, Fire Department.)

ough analysis of existing practices. Typically, the following questions will come to the surface:

1. How many staff members are assigned?
2. Is personnel time productive?
3. What is the cost of the program?
4. Is the program effective?
5. What are the physical limitations of the program?

These questions reflect only a few considerations; obviously, there are many more. In any event, a concise evaluation of the current inspection practices should be detailed carefully. At this juncture, and slightly before the decision, staff input would be extremely useful (Figure 8–1). For example, are staff members satisfied with the current process? If not, what changes would they like to see implemented? And do they have any suggestions for improving the quality and quantity of the work process?

Decision   Once these steps are completed, fire service managers should make their decision regarding the implementation of changes. Additionally, the go/no go is a decision point in its simplest form (Figure 8–1). The go situation might entail only slight modifications or changes to the existing inspection program. The no go situation might reflect a degree of comfort with the existing program. It is, however, difficult to imagine any existing inspection practice that would not lend itself to beneficial change.

Preparation   Should managers decide to alter the existing goals of inspection practices, it is important that they undertake a thorough preparation for these changes. Again, this is a point at which staff input is useful, both in itself and as a means of keeping the communication lines between managers and their staffs intact.

Documentation   Documentation for change is often overlooked, although it is an invaluable—and essential—tool for fire service managers. In this context two considerations are essential. The first is resource assessment. In simple terms this is a description of what the manager's inspection practices can and cannot physically accomplish with existing personnel and equipment. The second consideration is that of alternative methods. Again, in a simple format alternative methods are presented for providing certain desired levels of inspection services through the use of nontraditional roles. For example, would the inclusion of engine company personnel in an inspection program increase inspection activities to a desired level? Would the impact of outside agencies such as public utilities and planning departments accomplish prime objectives through increased inspection considerations contributed by each agency? Is there a role for the police department in inspection practices? These questions illustrate typical alternative delivery considerations, not only for inspection practices but for the fire service as a whole. Alternative delivery systems can serve as a managerial attempt to force the fire service out of its traditionally isolated position.

Decision It is at this point that the decision to implement changes in inspection practices is made. It is important to remember that a decision of this nature not only affects fire service personnel but could also affect both political and municipal thinking—a factor that could be most acute in terms of liability.

Implementation of the revised process When the decision has been made, the proper instruction and format for the revisions are implemented. The new, or altered, direction should be underscored by thorough homework and communication within the elements affected by it.

Process evaluation This phase serves to emphasize the need to constantly evaluate the programs that are being implemented. Cost–benefit analysis and performance measures (as discussed in Chapters 12 and 14) are two of the yardsticks of this stage—and, indeed, of the entire process, starting with determination of goals and objectives. The evaluation process will dictate modification on the basis of experience and practicality. There will, of course, be continuous feedback to earlier stages in the cycle.

Planning

Sound planning is the foundation of effective and productive management of inspection services. In the preceding section goals and objectives were discussed: this might be considered placing the cart before the horse. Planning is in fact an integral part, if not the first step, of the goals and objectives process. As such, the planning process will be used to examine the precise relationship of existing services within the fire service, as well as relationships with those agencies that affect that service. Such analysis is necessary to assure that sound methodologies appropriate to the task at hand are employed.

For example, a lack of understanding of building codes from the perspective of the building official could be counterproductive, at very least, to inspection services. And the impacts of land planning and use, utility maintenance and development, political climate, and pressure groups are aspects of sound planning that must be incorporated into effective management for inspection services.

As has been indicated, the broad range of factors affecting inspections should be analyzed in light of resources available, cost-effectiveness, and productivity. As regards this last factor, if planning indicates use of fire suppression forces, the fire service manager will need to examine traditional roles and the lack of training in inspection services, and then develop sound training programs and communication processes prior to implementing the suppression/inspection service. As a prime managerial consideration, the use of these fire suppression forces could be critically important in light of municipal practices for increasing the productivity of typical fire service delivery. It would obviously be far more productive for the fire service to have field personnel involved in fire-related programs as opposed to nonfire-related programs such as maintenance of parking meters and recording of water and electric meters. The latter type of activity often results from the failure of the fire service manager to demonstrate clearly the full and complex factors affecting productivity, and often is a response to the demands on the municipal dollar.

Alternative approaches, via the planning process, are again key aspects of sound managerial practices. This is not to suggest that traditional use of inspection services should be abandoned but rather that modern fire service managers need to examine these practices in light of the influences surrounding them now. Such examination might suggest a continuation of historical practices together with a development of nontraditional approaches to increase the effectiveness of the service. It is equally important to be able to present, via the budget structure, alternative programs that are within the municipality's funding ability. In this light, to approach a budget review with only one method of operation will, at best, be frustrating and will often result in municipal direction of fire inspection and suppression into other municipal activities.

Organization and staffing

Four organization models For purposes of comparison and discussion, four models of inspection service organization and staffing are presented in Figures 8–3 to 8–6. Figure 8–3 represents a town of approximately 15,000 with a paid

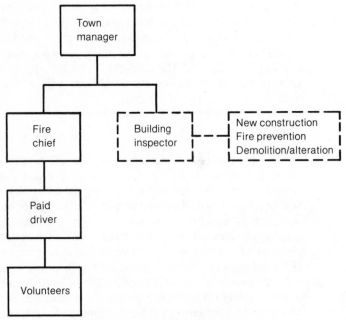

Figure 8–3 Organization chart for a city of 15,000 population.

chief and paid drivers, supplemented by a volunteer firefighting force. Inspection service, as an adjunct to the fire service, is illustrated by a nonconnecting block representing a civilian whose official title is building inspector but who must double up on fire prevention related matters.

This practice brings inspections under nonuniformed control as a totally separate function from typical fire department activities. Obviously, fire prevention and inspection practices must affect fire suppression and must be integrated with it on a day-to-day basis. In this organizational structure, a cooperative relationship must exist between the fire official and the building official.

Figure 8–4 represents an inspection service application in a city of approximately 75,000. Here, fire inspection services are also structured as a separate function from fire suppression and, in addition, the inspection services also include the city building inspection division. In this particular case, the head of the fire prevention division manages both uniform and civilian inspectors for an unusual approach to both building and fire prevention considerations. To quite a large extent this configuration allows some fire-related input into one and two family dwellings that, historically, prevention cannot address.

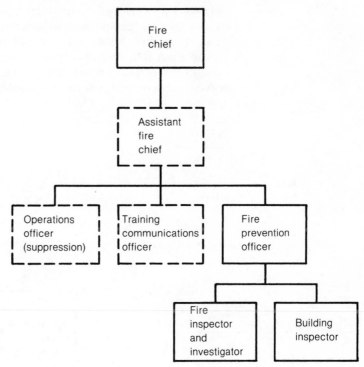

Figure 8–4 Organization chart for a city of 75,000 population.

In Figure 8–5 we have a community of approximately 750,000 people with a large inspection base structured as part of the operations division, which is headed by a deputy chief. Prevention is considered an equal and a parallel function with suppression and training. In some estimates, this configuration is one of the more objective in attempting to bring fire-related agencies together through some coordinating plan. Inspectors as well as field personnel (suppression) are engaged actively not only in ongoing inspections but also in public safety presentations, educational activities, and media contact.

While these three figures represent operations in their respective communities, it would be misleading to assume that these are the broad applications throughout the country. Many different configurations exist—or, in some cases, do not exist at all—with regard to inspection services. The size of the department has some bearing on the activities of inspection services, and it would be safe to assume that an equally important factor is the fire manager's concern for or understanding of the relationship between inspections and total fire service management. The two larger communities, shown as Figures 8–5 and 8–6, appear to represent progressive thinking in the area of a full-scope managerial approach (although their approaches are from slightly different directions).

Figure 8–6 depicts yet another approach to inspection services structure. In this example operations and inspections are directed by two senior officers accountable directly to the fire administrator. In this form of structure it is easy for the administrator to make assumptions of performance and reliability and not to take an active hand in inspections program development or application. In some cases this organizational structure has resulted in the isolation of inspection services because of the continuing needs of suppression. The key to avoiding this situation is the fire administrator's interest in and knowledge of inspections and their significant impact on other areas of consideration within the fire administrator's managerial scope.

Consolidation of services One of the fastest-growing trends in this area is the consolidation of fire and inspection services. The Institute for Local Self Government has done a substantial amount of research into the pros and cons of consolidation. The institute concludes that, given the proper development and management of such a program, it should increase productivity and fire service delivery capacity and reduce a community's fire loss.

Figure 8–5 Organization chart for a city of 750,000 population.

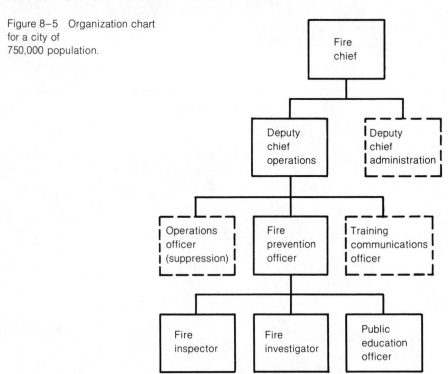

In a 1977 report, the institute warns of the need for careful thought, preplanning, and homework regarding all aspects of such a consolidation, and makes the following statement:

The most important elements to consider in order to achieve a successful program include:

—inherent organizational resistance to change
—existing legal constraints which may curtail the consolidation of inspection services
—development of program measurement criteria to monitor productivity continuously
—voluntary participation in the program
—necessity of strong commitment to training
—additional wages for the Firefighter/Inspector position.[3]

In addition, it is necessary to allow time to educate all levels of a community and its government to a major reorganization of a portion of that government's services. Fire service personnel, elected officials, and the citizens themselves should be made thoroughly familiar with the proposed innovation. The institute goes on to state the following:

Cooperation can be achieved most easily if the parties affected perceive a benefit to be gained from the change. Inspection consolidation appears to offer many inducements to the vested interest groups concerned with public safety. Firefighters could conceive of the changes as a further chance to professionalize their services and possibly increase their salaries.[4]

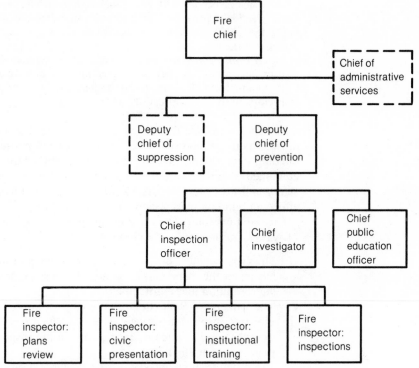

Figure 8–6   Organization chart for a city with two deputy chiefs for suppression and prevention, respectively.

Inspection consolidation is attractive to fire administrators because it is a cost-efficient means of improving fire protection. It is an inducement to city administrators and councils because they can demonstrate the delivery of a more effective service at a decreased cost at a time when the costs of local government operation are soaring. The institute goes on to say:

It is obvious that the decision to place inspection services under the purview of the fire department must constitute a heavy commitment to weather the stress that may occur to the governmental system. Evaluation of potential opponents of consolidation should be made prior to implementation, however, in order to assess their effect on the program. If the strength of the opposition is too great, it may be wiser to forego consolidation than to fight a battle which may not be won.[5]

To provide flexibility for a community interested in consolidation of inspection services, the institute, in its report, has reapplied terms from Harry More's book, *The New Era of Public Safety,*[6] to define the different types of consolidated fire safety inspection programs. The institute lists these as follows:

Nominal Consolidation: the placement of the two departments, fire and inspections, under one administrative head, e.g., Director of the Fire and Code Enforcement or

Director of Safety (excluding police). Each service reserves its individual and distinct identity operationally.

Functional Consolidation: a degree of consolidation in which separate fire and inspection services are retained but one or more duties, e.g., records, communications, scheduling, etc., normally performed by one department have been assigned to members of the other department.

Selected Area Consolidation: cross-training of some firefighters as generalist inspectors and assigning them to stations and specific geographic areas, e.g., residential areas, to perform combined duties, with either the retention of the separate identities of their fire and inspection departments or their unification into one department.

Partial Consolidation: creation of a third force by cross-training some firefighters as generalist inspectors with either the retention of the separate identities of the fire and inspection departments, or their unification into one department. Cross-trained firefighters perform a variety of inspection services out of their assigned fire stations throughout the city.

Totally Consolidated Services: a single unified force in which the fire and inspection services have been combined into one department, e.g., Fire Safety and Code Enforcement Department. All firefighters are cross-trained as generalist inspectors, assisted by specialists where necessary.[7]

A case study   In 1972 the city of Bellevue, Washington, consolidated and coordinated its inspection services. The functions of permit coordination, the city's building department, and the fire department's Fire Prevention Bureau were combined to ensure stricter code enforcement, stronger emphasis on the life safety and fire safety provisions of the code, and avoidance of duplication of efforts in building plan review and final field inspections.

City administrators say the consolidation has benefited Bellevue in a number of ways, among them the following:

1. The cross training of inspectors in building and fire and life safety codes has given the inspectors a broader knowledge and experience in code interpretation and enforcement.
2. The citizens of Bellevue are receiving an improved and more cost-effective inspection service. The city saved money in state pension expenses and salaries by hiring civilian fire inspectors at a lower wage than that of firefighters.
3. The cross training and day-to-day collaboration of inspectors has encouraged a feeling of teamwork instead of the traditional feeling of competition between the fire and building departments.

Strengths and weaknesses of types of programs

In order to discuss efficiently the strengths and weaknesses of the various inspection programs mentioned in this chapter, it is necessary to reduce those programs to their basic level. All inspection programs, whether simple or complex, are variations on the two basic models. They are either examples of separate building and fire departments or they are examples of consolidated inspection services.

It is interesting to note in comparing the two types of inspection services that the strengths of one are the weaknesses of the other and vice versa. Thus, any decision between the two should be as simple as deciding which strengths would be the more desirable for a given community.

When the building and fire departments are separate, it allows the inspectors to be specialists in their field. In a consolidated operation cross training breeds a generalization of skills and knowledge which could put the inspectors and their agency at a disadvantage when dealing with private sector specialists.

Each agency serves as a watchdog for the other in a dual department operation, thus decreasing the chances for corruption. In the combined agency there is no such watchdog function and so the possibility of graft and corruption increases in the total inspection system.

Firefighter involvement in the inspection process in a separate agency system tends to be more intense because of the personal safety factors inherent in the inspection of a building. Unfortunately, when the departments are consolidated there tends to be an intra-agency conflict between the uniformed firefighters and civilian inspectors.

One of the most obvious strengths of combining departments is the more effective use of personnel. Consolidating administrative personnel allows more budget money for field inspectors. More important, it allows local government to deliver a more effective service at a reduced price to the taxpayer. Consolidation of files contributes to this cost-effectiveness by cutting down on the paperwork and storage of building plans and charts.

When the departments are separate the potentials for duplication of effort and bureaucratic delay are great. For example, with a double layer of bureaucracy, personnel in both agencies will be performing similar administrative and field tasks. Productive time is lost because of interdepartmental conflicts on code interpretation. The different physical locations of the departments cause logistical problems for plans review and preconstruction conferences.

A consolidated inspection service centers accountability in one agency; there are no gray areas of responsibility. Of equal importance, it lessens the chance for conflicting decisions from local government because the architects and developers now have only one agency with which to deal. This saves the city administration valuable time because, when the agencies are separate, that administration often finds itself acting as referee for conflicting decisions between the departments.

The separate and consolidated inspection services also have their own unique strengths and weaknesses. For example, when the departments are separate the inspection function provides an opportunity for light duty assignments for injured or otherwise incapacitated firefighters. While this solves some personnel problems, it could create others.

One of the most serious problems in the combined departments system is in the consolidation process itself. During the transition period, questions of territory could cause major personality conflicts among the personnel of the new agency.

The Institute for Local Self Government makes a case for inspection consolidation.

The problems inherent in a decentralized inspection program . . . are many. These problems are largely attributable to the natural consequences associated with a bureaucratic organization and include:

—ad hoc proliferation and duplication of inspection services
—inefficient service delivery
—parochial interpretation of inspection codes
—absence of systematic inspection process
—uneven level of code enforcement.[8]

Coordination

Whether a community provides a separate inspection service or a consolidated inspection program, formal coordination within the organization and with outside bodies is absolutely necessary if the agency is going to provide effective service.

Assistant Fire Marshal H. D. Crossnine of Memphis, Tennessee, with fifteen years of experience in code enforcement as a fire prevention officer, has emphasized the need for fire officials to become directly involved in the review and approval of building plans. In an article in *The Building Official and Code Administrator,* Crossnine made the following statement:

To have a viable and progressive code enforcement program designed to fulfill the goals set forth in the building code, it is obvious that the influence of the Fire Official in matters of fire safety and fire suppression systems is desirable and necessary.

The Fire Official has a direct interest in the installation and location of standpipes, sprinkler systems . . . and similar fire protection devices, all of which are usually regulated by the building code. This acute interest is cultivated by experiences where his life and the lives and property of the people he is charged to serve have depended on these systems being installed and operating satisfactorily.

A Fire Official who believes that he can delegate his responsibility for direct involvement in Code Enforcement to the Building Official does not truly realize the injustice of this action. He has a duty and responsibility to share his expertise and knowledge, as well as to use them to ensure public safety from fires in his community. He can do this by active participation in plans review, code revisions and Code Enforcement. Being part of the plans review process gives the fire service some control over the installations of fire protection systems and of operations that present special problems to the fire service. It is obvious that the capabilities of the fire service will vary due to the size of the department and region, but there are few localities where someone has not been delegated to the responsibility of fire safety enforcements. This person must take a vigorous part in plans review rather than the secondary approach of approval. This author recommends a written set of administrative procedures, satisfactory to the Fire Official and Building Official, to ensure that areas of responsibility are well defined and do not create cause for conflicting orders.

Primary concern of both departments must be to ensure the public safety, health and welfare. This premise can be the foundation on which to build a system that utilizes the talents of both departments for the progressive Code Enforcement program that is necessary for efficient, high quality code application. For this to be effective, it must be approached with a positive attitude and mutual respect.[9]

The concern for cooperation and coordination within the agency and between the agencies responsible for providing inspection services is by no means a recent phenomenon. Over a decade ago in *Fire Journal* an editor's note made the following statement:

In too many communities the relationship between the fire and building departments displays serious deficiencies. The overlapping responsibilities for safety to life from fire in buildings often lead to misunderstandings, injured pride, friction and consequent loss of efficiency. Under such circumstances the community suffers, and the property owner may, to his sorrow, find himself caught in a cross fire between two powerful elements of a municipal government.[10]

That editor's note was the introduction to a panel discussion. The discussion documented the benefits enjoyed by the community when the Fire Prevention Bureau and the Building Inspection Division in Raleigh, North Carolina, began to work together.

As the result of a cooperative school on the state building code and the American Insurance Association's fire prevention code, there was better understanding and interpretation, so that a citizen could rely on getting the same information from inspectors with the Building Inspection Division and those with the Fire Prevention Bureau. Overall, the city of Raleigh enjoyed enforcement of its minimum housing ordinance, cooperation on inspections, cooperation by the plans examiner, and stronger certificates of occupancy as a result of this coordination.

The cooperative arrangement between the Fire Prevention Bureau and the building department in Memphis, Tennessee, has served as a model program for many communities. In a later article in *The Building Official and Code Adminis-trator,* H. D. Crossnine described this program:

The construction industry is advancing at a rapid rate in the field of fire protection. High-rise buildings, institutions, schools and large industrial complexes are just a few of the commercial projects presently being reviewed by the engineering section of the Memphis Fire Department.

With the advent of hydraulically calculated sprinkler systems, multi-story standpipe systems, computerized fire alarm systems and other highly technical fire protection systems, it became apparent that highly skilled and experienced personnel would be needed to police the ever expanding industry and seek effective Code Enforcement relating to built-in fire protection.

It should be pointed out here that in order for a plans review process to be effective and meaningful, there must be total cooperation between the fire and building departments. Through the coordinated effort of both the Fire and Building Official, the City of Memphis has provided a system by which construction projects are thoroughly examined for fire protection considerations, and areas of responsibility are well defined.

Applications for permits accompanied by working drawings for all occupancies except one and two family dwellings are received daily from the building department. The submitted drawing and specifications are reviewed by fire department personnel for code compliance utilizing the BOCA *Basic Fire Prevention Code* and other applicable codes and ordinances. Comments as well as recommendations are attached to the application for permit and returned to the building department. The process generally takes no longer than 48 hours depending on the size of the proposed construction project. While the submitted drawings are in the fire department's possession, it affords them the opportunity, if needed, to contact the architect and/or owner to discuss with him possible code deficiencies and make recommendations to improve the fire protection quality of the building.

The Building Official, upon completion of review of the submitted drawings, is now prepared to issue the construction permit. At this time our code-related comments are explained to the contractor individually to ensure that they are fully understood and incorporated into the construction project.

Building permits and fees are handled through the building department and the central permit office. This procedure means that the party applying for the permit does not have to go to each separate agency, such as electrical, plumbing, fire, health and other city inspection bureaus. . . .

This entire process must be well planned and coordinated so as not to delay the anticipated construction project. Additional personnel, such as secretaries and filing clerks, must be provided to ensure that efficient files are maintained and that all correspondence is recorded. The importance of accurate records cannot be emphasized enough in that these records become the legal history of the building and provide valuable information for future use. [See Figure 8–7 for an example of the inspection survey report of the Memphis fire department's Fire Prevention Bureau.]

During the time that the Memphis plans review process has been functioning, great strides in the improvement of fire protection have been made, and the cooperation and respect of architects, engineers and other professionals in the construction industry has been gained. It is this professional attitude and cooperation that makes the system work. The feeling in Memphis is that if the building and fire departments cooperate effectively in the plans review process, maybe the day will never come when the firefighter has to fight a fire in this building.[11]

Worthy of specific mention here is the problem of equal sign-off authority for the fire department on occupancy permits. Because of political considerations, local government is often reluctant to grant such authority to the fire department, traditionally a more politically independent local agency. In order to protect their own territory, many building departments do not want to give sign-off authority to fire departments. But sign-off authority (represented by the occupancy permit card in Figure 8–8) is exactly what a fire department must have in order to represent adequately the fire safety and life safety viewpoints.

INSPECTION SURVEY REPORT OCCUPANCY CODE NO.	MEMPHIS FIRE DEPARTMENT FIRE PREVENTION BUREAU	OFFICE OF FIRE MARSHAL 79 SOUTH FLICKER MEMPHIS, TENN. 38104 PHONE: 458-2724
LOCATION	FIRM NAME	OCCUPANCY
Indicate violations in check boxes relative to subject matter.	OWNER OR MANAGER	Statements are aids to memory only not quotations of the City Codes.

A. FLAMMABLE LIQUIDS - GASES - SOLIDS - EXPLOSIVES
1. ☐ Not properly stored - handled - processed
2. ☐ Excessive amounts on premises
3. ☐ Dip tanks, spray booth not properly separated or const.
4. ☐ Materials not stored to retard spread of fire
5. ☐ Storage rooms-premises not properly marked
6. ☐ Storage-prohibited except in fire resistive room or outside building
7. ☐ Tank location not in accord with applicable standards
8. ☐ Above ground tanks storage to be properly maintained, diked and marked
9. ☐ Valves-dispensing equipment to be approved type - maintained in good order
10. ☐ Electric wiring and appliances to be U.L. approved type
11. ☐ Misuse of materials subject to fire and injury to personnel

B. ELECTRIC DISTRIBUTION SYSTEM
1. ☐ Wiring - switches - plugs defective, to be replaced
2. ☐ Overload-fixtures-panel not in accord with M.E.C.

C. ELECTRIC APPLIANCES & EQUIPMENT
1. ☐ Appliances-motors to be maintained in working order
2. ☐ Wiring-improper and temporary, unsafe practice

D. FIRE PROTECTION SYSTEMS & APPLIANCES
1. ☐ Standpipe hose-cabinets-valves to be repaired, replaced, obstructed
2. ☐ Sprinkler system riser, valves, heads, siamese, hydrants, alarms repair, replace, inoperative, obstructed
3. ☐ First aid fire extinguishers,replace,recharge,test date tag
4. ☐ Stock-merchandise stored too close for system to operate efficiently

E. HEAT PRODUCING DEVICES
1. ☐ Defective-to be replaced-repaired
2. ☐ Improper-prohibited device, to be repaired or removed
3. ☐ Venting - improper, inadequate
4. ☐ Combustibles stored too close to appliance
5. ☐ Appliance not approved by A.G.A.
6. ☐ Clearance from appliance inadequate

F. EXITS, PASSAGEWAYS, LIFE SAFETY
1. ☐ Doors-locked,blocked,inoperative,swing wrong direction
2. ☐ Corridors-passageways,obstructed,improperly maintained
3. ☐ Stairs,towers,obstructed,defective,improperly maintained
4. ☐ Door devices - panic hardware, fusible links, defective, inadequate
5. ☐ Exit passageways-inadequately lighted,provide exit lights
6. ☐ Exit lights - to be lighted at all times
7. ☐ Exit signs - Markings, inadequate improper size
8. ☐ Exits - Inadequate, insufficient number

G. SIGNS - NOT POSTED - INADEQUATE   ☐

H. GENERAL HAZARDS
1. ☐ Hazardous accumulation rubbish,debris,waste materials to be removed
2. ☐ Stock-merchandise improperly stored to retard spread of fire
3. ☐ Interior finishes-decorations-tents,remove or flameproof
4. ☐ Piping, all improperly installed,comply with code
5. ☐ Smoke-heat detection-fire alarm systems inoperative, to be repaired
6. ☐ Ventilating systems to be cleaned, repaired, installed
7. ☐ Aisles,cross aisles to be maintained full width at all times
8. ☐ Combustible lint and dust to be removed from equipment, walls, beams, floor, disposed of in proper manner
9. ☐ Vacant Building - secure all openings until such time as the building is made safe or taken down and removed

I. OTHERS
1. ☐ A valid Fire Department permit will be required for the following_____
2. ☐ Premises and equipment in good order No visible hazards observed this date

J. REFERRAL ITEM(S)
1. ☐ Item(s)_____
   will be referred to_____
   Dept. for proper disposition

REMARKS_____
_____
_____
_____
_____
_____
_____
_____
_____
_____

Inspector	Copy Received By	Position

These above checked violations of the City of MEMPHIS Codes of Ordinances or other hazardous conditions as indicated were observed during an inspection survey of the above premises this date. Your cooperation in correcting the conditions enumerated will be appreciated. Continued violation will subject you to penalties as prescribed by said Code of Ordinances of Law.

Inspection Date_____ Time In_____ Time Out_____ Re-inspection Date_____

Figure 8-7   Memphis, Tennessee, Fire Prevention Bureau inspection survey report.

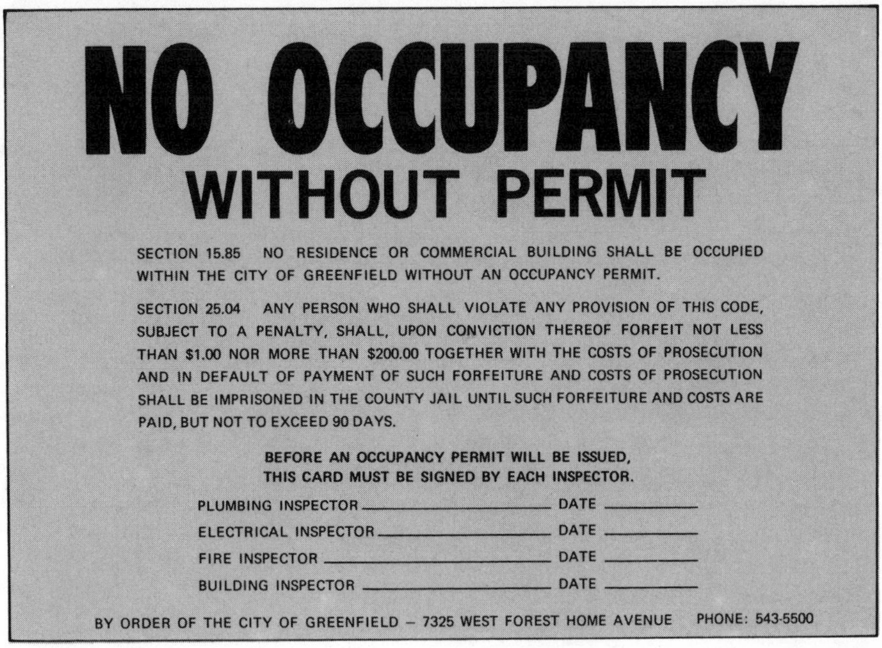

NO OCCUPANCY
WITHOUT PERMIT

SECTION 15.85 NO RESIDENCE OR COMMERCIAL BUILDING SHALL BE OCCUPIED WITHIN THE CITY OF GREENFIELD WITHOUT AN OCCUPANCY PERMIT.

SECTION 25.04 ANY PERSON WHO SHALL VIOLATE ANY PROVISION OF THIS CODE, SUBJECT TO A PENALTY, SHALL, UPON CONVICTION THEREOF FORFEIT NOT LESS THAN $1.00 NOR MORE THAN $200.00 TOGETHER WITH THE COSTS OF PROSECUTION AND IN DEFAULT OF PAYMENT OF SUCH FORFEITURE AND COSTS OF PROSECUTION SHALL BE IMPRISONED IN THE COUNTY JAIL UNTIL SUCH FORFEITURE AND COSTS ARE PAID, BUT NOT TO EXCEED 90 DAYS.

BEFORE AN OCCUPANCY PERMIT WILL BE ISSUED,
THIS CARD MUST BE SIGNED BY EACH INSPECTOR.

PLUMBING INSPECTOR ______ DATE ______
ELECTRICAL INSPECTOR ______ DATE ______
FIRE INSPECTOR ______ DATE ______
BUILDING INSPECTOR ______ DATE ______

BY ORDER OF THE CITY OF GREENFIELD – 7325 WEST FOREST HOME AVENUE PHONE: 543-5500

Figure 8–8 Occupancy permit card.

Control

The importance of measuring the effectiveness and success of any program has been mentioned earlier in this chapter. This measurement is necessary because proper management is an ongoing process. Specifically, for inspection services, some rationale to show the basic application and productivity of the inspector's time in relation to subsequent fire development is extremely important.

In a 1977 report, Philip Schaenman and others address this topic:

> An important gap in current measures of fire protection performance is the absence of measures of how well fire inspection programs perform in holding down fire incidence, fire loss, and fire casualties. While overall fire prevention measures like the fire rate reflect inspection program effects, these overall measures also reflect the effects of many other factors. Therefore, to distinguish between effective and ineffective prevention strategies and to develop priorities for the use of funds on inspections, specific measures of inspection program effectiveness are needed.
>
> To help fill the gap, fire departments should consider use of these additional procedures:
>
> —Measurement of the rate and percentage of fires that are "relatively preventable by inspection."
> —Comparisons of the fire rate in inspected households versus the fire rate in those same households prior to the inspection and versus the fire rate in households not inspected.
> —Measurement of the change in fire rate as the time since the occupancy's last inspection increases, for occupancies (usually nonresidential) covered by a program of regular inspections.[12]

The Institute for Local Self Government emphasizes the need to establish productivity measures to determine the impact of consolidated inspection programs. According to the institute these measures will allow community managers to determine the efficiency and effectiveness of the delivery of inspection services. Without such measures, an objective evaluation of the inspection program will be hindered if not made impossible. The institute elaborates as follows:

The National Commission on Productivity and Work Quality has developed various indicators that are useful to measure inspection program effectiveness. These indicators enable determination of (1) planned volume of inspections performed; (2) timeliness of inspections; (3) quality of inspections completed; and (4) the degree of code compliance. Efficiency is measured by determining the input compared to output. Such considerations relate to the number of inspections performed per manhour and/or miles traveled per number of inspections.

Taken together, effectiveness and efficiency measures gathered over time will provide objective determination of program productivity. Once standards have been established, steps can be taken by cities to initiate productivity bargaining.[13]

The same report warns of the pitfalls of the quantitative approach to measuring the success of an inspection program. Specifically discussing the Phoenix, Arizona, Generalist Inspector Program, the report states:

One of the standards used to measure [its] success . . . is the number of man hours required per inspection. On the basis of this quantified approach, the daily inspections per man increased from an average of 25.1 when the standards were first introduced to an average of 34.3 two years later. This amounted to a 37% increase and is attributed to a reduction in mileage and in travel time and to the less complex nature of the inspections made. A quantified measurement of inspection output, by itself, is an incomplete device for determinging productivity, since it omits the element of quality. The inspection/man/day criterion used by Phoenix does not address the question of whether the less complex inspection performed by the generalist is of comparable quality to that of several specialists on the same site. On the other hand, a related question also not approached is whether specialists who spend time conducting the more routine inspections produce any significant benefit to the public beyond what a generalist brings to the task. These questions remain to be answered.[14]

The quantitative approach, however, can be helpful in measuring one of the primary objectives of an inspection program, an increase in productivity. The Alexandria, Virginia, fire department finds it useful to compare all its inspections and code enforcement activities on a month-to-month and year-to-year basis.

As a final word, Schaenman and others have stated:

There is an increasing willingness and perceived need to devote more resources to fire prevention programs, such as pre-fire inspections. But because no satisfactory method has been available to measure the effectiveness of such programs in preventing fires, there has been no way to know whether the greatly increased resources being sought would produce the desired results.[15]

Specific effectiveness and productivity measurement tools are needed to fill this information gap.

Conclusion and outlook

This chapter has examined the management of fire inspection services in terms of the management cycle, emphasizing a systematic approach in which the setting of measurable objectives, their implementation, revision by the feedback process, and evaluation, have been noted. A brief initial overview made the point that even routine inspections have some educational or public relations aspect if they involve the public. The roles of planning, organization, and staffing, the strengths and weaknesses of various organizational approaches, and the coordination and control functions were also analyzed.

Turning again to the wider context, it is appropriate to take a look at the future. What are the major existing challenges? And what can be done about these challenges?

International statistics highlight vividly the failure of the United States fire service in the area of fire loss management. The most advanced and industrial nation in the world needs a new approach if it is to solve its fire loss problem. Obviously, the traditional approach is not doing the job.

Research into the socioeconomics of the fire problem is needed. There are numerous questions to be addressed, for example: What are the effects of poverty and education levels on the fire problem? Does home ownership increase fire safety awareness? What is the correlation between fire frequency in the single head of household family versus the traditional dual father/mother unit? What is the relationship of drug and alcohol abuse to fire deaths? At what point will the American public react to the high cost of fire in relation to life and property loss? How can we make the public as aware of fire safety as it has been of polio, traffic fatalities, and crime?

Should we attack the apathy of the American public with regard to fire by placing a social stigma or criminal penalty on fire safety negligence? Do we build in structural fire protection to a degree that will minimize losses and accept a high frequency rate? Is the fire service assuming too much of the burden for the fire loss management failure? Should we be looking to the behavioral sciences for answers?

Most fire managers would agree that, obviously, better codes must be enacted and enforced. Accountability for failure to perform job functions by elected officials, architects, builders, interior designers, and inspection services should be punished with severe fines and penalties. Special interest groups that ply their trade at the expense of the safety of the general public should be exposed by the news media.

Safety inspectors must strive for a higher degree of professionalism in order to compete with their better-educated adversaries in the private sector. Many cities facing productivity issues of the kind discussed in Chapter 14 would do well to thoroughly examine their code enforcement agencies with special regard to efficiency, cost-effectiveness, and duplication of effort.

1 See, for example: Research Triangle Institute, International City Management Association, and National Fire Protection Association, *Municipal Fire Service Workbook,* prepared for the National Science Foundation, Research Applied to National Needs (Washington, D.C.: Government Printing Office, 1977); Philip S. Schaenman and Joe Swartz, *Measuring Fire Protection Productivity in Local Government: Some Initial Thoughts,* report prepared by The Urban Institute and the National Fire Protection Association (Boston: National Fire Protection Association, 1974); and Philip S. Schaenman et al., *Procedures for Improving the Measurement of Local Fire Protection Effectiveness* (Boston: National Fire Protection Association, 1977).

2 See, for example: The Urban Institute and International City Management Association, *Measuring the Effectiveness of Basic Municipal Services: Initial Report* (Washington, D.C.: The Urban Institute and International City Management Association, 1974); and Harry P. Hatry et al., *How Effective Are Your Community Services? Procedures for Monitoring the Effectiveness of Municipal Services* (Washington, D.C.: The Urban Institute and International City Management Association, 1977).

3 Institute for Local Self Government, *Public Safety Inspection Consolidation: An Alternative to Divided Responsibility for Total Fire Protection,* Alternatives to Traditional Public Safety Delivery Systems, no. 3 (Berkeley, Calif.: Institute for Local Self Government, 1977), p. 87.

4 Ibid., pp. 87–88.

5 Ibid., p. 89.

6 Harry W. More, Jr., *The New Era of Public Safety* (Springfield, Ill.: Charles C Thomas, 1970).

7 Institute for Local Self Government, *Public Safety Inspection Consolidation,* p. x.

8 Ibid., p. 11.

9 H. D. Crossnine, "Why Fire Officials Need To Work with Building Officials," *The Building Official and Code Administrator,* September 1977, p. 5.

10 "Panel Discussion: Fire and Building Departments Develop a Working Relationship," *Fire Journal,* March 1967, p. 53.

11 H. D. Crossine, "Cooperation in Memphis," *The Building Official and Code Administrator,* November 1977, p. 15.

12 Schaenman et al., *Procedures for Improving the Measurement of Local Fire Protection Effectiveness,* pp. 73–74.

13 Institute for Local Self Government, *Public Safety Inspection Consolidation,* p. 82.

14 Ibid., p. 51.

15 Schaenman et al., *Procedures for Improving the Measurement of Local Fire Protection Effectiveness,* p. xi.

9 Managing fire control

The process of maintaining, modifying, or establishing a fire control or suppression and rescue division of an agency's fire department is challenging and complex. There are many disciplines involved in managing a fire control organization. Only a clear understanding of the management function, coupled with administrative ability backed up with proven technical background, will lead to the attainment of fire department and community goals and the accomplishment of objectives.

On the basis of an agency's goals, fire control strategies (objectives) should be established as prerequisites for determining requirements of a fire control organization.

In this light there are many items to be considered. The current system (base line) and the current organization, practices, and traditions are usually the most important factors. There is no absolute answer as to how and why an organization should change. The forces at play tend to prevail unless there is some overriding, compelling reason to press for change.

In some cases following current practices may be the most cost-effective method of achieving desired goals. In many cases, however, goals may need to be reassessed in view of today's requirements. History has shown that most fire control organizations have evidenced a continuing desire on the part of fire services managers to improve the level of service.

Lack of funds and budget restrictions are usually the major inhibitors to providing better levels of service through an expanding fire control organization. The Insurance Services Office (ISO) grading schedule or the grading engineers' recommendations and reports are normally used by fire chiefs as the basis for justification of the need for additional financial resources, on the traditional theory that more personnel and more equipment mean an improvement in the level of service.

The time has come for fire services managers to design the fire control system on the basis of the community's approved goals and objectives (measured with a sensitivity to probability of attainment) that have been established in the political arena and as expressed in a community fire protection master plan of the type described in Chapter 6. The grading schedule or insurance rates should be considered as secondary in the overall professional management and assessment of needs.

The fire control system is by far the most costly element of a fire department's operations and should be designed and operated in the most cost-effective fashion. (The value of "cost-effectiveness" is determined by definition at each local level of government and will vary from community to community. This variation results from the process of balancing the accepted or tolerated risk against the actual risk in each community.) One three or four man company costs several hundreds of thousands of dollars per year. A fire control company not needed or poorly utilized represents a significant financial waste. On the other hand, too few companies, or poorly manned ones, can result in property and life loss beyond community accepted norms. Also, the cost of a firefighter death or a disabling injury may far exceed the expense of a fire company. This is not to say that there is a fixed value on a life or injury. The point is that the firefighting forces are the asset that protects the community's economic and tax base as well as its health and welfare. This asset is a valuable one and must be carefully provided and wisely managed.

There is no single problem or solution to be found when a community's fire control system is designed, although many fire chiefs and managers are engaged in just such a search. But such an attempt merely illustrates a lack of understanding of the complexities of what constitutes an adequate fire protection delivery system.

In addition, the multiplicity of problems faced by fire control managers is compounded by serious financial considerations. Managers faced with demands to maintain a level of fire service, or in some cases a need to increase that level, must set goals and objectives in all areas of community expenditure and revenue. This procedure is required in order to properly determine the true importance and priority of fire control versus other community programs.

It might well be asked what the essence is of the effort or process of managing fire control. Most managers would agree that fire control is in direct relation to the fire problem and is essentially a community-wide problem. By definition, *community* is not necessarily limited to a single governmental jurisdictional boundary or political body. In most geographical areas, therefore, managing fire control encompasses far more than a specific city and/or a specific fire department.

Similarly, managing for fire control will in itself involve various segments of the community's government(s). The importance of this systematic approach to managing fire control is often overlooked. Much more is involved than just a single company of firefighters knocking down a fire at a single incident.

The fire control management process needs to be carefully designed to be flexible and to be capable of serving a variety of community and citizen needs. The organizational development should in fact be fully responsive to the many diverse duties and responsibilities that are required of fire departments if they are to deserve the "public trust" that the community places in them.

In addition to carrying out the daily administrative and management functions, as required of any organization, this responsibility generally means that managers of fire control systems must take into account both the interactions just mentioned and the extreme and adverse conditions of manual fire suppression in which fire control management generally takes place. There is a further challenge: to be effective, the elements that make up fire control management need to maintain a combat emergency readiness configuration twenty-four hours a day, 365 days a year.

Keeping this in mind (the commitment to a delivery system consisting of the fire department's responsibility and the community's master plan), it becomes clear that a whole range of fire protection activities is in fact interdependent. Some of these activities (discussed elsewhere in this book) are fire code enforcement, building inspection, public education, training, fire cause investigation, and arson investigation.

The essential principle is that it is best to reduce the need for fire control forces by minimizing the number of fire suppression emergency calls. The decision involved must, however, be balanced and based upon peak fire combat situations. A change in one or more of the constituent elements of the fire control system will of course modify the effect of the whole from an organizational standpoint.

The discussion in the remainder of this chapter, given the above background, takes the managerially-oriented reader through the crucial stages of the management cycle as they relate to the fire control function. The stages of the cycle are discussed under the following headings: planning, organizing, directing, coordinating, and controlling.

Planning

As has been mentioned, the community fire control system should be based on local philosophy and desires. The initiation of the planning for such a system usually comes about because of some problem or need. Generally, the local political force or fire administration expresses a desire to eliminate a problem or to make a change as a result of a fire or disaster that has just occurred locally or that could occur.

Community expressions such as, "That fire should never have occurred," or "The fire department lost the whole block," or "We should never have let the town become dependent on one industrial plant," or "They should never have lost all those people on the upper floors when the fire started on the first floor," all lead to some form of community need and suggested action.

These statements are all expressions related to desired community goals, acceptable risk, and level of service. The only missing element is a logical plan with alternatives which can—where possible—be costed out, for which an assessment of ability to pay can be determined, and for which decisions can be made on a selected objective.

Goals

Some fundamental fire control decisions required to determine what strategy or plan to follow are stated below:

1. Should fire control service be provided to protect all potential occurrences?
2. Should the service provided be provided equally to all properties?
3. Should public protection be provided only to an identified level and private protection be required above that level?
4. Should the level of service be limited only to exposure protection?
5. How much fire loading and fire area should be contained by the initial alarm, or the multi-alarm, or the mutual aid forces?
6. Should the occupancies that are economically essential to the community receive a higher level of protection than housing and ordinary commercial occupancies?
7. Should multiple services be provided with fire control forces (i.e., emergency medical, salvage, blight reduction, housing code enforcement)?

These basic concepts evolve into fundamental fire department goals and lead to the establishment of strategic and tactical fire control objectives. Examples of some potential fire control goals might read as follows:

1. To serve, without prejudice or favoritism, all of the community's citizens by safeguarding collectively and individually their lives against injurious effects of fire, explosions, and other related hazards (including all rescue operations).
2. To safeguard the general economy and welfare of the community by preventing major conflagrations and the destruction by fire of economically essential industries and businesses.
3. To serve all of the community's citizens and property owners by protecting their individual material wealth and economic well-being against the destructive effects of fire and explosions. All property deserves to have an equivalent degree of protection, commensurate with the actual property hazard involved and not with geographical location or monetary value.

The goal-oriented statement should be analyzed and professionally interpreted into a series of alternative objectives from which selections can be made. Various delivery systems, consisting of potential organizations which include the appropriate functions and elements, should be considered and cost of each should be assessed. The existing organization and system should be considered the base line.

The fire control organization needs to be kept dynamic and should continually be adjusted to meet changing fire problems, new technologies, new laws and regulations, modifications to the work rules, and changes occurring in the community. The manager should continually evaluate the objectives as to their continued viability (and the probability of attainment of goals). The manager should also consider whether they should be modified or maintained. If new goals or objectives are developed and they are political decisions, they must be submitted to the legislative policymakers for approval.

Once goals are established or reaffirmed, existing operational strategies (objectives) should be made to conform. Strategies and tactical management decisions should always be written in objective form, that is, in measurable statements which include units of time, quantity, and quality. Unless the operation of the fire control activity is measured, no one, including the fire control manager and the chief officers, will be able to measure the success or failure of the organizational endeavors.

Strategic objectives

Strategy should not be reserved for the fire ground but should be laid out for all elements of the fire control system. For example, do decision makers want a centralized and concentrated fire company deployment with heavy manning, or a decentralized system with many stations and fire companies and with light manning? Is the water system adequate to provide adequate fire flow or must a strategy be based on a tanker or relay system? Are the economics or traditions in the community such that a volunteer manning program is functional and cost-effective, or must a combination of daytime paid and nighttime volunteer be utilized?

Metropolitan or other areas with high rise buildings or industrial complexes with hazardous materials need to develop a strategy equal to the problem or hazard, or attendant risk. High rise fires may require substantial quantities of manpower as well as the logistical ability to assemble sufficient equipment and materials.

Operational strategy is so basic and so important to fire control that it is essential that community administrators and the legislative body be given professional advice as they consider, confirm, and authorize the appropriate budgetary and other supporting legislation and administrative procedures.

Tactical objectives as related to strategic objectives

Once strategic objectives have been laid out, the fire department manager develops tactical objectives to meet the overall approved plan. Again, these must be measurable and are usually formed and allocated to the preformed basic work unit in the fire department—the fire company.

What are some considerations to be kept in mind when determining tactical objectives? These considerations closely follow the sequence of events in the fire control cycle. The key element is time: the time of day, the fire spread rate, and the heat, smoke, and generation rate. The amount of fuel, the fire intensity, and the configuration of property at risk are also extremely important. Along with the property loss potential, the most critical factor is life safety. All this affects and delineates the response time and deployment of the fire companies. (This concept is referred to as *reflex time*, that is, the time span from the time of ignition to the first application of manual suppression by the fire department.)

As has been mentioned, tactical objectives are based on the strategic objectives that have been laid down. Some examples of strategic objectives might be the following:

1. To minimize the life loss potential and the fire spread factor by maintaining a strong and comprehensive fire prevention, occupancy, and building code enforcement program.
2. To reduce the long-range fire problem by requiring a comprehensive sprinkler ordinance (for example: to include all commercial occupancies of over 12,000 square feet, all housing occupancies of fifty or more units in one structure, and all structures over fifty-five feet in height). The intent is to lower the large life and property loss probability and to transfer the major cost of fire protection to the developer rather than allocating annual tax funds to support expensive "standing armies" for manual fire control.
3. To reduce undesirable fire ignitions by fully investigating the cause of each fire, developing a management information system, and establishing an action program to prevent further ignitions.
4. To consider placing the building and safety department under the control of the fire control manager (fire chief).
5. To shorten fire discovery and reporting times by maintaining a fire watch system and an effective emergency communications system.
6. To attempt to control all emergencies before they become large by attacking them quickly and aggressively with professionally trained and equipped fire and rescue attack teams.
7. To prevent conflagrations by controlling large emergencies with in-depth fire and rescue control forces and an adequate water supply.
8. To minimize the cost of municipal fire services by developing effective, on-duty, first-strike teams and backing them up with off-duty reserve forces and regional fire services.
9. To aid citizens in need of rescue or emergency medical attention. The intent is to utilize available fire control manpower for a needed service without compromising fire control priorities. Emergency medical manpower shall be primarily allocated to emergency medical priorities but shall also be utilized to perform fire protection and control duties.

On the basis of these strategic objectives, a further breakdown is made into the following suggested tactical objectives:

1. For all structural fires, to deploy one engine company within five (5) minutes and an additional engine company, one ladder company, one paramedic unit, and one chief officer within ten (10) minutes for 90 percent of all alarms in areas with a required fire flow of 4,500 gallons per minute (GPM) or less. For all areas over 4,500 GPM, the first engine and truck (ladder) must arrive within five (5) minutes for 90 percent of all alarms. The lapsed time (reflex time) is to include fire dispatch and response time. The objective is to control the fire before flashover (sudden spread), or before the fire has extended beyond the first (original) area of involvement. (Using the standard time versus temperature curve as a base, flashover is estimated to be eight [8] minutes after ignition in standard fuels.)
2. The general tactical objective is to develop an attack force that can aggressively advance two standard fire stream hand lines (or the equivalent). For major emergencies beyond the normal capability of the

first alarm assignment, the objective is to deploy a programmed reserve and automatic aid fire force of six (6) engine companies, three (3) truck (ladder) companies, and three (3) chief officers within fifteen (15) minutes of a third alarm. The objective is to prevent large fires from extending to other structures.

3. For all fire and emergencies (i.e., a probability of fire or explosion) in petroleum storage and production areas, to deploy, within ten (10) minutes, special light water or foam firefighting equipment and prepare for long relays and extended pumping operations. The objective is to provide engine companies with adequate petroleum fire firefighting equipment. For fires in water deficient areas, the objective is to deploy, within ten (10) minutes, a pumper–tanker and relay operation of adequate capacity to augment local supplies.

4. For fires in harbor areas, to deploy within five (5) minutes for 90 percent of all marine-oriented incidents adequate marine firefighting equipment of 500 GPM.

5. To maintain and deploy one engine company within five (5) minutes of notification in 90 percent of all light rescue emergencies. In addition, a paramedic unit shall be deployed within five (5) minutes 80 percent of the time. The objective is to provide emergency medical services (EMS) and rescue all trapped persons, including those who need to be extricated with forcible entry equipment.

6. To deploy a truck company in addition to an engine and paramedic unit on heavy rescue incidents. The truck shall arrive within ten (10) minutes 90 percent of the time. The objective is to rescue all trapped persons regardless of the situation.

Such a planning effort, when developed in measurable terms, can determine whether the existing fire control organization is deployed and operating satisfactorily or whether it should be modified to meet changing needs. The basis is the data that have been collected and evaluated over the years (see Chapter 18).

Organizing

The best method of ensuring success in the establishment of or in a modification of a fire control organization is to organize a limited-term project team. Selected members may be reassigned to special detail or, in smaller organizations, may wear two or more hats. Projects are restrictive and are limited to resources available. They last only until the objective is accomplished (a procedure known as the *sunset theory*).

Given an objective to organize, staff, equip, and station a planned number of fire companies at selected locations, the next step would be to develop a job and task list of items to be performed. This list is usually made in a chart sequence listing or along the lines of a flowchart, with both having completion times for each task. Each job would have a set of specifications to determine quality and quantity requirements. This process is true whether one is building fire stations; buying fire apparatus or equipment; or hiring, promoting, or training personnel. Large departments may have personnel permanently assigned to these duties but most departments would use the project team concept.

There are numerous types and sizes of fire control organizations, the smallest being a one or two company tactical operation with a fire officer in charge of each unit and a fire chief commanding operations and management administration. A slightly larger department might have an assistant fire chief and a second in command and perform staff functions such as training, communications, and personnel.

Volunteer departments may choose their own personnel and appoint their own officers. In some cases the rules and regulations of the department need to be approved by the city or village legislative body. This may also be true for personnel appointments.

Conflicts can occur when the volunteer organizations are not responsible to the city or village legislative body. Many state laws permit the formation of an independent fire company or department.

Fire districts in many states can form their own agency through a vote of the people and can levy and collect their own taxes. These districts are usually governed by an elected board of trustees.

Most volunteer departments are formed and managed by the community's most responsible citizens and are respected and appreciated by all. Some volunteer organizations have become the leading political force in a community.

Basic organization positions

The fire chief is the ranking administrative and fire combat officer. The only exception would be under a commission form of government; in this case the commissioner would be the chief administrative officer.

The assistant fire chief is also an administrative officer and is generally utilized in small departments to operationally cover in the absence of the fire chief, to act as a sector chief at emergencies, and to perform staff duties. (Depending on the personalities of those involved, a poor administrative situation can develop if the assistant fire chief is in the direct chain of command between the companies and the fire chief. This is usually rectified by forming the type of small organization illustrated in Figure 9–1.) A synonymous term for the assistant fire chief is deputy fire chief. However, this title is more prevalent in larger departments.

Figure 9–1   A small, simple fire organization.

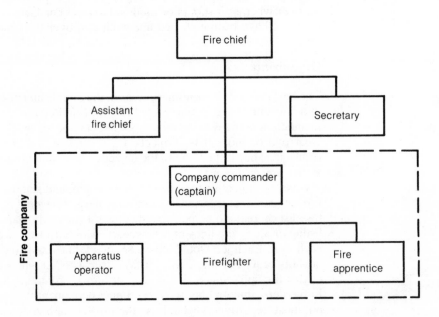

The company commander, usually a fire captain, is the ranking position in a fire company. The company commander's duties usually include the command of the on-duty fire company and the fire station to which he is assigned. A fire lieutenant, on the other hand, is in command of his company and receives coordinating instructions on station management from the station commander.

The apparatus operator or driver is usually a senior firefighter and is assigned to drive the fire truck. Some departments consider this position as a separate promotable classification and may use the title of fire engineer.

The position of firefighter is that of a journeyman who has completed all probationary assignments satisfactorily and by proven performance can carry out all tasks required.

A fire apprentice is an entry level position assigned to a fire company. This person in a small department will learn through on-the-job training. Larger departments will probably detail the trainee to a recruit academy for several weeks and then to a fire company for on-the-job training. Another title for this position is probationary firefighter.

The U.S. Department of Labor has model fire apprenticeship standards, developed jointly by the International Association of Fire Chiefs and the International Association of Fire Fighters,[1] that will be gaining more acceptance over the years. There are also state and national certification programs that validate job performance for the entry as well as other career positions (for further discussion of these subjects see Chapter 13).

Because the size of the organization is quite limited in Figure 9–1, fire prevention duties are carried out by fire control personnel, administrative or specialist, from other agencies such as the state or the county.

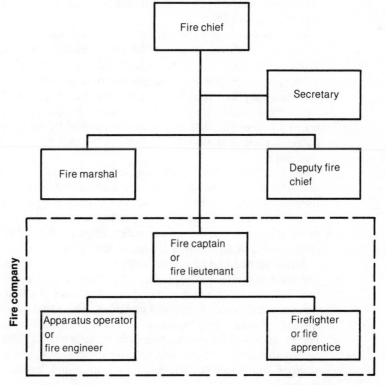

Figure 9–2 A small paid fire department with a fire marshal position.

Figure 9–2 represents a slight expansion over the department shown in Figure 9–1 and would be typical of a small paid fire department. The principal increase is in the position of fire marshal. Because paid departments handle most fire prevention, inspection, code enforcement, and public education duties, it is necessary to provide a person who can coordinate the fire prevention duties of the fire control forces and can undertake more complex inspections, plan checks, and administrative duties.

The premise of this chapter is that fire control personnel perform a wide range of duties which include firefighting; training; station, apparatus, and equipment maintenance; fire system inspection and testing; fire code enforcement; public education; rescue; salvage; and emergency medical and possibly some form of medical technician work. The cost of personnel and the desire on the part of all fire service personnel to professionalize the functions and activities carried out by the fire company members dictate a wide range of tasks, high technical skill, and full productive work during all available work time.

The top limit on the number of fire companies represented in Figure 9–2 is three. Any more would exceed the span of control of the fire chief. Because each company represents three or four separate shifts, much of the coordination between fire companies and the administration would have to be handled by the deputy fire chief.

Positions in larger organizations

Figure 9–3 represents an expanded organization and an improved span of control for the fire chief. The counterbalance is that the organization has one more level in the chain of command which increases the problems of communication.

This organizational structure would be suitable for three to five fire companies. Any more would tax the capacity of the operations officer. An expansion beyond this number would require an aide for the operations officer or a coordinator in the form of an assistant fire chief working as staff for the fire chief and operations officer.

There is no absolute rule to follow when determining the span of control or exact organizational structure. Much depends on the supervisory and managerial personalities and capacities of the personnel assigned to handle the job.

Most fire department organizations are based on a foundation of formal rank classifications (i.e., fire chief, deputy fire chief, assistant fire chief, fire battalion chief, fire captain, fire lieutenant, apparatus operator, firefighter, and fire apprentice). These classifications are determined by analyzing job duties and allocating formal common fire service job titles to the appropriate personnel groupings.

Once members have been assigned a formal job title, the fire administration may use allocated personnel, commensurate with their position, in various functional position assignments. When this occurs, the person is usually given a descriptive functional title (i.e., division fire chief, division commander, operations officer, battalion commander, district fire chief, fire marshal, shift commander, company officer, apparatus operator, driver, etc.).

These formal and functional titles have been intermixed in the examples for purposes of discussion. As a general principle, it is best to use a minimum number of formal titles and to provide organizational flexibility by assigning ranked personnel to various functional positions. This same concept carries through to the fire ground when functional combat assignments are used (i.e., incident commander, public information officer, safety officer, liaison officer, suppression and rescue section chief, division supervisor, planning section chief, resources status unit leader, situation status unit leader, water resources unit leader, etc.).

There is a general avoidance of a one-on-one chain of command relationship in the illustrated examples (i.e., when only one person reports to the boss). The principle is that all personnel are responsible for a work or program activity and it is best to fully assign persons to positions of measurable work effort rather than to one of singular assistance or singular supervision. This statement holds true for both day-to-day management and fire ground command.

Figure 9–4 is an example of a larger organization consisting of multiple battalions and requiring full command of fire control activities by a division fire chief. The size of the department may still grow through the addition of support divisions, but the operations division combat command is primarily considered as a separate program activity. If the department is so large as to require a multi-fire control division, a deputy fire chief would be inserted into the structure. This is not to say that firefighting personnel perform *only* fire combat duties. Productivity requirements still dictate a wide range of duties, such as code enforcement, public education, salvage, and emergency medical duties. It is only when personnel are called in to respond to ten or more incidents per working shift that a combat member can specialize in firefighting duties to the exclusion of other duties and/or programs.

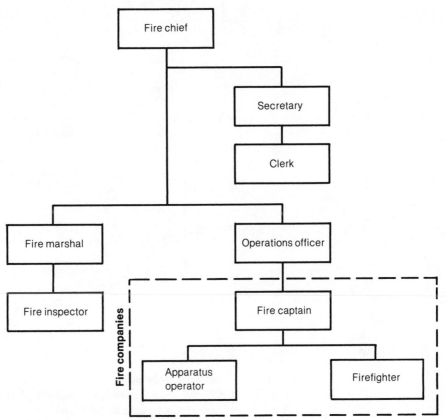

Figure 9–3   An expanded fire organization suitable for three to five companies.

The principle of authority commensurate with responsibility applies to all tasks performed by fire control personnel. The division fire chief in this example is responsible for all the assignments given to the operations division. This includes fire prevention and all other duties. To divide authority and control by function would fracture the organization, and officers in the fire prevention division should only be coordinators to fire company members in this case.

Many departments divide out functions when they become large. This is particularly true when members were hired and trained as firefighters. There is a general reluctance to take on additional tasks, but full productivity is vital to any organization and the fact that job titles imply firefighting should not preclude secondary performance tasks intended to eliminate fire hazards and provide emergency medical services.

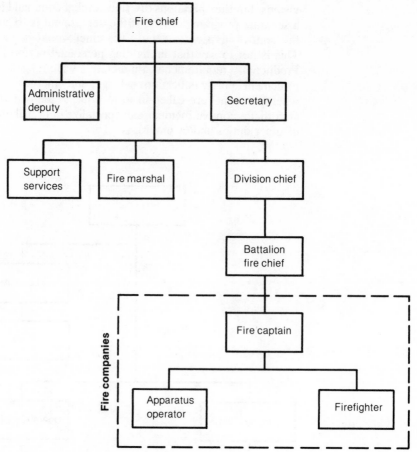

Figure 9–4   A large fire organization with multiple battalions.

Deployment of combat manpower

One of the most controversial organizational subjects is the question of how many fire combat members should be assigned to an engine or ladder company. The primary concerns or issues for the firefighter are safety and exhaustion. The basic answer to the safety question is that two or more persons should work together as a team when working in hazardous atmospheres and environments, and at least one person should be in a safe area ready to effect a rescue or call for help as required. (Also, it should be remembered that effective supervision is absolutely necessary at all times.)

On the question of exhaustion, much depends on the strength and condition of the member. Each department has different job-related performance standards, and these should be judged on the basis of local job requirements. A general guideline would be to lift, carry, and drag up to 150 pounds of equipment and have the stamina to run one and a half miles in twelve minutes. A specific job requirement would be to lift, carry, and raise a twenty-four foot extension ladder. (The National Fire Protection Association publishes a standard on the job performance requirements for firefighters.)[2] Fire department management has the same safety desires as labor. On the question of work effort, management is looking to effect the rescue of trapped persons and to apply a given amount of water to either contain or extinguish a fire.

Company members in good physical condition are generally expected to perform with concentrated effort in a hazardous environment for a maximum of thirty minutes without relief. In tactical terms this would relate to two fire-fighters advancing a single $1\frac{1}{2}$ or $1\frac{3}{4}$ inch hose line at ground level and applying 80 to 200 GPM of water. Three firefighters would be required to advance these charged lines up stairways. Three firefighters would be needed to advance a $2\frac{1}{2}$ inch charged hose at ground level and apply 200 to 300 GPM. Four firefighters would be required to advance the same hose lines up a stairway.

Various tactical manpower deployment systems can be devised to meet the safety, exhaustion, and advancing hose line criteria as stated above. The most efficient methodologies should be decided by the local fire chief, who can best evaluate the fire problem on alternative solutions.

Directing

The reverse organizational chart shown in Figure 9–5 illustrates the importance of the labor force in the fire company. The entire fire control organization exists for the purpose of controlling and extinguishing fire and performing related duties to prevent fire. All command and administrative personnel exist for the main purpose of supporting the field operations through directing, coordinating, and evaluating the effective use of the fire company. A lack of understanding of this relationship can lead to ineffective effort and an increased potential for life and property loss.

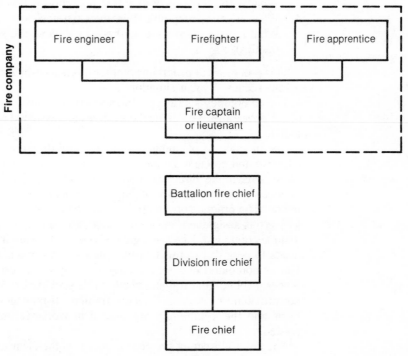

Figure 9–5 The importance of the labor force in the fire company.

Labor and management are equally important and equally needed to achieve fire control objectives. Anyone who loses sight of this balance and relationship will cause a disturbance in the motivational thrust of the fire department.

When directing a fire company or companies, it is important to remember that only the work produced by the unit is measurable and accountable. Conversely, only well-planned, directed, and coordinated efforts by a fire officer or chief officer will provide the leadership required to effect a successful operation.

There are many traits that make an excellent command officer. The first is the ability to be a good strategist. A well-planned action is essential. Only a department with excess resources can afford to attack a fire without a plan that leads to a defined direction. This is true no matter who is the incident officer. Departmental policies and procedures usually direct the highest ranking line or combat officer to be the incident officer. This procedure starts with the first arriving company officer and changes upon the arrival of subsequent superior officers. The rank or level of fire officer required to command multi-company forces on the fire ground depends on the magnitude of the emergency and the amount of resources to be deployed. Ability to exercise effective span of control tends to diminish as the magnitude increases, and this relationship is geometrical rather than arithmetical.

Many departments have a policy to only use line officers for fire duty. This practice of not using fire prevention or training officers is subject to question. Does any department have sufficient staff to be able to afford not to train staff officers for fire command duty during major emergencies? Personnel flexibility and an adequate number of qualified officers to direct operations are essential to any emergency organization. Any restrictions in this process can be a waste of manpower.

Essential to the function of directing are the following questions or elements:

1. What is the problem?
2. What are all the facts that can be obtained?
3. What is the forecast of events if no action is taken?
4. What are the acceptable objectives (strategies)?
5. What are the alternative methods to achieve the selected objectives (tactics)?

This process is appropriate whether this is a regular organizational problem or an emergency combat situation.

The emergency's strategic objectives (plan) must encompass the entire scope of the operations, and tactical objectives are assigned to fire companies (tactical units).

The practice of planning, organizing, and directing combat operations in an effective and efficient manner is both an art and a science. The time and hazard constraints make directing a very important and critical task. This is compounded with a progressive change in command as the operation builds in magnitude. The practice of directing cannot be left to chance and all personnel subject to this assignment must be trained, educated, and given the opportunity to assume command. Lives and great economic loss are at stake and consideration needs to be given to this fact by policymakers, managers, and administrators. Unless command officers are directing major fires on a daily basis, extensive officer level combat training needs to be provided. Too many departments are not providing professional quality training. If management cannot direct, then labor and the community are placed in jeopardy and organizational cost is wasted.

The key to directing fire control forces is the clear understanding on the part of all personnel of what is expected of them. Policies, procedures, and practices need to be identified and published in advance. This starts with the law needed to establish the organization and ends with the evaluation of the last combat performance. The foundation for directing is measurable performance standards.

There is no meaning to an established strategy (plan) or to tactical objectives (fire company combat assignments) unless the incident officer and the respective company officers *know* the *capability* of the tactical units (fire companies).

All officers must know the company's capacity, its ability to accomplish tasks, and how quickly it can carry out its mission and then be ready for another mission. Without this knowledge of company performance, the giving of orders will have no meaning and the mission will be inefficient in the application of resources. There are many case histories where resources were poorly allocated. One is where the emergency is overcome with excess resources, another is where the fire runs out of fuel, and there are many others where the strategy is changed to exposure protection rather than a save of a portion of the building or contents.

The best method of setting performance standards is to establish standard methods or evolutions that are in common with either engine or truck companies, or with task forces. The standard should be measurable in terms of time, quantity, quality, and ability to adjust to changing conditions (i.e., broken line, firefighter injury). For example, the need may be to determine how long it would take the first arriving company to place a single interior attack line in operation on the fifth floor. The established performance standard might finally be determined to be, for example, "A fire attack team (engine or truck company) shall be able to place a 100 foot, $1\frac{3}{4}$ inch attack line in operation at 100 pounds nozzle pressure on the fifth floor within fifteen minutes." The tasks and methods are assumed to be in compliance with those published in the operations or training manuals or those established by the department academy standards and programs.

The incident officer is now in a position to set a strategy to contain and extinguish a one or two room fire on the fifth floor of a building within twenty minutes, if the fire does not spread beyond the room or rooms before the first attacking company is in position.

Hypothetically, then, a scenario could be to set a strategy to attempt the containment and extinguishment of the fire with an aggressive interior attack, by the first alarm assignment, directly on the fifth floor. If this fails to check the spread of fire, reinforcements will be brought up for relief and to strengthen the attack, to ventilate as possible, to conduct surface rescue operations as needed, and to attack and extinguish the fire. The estimated control time is twenty minutes.

Continuing with the scenario and assuming a first alarm assignment of three engines and one truck (ladder) company, the tactical objectives (directions) given by the incident officer might be (hypothetically):

1. First engine, make a direct attack on the fifth floor (fire floor) with a $1\frac{3}{4}$ inch attack line, using wet standpipe system; if unable to extinguish with first fire attack team, then check extension. Your estimated control time is twenty (20) minutes.
2. Second engine, provide water supply to standpipe system, check extension to sixth floor, if any, and report. Supply to be provided in five (5) minutes.
3. Third engine, provide secondary attack on fifth floor, support first engine's attack, check any extension from assigned standpipe. The estimated control time is twenty (20) minutes.
4. First truck, support engine one's attack on fifth floor, conduct search and perform rescue as required; provide for ventilation and salvage operations. Check all possible extensions and report any extensions or strategic and tactical exceptions.
5. Incident command officer to establish command post, set strategy and tactical objectives, issue tactical orders, and call second alarm and subsequent alarms.

These are hypothetical examples, for illustrative purposes only, of the type of initial directions required from the incident officer. The initial decision may have been made by the first arriving company officer.

Commanding a fire or any other emergency operation is demanding and complex. The number of decisions to be made under emergency conditions is significant, and the consequences of error are enormous. Time management is essential, for the incident officer must have all the facts, be available at all times, and issue directions as required. The management techniques required between the incident commander and the company officers require considerable training and practice. Above all, there are no substitutes for professional management skills and abilities and the knowledge required on the fire ground.

Coordinating

The management/administrative process of coordinating fire control forces is just as vital in day-to-day operations as it is during emergency situations. The difficulty of coordinating can be eased if the functions of planning, organizing, and directing are properly addressed and carried out.

Once the plan has been placed in operation, the continued achievement of direction by all personnel and fire company units is a sign of good coordinating. Because typical American fire department organizational structures are decentralized, the necessity for coordination is even more of a factor.

Fire companies should be deployed in a strategic manner to provide the optimum response time to emergencies. The coordination of this activity cannot be left to chance or opinion. The fire administration manager establishes the general strategy and the actual day-to-day coordination is designed into the management system (i.e., is executed by the fire dispatchers working under some type of management authority). On a day-to-day nonemergency basis the units (companies) may be redeployed or taken out of service for various reasons. Fire prevention code enforcement, pre-fire planning, and fire control training are justifiable reasons for taking a calculated risk that may lead to a long response time. Also, because many emergencies require more than one fire company or unit, the calculated risk factor can quickly become compounded.

The question of risks

Fire officers are fire control risk managers. Much of the risk is preset by structural conditions or the fire problem in the community. Other risks are set when the operational fire defense system is organized (manning standards, adoption of fire codes, etc.). But much of the day-to-day risks are set by the operations managers who in reality play the percentages. Fire departments that are well staffed and equipped have a much easier time of it than do those that are operating with inadequate manpower and equipment.

It is easy for the fire chief to justify the absence or delay of a fire company because they were assigned to a prior emergency. But when is it more important to redeploy a company for training or fire prevention work than to maintain it in readiness within its response district? Of course, there is no risk when the company is in its district performing these tasks and on radio alert availability.

The answer to these questions lies in a professional opinion stating, "We will be in a position to better meet the department objectives when there are highly trained personnel in the fire company than when there are untrained personnel with a shorter response time." The same is true for fire prevention and the elimination of unwanted fire ignitions.

A manager can further minimize the risks if he knows the best time to take a chance (i.e., risk management). A good management information system that provides the data necessary to forecast the probabilities of a fire or other emergency is essential. For example, there may be less fire incidence and lower loss (life and/or property) ratios during the morning hours than at other times.

The next question is, "If the risk is acceptable, then how large a risk or how many companies or units, in what configuration, am I willing to pull off district assignments and redeploy or rearrange?" This process is management by design to meet objectives.

The objective is always the key issue when making any kind of management decision. "Is this action the most cost-effective method of achieving policy set through the goals and objectives process?'' If not, then the action should not be taken. Some communities may pull as much as one-third of their fire control forces off line during low incident periods for fire training and fire prevention purposes. Timing is the essential element when making these decisions. (Fire loss can be equated to time and quality of training—as can manning standards and fire station location.)

On the fire ground

On the fire ground, coordination makes the difference between a well-run and a poor operation and thus between an increase and a decrease in the fire loss. Again, the key is good planning, organization, and direction. But once the direction has been given, timing and coordination between the operating units is essential.

A structural fire of any consequence would require the minimum deployment of two engines, one truck (ladder), and a chief officer. Tactical considerations are always given in terms of the capability(ies) of the company(ies) and the support required by other units; that is to say, the synergistic effect is most important in accomplishing the mission (i.e., multi-company concerted action is more effective than single company independent action).

A simple hypothetical strategy on a fully involved two story residence fire would be to check for exposure problems; attack and control the fire on the first floor; proceed to the second and attack and control; perform rescue as the companies proceed and perform ventilation as required; complete extinguishment and perform salvage as needed.

Tactically, then, engine one would be given an objective to secure an adequate water supply, check for exposure problems, force entry, and control and extinguish the fire on the first floor with an interior attack, picking up any rescue as they proceed. (For purposes of discussion, this example has been kept simplified—i.e., no direction of attack, etc.)

Truck one would be given a tactical objective to support the engine companies by forcing entry, ventilating, laddering, performing search and rescue, opening concealed spaces, ensuring advancement of hose lines through support action, and providing salvage as priorities permit.

Engine two would be given a tactical objective to provide attack support to engine one on the first floor and, when safety is ensured, to control and extinguish the fire on the second floor with an interior attack and also pick up surface rescue.

These are limited objectives and, as they are completed, the officers would be expected to report for new assignments. Also, if conditions should change or if the objective cannot be met in a reasonable time frame, then a new strategy might be in order and revised tactical objectives would be allocated (for example, to declare the structure unsafe for firefighters, have hand lines withdrawn, and set up for heavy stream appliance).

In the hypothetical example given above, the units had their individual assignments but each played a role in the total objective. Each assignment was integrated into the overall operation. Coordination and timing are vital to providing the balance required to make the most of the assignments given and of the type of units deployed.

Controlling

Control is the final function relating to managing fire control services. All functions are equally important and controlling is no exception. Controlling is based on the feedback that determines progress toward the objective and provides indicators for possible change.

Fire control forces operate in an environment of many disciplines. At one moment the fire company is in a state of emergency readiness that requires little on-line control; the next moment it may be involved in an all out effort to save life and property.

It is only through well-established policies and procedures, determined in advance of the activity, that the organization can function effectively. Unless there are measurable standards against which productive effort can be evaluated, the fire manager will have merely a subjective opinion of whether assigned tasks were completed on time, in sufficient quantity, and with the quality desired. These points are true of any organization (and they are true of both emergency and nonemergency situations).

Fire suppression should never be disorganized. Fire suppression is much more than just putting the fire out. Because life and property are at risk and because firefighting is so hazardous, the practices, procedures, and techniques used by individuals or by fire companies must be under the confirmed control of chief officers at all times.

Because actual firefighting operations are not usually measured in terms of cost, pre-prescribed performance standards need to be established for individuals and fire companies. It is these identified standards that give individuals and companies the satisfaction of a job well done. (Much of the individual commitment of the firefighter in fact stems from morale.)

Day-to-day individual performance is based on a list of job duties prescribed for a given classification. This is reinforced in training sessions and evaluations of on-the-job performance.

Company performance is usually measured against some type of fire ground hose or ladder evolution that has become standard operational procedure over the years.

Fire critiques or analyses of combat and emergency operations are usually subjective activities based on past history and on the professionals conducting the evaluations. Evaluating is complex because no two fires or emergencies are alike and it is a very dynamic process. Also, the periods between preparation and actual control are relatively short.

It is important that fire and emergency control forces arrive at the scene procedurally proficient, properly motivated, and instructed in the objective (and with competent leadership).

Once direction is given, control is exercised by the command officer in many ways. First, the command officer should position the command post at a location where the greatest observation can be made of the entire fire ground. Second, all officers should report when they achieve objective or as soon as they become aware that they will not meet objective. This aids in time management and supports control. Also, this establishes tactical points for time of the required feedback.

Post-fire operations control is usually reserved until all the reports are in and adequate summaries can be prepared. However, the critique should not be delayed any longer than necessary, so that minds are still fresh. It should be remembered that the purpose of the evaluation is to find problems, establish corrective action, and give recognition to the success of the operation and the participants. The fire control management cycle of planning, organizing, directing, coordinating, and controlling is an ongoing and never-ending process.

1   International Association of Fire Chiefs and International Association of Fire Fighters, *National Apprenticeship and Training Standards for the Fire Fighter* (Washington, D.C.: U.S. Department of Labor, 1976). These standards are available from: U.S. Department of Labor, Bureau of Apprenticeship and Training, Patrick Henry Building, Room 5414, 601 D Street, N.W., Washington, D.C. 20213.

2   National Fire Protection Association, *Fire Fighter Professional Qualifications*, NFPA no. 1001 (Boston: National Fire Protection Association, 1974).

Managing emergency medical and rescue services

What do we mean when we use the term *emergency medical services?* In recent years, largely owing to federal initiatives, the term has taken on a new and much broader meaning. Formerly it was synonymous with an ambulance service or with a local hospital emergency room. The lack of an emergency medical services (EMS) *system,* however, began to be identified as a cause of excessive mortality among victims of accidental illness and injury.[1]

With the enactment of the Highway Safety Act of 1966 (P.L. 89–564) the picture began to change, as federal resources became available to improve several aspects of prehospital emergency medical care. Channeled through state highway safety agencies, these funds were committed to upgrading ambulance attendant training, radio communications, and ambulance vehicles. Considerable progress was made in the subsequent years, during which time standard training programs were developed for emergency medical technicians (EMTs) and EMT–paramedics.

In 1973 the Congress enacted the Emergency Medical Services Systems Act (P.L. 93–154) and authorized $185 million during the first three years for the planning and implementation of regional EMS systems in numerous areas of the country. This law and the program regulations it authorized placed major emphasis on EMS as a system. In the process, the law and its regulations defined many of the roles and responsibilities attendant on participation in an EMS system as a provider of services. Thus, EMS was an idea whose time had come.

What definition does the federal legislation offer? A comprehensive EMS system as defined by federal law is regional in nature (covering a medical service area as opposed to a specific geopolitical jurisdiction) and encompasses fifteen basic system components, ranging from citizen access, transportation, personnel training, communications, and hospital categorization to public education, consumer participation, specialized treatment facilities, critical patient transfers, and patient rehabilitation. The fire service role in the system generally is limited to the prehospital phases. (It should be borne in mind that other local government employees—notably in the police department—and various private sector groups also are trained in some elements of EMS techniques.)

The above description is intended as a brief background to the management of emergency medical and rescue services today. This chapter presents an extended analysis of these services from the managerial perspective, that is, from the viewpoint of key decision makers within and without a local government fire department.

The following section outlines the main dimensions of the managerial challenges presented by EMS functions as they relate to the overall fire services area and also to other organizational elements within and without the local government structure. The overview presented in this first section is divided into two parts: the evolution of fire service involvement in EMS, and the management challenges that have arisen as a result of this expansion of the traditional fire services field.

The second main section forms the core of the chapter. It presents a detailed analysis of the EMS function from the perspective of a management cycle, running from the setting of goals and objectives to the process of evaluation that completes the cycle by facilitative feedback to the goal-setting process. The first of the six subdivisions to this section suggests a management approach to the setting of goals and objectives. The second emphasizes the theme of planning as a cyclical process. The third gets to the heart of the matter by discussing the selection of alternative management approaches in terms of six different operational profiles. It is important to emphasize at the outset what is spelled out later in the chapter, namely, that the six operational profiles presented are composites of actual fire service experience in a number of communities, and that any resemblance to a specific fire department is coincidental. The author has extensive nationwide experience in this area, however, and is hopeful that the profiles are sufficiently realistic to be of use to fire service decision makers.

The third component of the second section also presents a managerial assessment of the operational profiles just analyzed. The fourth addresses the question of direction—"Who's in charge?" The fifth takes a look at the specific managerial challenges presented by the unusual features found in EMS services. The sixth section completes the management cycle by discussing the difficult question of evaluation.

The third and final section of the chapter is a conclusion and a brief outlook, assessing what may be the shape of things to come in this fast-developing area.

It should be emphasized that the approach throughout the chapter is to identify the structural and operational elements involved that present challenges to the fire services manager. It is hoped that managers will regard these elements as tools with which they can fashion a chain of command and an implementation process appropriate to the circumstances of a particular fire department and a specific community. As has been stressed throughout this book, there is no "one best way"—there is only the approach that proves managerially, politically, and administratively viable in a specific jurisdiction.

EMS as a challenge to management: an overview

The evolution of fire service involvement

Fire department participation in EMS varies greatly throughout the United States. It can include maintenance and operation of a dispatch and communications facility, training of personnel in basic life support, operation of first-responder units (including pumper or ladder companies), basic life support units (with or without patient transportation), advanced life support units (involving firefighter or civilian paramedics), and public education (including blood pressure screening programs and training of citizens in the technique of cardiopulmonary resuscitation [CPR]).

The historical background　How did this involvement come about? Fire service involvement in EMS has been evolutionary. As early as 1928 a few fire departments began to provide first aid services to citizens suffering from breathing difficulties and heart attack symptoms. Primitive resuscitator–inhalator devices used by fire departments to assist firefighters in cases of smoke inhalation became the standard equipment for aiding the public in medical episodes. As early as 1930 fire departments began to develop special vehicles for this function; these often included heavy rescue and extrication equipment for specialized rescue and firefighting situations.

Equipment, medical aid training, and operational procedures improved very little over a period of three decades. In the early 1960s, however, new techniques in artificial breathing and circulation were devised, leading to the technique of CPR. (Some fire departments had adopted this technique even before it was officially adopted by the American Red Cross.) Also during this time, resuscitation equipment was redesigned to be more compact and portable. At the same time, public demand for fire department first aid services was steadily, if slowly, increasing.

In the late 1960s medical journals began to report the dramatic results of European mobile intensive care programs.[2] These revolutionary operations reversed the traditional approach of emergency care and actually took the medical team from the hospital to the location of the patient suffering from, for example, an acute heart attack. A few pioneering medical doctors began the development of similar systems in several locations across the United States. Almost without exception, firefighters were chosen to be trained as the specialized paramedic technicians to serve on these early units.[3]

In Miami, Columbus, Los Angeles, Seattle, and Jacksonville, fire department paramedics quickly earned the vocal support of their medical mentors as they jumped from the basic first aid function to sophisticated medical care functions. One of the pioneering physicians referred to Miami firefighter paramedics as practitioners of "gutter medicine."

By 1971 there were at least twenty-four mobile intensive care units in operation in the United States.[4] In that year a popular television series opened which depicted the adventures of a team of Los Angeles County fire department paramedics. Fire department EMS interest increased significantly as citizens became curious as to why their local fire department did not provide the sort of services depicted in the television series. As of 1977, advanced life support systems (using paramedics) were operational in at least 310 American communities. An estimated 33 percent (102) were operated by the local fire department.[5] The number has grown since.

New services, training, and equipment In the backwash of paramedic services there has been widespread development of first-responder and basic life support services. During 1977 one source reported that 56.1 percent of all fire departments in the United States were providing some level of emergency medical services and that an additional 2,087 departments were planning for implementation of emergency medical services in the subsequent twelve month period.[6]

The prehospital care and transportation components of an EMS system often involve not only a variety of services but also a variety of resources. For example, a fire department may provide first-response basic life support with pumper, ladder, or special rescue companies while relying on a private ambulance service for advanced life support (paramedic) services and ambulance transportation. In other instances police and fire agencies may provide first-response services, with fire department paramedics providing advanced life support and private ambulances providing patient transportation. One survey disclosed at least ten different profiles involving fire, police, volunteer ambulance, private ambulance, separate municipal ambulance, and hospital operated ambulance services.[7]

Intensive care of trauma victims is an area that has been given special attention by some fire departments. It should be borne in mind that public demand for improved services is built largely on public expectations that the improvements will result in a greater likelihood of patient survival. Well-publicized reports (and graphic television coverage) on the Vietnam experience showed that prompt and correct handling of all sorts of injuries in the field—*before* the victim is moved—can prevent shock, reduce the severity of injuries, shorten the patient's confinement to a hospital, and reduce the potential for permanent disability.

In Maryland and Illinois statewide EMS systems have been developed with special emphasis on intensive care of trauma victims. Evaluation of these programs disclose greatly improved survival potential for critical patients treated in

Glossary

Ambulance: A vehicular conveyance designed and operated for transportation of ill and injured persons in a prone or supine position, equipped and staffed to provide for first aid or life support measures to be applied during transportation.

Backboards: Rigid support devices (usually constructed of wood) which are affixed to a patient's posterior torso (by means of straps, belts, or adhesive tape) in all cases of confirmed or suspected spinal injury, including all cases where the patient is unconscious. When properly applied, these devices can avoid aggravating or causing spinal injury and neurological injury during prehospital extrication and transportation.

CPR (Cardiopulmonary resuscitation): A combination of artificial respiration and closed-chest cardiac massage, performed by either one or two rescuers on a patient who is pulseless and nonbreathing. When promptly and properly applied, CPR has been shown to be an effective method for preventing deterioration of vital organs in patients who are without natural circulation and respiration. This rescue technique is generally recognized as a "holding action" which merely sustains the patient until advanced life support measures can be applied to restore natural pulse and breathing. Where large numbers of citizens in a community have been trained to perform CPR, statistical evidence shows substantial improvement in the long-term survival of persons who suffer from out-of-hospital cardiac arrest.

Advanced life support: All basic life support measures, plus invasive medical procedures, including: intravenous therapy; cardiac defibrillation; administration of antiarrhythmic medications and other specified drugs, medications, and solutions; use of adjunctive ventilation devices; and other procedures which may be authorized by state law and performed under medical control.

Basic life support: Generally limited to airway maintenance, ventilatory (breathing) support, CPR, hemorrhage control, splinting of fractures, management of spinal injury, protection and transportation of the patient in accord with accepted procedures.

EMT (emergency medical technician): A generic term referring to at least two emergency care positions: (1) EMT (sometimes known as EMT–Ambulance), a person who has been trained in a program of at least eighty-one hours in length and who has been appropriately certified as proficient in basic life support; (2) EMT–Paramedic (sometimes known as EMT–P), a person who has been trained in a program which includes, as a minimum, all fifteen modules of the U.S. Department of Transportation's National Training Course for the EMT–Paramedic, and who has been appropriately certified as proficient in advanced life support.

Medical control: A planned approach to the provision of advanced life support services in an out-of-hospital setting. Under this approach paramedic personnel are viewed as surrogates of a designated resource hospital and a designated medical director in that hospital (regardless of other employer–employee relationships).

Triage: A military term referring to the process of sorting the sick and wounded on the basis of severity of condition and urgency. In modern EMS systems triage occurs as calls are screened by a dispatcher, as first-responders determine the need for basic and/or advanced life support personnel, as basic life support units determine whether advanced life support personnel will be needed, and where decisions are made concerning transportation (emergency or nonemergency; private or public).

the system.[8] In Seattle a multiple-tiered emergency response system (involving trained citizens, fire department basic and advanced life support units, and a major medical center) resulted in a tripling of the long-term survival rate for victims of the cardiac malfunction often referred to as *sudden death* (ventricular fibrillation).[9] In Jacksonville, Florida, between 1968 and 1971, the local EMS system registered a 24 percent improvement in fatality rates connected with automobile accidents.[10] In reaction to reports of these dramatic successes the public has tended to question why similar programs are not possible in every community.

Greater public demand for state-of-the-art emergency medical services has brought about major changes in training, equipment, and operational profiles for all EMS providers. This factor has affected the fire department by challenging several decades of tradition. In many departments the basic Red Cross first aid training programs have been replaced by the minimum eighty-one hour EMT training program or by the more thorough U.S. Department of Labor EMT apprenticeship programs. The traditional positive/negative pressure cycled oxygen powered resuscitators have been replaced with positive pressure ventilation valves to facilitate advanced resuscitation techniques. Where fire departments have assumed advanced life support responsibility, selected personnel have been committed to intensive months-long paramedic training programs. In many cases all fire apparatus and other vehicles have been equipped with a minimum complement of backboards and other basic life support equipment. And many fire companies have been assigned to serve as the first assault on medical emergency problems, which drastically increases their alarm frequency.

The organizational responsibility for EMS   The tradition of an organized response to individual medical emergencies is rooted in military history. As early as the Napoleonic Wars special conveyances were committed to the task of moving the injured from the battlefront to treatment areas behind the lines. In the United States early ambulance services were operated by hospitals. As time progressed, the function became the province of funeral directors, police and fire departments, private ambulance operators, and volunteers.

A number of factors, including major changes in the traditional practice of medicine, contributed to public expectations for services and ambulance transportation. As physicians discontinued the practice of house calls, the need for specialized transport to a hospital became more significant. Also, as Americans became more mobile, long-term relationships with a family physician became a rarity. The hospital emergency room became the primary medical care location for increasing numbers of citizens. A growing tendency to depend on government for services emerged in the field of ambulance transportation with a consequent increase in local government involvement, including financial subsidies to private services and outright assumption of ambulance service responsibility by some public agencies.

With a sizable body of reliable trained and disciplined personnel, operating within an existing command structure, possessing vehicular and communications resources, operating from structural facilities located throughout the community, and holding the confidence of the public, the local fire department often seemed a natural source of medical aid responsibility. Also affecting this trend was the fact that most firefighting personnel were actually engaged in emergency activity for only a small percentage of their total available on-duty time.

Fire department willingness to assume this new and greater responsibility has not always been universal. In a number of communities fire officials have resisted efforts to utilize their personnel and other resources for EMS. In these locations the improvements of recent years have generally involved the upgrading of private ambulance services or the development of a new and independent municipal agency.

Development of the early mobile coronary care units in the United States seems to have occurred in areas in which the local fire department has willingly assumed the challenge of expanding its services. It was this service-minded orientation that attracted the attention of those medical doctors who sought to develop pilot programs in advanced life support. The consensus among this medical group was that their experience ideally fitted firefighters for the role of physician surrogates in taking advanced life support to the streets in the critical early stages of a medical emergency.

Despite severe financial difficulties experienced by most local governments during the middle and later 1970s, public opinion has tended to support government's role as a provider of prehospital emergency medical services. Indeed, voters in several locations have authorized tax levies to support local government operated paramedic services when tax levy authorizations for a variety of other functions were turned down.

With public support, availability, trainability, and tradition in its favor, then, the fire service has generally moved toward a dual function—provision of fire protection services and provision of some form of prehospital emergency medical care and/or transportation. Increased public utilization has resulted in alarm ratios which produce two emergency medical calls for every fire alarm in a majority of communities where the fire department is a part of the EMS system; at the same time, in many locations expansion of traditional fire department services to include EMS has been accomplished without major increases in total staffing costs.

The challenge to management

As local government decision makers well know, in any management environment expansion of services tends to present problems. This is especially true where the new and expanded service varies significantly in nature and dimension from the traditional functions of the managed entity. Fire service involvement in EMS carries an array of potential problems that have tested the management skills of many municipal officials in recent years.

This involvement in comprehensive EMS systems comes at a time when the topic of planning as a management function has taken on major significance for fire officials. Although, as has been pointed out in Chapter 6, planning concepts and methods should be viewed as a key to problem prevention and management, the relative newness of planning to many fire departments tends to cast this subject within the general perception of "problems." Health care planning, as a discipline, has a lengthy history flowing from federal initiatives to increase the availability of health care while restraining costs. To the extent that prehospital care is a part of the total health care system, organized planning of fire service involvement is basic to the endeavor.

Among the essential planning considerations are the staffing and organizational requirements of the fire department's prehospital component. In most cases this will involve concern for organizing and implementing the service for the most cost-effective use of existing personnel. Lengthy training programs for basic and advanced life support personnel require appropriate planning for consequent special staffing needs. The upgrading of a department's recruitment standards may be necessary to reflect the special intellectual requirements of emergency medical training programs, although appropriately recruited firefighters can satisfy the intellectual needs of the most demanding paramedic programs. Planning should also take into account the need for maintenance of skills and the need for personnel to replace those lost to attrition or promotion. And the planning effort should include consideration of appropriate levels and styles of supervision of personnel committed to the EMS function.

A concentrated effort to gather planning data should include seeking out in-

EMS planning goals and objectives

For the fire department planning the development of an EMS component the following set of goals and objectives might be typical:

Goal I: Provide first-response and basic life support services in cases of medical emergency

Objectives:

1. Develop operational policies in coordination with hospital, medical director, police agencies, and ambulance services
2. Design, purchase, and install radio and telephone communications equipment to permit public access to emergency medical services and to permit coordination between EMTs, public safety agencies, ambulance services, and hospitals
3. Equip designated apparatus and rescue vehicles with basic life support equipment and supplies
4. Modify departmental training programs to provide continuing education of EMTs and maintenance of basic life support skills
5. Train [number to be inserted] fire-fighters to level of EMT
6. Initiate service.

Goal II: Provide advanced life support services and emergency ambulance transportation in cases of life-threatening medical emergency

Objectives:

1. Establish contractual relationship with medical control hospital for training of [number to be inserted] personnel as mobile intensive care paramedics and for continuing education, skill maintenance, and medical control functions
2. Establish selection criteria and solicit paramedic training applications from among personnel previously trained to EMT level
3. In coordination with medical control hospital, establish commencement date for paramedic training and arrange for appropriate staffing to replace personnel assigned to training program
4. Establish specifications for mobile intensive care vehicles, equipment, and communications hardware and commence purchasing procedures
5. Initiate paramedic training program
6. Develop operational policies in coordination with medical control hospital, medical director, police agencies, and ambulance services
7. Conduct community public education/orientation program in preparation for initiation of mobile intensive care service
8. Take delivery of vehicles, equipment, and communications hardware and prepare for service
9. In coordination with medical control hospital, medical director, and appropriate health-related agencies, prepare reporting instruments and procedures to facilitate ongoing evaluation of mobile intensive care program
10. Conduct paramedic graduation exercises and initiate service.

The foregoing goals and objectives are not intended as a complete list of planning considerations for the respective programs; they merely illustrate the distinction between generalized goals and specific objectives.

formation from other agencies and programs to anticipate such factors as employee fatigue and a phenomenon referred to as *paramedic burnout* (discussed later in this chapter). Alteration of the department's response profiles may be necessary to meet the need for shortest possible response times. The accommodation of both fire protection and EMS functions should be the subject of intensive planning to enhance the potential for excellence in both functions without compromise to either.

Another essential planning consideration would relate to labor–management relations in many areas. Through the planning process, efforts should be undertaken to anticipate and overcome possible resistance to increases in work load and responsibility. Where new organizational profiles and staffing patterns are deemed necessary for desired operational flexibility, employee consensus should be a goal pursued through the planning process. Potential budget impact should also be explored through detailed planning. For example, increases in demand for services should be anticipated from the standpoint of increased costs to the agency; thus, the potentially greater use of vehicular resources, operating costs, and supplies would be a planning consideration.

Involvement in an EMS system requires ongoing coordination with other community agencies, services, and institutions. The first step toward such coordination can be taken through the planning process. Thus, the local medical community, the hospitals, the other public safety agencies, the training facilities, and the program's medical director should be included in the planning process from its beginnings.

The above discussion has outlined the managerial challenges presented by EMS. The next section takes a detailed look at how this important function can fit into the framework of the familiar management cycle of problem identification, control, and resolution.

The management cycle and emergency medical and rescue services

The setting of goals and objectives

As experienced local government managers recognize, a fire department's delivery of EMS services, as part of an EMS system, should be conceptualized and implemented through measurable and manageable goals and objectives. Goals should be stated in somewhat generalized terms, while objectives should be more definitive and specific.

The identification and formulation of goals is a part of the planning process. The development of objectives relevant to the goals is also a planning function. Through planning, desired future events (goals) can be identified and articulated. Through planning, too, effective ways of accomplishing these desired future events (objectives) can also be identified and articulated. Planning is directed toward producing a desired future situation which is not expected to occur unless something is done to ensure that it occurs.

Planning as a cyclical process

Planning should be viewed as a cyclical process, as opposed to a technique for accomplishing an endpoint result. An organization's services and functions should be evaluated continuously, with results being measured against original goals and objectives. Thus failure to fully achieve goals can serve as the signal to revise objectives accordingly in a continuing effort to control events rather than be controlled by them.

The process Figure 10–1 shows continuous, cyclical planning as it is related to EMS. The process commences with general goals. (What do we want to accomplish?) It then proceeds to the development of specific objectives. (How are we going to do it?) In the process of developing these objectives, system descriptive studies should be used. This can be referred to as a *planning data base* —a compilation of all relevant information necessary to formulating practical and achievable objectives. (What do we have to work with and what potential obstacles do we face?) A detailed example of this is given in Figure 10–2.

It is seldom that a single approach can be agreed upon in planning efforts to achieve a goal. Two or more alternative approaches may be developed as objectives. Implementers of the program then have the task of choosing from among the alternatives and developing programs based on the selected objectives (Figure 10–1). After implementation, the service will produce reported information (data) which can be referred to as *system outcomes*. Evaluation of this data should be continuous. Where the evaluation discloses excessive deviation from the original objectives, these objectives should be revised to correct the deviation.

It is the evaluation of system outcomes and the revision of objectives that make planning continuous and cyclical. Without this evaluation, deviations are likely to go undetected until a crisis occurs. Continuous and cyclical planning provides an opportunity to monitor the activity and prevent crisis: it is a practical method of controlling events rather than being controlled by them.

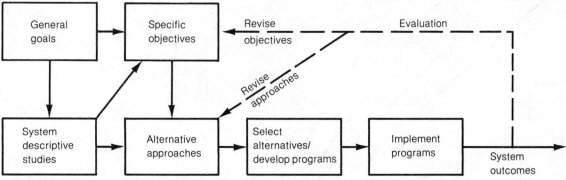

Figure 10–1   EMS planning as a continuous, cyclical process.

The program planner and the community planner   In planning for EMS involvement the fire official is not likely to be alone in the process. The health care system in any community or region may be likened to an artist's suspended mobile: touch it here and it jiggles over there. Thus, it is important that any prehospital care service be planned in concert with the total health care system.

Throughout the nation, as a result of the National Health Planning and Resources Development Act of 1974 (P.L. 93-641), overall health planning activities are designated to a network of organizations known as *Health Systems Agencies* (HSAs).[11] These relatively new agencies employ health planners to assist in planning health-related programs and to control overly expensive growth of health care institutions and resources.

Another federal law, the Emergency Medical Services Systems Act of 1973, provides funding for hundreds of regional emergency medical services projects throughout the United States. This funding authority was extended by congressional act in 1976. Eventually, more than 300 regional EMS management entities will have been established throughout the country. All of these organizations employ personnel with some degree of health planning experience.

The fire official who will be planning an EMS activity needs to seek out a local or regional EMS planner at the HSA or the regional EMS entity, or both. The regional EMS entity may be affiliated with the state health department, a regional council, a council of governments, a regional planning board or commission, or a nonprofit corporation. The U.S. Department of Health, Education, and Welfare (HEW) has funded all of these types of organizations for EMS planning and implementation activities.

Once the appropriate planner, or planners, are located and introduced to the proposed fire department EMS activity, it is important to recognize the extent and limits of their authority and responsibility. For purposes of this discussion, these health planners should be viewed as "community planners." By contrast,

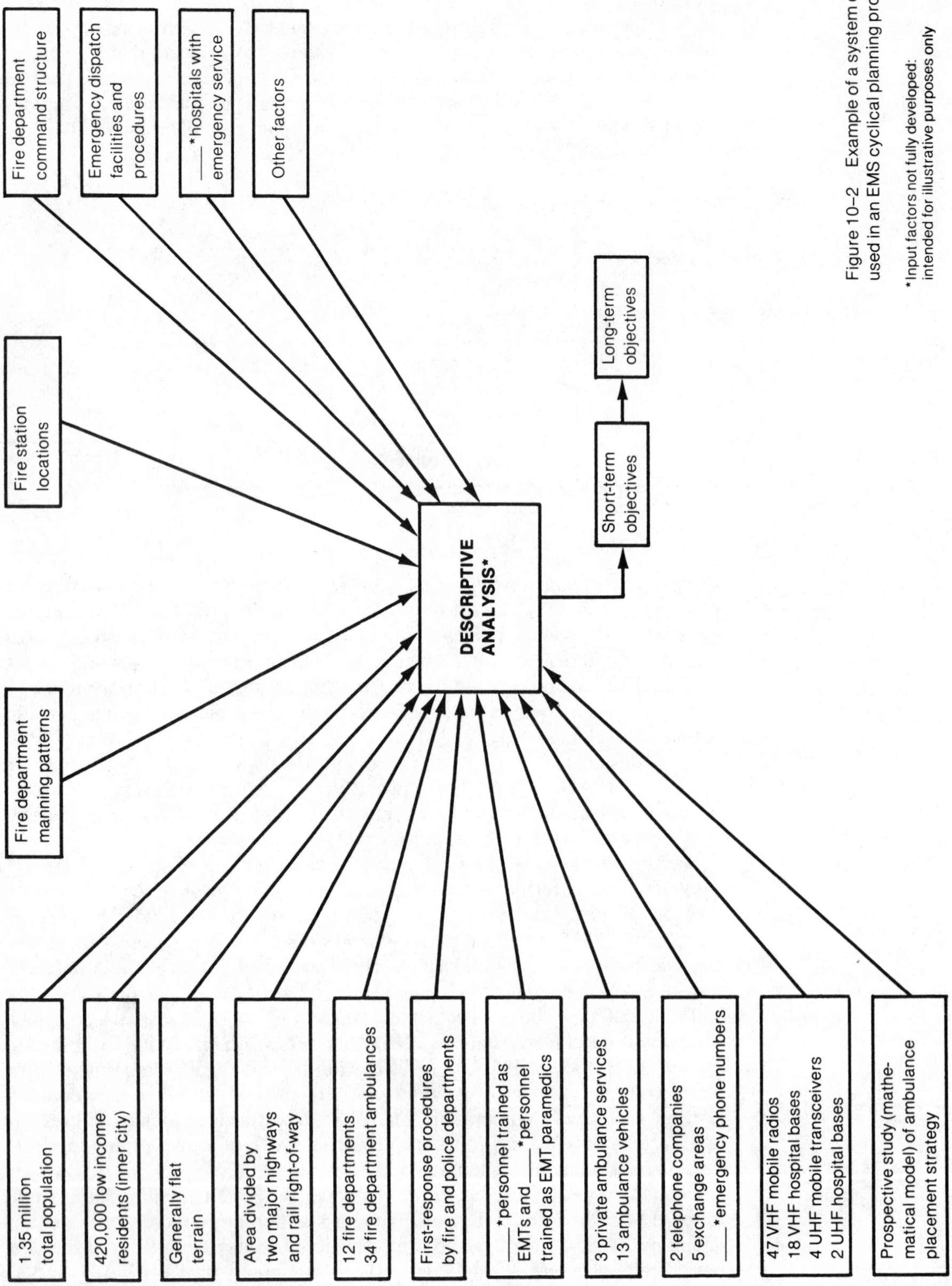

Figure 10–2   Example of a system descriptive study used in an EMS cyclical planning process.

*Input factors not fully developed: intended for illustrative purposes only

the fire official who plans for EMS involvement should be viewed as a "program planner." In order to avoid conflict, there should be a clearly defined division between the responsibilities of the community planner and those of the program planner. This division is shown in Figure 10–3.

As indicated, identification of the problem falls within the province of the community planner (Figure 10–3). In reality, however, it may be necessary to guide an HSA-based planner to the fact that a community's emergency care resources are less than adequate. For example, an unreliable ambulance service with poorly trained attendants produces a reasonable assumption that survivable emergency patients are dying for lack of a modern and efficient prehospital care system. Even a competent basic life support system that lacks the backup of advanced life support (paramedic) services suggests that improvements are called for. The HSA-based planner is likely to be involved in a broader scope of health-related planning activities, and so may have little familiarity with specific EMS considerations. This community planner can be assisted in identifying the problem through published reports and statistics concerning those localities with fully developed prehospital care systems.

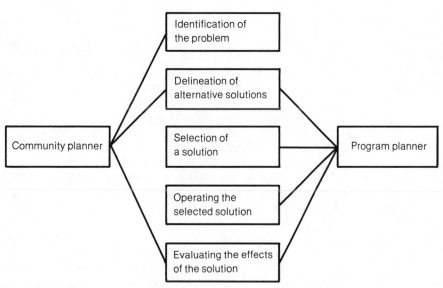

Figure 10–3 Division of the responsibilities of the community planner and the program planner.

While the HSA-based planner may need some guidance to identify the problem, the regional EMS planner (employed by an HEW-funded EMS project) is likely to be quite familiar with the local and regional EMS problems, as identification of those problems is a necessary part of applying for the federal funds that support the organization he or she works for.

Once the problem has been identified (the need for improvements in prehospital emergency care and transportation), the community planner and the fire official/program planner should collaborate on delineating alternative solutions to the problem (Figure 10–3). Selecting solutions, however, should be the province of the program planner. Operating the selected solution (implementation) should, in turn, be the responsibility of the program planner. In making the process continuous and cyclical (through evaluation and possible modification of objectives), however, the community planner and the program planner should work in concert.

The selection of alternative approaches: operational profiles

As has been mentioned earlier in this chapter, one survey has identified at least ten different profiles of operation for prehospital advanced life support programs. Within the fire service component of such programs, there are equally diverse operational profiles. In the planning process alternative approaches will be identified, and the program planner (as mentioned above) will need to select from among these alternatives.

Figure 10–4 gives samples of some considerations for six distinct operational profiles. The factors illustrated are not intended as a complete list. They may, however, be used by management as a planning base in designing a fire department EMS program or in modifying or expanding an existing service. Characteristics of each of the illustrated profiles (Profiles A–F) are discussed immediately below. (As mentioned early in this chapter, the six profiles represent composites of actual fire service experiences in a number of locations in the United States. Any resemblance to a specific fire department is coincidental. Despite the anonymity, the profiles are close enough to actual experiences to produce some valuable lessons.)

Profile A The first-response function recognizes that no other qualified emergency service can reach the scene of most medical emergencies faster than the nearest engine or truck company can. Thus, at least two members of each of these companies are trained to the level of *first-responder* or *emergency medical technician* (both training programs developed by the U.S. Department of Transportation).

When the fire department dispatcher receives a report of a medical emergency, the nearest unit (engine or truck company, whether located in a fire station or available by radio in the field) is dispatched simultaneously with the nearest available mobile intensive care (paramedic) unit. In the department discussed here a number of paramedic firefighters have been promoted to driver or company officer positions. By assigning these individuals to districts with high frequencies of medical emergencies and by equipping their fire apparatus with paramedic equipment and supplies, the department has been able to ease the burden on its busy rescue units. Thus, in some cases the first-responder unit will actually be a paramedic pumper or truck.

The first crew to arrive at the scene of the medical emergency will immediately assess the situation and determine the need for the paramedic rescue unit (which usually responds from a more distant location). If it can be determined that advanced life support services will not be needed, the first-response unit can cancel the paramedic unit's emergency response by radio or telephone contact with the dispatcher. This action makes the paramedic unit immediately available for another response (fire or medical emergency). In such instances it is important that such a medical *triage* decision be made by individuals adequately trained in basic life support (EMT training, as a minimum). Where there is any doubt, such as potential for deterioration of the patient's condition, the paramedic unit should be allowed to continue to the scene.

In this profile firefighters are used in a dual role. That is, first-response, basic life support, and advanced life support (paramedic) personnel are fully qualified firefighters who have been specially trained for emergency medical care functions after completing a period of service as firefighters. These paramedic personnel respond to fire alarms as well as to medical emergencies. In firefighting operations their assignments can range from search and rescue, forcible entry, and salvage operations to actual fire suppression functions and overhaul of the fire building. Obviously, their presence at the scene of a fire is valuable in the event of casualties. In most cases they are employed in fire operations in such a

Program considerations	Profiles					
	A	B	C	D	E	F
Level of service/training						
First-response	X	X	X	X	X	X
Basic life support	X	X	X	X	X	X
Advanced life support	X	X		X	X	X
Operational profile						
Engine companies	X	X	X	X	X	X
Truck companies	X	X				X
Rescue vehicles (nontransporting)	X		X			
Rescue ambulances (transporting)		X		X		X
Paramedic pumper/truck	X					
"Medic company"					X	
EMS personnel						
Civilian employees of fire department				X		
Firefighters (dual role)	X	X	X	X	X	
Firefighters (limited first-responder role)						X
Volunteer members						X
Patient transportation						
Transport all cases						X
Transport only emergencies		X		X	X	
Transport only in special cases						
Nontransport	X		X			
Dispatch locations						
Respond from hospital		X				X
Respond from fire stations (or field)	X	X	X	X	X	X
Supervision of EMS personnel						
Designated field EMS supervisors				X		
Fire company officers	X	X	X	X	X	X
EMS units dispatched by						
Fire department dispatcher	X	X	X	X	X	X
Police department dispatcher						
911 or public safety dispatcher		X	X			X
Hospital		X				X
Cooperation with ambulance service						
Private ambulance service(s)	X	X	X	X	X	
Municipal (government) ambulance			X			
Police ambulance						
Volunteer ambulance						X
Training of EMS personnel						
Fire department training staff		X	X	X		X
College or university	X		X	X	X	X
Hospital	X	X		X	X	X
State agency						X
Finance						
Fire department budget only		X	X	X	X	X
F.D. budget and supplemental funds	X					
Special tax revenue						
State or federal assistance	X					X
Charge for service		X		X		
Community fundraising						X

Figure 10–4   Six sample operational profiles for fire department EMS programs.

manner as to to maintain reasonable readiness to respond to a medical emergency if necessary. Thus, they are seldom fully committed to a fire suppression operation.

Several jurisdictions have utilized the dual role concept with success; this profile permits the implementation of advanced life support services with minimal increases in total manpower. There have been no reports that either function has been compromised by the use of personnel in both roles. However, the willingness of individuals to serve in both capacities seems to depend on such factors as the history and tradition of the agency, the quality and style of the department's management, and the relative work load of the department.

In Profile A all units respond from fire stations or from field assignments where they are available by radio. All personnel, including the paramedics, are supervised by fire company officers. This supervision, however, never extends to medical judgments, which are the responsibility of the medical control hospital and its authorized staff. Even where the company officer may have once served as a paramedic, the advanced life support program should be viewed as a hospital outreach program, with medical judgments by the hospital in consultation with paramedics over communications linkages. Although this split in supervisory responsibility has been troublesome for some departments in the early stages of their program, it is entirely workable and tends to smooth out with frequent contact and coordination between department officials and hospital personnel.

All calls for assistance in Profile A are conveyed to department units by the fire department dispatcher; however, the dispatcher receives the calls from a number of sources, including the local police department and local ambulance services (by means of telephone hot lines). This arrangement stems largely from tradition. Long before the advent of the paramedic service, the public had grown accustomed to calling the fire department for first aid assistance.

An important element in Profile A is the use of private ambulance services to provide patient transportation where needed. Although this feature tends to produce a clutter of emergency vehicles at the scene, it is a critical factor in the dual role use of firefighting personnel. In cases which are not life threatening the private ambulance services transport the patient to a hospital; thus, fire department units become available again upon arrival of the ambulance. In cases involving life-threatening medical problems one or both of the paramedics will accompany the patient in the ambulance with the ambulance crew. A member of the local engine or truck company will follow the ambulance to the hospital in the paramedic rescue vehicle.

At least one study has measured time factors involved in the transportation modes (where the fire department transports patients to the hospital) against time factors in the nontransporting mode (where private ambulances are used). Where a fire department rescue unit provided transport, the average time out of service per transport exceeded one hour. By contrast, the average time out of service where they were not obligated to transport was only twenty-three minutes.[12]

A viable private ambulance service is essential to a community's total health care needs. In the absence of this service, a public agency would be obligated to provide all nonemergency medical transportation, including convalescent transfers, interhospital transfers, and transportation of nonambulatory outpatients for periodic clinic appointments. These transportation functions can overwhelm an emergency rescue service very quickly. The financial stability of a private service can be strengthened if the service is used as a supplement to the fire department's EMS program.

Very few private ambulance services, however, can match the features of a fire department in delivering prehospital care. Troubled by excessive personnel turnover, a fragile economic base, and limited dispatch locations, most private ambulance services cannot serve a community's needs for first-response within five minutes of alarm and for the sequential delivery of sophisticated emergency medical services and personnel available through Profile A.

Training of EMS personnel in Profile A was conducted by the medical control hospital, which is affiliated with a university medical school. This training function is the primary responsibility of a qualified emergency physician (referred to as the *project medical director*) and of the medical education staff of the hospital. Training is continuous for paramedics, with daily reviews of medical incidents and monthly continuing education programs. By constantly monitoring performance, the project medical director has detected some instances of serious skill decay. In those cases, the director has mandated a period of retraining for those individuals—which has caused some extra salary expenses for the fire department. In a few instances the project medical director determined that a paramedic was "burned out" and has ordered that person removed from active duty as a paramedic. In such a case the individual has been reassigned to an engine or truck company. Under a contract between the hospital and the fire department such a decision is the sole responsibility of the project medical director and requires immediate compliance by the fire department. (The syndrome known as *paramedic burnout* is further discussed under Profile D.)

Financing of Profile A comes from the fire department budget, supplemented by funds generated from a federal grant. The dual role feature of this profile allows for the expanded service without involving an appreciable increase in the department's total budget. The supplemental funds have provided partial support for the purchase of medical care and communications equipment and of some rescue vehicles, and have helped with training costs incurred by the hospital.

Profile B Most of the features of Profile A are present in ths second operational alternative, with the main difference being the use in Profile B of transporting rescue ambulance vehicles. This feature has an impact on the entire service.

Although the department discussed here provides first-response and basic life support services in addition to the rescue ambulances staffed by paramedics, the out-of-service time for each incident tends to be longer. This is true for both the paramedic units and the engine or truck companies that may be first to arrive at the scene in most cases.

In addition to the greater out-of-service time (also mentioned under Profile A) the availability of public ambulance service tends to encourage greater public use of the service (including some degree of calculated abuse). Although Profiles A and B involve nearly identical population bases the department in Profile B can expect to receive nearly double the number of calls for assistance. (There is a charge for this service, but it has not discouraged inappropriate use of the system.)

Because of excess public demand, the fire department ambulance service is sometimes not available for immediate dispatch. This leaves the patient in the custody of the first-response engine or truck company until alternative arrangements for transportation can be made. This involves waiting for an available fire department rescue ambulance or calling a private ambulance. However, local private ambulance operators, because of loss of income, sharply reduced their number of vehicles in the area shortly after the fire department implemented its ambulance service, and delays often occur when the private units are called. This extended waiting period means that the engine or truck company at the scene is not available for either fire or medical emergency calls.

Technically the rescue ambulance paramedics are classed as dual role personnel: they are qualified firefighters who have been trained and certified as paramedics. In reality, however, they are seldom used in a firefighting capacity. The frequency of their medical calls makes it difficult to rely on their availability for fire suppression duties; furthermore, their vehicle is not equipped with ancillary fire protection equipment. However, they are eligible for promotion to higher ranks within the fire department and they may voluntarily leave their paramedic function for return to firefighter duty with an engine or truck company. This alternative has proved valuable to those individuals who have suffered the effects of nonstop alarm activity while serving as paramedics.

Although most of the rescue ambulances in Profile B respond from fire stations or from field assignments where they are available by radio, a few of the units are dispatched from medical control hospitals. This enables the paramedics to be involved in patient care functions and continuing education programs between alarms. In some localities operating under this profile, paramedics are rotated through assignments to hospital based units as a means of balancing the experience and education of the entire paramedic staff over a period of time. Although all EMS personnel in this profile are technically supervised by their respective fire company officers, those assigned to hospital based units are in fact quite detached from their supervisor. This detachment can create management problems and further supports the policy of rotating personnel through the hospital based units.

Although there are three methods of dispatch in this profile (hospital, public safety dispatcher, and fire department dispatcher), contact with EMS units and personnel comes from only two sources. The 911 or public safety dispatcher shares a dispatching facility with the fire dispatcher. When a call is received on the universal number (9–1–1) it is automatically referred to the fire dispatcher who then notifies the appropriate units. When hospital based paramedics are working or training within the hospitals, calls are relayed to them by the fire department dispatcher through the hospital operator and intercom system.

In the Profile B system the fire department training staff conducts basic life support (EMT) training programs in an attempt to train and certify every member of the department eventually. The medical control hospital cooperates with this program by providing a ten hour orientation in its emergency department for each trainee. The hospital assumes entire responsibility for paramedic training. As in Profile A, a medical director oversees the program and the continuing medical education staff of the hospital coordinates training and retraining programs for the paramedics.

The fire department's EMS program in Profile B is financed entirely by its budget. The establishment of the program was widely supported by the city council and budget increases were authorized accordingly. The hospital has been designated by the state as an official training center for paramedic training; in connection with this designation, it receives funding assistance from the state. The charge for ambulance service is collectible in less than 50 percent of all billings. Collectible revenue is deposited to the city's general fund.

Profile C   In this third profile the fire department does not provide advanced life support (paramedic) services; instead, it complements a municipal ambulance service and private ambulance services through immediate response of fire department units when a call for emergency medical assistance is received.

The limited nature of this fire department's services is a product of local history. Until recent years the fire department was headed by a fire chief who had spent many years in the department and was approaching retirement. Opportunities to add EMS to his department's responsibility were either spurned or ignored. In the meantime an election referendum was sponsored to provide tax resources for development of a separate municipal ambulance service which would include the training and implementation of paramedics. The issue was approved by voters and the municipal ambulance service was established as a separate branch of local government.

Although the municipal ambulance service is operational at the advanced life support level, it is limited to emergency care and transportation only. Thus, private ambulance services continue to provide nonemergency medical transportation. Despite authorized tax revenues for operation of the municipal ambulance service the number of available units is not adequate to provide consistent response times of five minutes or less to all sections of the jurisdiction.

With a change in fire department leadership came a greater willingness to accept EMS responsibility. The new fire chief recommended that his agency supplement the municipal ambulance service with first-response and basic life support services. Through mutual planning, an effective system of dual agency response has evolved.

In Profile C most calls for medical emergency assistance are received by the countywide public safety communications center (which utilizes the 911 emergency telephone number as well as seven-digit emergency numbers). The dispatcher simultaneously sends out the municipal ambulance service and notifies the fire dispatcher. The latter, in turn, notifies the fire station nearest the address of the emergency. Where the reported information suggests the need for extra manpower or special equipment, the fire department's special rescue vehicle is also dispatched.

In a majority of cases the local engine company will arrive first at the scene of the emergency. At least two members of each company have been trained to the level of emergency medical technician in eighty-one hour basic life support training programs. Where needed, basic life support is initiated by these personnel pending the arrival of the municipal ambulance with its paramedic unit. Through a common radio frequency the fire unit can communicate with the responding paramedics to advise them of conditions at the scene. Where the patient is stable and an emergency response is not warranted, this information is radioed to the paramedics and they proceed to the scene at normal traffic speeds.

Where the first arriving engine company determines that the case is nonemergency, the company officer is authorized to cancel the response of the paramedic unit. In such an instance a private ambulance is called to the scene and transportation must be paid for by the patient or the patient's insurer. A majority of cases are in fact nonemergency, and company officers have received special training to assist them in diplomatically handling those who may be distressed by the refusal to provide public ambulance service. In a case where there might be any question concerning the patient's true medical condition, the municipal ambulance paramedics continue to the scene and make a medical evaluation in communication with their medical control hospital.

Training of the fire department personnel has been accomplished through an arrangement between the fire department and a local community college. Fire department training officers were first trained and certified as EMT instructors. This training also included their certification as community college instructors. Thus, although the training is conducted on-duty in fire department facilities (except for the ten hour hospital internship), firefighters trained as EMTs in this program also receive college credit.

Since the fire department provides its first-response and basic life support services with dual role personnel, there has been no addition to its staff nor to its personnel budget. However, alarm activity has increased threefold since the cooperative program commenced. This has had some impact on vehicle replacement, vehicle maintenance, and operating budgets. All necessary basic life support equipment is purchased and maintained through the fire department budget.

A management problem peculiar to this profile concerns the frustration of firefighters who would prefer to operate at the advanced life support (paramedic) level. Many of the younger personnel express bitterness because their former chief did not pursue this possibility during his tenure. Though they realize that the municipal ambulance service (and its paramedic staff) is permanently in place they continue to push for an expansion in their role in EMS. In the early stages of the program this morale problem produced some personal confrontations between employees of the respective municipal agencies. Circumstances have improved, however, through skillful personnel management by administrators of both agencies.

Another factor in the resolution of firefighter impatience has been the gradual expansion of their training and skills to permit their active involvement in life-threatening medical emergencies. Training exercises conducted by the municipal ambulance paramedics at fire stations have been a major factor. Consequently, in most instances of cardiac arrest, severe trauma, or other serious emergencies the basic life support firefighters tend to serve as adjuncts to the paramedics, setting up intravenous equipment, manning the radiotelemetry unit, operating suction units, retrieving equipment, etc.

Profile D   This fourth example is the only fire department in the six profiles to use civilian (nonfirefighter) employees. The decision to establish an EMS service in the fire department was made by the mayor and the city council. The fire chief, responding to the mandate, recommended the establishment of a separate civilian-staffed EMS service within his department.

The factors leading to the fire chief's recommendation were several; among them was the department's high rating from the insurance industry's rating service. This rating was grounded largely on relatively heavy manning standards. The chief was adamant in maintaining his manpower complement and was unwilling to compromise by otherwise using those personnel committed to fire protection. He contended that acceptance of responsibility for the ambulance service would require him to employ additional personnel for that service (as opposed to using existing firefighters in a dual role).

The choice was narrowed down to the hiring of additional firefighters (to be committed to operating the ambulance service) or the hiring of civilians. Cost became the major factor in the ultimate decision. The chief concluded that he could employ civilians, have them trained to the paramedic level, and compensate them at a rate somewhat less than that paid his firefighters. His recommendations were accepted by the fire commission and the city council.

Exceptionally high quality recruits were obtained after a period of advertising and selection. Their initial training included a period of orientation conducted by the fire department's training staff. This was followed by a community college training program leading to certification as basic level EMTs. Finally, the trainees were committed to an extensive paramedic training program conducted by a university medical center hospital.

Existing fire stations were utilized as dispatch locations after systems analysis had determined optimum locations for the new ambulance units. The civilian paramedics were assigned to be supervised by fire company officers in those stations, although several veteran paramedics were recruited and employed as field EMS supervisors. A clear definition of the roles of those supervisors was never established.

In Profile D all alarms are transmitted to the paramedic units by the fire dispatcher, although some my originate with other public safety agencies that have telephone contact with the fire dispatcher. The paramedics operate rescue ambulances with patient transport capability. They respond from their respective fire station bases or in response to radio assignments from the fire dispatcher if they are in the field and available for calls.

If one of the paramedic ambulances is as close to the location of a reported emergency as the local engine company, or closer, then that ambulance is dispatched alone. If it is unavailable for a response or if a local engine company is closer to the scene, then the engine company is dispatched. However, engine

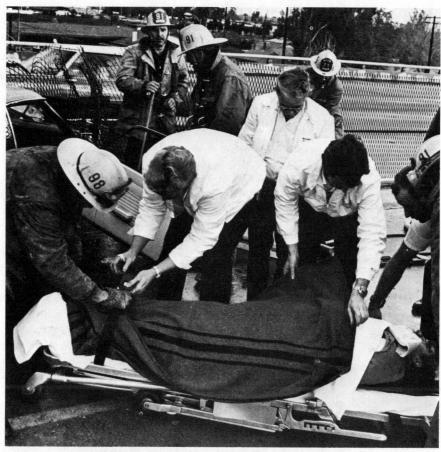

Figure 10–5   Close cooperation between paramedics and fire company personnel is important to patient care in many medical emergency situations. (Source: Mike Meadows photograph.)

company personnel are trained only to the level of Red Cross first aid. Although the department's firefighters are being trained in cardiopulmonary resuscitation, their skills in initial management of most critical cases are highly limited.

The dispatch profile of this department creates difficulties for the paramedic teams. For example, when they respond to a case of cardiac arrest without additional manpower assistance they have great difficulty in accomplishing the important invasive medical techniques required in the initial stages of the rescue effort. Recommendations for a universal medical emergency response by engine companies have not been accepted.

As with Profile B, the availability of public ambulance service tends to encourage greater public use and abuse of the service. And here, too, the charge for ambulance service does not appear to minimize this factor.

Again, as with Profile B, excess demand for the service produces frequent instances when an ambulance is not available for immediate dispatch. This leaves the patient in the custody of the local engine company personnel, who are limited by their marginal emergency care training. Transportation of the patient in such cases depends on the eventual arrival of a fire department ambulance unit or private ambulance called by the fire dispatcher. Until the arrival of an ambulance the engine company is unavailable for fire or medical emergency calls.

The fire department finances its paramedic ambulance service through its fire department budget, although initially supplemental funding was obtained from federal grant sources to train the personnel and equip their ambulance vehicles.

Although there is a charge for ambulance service, revenue derived from this charge recovers less than 30 percent of the costs of operation (owing to a relatively small charge and poor collection experience).

Although cost was a major factor in electing to employ civilians any salary savings have been erased by subsequent events. Early in their experience the civilian paramedics observed that their work load was considerably greater than that of their firefighter counterparts, and that their paramedic training was longer and more demanding than the recruit training of the firefighters who were compensated at a higher rate. The detached nature of the separate service was accompanied by a detached style of management on the part of the fire department. Paramedic equipment repairs were afforded a low priority. Paramedic grievances went without answer. Frustration rose as morale plummeted. In desperation and in anger the paramedics formed their own union and affiliated with a militant labor organization. The fire department was forced to deal with another bargaining agent. The paramedics' union successfully negotiated salaries which now exceed those of the firefighters.

In the meantime financial pressure has caused the city council to order across-the-board cuts in municipal agency budgets. In setting budget priorities the fire chief is aware that no cuts can be made in the overworked paramedic ambulance service. On the other hand his heavily manned fire companies are limited to the primary function of fire protection. Despite their responses as an adjunct to the paramedic units, the firefighting staff is in fact occupied by emergency activity for less than 5 percent of its on-duty time. As financial pressure increases, political enthusiasm for insurance rating designation weakens. Without the opportunity to make his firefighting staff more cost-effective, lacking the option of eliminating the paramedic ambulance service, and facing little political support for heavy manning of fire companies, the chief may be forced to reduce his manning standards as the only means of balancing a reduced budget.

The problems experienced by this department and its EMS service include underdesign, defective political and financial planning, negligent management of human resources, and lack of an escape route for overworked paramedics. Some sophisticated planning was undertaken to determine appropriate numbers and locations of paramedic ambulances, but political considerations were not included in the planning. It was presumed that all members of the city council would accept the limitation of service to true emergencies. In reality, political undercutting has limited the department in its efforts to operate the service as designed. To avoid political and budgetary retribution from council members (who express anger when a constituent is denied service) the service is forced to operate beyond its designed capacity. Inadequate numbers of ambulances and personnel are attempting to handle an excessive number of calls.

Failure to seriously plan for the special management problems of an EMS service have contributed to the poor morale and the labor–management turmoil evident in this example. (From the beginning there has been a presumption that the EMS service could be managed as the fire protection function has been for generations. No effort was made to consult with other fire departments that had experience in management of an EMS operation.) But nonstop emergency activity tends to limit the individual and collective tolerance and motivation of these paramedics. Attitude defects affect their handling of the public and tend to encourage lawsuits against the municipality for perceived negligence. Since the paramedics are civilian employees, they cannot transfer to a firefighting assignment. In essence, they have no escape route other than resignation from the department. The consequent syndrome has been described as *paramedic burnout*.[13]

Profile E   The fifth profile combines fire protection and emergency medical services in a unique blend of personnel and vehicle resources. The structure is

Paramedic burnout As fire departments have become involved in advanced life support programs, wherein firefighters have been trained to serve as paramedics, a number of new and unfamiliar problems have been experienced by program managers. Among the more perplexing of these is the problem generally referred to as *paramedic burnout.* However, the problem is not unique to fire departments nor to paramedics.

Burnout is an attitudinal syndrome frequently observed among allied health care workers whose duties include frequent responsibility for seriously ill or injured patients. It seems to be most frequent and pronounced among those workers whose occupational environment requires prompt actions, decisions, and judgments which may have life–death consequences for patients. Among nurses, for example, burnout appears to occur most frequently among those working in burn units, intensive care units, and emergency departments.

Among paramedics, symptoms of burnout generally include deterioration in job interest and in organizational loyalty. Abnormally low tolerance for management or supervisory judgments has been noted as a symptom, as well as increasing use of sick leave. A tendency to refer to certain patients in derogatory terms may signify elements of burnout, as may consistent failure to satisfy reporting requirements. One of the most serious symptoms appears to be a lessening of intellectual curiosity, as signified by diminished interest and reluctant participation in continuing education programs.

Among fire department paramedics the syndrome seems to be an individual phenomenon, with some individuals more susceptible than others. Although there has been no conclusive research on the syndrome at least one study identified stress among paramedics to be significantly higher than among their nonparamedic firefighter counterparts.[1]

It has been observed that management styles and internal organizational conflicts may contribute to the burnout syndrome. Where management has failed to communicate a strong commitment to the department's EMS program, paramedics may be subject to abusive comments and actions by their nonparamedic counterparts. Thus, while they are committed to a heavy work load and stressful performance in an emotion-charged atmosphere, they may be chided at the fire station for disrupting sleep, meals, and routine duties with their frequent alarms and responses.[2] As EMS becomes more of a traditional fire department function, this problem may decrease. In the meantime, management could help minimize the conflict by consistent and visible support for the EMS program.

Paramedic burnout challenges the perception that paramedics can and should serve in this role for their entire career. The lessons of nursing indicate that such a health care role may be relatively short. Fire department managers should consider this factor in designing a system profile that allows for a career escape route (i.e., an opportunity to promote or transfer) for paramedic personnel who suffer the syndrome. Also, it would seem advisable to budget for replacement personnel and training costs.

Source: The two references cited above are: (1) LaVerne M. Dutton et al., *Emergency Medical Services* 7 (September/October 1978): 88–95; (2) James O. Page, "Suddenly It's 1980," *Fire Chief,* June 1978, p. 48.

based on a selected number of fire stations designated to house *medic companies.* Each of these companies consists of a four person crew, with at least two trained and certified as advanced life support paramedics and the remaining members trained to the basic life support level. Each medic company is equipped with a standard fire pumper and a fully equipped paramedic ambulance vehicle. In addition to their medical care training, all assigned personnel are fully qualified firefighters. One of the four serves as the company officer while another serves as the assigned driver (classed as *engineer*).

All alarms received by medic companies are transmitted through the fire dispatcher, although some calls are forwarded to the fire dispatcher by a public safety communications center. In the event of a fire alarm all four members of a medic company respond on the pumper, leaving the ambulance in the station unmanned. During the period of unavailability, any fire or medical emergencies occurring within the medic company's first-in district are handled by adjacent companies.

In the event of a medical emergency all four members of the medic company respond on the paramedic ambulance. Again, any emergencies occurring in their district while they are unavailable are handled by adjacent companies.

This profile has several advantageous features. For example, it provides a full four person crew for handling medical emergencies (which outnumber fire alarms on a three to one basis). In addition, the system was implemented without additional personnel. Also, it allows paramedics to achieve promotions without leaving the advanced life support service. In this way it is possible for the company officer and the driver of a medic company to be paramedics (having been promoted from the firefighter ranks).

The medic company profile may be limited in its application to those locales with dense populations and compact boundaries. It depends on the availability of prompt response by fire companies in adjacent districts. To avoid overuse it should be limited to emergency cases only. Private ambulance services should be available to transport nonemergency cases, to allow prompt availability of medic companies at the conclusion of a medical emergency response.

This city also operates a number of standard fire companies. When medical emergencies occur in the districts of those companies, the medic company must respond from a distant location. Where that response is likely to take more than four minutes, it is recommended that the standard fire company be trained and equipped to serve in a first-response role. Upon arrival of the medic company the first-response unit would be immediately available (owing to the four person staff on the paramedic ambulance). When personnel of the first-response company are trained to the EMT level they may be capable of triage, which would enable them to cancel the response of the medic company where the case did not require emergency assistance.

Personnel in this system have been trained in a program conducted by a local hospital which is affiliated with a university medical school. The physician who supervised the training is on the faculty of the medical school and serves as the fire department's medical adviser. His authority to monitor paramedic skills and correct apparent deficiencies is informal but is readily acknowledged by the administration of the fire department.

Budgetary requirements related to the EMS service include the salaries of individuals working in the place of trainees during the paramedic training program. Otherwise, no additional personnel have been hired. Purchase, maintenance, and replacement of vehicles are costs borne by the fire department budget. Training costs (other than trainee salaries) are absorbed by the medical school, which is funded by state government. Overall, the cost of the EMS service is less than 5 percent of the total fire department budget.

Profile F This last example is the only one of the six profiles to use the services of volunteers. In this particular community the volunteer ambulance service is an ingrained element of local tradition. The volunteer organization enjoys the respect and financial support of the community. It has provided ambulance service for nearly twenty-five years and in recent years has expanded that service to include mobile intensive care given by certain of its members who have been trained as paramedics.

Until recent years the fire department was a separate and distinct volunteer entity. However, with rapid growth of the population and tax base the department has been converted to a paid fire service, supplemented by volunteers in cases of major fires.

Until the volunteer ambulance service was upgraded to the paramedic level, there was no cooperative arrangement between that group and the fire department. Calls for medical assistance were handled exclusively by the ambulance service. From its beginnings the volunteer service has provided both emergency and nonemergency medical transportation. This factor is related to the relative success of the volunteers' annual fund drive, which involves door-to-door solicitations.

As the ambulance service became more sophisticated its medical director recognized the need for basic life support service as an adjunct to the paramedic service. All of the volunteer service's ambulances respond from a single central location (either a fire station or a hospital). Average response times to some locations in the community exceed eight minutes. On the advice of the medical director the fire department was approached with the proposal that its units be used for a first-response function in cooperation with the volunteers.

The fire department responded positively to the proposal and has trained its entire staff to the level of EMT. Dispatch procedures have been revised to provide for an immediate response by the nearest engine or truck company simultaneous with the dispatch of the volunteer ambulance service. Upon arrival at the scene firefighter EMTs commence basic life support actions where necessary. Since the volunteers transport in cases of both emergency and nonemergency, the fire companies will cancel the ambulance response only in the event of a false alarm.

The volunteers' skill maintenance program requires each paramedic to engage in continuing education programs at his or her medical control hospital. While engaged in these programs they are available for emergency response from that location. Fire department first-response units, however, are dispatched from their fire stations or from the field when notified by radio.

The volunteers are dispatched by a public safety communications center which is accessible through a 911 emergency telephone number. Since the fire department has commenced its first-response function, citizens have increasingly tended to call the fire dispatcher to report medical emergencies. Cooperative arrangements have been developed to relay calls immediately and facilitate dispatch of appropriate units without delay.

Training of the firefighters to the EMT level has been conducted jointly by the fire department training staff and a local community college. The paramedics' medical control hospital provides the ten hour clinical experience for the trainees and has developed a continuing education program to prepare the firefighter EMTs for periodic recertification, as required by state law. Training of the fire department personnel has been complemented by the state government. Programs conducted by the state EMS agency include special extrication courses and refresher training for EMTs. These programs are mobile and are conducted while the firefighters are on duty.

The fire department's EMS component has required no additional personnel. Costs for the service are limited to increases in vehicle and equipment replacement, in maintenance, and in operational budgets. Basic life support equipment used by the firefighter EMTs has been provided by the state EMS agency.

In the early stages of the program the firefighters and the volunteers experienced occasional divisiveness over their respective roles. Some of the younger firefighters were frustrated by the limits of their basic life support service. Later, however, they were given the opportunity to join the volunteer unit and train as paramedics in their off-duty time. Several accepted the offer. When these firefighters are on duty with the fire department their role is limited to basic life support, but their specialized knowledge and skills are valuable to the volunteer paramedics when both agencies are present at the scene of a life-threatening emergency.

In recent years many volunteer organizations have shown a strong interest in providing advanced life support services with specially trained volunteer paramedics. However, competent and experienced advice would point to some sobering realities.

For example, most volunteer fire or ambulance organizations must maintain a large roster of personnel in order to provide adequate emergency response coverage. Volunteer services usually exist in rural or suburban areas with a relatively low volume of calls for emergency services. The combination of large numbers of volunteers and a relatively low call volume results in a limited number of actual emergency events for each volunteer member.

Initial training of volunteers as paramedics is another limiting factor. Despite some early training programs that were short in duration and limited to cardiac problems, a national standard for paramedic training has evolved which calls for in-depth training in a variety of medical emergency disciplines.[14] Deviation from this standard presents serious potential for legal problems and also undermines a local community's potential for federal EMS funding assistance.

The national experience with paramedics has clearly demonstrated that the important skills of well-trained paramedics diminish quickly without frequent involvement in significant medical emergency situations. The typical demographic environment in which volunteers work seldom presents opportunities for such frequent involvement. Furthermore, a large number of trained volunteers must share those infrequent opportunities, which limits individual experience. Although less desirable than actual field experience, ongoing training in a hospital is used to counter skill decay among underutilized paramedics in some locations. However, since volunteers are already committed to their primary employment—not to mention responsibilities to home and family—the burden of such ongoing training is unacceptable in many cases. Finally, the stability of a volunteer organization is affected by extraneous factors: for example, transfers or changes of employment can remove a trained volunteer from the community after considerable time and resources have been devoted to his or her training.

All in all, it is a rare community that can implement an advanced life support service with volunteers, but, on the other hand, enough communities have succeeded in this task to prove that it is possible.

An assessment of the sample operational profiles   From the foregoing analysis of six distinct profiles of EMS involvement for fire departments, managers will recognize that there is no single set of features that is appropriate for all agencies. Community history and tradition tend to affect the design of EMS within a local fire department. Other organizations and agencies may have preempted the field of service or parts of it. Design may be affected by the availability of ancillary services such as dispatching by a public safety communications center. The size, shape, and function of a fire department EMS component may be affected by the size, strength, and affiliation of local hospitals. Political influences are likely to affect the design where decisions must receive the sanction of a city council or other policymaking body. The nature and availability of supplemental funding would be yet another influential factor.

While, as mentioned earlier, the six profiles represent composites of actual fire service experiences, the profiles come close enough to actual experiences to furnish some valuable lessons.

Level of service/training   For example, it should be noted that each of the six examples provides first-response and basic life support services. This factor is related to location and mobility of fire department resources. Although some police agencies have trained and equipped their officers and patrol units for this function, a paid fire department is difficult to match in its ability to deliver trained personnel to the scene of a medical emergency within a very few minutes.

In all but one of the examples fire departments provide advanced life support services as well. This does not reflect actual national ratios; however, during the late 1970s increasing numbers of fire departments were upgrading their EMS response to include the paramedic level of service. As indicated in the examples, this move changes the entire complexion of a department's EMS responsibilities. Inherent in this move is the requirement for medical control (discussed in greater detail later in this chapter).

Response vehicles The use of fire apparatus (pumpers and trucks) for EMS response has increased greatly in recent years. As indicated in Profile A, paramedic pumpers are a feasible approach. In at least one location small rescue vehicles were eliminated and the department placed its paramedics and their equipment on aerial ladder trucks. According to the chief of that department, numerous advantages are available in this approach.[15] However, in this and other nontransporting modes cooperative arrangements with private ambulance services are necessary.

Figure 10–6 Nontransporting rescue vehicles used in some locations are equipped for medical emergencies, rescue operations, and fire protection functions.

The issue of patient transportation is critical to every EMS operation. As indicated by the examples, a fire department's assumption of patient transport responsibility includes some serious burdens. In nearly every location the provision of public ambulance service is hindered by public abuse. This abuse includes demand for service in cases where a true emergency does not exist. It is also found in widespread refusal to pay a charge (however minimal) for the service. There appears to be a public attitude that the service should be freely available and should be fully supported by tax sources.

The fire department assumption of emergency ambulance service requires clearly articulated policy from the local body of elected policymakers. In seeking a statement of policy, city management should be very candid as to the nature and intent of the service and the potential for constituent complaints when transportation service is denied in nonemergency cases. A lack of political commitment signals the potential for an overused service that will produce innumerable management and operational problems.

In five of the six profiles, private ambulance services are used (in varying degrees) for patient transportation. Such a cooperative arrangement can serve a variety of needs although the response pattern may appear uncoordinated. In addition to the advantages of cooperation with private ambulance services, there are a number of problems to be anticipated.

Generally speaking, private ambulance services are marginal business enterprises. Often they are owned and operated by individuals with limited management competence. Ambulance attendants employed by private services usually work very long weeks for little more than a legal minimum wage. Generally they tend to be young people who depart the field of ambulance service when an opportunity for higher income appears. Personnel turnover among private ambulance services ranges from 20 percent to 100 percent per year. Throughout the nation, cooperative arrangements between fire departments and private ambulance services have been tenuous at best. On an organized basis, the private ambulance industry has consistently and vocally opposed fire service involvement in EMS. That animosity has been carried into the working environment, resulting in detrimental confrontations while the parties have been engaged in patient care and transportation.

Difficulties between the two sectors have led some jurisdictions to completely displace the private services with a public ambulance service. However, as indicated by the foregoing profiles, the burdens inherent in such an endeavor tend to outweigh any benefits. In a few locations enlightened fire service administrators have pursued better working relations with private ambulance providers despite periodic eruptions. Where an appropriate attitude of maturity and common sense can be instilled throughout the fire department, the attitudinal flaws in a public–private cooperative arrangement are surmountable.

Civilian employees Among the examples presented, the most perplexing set of difficulties is to be found in Profile D, the only example to use civilian employees of the fire department. This should not suggest that use of civilian employees is universally unwise. However, it points to several problems that arise from such a situation.

One problem is that there can be little justification for limiting full-time paid firefighters to the single role of firefighting. Contemporary economics in local government would demand that optimum use be made of public employees' available time. There is abundant evidence that properly trained and motivated firefighters can be trained to provide both fire protection and EMS services without compromise to either.[16] In one location, which operates one of the nation's busiest fire rescue units (staffed by dual role firefighters trained as paramedics), the combination of fire and EMS activity occupies only 13.3 percent of the on-duty time of the personnel assigned to the unit.[17] Where EMS activity is specifically assigned to an entire new body of civilian personnel, questions remain concerning justification for the unproductive time of the single role force of firefighters.

In some locations the thrust for civilian EMS employees has been fed by discussion of the need for a career ladder. Presumably, a new administrative structure within the fire department would provide promotional opportunities for the civilian employees while maintaining their occupational involvement in the emergency care service. In reality, however, supervisory vacancies would occur only in the event of death, discharge, or retirement. The vast majority of personnel would remain at the working level throughout their career.

The special position of paramedics Long-term commitment to the working level has special significance for a paramedic operating in an urban environment. Growing public awareness and demand for advanced life support services means that most urban paramedics are engaged in nonstop emergency activity during almost every duty shift. The realities of this duty involve high levels of stress for most paramedics. It is believed that this stress is the product of frequent operation of an EMS vehicle under emergency conditions, operation in the undisciplined and emotional environment of an emergency scene under the watchful eyes of numerous observers, the need for uncommon skill in dealing with distraught patients and their families, and the requirement for immediate life or death judgments in handling serious medical emergencies. Stress is compounded where paramedics are subject to physical abuse and injury when dealing with drug and intoxication cases or while operating amid crowds of unruly spectators. Stress is aggravated when fire department administration fails to be sensitive to paramedics' special needs, or when their medical control hospital is unresponsive.

The problems of the urban paramedic may be likened to those of a critical care or burn care nurse. In those occupations there is a common syndrome which limits the duration of viable performance in a stressful environment. During the late 1970s, urban paramedics began to display symptoms referred to as paramedic burnout (discussed earlier in this chapter). For those paramedics so affected who are committed to a dual role an escape route exists through reassignment to a firefighting role. Others escape the rigors of their paramedic assignment through successful competition in promotional exams. Civilian paramedics employed by a fire department, on the other hand, seldom have an effective escape route other than resignation from the department.

It might be suggested that there is some degree of waste in training personnel for a paramedic role that may be limited to a few years of performance. However, as in the nursing profession, the cost of training replacement paramedics may reveal itself as a cost of doing business. Most important is the fallacy of retaining personnel in a stressful role after they have begun to exhibit irreversible signs of burnout. To the extent that the dual role approach provides an occupational avenue of escape without complete severance of a career it may be seen as preferable to the civilian paramedic concept.

Where paramedics are removed from their emergency care role (by promotion or reassignment), the question will occur as to the relative wisdom of expensive training programs in preparation for short tenure. However, where a fire department's EMS response resembles any of the six profiles described above, the suspicion of waste can be qualified.

When a firefighter paramedic is promoted to an officer's position, assignment is likely to be made to a local fire company. If that company is involved in first-response activities the promoted paramedic will bring an extra degree of skill and experience to the job. Those skills and that experience will have relevance to the provision of basic life support pending arrival of a paramedic unit, and they will be helpful in the form of another set of trained hands to assist paramedics after their arrival at the scene. The same benefits can accrue in the case of paramedics who have burned out and are reassigned to fire companies.

As evidenced by Profiles A and E, there exists an opportunity in some departments to reorganize in an effort to retain the value of paramedic training and experience after promotions occur. This can occur through assignment of promoted paramedics to paramedic pumper/truck companies or to a medic company. In considering profiles for optimum use of skill and experience, it is important to note that most fire departments with EMS involvement find that medical emergencies represent the majority of alarms received. Although the agency may be officially designated as a fire department, the community sees its service role as being much broader. Many of the EMS implementation and management difficulties experienced by fire departments relate to a lack of relevant background on the part of fire department administrators. The situation is analogous to that of fire protection services that are organized and managed by a medical doctor who has no background in firefighting. In the future, however, if promotional opportunities are afforded to firefighter EMTs and paramedics they will become the next generation of fire chiefs and they will bring to their position relevant experience in both fire protection and emergency medical care.

The question of direction

Direction of a fire department's EMS functions is one of the most sensitive issues to be dealt with by local government decision makers. In many instances direction is split between medical considerations and operational prerogatives. This split is most significant with regard to advanced life support services delivered by paramedics. In order to understand the points of division it is necessary to clearly recognize prehospital advanced life support services as an outreach function of the medical control hospital. This perception should be distinguished from the view of paramedic services as a local government or private ambulance function which merely uses a hospital for guidance.

The concept of medical control The current concept of medical control in EMS has grown from the actual experience of paramedic operations throughout the country. Many of the earlier programs were established without the advantage of clear conceptual understanding. Medical and operational problems growing out of those operations resulted in federal and state requirements for medical control of paramedic operations. Subsequently, most such operations have been developed as hospital outreach programs, using employees of another agency (such as a fire department) as surrogates of a designated physician at the medical control hospital (or as that physician's authorized representatives).

The concept of medical control has created some discomfort for fire officials, hospitals, and physicians. In essence, fire chiefs are required to relinquish some degree of control over their employees. The physician at the medical control hospital (often referred to as the project medical director) is required to assume responsibility for someone else's employees in certain situations. The hospital itself may be required to stand behind the fire department's paramedics and even insure against any possible negligence in their medical performances. In addition, the hospital may find it necessary to devote some of its personnel and resources to training paramedics who are not on the hospital's payroll.

Despite its unorthodox aspect, the concept of medical control has proved itself in locations throughout the United States. Moreover, it is a reflection of long-established legal principles. Legal precedents dating back to 1826 have dealt with the issues of vicarious liability,[18] respondeat superior (employer responsibility for employee negligence),[19] and the ''borrowed servant'' (borrowed employee; discussed later in this section)[20] situations found in the concept of medical control.

The medical control hospital A major element in the modern concept of medical control is the designation of one or more hospitals in a community to serve as medical control hospitals (often referred to as resource hospitals or base station hospitals). Given the responsibilities attached to such a designation, it is important that a hospital be so designated solely on the basis of its ability and willingness to carry out those responsibilities. In some of the earlier EMS programs excessive numbers of hospitals were equipped with radio and telemetry gear and were then presumed to be fulfilling their role by merely communicating with

EMTs and paramedics during the management of medical emergencies. The flaws in this perception were revealed as it became obvious that no single hospital or medical professional had the ultimate responsibility for training, skill maintenance, continuing education, medical auditing, and system coordination. Moreover, in such a situation no single hospital had come to grips with the issue of legal and financial indemnification of paramedics who might be charged with negligence by civil litigants.

Designation as a medical control hospital tends to carry a degree of prestige, even though the burdens of the designation generally outweigh any benefits. Thus, in most communities there is intense competition among hospitals for this role. The actual designation process should be conducted by a regional or community EMS coordinating agency, using appropriate criteria.[21] The final designation of one or more hospitals should be made by a broad-based health-related committee or council after review of written proposals submitted by each of the competing hospitals. This final designation should be based entirely on the relative ability of the hospital or hospitals to meet or exceed the criteria established for the medical control function.

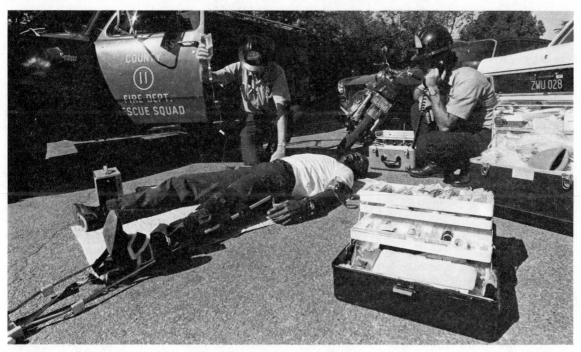

Figure 10–7   In cases of traumatic injury, paramedics must be trained to immobilize fractures and treat shock under orders of their medical control hospital.

The project medical director   Another major element in the medical control concept is the designation of a fully qualified physician to serve as project medical director at the medical control hospital. In this regard, fully qualified should include unquestionable competence and experience in all phases of emergency medicine. Preferably this person should be a full-time emergency physician and should have department head status over the emergency department at the medical control hospital.

The project medical director needs to be armed with sufficient authority to effect necessary changes in the hospital's operations, including the mandating of improved emergency care skills on the part of physicians and nurses working in the emergency department. The authority should extend to coordination with other hospitals in the community to assure that patients treated by paramedics and transported to these other hospitals receive appropriate care in all cases.

The project medical director will need full access to the resources necessary for initial training of EMTs and paramedics, and for skill maintenance and continuing education programs. Through daily reviews of run reports and medical records, the project medical director needs to make every effort to detect faulty care or defective skills or judgment on the part of prehospital and in-hospital personnel, and he or she should have the authority for such review and for correcting any deficiencies.

Through formal contracts with prehospital provider agencies (such as the local fire department), the project medical director should be given authority to direct EMTs and paramedics into retraining programs where these are deemed necessary. Such contracts should also authorize the director to mandate the removal of personnel from emergency care positions where their skills, knowledge, attitudes, or performances are deemed medically inappropriate to the responsibilities.

The legal principles Under the concept of medical control, service providers and the medical control hospital are governed by the legal principles referred to above (vicarious liability, respondeat superior, the "borrowed servant"). One authoritative source has described the basic principle as follows:

A servant (employee) directed or permitted by his master (employer) to perform services for another may become the servant (employee) of such other in performing the services. He may become the other's servant (employee) as to some acts and not as to others.[22]

Restated in contemporary terms, it may be said that the medical control hospital desires to improve its service to the community by providing prehospital care in the form of advanced life support performed by paramedics. However, in that the hospital lacks the resources to actually deliver those prehospital services, it must rely on another agency to provide the necessary personnel, dispatching, vehicle, and structural resources (such as the local department). When the employees of that other agency are engaged in patient evaluation and care functions they are performing as "servants" (employees) of the hospital. Thus, as with all of its own agents and employees, the hospital has a need to protect its patients and itself against negligent or otherwise defective performance. This reality supports the medical control hospital's right to assert its standards of quality through the training, monitoring, and continuing education of paramedics employed by another agency.

The guiding legal principles, then, hold that one may become the "servant" of another as to some acts and not others. It is obvious that fire department paramedics would not be under appropriate control of the medical control hospital other than when they were in direct contact with patients, or during preparation for their patient care role (training). At all other times these personnel should be viewed as being within the operational control of their principal employer (the fire department).

Supporting the applicable legal principles is the persuasive fact of community reliance on its hospitals as the focal point of health care quality. Certainly no informed citizen would expect its fire department or private ambulance service to make judgments as to the relative quality of emergency health care performance. In the same way a firefighters' labor organization which might be offended by the power of the project medical director should be reminded that that physician and the hospital he or she is responsible to have the ultimate legal, moral, and professional responsibility for health care quality. No other public agency, committee, community organization, or employee representative group is qualified to make judgments as to the quality of medical professional or paraprofessional performance. Even if such an entity were to assert itself in this role of monitoring quality, it undoubtedly would not wish to be in the role of civil defendant when a performance defect results in injury or death.

The need for adjustment   In the six system profiles presented in this chapter, the operational direction of the fire department paramedics is delegated to the company officer. There is abundant evidence that company officers—even without paramedic training—can adequately perform this supervisory task.

Traditional approaches to fire department and fire company supervision may need to be altered to some degree to meet the special requirements of an EMS program. The nature of most fire department EMS operations will tend to reduce the traditional close contact between company officers and their subordinates. This factor together with the division of loyalties between the fire department and the medical control hospital may prove a disturbing experience for company officers and their supervisors.

Overall, it would appear that operational difficulties have been generated by one or the other of two extreme approaches. In one such approach there is an effort to oversupervise the EMS personnel: for example, an officer may interfere in patient care situations for which the officer is neither qualified nor trained. Occasionally such an attitude manifests itself in the restrictive tethering of EMS personnel to the fire company: refusing to allow paramedics to leave the station with their vehicle to attend an interesting continuing education program at the hospital would be an example. Another example would be making paramedics responsible for station maintenance chores despite their obligation to answer many more alarms than their firefighter counterparts answer.

The other extreme approach appears to be an attitude of official insulation from those personnel assigned to the EMS function. This attitude was inherent in the problems discussed in Profile D. Where the department's administrators fail to communicate the importance of the EMS component, disregard and contempt are likely to filter down through the ranks. In such instances the EMS personnel tend to feel rejected by their department and an imbalance of loyalties is a common result.

Despite such difficulties the national experience suggests that the majority of fire departments involved in EMS have succeeded in mastering appropriate direction of the operational aspects of the program. As more firefighter EMTs and paramedics rise through the promotional ranks it is likely that their supervisory and management techniques will reflect their background and experience in both aspects of their department's mission.

A political and professional minefield?

In 1977 a prestigious national publication referred to emergency medical services as a "political and professional minefield."[23] Those who have labored in the EMS field will recognize that assessment as reasonably accurate. EMS, in the context of a comprehensive emergency care system, usually involves some reorganization of existing roles, territories, and procedures. The comfort and security of tradition and status quo are often disturbed by the organizational and operational needs of an EMS system.

A diverse set of elements   EMS involves a diverse set of individuals, agencies, organizations, and institutions. There is no single organizational umbrella that employs and directs every person who must serve the immediate needs of an emergency patient throughout the sequence of emergency care and transportation. For example, a public utility telephone company may be responsible for establishing and maintaining an emergency telephone system. Calls generated by that service may be received by employees of a public agency not affiliated with the telephone company. That public agency may, upon receipt of a call for assistance, activate the response of one or more other organizations (such as a fire department, a police department, and a private ambulance company). The roles of the respective response agencies must be predetermined and the employees of those agencies must be adequately skilled in those roles.

Training of the prehospital emergency personnel may be the assigned role of still another organization or institution. Medical direction of these personnel, as well as monitoring of their medical performance, is likely to be the responsibility of a private physician who may be bound by contract to a hospital. That hospital is still another entity in the scenario. Its roles are likely to be multiple and can encompass provision of acute emergency care, ambulatory care for the less-than-acute emergency patient, long-term care for the seriously ill or injured, and rehabilitation services for those who survive their medical crises.

To the extent that local government perceives a responsibility in EMS, elected officials may assert their collective will on the system from time to time. In addition, they may be expected to provide financial resources to support certain segments of the EMS system.

Local health planning agencies are still another element in the system, as they seek to assure maximum public access to emergency care services within reasonable cost limits. Where a locality is within a federally funded EMS project area, another entity will be working to influence the size, shape, and function of the system and its many elements.

In most communities there is little chance that so many diverse elements would ever come under a single management entity—nor is there any valid reason to believe that long-term benefits would result from such a consolidation. It is all the more important, then, that these various elements be coordinated toward the essential focal point—the needs of the emergency patient. In most cases the relative success of such coordination will determine the relative success of the EMS system in reaching its performance goals.

Coordination: the need for planning   Cooperation in EMS is fragile and requires constant attention. When it is a planned endeavor, pursued on a regular basis, coordination can become a method of controlling events rather than being controlled by them. But when coordination is viewed merely as a response to crisis, it is likely to affect emergency care services adversely while, at the same time, continually diverting key policymakers and managers from the goals of creativity and stability.

In smaller fire departments coordination of the department's EMS functions within the community is likely to be the responsibility of the chief or one of the chief's key subordinates. In many larger departments the coordination function may be assigned to an EMT or paramedic who has been promoted to the rank of officer. Although it is not absolutely necessary, it has proved of value to assign the coordination function to individuals who have served (or are currently serving) in an actual patient care role. Such experience in the system lends credibility to the individual in his or her efforts to coordinate with other service providers.

Where a fire department assigns one of its members to coordinate its EMS function with the rest of the EMS community, it is essential that that individual possess authority commensurate with responsibility. Diligent commitment to planning is of great help in this regard. Where a department's EMS planning is thorough and continuous, all potential policy conflicts will be anticipated and strategies can be devised in advance for use by the EMS coordinator. On the other hand, a crisis-oriented approach to EMS coordination will leave the fire department's coordinator without any guidance in dealing with the day-to-day ebb and flow of organizational interrelationships; instead, the coordinator will be obligated to serve as a messenger of crisis and reaction between the fire department and the other elements of the system.

The fire department–hospital relationship   One of the key roles of the fire department's EMS coordinator stems from the department's unique relationship with the medical control hospital and the project medical director. The potential problems of perception and cooperation are endless. To compound the difficulties, the project medical director may take a possessive stance with regard to fire department employees trained as paramedics. In such circumstances the paramedics often become pawns in a reactionary battle for loyalty and operational prerogatives. Where this situation is not appropriately managed the fire department may tend to step into the arena of medical judgments and the project medical director may tend to venture into operational policy. A most effective means of preventing such a dilemma lies in role sharing.

In some of the more successful EMS programs emergency physicians are given frequent opportunities to spend periods of duty with paramedics in their operational environment. For an emergency physician concerned with fire department paramedics, this experience should include spending time at fire stations between alarms, as well as watching dual role paramedics performing as firefighters in actual situations. After such experience a physician may find most of the fire department's policy prerogatives reasonable and acceptable.

Where a fire department's EMS personnel must rely on emergency nurses in their relationships with hospitals, these nurses should also be given the opportunity to join the paramedics in their environment. In addition contributing to mutual understanding, the physician–nurse "ride-along" programs provide an opportunity for assessment of their own skills in the real world of prehospital care.

Fire service administrators may also find their relations with medical control hospitals and medical professionals strained by seemingly worthless mandates issued by those sources. Those fire service administrators would do well to orient themselves to the operational environment of the hospital emergency department and its staff. Basic level EMTs must spend at least ten hours in an emergency department internship as part of their training. Paramedic trainees often spend hundreds of hours in their clinical internship. Their fire department superiors would benefit from such first-hand observation, and could gain a better understanding of the circumstances which produce conflicting views on how best to deliver services. In EMS, as in all areas of interpersonal relationships, merely talking to a potential adversary on his or her own turf can be a simple and effective method of preventing conflict.

Planning as an essential management function   Where EMS is a solid commitment of a fire department, and where that commitment is clearly communicated from the top, coordination of the function within the department should operate as a matter of course.

Once again, planning is an essential ingredient. If used before implementation of the EMS service and on a continuous basis after implementation, planning can identify potential conflicts within the agency and strategies can be effected to minimize or prevent such conflicts. This is largely a matter of organizational attitude. In nearly every fire department there will be personnel who strongly believe that a fire department's role should be limited to fire protection. Unless there is strong and consistent evidence of top level policy to the contrary, pockets of resistance and interference will surface to produce problems that could have been prevented.

While some of the most vocal opponents of fire department EMS programs have been found within the fire service, experience has shown that such resistance can be penetrated and that equally strong supporters can arise from the ranks of the resistants. Such a conversion can result from a program of internal orientation. The command structure of a fire department can serve as the most effective mechanism for such orientation. (It may be found necessary to conduct training programs for management employees to prepare them for the orientation task.) It is important for managers to always keep in mind the fact that support and clarity will have to flow from the top if the program is to function successfully.

Evaluation

One of the words heard most frequently in the EMS field is *evaluation*. In essence, it merely means the examination of a specific function to determine whether that function is producing the desired results. It is obvious, then, that *the desired results* must be identified. These results will have been stated as goals (What do we want to accomplish?) in the initial stages of the planning process (Figure 10–1). Also, it is obvious that reported information (data) will be necessary to measure performance. When the data (in the form of system outcomes) are measured against the goals (and the objectives formulated under those goals), there will be an opportunity to evaluate the program and its performance.

The primary goal of a comprehensive EMS system is to reduce unnecessary death and disability through improved emergency care and transportation. The measurement of performance against this goal is referred to as *patient outcomes:* that is, How many patients survived who would have died without the proper functioning of the system? There are many sophisticated variables in this form of system evaluation and they tend to be beyond the scope of a fire department's effort to evaluate its components of the system.

Factors for evaluation in the fire department's EMS component would include average response times for EMS units, relative availability of units to respond when needed, safety and maintenance factors in the operations of department vehicles in EMS activity, relative performance of department employees in EMS training programs, and relative durability of department employees in their respective EMS-related roles. However, for purposes of evaluation these and other factors must be stated in terms of measurable goals and objectives from the outset. To measure an end product or result without a starting-point reference is one dimensional and offers no basis for comparison.

Evaluation is represented by the broken line segment of the continuous planning process illustrated in Figure 10–1. It is the segment of the process that makes it cyclical and continuous. For example, if a fire department's goal is to provide an average response time of four minutes or less for all medical emergencies, that goal should be identified from the outset. If the first year's performance discloses an average response time of 4.5 minutes, either the objective or the approach to achieving that objective must be revised. Or if a department's goal is to graduate 80 percent of all paramedic trainees from the paramedic training program, that goal should be identified and stated prior to initiating the program. If the experience discloses that only 75 percent of all trainees are graduating, it may be a sign that admission criteria need to be strengthened or that the department's recruitment standards are inappropriate to its full range of emergency services. On the other hand, such a disclosure may indicate defects in the training program or in its testing procedures. In any event, either the objective or the approach to achieving the objective must be revised as a planning function.

As has been mentioned, continuous planning is at the heart of a well-designed and properly functioning EMS system or component of that system. And it should be noted that the planning techniques employed in the EMS activity are fully applicable to all fire department functions. The successful manager is a successful planner who controls events instead of being controlled by them.

Conclusion and outlook

In recent years the role of the American fire service has expanded to meet community needs for improved emergency medical services. This development coincides with and is related to advancements in emergency medical technology and the modern philosophy of delivering sophisticated life support services at the scene of the medical emergency and during transportation of the patient to a medical facility. The expansion of the fire service role also coincides with growing economic pressure to use the available time of fire protection personnel more effectively. Although numerous problems arise in this evolutionary process, skillful planning and good management can produce optimum results in improved public service.

The future is not likely to hold any relief from the pressure of limited municipal finances. Public demand for increased services is likely to continue, placing responsibility on local government to make cost-effective use of public employees. Use of fire department resources, including personnel, in the delivery of prehospital emergency care and transportation services is likely to increase as a result of these conflicting pressures.

A new generation of fire service managers can be expected to emerge as dual role personnel rise through the ranks with broadened expectations and abundant practical experience in service delivery. Properly managed, the merger of EMS with traditional fire service responsibilities can contribute to a healthy future for tomorrow's fire departments.

1 See: National Academy of Sciences, National Research Council, *Accidental Death and Disability: The Neglected Disease of Modern Society* (Washington, D.C.: National Academy of Sciences, September 1966).

2 J. Frank Pantridge, "A Mobile-Intensive Care Unit in the Management of Myocardial Infaction," *Lancet* (2: 1967): 271.

3 James O. Page, "Why Fire Fighters?" *Fire Command,* August 1972, pp. 28–31.

4 Leonard B. Rose and Edward Press, "Cardiac Defibrillation by Ambulance Attendants," *Journal of the American Medical Association* 219 (3 January 1972): 64.

5 "'3rd Services' Giving 31% of Paramedic Care," *Emergency Care News* [Published monthly by Public Technology, Inc., Washington, D.C., for the Emergency Medical Services Technical Assistance Program], October 1977, p. 1.

6 Research report prepared by the Harold Hayes Research Organization for *Fire Chief,* 1977.

7 Joe Slotkin and Elliot Salenger, "National 'Paramedic' Survey," *Paramedics international* 1 (Summer 1976): 14.

8 See: R. Adams Cowley, "The Resuscitation and Stabilization of Major Multiple Trauma Patients in a Trauma Center Environment," *Clinical Medicine* 83 (January 1976): 14–23; and Ross Mullner and Jack Goldberg, "The Illinois Trauma System: Changes in Patient Survival Patterns following Vehicular Injuries," *Journal of the American College of Emergency Physicians* 6 (September 1977): 393–96.

9 Leonard A. Cobb, Hernán Alvarez III, and Michael K. Copass, "A Rapid Response System for Out-of-Hospital Cardiac Emergencies," *Medical Clinics of North America* 60 (March 1976): 283–90.

10 John M. Waters and C. H. Wells, "The Effects of a Modern Emergency Medical Care System in Reducing Automobile Crash Deaths," *Journal of Trauma* 13 (July 1973): 645–47.

11 Provided for in the National Health Planning and Resources Development Act of 1974 (P.L. 93–641). See: Aileen R. Lotz, "Health Services Management," in *Managing Human Services,* ed. Wayne F. Anderson, Bernard J. Frieden, and Michael J. Murphy (Washington, D.C.: International City Management Association, 1977), pp. 390–91, for a detailed discussion of HSAs.

12 Report issued by the city Department of Budget and Research, City of Long Beach, California, 1973.

13 James O. Page, "The Graying of Paramedics," *Paramedics international* 2 (Summer 1977): 14–17.

14 U.S., Department of Transportation, National Highway Traffic Safety Administration, *National Training Course for the Emergency Medical Technician–Paramedic* (Washington, D.C.: U.S. Department of Transportation, 1977).

15 See: Dorothy Coxe, "Five Approaches to Fire Department EMS," *Fire Chief,* November 1977, p. 37.

16 Ibid.

17 "Planning Your EMS Workload," *Fire Command,* August 1977, pp. 20–22.

18 *Laugher* v. *Pointer* (1826, King's Bench) 5 B. & C. 547, 108 Eng. Repr. 204.

19 *McFarland* v. *Dixie Machinery & Equipment Company,* 348 Mo. 341, 153 S.W.2d. 67 (1953).

20 *Mature* v. *Angelo,* 373 Pa. 593, 97 A2d. 59, 60 (1953).

21 An example of criteria to be used in selecting and designating medical control hospitals is available from ACT Foundation, Basking Ridge, New Jersey 07920.

22 American Law Institute, *Restatement of Agency* (Philadelphia: American Law Institute), sec. 227.

23 "In a Medical Emergency, Can You Get Help Fast?" *Changing Times* [The Kiplinger Magazine], October 1977, p. 24.

11 Managing fire and arson investigation

"The sky is red." In this cryptic phrase a professional arsonist, or "torch," advises his client that a contract has been fulfilled and an agreed-upon piece of property has been destroyed. Unfortunately, as Table 11–1 shows, the sky is indeed red from incendiary fires in the United States today—fires which are attributable not only to the professional torch but to all types of fire-setters.

For the fire chief, and indeed for all local government decision makers involved with the management of fire services, the investigation of all fires to determine the cause—and the investigation of incidents of arson in particular—is a central issue. The arson problem is a major one. And it will not go away easily. To bring it under control will demand the best in management.

The problem is technically difficult. The successful arsonist may destroy vital evidence in the process; this, indeed, will be the arsonist's aim—and the specialized criminals operating in this area are sophisticated and well equipped. Moreover, the successful detection and prosecution of arson requires careful and diplomatic liaison with a number of administrative entities. The successful fire and arson investigation manager must therefore possess skills in facilitating communication with other public safety entities and other levels of jurisdictions as well as in assembling and administering a specialized operation demanding a high degree of technical knowledge.

It is the purpose of this chapter, then, to present to fire officials some approaches to the problems they may face in organizing and managing the fire and arson investigation effort.

The chapter, which is divided into five main sections, opens with the question of organization. Emphasizing a managerial perspective, this section offers an overview of the problem to be addressed (in terms of the purpose and responsibility of the arson control entity, as well as its organization and procedures) and also examines the utility of the role of the arson task force.

The next section of this chapter looks at the arson unit's relations with the prosecutor's office. The third section, after discussing the importance of police/fire cooperation, and the role of the fire marshal, analyzes five elements of the investigative process: personnel, location, operations, training, and records. The fourth section describes the arson strike force experience, and the fifth details the coordination process with other groups (police and fire departments, adjacent jurisdictions, states, private investigative agencies, the insurance industry, etc.). There is a brief summary and conclusion.

It is important to emphasize at the outset a theme to be taken up in the first section: that while the arson challenge may achieve its most dramatic expression in larger jurisdictions, particularly in physically deteriorating urban cores including industrial zones and waterside areas, it is also a challenge in the smallest of rural jurisdictions. Indeed, smaller communities make up the bulk of local government jurisdictions in our country. Patient and undramatic cooperation among individuals is likely to be the norm in such communities, rather than highly organized (and highly visible) task forces with specialized components. Nevertheless, the principles of good management—emphasized in this chapter and throughout this book—are applicable in both instances.

Organization

Attacking the problem: a managerial overview

Discussion of the organization of fire and arson investigation from the management perspective tends to focus on larger municipalities. It should be kept in mind at the outset, however, that when local government sets about to organize for arson suppression the basic principles and operational concepts are similar, regardless of the size of the jurisdiction involved. The differences among city, town, and rural approaches to organization are confined principally to titles or official designations of individuals and to the size and scope of the operation.

Purpose and responsibility Whether the local official is called mayor, city or town manager, or county administrator, his or her responsibilities are similar—to organize an arson control entity and to secure cooperation from the members of this group. And the decision-making arm of the local government, whether

Table 11–1 Incendiary and suspicious fires in the United States.[1]

Year	Number of fires	Monetary loss
1977	177,000	$1,159,000,000
1975	144,100	633,900,000
1973	94,300	320,000,000
1971	72,100	233,000,000
1969	56,300	179,000,000
1967	44,100	141,700,000
1965	33,900	74,000,000
1963	30,900	55,000,000
1961	21,400	38,400,000
1959	20,300	27,730,000
1957	15,000	26,730,000
1955	9,600	27,100,000
1953	7,500	22,000,000
1951	5,600	16,100,000

Source: National Fire Protection Association, issues of *Fire Journal* from 1952 to 1978. Reprinted by permission.

1 Results for 1977 are for structure fires; results for earlier years are for building fires. In addition to buildings the structure category includes principally open platforms, bridges, roof assemblies over open areas, tents, air supported structures, and grandstands.

The 1977 results, in addition to being for structure rather than building fires, are based on significantly improved statistical methods and are therefore not strictly comparable to the estimates for earlier years. However, the 1977 statistics do reflect the overall trend of the arson problem in the United States. It was also estimated that 700 deaths resulted from incendiary and suspicious fires in 1977.

city or town council, or board of supervisors in a rural area, should fully support the effort to combat arson by authorizing and allocating the necessary funds.

The role of the office of management and budget, whether that department is called finance office or fiscal office, is also the same regardless of the type of jurisdiction. The recommendations of this office will have a heavy impact on the actions taken by the executive and the decision-making bodies.

The role of the prosecutor (discussed later in this chapter) is, again, similar, regardless of size of jurisdiction. The difference in smaller cities and counties is basically numerical—the prosecutor's office having only a small staff or perhaps one person. Whatever the size of the jurisdiction, these individuals will need to become knowledgeable in the arson field, to work with enforcement people throughout the investigation, and to prepare cases for prosecution thoroughly and competently.

Organization and procedures The organization for the actual investigation of fires bears many similar features among jurisdictions yet will, of necessity, vary with size of jurisdiction. For example, an arson squad (discussed below) may not be justified in small or even medium-sized cities and counties, but there must still be a clearly identified system for fire and arson investigation that is acceptable to both fire and police officials. For this purpose, there are several alternative procedures that deserve consideration.

In some localities fire prevention personnel examine every fire scene to determine origin and cause, with the assistance and cooperation of the fire suppression forces. If this preliminary investigation, which also involves interviewing key witnesses, indicates that the fire is of suspicious origin, assistance from local police agencies is requested, and state arson investigators, if available, become involved in the case. There are both strengths and weaknesses in this system. On the positive side there is the reasonable assurance that the origin and cause of every fire in the jurisdiction will be the subject of inquiry. On the negative side fire prevention personnel without police powers are severely handicapped in their investigative efforts. Problems arise when local enforcement personnel lack the experience, expertise, or time to participate effectively in the investigation. Sometimes because of a shortage of personnel state investigators cannot join in the case for several days. This system often results in a somewhat disjointed investigation, with repetition and duplication of effort.

Another procedure involves the formation of an arson investigation team consisting of fire prevention and permanently assigned police personnel working in pairs. This organization resembles a miniature arson squad, with the size of the team dependent upon the needs of the locality. Once again, the appropriate state agency may be requested to enter the case. This system has proved highly effective in some jurisdictions.

Some local governments place the entire responsibility for fire and arson investigation in the fire department. An essential requirement for the success of this system is the possession of police powers by the fire personnel conducting investigations. Often, these individuals are designated as fire marshals and, after completing certain required training in police procedures and investigative techniques, are granted full police powers. Either working within their own organization or teaming up with state investigators these officers can operate very effectively.

The key to the success of the systems cited above is complete cooperation and understanding between police and fire officials at the highest level. The roles and responsibilities of personnel from each organization should be clearly identified in written rules and regulations.

In rural areas, where fire protection is provided almost entirely by volunteer or on-call departments, the investigation of fires is an acute problem. Again, there are several alternative procedures to be considered.

Regardless of the system adopted in any rural jurisdiction, the fire department—whether volunteer, on-call, partially paid, or fully paid—bears the responsibility for determining that a fire is suspicious. Without this action it is probable that no investigation will be requested and therefore none will be made. For this reason the training of all fire department members in basic arson detection and of certain selected members of each department in fire cause determination is mandatory.

After the fire department determines that a fire is suspicious, or at least warrants further investigation, there are several alternative procedures. The fire chief or fire officer-in-charge can call for immediate assistance from the local law enforcement agency, which may be the county police or the county sheriff's office. Again, certain problems can arise when there is lack of expertise and experience on the part of local enforcement agencies. If these organizations are held responsible for making fire and arson investigations, it is necessary that at least one member be designated as the arson investigation specialist and receive training commensurate with this assignment.

Another alternative is for the fire department, upon determining that a fire is suspicious, to call for an investigation by an appointed county fire marshal. This person should not be a political hack appointed because of a position of prominence or connections in the community to carry out hazily identified duties. The local fire marshal should be a full-time employee whose duties and responsibilities are specified and who is qualified by experience and training to conduct arson investigations. This officer can pair up with state investigators as the need arises.

In some jurisdictions the fire chief calls on the state investigative agency directly if a fire is deemed suspicious. There are several disadvantages to this procedure. First, the state arson investigation unit will seldom be sufficiently staffed to respond on a timely basis to every such request. As a result, several days or more may elapse before an investigator arrives at the fire scene. During this time the scene is normally not secured and may be altered by trespassers, thus negating the admissibility of any physical evidence discovered. Second, the effectiveness of the investigation is diminished if local authorities are not involved, as these people possess information on suspects and witnesses that can be extremely valuable to the state investigator. If the state representative contacts the local official on arrival several days later, valuable investigative time has been lost.

In summary, in rural areas experience points to the fact that fire suppression personnel must be trained in basic arson detection; selected individuals in the fire department must be qualified to make fire cause determination; and a local official should be designated and trained to make at least preliminary investigations pending the arrival of a state investigator. Once again, it is important that all involved agencies should participate and cooperate throughout the investigation.

The insurance industry and the Chamber of Commerce have equally important roles in arson control in small and medium-sized cities and towns and in rural areas. Their contributions to arson control are basically the same as in large metropolitan areas but on a smaller scale. The same is true of such entities as the housing authority, the building department and its officials, and the welfare department. Finally, the full participation of the news media is equally vital in the arson control program regardless of the size of the jurisdiction.

The arson task force

From the mid-1970s, the concept of an arson task force attracted much attention in the national media, in fire service professional literature, and at national conferences of organizations working in the fire field. The experience of Seattle and other areas in combating arson has become quite well known.[1] While all of our major metropolitan areas do not necessarily have severe arson problems, these metropolitan areas do present challenges that are in many respects quite different from the problems of smaller municipalities, townships, and counties across the nation.

Whether or not an arson task force is suitable for a jurisdiction, the managerial principles inherent in this task force are of interest on two grounds: first, as examples of an effective approach to the national arson problem; and second, as examples of the managerial perspective that local government decision makers addressing the arson problem need to cultivate.

Assembling the task force The arson task force may be comprised of representatives of the executive branch of the municipality (the mayor or the city manager), the elected decision-making arm (the city council, town council, or board of supervisors), the office of management and budget, the prosecutor's office, the fire chief, the police chief, a representative of the insurance industry, and a representative of the Chamber of Commerce. The task force would include in its meetings and deliberations, as the occasion dictates, representatives of other interests, such as the housing authority, building officials, and welfare organizations. After high incident arson areas are identified, members of groups that may comprise the majority of the population in those areas may become involved in the task force efforts. The setting up of an arson task force is thus a major management challenge.

A key group upon which the success of the arson suppression effort will depend is the news media. Without support from newspapers, radio, and television the program will have little chance of acquiring public support and participation, and such support should be sought actively.

It should be kept in mind that the fire and police chiefs, either or both of whom may be actively involved in the investigation of fires, are merely members of the task force. Arson fires can be reduced by effective investigations, but a significant reduction cannot be accomplished without a concerted effort on the part of *all* those mentioned above. The objectives of the task force are clear—to prevent incendiary fires and to assure that they are properly investigated if they occur.

The task force carries out its mission in three phases: first, identifying the arson problem; second, determining its causes; and third, developing strategies for combating the problem, and defining strategic roles.

Identifying the problem The first phase mentioned above is essential to the success of the effort. Under the most adverse conditions, no fire loss facts and figures are available in the jurisdiction. While this is the exception rather than the rule, such situations do exist. Without records, and without adequate records, it is difficult for the task force to begin to identify the problem. A better grasp of the problem is possible if records are kept of all fires and their causes. (This immediately raises the question: What group determines the origins and causes of fires? If it is fire department personnel, how well qualified are these individuals for the assignment? Is this determination of origins and causes to be made by trained persons in cooperation with all fire department personnel? In other words, are the facts and figures on fire causes only as accurate as the people keeping them are experienced?)

Another problem that arises is that where this information is available the usual format consists of mass totals: for example, number of responses, number of fires; monetary losses, causes of fires—per month and perhaps annually. Except in very general terms, this type of report provides only sketchy information with which to analyze the arson problem. It does, however, provide a broad base for determining that a problem actually exists. The initial assignment of the task force, then, is to develop a system whereby detailed information on incendiary fires is readily available—a system with records that identify types of property involved, time frames within which arson occurs, and high arson incident areas. (Techniques in the area of record keeping are discussed in detail in Chapter 18.)

Determining the causes When the task force accepts, on the basis of general information available, the existence of an incendiary fire problem, the second phase of activity begins—that of determining its causes: in short, answering the question, Why do we have arson in our community? A review of fire department records might provide the answer. Why, for example, do the suspicious fire losses in a certain section of the municipality involve apartment houses? Do the property owners have a motive? Would the occupants want to burn the property? And if taverns or bars are high on the list of suspicious/incendiary fires, why is this so? Have recent ordinances on topless dancers affected the

---

Why arson? In contrast to the fire accidents difficult to prevent are the fires set on purpose. In 1971, among fires reported to the National Fire Protection Association, about 7 percent were classified as incendiary; an additional 17 percent were "of unknown origin." Arsonists pick expensive targets: Among the 1971 fires in which losses exceeded $250,000, 27 percent were classified as incendiary, another 47 percent as of unknown origin. In many large cities, fire chiefs believe that almost half of all fires in their experience have been deliberately set.

Fire has always held an attraction for demented thrillseekers. That fire is a way of attacking authority is indicated by the fact that in 1971 26 percent of the large-loss school fires and 44 percent of the large-loss church fires were incendiary. . . .

Not all deliberately set fires stem from

malice or thrillseeking; an increasing number are set for profit. A number of building owners have been setting their properties afire to reap insurance benefits and tax write-offs in excess of market value, delinquent taxes, or demolition costs. In the troubled city of Newark, N.J., where the number of vacated buildings increased by 300 percent between 1965 and 1971, the number of fires in these structures increased by over 500 percent. There is evidence that the Fair Access to Insurance Requirements (FAIR) plan, designed to provide insurance on properties not qualified under normal company standards, is being used by some owners of deteriorating buildings to burn for profit.

Source: National Commission on Fire Prevention and Control, *America Burning: The Report of the National Commission on Fire Prevention and Control* (Washington, D.C.: Government Printing Office, 1973), p. 4.

---

business to the extent that the owner burns or has the building torched? Is "the organization" taking over all tavern operations and using fire and/or bombings to bring reluctant owners in line and to intimidate others? In summary, if the task force is to analyze the arson situation properly, accurate and detailed information must be available not only on the numbers of incendiary/suspicious fires but also on the types of property involved, so that the underlying motives for fire-setting in the community can be identified.

Developing strategies and defining roles The task force now faces its final and most important challenge—that of developing strategies for combating the arson problem. The mechanics of developing these strategies are reasonably simple and involve, initially, a series of scheduled conferences for task force members. The frequency of such meetings depends on three factors: (1) the seriousness of the arson problem; (2) the degree of participation by task force representatives; and (3) the effectiveness of the leadership of the mayor and/or city manager.

Mayors and/or city managers are key leadership figures in the early stages of the task force operation. They should publicly and privately express full support for the task force. It is most important that concern over the arson situation in the community be conveyed to the public: citizen understanding of the need for and purposes of the task force is essential. But the most important function of the mayor or city manager is to secure the full cooperation of all members of the task force: without strong, positive leadership the task force can become an organization on paper only.

The function of the city or town council in relation to the task force is two-fold: it plays a supportive and a decision-making role. While the mayor or manager may be convinced of the need for a thoroughgoing attack on arson, the support of the local government body is essential to the success of the program. It is necessary for the council to recognize and accept the need for positive action, and to make decisions concerning personnel and funds for executing such action. Without this active support, once again the task force could become merely a symbolic organization.

Without adequate funding and personnel the arson control effort will fail; therefore, the office of management and budget is a key organization within the task force. This office, together with the director of personnel, will supply vital facts and figures to the city or town council. If these key officials are not convinced that the arson problem in the community warrants additional funding and personnel, this will have a strong influence on the council. It should be clearly pointed out that the community cannot—and is not willing to—tolerate the financial losses from arson. Loss of income because of industrial, commercial, and multiple or single occupancy fires may be creating severe financial problems for a municipality. In some areas between a third and half of the businesses and industries that have suffered a major fire have not rebuilt or reopened. Loss of income in the form of taxes, salaries, and overall revenue in such cases has a significant financial impact on an area. In short, the expenditure of several hundred thousand dollars annually to combat arson must be compared with the loss of several million dollars annually in lost revenue, both direct and indirect.

The role of the prosecutor

The preceding section has outlined, in broad terms, the managerial options available to local governments seeking an overall approach to their arson problems. The discussion now focuses in detail on the arson investigation process. As the operations of the arson investigative unit are ultimately directed toward bringing the accused to trial and securing a successful outcome of that trial, the relationship with the prosecutor and the prosecutor's office is an important consideration. This relationship is treated immediately below, as prefatory to the discussion of investigation. The overall framework of an arson task force will be used as a convenient benchmark, although it is recognized that the managerial principles involved will often have to be adapted to jurisdictions that have not accepted the task force concept in its entirety.

The individuals and organizations whose roles have been discussed up to this point are not actual participants in the arson control effort; rather, they provide the necessary support at the executive, decision-making, and financial levels. The role of the prosecutor, however, is a different matter. The prosecutor plays an important role in bringing the criminal or criminals to justice in this extremely difficult type of criminal court case. His or her cooperation with the arson investigative unit can be most important to the outcome of a case. The prosecutor's knowledge and expertise can be of valuable assistance to the arson investigative unit. At various stages of the investigation legal problems (perhaps unprecedented) will arise on which the arson investigators need guidance and advice. If relations between the investigators and the prosecutor's office are good, this guidance and advice will be forthcoming. It often happens, however, that, because of excessive case loads, no representative of the prosecutor's office is available to meet with the investigators and help resolve their problems. When such individuals are available and are given this assignment, their experience and expertise are often limited. (This may well be because [1] arson cases and prosecutions are rare in the community and [2] all members of the prosecutor's office may handle criminal cases across the board on a rotating basis and assignments are not made on the basis of the offense involved.)

Another problem often referred to by investigators is that no pretrial conference is conducted. Investigators state that their only contact with a prosecutor occurs on the courthouse steps ten minutes before the trial, or on the elevator going up to the courtroom. Under these circumstances many arson cases which are effectively investigated are lost because of ineffective prosecution. Clearly, there is a communication problem of major proportions if such circumstances exist.

To correct such deficiencies, changes in attitude and in procedure are necessary on both sides. Initially, fire department management should help make the prosecutor's office aware of the seriousness to the community of the arson problem. Secondly, it will be mutually beneficial if selected persons within the prosecutor's office are specifically assigned to arson investigation and prosecution. The crime of arson is technical and complex; extensive study and research on court cases and significant decisions are required. If several individuals are assigned to the prosecution of arson, then one of them should be designated as the team leader.

The organization of such a group in the prosecutor's office helps develop a close working relationship between that office and the arson investigators; this, in turn, serves a dual purpose: it enables the prosecutor to keep abreast of developments, and it provides a source of advice and guidance to the investigators. The prosecutor can recommend courses of action and investigative steps to enforcement personnel as well as specifying what additional evidence is needed to bring charges against an individual, and the investigator is advised of deficiencies which exist which will make successful prosecution difficult and a conviction unlikely. (In the case of a small jurisdiction, this same close working relationship can exist involving only two persons.)

If liaison has existed between prosecutor and investigator from the beginning of the investigation, the pretrial conference is routine and uncomplicated. Nevertheless, this meeting must be conducted efficiently and the testimony of the investigator reviewed in detail. The exact location of physical evidence, its significance, and who will present it should be established. It is essential that the investigation report be reviewed carefully to ensure that the contents are consistent with the testimony to be offered. The reliability and credibility of other witnesses and their anticipated testimony should be discussed. The tactics and strategies of defense counsel will need to be considered, as well as the possible approaches which may be employed in cross-examining the investigators. Means of diminishing the impact of the testimony of defense witnesses, hostile witnesses, and, perhaps, surprise witnesses should be developed. In all, every contingency should be anticipated, and preparation should encompass the most minute detail.

When teamwork between prosecutor and investigator has been perfected, a major step has been taken towards eliminating light or suspended sentences for arsonists. When prosecutors are familiar with all the facts and know that the prosecution has a strong case, they will be unwilling to settle for anything less than punishment that takes into account the seriousness of this crime.

As an additional deterrent to the would-be arsonist, the prosecutor's office can make it known to the public that convicted arsonists will be dealt with harshly and that realistic sentences will be vigorously sought. Widely publicized convictions and the prospect of more to follow may well cause many potential fire-setters to have second thoughts.[2]

Investigation

Before prosecution comes investigation, and many authorities would agree that the most important segment of the arson control effort is the investigative unit. While the total attack on arson is a task force responsibility, it is upon the investigators "in the trenches" that the ultimate success of the program will depend.

The importance of police/fire cooperation

The composition of the investigative unit should not pose a problem and yet it frequently does. Historically, rivalry and jealousy between police and fire personnel have existed in varying degrees over a variety of matters—salaries, working conditions, hours, job safety, fringe benefits, and a general lack of mutual respect.

In fire and arson investigation further confusion and misunderstanding arise because of the nature of the offense or suspected offense. When a fire occurs, it is a fire department function to extinguish the blaze with the least possible loss of life and property. When a crime is committed, it is a police department function to investigate the crime and apprehend the perpetrator. The conflict over which agency has jurisdiction arises when a fire occurs as the result of a criminal act.

Occasionally, in some localities fire officials will insist that, since fire is involved, the investigation of suspicious fires is the responsibility of their department. In the same communities the police will maintain that, since a crime may have been committed, investigation of suspicious fires is a function of law enforcement personnel. Each organization insists that the investigative authority is theirs and each may actually conduct separate and concurrent probes of the same fire, with no cooperation, coordination, or exchange of information. Effective investigation of suspicious fires under these conditions is impossible—and the party that benefits is the arsonist.

A contrary situation occasionally occurs in which the fire chief will maintain that investigation of crimes is a police function and therefore the fire department will not investigate suspected arson fires. In the same community the police chief will insist that fire is a fire department function and therefore investigation of suspicious fires is not the responsibility of the police department.

The result can be a stalemate, with no fire investigations being conducted. If the arsonist benefits from dual, separate investigations by fire and police officials, imagine the position of an arsonist in a community where no investigations are conducted.

While the conditions cited above are extremely rare, certain other nonproductive procedures are encountered somewhat more frequently. For example, some localities may place fire/arson investigative responsibilities entirely within the fire prevention bureau or similar entity. The city/town code will read: "The Fire Prevention Bureau within the Bureau of Fire shall determine the origin and cause of all fires occurring within the city" (an impressive but relatively meaningless declaration, since the authority to carry out this assignment does not accompany the responsibility). The result is a group of inspectors and fire prevention people in uniform without authority and without police powers attempting to conduct productive fire/arson investigations. Under this procedure, there may be agreement, either written or verbal, that if the origin of a fire is determined to be suspicious fire prevention personnel will call for police assistance— usually from the detective division.

This can pose several problems. First, detectives assigned on a case-by-case basis may have little or no experience in arson and may thus be challenged in court as to their expert witness status. Second, other case assignments may make it impossible for the detective to spend the days or weeks sometimes required on an arson investigation. Third, the police representative may be pulled off the case at a crucial point in the investigation to respond to a police emergency. Fourth, the work schedules of the fire and police representatives may not coincide. The result of these conditions is an uncoordinated, piecemeal investigation that never reaches a satisfactory conclusion. Ultimately, the fire prevention people decide that it has been a waste of time, and the fire is "determined" to be of accidental origin. In those instances where the evidence of incendiarism is too weighty to be ignored, fire personnel decide to conduct the investigation themselves and no enforcement agency is involved.

It is the responsibility, then, of fire managerial personnel to ensure cooperation between police and fire departments in this matter of fire/arson investigation, and to see that the responsibilities of both departments are coordinated. The use of personnel from both departments in the investigative process is discussed in greater detail later in this section.

The fire marshal

In many cities, towns, and other local jurisdictions there exist individuals entitled *fire marshals*. What is a fire marshal? A well-known national organization has been wrestling with this question without success for years. Governing bodies appoint fire marshals without defining their duties, responsibilities, authority, to whom they report, who reports to them, or their relationship with the fire chief. Among the nebulous assignments given to fire marshals, some reference to investigating the origins and causes of fires in the jurisdiction may be included. If fire marshals are to serve productively, their role in the fire department organization and operation should be clearly defined. It is especially important that their duties in the arson investigation effort be clearly delineated, otherwise their presence merely complicates the process further. The various functions in which the fire marshal may be involved will be discussed later in the chapter.

Personnel

Size of the unit The number of personnel assigned to the arson investigation unit depends to a large degree on the population of the jurisdiction and the extent of the recognized arson problem. Obviously, a squad of fifteen to eighteen members is not financially practical in a city of 15,000 to 20,000 population (although the loss from incendiary fires might justify a unit of this size). Consideration must be given to a number of factors, including evaluation of results and financial constraints. Is the number of investigators sufficient to handle the case load or is every investigator attempting to work ten or twelve fire losses at one time? Are fires of questionable origin being glossed over and are incomplete investigations being closed out to prevent a backlog? Is the average workweek for squad personnel fifty to sixty hours? Is response time to a request for investigation three or four days? If the answer to any of these questions is affirmative, the unit is too small and additional personnel should be added. The investigation of fires, even for cause determination, is a slow, tedious, and time-consuming process and individuals assigned to it need to be given ample time to do their jobs properly.

Monitoring and evaluation It is important that the operation of the squad be monitored and evaluated frequently. Detailed records should be kept that indicate case assignments, hours of work, response time, and results attained. Exhausted, overworked, frustrated, and ignored investigators will be tempted to go through the motions of carrying out their duties—a condition which should not be allowed to develop.

Selection The composition of the arson unit can and often does vary, with personnel assigned from either the police or the fire department exclusively, or from each department. Experience has shown that a combination of fire and police personnel is the most effective approach, as it combines the expertise of fire personnel in the technical aspects of fire with that of police personnel in investigative techniques.

While professional background is a significant consideration in selecting individuals for the unit, it should not be the sole criterion. Another factor to be weighed is the potential capability of the persons under consideration. Interest and motivation are essential qualities for a good investigator, and for this reason only those who volunteer for the unit should be accepted. Arson investigation is extremely difficult and discouraging, and some individuals may not be suited either psychologically or physically for the job. Another consideration is that those assigned to the arson unit should have the option of requesting return to their former position with their parent organization. It is important for the fire official to remember that a member of the squad who is dissatisfied and disgruntled will not only perform poorly but will also have a demoralizing effect on others.

The arson squad should not be used as a dumping ground for persons who cannot perform satisfactorily in other capacities within their own organizations. On occasion, an individual may suffer a disabling injury while serving as a member of either the police or the fire department. There is a tendency to assign that person either to training or to the arson squad, a situation which should be avoided. (This is not to say that an individual who is slightly disabled in the line of duty should never be assigned to investigation, but that the deciding factor should be the ability to perform competently in an investigative capacity.)

Police department personnel Concerning police department members of the arson squad, experience has shown that these individuals should come from the detective division. The uniformed officer has not acquired the skills necessary for conducting investigations and the arson squad should not serve as a training ground. Arson is considered by many to be the most difficult of all crimes to investigate; therefore, it demands the use of every skill previously acquired plus techniques peculiar to arson cases. The detectives selected for the squad must already possess expertise in the areas of interviewing, of collection, preservation, and evaluation of evidence, of interrogation, of case preparation, and of testifying in court.

Before an applicant is selected for the arson unit, department records should be reviewed carefully, with particular attention to evaluation reports. This will generally indicate the extent of the applicant's professional competence, and—of great importance—the extent of the person's ability to work with others. An essential part of the selection process is a personal interview; while this can be done by one person, it is preferable that it be held by a board of qualified individuals. These board members should have some basic knowledge of arson investigation and, in particular, of the qualities the applicants should possess. An opening question to consider is why they want to become members of the unit. Any response which lacks strong indications of motivation and interest should receive cautious consideration. Do they work well with others? As stated previously, perhaps this information will be reflected in departmental reports, but often the board may be able to observe behavioral characteristics which might indicate whether or not an applicant is a person who works well in a group. The arson squad is a closely knit group, although composed of people with different job-related backgrounds—fire and police. For the squad to function effectively, all members will need to work together, sharing experience and information which will benefit the entire unit, not just one individual. There is no place for a loner—or a dissatisfied person—in a group which depends so heavily for success on cooperation among its members.

Fire department personnel Concerning fire department personnel in the investigation unit, in all probability there are individuals in the fire department who are assigned to fire investigation and to determination of causes. These individuals may have attained a high degree of skill in these areas but, through no fault of their own, they may completely lack basic investigative skills. It must be understood that this expertise will not be acquired overnight, and that it will come from two sources: training and field experience with qualified police-oriented individuals in the arson unit.[3]

Selection of fire department personnel for the arson squad should follow the same general guidelines discussed for selection of police personnel. An additional consideration is the educational level of fire department applicants: it is important to keep in mind the functions these individuals will perform as arson investigators which were not required in fire cause determination and fire investigation. Members of the arson unit will in the course of their duties review insurance policies and records, financial and medical reports, and legal and technical documents. In addition, preparation of case reports and testifying in court demand a reasonable command of the English language and the ability to express oneself. This is not to imply that investigators must be college graduates, but certain academic standards should be established.

As with police department personnel, fire department members of the arson unit should possess the ability to work with others. They should be willing and able to share their knowledge of the technical and behavioral aspects of fire, as it is through such sharing that police-oriented individuals will acquire expertise in this area.

As stated previously, high individual morale and unit esprit de corps are essential to the successful operation of the arson unit. A key point for managers to remember is that the spirit of this organization can be destroyed by poor administrative planning, specifically as regards the salary scale of unit members. Situations exist in which fire department members of an arson squad carry the title and rank of firefighter, with a commensurate salary, while police department members may be detective sergeants or lieutenants with a much higher pay scale. The effect on morale is disastrous when two people working side by side and performing the same basic functions have a 15 to 30 percent difference in pay. A standard salary scale commensurate with the requirements of the job and high enough to attract and hold the most qualified individuals from both the fire and police departments is necessary. The arson squad should thus be an elite organization comprised of top performance people carefully selected from both fire and police departments.

Location

A most important decision needs to be made as to whether the arson squad is to be located in the fire department or the police department. In the majority of municipalities the fire department exercises operational control of the unit, with administrative control retained by the parent organization. For example, if the squad includes police personnel and functions under the fire chief, this individual supervises the routine daily operations such as case assignments and hours of work while the police chief maintains administrative control concerning discipline, payroll, and similar matters. If the squad is under the police chief, a like procedure exists relative to fire department personnel in the unit.

When the arson squad is located within the fire department a determination must be made of where the unit fits into the organization. In some localities the fire chief assumes direct command, a procedure which offers both advantages and disadvantages. This direct command assures the squad members of communication with the chief and of a high degree of visibility and recognition. A disadvantage is the possibility of overemphasis of the arson investigation effort, with the resultant neglect of other important phases of fire department operation, specifically suppression and prevention. A more logical approach may be to assign the supervision of the arson squad to a fire marshal who is directly answerable to the chief. The duties, responsibilities, and authority of this individual must be clearly defined, including relationships with supervisors in other operational branches of the fire department. The important point is that the arson squad should operate under the control of a qualified person whose duties are clear and who is knowledgeable on the subject of arson. Fire prevention, inspections, and public fire safety education should not be assigned to the supervisor of the arson squad, as these add many and perhaps conflicting responsibilities. The successful operation of the arson unit demands effective leadership, which must be strong and dynamic, and uninhibited by involvement in other department functions.

When the arson squad is located in the police department there is always the possibility that the unit will be lost in the vast complex of department operations. Furthermore, law enforcement organizations across the nation have recently been engulfed by a rising tide of crime. Under these conditions it is unlikely that the chief of the department or the head of the detective division could devote the time necessary to properly supervise the activities of the arson unit. If the squad is located in the detective division along with other specialty squads such as auto and bicycle theft, vice, etc., the arson effort might well become a low priority item. Also, there is the possibility that members of the arson organization might be drained off occasionally to assist in emergencies arising within that division, thus jeopardizing unit integrity and continuity of operation. In summary (although police chiefs might disagree with this statement), the arson squad can function in the police department, but fire department experience indicates that it operates more effectively when located in the fire department.

Operations

The day-to-day operation of the arson unit is beyond the scope of this chapter, but some general guidelines may be presented here.[4]

An essential consideration is that all members of the unit should be qualified to conduct a complete investigation, from fire scene examination to determination of origin and cause through the interrogation and courtroom testimony. While it is recognized that some squad members will be more qualified than others in certain specific areas, it is nevertheless ineffective to segregate investigative activities. Fire department personnel may be superior to police personnel in fire scene examination, but this function should not be relegated exclusively to fire personnel. By the same token interrogations should not be conducted entirely by police personnel. Through field experience, plus training, in those areas to which they have not previously been exposed, every member of the unit can attain expertise in all phases of investigation.

Work schedule The work schedule of the unit should be designed so that at least one investigator is on duty at all times. The seriousness of the arson problem will dictate when and under what circumstances squad members will be called to the fire scene. The availability of squad members is largely dependent on the number of people in the unit on duty at any particular time. In some jurisdictions investigators answer every alarm, but obviously this is not always possible or practical. Response to major and to multiple alarm fires is a more reasonable procedure. An investigator might best be called only when the fire department suspects arson because of certain physical observations on arrival at the fire scene, or when a qualified fire officer cannot determine an accidental cause for the fire. Caution must be used in calling for investigators, otherwise a situation could develop in which squad personnel dash from fire scene to fire scene, accomplishing very little at each.

Communication   Radio communication is necessary if squad members are to operate efficiently. Equipment that permits communication with both fire and police headquarters should be provided in squad vehicles. Portable hand carried sets or walkie-talkies through which squad members can communicate are also necessary, particularly when the squad is conducting stakeouts and surveillances. The need for adequate communication equipment for every squad member at all times cannot be emphasized too strongly.

Vehicles and equipment   Concerning motor vehicles operated by the unit, experience has shown that most of the squad personnel should be issued plain unmarked cars with blind tags. Each investigator should be issued a car which is assigned exclusively and permanently and kept at all times, both on and off duty. This procedure assures that the entire squad can be called and will respond during an emergency. Another consideration is that the preservation of the chain of custody of physical evidence becomes more difficult if many people have access to the trunk of an arson unit automobile. The investigator should be

---

Investigation equipment   An individual investigator in the arson investigative unit will need to have the following equipment available in his or her vehicle at all times:

Axe
Camera
Cardboard boxes
Claw hammer
Combustible gas detector
Cultivator
Film
Flashbulbs
Hacksaw
Handsaw
Hoe, short handle
Knife
Labels
Lights (2)
Magnifying glass
Marking pencil
Mason jars, various sizes

Metal cans, various sizes
Notepaper
Paper towels
Pen and pencils
Plastic bags
Portable gas chromatograph
Pry bar
Rags
Rake, short handle
Ruler and yardstick
Screen
Screwdriver
Sealers
Shears
Shovel, short handle, square point
Small hand shovel
Sponge
Staple gun
Tape measure
Tape recorder
Tin snips
Wire cutter
Wrench.

---

able to testify that no other person had keys to the trunk of the vehicle in which the evidence was locked when it was being transported to the evidence storage locker or to the laboratory. Under these conditions, allegations that the evidence was altered or tampered with while under the control of the investigator have no validity or substance.

The issuing of individual cars also enables investigators to keep in their control the tools and equipment necessary for conducting a thorough fire scene examination. It is a handicap to an investigator to prepare to enter a fire scene and to discover, on opening the trunk of the squad car, that the investigator who used the vehicle previously has removed the lights, the camera, and the entire evidence collection kit. In addition, if the care and maintenance of this equipment become one person's responsibility and that person fails to replace the batteries in the lights or restock the supply of film, there is no one else to blame.

Concerning equipment, the manager should not lose sight of the fact that new appliances and devices continue to appear that can materially assist arson investigators in their job, particularly in fire scene examination. It is important for the manager to keep abreast of these new appliances, and of those that have been proved of value. Fire scene examination is a difficult task under any conditions and the investigator needs every technical and scientific aid available. In fact, a mobile crime scene search vehicle designed and equipped for use by the arson squad could provide additional technical and scientific aids.

Training

General considerations After the arson squad is organized, its members selected and assigned, and orientation and indoctrination sessions held, the next step is the training of the personnel involved. In planning a program that will benefit all unit personnel, it is important for the manager to remember that the professional experience of the individuals differs.

Fire department personnel should receive basic and advanced training in police procedures and investigative techniques, which include the interviewing process, criminal law, the judicial system, note taking, report writing, arrest procedures, use of firearms, rules of evidence, search and seizure, interrogation, criminal investigation, and courtroom testimony.

Instruction in these subjects will give fire investigators at least the fundamentals of police procedures which, combined with field experience, will enable them to function effectively as arson investigators. In addition to skill and knowledge training, instruction should be provided which will result in a change in attitude and philosophy on the part of these fire personnel. They will need to realize that they are no longer in the role of the friendly inspector or fire prevention officer dealing with store owners, restaurant operators, and school principals. As investigators they will encounter criminals involved in the commission of a major crime, who will lie to preserve their freedom and will resort to physical violence on occasion to prevent being arrested. The importance of an investigator's understanding the threat to his or her safety cannot be emphasized too strongly.

Training for police personnel in the arson unit should center on subjects such as fire department operations, basic fire ground strategy and tactics, firefighting equipment and its utilization, fire terminology, the chemistry of fire, fire behavior, fire origin and cause, and fire scene examination. Supplemented by field experience and by work with fire personnel, this training will enable police investigators to develop skills and knowledge in these areas.

Whether all members of the arson squad receive all the training listed above will depend on individual needs. However, advanced instruction should be directed to the entire squad, who should attend a course as a unit if this is at all possible. These classes should be conducted primarily in the field at fire scenes, and should involve practical application of skills and knowledge previously acquired. Fire scenes examined need not necessarily be confined to suspicious fires—any fire will serve the purpose, as long as it is instructive. This on-the-scene training is far more productive than classroom instruction utilizing photographs, slides, and other single dimension training aids.

The objective of this training is to enable all members of the arson unit to carry out their duties as squad members from the beginning to the conclusion of any investigation. Training and learning should never cease; retraining classes are necessary on a regular basis to reestablish fundamentals and to provide additional skills and knowledge, as well as innovative concepts.

Detection and observation To ensure the success of the arson control effort, it is necessary that training encompass the areas of arson detection and fire cause determination. Courses in detection should be conducted for all fire department personnel, and the training should be confined primarily to observation—what the firefighter should look for which may indicate arson.

The reasons for this involvement should be understood. First, many fires will never be investigated if firefighters do not observe conditions and circumstances which indicate that the fire is suspicious and that an investigation should be requested. Second, the observant firefighter can convey significant information to the investigating officers. Third, firefighters can assist in establishing the incendiary origin of the fire by courtroom testimony, not as expert witnesses expressing opinions but as experienced firefighters testifying on their observations.

No attempt is made here to outline a complete training course for firefighters, but general recommendations on broad subject areas seem appropriate. On the way to the fire, suppression personnel should observe the general weather conditions, the direction and approximate velocity of the wind, and certain natural conditions such as snow and ice on the highway and manmade barriers which impede the progress of apparatus responding to the alarm. People leaving the fire scene either on foot or in vehicles should be noted, particularly when fires are occurring in a series.

Figure 11–1 To the observant investigator, excessive burning at floor level in the corner of a room (normally a cool area) suggests that the fire may have been set.

Upon arrival at the fire, firefighters should note the means of gaining entry into the structure, as well as any cover, such as blankets, over the windows and doors. Of great importance to the investigators is the exact location of the fire as observed by the firefighters. If the structure is completely destroyed, the precise location of the fire in its early stages will enable the investigators to concentrate their fire scene search in this area.

Firefighters should be observant of smoke and flame of unusual color, not associated with normal burning, and of unusual odors. Notice should also be taken of the presence of separate and unconnected fires in a structure, as well as "streamers" of combustible materials or flammable liquids which aid the spread of fire from room to room. Firefighters may also observe other efforts intended to assist the fire spread, such as holes punched in walls, exposed wood lathing, and interior doors propped open. Suppression personnel should also note any unusual behavior of the fire; for example, if the fire increases rather than decreases when water is applied, or if it rekindles several times, the presence of an accelerant is indicated.

The absence of furniture, clothing, and personal effects in an occupied house is significant, as it may indicate that these items were removed by the occupants prior to the setting of a fraud fire. The presence of household effects in great numbers and of substantial size outside the dwelling presents the distinct possibility that they were removed prior to the torching of the structure. These same items may appear later in the claim submitted by the arsonist in an effort to defraud the insurance company.

In mercantile, industrial, and manufacturing buildings, preparation for an incendiary fire should be noted by the firefighter. Fire doors that are propped open and inoperative sprinkler systems should attract the attention of fire department personnel. A technique of totally incapitating a sprinkler system is the use of dry ice to freeze the water. The ice in the pipes does not melt until the fire is well under way in the areas protected by individual sprinkler heads. The dry ice dissipates in the heat, leaving no trace of its presence apart from the wire, string, or tape used to affix it to the pipe.

During the later stages of the fire, firefighters should observe the manner and dress of the occupants of an involved dwelling. People who watch their worldly possessions being destroyed in a state of calm composure indicate the possibility of a deliberately executed fraud fire. If occupants who have allegedly been aroused from a sound sleep by smoke and flames appear fully clothed this is a suspicious circumstance.

At this time firefighters may have an opportunity to observe the crowd gathered at the scene and to look for individuals whose appearance or actions are unusual. Included in this group is the "eager beaver" who dashes around the fire scene shouting orders and giving directions, and supposedly assisting the firefighters. This same person may have been observed waiting for the arrival of the apparatus, pointing out to the firefighters the exact location of the fire. Later this individual may visit the fire station, asking questions and showing a great interest in a fire or in fires in general. When fires of a suspicious nature are occurring frequently in a community, the continued appearance of this person at a number of these fires and his or her unusual actions should be noted by firefighters and this information conveyed to the investigators.

Cause determination and the fire officer   Training in the subject areas discussed above should be directed to all fire department personnel, but fire cause determination instruction is provided only for certain fire personnel. These individuals are determined by the standing operating procedure of the fire department. That is, when a fire has been extinguished, in some jurisdictions prevention personnel (not members of the arson squad) are called to the scene to make cause determination. This may result in an unnecessary duplication of effort by prevention personnel and the arson squad members who enter the investigation later, since the scene must be reexamined by the investigator (who must interview witnesses so that he or she can testify in court on the basis of actual findings at the scene). Thus another step has been added to the investigative process, with a consequent delay in completing the case.

If the arson squad is of sufficient size, an investigator is notified of the fire and responds while the fire is in progress. (Normally it is not feasible for arson squad members to answer all alarms, as this procedure necessitates a great amount of traveling from fire scene to fire scene and disrupts orderly investigation of established arson fires.)

Probably the most practical procedure is to use the services of company officers for on-the-spot cause determination. The training of fire officers, then, entails instruction in determining origin and cause; however, it should be clearly established that they are not arson investigators, but "cause determiners." Instruction, therefore, is limited to company officers' actions during the scene examination which takes place at the earliest logical time following the fire.

These fire officers must be trained to look for the indications of arson previously mentioned (unusual odors, multiple fires, streamers, unusual and uneven burning, and possible containers of accelerants in unusual locations). These officers should be given basic instruction in examining the heating system—to determine the position of draft controls, to locate mechanical malfunctions in the system, to note defects in the flue and exhaust pipes, and to spot breaks in oil and gas lines.

Figure 11–2 Investigators of a suspicious fire in this building found this trash material, only slightly burned, which had been placed near the furnace to give the impression that the fire originated from accidental causes.

Training should also be provided in routine examination of the electrical system, particularly in the apparent area of fire origin. Burn patterns in the vicinity of wiring in poor condition and electrical outlets and appliances may indicate a fire of accidental cause. Instruction in the procedure for examining fuse boxes should be offered, including how to check for oversized and blown fuses, pennies behind the fuse, and fuses "jumped" by some other means. The fire department officer may require only minimum instruction to become skilled in recognizing various types of fires from examining burn and char patterns. The baked effect created by a slow, smoldering fire must be contrasted to the deep burn pattern which normally accompanies a rapidly developing intense flame.

Instruction must emphasize the need for close examination of the fire scene to establish the absence of clothing, furniture, and personal effects in residential fires, and the absence of fixtures, stock, and machinery in mercantile, industrial, and manufacturing fires. Fire officers should be trained to look for the unusual, such as numerous For Rent or For Sale signs on the premises, auction posters, and condemnation notices, as well as uninhabitable condition of the property. There may exist certain intangibles which give the fire officer an instinctive feeling that the fire is suspicious. Under these conditions the fire officer should be taught to weigh the total circumstances of the fire, evaluating such factors as motive, owner demeanor, and logical cause.

There are three particularly important managerial points which should be incorporated into the fire officers' training program. First, no cleanup operations should be conducted until the fire scene examination for origin and cause has been completed. If no reasonable point of origin and probable cause can be established following the examination, then no cleanup should be made prior to the arrival of arson squad personnel. It is important that fire officers understand the need to preserve the fire scene as far as possible. Second, training should include emphasis on the necessity of securing the fire scene pending the arrival of arson unit personnel. If this is not done, curious trespassers may trample and/or remove physical evidence of an incendiary fire. The involved structure must be cordoned off and everyone kept out except persons who are authorized by the officer in charge to enter the building for a specific purpose. No one should be allowed to remove any item from the premises without the permission of the fire officer. Third, the responsibility and the involvement of suppression personnel in the arson control effort should be made crystal clear to fire department officers. Without the assistance and cooperation of suppression forces, any significant progress towards reduction of arson fires will be impossible.

Record keeping

The subject of maintenance of records on fire losses—particularly as they relate to suspicious fires—has been referred to briefly earlier in the chapter. As these records involve far more than a mere listing of fires, perhaps a more accurate description would be an intelligence file. Before discussing how such a file might be developed, it is appropriate to point out that such records do not necessarily have to be computerized, although this is desirable. A viable alternative to setting up a separate computer operation in the fire department is to use the existing facilities in the police department. In all probability this equipment is highly sophisticated, with extensive capabilities, and only minimum modifications would be required to handle fire loss information along with that on burglaries, auto thefts, and other criminal offenses.

What is the potential value of a complete records system in the arson control effort? If the records reflect nothing more than the location, type of property, and date and time of suspicious fires, high frequency arson areas can be pinpointed. In addition to identifying these areas, properties subject to set fires can be noted, along with the hours during which the majority of these offenses occur. This information enables the arson squad to concentrate its efforts in these areas at the appropriate times. Equally important, it points out the need for an arson strike force and the target locations and time frames in which this group can operate with maximum impact. As has been stated previously, one of the most effective methods of controlling arson is to prevent it, and when information, computerized or not, is readily available as to where and when arson fires may occur, a significant step has been taken.

The principal value of an intelligence file is that it provides the arson squad with names, not only of individuals but also of real estate and insurance agents, lending institutions, contracting and demolition firms, salvage companies, adjusters, and any other individuals or concerns that might be involved in arson for fraud.

A word of caution is necessary at this juncture. In view of public attitudes regarding intelligence files, and, even more pertinent, with the existence of federal and state legislation governing such records, the prudent manager will see to it that due weight is given to the obvious arguments against, as well as for, such a procedure. If such a file is established, legal advice should be sought as to assurances regarding the confidentiality of information contained therein, particularly in the light of "sunshine laws" making many public documents open to scrutiny by the media, concerned taxpayers, and others.

Given this background, it is also necessary to state that, in the opinion of many persons active in the arson investigation field, the need for a file on such people and businesses can be justified by a brief résumé of just how the entities mentioned above may be involved in an arson scam. The entire operation is a well-designed and well-planned conspiracy, with each entity mentioned above an integral part thereof. The property involved, for example, a run-down apartment building or a vacant warehouse, generally has a relatively low market value. The purchase of the property, perhaps through a dummy corporation, is arranged and executed by the real estate agent. Funds for the purchase are acquired through a lending agency which is fully aware of the whole scheme. Insurance is placed on the property and contents far in excess of their value by the insurance agent, who is also a conspirator. At this point occasionally a contractor is involved, who is allegedly employed to renovate the structure. The contractor's role is to make a few token repairs to the building prior to the fire and after the fire to cite extensive improvements which were accomplished, thus justifying the insurance claim. The demolition firm may be nothing more than a silent conspirator, agreeing to kickbacks to each of the co-conspirators if the demolition job is awarded to the company after the fire.

The key figure in the entire scheme is the insurance adjuster, who, after the fire, submits an exorbitant claim to the company or companies that have coverage on the loss. The salvage company may benefit in two ways: first, from contents which are stealthily removed from the structure before the fire, and second, from salvage rights awarded after the fire for token payment only. The final reward for all the conspirators is a share in the insurance checks, which will far exceed any investment. Unfortunately, a few documented cases also show that on rare occasions there can be another participant in the conspiracy—namely an investigator who officially reports that the fire was of accidental origin.

With this type of fraud becoming more frequent, the need for an intelligence file, with names of individuals and businesses clearly identified, becomes increasingly obvious. These individuals and businesses will frequently use aliases, will change names of involved companies, will set up paper corporations, and will resort to all manner of other deceptions to conceal their participation in the scheme. It is a challenging assignment to the arson squad to keep up with the activities of such people through its own efforts and through the computerized record system and intelligence file, but this is an integral part of the arson prevention and control effort.

In addition to revealing information relative to such schemes, the records will identify property owners who have had previous suspicious fires. Names of and pertinent information on suspected fire-setters, professional torches, and the so-called pyromaniacs will be integrated into the system. The modus operandi connected with a suspicious fire will often lead to suspects who have developed an unconscious pattern for their fire-setting. Again, close liaison with the city attorney or other competent legal authority is mandatory if such an assignment is being considered.

The arson strike force and its applications

An operation that is proving highly effective in the arson prevention effort is the arson strike force. In Seattle, Washington, this activity has produced meaningful reductions in incendiary fires. As noted earlier in the chapter, however, the arson strike force may not be applicable outside of large metropolitan jurisdictions.

In Seattle the fire prevention patrols developed by Fire Chief Frank R. Hanson employ combat firefighters. Chief Hanson states that the fire prevention patrol "was formed with the belief that placing uniformed fire personnel and equipment in selected problem areas would be the most direct and visual method of offering community support in dealing with problems related to the service we provide—primarily the protection of lives and property."[5]

Perhaps the most unusual aspect of the Seattle program is that in most cases no effort is made to conceal the fact that the patrol is in action in a specific area. Firefighters in obviously identifiable fire department vehicles cover certain assigned areas during hours when numerous arson fires have occurred, as identified by the computerized records system. In addition to visibility, these personnel also make their presence known by conducting inspections and performing other fire prevention activities while on patrol. When data analyses taken from the computer indicate that certain types of businesses have become or may become high arson incident targets, these businesses are given special attention by patrol members. Frequent inspections of the property and visible stakeouts are conducted, with the result that the property owner is keenly aware of this special attention. The combat firefighter is not a police officer, and is instructed to call for law enforcement assistance when it is required. According to Chief Hanson the fire prevention patrol has received wide support from the community, and this support has materially increased its effectiveness and has significantly reduced arson fires in Seattle.

Three features of the Seattle arson strike force seem worth pointing to at this juncture. First, those in charge agree that the operation should be left entirely up to the fire department. When a team comprised of a police officer and a fire department representative is sent out on patrol, the normal duties to which the police personnel may be called make it impossible for the team to function effectively. Additionally, people in the community will provide more information to fire department personnel than they will to the police, as the firefighters generally have a better relationship with the citizenry.

Second, the strike force members attempt to convey to the community the message that they are there to help. This objective can be accomplished only through communicating with the people—explaining the strike force's mission and seeking citizens' help in preserving their neighborhoods.

Third, the ultimate objective of the strike force is to prevent arson and by its presence to act as a deterrent. The most important factor in the operation is success—the number of arson fires is being reduced. At a time when many major cities across the country are being overwhelmed by incendiary fires, the Seattle program provides a clear illustration that an arson strike force or fire prevention patrol can contribute materially to the arson suppression effort.

Cooperative efforts in combating arson

The arson unit and the police and fire departments

A determination needs to be made as to the relationship that should exist between the arson investigation unit (as described earlier in this chapter) and other agencies within the municipality, particularly the fire and police departments. An atmosphere of mutual respect must be developed between the arson unit and combat firefighters, as their assistance and cooperation are necessary if the investigation is to be successful. The areas in the investigative process which involve the firefighters have already been discussed, but the need for a sound working relationship is worth repeating here. Of equal importance, too, as previously stated, is close liaison with the police department, particularly the detective division, as arson fires are often connected with other crimes such as burglaries, breaking and entering, and sex offenses.

Neighboring jurisdictions

The arson squad should maintain lines of communication with jurisdictions bordering the municipality, as the arsonist is not concerned with jurisdictional boundaries when setting fires. Often suburban communities do not have the capability to conduct their own arson training programs, whether for firefighters, fire officers, or investigators, and will welcome the opportunity to attend a course conducted by the municipality for its own personnel. Joint participation in such training leads to an exchange of information concerning techniques, procedures, problems, suspects, and other mutually beneficial matters. A procedure which has proved effective is to conduct regularly scheduled meetings of fire and police officials involved in fire and arson investigation. The purpose of these conferences is to give attendees the opportunity to report informally on arson trends, patterns, and specific cases in their jurisdiction. This communication can lead to the apprehension of a fire-setter because of some common denominator such as types of buildings burned; dates, days of week, and times of the offenses; or modus operandi.

States

Most states have some entity in the state government charged with the responsibility for investigating arson or suspicious fires, usually upon request from a locality. This organization is usually located in a state agency such as the fire marshal's office, the state police, or the state bureau of investigation. With the present severe arson problem, the majority of state arson investigative agencies do not have sufficient personnel to actively participate in investigations in large municipalities.

Even though state and local investigators may not be working jointly on cases, there should be communication between the two groups. Arson arrests and convictions in the municipality should be reported to the state agency so that accurate incendiary fire facts and figures are available on a state level. Information obtained from the state agency on arson incidents in other areas may be of assistance to municipal investigators. In substance, the arson unit should not operate in isolation.

Private investigative agencies

Over the years a number of private investigative agencies have come into being. Some are supported in some form by the insurance industry on a continuous basis, while others are retained by a company or companies on an individual case basis. In most instances these people are completely ethical and can be of assistance to the local investigator in certain specific phases of the case, particularly as regards providing insurance information. Arson squad members should thoroughly check the credentials and the past reputation of any person who claims to represent an insurance company's interest.

The insurance industry

Earlier in this chapter, in connection with the arson task force, the insurance industry was cited as a resource in the effort to combat arson. As members of the arson task force, local representatives of the insurance industry can contribute to the arson control effort in several significant ways. First, individual agents should exercise care in writing insurance and in not grossly overinsuring property. Second, agents should not demand immediate settlement of a claim following a fire of questionable origin. (Instances in which insurance settlements are made while investigations are still in progress are not unusual.) Third, agents should inform the arson unit of any activity—such as increased insurance or new policies—involving individuals who have a history of fires, suspicious or otherwise. Fourth, and perhaps most important, representatives of the insurance industry can create within the insurance agencies and companies a sense of awareness and concern over the arson problem in the community. As a result, an atmosphere of mutual cooperation between the local government investigators and the insurance people can be developed.

While not directly related to arson task force activities, an action taken by the insurance industry in several states is producing meaningful results in reducing arson fires. The industry is funding programs in which rewards varying from $1,000 to $10,000 are being offered for information on incendiary fires. Large dramatic signs are posted on fire damaged property where arson is suspected, informing the public that rewards will be paid for information leading to the arrest and/or conviction of the arsonist or arsonists. Persons providing information can remain anonymous, and their identity and information will be given every protection. Such reward programs are in effect in Michigan, Ohio, and Washington, and arson investigation experts in each of these states report significant results.

On the national level the insurance industry is displaying an increased awareness and concern over the spiraling costs of arson. Full-page advertisements in national magazines, paid for by individual insurance companies, call the public's attention to the arson problem and its significance for all property owners in that it causes their fire insurance premiums to increase. A national clearinghouse that records considerable data on property insurance loss, for purposes of comparison, has been implemented by the American Insurance Association; it is available, by subscription service, to individual insurance companies.[6] These actions, and others that are contemplated, indicate that insurance groups are making genuine efforts to become involved in the national arson control program.

Housing authorities

An entity also previously mentioned in connection with the arson task force is the local housing authority. This involvement in fact moves beyond the local level, as federal authorities also enter the picture. It is normally the function of local building officials or the housing authority to restrict occupancy or to condemn property. When property owners are informed that buildings can no longer be occupied or used for any profitable purpose, the property becomes a financial burden. The fact that a successful fire with more than adequate insurance monies collected is a solution to the problem is quite obvious to the owners of such properties. Building officials, inspectors, and the housing authority should keep the arson unit informed of occupancy restrictions or condemnations, as the potential for incendiary fires under these circumstances is great.

On the federal level a situation exists relative to housing that is causing numerous arson fires. For a number of years in an effort to provide low cost housing for low income families the federal government subsidized the construction of single family dwellings in urban areas. Unfortunately, many of these houses were poorly constructed of inferior materials, with inadequate heating systems, faulty plumbing, and major structural weaknesses. When these units literally began to fall apart, the occupants refused to make any further payments and simply moved out, causing the housing to revert back to the government. Stuck with many thousands of such units in urban areas across the country, federal authorities were forced to sell these houses—in some cases for as little as $100! The purchasers in many instances had only one thought in mind—to buy for a song, insure for $10,000 or $12,000, and burn to collect. While this incentive to buy and burn has eased up to some extent, the opportunity to make such easy money is still available in certain areas of the country. Federal housing officials, through the efforts of the arson task force, should be made to realize the seriousness of this problem and to accept the responsibility for initiating corrective action.[7]

A contributing factor to the number of urban arson fires is a procedure in which the housing authorities and the welfare departments are participants. In many urban communities, if a family on welfare has a fire they are paid up to $2,000 to purchase furniture, clothing, and household necessities to replace those destroyed. In addition, they are moved to the top of the list of those waiting for newer, more adequate housing provided by the local government. This double benefit has been the catalyst for many set fires, and both the housing and welfare departments, as members of the arson task force, must be persuaded to take the necessary steps to correct this situation.

The Chamber of Commerce

An organization that can make a significant contribution to the arson task force is the local Chamber of Commerce, particularly on the following three counts. First, through its contact with the business interests in the community the Chamber of Commerce can encourage participation by businesses of all types in the arson control effort. Second, the Chamber of Commerce can supply information on business and economic trends, on migratory patterns within the city, on employment and unemployment figures, and on specific businesses or types of businesses in financial trouble. A correlation between this information and suspected arson fires may be possible. Third, through its various lines of communication the Chamber of Commerce can create in the community an awareness of the arson problem and its economic impact on the community.

The media

While not actually included on the arson task force, the news media is a most important ingredient in a successful arson control effort. The public needs to be informed of the creation of the task force, of its purposes and objectives, and of what it hopes to accomplish in the interest of the community. Also, the media— radio, television, and newspapers—can convey to the general public the seriousness of the arson problem and its impact on every citizen. Spot announcements on radio relating arson loss figures and urging citizen cooperation are most effective. Television coverage of final results of investigative efforts arouse public interest and concern over arson losses. Television audiences in general are interested in crime-oriented programs, and when such programs are oriented to the locality they have an even greater attraction. Newspaper coverage of the effort to combat arson and the success of the arson investigative unit generate community support. Through the media the public can be made to realize that every citizen is a participant in the arson control effort. Without this feeling of being involved, the average person will view the entire program with indifference and apathy. This attitude can be overcome with the cooperation of the media; if it is not, the entire effort can end in failure.[8]

Conclusion

This chapter has stressed the managerial and organizational aspects of the attack on the arson problem at the local government level. It has looked at major organizational options available to local government managers and fire managers and has emphasized such operational aspects as the task force approach; the relationship with the prosecutor; and the arson investigative unit and its personnel, operations, training, and record keeping. It has also described something of the experience of arson strike forces as used in Seattle.

The chapter has stressed the need to make managers—whether inside or outside of the fire department—aware of the arson problem and of what they can do to combat it. Arson has an impact in every area of the country, and local governments and their professional staffs, regardless of size, have the choice of either curbing this crime or living with the consequences for their community. As innumerable reports and conferences have made clear, arson is one of the most costly (and one of the most rapidly growing) crimes in the United States; it represents a dollar cost four to eight times greater than that of any other individual crime. Any successful attempt to control this problem will have a demonstrable payoff for the cost-conscious taxpayers of our communities.

1 City of Seattle Fire Department, *Seattle Arson Task Force: Implementation Program* (Seattle, Wash.: City of Seattle Fire Department, 1977). The Seattle experience has been written up in a special issue, devoted to arson, of *Target* (the monthly newsletter of the Criminal Justice Project of the International City Management Association), for January 1978.

2 The subject of cooperation between the prosecutor's office and the arson investigation unit is discussed in: Robert C. McGann, "DAs Are Urged To Become Involved in Early Stage of Fire Investigations," *Fire Engineering* 131 (August 1978): 66–70.

3 For detailed information on the management of police criminal investigation, see Thomas F. Hastings, "Criminal Investigation," in *Local Government Police Management,* ed. Bernard L. Garmire (Washington, D.C.: International City Management Association, 1977), pp. 211–31.

4 For detailed coverage of arson unit operations, see: Benjamin S. Huron, *Elements of Arson Investigation* (New York: Dun · Donnelley Corporation, 1976).

5 Seattle Fire Department, *Seattle Arson Task Force,* Part VII.

6 Further information on this service can be obtained from: American Insurance Association, 85 John Street, New York, New York 10038.

7 A full discussion of federal housing options and their costs, with references to the literature on the subject, can be found in the following publications: James Follain, Jane Katz, and Raymond J. Struyk, *Programmatic Options To Encourage Home-ownership* (Washington, D.C.: U.S. Department of Housing and Urban Development, Office of Policy Development and Research, 1978); U.S., Department of Housing and Urban Development, Task Force on Housing Costs, *Final Report of the Task Force on Housing Costs* (Washington, D.C.: U.S. Department of Housing and Urban Development, 1978); and Irving H. Welfeld et al., *Perspectives on Housing and Urban Renewal* (New York: Praeger Publishers, 1974).

8 For information on managing community public relations, including working with the media, see: William H. Gilbert, ed., *Public Relations in Local Government* (Washington, D.C.: International City Management Association, 1975).

Part three:
Personnel,
the budget,
and productivity

12 The budgetary process

What is public budgeting? What do decision makers both inside and outside of the fire department need to know about the elements making up the budgetary process in their jurisdictions? How does the fire department fit into this process? What are the types of budgets? How is an adopted budget controlled?

In the political and administrative climate of the late 1970s these are questions that fire chiefs and other managers (and all those who aspire to such positions) must address if they are to be effective. Taken together, these questions—and some of the answers to them—form the basis of this chapter.

The chapter is organized into seven sections. The first three take a look at the theory and practice of budgeting—and at the resources to budget. The fourth section focuses on eight types of budget, and their strengths and weaknesses. This is followed by a section that outlines and assesses the budgetary controls so important to successful management: this fifth section covers such traditional devices as percentage deviation reports and allotments, but also covers various behavioral and human relations controls, such as management by objectives and job enrichment. The sixth section takes a brief look at retirement systems budgeting, and the seventh provides a short summary of, and conclusion to, the discussion. Throughout the chapter the authors—who combine both managerial and teaching experience—have sought to provide a straightforward and realistic discussion that will be useful to those in fire departments and those in appropriate college and university courses who may not have an extensive background in economics or public finance. For those seeking to further explore the theoretical underpinnings of the discussion, another volume in the Municipal Management Series is available and recommended.[1]

By way of overview let us return to the question posed at the beginning of this chapter: What is public budgeting? Those with experience in this area might describe public budgeting as a strange combination of the political and the administrative. A public budgeting "system" consists of the following three seemingly disconnected but carefully intertwined elements:

1. The mechanical system, whereby the accountants and financially-oriented types make sure that all the figures add up and are entered in the proper spaces in the correct forms.
2. The systemic technicians, who "massage" the mechanically derived data to assure that the "most efficient and effective" alternatives are chosen. The tools of this group are the analytical tools of cost–benefit analysis, managerial analysis, alternative studies, reorganization plans, and other similar approaches.
3. The political element, whereby the elected officials are "educated" by inputs from special interest groups, the general public (who also usually are members of various special interest groups), and the staff. Included among the last group are those who are requesting appropriations for their governmental operations, such as fire chiefs.

Such is the setting of any—and every—budget system, no matter how small, or how gigantic, the jurisdiction.

Budgeting for a public jurisdiction can be defined as the development and execution of a plan for effective use of financial resources in carrying out policies for a fiscal period. *Public budgeting* is the expression in financial terms of the cumulative policies of the jurisdiction for the impending fiscal year.

The theory of budgeting

Public budgeting theory holds that there are four basic reasons for adoption of the public budget, namely:

1. Policymaking, which is intended to express policy financially. It is a kind of scorekeeping of priorities by dollar allocations to agencies or functions.
2. Supplying information to the policymakers and the public, so that they may more intelligently distribute scarce public dollars among competing governmental uses. Also through the budget, the public is to be informed as to the collecting and setting of priorities for their collective public assets and the services provided therewith.
3. Supplying specific data to operational managers within the component parts of the jurisdiction, so that they may fine tune their operations as the fiscal year progresses. Such operational decision making, of course, presupposes that there is an accurate and timely budgetary accounting system with which to track revenues and expenditures as the fiscal year unfolds.
4. Controlling objectives and expenditures. Unfortunately, this fourth reason at times consumes the other, more theoretical, reasons and tends to become the be-all and end-all of the budgetary process.

The resources for budgeting

It is axiomatic, as proved in the mid-1970s by the unhappy experience of the city of New York, that annual revenues must at least equal—and should usually exceed—budgeted appropriations and the expenditure of public monies at the local level.

Since World War II, local expenditures and the revenues which give rise to them have expanded at a higher average annual rate than either the gross national product (GNP) or the expenditures of the federal government.[2] Grants from the federal government have accounted for an increasing share of state and local expenditures, amounting to some $7 billion in 1960 and growing to $41.8 billion by 1974.[3] Over the same time span combined state and local sources of funds, apart from federal grants, grew from $53.3 billion to $196.1 billion or 368 percent as compared to the 597 percent grant growth.[4]

City financial resources

From 1960 to 1974 city government diversified considerably and rapidly out of the property tax, which in 1960 accounted for $5.2 billion or 34.9 percent of city revenues. By 1974, while the amount had risen to $12.2 billion the percentage had declined to 23.1 percent.[5] The balance was more than made up by the increase in intergovernmental transfers from state and, increasingly, federal sources—from $2.3 billion (15.4 percent) in 1960 to $16.6 billion (31.4 percent) in 1974.[6] And the trend continues.

Charges and miscellaneous revenues have risen only proportionately as many cities seek to diversify their revenue base. In the decade and a half from 1960 to 1974 such sources have risen from $2.2 billion of the total $14.9 billion revenue (or 14.8 percent) to $8.1 billion of $52.8 billion (15.3 percent). Coincidentally, this revenue source in 1960 just equaled the $2.2 billion expended also in 1960 for police and fire protection, while such combined public safety expenditures had reached only $7.2 billion by 1974.[7] It appears, then, that expenditures for public safety have not increased as rapidly as the revenue base expansion.

Fire department revenues

Fire departments other than volunteer departments, whose importance should not be overlooked, have usually not generated funds for their own direct support, as the nature of fire protection is a community-wide service. The service charges which, historically, helped to support fire protection and which were levied after the fire had started, were, typically, disastrous, since they were hard to collect. The fire services have usually been supported by the general fund of the local agency. Special tax districts created for a single purpose, such as fire protection, sewers, libraries, and similar services, have relied on the property tax.

In 1978 California voted in Proposition 13, which generally limited property taxes to 1 percent of market value. This limitation has seriously restricted the revenues for special tax district fire departments in California (and the message of the voters in that state has not been lost elsewhere). In addition, the limitation on property tax revenues has created higher levels of intense competition for already scarce resources. The fire department managers in California face an array of alternatives that range from severe cuts to moderate cuts, and also face continuation of current levels of services with probably little option for increased levels of budget allocation.

Some fire departments charge fees for specific services, especially such services as fire inspection and plan checking. These fees are intended to support the inspection services that are regulatory for the hazardous materials and processes. In response to Proposition 13 numerous suggestions were made for service charges that would bring in funds for the operation of fire departments. Some of these service charges were adopted in Inglewood and in San Clemente for rescue calls and transport service by paramedics, for buildings of excessive size having service demands larger than an average home, and for clearance of fire debris.

Fire department expenditures

Fire departments have usually expended in proportion to available total local revenues. In recent years fire department managers have been confronted with restrictions of available revenues—often to their dismay after years of constantly increasing levels of service in our urban regional expansions. In the 1970s efforts have been made to increase levels of technical efficiency; these efforts have been augmented by scientific methodology. Public Technology, Inc. (PTI), the International City Management Association (ICMA), the National Aeronautics and Space Administration (NASA), the U.S. Fire Administration (USFA; formerly the National Fire Prevention and Control Administration [NFPCA]), the National Fire Protection Association (NFPA), the International Association of Fire Chiefs (IAFC), the International Association of Fire Fighters (IAFF), and private vendors have all participated in manpower studies and equipment development in an attempt to reach higher levels of efficiency.

Unfortunately, little data have been developed or collected in a systematic, reliable way to date. ICMA's *Municipal Year Book* and its Urban Data Service Reports annually present data on fire department expenditures, but these data are grouped together for classes of municipalities and are not broken out for individual fire departments; therefore, they do not allow comparability. Researchers would need to seek out specific details from each fire agency and construct comparable tables which reflect realistic and accurate data.

As a consequence of the absence of reliable data on budgetary expenditures for fire protection, it can only be determined that most fire departments are managed in rational coordination with the Insurance Services Office (ISO) grading schedule (see Chapter 4) and according to traditional concepts of consensus budgets determined by the past year's budget allocation plus incremental changes.

The emerging theory of fire loss management budgeting

Efforts to collect systemic data are being made by the National Fire Data Center of the U.S. Fire Administration. Earlier efforts made in 1970—funded by grants from the U.S. Department of Housing and Urban Development (HUD) to NFPA—assisted in the development of the Uniform Fire Incident Reporting System (UFIRS), using the NFPA 901 format. The USFA, assisted by NFPA, later developed NFIRS (National Fire Incident Reporting System), which also uses the NFPA 901 format. NFIRS provides the data collection system for understanding the nature and scope of the actual fire problems in the United States. As of 1979 approximately thirty states had agreed to use the NFIRS format and transmit the data to the National Fire Data Center of the U.S. Fire Administration. (This topic is explored further in Chapter 18.)

Concurrent with these developments, creative thinking by fire department managers was being directed at the traditional concepts of *efficiency* in fire departments. Public demands for continued increases in services were inconsistent with restricted budget allocations throughout the country. In 1969 Charles Rule, then fire chief of Greenfield, Wisconsin, proposed, and was successful in obtaining, legislation to require automatic sprinkler systems in all buildings over 10,000 square feet of total floor space. This same concept was advocated in Mountain View, California, by Byron Chaney, when he was fire chief there, to cope with increased service demands and restricted budget allocations. In 1972 the city of Mountain View enacted legislation requiring automatic sprinkler systems in buildings over 10,000 total square feet and smoke detectors or automatic sprinkler systems in buildings over 5,000 total square feet. This attack on the maximum size of potential fires was a strategic shift from technical definitions of *efficiency* to measures of *effectiveness* in fire loss management.

This automatic sprinkler system law was soon adopted by all the nearby cities in Santa Clara County, and by Santa Clara County itself, in 1973–74. The concept was quickly supported by Bernard Levin at the National Bureau of Standards in May 1973. As program manager of the Fire Services Program, he agreed to fund the Master Planning for Fire Protection study in fiscal 1973–74. This study was transferred to the NFPCA in 1975 after NFPCA's creation by Public Law 93–498 in late 1974.

Increased effectiveness in the life safety aspects of the fire problem were initiated in the city of San Carlos, California, in 1973 by the then fire chief, Richard Bosted, who advocated and saw the adoption of legislation for the mandatory installation of smoke detectors. (The U.S. Department of Housing and Urban Development issued regulations requiring smoke detectors in all residential buildings funded or guaranteed by the federal government after 1 April 1974.)

A 1971 staff report of the San Jose, California, fire department indicated that Chicago and Seattle were using fire protection engineers to assist in the planning of fire protection. A number of fire departments soon followed this lead, and by the late 1970s the list included San Jose, Los Angeles, Santa Monica, Costa Mesa, and Orange County, all in California, as well as Jacksonville, Florida, Alexandria, Virginia, New York City, and numerous other fire departments throughout the United States.

Out of these shifts from technical efficiency to strategic effectiveness, the methodology for budget preparation for the fire problem has developed. The concept of reduction of the size of fires to maximum areas of 10,000 square feet by mandatory automatic sprinkler systems has the correlated reduction of required fire flow and required fire companies necessary to control that magnitude of fire. (Required fire flow—the amount of water needed to provide adequate fire protection—is discussed in Chapter 9, together with other control methods.) This shift in attacking the size of the fire problem potential is recognized and is part of the ISO grading schedule, 1974 edition. This increased effectiveness should be part of the fire department manager's approach to development of the budget.

The early detection of smoke enables people to rescue themselves in the early stages of the fire cycle and to call the fire department while the fire is still small. This represents both increased efficiency and increased effectiveness.

The concept that budget allocations should be predominantly for fire suppression is often attacked on the basis that fire prevention has a higher cost–benefit ratio than fire suppression has. While this is true, it is misleading because of inadequate analysis.

Fire department revenues are usually calculated as minor levels of cash receipts. This has face validity but ignores the true value of an organized fire department, which is to preserve the community of people and the economy. It is difficult to think in terms of a loss of the economy because it is not usually totally destroyed. We pay for fire losses by suffering losses directly or by paying for the preventive efforts on the part of fire departments that are made to minimize direct fire losses. Even though the prevented losses cannot be seen, it is essential to analyze the saving of buildings and contents at risk to fire losses as revenues generated by the fire department.

The entire economy relies on the fire suppression capability of fire departments; this includes the fire prevention programs. These fire prevention efforts include the concepts of management of fire losses by mandatory automatic sprinkler systems and mandatory smoke detectors in all buildings—to reduce the size of fires and to reduce the costs of providing fire suppression forces.

The need for providing adequate fire protection through fire suppression is due to the fact that an industrial economy depends on large concentrations of combustible materials and buildings. Random events create fires in these situations and the resulting fires are either controlled while small or burn the entire amount of combustibles at risk. This fire risk is so high that investors will not commit their financial resources unless the fire losses are spread over the entire economy through fire insurance.

The history of bankrupt fire insurance companies has been such that it has been necessary to develop reliable and adequate fire control forces and built-in fire protection equipment and systems, so that the fire insurance industry can provide financial protection to investors; therefore, the fire suppression forces, including the fire prevention efforts, are a mandatory feature of the industrial economy. The significant point is to manage the total fire problem instead of reacting to individual fires only.

It has been advocated that the financial support of fire departments should be provided by the fire insurance industry. This could be accomplished by a fire insurance tax or service fee and could be scaled to some measure of private built-in fire protection such as automatic sprinkler systems and smoke detectors. This concept deserves funded research and study by the U.S. Fire Administration, as it applies across state lines and involves interstate commerce.

The practice of budgeting

Experience unfortunately demonstrates that many budgetary systems are operated in such a way that the theory of budgeting has long since been ignored—if it was ever known.

Some characteristics

The policymaking decision process   The nature of the policymaking decision process is such that the seemingly objective process of deciding budgetary priorities is, in fact, anything but objective. Since the turn of the century various budgetary systems, approaches, and format types have been developed in the continuing quest for objectivity. It would appear that the very nature of democracy, and its linchpin of representative elections and the inherent "politics," militates against objectivity in the usual sense. Budgeting could be additionally defined as a rational decision-making mechanical system working within a larger irrational process (although politicians might object to such a characterization).

The management control system   The management control system of assuring that monies are not expended for purposes and objectives not intended, and that overexpenditures are not incurred, is that part of the total budgetary process that most governmental employees experience. Most such "systems" are based on the assumption (an erroneous one, as will be later described) that a small group of strategically placed persons in the organization can control the behavior, and the expenditure patterns, of vast numbers of persons and great sums of money. Thus, many budgets are almost solely control documents. As such they are short on objectives and long on obsessive monetary strictures.

Conflicts between policymaking and management control   Inherent conflicts exist between the policymaking process and the management control devices. A budgetary format and system that concentrates on the broad picture of programs and objectives usually is lacking in details sufficient to be useful as a day-to-day management information and control tool. On the other hand, a financial decision-making approach that relies heavily on detailed data sufficient to meet operational needs usually degenerates into the ubiquitous "pencil counting" decision process. The latter approach guarantees loss of vision as to the overall objectives of the expenditure of public monies. Thus, any budgeting system is seemingly caught between the two conflicting needs and must be a compromise between them. While these needs can be reconciled, such reconciliation is extremely difficult to accomplish and is in fact a rare occurrence.[8]

A variety of systems

Several budgeting systems are described in the section that immediately follows. While some approach operational needs and others approach policymaking decision capability, none addresses both of these needs. Such are the anomalies of the public budgetary process. This, perhaps, is also why each of the public elected and appointed policy officials and the operating personnel usually damn the budget process and wonder what is happening to the citizen's tax money.

Types of budgets

Since the late nineteenth century eight basic budgetary systems or formats have been developed and, to a greater or lesser degree, installed in and used by governmental jurisdictions. In the following discussion each is described briefly. The more useful of these are illustrated by figures.

The lump sum budget

Before the governmental reform movement which began around the turn of the century, most fire departments were appropriated a lump sum of money considered adequate for their needs. The fire chief, who was usually politically appointed by the city council and its fire committee, would recommend the amount to the fire committee. The fire committee, which consisted of council members, would review this recommendation and would, in turn, recommend an amount to the full city council. The finance committee of the council would add up all such amounts for all such committees and would adopt the budget and tax rate to finance the fire department.

The fire chief, subject to the month-to-month general supervision of the fire committee, would dole out the money pretty much as he and the fire committee saw fit. Obviously there was considerable opportunity for mismanagement and diversion of monies. When such problems reached the epidemic level the reformers appropriately sought major changes. One of these revisions was a strictly controlled budget, the line item budget.

The line item budget

By far the most prevalent budgetary format, and the original "reform" budgetary format, the line item budget (Figure 12–1) is basically a listing of items of purchase and acquisition, by department, by agency, or, in some cases, by a lesser organizational unit within the larger component. The concentration on object of expenditure (line item) in considerable detail often results in a lengthy document.

Figure 12–1 A typical line item budget. (Source: City of Laguna Beach, California.)

CITY OF LAGUNA BEACH
DETAIL OF EXPENDITURES

FUND GENERAL	DEPARTMENT FIRE	DIVISION	ACCOUNT NO. 11-151

Object No.	Account Title	1974-75 Actual	1975-76 Budget	1976-77 Department Request	1976-77 Manager Recommends	1976-77 Council Adopted
	SALARIES AND BENEFITS					
101	Salaries, Full Time	487,597	507,802	515,100	515,100	528,586
102	Salaries, Part Time					
103	Salaries, Overtime	12,662	6,290	25,000	12,500	12,813
105	Salaries, Redistributed	200	220			
201	Retirement	46,843	49,700	57,800	57,800	59,070
202	Workmens Compensation	29,498	43,100	57,446	56,514	56,381
203	Medical/Life Insurance	11,447	14,592	14,231	14,231	18,462
	Sub-Total	588,247	621,704	669,577	656,145	675,312
	MAINTENANCE & OPERATION					
301	Uniforms	5,682	9,955	7,700	7,700	7,700
302	Training, Travel, Dues	731	890	855	855	855
'05	Gas & Lubricants	2,042	2,444	2,600	2,600	2,600
	Materials & Supplies	4,920	6,190	7,500		700

Advantages The advantages of the line item budget are simple. First, owing to the ease of adding up the lists of items to be purchased and services to be acquired, a budget total is easy to derive. When all such organizational monetary lists are added up and compared to total revenues, the amount "out of balance" or, rarely, that which is left over, makes it relatively easy to assure a balanced budget. (Historically, the difference was made up in property taxes, and the budget was "balanced" by calculating the "out of balance" amount in terms of cents per hundred of assessed valuation.) Unfortunately, the balancing process is such that it looks easy to cut and balance, since little if any implications are indicated resulting from the reduction in items. But the absolute ability to balance is a significant advantage.

A second advantage—at least most consider it such—is that, since dollars are appropriated for the specific items, and failure to expend would be considered a lack of need for such monies, then absolute expenditure of all appropriations is an almost inevitable outcome. If such monies are not spent then invariably the unexpended amount for the current fiscal year is lost, as is an equal amount for succeeding years.

A third advantage is the provision of the level of operational detail needed by departmental supervisors for timing, revising, and controlling their internal day-to-day operations. Such listings are also vital to the preparation and justification of the next year's budget and as an estimating base for the component parts for any fire department modifications or additions.

Disadvantages The major disadvantages of the line item budget are numerous—so much so that most jurisdictions and all budget theoreticians have at one time or another attempted to switch away from it to another form. Most have been unsuccessful because of the first of these major disadvantages, which stems from the fact that a line item budget, by its very nature, permits a direct and absolute linkage between the budgetary control accounting system and the budget. The recordation of invoices and payrolls directly against specific line items within organizational components is simple and is easily systematized and—even more important—it meets the control needs of those in charge of most budgetary processes. Thus, the small control group, or individual, can easily spot who is tending to overspend and can deal as harshly as need be to assure that such overexpenditure occurs only once (in fact, the control group or individual may even spot such expenditure prior to consummation). This direct ability to tightly—most say overly—control the operational officials acts effectively and generally to stifle innovation and enthusiasm. It also assures maximum spending of appropriations, whether such spending is needed or not.

Another drawback to the line item budget is the emphasis it places on objects of expenditure (inputs) rather than on results of expenditure (outputs). Because of the line item budget's emphasis on detail, most discussion held by policy officials on this budget form is aimed at "cutting out the fat" rather than at substantively exploring alternative methodologies for using the line item amount of dollars to secure the same objective. A phenomenon accompanying the above is usually a lack of operational flexibility. Monies are appropriated for the specific item; should events change between preparation and execution, approval by a budgetary official or even the city council is frequently needed to transfer monies between line items. This review process often amounts to double jeopardy: thus, other devices are often resorted to by the operating official to secure operating flexibility in use of appropriated resources.

The performance budget

Periodically, since the late 1920s, governmental budget analysts have attempted in one way or another and with varying degrees of finesse to apply the scientific management principles of industrial engineer Frederick W. Taylor to governmental operations and budgeting.[9] The performance budget (Figure 12–2) is one attempt at such an application.

The features of the performance budget are basically that (1) standards of performance are set for each organizational unit, (2) compliance is measured against those standards, and (3) those standards as units of work are divided by

CITY OF LONG BEACH, CALIFORNIA

COMMENTARY

1. FUND	2. FUNCTION	3. ACCOUNT	4. DEPARTMENT
GENERAL PURPOSE		1-22	FIRE

GOAL: To maintain a physical environment within the City wherein the incidence of fires will be at a minimum. When fires do occur, to detect them in their incipiency and control them with a minimum loss of life and property. To provide emergency medical service, to stabilize the condition of sick and injured persons in the field and ensure their delivery to a medical facility with minimum effects of trauma.

Programs	Performance Indicators
2.0 Fire Suppression and Rescue	
2.1 Alarm/Communications	Number of calls for emergency service
	Percentage of emergency calls received via fire alarm box
	Percentage of emergency calls received via telephone
	Percentage of emergency calls received via other sources
	Ratio of defects found to alarm/communication systems tests conducted
2.2 Dispatching	Number and type of calls dispatched
	Percent of calls dispatched in less than designated target time
2.3 Firefighting	Number of fire alarms
	Percent of first-in response times less than designated target time
2.4 Emergency Medical Services	Number of paramedic service responses
	Percent of service responses in less than designated target time
	Number of cardiac arrest victims sustained by paramedics
	Percent of non-paramedic first aid responses in less than designated target time
2.5 Technical Services Support	Total hours downtime of emergency equipment
	Major equipment repair costs
	Major equipment replacement costs

Figure 12-2 A performance budget. (Source: City of Long Beach, California.)

the dollars allocated and a unit cost is derived. The goal is to reduce, or at least to hold steady, the unit cost.

Advantages The advantages of this budget system have to be viewed in historical perspective. As the line item budget does not normally consider results or outputs, institution of the performance budget system has made a major change in that results are at least viewed. Goals are set in the form of desired outputs and a measurement system is developed to quantify the degree to which these desired objectives are reached. A jurisdiction changing from the line item to performance budgeting is automatically forced, for the first time, to look beyond the immediate dollar amounts in the line items and to attempt to see what the money is buying in terms of service.

Disadvantages The disadvantages of the performance budget, however, have universally outweighed the advantages; therefore, few conversions have been attempted since the late 1950s, and those generally have been unsuccessful and short-lived. Primary among the problems is that the entire presumption of Taylorism has been disproved totally by social psychologist researchers who have applied their work to governmental management.

In this type of budget system, development of the performance standards is usually authoritarian, with a small group of "efficiency experts" determining both what the appropriate unit of measurement for each work (budget) group will be and how many units of output should be secured. This "big brother" approach, with little or no meaningful participation on the part of those to be measured, is inherently behaviorally invalid. Because of its imposed nature, the unit measurements and costs are notoriously unreliable and soon prove self-destructive.

Furthermore, personnel are needed to count and maintain the work statistics, and the doom of many performance budgets has been caused by the tendency to add personnel to count and control, thereby adding to both expense and annoyance. Also, a marked tendency has been observed to turn the measurement process from a means into an end in itself.

In addition, a problem of performance measurement, upon which performance budgeting is based, is the inherent problem of quantifying quality and of measuring many types of less physically-oriented governmental services. The entire evaluation movement has been built on this need (and on the failure to meet it).

The "classical" program budget

Since the end of World War II jurisdictions have attempted to simplify the line item budget process and to make it more conducive to goal setting and less subject to overcontrol by volume of detail. Lakewood, Colorado, presents one of the latest, and probably one of the most successful, attempts at what at one time was loosely called program budgeting (Figure 12–3). This term covers a multitude of approaches. (The example given here of this excellent system is not for a fire department, since Lakewood is served by an areawide fire organization not under its budget system; however, the format can be readily seen from Figure 12–3.)

In so-called classical program budgets, most line items either are wholly abandoned or are greatly reduced in number. Appropriations are by organizational unit and are determined by supervisorial responsibility. Within the so-called program, appropriations are made by lump sums to so-called major objects. These usually are: (1) personal services (salaries, wages, and fringe benefits); (2) services and supplies (everything not covered by 1, 3, and 4); (3) capital outlay and improvement of locally defined "major" acquisitions of real or personal property or construction; and (4) interfund transfers (accounting jargon for shifting monies from one restricted "pot" to another). Sometimes some limited detail is provided, but generally the thesis is that, without line item detail as a distraction, goals and service levels can be discussed. That type of circular logic eventually inexorably leads to the demise of most such lump sum budgetary systems.

Advantages The major advantage of the classical program budget approach is the obvious concentration on programs and service levels rather than on the inputs of dollar amounts and line item objects. Such an approach does require some analysis of the organizational supervision pattern and, as a result, may force some reorganization in order to combine any duplicating or overlapping programs that may become apparent through this approach. Once this hurdle has been overcome, the policymakers will need to reach some hard decisions as to how much dollar emphasis they wish to place on each program. Sometimes such decisions are difficult to make without some measurement of work load; in

LEISURE	**PARKS**

PROGRAM	PARK PLANNING AND LAND ACQUISITION
PROGRAM DESCRIPTION	Planning, analyzing, and negotiating parkland purchases; reviewing, evaluating, and negotiating park dedications relative to platting. Correct title errors in incorporated County park lands.

PERFORMANCE OBJECTIVES

1. To acquire six sites of proposed park land consisting of 164 acres for public park, open space, and recreational use.
2. To improve the productivity of parkland acquisition by reducing appraisal and research/planning costs per acre, and by keeping legal and negotiation costs below 1974 levels.
3. To improve the effectiveness of the land acquisition program by reducing elapsed time to acquire parcels through voluntary sale to four months, and through condemnation to six months.
4. To establish and maintain a current survey and inventory of all City parklands for the staff and public.

INDICATORS OF PERFORMANCE

MEASUREMENT	Objective	1974 Actual	1975 Estimate	1976 Projected
Demand				
Acres of Parkland Recommended for Population (DRCOG)		2,079	2,154	1,773
Acres of Parkland Budgeted for Acquisition	1	266.6	230	164
Sites Planned for Acquisition	1	18	12	6
PAR Reviews Requested		10	91	100
Workload				
Acres Reviewed/Investigated		2,889	2,600	2,000
Negotiation Sessions		200	326	120
Contracts Developed		21	36	18
Acres Acquired	1	75.22	381.9	164
Productivity				
Appraisal Cost per Acre	2	$ 64.01	$ 47.63	$ 35.25
Legal Cost per Acre	2	$ 73.04	$ 54.98	$ 65.07
Research and Planning Cost per Acre	2	$ 48.58	$ 40.52	$ 38.09
Negotiation Cost per Acre	2	$ 163.72	$ 29.22	$ 34.08
Effectiveness				
Months Elapsed to Acquire, Voluntary Sale	3	9.6	4.25	4
Months Elapsed to Acquire, Condemnation	3	14.0	6.5	6
Acres Remaining to be Acquired		2,154	1,773	1,578
Percent of Budgeted Acres Acquired		28.21%	166%	100%

ANALYSIS

City Council directives for park land acquisition from the 1976-1980 Capital Improvement Program will be implemented by this program. This program will be funded by capital improvement revenue sources as shown in the CIP budget (page 333). Increases in personnel costs are primarily due to the addition of a park planner to assist in conceptual design and site analysis. Park land acquisitions for 1976 include Bear Creek (Hiwan), 13th & Carr, First & Teller, Addenbrooke, Robbins-Dasher, Maple Grove, and Welchester.

RESOURCES

CATEGORY	1974 Actual	1975 Budget	1975 Revised	1976 Budget
Personnel	$ 16,353	$ 19,981	$ 16,283	33,785
Operating/Maintenance Supplies		350	300	1,550
Charges & Services	1,487	16,690	11,940	6,665
Capital Outlay	796,450	1,628,327	265,051	1,943,555
TOTAL	$ 814,290	$ 1,665,368	$ 293,574	1,985,555

Figure 12–3 A program budget. (Source: Department of Parks, City of Lakewood, Colorado.)

such a case some of the elements of the performance budget often are grafted onto this original approach to program budgeting. If the "controllers" of the line item detail (so frequently seen as being ascendant in that type of budget) have become overly control-oriented, then a "classical" program approach to budgeting will return the decision making to policymakers and management people. In other words, if there are no minute details to provide the control-oriented personnel with data with which to pick away at line management personnel, then the policymakers will return to the ascendancy.

Anyone who works in the field of budgeting will recognize that the term *program*, when used as a description of a budgeting system, becomes increasingly problematical the more precise one's definition of *program* becomes. This is one of the other disadvantages stemming from the advantages of the program approach to budgeting.

Disadvantages Major disadvantages of the classical program approach are those alluded to above, plus the generally inherent loss of line item detail. Hard operational experience has shown that this last is essential for effective day-to-day management decision making regarding the use of monetary resources. But, when such details exist, there is an almost irresistible backward pull toward the detailed decision making of the line item budget and its strict controls. Simply put, it is easier to count pencils, axes, nozzles, and feet of hose used than to decide upon service levels among competing programs all of which have been instituted at the insistent request of some interest group.

This is one of the major problems in any approach to budgeting. It seems to come into focus more rapidly and more concentratedly in the classical program budget approach to the division of scarce governmental revenues. This is why few such budgets remain and why many "modified" program budgets exist.

The pure program budget

One of the better modified program budgets is one in which all costs are summarized in each program rather than being placed under "overhead" expenses, fringe benefits, and other government-wide categories having their own line items. Such "pure" program budgets are quite rare, owing, in great part, to the complexities of accounting system construction and maintenance that would be sufficient to distribute all such indirect costs to and among all direct operational programs.

Advantages Advantages of the pure program budget are few, but they are major ones. First, as is shown in Figure 12–4, when a program is considered, *all* costs (direct, one time, and indirect) as well as overhead are charged to the program through a cost distribution accounting system. Thus the *true cost* of any change

	Costs ($)		
Factor	Continuous	One time	Ten inspectors
Salary	12,000		120,000
Fringe benefits	5,000		50,000
Car		6,000	
Operating car	5,000		50,000
Radio/equipment		2,000	
Maintenance of radio/ equipment	500		5,000
Uniforms/equipment	500	1,000	5,000
Dispatching and support	13,000	9,000	130,000
General overhead @ 20%	4,600	3,000	
Total	40,600	21,000	360,000

Figure 12–4   Cost distribution accounting system for a pure program budget: cost of fire inspector services.

in service level is fully known. This prevents accumulated hidden overhead and support expenses, which invariably (though this is often unrecognized) rise with the enhancement of any governmental direct service effort.

A second, but allied, advantage is the inexorable requirement of such a budgeting system for uniformity in determining true costs, to assure that they are not arbitrarily applied, that they are equitably distributed across all operational programs, and that support and staff functions are adequately oriented to their support role rather than being oriented to a control role.

Disadvantages   A significant disadvantage arises from the latter requirement in that a certain openness of management philosophy is required to place operational responsibility and flexibility in the hands of "program" managers. Many governmental organizations are still too control-oriented to permit, much less systematize, such decentralized authority to match assigned responsibilities.

The other disadvantage is an obvious one—the requirement of a comprehensive cost distribution accounting system. With the advent of low cost computers neither hardware nor implementing software are the problems; only the willingness to design and implement complete cost distributional systems inherent in pure program budgeting is lacking. One suspects that there is a direct causal link between the loss of central dominance and the lack of willingness. This is an area which suggests research into and development of a uniform cost accounting methodology for fire department managers; it could be part of an executive development curriculum at the National Fire Academy.

The planning-programming-budgeting system (PPBS)

Much has been written about this approach to budgeting since its adoption by the U.S. Department of Defense in 1962. Its quiet abandonment by the balance of the federal government in 1972 was not so well advertised.

PPBS is based on a chain of events with a flawed end link. First, programs are identified and objectives are set. Then numerous alternative routes to reaching the goal are catalogued, and a cost–benefit study is made of each alternative so identified. These alternative studies are undertaken by a centralized staff of independent analysts. The solution that proves to be the most cost-beneficial is adopted and a multiyear plan is derived. Each year of the plan is programmed into the current budget; this assures continuity of effort. Figure 12–5 illustrates the use of PPBS at the local level.

Advantages   Major advantages are, first of all, the systematic examination of a wide range of alternatives and, secondly, assurance of some year-to-year consistency in following an adopted plan to secure governmental program objectives. Thus, budgetary decisions are made on cost-effectiveness measures that provide the highest level of service for the lowest cost.

Disadvantages   The disadvantages of PPBS have apparently much outweighed the advantages, for relatively few such budget systems remain and most of these show signs of heavy stress and significant modification. Perhaps the most serious problem was the weak end link in the above-mentioned chain of events: namely, the prediction that the most cost-effective alternative would be the one chosen by the elected representatives. This has usually not been the case; in actual fact, political acceptability and constituent/special interest group support have been far more important deciding factors than mere cost-effectiveness. The PPBS approach thus exposed a hypocrisy inherent in governmental decision making—the tendency to make it appear that economy and efficiency are paramount when, in fact, they are not. Thus, the system had to be modified. In most instances it was abandoned and the line item approach was reinstituted or another system was devised.

Yet another disadvantage of PPBS was a tendency to define programs in such a way that they cut horizontally across supervisory lines, dividing program execution between operational officials and the deciding program analysts. The resultant stalemate was unacceptable in practice although avoidable in theory.

Critics of PPBS also point to the volume of cost–benefit analyses produced, the loss of operational line item details in the drive for cost–benefit studies, the lack of adequate numbers of analysts, and the problem of untrained analysts, as well as the mind-boggling problem of measuring every possible alternative to

City of San Diego, California **PROGRAM BUDGET**	DEPARTMENT/DIVISION Fire Department			NO. 16.00
	Actual FY 1975	Current FY 1976	Proposed FY 1977	Final FY 1977
Input				
Staffing (Position-Years) (PEP, CETA, etc.)	28.00 (4.00)	28.00 (4.00)	28.00 (-0-)	28.00 (-0-)
Personnel Expense Non-Personnel Expense TOTAL	$634,932 28,460 $663,392	$582,169 23,471 $605,640	$595,170 25,321 $620,491	$648,435 25,321 $673,756
Output				
Number of annual inspections required	6,917	6,920	2,980(1)	2,980(1)
Number of inspections per- formed (total)	2,300	2,400	2,400	2,400
Percent of required annual inspections performed - %	33	35	81	81
Number of permit renewal inspections required	N/A	250	0	0
Number of fires requiring investigation	1,400	1,500	1,600	1,600
Number of investigations performed Position hours per investi- gation performed	808 2.1	900 5.0	900 5.0	900 5.0
Number of arson related arrests	53	55	60	60
Number of arson related convictions	43	45	50	50
Number of fire hazard complaints received	2,189	2,300	2,400	2,400
Number of fire hazard complaints resolved	1,813	1,900	2,000	2,000
Number of plans checked Position hours per plan check	1,383 1.61	1,200 5.0	1,200 5.0	1,200 5.0

(1) Based on anticipated revision to Uniform Code to limit required inspections to schools, care facilities, and public assembly areas.

Figure 12–5 A planning-programming-budgeting system adapted for a fire department. (Source: City of San Diego, California.)

every possible governmental problem on which budget resources are spent or are proposed to be spent.

The integrative budgeting system (IBS)

Several jurisdictions have taken an eclectic approach to governmental budgeting and have devised their own systems, choosing those elements that seem to work and discarding the problematical parts of all of the previously described systems. This approach to public priority setting is known as an integrative budgeting system (see Figure 12–6).

Essentially line item based but computer-driven, the IBS approach uses only the three major objects of personal services, maintenance and operation, and capital outlay and improvement within each program for policymaking and service level determination. The line item details are for operational use only. The detailed line item budgets can be used to develop the "totals" for program budgets. The totals are appropriated without detailed control and are subjected to post-audit and critique. A diligent effort is needed in selecting the "best" alternative when such a post-audit criticism takes place.

Under this system, programs are defined as the lowest level of supervision or responsibility; they are aggregated upward, with absolutely all overhead and support costs distributed across all programs. Performance "indicators," not hard and fast measurements, are collegially arrived at but are used only by the program managers for self-measurement purposes. Cost–benefit principles are adapted from PPBS but are applied only where preliminary study indicates that the effort would be both productive and politically acceptable. Controls are limited, being primarily behavioral in nature and not predicated upon an authoritarian punishment system.

Advantages Major advantages are the proved nature of those elements that have been incorporated into IBS. The flexibility that comes from the computerization of the entire system and the behaviorally invalidated nature of the few controls can also be numbered among the good points.

CITY OF INGLEWOOD California — 213

LINE ITEM BUDGET AND PROJECTIONS

CODE + 04-40-30

FUND: PUBLIC SAFETY 04 | DEPARTMENT: FIRE | DIVISION: FIRE SUPPRESSION | SECTION: | UNIT:

ACTUAL EXPENDITURES		APPROPRIATION	CODE	OBJECT DESCRIPTION	RECOMMENDED	+ (-)	APPROVED	PROJECTIONS			
FY 72-73	FY 73-74	FY 74-75			FY1975-76		FY 1975-76	FY 1976-77	FY 1977-78	FY 1978-79	FY 1979-80
				PERSONAL SERVICES							
95	97	97	10000	FULL TIME POSITIONS	97			97	97	97	97
858	722	722	11000	REGULAR OVERTIME HOURS	650	72-		650	650	650	650
858	722	722		TOTAL HOURS REQUIRED	650	72-		650	650	650	650
				PERSONNEL COSTS							
1464667	1529103	1701871	10000	SALARIES	1731474	29603		1818048	1908950	2004398	2104618
95	946	39570	10003	SUPPLEMENTAL PAY	43980	4410		46179	48488	50912	53458
1218	306	10362	11000	REGULAR OVERTIME	9329	1033-		9795	10285	10799	11339
		3012	11001	PARAMEDIC OVERTIME	3012			3163	3321	3487	3661
6355	8321	15000	11010	CONSTANT MANNING	10000	5000-		10500	11025	11576	12155
1773			13000	PART TIME							
59216	61292	66675	14000	SPECIAL PAY	75000	8325		78750	82688	86822	91163
329701	345005	399346	15001	RETIREMENT	406222	6876		426533	447860	470253	493766
	209	374	15002	SUPPLEMENTAL RETIREMENT	404	30		424	445	467	490
	9320	27214	16000	INJURY PAY	20843	6371-		21885	22979	24128	25334
40691	45593	52081	16001	HEALTH INSURANCE	70584	18503		74113	77819	81710	85796
10887	10921	11475	16002	LIFE INSURANCE	12250	775		12863	13506	14181	14890
66366	42437	108855	16003	WORKERS COMPENSATION	59550	49305-		62528	65654	68937	72384
7644	7715	10296	16004	DENTAL INSURANCE	10296			10811	11352	11920	12516
17694	24187	26183	16007	SICK LEAVE RESERVE	26435	252		27757	29145	30602	32132
			16008	VACATION RESERVE	13217	13217		13878	14572	15301	16066
2006307	2085355	2472314		TOTAL PERSONAL SERVICES	2492596	20282		2617227	2748089	2885493	3029768
				MAINTENANCE & OPERATION							
13604	18821	21840	21000	UTILITIES	24000	2160		25200	26460	27783	29172
51736	51736	53618	21001	HYDRANT RENTAL	9118	44500-		9574	10053	10556	11084
1338	1860	1838	24000	OFFICE SUPPLIES	1930	92		2027	2128	2234	2346
933	941	960	27000	OFFICE EQUIPMENT EXPENSE	960			1008	1058	1111	1167
12520	10895	12950	28000	UNIFORMS	13500	550		14175	14884	15628	16409
74640	75334	87121	29000	EQUIPMENT EXPENSE	100065	12944		105068	110321	115837	121629
59	438	473	34000	SMALL TOOLS	373	100-		392	412	433	455
107	415	378	35000	TRAVEL & SUBSISTENCE	378			397	417	438	460
330	370	420	36000	TRAINING	420			441	463	486	510
		1000	36001	FIREMENS OLYMPICS	1000			1050	1103	1158	1216
104	61	289	37000	DUES & SUBSCRIPTIONS	289			303	318	334	351
8583	18907	13650	40000	SPECIAL EXPENSE	13650			14333	15050	15803	16593
587	799	2000	40001	PARAMEDIC PROGRAM	2000			2100	2205	2315	2431
199718	219341	296242	59999	OVERHEAD	295291	951-		310056	325559	341837	358929
364259	400918	492779		TOTAL MAINTENANCE & OPER	462974	29805-		486124	510431	535953	562752
				CAPITAL OUTLAY & IMPROVEMNT							
			70000	FIRE HOSE	8000	8000					
			71000	BREATHING APPARATUS	1620	1620					
			76000	FIRE FIGHTING TOOLS	750	750					
20436	28589	15820	99999	PRIOR YEAR/PROJECTIONS		15820-					
20436	28589	15820		TOTAL CAPITAL OUTLAY & IMPR	10370	5450-					
2391002	2514862	2980913		TOTAL APPROPRIATIONS	2965940	14973-		3103351	3258520	3421446	3592520

Figure 12-6   Major elements of an integrative budgeting system.
(Source: City of Inglewood, California.)

Disadvantages Significant disadvantages exist, however, in the integrative budgeting system. Primary among these is the behavioral nature of the controls, resting on the techniques of management by objectives (MBO) and organization development (OD)—techniques which are time-consuming and are threatening to the authoritarian manager or management philosophy or system. Furthermore, in this approach the entire budgetary system must be completely rebuilt and computerized. This requires a complex schedule of centralization, redesign, training, and decentralization concurrent with the MBO/OD efforts. In addition, the system has proved to have worked best in conjunction with a true merit pay plan for management personnel.

An equally important drawback is that the system supplies information that

6

requires that policy officials make hard decisions as regards service level bases, something that many, if not most, policy officials are ill-prepared to do. Finally, three to four years, optimally, would be required for design and implementation of the IBS approach for public budgeting in any specific jurisdiction.

Zero-based budgeting (ZBB)

No discussion of governmental budgeting systems would be complete without some discussion of the latest of the approaches described here—namely, zero-based budgeting. First developed by industry, zero-based budgeting was later applied to several jurisdictions and then to the federal government.

The basic elements of ZBB are: (1) identifying decision units (programs) within the jurisdiction; (2) analyzing each decision unit in a decision package; (3) evaluating and rank ordering all decision packages; and (4) preparing the detailed operating budget on the basis of the approved decision packages.

A decision package consists of several parts: (1) a statement of purpose and objective; (2) a description of actions proposed; (3) costs and benefits of the package and the proposed actions; (4) work load and performance measures; (5) alternative means of accomplishing the objectives; and (6) various levels of efforts. These last are analyzed, costed, and ranked through the use of the following basic levels: (1) program elimination; (2) reduced level of activity; (3) current level maintained; and (4) increased level of effort. Increases and decreases

City of Huntington Beach
FY 1978 Zero Base Budget
(33)
CONTINUATION FUNDING LEVEL   2 of 4

PROGRAM	DEPARTMENT	ACCOUNT NO.	RANK: MGR.	RANK: DEPT. HEAD	RANK: ADMIN.	RANK: COUNCIL
Fire Prevention	Fire	301	2 of 4	7 of 22	59 of 309	59 of 309

PROGRAM GOAL:

To protect life and property by preventing unfriendly fires from starting and to maintain a construction and fire loading system that will keep potential fire problems within the manageable limits of the fire control system.

DESCRIPTION OF PROGRAM ACTIVITIES IN FY 76/77:

- Perform fire investigations to determine causes for fire prevention purposes and to deter the malicious setting of fires.
- Provide for elimination of future fire hazards and to insure access and firefighting capability through planning and plan checks.
- Eliminate fire hazards through code enforcement.
- Provide public information and education to inform and motivate the public of the need to:
  A. Eliminate fire hazards
  B. Become fire safety conscious

ACCOUNT FOR COST INCREASE WITH CONTINUATION FUNDING OVER FY 76/77:

The personnel costs have been increased due to salary increases per association agreements.

QUANTITATIVE MEASURES	FY 76-77	FY 77-78 Cont. Level
Number of fires investigated with necessary follow-up	150	150
Number of development plans checked for access, water, fire protection systems and State code compliance	1,404	1,404
Inspections for code compliance	3,070	3,070
Public information and education lectures and demonstrations to inform community of fire and other life saving hazards	820	820

COST SUMMARY	FY 76-77	FY 77-78 Cont. Level
Personnel Costs	214,931	245,833
Operating Expenses	8,923	8,613
Capital Outlay		
Total	223,854	254,446
No. of Personnel Permanent/CETA	7 0	7 0

Figure 12–7 Zero-based budgeting sample.
(Source: City of Huntington Beach, California.)

are usually at set percentages, for example, 10 percent and/or 25 percent—up and down.

While examples of ZBB in action were as yet limited in the late 1970s, Huntington Beach, California, seemed to have had more success than most with ZBB, owing to an extreme financial squeeze which forced its staff and city council to recost and review programs in order to make retrenchment decisions (see Figure 12–7).

Advantages   Some advantages of ZBB are that it requires a complete and orderly review of all governmental efforts, as well as an attempt to place them in priority order in view of current beliefs and needs. Furthermore, exploration of new ways to accomplish old objectives is encouraged, as is an inherent decentralization of authority and decision making.

Disadvantages   The disadvantages are less than objectively derived, since not enough experience has been gained to determine whether truly valid criticism is involved. But one significant problem already seen to be evolving is the inherent subjectivity in the ranking process. What one person from one viewpoint might rank as high, another person, with a different position and orientation, might rank as quite low or might even eliminate. Thus, size of jurisdiction and number of decision packages beyond the purview of a relatively small group of persons make such rankings suspect of subjectivity.

Another disadvantage is found in defining decision units. The same problems exist here as in pure program budgeting: What is the composition of the program as defined? And are all costs included therein or are some cost elements centralized elsewhere and not distributed across the programs (decision units)?

Zero-based budgeting may only strive to ensure that there is continuing, adequate justification for operations already in existence. Unless the fire official using ZBB is truly firm about what constitutes adequate justification, all current operations are probably justifiable.

Budget controls

The term *control* has unfortunately become almost synonymous with the word *budget*. While there is no doubt that budgets must be controlled to assure that adopted policy objectives, spending priorities, and spending limits are adhered to, overcontrol has become almost endemic. Those controls applied to public budgets can be divided into two broad categories—traditional controls and behavioral controls—each of which can be divided into subcategories. These categories and their subdivisions are discussed below.

Traditional controls

Those controls usually associated with a line item type of budget are the most prevalent, overworked, and overemphasized. First and foremost among these is line item accounting.

Line item accounting   Line item accounting control is the essence of and the reason for line item budgeting. Each and every payroll, purchase order, contract award, and invoice is charged against the appropriate line item, and the amount remaining available in that specific budgetary line item is reduced by the amount of the payroll entry, purchase order or contract award, or invoice if no encumbrance system is in place. Thus, the burden is on operational personnel not to exceed their spending authority by specific line. But there must also be assurance that dollar amounts and accounting routine and recordation are accurately done and are reported in a timely manner. In other words, timeliness and accuracy of the budgetary accounting system are of vital importance to the operating official. Thus "control" is out of the hands of (and out of the direct control of) the operating official, but that employee is still held responsible for results and for nonexpenditure.

Budgetary accounting reports Budgetary accounting reports provide operating personnel, as well as the budgetary control person or group, with monthly or sometimes quarterly reports showing the balances remaining unexpended and/or unencumbered in each account. These reports are usually line item in nature, as they are of great utility to operating personnel in such format. It is an unfortunate fact, however, that the control group or person will sometimes require strict adherence to the dollar limits of each line item, and either will not permit monetary transfers between items or will require extensive justification or even governing body approval. These extremely tight dollar controls are usually counterproductive, forcing the operating official to make a choice between concentrating on the job or subverting the controls so that financial and operational flexibility sufficient to "get the job done" can be achieved. This almost forced subversion is probably the greatest flaw in line item budgeting.

Percentage deviation reports While percentage deviation reports are helpful budgetary management devices, they are subject to the same overuse and misuse as line item and budgetary accounting reports. Percentage deviation reports provide operating personnel—and the budget control forces—with line item data in terms of dollar amounts expended or encumbered and as a percentage of the budget. When these reports are matched against the "normal" rate of expenditure (e.g., 33 percent for four months, 50 percent for a half year, 67 percent for eight months), all those concerned can see what degree of controls or sanctions should be applied against any offending overspender. Unfortunately, however, all fire department expenditures will not fall within neat calendar patterns. This leads to the next control.

Allotments An allotment system literally subdivides the budget for each unit into quarterly or monthly (usually the former) allotments. That amount cannot be exceeded for the time period. To further complicate matters, allotment systems have to be predicated on seasonal differences in expenditure rates and then controlled to assure that the quarterly or monthly allotment is not exceeded.

When coupled with line item controls allotments can almost literally force an operating official to pay more heed to the budget management and control system than to the primary public service responsibilities of the operating unit.

Position controls Position controls are essential in that most governmental jurisdictions expend from 60 percent to 90 percent of their budgets on the personal services of salaries, wages, and direct fringe benefits. For this reason, controlling the number of positions (by means of position classification and, through this means, by the steps between minimum and maximum salary) limits budgetary expenditures. It is probably equally important to assure some equity and consistency between organizational units, both as to pay ranges and as to number of personnel by classification category. Budgeting a lump sum for personnel without such limits would be an open invitation to position favoritism and to eventual deteriorating organizational morale—and to subsequent budgetary difficulties of major magnitude.

Part-time positions are usually budgeted and controlled by the number of hours of service permitted for each part-time classification. Overtime and fringe benefits can only be controlled by dollar limits through the budget system.

Purchase order and contract award review This is a type of budgetary control almost guaranteeing fierce conflict between the "controllers" and the operational officers. The "normal" course of events within a governmental jurisdiction would route a requisition for a purchase from the fire department to the purchasing agency. After the budget has been adopted and the amounts and/or specific items being requisitioned are included in it, fire chiefs can requisition approved items when they determine that these items are necessary. But in some agencies utilizing this type of control—and in spite of budget adoption—the routing system for requisitions requires that the central budget office re-review and reapprove the specific item or contract *before* it can even be received by the purchasing office for call for bids or for institution of other acquisition methodology. Thus, a double jeopardy conflict would be set up between the requisitioning fire agency and the budget controllers as regards the need for the item or service. The unfortunate aspect of this control is the inevitable separation of responsibility for operating results from the authority to expend appropriated amounts so as to secure promised results. Denial of purchasing authorization by a budget authority can lead to special efforts on the part of the operating person to assure that the worst predictions made immediately after the denial in fact come true.

Performance statistics review Performance statistics review is another budgetary type of review used especially stringently where units "produced" lend themselves to division into amounts budgeted or expended, which results in a unit cost. Any use of such controls must always take cognizance of the flaws in reporting: (1) "production," (2) seasonality of outputs and expenditures, and (3) time lags. As such control devices are notoriously unreliable because they are behaviorally invalid (as was discussed earlier in the section on performance budgeting), any such device should be approached with extreme caution and used only after repeated and continued verification of all elements and data inputs.

Travel and subsistence Travel and subsistence reports and reviews are periodic political targets for tirades, ostensibly to prevent "junkets at the taxpayer's expense." Whether the public in general or a mere vocal few are interested in such matters, it is a fact that these items have been singled out for special justification and control. Some limitation systems go so far as to require prior governing body approval for trips, which guarantees massive attention, publicity, and the inevitable additional controls of a like nature over other suspect items.

Training, dues, and subscriptions These expenses are among those added to the control list for special attention. Elaborate and time-consuming (and expensive) justifications, reviews, multilevel approvals, and other control systems and procedures for the five items of travel, subsistence, training, dues, and subscriptions make one suspect that the costs, confusions, and displaced priorities in such a review system place governments in the proverbial position of being penny-wise and pound-foolish.

Behavioral controls

Amazingly enough, despite the recognition in organizations today of the research done in the field of human behavior, most budgetary controls are still based on authoritarian behavioral premises. As invalid as these premises are, they prevail at present. The relatively few governmental agencies that have applied behavioral science to their internal motivation and management systems have found self-control to be a much more viable and powerful limit to spending and goad to goal achievement than all the absolutist central dominance controls ever devised. Although this chapter focuses on budgeting, a mention of a few of the behavioral modification approaches that are useful in budget administration is in order.

Motivation   Motivation is perhaps the leading basis for applying behavioral science to budgeting. A basic motivator of governmental employees is participation, something that generally is sadly lacking in the preparation and administration of a budget. Approaching budget preparation from the top of the hierarchy downward, rather than from the bottom up, is guaranteed to be countermotivational as well as more difficult to control. If someone participates in an activity then that person has some vested interest in the development and execution process and is more easily motivated. The basis of motivation is to influence individual—and thereby group—behaviors by working on existing desires, whether overt or hidden.

Management by objectives (MBO)   This approach can be employed as a fairly direct budgeting control because individuals work more effectively when they clearly understand the goal or objective toward which they are working. Furthermore, people perform better and are more cooperative when they have helped establish the goals and are at least marginally free to select the means by which the goals are to be secured. In other words, many of the traditional controls discussed earlier are invalidated by human behavior, and a recognized MBO process can be a much more powerful control than these traditional and imposed controls.

Organization development (OD)   This is a continuing process, not just a project; in effect, it institutionalizes and thereby perpetuates the behavioral controls. Organization development is a team building approach to facilitating planned change; among other things it provides a sense of ownership among those implementing the objectives of the organization. Self-control and self-direction, which are important end results of an OD process, are essential elements in an internalized budget control system. But if OD is to succeed, the climate should be such that it is encouraged; this means that authoritarianism and the exactitude of scientific management have to be abandoned. Many—if not most—public organizations have not yet reached that point.

Job enrichment   Job enrichment as a form of budget control implants the MBO/OD processes more deeply into the organization by means of designing a job vertically to make it more psychologically meaningful. The employee has more extensive control over his or her own job and can assume much of the credit (or blame) for results. Thus, placement of responsibility is direct, and budget control is far easier to achieve.

Self-actualization   Self-actualization is the ultimate control sought in an organization; through this means, each employee fulfills his or her individual potential after having progressed through and achieved the lower ranks of the hierarchy of needs: physiological needs, safety needs, belongingness needs, and the need for esteem.[10]

A comprehensive effort aimed at motivating employees and a full progression of behavioral controls as listed above would probably be less expensive and infinitely more effective for the chief fire official than would be the elaborate centralized traditional controls, based on dominance, that were enumerated earlier in this chapter. Experience has shown that those organizations that have tried behavioral controls have experienced increased levels of efficiency and effectiveness.

Retirement systems budgeting

The fire services participate in numerous retirement systems. These retirement systems must provide the monies, when needed, for a number of retirement benefits which normally include service retirement after a specific number of years of service (such as twenty, twenty-five, or thirty years) or at a specific age (such as fifty or fifty-five).

Most retirement systems provide additional benefits which achieve social protection for the individual and achieve personnel administration goals for the fire department. These additional benefits include such areas as service-connected disability, nonservice-connected disability, and survivor allowances for widows and orphans for service-connected death before retirement, nonservice-connected death before retirement, and death after all retirements.

All retirement systems have two general areas of costs which are (1) for the benefits paid, and (2) for the administrative expenses of operations and investment counsel. Most boards of trustees of retirement funds are provided by local or state laws and often include persons who are limited in technical expertise in money management. Experts in fund investment management should be obtained on a contractual basis with an annual retainer. The contract should be renewed every few years to ensure prudent management of these funds. Retirement funds are fiduciary in nature and should provide for a prudent level of security and management. Security can be achieved by insurance and by custodial possession in large banks. Regular independent audits and actuarial evaluations are an absolute necessity.

For budgetary purposes it should be clearly understood that the retirement system has to pay the vested benefits. To be sure that the necessary money will be available when demanded, it is essential to plan for decades into the future. Again, expert assistance is mandatory and is easily obtained by employing on a contractual basis a member of the Society of Actuaries. The actuary can calculate the probable cost of the benefits by determining the many variables associated with the members of the retirement system (and their dependents), such as ages of entry, exit, death, and/or disability. The actuary evaluates and analyzes the assets on hand, the estimated interest rates, and the estimated refunds to determine the necessary rates of future contributions to fund the estimated costs for the current and future vested benefits.

Other aspects of budgeting for retirement system costs should include consideration of personnel management. Some provisions of modern retirement systems provide for early vesting of benefits earned to date, instead of postponement to the actual date of retirement. This avoids retention of dissatisfied employees.

Age of entry should be open instead of being limited as it now is for most fire and police department retirement systems. Fixed entry ages are a historical accident which should be changed to allow personnel transfers and career mobility among local agencies and from local to state to federal service.

The Intergovernmental Personnel Act of 1970 (discussed in Chapter 13) provides direction and assistance in career mobility to federal, state, and local government personnel and includes academic personnel and faculties for short-term assignments up to two years. Early vesting of benefits and reciprocity of retirement credits among retirement systems—local, state, and federal government and academic private systems—will assist the fire services to provide modern personnel management to achieve professional career mobility. Unified and integrated retirement systems that provide for early vesting and reciprocity will assist in avoiding "double dipping" problems and will increase the efficient and effective use of personnel.

Numerous retirement systems become underfunded because of granting increased benefits that are retroactive to date of entry for current employees. This creates an "instant" unfunded liability. Provisions for fully funding these "actuarial debts" are calculated by the actuary and are usually funded over a long term such as thirty or forty years. This is consistent with the life spans of the members and dependents that receive these retroactive benefits. These contribution rates are termed *prior service* and are in addition to the contribution rates for current service.

Recent policy changes have required the actuarial evaluations to consider and to report the effects of long-term inflation, especially as it affects the benefits to be paid in the future. Long-term inflation at relatively high rates has high costs. Contribution rates must be adjusted to provide for the required monies so that financial chaos and bankruptcy are avoided in the future.

Summary and conclusion

This chapter has attempted to provide a basic but comprehensive coverage of the complex political flows and conflicts that are associated with the budgetary process in local governments. All who have worked in local government will recognize that budget-related matters consume a high proportion of staff time and effort throughout the fiscal year—the more so in times of public disenchantment and associated fiscal pressures. Professional managers within and without the fire service should be aware of, and remain on top of, these trends if they are to provide effective and professional service, and if they are to maintain their department's position in the contemporary scramble for the allocation of scarce resources. The discussion throughout has therefore remained close to the realities of the profession, and is based on the experience of the authors and on real world situations. The authors have, therefore attempted to outline the following basic topics: the theory and the practice of budgeting and their underpinnings in the way of resources; the main types of budgeting and their advantages and disadvantages; and the main types of budgetary controls, both traditional and modern. A look has also been taken at some of the problems associated with the increasingly important topic of retirement system budgeting.

The chapter, then, represents a starting point. Individual fire service managers will find, like generations of their predecessors, that there is no substitute for real-life experience in grappling with the specifics of a fire department in a particular community with its own particular economic, social, and political characteristics.

1   J. Richard Aronson and Eli Schwartz, eds., *Management Policies in Local Government Finance* (Washington, D.C.: International City Management Association, 1975).

2   U.S., Department of Commerce, Bureau of the Census, *Pocket Data Book USA 1976*, 5th ed. (Washington, D.C.: Government Printing Office, 1976), p. 98.

3   Ibid., p. 106.

4   Ibid.

5   Ibid., p. 110.

6   Ibid.

7   Ibid.

8   See: Douglas W. Ayres, *Integrative Budgeting System: A New Approach from Old Failures* (San Juan Capistrano, Calif.: By the Author, 25572 Purple Sage, 1977). This is perhaps the closest approach made to such reconciliation between the broad policymaking process and the needs of the day-to-day operational officials.

9   For a discussion of some of Taylor's theories, see: Stanley Piazza Powers, F. Gerald Brown, and David S. Arnold, eds., *Developing the Municipal Organization* (Washington, D.C.: International City Management Association, 1974), pp. 36–41; for further reading, see also: Frederick Winslow Taylor, *The Principles of Scientific Management* (New York: Harper & Brothers, Publishers, 1947).

10 Abraham H. Maslow, *Motivation and Personality* (New York: Harper & Row, Publishers, 1954).

13 Personnel management and labor relations

Personnel costs, as this chapter points out, can account for more than ninety out of every hundred taxpayer dollars expended in a fire department budget. Thus, personnel management in the fire service is a crucial area of responsibility for managers both inside and outside of the department.[1] The first part of this chapter, then, presents a detailed assessment of personnel management practices from the perspective of chief decision makers. (This section may be read in conjunction with Chapter 12, which discusses some of the financial underpinnings of personnel systems, and also with Chapter 15, which covers training and education.)

Labor relations in local government fire departments is rapidly becoming the other side of the coin to personnel management, and the authors of the second part of this chapter take the reader through the important stages of the collective bargaining process—which today is a fact of managerial life in the area of local government.

Each of the two main divisions of this chapter opens with a brief overview and a discussion intended to put the subject into perspective, and each concludes with a brief look into the future.

A: Personnel management

Overview

The first division of this chapter is organized into ten parts. First, there is a discussion of the changes and challenges facing the manager in this field. Second, the subject of organizing for personnel management is discussed. This is followed by a brief description of manpower planning. The fourth section addresses equal employment opportunity and affirmative action, while the fifth analyzes the managerial options for recruitment. The sixth surveys the selection process, from traditional testing procedures to assessment centers, and the seventh takes a look at some of the challenges involved in performance appraisal. The eighth assesses the professional responsibilities involved in staff inspections, the ninth looks at the crucial area of personnel development, and the tenth provides an overview of some future prospects and also points to the fact that the past is not necessarily prologue to the future.

The coverage is aimed at elucidating the principles involved in personnel management in the fire services. It is intended that the principles discussed should have application to small as well as large departments, and to volunteer professionals as well as those who are fully paid professionals, although the discussion of necessity tends to concentrate on the challenges presented by the complex organizations of the larger, fully paid, fire departments.

A final point is that, in our changing legislative and judicial environments, managers would do well to keep abreast of new developments through referring to standard sources.[2]

Changes and challenges

Peter F. Drucker, management consultant and professor, has pointed out that managers are fond of saying, "Our greatest asset is people." He went on to add, however, that "most managers know perfectly well that of all the resources, people are the least utilized and that little of the human potential of any organization is tapped and put to work."[3] Indeed, he proposes that managers—private and public alike—in reality view their personnel in terms of problems, procedures, and costs, and he adds that contemporary personnel management has been heavily imbued with such thinking. As a result, personnel management policies and practices typically have been designed to categorize and control employees. Drucker concludes that, while the traditional approach has its place, personnel management should begin to lead and to train in light of the new challenges confronting public organizations.[4] Clearly such a recommendation, if implemented, would measurably stand to benefit the fire service and, significantly, would be of benefit during a period of unprecedented inquiry and concern over increasing the cost-effectiveness of the fire service.

A brief review of the literature or a casual conversation with someone involved in public personnel will quickly reveal the fact that the field is a cauldron of complex changes and challenges. (While this applies to the public sector generally, it can be applied particularly to the fire service.) Regardless of the types of changes—whether evolutionary, like the lessening of authority or numbers of civil service commissions, or more or less revolutionary, like affirmative action—they all present a challenge in adaptation and coping. The changes could be more easily handled if only they did not conflict. The changes now transforming public personnel actually present a dual challenge: first, the resolution of conflicting demands for change; and second, the implementation of new policies and practices that comply with that resolution. For the personnel manager who sees challenges as opportunities there are a multitude to choose from.

Let us examine five such changes or issues that loom large in the minds of today's fire service personnel managers. Obviously there are many more, but the five issues covered here have been chosen because of their prominence and the conflicts they pose. Each issue may be described in relation to its opposing position.

Merit versus representation First there is the issue of merit versus representation. Simply stated, merit denotes in personnel parlance the principle that only "the best shall serve." This tenet was advanced by the National Civil Service League in 1881 and was promulgated by Congress in the benchmark Pendleton Act of 1883. Shortly before 1900 most local governments had followed by establishing similar charters or statutes. In 1970 Congress established as national policy six merit principles under the Intergovernmental Personnel Act, which stated:

The quality of public service at all levels of government can be improved by the development of systems of personnel administration consistent with such merit principles as—

1. Recruiting, selecting, and advancing employees on the basis of their relative ability, knowledge, and skills, including open consideration of qualified applicants for initial appointment;
2. Providing equitable and adequate compensation;
3. Training employees, as needed, to assure high-quality performance;
4. Retaining employees on the basis of the adequacy of their performance, correcting inadequate performance, and separating employees whose inadequate performance cannot be corrected;
5. Assuring fair treatment of applicants and employees in all aspects of personnel administration without regard to political affiliation, race, color, national

origin, sex, or religious creed and with proper regard for their privacy and constitutional rights as citizens; and

6. Assuring that employees are protected against coercion for partisan political purposes and are prohibited from using their official authority for the purpose of interfering with or affecting the result of an election or a nomination for office.

The 1960s (particularly with the enactment of the Civil Rights Act of 1964) gave impetus to increasing the representation of minorities in private and public organizations. The term *affirmative action* (discussed in detail later in this chapter) is omnipresent in the minds of personnel managers. Today, to "the best shall serve" the words "on a representative basis" have been added. The theory and ethics involved are sound and are commendable, but the application of the principle has been filled with ambiguity and argument. In 1970 the National Civil Service League produced the sixth edition of its *Model Public Personnel Administration Law,* which contained the following recommendations (number 1 should be noted particularly):

1. The establishment of programs, including trainee programs, designed to attract and utilize persons with minimal qualifications, but with potential for development, in order to provide career development opportunities among members of disadvantaged groups, handicapped persons, and returning veterans. Such programs may provide for permanent appointment upon the satisfactory completion of the training period without further examination. . . . Just as the public jurisdictions helped the nation to repay the debt to returning war veterans it is important now that they help repay a debt resulting from years of public employment deprivation for minority group members, by giving preferential treatment to members of minority groups. . . .

2. [The establishment and publicizing of] fringe benefits such as insurance programs, retirement and leave policies.

3. Development and operation of programs to improve work effectiveness, including training, safety, health, welfare, counseling, recreation and employee relations. . . .

4. The establishment of the position of hearing officer to respond to employee grievances and appeals, after other normal administrative appeals have been exhausted, will help to create a system that has both the support and respect of all those persons affected by it. . . .

5. In addition to agreements that facilitate personnel mobility, state and local governments should enter into arrangements with each other for personnel services and facilities. Agreements of this type will enable a jurisdiction to make the most efficient use of its resources. They will be particularly beneficial to the small political subdivision that does not always have sufficient resources to provide the full range of personnel services and facilities.[5]

Civil service commissions versus personnel departments The proposed model law sets the stage for a second dispute—that of civil service commissions versus personnel departments. More will be said about the roles and the functions of these two organizations later in this chapter. Those defending the retention of civil service commissions underscore their past successes and the threat of political patronage. In turn, those advocating strong personnel agencies emphasize the increasing legal and administrative requirements for bureaucratic change. It appears that the trend is in favor of the model law mentioned above, and thus the responsibility (if not the number) of commissions has been on the decline.[6]

Home rule versus the law The third controversy roughly encompasses the claims of local autonomy (home rule) versus those of legal and/or statutory decisions. On the one hand we see the closely guarded sovereignty of state and local government; on the other we observe legalistic reforms emanating from the courts and political bodies—reforms that explicitly question the authority and independence of home rule. Chester Newland sums up this dilemma as follows:

The feature of populist-oriented 1970s legislation which may be most disruptive of highly legalistic, bureaucratic organizations—whether personnel or program agencies—is its tendency to drive public administrators to even greater legalistic extremes. Instead of selective enforcement of laws and provision of public services, agencies are increasingly forced into 100 per cent performance of a multitude of legal provisions. With respect to public personnel, for example, there has been a tendency to require different agency action programs to implement each of the multitude of special interest employment provisions adopted in recent years. In a litigious environment this may be hostile to selective and coordinated enforcement which has been the classic approach to reasonable execution of law under the consent system of American constitutional government.[7]

The question thus basically revolves around a matrix of administrative objectives (effectiveness) and legal requirements (social equity).

Labor relations versus collective bargaining   The fourth debate is the most overt of the five—labor relations versus collective bargaining, a subject fully explored in the second part of this chapter. The significance of this debate has grown from the past decision on whether public employees should unionize to the current situation of determining what is bargainable. We frequently see employee demands invading the domain of management prerogatives. At times the very essence of the merit principle has come under attack. Douglas McIntyre has described this situation in the following words:

There are few more provocative subjects in public personnel administration today than the relations between collective bargaining and merit. The possibility of some alleged inevitable conflict between these two systems has hung like a dark cloud over the new collective bargaining systems in public jurisdictions. Since both systems have irreproachable objectives—in the case of collective bargaining the participation by employees in setting the terms and conditions of their work, and in the case of merit principles the staffing of public agencies with the most able persons from all parts of our society—it is certainly in the public interest to bring about a marriage of the two which will make the progeny legitimate. . . .But most progressive public personnel administrators, like most responsible union officials, find no essential conflict between the concepts of merit-based personnel administration and collective bargaining.

Differences usually arise from differing emphases and methodologies in the systems rather than opposition to the basic principles and philosophies. One way to forestall conflict or divorce, therefore, is to recognize from the beginning the similarities and common aims and seek to minimize the differences.[8]

In addition, public labor unions are frequently at odds with affirmative action laws; Garry Whalen and Richard Rubin have referred to this as follows:

A tug-of-war is developing between the new laws forbidding discrimination in employment and such long-accepted labor union practices as seniority and fair representation. The growing body of laws prohibiting discrimination is now challenging public managers and employee organizations. For instance, seniority provisions, long considered a mainstay of the union contract, can be construed as inhibiting women and minorities from advancing up the ladder. Affirmative action plans to eliminate employment discrimination conflict in some cases with the rights and interests of employers and unions as stated in contract negotiations and in labor agreements.[9]

In summary, the public sector union movement has generated a host of considerations for the personnel manager; the fire personnel specialist is intimately involved in dealing with them.

Central personnel agency versus departmental unit   The last of the five issues focuses on the respective roles and responsibilities of the central personnel agency (CPA) and the departmental personnel unit (DPU) or specialist.

Both should address the four subject areas just described plus the following: recruitment and selection of employees on a merit basis; training programs at both recruit and in-service levels; a promotion program; an equitable system of evaluating job performance; job classification; salary plan administration; a comprehensive plan for conditions of service (to include vacation, sick leave, attendance, working hours, overtime, and transfer policies); an employee relations program (including grievance procedures); a safety program; medical and insurance programs; a retirement program; and a labor–management relations program.[10]

Organizing for personnel management

Organizing for personnel management is primarily shaped by personnel policy, the genesis of which may be described as follows:

Public personnel policy stems basically from statutes, charters, ordinances, and rules which reflect an amalgam of ideologies and interests championed by interest groups. At the same time, much of local government personnel policy is the product of negotiations between officers representing the public as the employer and representatives for organized public employees. This product materializes as written contracts, memoranda, or as formal policies.[11]

Policy, too, will help determine whether a departmental personnel unit (DPU) should exist in a fire department and, if so, what its role should be compared with that of a central personnel agency (CPA). Four other factors also assist in making this determination. They are:

1. Legal requirements for centralization: Those jurisdictions with independent civil service commissions may find that the basic laws establishing the commission assign specific functions to it.
2. Size of jurisdiction and size of departments: Relatively small jurisdictions are likely to centralize personnel operations in order to achieve economy of scale. On the other hand, larger jurisdictions with large departments may find it expeditious to decentralize some personnel operations.
3. Existence of qualified operating department personnel offices: This factor is closely related to jurisdictional size. It is very unlikely that small jurisdictions can afford a departmental personnel office. . . .
4. Tradition: Some agencies have operated traditionally on a centralized or a decentralized basis.[12]

The central personnel agency   There are two basic forms of CPA: the civil service commission and the staff personnel department. The commission is comprised of three to five members that are usually appointed (for four to six year terms) by a mayor or an elected body. The commission performs the following functions: testing, certification of appointments, and hearing of employee appeals (in some instances the commission may become engaged in job classification and pay plan administration).

The staff personnel department may operate in conjunction with a civil service commission or alone. The personnel director or manager serves as a department head and is appointed by the mayor or city manager/county administrative officer. (There are variations to the two models, such as a public safety or fire civil service commission, which, of course, would have a limited purview.) This type of CPA is specifically responsible for recruitment, certification, classification, pay plan administration, manpower planning, employee development and training, labor relations, productivity programs, and other elements of a comprehensive personnel program.[13]

In general, the CPA is expected to meet the following goals:

1. *Legal requirements:* to perform certain specific functions as required by state and local statutes, such as the administration of civil service examinations for municipal employment
2. *Citywide uniformity:* to provide consistency in personnel practices, avoiding arbitrary treatment of all municipal employees, in such areas as fringe benefits, job classifications, salary administration, vacation, and sick leave
3. *Economy:* to eliminate duplication of activities and provide a more effective means of handling similar functions of all city agencies
4. *Expertise:* to provide competent personnel technicians to all city agencies, particularly in the areas of personnel testing, position classification, and labor relations
5. *Public convenience:* to provide a centralized point within a municipality to furnish the public with information concerning job qualifications and vacancies.[14]

It should be remembered that the authority of the CPA varies greatly from city to city, from county to county, and from state to state. In smaller government jurisdictions such an agency is not likely to have professional staff. Therefore, the entire personnel function as it relates to the fire agency is the responsibility of the fire chief. Normally, as the size of the jurisdiction increases the CPA evolves first as part of the duties of an individual, then as a full-time job, and, finally, as a highly structured organization with skilled technicians and administrators. Also, with growth in size of jurisdiction, the fire agency's personnel functions become assigned to a particular person or unit.

The departmental unit　In most medium to large local governments we find that the authority for personnel management is divided between the fire chief and the CPA. With increasing and conflicting demands being made on the fire service and, in turn, on fire management, it becomes all the more critical that the fire agency actively pursue a greater involvement in personnel decisions. To put it bluntly, when policy or procedural personnel decisions are being made concerning the fire agency the agency should *directly and meaningfully participate in the decision-making process.* Consequently, it seems most prudent that a fire agency assign personnel management responsibility to a particular unit or to a specific person, or else divide it among a group of fire managers and/or supervisors. Regardless of the format adopted, it remains essential now (and should be even more so in the near future) that fire management build a personnel management capability.

The above comments are not intended to diminish the central authority or criticize the prime responsibility of the city/county personnel department. It is hoped this department will conduct its business in a coordinative and facilitative style while concurrently providing leadership in personnel matters in the form of expertise and advice to the so-called line (program) agencies (fire, police, public works, recreation, etc.). The fire agency will be expected to support the personnel department by participating in decisions that affect its operations and by taking broad personnel directives and implementing them in ways that are specifically effective to the agency. The following personnel functions should be considered as falling within the purview of the fire agency:

1. Development of policies and instructions in all areas of [fire] human resources administration, subject to approval of the chief.
2. Service as advisor to the chief and other line officials on personnel matters.
3. Development of an integrated management information system which includes all necessary personnel data, such as reporting of individual activity or performance.
4. Development of programs for the effective recruitment of qualified [firefighting] applicants, including women and minorities.
5. Development and administration of systems of selection for appointment to the

[fire] service, including a program of background investigation and possibly psychiatric appraisals.

6. Development of criteria for promotion and a system of determining the relative qualifications of eligible [fire service] officers in accordance with these criteria.

7. Administration of a training program for all [fire] ranks, including entry training of recruits, in-service training of experienced officers, and training for advancement.

8. Development of a system of performance evaluation, including, where legal, an evaluation of promotion potential.

9. Development and administration of a system of position classification and assignment analysis, to assure equal pay for equal work as well as to form the basis for staff assignment and evaluation.

10. Development of a plan of adequate compensation, fairly distributed among ranks and assignments . . . including provision for differentials based on special hazards, shifts, or outstanding performance.

11. Representation of the [fire] agency in negotiations or other meetings with representatives of organized employees, and development of a grievance procedure to minimize conflict within the agency.

12. The administration of a program of exit interviews of resigning [fire] officers, using information thus gathered to adjust unsatisfactory working conditions. [Note: this source should be cited with caution.]

13. Development of a high level of morale and strong motivation among [fire personnel] in order to obtain [their] greatest commitment . . . to the goals of the agency.

14. Provision of advice to line managers at all levels concerning human resources problems, with special attention to leadership and disciplinary problems; and the administration of a program review of disciplinary actions and appeals.

15. Conduct of a personnel research program.

16. Representation of the [fire] agency to the central personnel agency or civil service commission.[15]

Manpower planning

Manpower planning includes the development, maintenance, and utilization of the skills of actual and potential members of the fire agency. Moreover, it addresses the bottom line question of *how many* actual and potential employees ought to be selected, trained, and utilized. The number of fire personnel quite obviously influences the costs of providing fire services. A recent Urban Data Service Report made the following comment:

Nearly all municipal fire services are being forced to make certain cutbacks because of current fiscal problems. And with costs increasing for buildings, equipment, and personnel (the last accounting for approximately 90% of the typical fire department budget), fire service management is hard pressed to maintain adequate levels of fire protection.[16]

In the vast majority of fire agencies the manpower planning process is divided between training of actual employees and personnel management of potential employees. While it is not essential that the process be performed by a single unit, the overall manpower policy should control and coordinate the individual activities.

The following statement regarding the location of the manpower planning function should be noted carefully:

One final concern deserves attention: the locus of the manpower planning function within the jurisdiction. Restated, this concern is a question of whether to delegate all or part of the manpower planning function to the operative agencies within a jurisdiction or to centralize that function at a point organizationally close to the chief executive. In smaller jurisdictions the problem usually is resolved by assigning all manpower planning responsibilities to the persons who have assumed the personnel function.[17]

Hence, it would appear that most often the fire personnel manager will be accountable for manpower planning.

Both training and personnel management require policy direction on at least three important issues. The first of these is the upgrading of the work force (e.g., upgrading the amount of in-service skill level training, the minimum entry level educational requirement, and the job-related physical strength standards). The second is the development and maintenance of a viable manpower resource pool (e.g., qualified and certified fire service candidates immediately ready to enter and effectively serve the agency on a full-time basis). The third is the implementation of equal employment opportunity programs (e.g., job-related testing; elimination of cultural biases in recruitment, selection, assignment, and promotion). With all of this in mind, fire service manpower planners have a major responsibility to have the *right number* of qualified people available to be hired and deployed at the *right time*.

To establish manpower needs, the fire personnel manager needs to be able to forecast employee attrition, to estimate specific fire protection requirements, and to predict the availability of qualified manpower. No simple model or rule of thumb exists to help the fire personnel manager fulfill these manpower planning tasks. And manpower needs differ considerably among local governments. Even in cities and counties of similar geographical and population sizes the number of fire employees required to deliver appropriate fire services will differ. A few of the reasons for such variations are: type of land area, density, degree of industrialization, amount of property to be protected, number and types of fire risks, average number of working hours per week, arrangements for recall of off-duty personnel, type of personnel (paid as compared to volunteer), and citizen expectations of the fire service.

Manning has taken on new significance owing to the substantial costs connected with fire employees. Fire agency budgets are frequently 90 percent and above in dollars allocated to personnel. Many local governments have been compelled to modernize their equipment, improve their methods, and streamline their operations in order to increase productivity. An important decision invariably involves the employment of fewer fire personnel. Paradoxically, we see fire chiefs confronted with their agency's evaluation on the basis of the number of personnel riding on a type of apparatus rather than on the basis of firefighting strength and demonstrated experience.

Equal employment opportunity: affirmative action

The current state-of-the-art in affirmative action has resulted, ironically, in a "damned if you do, damned if you don't" situation. Most fire agencies have developed active support for equal employment opportunity—as have firefighter unions.[18] In many cases this active support has been genuine and persistent. Unfortunately, in a few instances this has taken the form of cosmetic slogans, with very little substantive progress. So much of personnel management today (and this will apply well into the future) is affected by explicit affirmative action requirements that this subject is best discussed before other more traditional components. Indeed, nondiscriminatory hiring, assignment, discipline, and promotion procedures are judged by many fire personnel managers as the most perplexing and frustrating of administrative decisions.

In the majority of situations a simple count of fire personnel reveals that minorities are inadequately represented. The fire service is primarily the domain of white males. This nation has challenged this condition as being wrong, unless proved to the contrary. And the evidence, while contradictory, seems to underpin the value of "equal" opportunities.

In the main, three federal laws have championed the affirmative action cause: Section 1981 of the Civil Rights Act of 1866; the Fourteenth Amendment to the

Constitution; and Title VII of the Civil Rights Act of 1964, as amended by the Equal Employment Opportunity Act of 1972.[19]

Title VII has become the modern civil rights muscle. Both its congressional history and its ramifications should be understood by fire administrators when they formulate affirmative action policies, goals, and programs. Significantly, Title VII prohibits any discrimination on the basis of race, color, religion, sex, or national origin in all employment practices (including hiring, promotion, firing, compensation, and various other terms and conditions of employment) for employers having fifteen or more employees. In 1964 the U.S. Equal Employment Opportunity Commission (EEOC) was established to investigate violations of the Civil Rights Act of 1964.[20] These guidelines became applicable to the public sector in 1972.

Equal employment laws, policies, and practices were originally promulgated to eradicate intentional and unethical acts of job discrimination. Title VII, nevertheless, recognized that much discrimination emanated from normal, frequently unbiased, employment practices. Many practices have in fact unintentionally perpetuated discrimination against minorities and women, and these practices have been challenged in the courts. Both court decisions and employment laws in recent years have clearly stated that the status quo must change and that minorities and women will not only be employed but will be actively recruited and appropriately selected. Anything to the contrary will be permissible only upon irrefutable evidence that a particular person is incapable of performing *validated* job-related tasks. As an example, the mere supposition that men and women cannot maintain their professional integrity through using the same lavatory or sleeping facilities is presently unacceptable.[21] Management should also be aware that there are regulations and guidelines designed to ensure that government sponsored activities are free of unfair discrimination on the basis of physical or mental handicaps. The following sums up the thinking in this matter:

The Supreme Court in the 1971 landmark ruling *Griggs* v. *Duke Power Company*, followed in 1975 by the *Albemarle* v. *Moody* decision, established a formula: employment selection procedures, whether at the entry or promotional level, are vulnerable to legal assault by a plaintiff charging racial or sexual discrimination if the procedure involves use of an unvalidated test and criteria and if the process results in a disproportionately low number from the plaintiff's class who achieve placement on the eligibility list. In order to establish a prima facie case of discrimination, a plaintiff has only to show that the "consequences" of the defendant's employment standard or practice is a work force which is racially or sexually disproportionate to the labor pool it draws from. All that need be shown is that a higher percentage of minorities or women than Caucasian males failed the examination process and that the percentage of women or minorities employed is less than the source. Once the plaintiff has made the requisite preliminary showing of disparate results in the selection process, the burden shifts to the hiring agency, which must prove that the examination process has been validated (i.e., that the standard has a substantial proven business purpose).[22]

Minorities and equal opportunity   The initial thrust of the equal employment legislation primarily sought to eliminate unfair and discriminatory job practices where minorities were concerned. As a reaction to this emphasis we have found some members of the majority crying out, "Reverse discrimination!" The most outstanding illustration of this was seen in the well-known case of *University of California* v. *Bakke* (46 U.S.L.W. 4896 [1978]), which raised questions that are exquisitely complex. A few of these are: What is the meaning of equal opportunity? How much help should any person or race receive from the government to atone for past disadvantage? Can any citizen be held back so that others can catch up? And are the courts best fitted to settle these questions? In spite of the 1978 Supreme Court decision in the *Bakke* case, many problems still remain to be resolved through the creativity and goodwill of a society committed to equality for all its citizens.[23]

Test validation   At the heart of the continuing controversy lies test validation. Test validation means that documented proof exists that the test does in fact examine for job-related skills, knowledge, and abilities and for job behavior (SKA/JB).[24] Selection criteria, methods, and instruments are being challenged in the courts: in other words, the validity of the tests used in selecting, assigning, and promoting employees is under close scrutiny. Validity may be stated as: Does the test in reality measure what it was intended to measure? One does not measure weight with a yardstick. Associated with the concept of validity are the equally important subjects of job task analysis and cultural impartiality.

There are various types of validity: face, concurrent, construct, criterion, and content. (Face validity is based on the reasonableness of the criteria; in concurrent validity, validation studies are conducted on the basis of ongoing personnel processes.) These first two types have a number of inherent inadequacies and will not be discussed here.

Construct validity involves the analysis of a measure with respect to several propositions that are a part of the construct.[25] Criterion validity is founded on a time-tested and proved measure or standard. Unfortunately, the public service has few criteria that it can employ for purposes of test construction. Compounding this problem is the propensity on the part of the courts to require criterion test validation.

Alternatively, the Equal Employment Opportunity Commission permits content validation *if* the test is designed to examine for job-related SKA/JBs. There are strong and convincing arguments in favor of using content validation *if* the test: (1) is internally sound (logical), (2) is founded on a job analysis, (3) is patently job-related (test content = job content), and (4) is used for measuring existing levels of achievement. Broad-based predictive and abstract (e.g., personality) tests would not meet these conditions and thus would require criterion forms of validation. Stephen Wollack has said that "the important principle here is that content validation is a rational process requiring some precise, though not necessarily quantitative, procedure for establishing that the content of the test does, in fact, correspond to the job content domain."[26]

Job analysis links together the entire process of establishing and documenting job-relatedness in employment procedures. To begin with, pertinent information about the tasks/duties of the job is gathered by one or more of the following methods: individual interviews, group interviews, supervisory interviews, direct observation, participant logs, and questionnaires. Subsequently, the required SKA/JBs are derived by the job analyst's critical analysis of the various tasks that constitute the job. Each SKA/JB must have a logical relationship to one or more job tasks/duties. From here, expert opinion and tested experience are used to categorize and/or give priority order to the following: relative importance of the tasks; level of proficiency in performing the SKA/JBs; how SKA/JBs may be acquired; minimum qualifications; and methods of measuring (testing) the SKA/JBs.[27]

Obviously, any culturally biased tests or test items must be excluded if a validation is to be technically sound and socially fair. A nonessential minimum height requirement is a case in point in that if set too high it would tend to adversely affect Hispanic and Oriental groups. Also certain words and language usages may have different connotations for different groups. It should be borne in mind, as well, that physical testing should encompass only those activities and features that are required on the job. Field testing of all selection instruments and constant surveillance of their content are procedures for detecting such inequities. It is important to emphasize, however, that in the end, only the courts can validate a test.

Recommendations for increasing the representativeness of the fire agency   Programs designed to make a fire agency more representative in manpower policies are best adapted to the particular characteristics of the department, the governmental jurisdiction, and the community it serves. The recommended steps that follow will be useless unless a sincere and sustained *public commitment* is made on the part of fire chiefs, with the total endorsement of their superiors, to the agency's active involvement in being a practicing equal opportunity employer.[28] The following steps are recommended:

1. All job announcements should state that the agency is "an equal opportunity employer"
2. The affirmative action responsibility should be assigned to a particular individual of management rank and authority
3. Specially trained recruitment task forces should be developed and put into operation.
4. Referral sources (e.g., colleges, military services, other government agencies, ethnic organizations) should be identified and continuous liaison with them should be maintained
5. Full use of the media should be sought
6. Walk-in recruitment counseling plus site visits to colleges and also to neighborhood centers should be provided by each fire station
7. The time period from recruitment to selection should be kept to a minimum
8. All tests should be validated and based on the SKA/JBs as determined by periodic job analyses
9. All fire personnel should participate in in-service training programs that develop their understanding of the need for representation and that elicit their involvement in the course of this.

Recruitment: attracting qualified resources

The fundamental goal of recruitment is to attract qualified individuals to serve as firefighters. The term *qualified* denotes persons who possess, or can acquire through entry level training, the requisite SKA/JBs to effectively perform the tasks/duties of a firefighter. When there are difficulties with the image of the fire agency and when there are low salaries and fringe benefits, a shortage of people with existing or innate qualifications, constraining residency requirements, and complicated administrative procedures, quite obviously there will be major hurdles confronting any recruitment effort.

Fortunately, the fire service is looked upon as the source of a highly important helping activity—the protection of life and property. Thus, any potential limitations on a successful recruitment program may be offset by the following incentives: a purposeful job; a stimulating set of responsibilities; a collegial working environment; reasonable pay and benefits; opportunities for career advancement; and job security. The late 1970s and the 1980s should see more qualified people applying for firefighter positions than there are job openings. The key, therefore, will be to attempt to attract the *most qualified* for purposes of the next phase—selection: hence the continuing paramount significance of recruitment. The quality and the effectiveness of the fire service, then, starts with recruitment.

Sources of the resources[29]   Those responsible for recruiting may find potential applicants through a variety of sources, including: current fire employees and other employees; walk-ins and write-ins; educational institutions; employment services; and consultants and professional job recruiters. Attractive, imaginative, and current literature and application forms should be available at all times.

(It should be remembered that such initial contact can either motivate an individual toward a career in the fire service or discourage that person from competing in the selection process.) Although job opportunities may not be continuously present, clear and appealing brochures and other handouts should be readily obtainable from central personnel and from all fire stations and fire personnel. (Such material can also help to augment fire/community relations.) Steps should be taken, of course, to ensure that fire personnel bring in genuinely qualified applicants.

Interaction with the resources[30] Among the ways of making contact with potential firefighters are the following: posted and mailed job vacancy announcements; advertising (newspapers, radio, and television); recruitment task force teams; visits, displays and open houses; work-study programs and internships; cooperative recruiting efforts; and professional associations. These techniques are equally applicable to recruiting for entry level and supervisory and management fire personnel. In addition to making any printed information attractive, it is important that such information clearly expresses minimum job requirements, the duties/tasks of a firefighter, the working environment, the pay and benefits, and other relevant employment conditions and expectations.

The management responsibility The recruitment and selection of personnel for the fire service is a basic responsibility of management. This responsibility can no more be farmed out to other government agencies than can management's responsibility to organize, plan, or budget. To do so is to abdicate a management function that is crucial to the proper operation of any organization.

The primary concern of fire agencies should be the quality rather than the residency of fire personnel. Artificial preemployment residency requirements limit the number of applicants from among whom qualified candidates may be selected.

One of the most effective recruiting techniques is to involve all fire agency personnel in recruitment activities by providing incentives for their participation. The benefits of such a program are twofold: more personnel become involved in recruiting than could be assigned specifically to such duties by the agency, and, because of their professional interest, fire personnel generally recruit better qualified candidates.

Selection and assignment

Fire personnel selection denotes the preferential choosing of human talent for the fire service in accordance with the tasks/duties of the job. As has been mentioned earlier, the selection process actually begins with recruitment. The succeeding stages are: examination, certification, and assignment (placement). The traditional point of emphasis, as it will be here, is examination. The primary intent of an examination or test is to identify those applicants who possess or are likely to possess the highest degree of SKA/JBs needed to fulfill the job requirements. (It should be remembered that tests throughout the recruitment sequence—both before and after the training or academy program—must be validated, and must be planned in relation to the training skills taught.)

As has been mentioned earlier, the purpose of the test is the key to deciding what type, format, and content to administer. A brief discussion of traditional merit system tests appears immediately below. Following this, a newer method of examining is explored—the use of assessment centers.

Traditional testing The four major categories of testing in terms of fire agency personnel decisions are the following: (1) entry level (for new employees); (2) lateral entry (for experienced fire personnel acquired from other fire agencies—

for the same position and for promotion); (3) promotional (open or closed to external competition); and (4) specialized assignments (e.g., fire prevention and arson). Figure 13–1 shows the typical examination techniques as they relate to these four categories.

	Category of testing			
Selection technique	Entry level	Lateral entry	Promo- tional	Specialized assignments
Application verification	F	F	F	R
Paper and pencil test	F	F	F	O
Physical agility	F	O	R	R
Panel interview (oral board)	F	F	F	O
Medical	F	F	O	R
Psychiatric	F	O	O	R
Background inquiry	F	F	F	R
Performance ratings	N/A	F	F	F
Appraisal of promotability, assignment	N/A	N/A	F	F
Rating of résumé	N/A	F	F	O
Professional search agency	R	R	O	R
Exempt appointment	R	R	O	F
Training	F	R	R	R
Probationary period	O	R	R	R

Key
F = frequently
O = occasionally
R = rarely
N/A = not applicable

Figure 13–1 Types of selection techniques as applied to testing categories.

It is significant to note the last two techniques cited in Figure 13–1: training and probation. The frequency of application is poor except under entry level decisions. Ironically, these techniques have consistently demonstrated their highest reliability in predicting a new employee's job effectiveness (the main reason being that there is a much longer exposure to an individual's SKA/JBs in a learning and job-related environment—or training—and in actual on-the-job performance). Fortunately, some fire agencies have recognized the immense utility of training and probation as mechanisms for selection. Applied in tandem they significantly increase a department's accuracy about a person's talent to successfully perform the duties/tasks of a firefighter.

Assessment centers Briefly, an assessment center (AC) is a carefully planned process comprised of situation based tests that are clearly job-related and are administered in a single and expanded time frame. Some of the traditional techniques of testing are also present in an AC.[31] Figures 13–2 and 13–3 illustrate the differences between traditional and AC methods of testing. The value of the use of ACs may be summed up as follows:

The answer to the query "Why AC's?" seems self-evident. First, and foremost, the traditional civil service paper/pencil and oral board interviews and other appraisal processes are just not cutting it. Concisely put, they inculcate too many inadequacies. In fact, some have accused the present system of inadvertently fostering the Peter Principle (promoting—or in some cases retaining—people to their highest level of incompetency). Second, the majority of those who have experienced the traditional means of demonstrating one's skills are vociferously asking for a more

Description of Exercises

Assigned Role Group Discussion

In this leaderless group discussion, participants, acting as a city council of a hypothetical city, must allocate a one-million-dollar federal grant in the time allotted or make other judgments on the varying proposals offered. Each participant is assigned a point of view to sell to the other team members and is provided with a choice of projects to back and the opportunity to bargain and trade off projects for support.

Non-assigned Role Group Discussion

This exercise is a cooperative, leaderless group discussion in which four short case studies dealing with problems faced by executives working in state government agencies are presented to a group of six participants. The participants act as consultants who must make group recommendations on each of the problems. Assessors observe the participant's role in the group and the handling of the content of the discussion.

In-basket Exercise

Problems that challenge middle- and upper-level executives in state government are simulated in the in-basket exercise. These include relationships with departmental superiors, subordinates and peers, representatives of other departments, representatives of executive and legislative branches, the public, and the news media. Taking over a new job, the participant must deal with memos, letters, policies, bills, etc., found in the in-basket. After the in-basket has been completed, the participant is interviewed by an assessor concerning his/her handling of the various in-basket items.

Speech and Writing Exercises

Each participant is given a written, narrative description of a policy, event, situation, etc. and three specific situational problems related to the narrative, each requiring a written response. The participant is also required to make a formal oral presentation, based upon the background narrative description, before a simulated news conference attended by the Capitol Press Corps and interested government officials and citizens (assessors).

Analysis Problem

The analysis problem is an individual analysis exercise. The participant is given a considerable amount of data regarding a state agency's field operations, which he/she must analyze and about which he/she must make a number of management recommendations. The exercise is designed to elicit behaviors related to various dimensions of managerial effectiveness. The primary area of behavior evaluated in this exercise is the ability to sift through data and find pertinent information to reach a logical and practical conclusion.

Paper and Pencil Tests

Three different commercially-available objectively scoreable tests are included in the assessment: a reading test used for self-development purposes, a reasoning-ability test, and a personality test. The latter two are being used experimentally at present, and as with the reading test, are not made available during assessor discussions.

Figure 13-2 Exercises used in a two day assessment program by the state of Wisconsin. (Source: William C. Byham and Carl K. Wettengel, "Assessment Centers for Supervisors and Managers: An Introduction and Overview," *Public Personnel Management* 3 [September–October 1974]: 355.)

accurate method of doing so. Third, to these two concerns, we would add those of the manager which can be posed as follows, "I am in need of a decidedly better process—legally, ethically, and politically—for making personnel decisions. Decisions that, in turn, explicitly impact such organization-wide concerns as 'affirmative action,' 'productivity,' and 'social equity.' "[32]

An AC can be used for a variety of purposes and structured in an infinite number of ways. Typically, however, it spans one to three days. The latter is preferable in that the candidates spend more time with the assessors. The ratio of assessor to candidate is important: the more assessors to the assessees, the better. One assessor per two candidates is ideal, although in some cases a higher ratio—if carefully planned and if the assessors are experienced—can be effective. Basically, there are five major considerations to be dealt with in establishing an AC: (1) job requirements—skills, knowledge, and abilities; (2) methodology—exercises and instruments; (3) training of assessors; (4) time frame; and (5) ratio of assessors to candidates. Decisions on these elements directly and primarily influence the costs and benefits of an AC, which is clearly most cost-effective for higher level positions.

A two day AC might be arranged as follows. The first day prior to the AC, the AC administrator and the agency representative meet with the assessors for an orientation session. The focal point of discussion is the particular job requirements and the agency expectations. The latter part of the day involves the training of the assessors in the use of the role playing exercises and test instruments. The center begins with a background interview that affords assessors and candidates an opportunity to become acquainted with each other's professional and personal history. Thereafter the candidates would probably be given a management exercise, an in-basket test, leaderless group discussions (nonassigned and assigned roles), an analytical problem-solving game, a fact-finding mission, an interview simulation, a written presentation, and an oral presentation. The assessors are rotated according to a schedule that ensures that each has equal time with the individual candidates. The day after the AC has been completed, the assessors finalize their reports and present their findings and recommendations to the AC administrator. The latter, in turn, verifies the data and then transmits the results to the client agency. Once the candidates have been informed of their ratings they can often elicit feedback, if they wish to do so, from the AC administrator (or, in some instances, the assessors).

An evaluation of the AC process can be stated as follows:

We are quick to admit that AC's have not been proven beyond a shadow of a doubt. Although, we can report that all the research and court cases thus far [have] expressed that it is more accurate and valid than other available methods. Further, comparatively, it is not expensive. In fact, we believe that you will find, as we did, that the benefits will exceed the costs. One of the pioneers in developing and using the AC technique, William C. Byham, sums it up for us by writing, "Granted that it is not perfect, however, it seems using an assessment center for identifying management potential is a sounder and fairer method than those traditionally used by management."[33]

Problems of some procedures Certain traditional selection methods may adversely affect the induction of some applicants and at the same time may be ineffective in identifying qualified candidates. While the mental demands of firefighting are unquestionably severe, the measurement of mental suitability frequently disqualifies a disproportionate number of minorities while its accuracy in predicting job performance is highly questionable. Fire agencies that use unvalidated tests of mental ability or aptitude are liable to court action brought by the U.S. Department of Justice. Fire administrators should retain the management of their own hiring practices by ensuring that the selection procedures are legal. This is not to suggest that an agency should abandon all formal tests of

Figure 13–3   Comparison of assessment center method with typical use of panel interviews and paper and pencil testing. (Source: Byham and Wettengel, "Assessment Centers for Supervisors and Managers: 359–60.)

Assessment Center	Panel Interviews	Paper & Pencil Tests
Built around dimensions carefully defined through job analysis, and all dimensions are systematically covered.	While dimensions from research may be used, more often no list is used or an inadequate list is used. No real attempt to cover all of the dimensions is made in the interview due to the usual lack of structure.	Tests may be selected by job analysis but tests only attempt to predict certain of the dimensions. For example, tests are poor at determining interpersonal dimensions.
Dimensions are agreed upon by management before use. This creates an acceptance and understanding of them.	Usually not the case.	Usually not the case.
The involvement of higher-level managers in the selection of assessment center dimensions and as assessors allows them to make effective use of assessment center reports and to believe in the results because they understand the system.	Membership of higher-level managers on interview panels often increases their distrust of the Panel Interview process as they feel it is unreliable. Thus they discount the results.	Unless a specific cut-off score is used as in Civil Service Examinations, the users of the test results seldom know how to integrate the test results with other performance data.
Multiple exercises are used. The participant can be observed in different situations: group and non-group; small and large group exercises that require preparation and those that do not; exercises where the participant is a subordinate, peer, supervisor; exercises requiring oral, written and other skills.	Single exercise.	Tests may be slightly different depending on tests used but all generally emphasize written and cognitive skills.
Uses multiple judgments (3 to 6 assessors) which increase accuracy and decrease bias.	Uses multiple judgments.	Quantitative score. Use of score may be judgmental.
Trained observers are used.	Participants in panel interviews are seldom trained and seldom have adequate time to plan the interview.	
Assessors usually do not know participants.	Interviewers usually do not know participants.	
Assessors are several levels above participants and thoroughly know the target-level job.	Interviewers are several levels above participants and thoroughly know the target-level job.	
Real behaviors observed.	What a participant says he would do or has done is determined. Follow-up of important areas possible.	Participants often say what they think will get a high score in nonability tests.
Formal method of recording observations used.	Usually no formal method of recording observations of behavior or insights.	Formal method of collecting data used.
Large amount of data on participant obtained.	Small amount.	Small amount.
Procedure delays final decision until all information about participant is obtained.	Research indicates that interviewers quickly jump to a decision and their subsequent questions are often an attempt to reinforce the first decision.	Highly quantitative.
Highly-structured program producing quantitative results.	Low in structure. Low in quantitative results.	Highly quantitative
High reliability.	Low reliability.	High reliability.
Validities usually around 4 to 5.	Little known about validity.	Seldom above 3.
Technique flexible to various jobs.	Technique flexible to various jobs.	Less flexible because content validation for supervisory and managerial jobs is more difficult to achieve.
Relatively easy to establish content validity (job-relatedness).	Difficult to establish content validity (job-relatedness).	Difficult to establish content validity (job-relatedness).
Criterion-related validity research should be conducted.	Criterion-related validity research should be conducted.	Criterion-related validity research should be conducted.
Produces insights into development needs that can be beneficial whether or not the participant is promoted.	Not usually the case.	Not usually the case.
Process is understandable to participants, they see it as a fair means of evaluating all areas of management potential.	Participant evaluation of fairness depends on interviewers. Most interviewees feel interview covers only a portion of important management skills.	Often misunderstood, biases carried over from negative school experiences.

mental and physical ability, but rather to say that an agency should validate current selection devices or, if they cannot be validated, should replace them with some more appropriate technique.[34]

Performance appraisal

The appraisal of performance in the fire service must center on *achieved results* as compared to *initial objectives*. Employee evaluation has taken on enhanced importance owing to the growing stress on *cost reduction* and *productivity improvement* in government. A number of movements have been implemented in support of greater cost-effectiveness, such as worker motivation, management by objectives (MBO), organization development (OD), and participative management. Thus, one sees that personnel management of necessity must operate in concert with fire management and vice versa.

Appraisal techniques vary from a single sheet of plain white paper to highly structured numerical reports. Similarly, the frequency can vary from monthly to never (although the usual appraisal period is six months or one year).

Space does not permit more than an overview of the appraisal process here. The process used, of course, will depend on the kinds of employees to be evaluated and on their duties. In the fire service, the objectives of employee appraisal are: (1) to provide evaluative feedback to management and the firefighter on the latter's compliance with rules and with productivity expectations; (2) to serve as a foundation for employee guidance and for needed areas of future professional development; (3) to discover fire personnel with talent for management or special assignment positions; (4) to justify adjustments in compensation or position classification; and (5) to foster an MBO program.[35]

Performance rating techniques include work activity records (e.g., number of fire suppression calls), graphic rating scales (very common in the fire service—numbers and alphabetic characters to encircle or check), multiple-rater group evaluations, open-ended written essays, an important incident file (e.g., three by five inch cards or a log on unusual events), self-evaluation, peer review, subordinate appraisal, and assessment centers.[36]

A general set of dos   First, all appraisal efforts must be thoroughly documented. Arriving at bottom line figures or check marks at the end of six to twelve months without obtaining supporting *recorded* facts is both unfair and open to grievances. Hence, an important incident file should be maintained by all supervisory personnel. What constitutes an important incident should be clearly defined in an appraisal guideline. Second, in reference to a guideline both supervisory and line personnel should read the guidelines once a year. The guideline should explain the intent and content of the rating process. Also, it should contain definitions of all terms used in the process.

Third, the raters should be periodically trained and evaluated in appraising an employee's performance. In essence, their performance appraisal should be partially judged on their knowledge and execution of their rating skills. Fourth, multiple raters should be used to evaluate each person. In this way rater bias and rating avoidance are significantly reduced.

Fifth, the rating form should be job-related. Similar forms should be designed for supervisors and managers. Sixth, the employee should be required to set individual objectives for accomplishment (MBO) during the subsequent time period.

In summary, the accumulation of important incidents is assessed by a group of raters to assist in the completion of the periodic appriasal and the MBO process. All of this, in turn, serves as a justification for salary, promotional, and training decisions. Moreover, it acts as a major cornerstone for a career development program. The very nature of such decisions—decisions that affect 90 percent of the budget—demands top priority in time and expenditure. Anything less would be foolish.

A final word Evaluation of fire personnel for advancement and promotion should not be limited to initial assessment of the individual's qualifications and abilities. Evaluation and selection of personnel for promotion and advancement should be an integral part of the personnel development process, beginning with identification of personnel who appear to have the potential for intensive development, continuing with assessment of their progress, and culminating with their final evaluation for advancement or promotion.

Staff inspections

The purpose of inspection and control is the monitoring of operational efficiency and effectiveness. It is best approached in a positive manner with the goal of revealing needed areas of program and employee improvement.

The two types of inspections There are two types of inspections. The first, line inspection, is achieved by routine ongoing supervisory policies and practices. Authoritative inspection responsibilities should include personal inspection of employees, as well as inspection of the equipment they use and how they use and care for it, how employees perform their duties, and the results of their efforts. The directive establishing the inspection duty of the manager and supervisor also should make it clear that this duty includes the responsibility to take the immediate action indicated by the inspection. Such action should include commendations for exemplary performance and corrective action for deficiencies.

The second type of inspection is staff inspection—that conducted by persons who, having no direct authority over the subject of the inspection, normally can only report upon the results. The need for staff inspection increases with the size of the fire agency and the complexity of its organizational structure and operations. When fire chiefs cannot conduct their own line inspections with the necessary frequency, they should provide for staff inspections.

A final word The fire chief is responsible for establishing and maintaining a system of inspection to obtain the information needed to direct and control the fire agency. Although the ultimate responsibility for inspection and control rests with the fire chief, it should be carried out continually at all levels of command and supervision.

Personnel development

A personnel development program essentially integrates recruitment, selection, training and education, career planning, career counseling, performance appraisal, and all other human resource considerations (health, safety, etc.) into a single system and unit. As a consequence, we find the traditional responsibilities of the fire personnel manager enlarged to those of a manager of personnel development. In addition to personnel development, what might be considered a careful program of management development for top decision makers is also of vital significance, especially in the fire service.

Personnel development is directed not only toward improving the performance of incumbent personnel but also toward creating a pool of personnel qualified for the positions of advanced generalists, specialists, supervisors, managers, and executives. Personnel development incorporates the concepts of career development and management development.

The value of internships with other organizations—public or private, law enforcement or another function—lies in the opportunity for the intern to observe the management and operation of agencies facing problems similar to those of his or her own. Such an exchange of personnel is beneficial on any level but perhaps most helpful to specialists and managers.

No one can develop judgment and learn how to make good decisions except by making decisions. Participation on management committees and boards is one technique of developing this ability. Such an opportunity to examine incidents from management's viewpoint has been found to broaden a participant's perspective.

The rotation of personnel for training and development is well established in private organizations as well as in the public service. The benefits to new employees include broadening their perspective of the entire fire service and agency and introducing them to the type of fire service work they particularly might like to do.

The past is not necessarily prologue

An often proved cliché may well prove applicable for fire personnel management: "If you want to know what the next five years will be like, merely look at the last five years." The reactive posture and mistakes of the past will be all the more costly in the future. The promise of the coming years for those in fire and fire personnel management is increased complexity and change. For example, how does one maintain existing or even lower costs for fire services while maintaining present service levels or expanding them? Fresh answers unencumbered by the stale prescriptions of the past must be sought.

The fire personnel manager will be confronted with decisions that must be made on cost reduction, service increases, public unions, equal employment opportunity, changing case law, new management techniques and tools, political pressures, and intergovernmental relations. At first glance this list may cause the manager to comment, "There's nothing new about these decisions." The novelty resides in the changing conflicting demands, changing constraints, and changing intricacies inherent in each of the problems. In the coming years adaptation, innovation, and commitment will become three bywords that fire chiefs and those responsible for fire personnel management will find most pervasive in accomplishing their duties and tasks.

B: Labor relations: no arena for amateurs

One infallible way of ensuring that a local government and its decision makers will become the focus of the most intensive and most unwelcome public scrutiny is to have public services break down through a strike of public employees. Examples of this were not lacking as the 1970s drew to a close. One overseas example makes the point: in late 1977 and early 1978 the world watched as England burned. As fire losses are common in industrialized nations, why did this matter receive extra attention? The answer was simple: the nationally organized fire union was on strike. As deaths, injuries, and property damage mounted, government leaders blamed the firefighters and the firefighters blamed an inflexible bureaucracy for tying their hands. The labor relations machinery—which had worked quietly for years with little attention from the media—had broken down hopelessly.

The British experience is not without its counterpart in the United States. Strikes among public service workers in general, and among professional or, more accurately, fully paid fire departments (for volunteer departments, too, can be professional), in particular, are now commonplace in the United States. Media coverage of the kind that focused on England has been focused on communities in the United States, and the attention, though unwelcome, is justified: the strike is the ultimate failure in employee relations, for it causes management, labor, and the public to pay a heavy toll. The strike is just one example—though certainly the most visible—of the great need for sound management practices and professional attitudes in labor relations. Labor and management experts alike would emphatically agree that this is no arena for amateurs.

The following discussion, which deals with the management of fire department labor relations, is divided into five parts. The first places labor relations in its historical context so that its contemporary aspects can be better understood. The second places labor relations in its fire department context by identifying key characteristics of fire department organization. The third—the heart of the discussion—takes a careful stage-by-stage look at the collective bargaining process with emphasis on those points that labor and management professionals alike agree need particular attention. The fourth part discusses contract administration and grievance procedures applicable after the contract has been signed, and the fifth provides a brief conclusion and outlook.

Throughout the discussion attention is given to identifying what experience and the consensus of management and labor specialists have shown to be areas of key concern for decision makers. To supplement this discussion of sound principles and procedures the reader is referred to appropriate publications for the latest statistics on labor relations activities and for the latest developments in the changing legislative and judicial arenas.[37] While the focus of the discussion is primarily on fully paid fire departments, it is intended that the principles identified should be adaptable to volunteer departments and smaller communities which may not have been confronted with the challenge of collective bargaining but are interested in sound, professional labor relations.

Labor relations in historical perspective

As labor relations, unionization, and collective bargaining in the American public sector seem to be imitating a cycle which has already run through private industry, and as it is difficult to appreciate the current state of labor relations in the United States without a look at the past, a brief overview of labor relations history is presented immediately below.

A brief history of labor legislation   Prior to 1932 the entrepreneurial spirit was strong in the United States. Since business and industrial leaders had wealth, influence, and the sympathy of the courts, unionizing efforts—though deeply rooted—remained relatively insignificant as a mass movement.

In the early days of the union movement employers capitalized on a general national feeling that the economy would function best if it were free of organizations that imposed restrictions—a classification that included unions. Unions were considered conspiracies, and injunctions against them were summarily issued. At the turn of the century big business dominated the American economic picture. The Sherman Anti-Trust Act, passed by Congress in 1890, was designed to encourage competition. While it had little effect on regulating the growth of individual firms or industries, the act did severely limit the growth of unionism. Virtually all unionism was ruled in violation of the antitrust provisions of the act.

The repression of unionism persisted until the Great Depression turned the general public against big business. The Norris–LaGuardia Act (1932) was the first legislative attempt to give legitimate unionism a chance to succeed. The new philosophy was that collective bargaining would ensure proper rights for both employers and employees and that the public interest would also be better served. The law ensured that labor unions would not be restrained by antitrust provisions of the Sherman act, and the 1932 law neutralized the power of the federal courts in labor cases.[38]

Learning the hard way If 1933 seemed like a dream year, 1934 was the year of awakening. Drafting NLRA was the work of many hands with not much time to pause over details. Along with its guarantees to labor, Section 7(a) conceded to employers that where existing employee organizations were satisfactorily representing employees, they could be recognized. That opened the way to company unions. Just as serious, the act established no congressionally sanctioned way of enforcing the section, opening a loophole that Roosevelt sought to plug by creating, by executive order, a National Labor [Relations] Board.

It was becoming clear that most employers had no intention of complying with Section 7(a). As newly organized unions confronted management with demands, they were met by blunt refusals to bargain. Strikes were called. The Labor Board responded gallantly and was developing "a common law" applying to the resolution of such confrontations, when it was challenged for lack of statutory authority by Weirton Steel and Budd Manufacturing. The board was brought to its knees. The final blow came from the President himself. Fearful that a looming strike in the fledgling auto industry would jeopardize national economic recovery, Roosevelt exempted that industry from the requirements of Section 7(a). The message was clear: Employers would not obey the law, and the government could not make them.

Bitterly awakened from the dream of 1933, the unions determined to rely only on their own strength—the strike —to combat the employers' strength —the dollar—and to establish for themselves the right to collective bargaining.

In the spring and summer of 1934 a wave of strikes washed across the country. In Toledo the unemployed— normally the pool from which management recruited strike-breakers— supported a new union of Auto-Lite workers and stayed with them through tear gas, bullets, and an assault by the National Guard until the company agreed to collective bargaining. Two persons died.

In Minneapolis truckers used brilliant planning and organizing to make good on their promise that "not a wheel will roll" until the union was recognized and bargaining begun. Through 36 days of violence on a grand scale, they made it stick and won recognition and wage increases. Five persons died.

On the West Coast, longshoremen closed down every major port and in San Francisco sparked one of the few general strikes in the nation's history before a bitterly anti-union business establishment agreed to terms that ended the loathsome "shape-up" method of hiring dock labor. Two persons were killed.

Source: Ralph J. Flynn, *Public Work, Public Workers* (Washington, D.C.: The New Republic Book Co., 1975), pp. 7–8.

While the unions of the nation were enjoying the organizational freedom afforded by the Norris–LaGuardia Act, business organizations were using infiltration, company unions, and ''sweetheart contracts'' as means of countering the new union efforts. Long and costly strikes ensued. New pro-union legislation was needed to promote effective collective bargaining.

In 1935 the National Labor Relations Act (NLRA), commonly called the Wagner Act, was passed and guaranteed the right of workers to organize and to bargain collectively. Industrial harmony and a stable economy were the desired by-products. Employers openly resisted the new law and forced the Wagner Act to a test in the Supreme Court. In 1937 in a five to four decision the justices of the Court upheld the law's constitutionality and allowed its broad application in the landmark *Jones and Laughlin* case.[39]

The National Labor Relations Board (NLRB) was created to administer and enforce the act and thereby to serve as a mechanism for ensuring industrial harmony. The act was successful in minimizing the number of organizational strikes and promoting the growth of unionism in industries. Between 1935 and 1948 union membership quadrupled from 4 million to 16 million.[40] Business and industry had lost their upper hand and unions had gained so much power that legislation was called for to create a balance more favorable to business and industry. This came in the form of the 1947 Labor–Management Relations Act, commonly known as the Taft–Hartley Act.

Since the Taft–Hartley Act placed new controls and restrictions on unions, it was openly supported by management and was perceived as a threat by unions; the then separate American Federation of Labor (AFL) and Congress of Industrial Organizations (CIO) vehemently opposed it. Ultimately, however, it placed management and unions on a more equal footing.

The last significant piece of labor legislation was the Landrum–Griffin Act (1959), which detailed regulations in certain phases of labor relations, put new restrictions on the activities of unions, and required additional accountability from employers. These various laws were enacted and were interpreted in the courts with a view toward economic stability and industrial harmony—all in all, with relative success.

Labor law and the public sector   All of this significant labor relations legislation was enacted, modified, and updated in the arena of the private sector, and public employees were excluded. It was thought that the public employee worked in an environment that was insulated from the entrepreneurial attitudes and the competition that had produced labor inequities and the rise of unionism in the private sector.

While, as we have seen, labor relations in private industry has become much more stabilized, public sector employees have become more vocal and the labor relations climate more volatile. Ralph Flynn has traced the official beginnings of the public sector labor movement to Executive Order 10988, issued in January 1962:

President John Kennedy extended the rights of union organization and a truncated system of collective bargaining to federal employees. This action exerted pressure at the state level and laws giving public employees the right of union organization and collective bargaining soon were enacted in major states.[41]

Even without the federal impetus it is quite probable that public employee unions and corresponding organizational attitudes would be just as evident today. The separate private and public modes of employment that have persisted since the Industrial Revolution are being drawn together, particularly for the following two reasons:

1. Public organizations are being continually forced through fiscal pressures to operate more like competitive businesses
2. The common denominator in employment is the employee—a human being with needs, desires, and aspirations which transcend the traditional public–private barrier.

When we speak of the *public employee* today, we should emphasize the word *employee* and give less emphasis to the word *public*.

The scope of the NLRA   The National Labor Relations Act, including the original Wagner Act as well as the Taft–Hartley and Landrum–Griffin amendments, is designed to make it

the policy of the United States to eliminate the causes of certain substantial obstructions to the free flow of commerce and to mitigate and eliminate these obstructions when they have occurred by encouraging the practice and procedure of collective bargaining and by protecting the exercise by workers of full freedom of association, self-organization and designation of representatives of their own choosing, for the purpose of negotiating the terms and conditions of their employment or other mutual aid or protection.

This official legal language, which caused "collective bargaining" to be part of "the policy of the United States," gave the official sanction needed for the actions of millions of union members. The jurisdiction of the NLRA, however, does not extend to the 14 million public employees in federal, state, and local governments. The intense interest of the federal government in the field of labor relations—and the extensive legislation which has resulted—nevertheless belies the limited range of its jurisdiction.

Some states have enacted legislation to cover the field of public employees. These laws vary widely from one state to the next, which adds to the confusion and the inequities of varying state controls. A strong undercurrent pointing to change is well under way, however, at the national level. Ralph Flynn makes the following comment:

It took the better part of a century to achieve the original Wagner Act. No one believes that it will take anywhere near that long to get federal legislation establishing the ground rules for civil conduct between labor and management in the public sector. Change has reached a velocity too great to make that kind of wait necessary. Because this is the case, the historical parallel between the Wagner Act and the present situation is, in terms of the legislative gestation period, inexact.

But in terms of the possible costs to the nation of achieving the needed breakthrough, the historical parallel has a chilling exactness. We can wait, keeping the question of public sector labor reform low on the legislative priority list, and see whether it takes a long, harsh wave of strikes and counter-repression to force action. Or, we can take heed of our history and act to make that expensive gamble unnecessary. We have it in our power, for a while at least, to set the price we are willing to pay for the inevitable.[42]

If a comparison is made between where the private labor movement was in 1935 when the Wagner Act was passed and where the public labor sector is today, some striking similarities are evident. The growing unrest, the increase in organizing, and the frequency of public employee strikes are all indications that legislation similar to the Wagner Act is due for the public sector. Many public administrators, union executives, and political leaders throughout the country feel that new federal legislation will be an absolute requirement to obtain labor relations harmony in the public sector.

The National League of Cities, among other groups, is making a strong case for a federal public labor law. Its action, along with that of others, is strongly influencing the quest for federal legislation.

It is possible that strong state legislation may provide the desired stability. Although state laws will not have the impact of federal laws, they will provide a needed measure of control. Those states that have faced public employee organization realistically are aware of an era sensitive to change and recognize that the change must be in both laws and attitudes. Figure 13–4 briefly outlines the history of labor legislation and the parallel cycle which is emerging in the public sector.

Labor relations in fire departments The fire department is a special type of public service agency and, whether its employees are union members or not, good labor relations is possible for the fire administrator who is willing to adequately research labor relations issues and to exercise professional understanding in dealing with employees.

In both unionized and nonunionized fire departments there is a contractual relationship between employer and employee. It is usually desirable for both

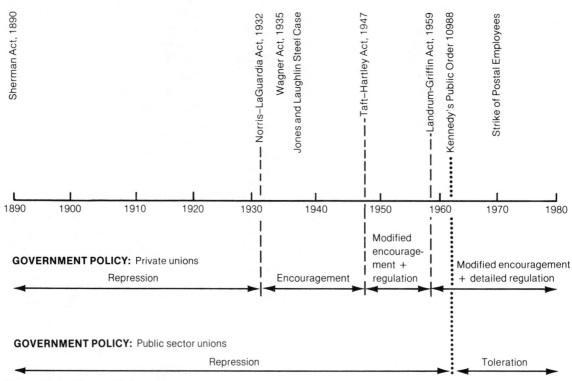

Figure 13–4   History of labor relations.

employees and administrators to have labor agreements formalized in writing. Nonunion fire departments should have at least a basic set of written guidelines. A wholesome atmosphere and a productive working relationship for both management and employees is the result of well-engineered labor relations.

Management maintains the upper hand and retains most of the prerogatives in a nonunionized setting. Currently, it must satisfy the same human needs and desires that serve as the foundation for union demands—high wages, fringes, good working conditions, and job security. The alternative is to face organizing attempts either from within the department or by outside labor organizations.

It is unwise for fire department management to overreact defensively when faced with employee attempts to organize. It is far better for all concerned (especially the public) if management recognizes the current wave of organization as an irreversible social trend which must be dealt with calmly and professionally. Serious appraisals of the earlier aggressive actions of private employers against private sector employee attempts to organize have shown these employer actions to have been negative, expensive, and futile.

A text on fire service management published by the National Fire Protection Association (NFPA) contains the following list of major sources of dissatisfaction which cause employees in general and firefighters in particular to organize:

1. Threats to security of job or position
2. Wages, salaries, benefits, promotions
3. Employees not knowing where they stand with management
4. Lack of involvement of employees in policy and decision making
5. Poor working conditions
6. Discrimination.[43]

The standard of professionalism in labor relations should be the same in both union and nonunion organizations. And where a fire department is in the transition stage of acquiring a formal union organization, the burden is on management to realize that the effects will not be devastating, to maintain a flexible attitude, and to seek ways of using the new union to strengthen its own managerial effectiveness.

With the advent of the era of public service labor organization, public administrators are faced increasingly with the obligation to deal either with new unions or with increasingly complex demands from existing unions. A simple change model (Figure 13–5) shows how time permits the reestablishment of equilibrium. The threat stage corresponds to the first inclination toward organizing—a period of intense anxiety for management. The reaction stage corresponds to the actual organizing—to the formation of a union or labor organization. Finally, the implementation stage shows the union organization integrated into the fire department. The implication is that management should make every effort to weather the storm, for equilibrium will ultimately be restored.

Figure 13–5 The unionizing change model.

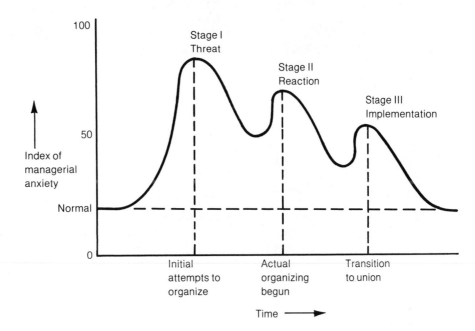

A powerful tool for a group of workers, unionized or not, is the strike. Before 1970 the strike was illegal for all public employees (and it still is for many), and they were effectively denied their most powerful weapon. Nonetheless, consistent with the trend mentioned earlier, strikes began to occur in the 1960s among federal, state, and local employees, despite legislative prohibitions.

When in 1970 a massive strike among postal employees caused all mail deliveries to be cancelled for several weeks, Congress agreed for the first time to recognize the union for collective bargaining negotiations. This trend has continued at all government levels.

The role of the IAFF As public employee unionism grew, the International Association of Fire Fighters (IAFF) grew in equal measure. By 1978 this union represented over 80 percent of the full-time paid firefighters in the country and its membership included some 1,900 local union organizations. (Some other paid firefighters—less than 0.5 percent—have affiliated with the International Brotherhood of Teamsters or another national organization.) A 1977 publication has given the following description of the IAFF:

Unlike most unions, local unions in the IAFF usually include fire department chiefs and officers (managers) among their membership. This situation has created the opportunity for conflict where effective management decisions mean fewer or more demanding jobs for rank and file members. On the other hand, this unique condition has permitted cooperation and industrial harmony between chiefs and union leaders, and has allowed executive officers of the IAFF to serve on national committees in the NFPA [National Fire Protection Association] and National Fire Prevention and Control Administration [now the U.S. Fire Administration].[44]

Union leadership in the public sector is often composed of well-educated persons who are as knowledgeable and professional in labor relations as are their management counterparts. The IAFF offers assistance and guidance to its many local organizations, small and large, scattered throughout the country. It is often influential in resolving labor disputes at the local level. Administrators who must negotiate with IAFF locals are actually dealing with the professional international union officers.

The history of the IAFF shows that it has usually had capable and knowledgeable leadership at the national level. The IAFF has supported technological advances and modern management practices and has cooperated with the U.S. Fire Administration (formerly the National Fire Prevention and Control Administration [NFPCA]) and the National Fire Protection Association (NFPA). Consistent with the national trend, however, the IAFF has become more militant, and in 1968 it removed a no strike rule which has lasted fifty years.[45]

Key aspects of fire department organization

An accurate perspective of labor relations in a fire department requires an understanding of the unique and complex characteristics which make fire departments a special type of public service organization (a subject discussed in detail in Chapters 2 and 3).

In a text by William Glueck, six factors, three internal and three external, were shown to be key characteristics of any organization. The internal factors are size, employee characteristics, and complexity, and the external factors are dependence, technology, and volatility.[46] Each of these six is relevant to an understanding of fire department labor relations.

	Listing by Glueck	Relevance for fire departments
I Internal factors	A. Size	Demographic differences, structure, number of employees
	B. Employee characteristics	Unique labor unions, civil service system, hazardous nature of profession
	C. Complexity	Increasing number of responsibilities, increasing number of hazards
II External factors	A. Dependence	Government agencies, public support
	B. Technology	Synthetic combustibles, extinguishing equipment
	C. Volatility	New focuses in fire department obligations

Figure 13–6 The relationship between six organizational factors and municipal fire departments. (Source: William M. Kramer, *A Managerial Analysis of Municipal Fire Departments,* Cincinnati: University of Cincinnati Press, 1977, p. 75.)

A national research report by William Kramer was built upon information submitted by 83.5 percent of the fire chiefs in United States cities of 100,000 or more population. Although this report's conclusions may not necessarily be valid for smaller jurisdictions, some points are of general interest. For example, the report discusses the relationship to fire department organizations of each of the six characteristics cited by Glueck.[47] Figure 13–6 summarizes the relevant information.

As an aid to understanding the fire department organizational setting in which labor negotiations are conducted and in which the labor function is carried out, an analysis of the six factors is given immediately below.

Size   The first factor, the size of the fire department, is an obviously necessary consideration. Not only does the smaller fire department have fewer members to placate, but it also usually has fewer work categories and job descriptions.

The size of a fire department was shown by Kramer to have an extremely close correlation with the size of the population of a protected municipality. In addition, highly accurate figures were compiled in the study giving both the average number of firefighters per 1,000 population and the percentages of promoted supervisory positions. Since these two subjects are often subjects in collective bargaining, they are summarized in Table 13–1.[48]

Table 13–1   Average number of firefighters and average percentage of supervisory firefighters for cities 100,000 and over, by population size.

Population size	No. of firefighters per 1,000 population	% firefighters who are supervisory
100,000–249,999	1.89	20.4
250,000–499,999	1.84	25.5
500,000 and over	1.53	21.7
Overall	1.81	21.8

Source: Taken, with minor adaptations, from William M. Kramer, *A Managerial Analysis of Municipal Fire Departments* (Cincinnati: University of Cincinnati Press, 1977), p. 77.

Employee characteristics   In fire department labor relations the central figure is the professional firefighter, an individual who is simultaneously an employee of the fire department and a member of a firefighters' union. As a class, firefighters cannot be taken lightly since they are a hardy group practicing one of the most hazardous of professions. According to the IAFF they far surpass police officers and other law enforcement personnel in deaths per 1,000.[49] In injuries per 1,000 they surpass police officers to an even greater extent.

Complexity   As other chapters in this book clearly indicate, the functions performed by members of a modern municipal fire department are being broadened to include many new tasks in the fields of fire suppression, fire prevention, and public education. Firefighters today deal with radioactivity, toxic chemicals, the hazards of high rise buildings, paramedic duties, and a multitude of complicating factors unknown a few years ago.

Dependence   This external factor can serve as a moderating influence on labor negotiations. Since management and labor both realize that the public, the government, and other groups can provide or withhold support and influence, negotiations tend to be conducted more realistically, and the labor–management negotiating committee is not an isolated entity.

Technology　As in private industry, technological advances are periodically introduced into the fire service. Many of them directly affect the nature of the firefighter's job. (Later in this chapter it is shown that the IAFF supports innovation and technological progress and that union officials at the local level are generally positive in their acceptance of the same.) The introduction of new technology in the fire service has faced as much opposition from conservative administrators as it has from unions. The best attitude for management is one of joint discussion and cooperation.

Volatility　The final factor is volatility—the degree of change in the environment. Fire departments today exist in an era of rapid development in which hazards are growing, technology is moving swiftly, and pressure is being applied for new thrusts in fire prevention and education. This volatility serves to expand both the number of negotiable issues and the complexity of long negotiated issues from the past.

The collective bargaining process

Overview　Although the term *collective bargaining* has become a household word, it does have a precise definition. Section 7(d) of the Taft–Hartley Act describes it in the following way:

For the purposes of this section, to bargain collectively is the performance of the mutual obligation of the employer and the representative of the employees to meet at reasonable times and confer in good faith with respect to wages, hours, and other terms and conditions of employment, or the negotiation of an agreement, or any question arising thereunder, and the execution of a written contract incorporating any agreement reached if requested by either party, but such obligation does not compel either party to agree to a proposal or require the making of a concession.

It is important to note that throughout the history of labor relations public employees, whatever their status, have always felt the effects of labor legislation. As conditions of employment changed in the private sector because of legislation they changed also in the public sector, which of necessity competes for labor from the same pool. Public employees have received a measure of shelter from the umbrella of private labor law.

It should be noted that collective bargaining in the public sector has a complexity which is often not found in private industry. Agreements which are reached in private sector industrial settings are often final and binding if ratified by employees. In the public sector, however, an agreement is often subject to approval by a city council, a state legislative committee, or a similar group. This additional step may range from a rubber-stamp formality to a jealously guarded system of control. In some jurisdictions the voters themselves must ratify public labor agreements.

Within the framework of the collective bargaining process, an agreement is reached between management and the union. In fire departments, according to the NFPA, this formal written agreement ordinarily covers five areas: (1) routine clauses, (2) union security, (3) the rights of management, (4) grievance procedure, and (5) conditions of employment.[50]

The NFPA goes on to explain that routine clauses are those which contain constitutional items, composition of the bargaining unit, reopening conditions, and amendments. Union security clauses contain a definition of the bargaining unit and provisions for union recognition. The management rights clauses list specific prerogatives retained by management, and the grievance procedure clauses spell out the details of the grievance and arbitration procedures. Finally, clauses regarding conditions of employment provide lengthy details concerning wages, hours, strikes, vacations, discharges, benefits, and similar matters.[51]

The detailed contract format is a further indication of the complexity of labor relations in the modern fire department. The complicated picture of today, however, had very different beginnings, which Donald Favreau has described as follows:

Fire fighters pioneered in demanding recognition from municipalities and in the effective use of the strike. The first collective bargaining contract between a municipality and its public employees in North America was recorded in 1674, about 100 years before the founding of the United States. The contract was signed by the mayor of the village of Ville-Marie, now the City of Montreal, and two fire fighters. It provided for a work week of seven 24-hour days, 50 cents per month salary, plus room and board. Included in the fringe benefit clause was the issuance of a pair of red trousers.[52]

Today elected officials and appointed administrators find that they must face demands from the union which far exceed a monthly salary of fifty cents and a fringe benefit package consisting of a pair of red trousers.

The position of elected officials The elected officials in a municipality, usually council members and perhaps a mayor, are obliged to answer to their constituencies. The voters who elect them and entrust them with a measure of control over local tax dollars demand that they do what is possible to keep the cost of public employees within reason. At the same time, these same officials are often elected through the public support and endorsement of powerful political cadres, including firefighter unions.

Automatically, the elected official is faced with the difficult task of answering to the voter who says, "I gave you my trust," and analyzing the needs of the firefighter who claims, "My union got you elected." The most respected elected officials seem to possess sound preelection knowledge and offer platforms that can be implemented. Quite often, realistic compromises can be achieved in labor negotiations—compromises which will suit both the union and the taxpayer who ultimately pays for the services rendered by the union.

The position of appointed officials Appointed officials often have a more effective hand in the control of labor negotiations since they do not have a voting constituency to satisfy and are actually "hired" by the elected officials to serve as effective business administrators. However, the appointed officials—city managers, safety directors, department heads—must of necessity be attuned to the policy requirements of the political leaders. This causes the same pressures to be placed indirectly on appointed officials that are placed directly on elected officials.

The role of the fire chief The role of the fire chief in labor negotiations can be pivotal, although historically fire chiefs may have had a small voice. As chief administrators of a fire department, there is the probability that fire chiefs will be sympathetic to the firefighters from whose ranks they have been promoted, especially if they retain brotherhood with their firefighters as a fraternal member of their union (a unique situation that has been a constant irritant to city managers and other similar officials). On the other hand, fire chiefs may be able to provide valuable insight for management.

One book on fire service management shows a sketch of a collective bargaining session, with the city council and the city manager facing the local union and the international union representative. The caption reads, "Where is the chief of department?"[53] The author goes on to make a valid argument to the effect that, while the chief should not be a member of the negotiating team, the chief should be present as a consultant to city officials.[54] The minimum prerequisite for this capacity, however, includes a knowledge of labor legislation and labor practices at the national, state, and local levels. Also required is a knowledge of the existing labor agreement and past practices in local negotiations. The remainder of this section, then, discusses the stages and various aspects of the collective bargaining process from the managerial perspective.

The negotiating teams   Usually both city management and the union will appoint negotiating teams. Since the local union team would be expected to include the local president, the best union minds, and legal counsel, management is compelled to present a similar makeup and caliber of negotiators. The alternative is to be out-negotiated. Gone are the days when "the brains of management" were pitted against "the brawn of the union." Today brainpower and sophistication are found on both sides of the negotiating table. The union leaders of today are usually educated and well versed in the laws of economics and finance, and the best approach for management is a cool head, aboveboard negotiating, and an ability to talk and listen with equal facility.

The negotiating team for management should realize that management offers less than it can afford to give and the union demands more than it expects to receive. The ensuing negotiating game causes inevitable tensions. This fact underscores the need for skilled persons on the negotiating team as well as a clearly designated leader.

The ideal negotiating team should include a high ranking personnel officer, a city financial expert or budget analyst, and a lawyer. No more than one additional member—perhaps someone with a special expertise—should be added to the team. Since this group is entrusted with the responsibility of representing the city administration, it should be given direct access, at least through its chairperson, to high ranking appointed and elected city officials. A city manager and/or a mayor can often use the influence of office to facilitate settlements.

Preparation for negotiations   Labor negotiations always deserve and often demand year-round attention, even though the specific negotiating period only occupies a part of the year—usually annually (sometimes less frequently for multiyear contracts). Everything that happens during the year in the field of employee relations will become a cumulative base upon which the next formal negotiating session will rest. Indefensible and unworkable (usually outmoded) items from earlier contracts and grievances may give roots to new demands on the part of the union or of management. W. D. Heisel, director of the Institute of Governmental Research at the University of Cincinnati, has made the important point that "thorough knowledge of strong and weak points in one agreement is important in writing its successor. This type information is gathered year round, not in a crash program just before negotiations begin."[55]

Since the climate of labor negotiations is established during the daily administration of previous labor agreements and not merely at the bargaining table, management should ensure that there is a cooperative and communicative attitude in labor relations throughout the year. If this has been successfully accomplished management will start a formal negotiating session from a relatively secure and comfortable position.

In preparing for negotiation management should realize in advance that the union will be presenting demands which can be classified as follows:

1. Items for which the local union has mandated its negotiating team to exercise the hardest kind of bargaining (pay raises, hours, and important fringe benefits that affect all members)
2. Items which affect all members but which are considered by the union body as "nice to have," or "a good way to break new ice"
3. Items which affect only small groups or classifications of union members;

these will be those items most readily conceded by the union as a settlement is reached (and these are usually the least expensive)
4. Items for which the union feels compelled to negotiate because of some outside thrust (e.g., from the IAFF).

This breakdown, combined with the history of previous negotiating sessions and an analysis of the existing contract, provides the fundamental knowledge management needs to have for successful negotiations.

Management should learn in advance all it can about the local union officers and other members of the union team who will be involved in labor negotiations. This information provides the management team with insight into individual personalities and the following they have in the union body.

If management is thoroughly familiar with the internal politics of the local union it can avoid problems in the following two areas:

1. Items presented for negotiation which represent the official will of the union can be distinguished from those presented as a special interest or pet project of an influential individual
2. The degree of control over the membership possessed by the existing leadership can be analyzed so that costly power plays (designed more to strengthen the position of the union leaders than to obtain a fair settlement) can be avoided.

Management proposals   Since the union will enter formal negotiations with a lengthy list of new and continuing demands, management should do the same. The best defense is a good offense. Not only is it proper for management to make proposals to the union—it is essential. By looking forward to anticipated problem areas management can often take the initiative to ensure that key topics will be discussed satisfactorily.

A comprehensive, well-organized plan of procedure and a sizable list of proposals by management must be devised to make sure that (1) the management negotiating team can operate from a position of power equal to that of the union, and (2) the management negotiating team will have proposals which can be traded off for union demands throughout the negotiation meetings.

High ranking fire department officials who routinely handle personnel problems can provide information which will indicate needed areas of improvement in the new contract. Further helpful information might also be available from a well-established personnel department. Past incidents, grievances, and arbitrated issues provide an excellent source of such material.

Necessary data   The central focus of negotiations will be wages and other direct monetary issues. Hence it is essential for management to have accurate statistical data which can be used either for initial bargaining or for comparison with similar data presented by a union team. The following list provides guidelines for the types of data needed:

1. National average wages for fire departments in general
2. National average wages for fire departments of similar size
3. Wage rates in local industry for positions requiring similar risks, skills, and education
4. National industrial wage rates
5. Cost of living indices
6. Patterns of increase or decline in city revenues
7. Patterns of increase or decline in city expenditures
8. Fire department personnel retention or attrition rates.

Some would say that low turnover could be correlated with general satisfaction with pay rates and working conditions, although others would hold that, as firefighters are career employees who have generally chosen their profession with security and retirement goals in mind, firefighters would work toward change of such conditions from within rather than terminate their positions.

At the bargaining table All of the preparation by management and the union becomes increasingly significant as the official negotiating period approaches (it is usually an annual event). Usually, both sides are filled with anticipation and determination and have a list of what is sought or demanded and a rough idea of the range in which a settlement can be reached.

At a specified time of the year either management or the union will make a formal overture for reopening the contract and scheduling negotiations. Since the absence of formal notification often means the continuation of the existing contract, the union will usually take the initiative. Their formal overture comes well in advance as a minimum of sixty days' notice is a usual requirement.

City administrators should then concentrate on establishing a workable schedule for formal negotiating sessions. Care should be taken to assure that sessions will be scheduled so as not to conflict with major functions (such as city council meetings) and not to interfere with the schedules of key personnel required on the city negotiating team. It is quite important to be prompt in setting up and carrying out full scale negotiations—anything less will be construed as stalling.

The city that has established a working collective bargaining procedure with its firefighters can expect (and will need) numerous and lengthy negotiating sessions. Only the insignificant, inexpensive items can be handled in single sessions. Each side must then allow the other sufficient time to consider proposals and counterproposals and to conduct necessary research. Also, the union team may require time to confer with its general membership while the management team conducts its own conferences and consults with elected and appointed officials involved in the labor negotiations. The negotiating team may be dealing with potential major changes already in the hands of long-standing committees and time for liaison will usually be necessary.

W. D. Heisel has produced a set of questions and answers which can serve as a guideline for effective behavior at the bargaining table; the following list of dos and don'ts is based primarily on Heisel's recommendations:

1. Management should avoid countering unreasonable union demands with unreasonable offers (e.g., pay reduction, elimination of fringes). This plays into the hands of militant union employees.
2. Management should always maintain a posture worthy of the respect of the union negotiating team *and* of the entire work force represented.
3. Management should avoid attacks on union security, such as reduction of the bargaining unit or termination of dues checkoff. (This will solidify union rank and file and give union leadership a strengthened bargaining position.)
4. Management should be willing to make some tentative concessions early to display good faith but not to such an extent that the bargaining position is weakened.
5. A formalized columnar work sheet should be used to record union demands, management proposals, and agreements reached.
6. Management should get agreement on items as soon as possible after their introduction. (A continuous tabling of topics heightens confusion and delays the ultimate settlement.)
7. When a completed package is submitted early and is rejected by the union, management should try to modify it by eliminating problem areas without significantly changing its cost and content.

8. When a completed package is submitted late and anticipated acceptance turns to rejection, a mediator may become necessary.
9. Words such as *never* and *final* should be avoided until they are actually meant and either side is prepared for any resulting difficulties.[56]

Mediation When labor relations break down a neutral third party is often required to resolve disputes. Just as the marriage counselor is often effective in domestic relations, so a neutral third party can play a vital role in labor negotiations when the two parties are diametrically opposed on an issue or issues. The third party in labor negotiations is the mediator, who is usually a member of the Federal Mediation and Conciliation Service or some similar state level agency. In an effort to achieve conciliation the mediator maintains harmony, clarifies misconceptions, and facilitates communication. The mediator's role is usually a helpful one and is often a vital one. Heisel has remarked that "an experienced mediator who is objective can usually sense the area in which the final settlement is likely to be made and lead the parties there."[57]

The mediator has a unique opportunity to reconcile differences by talking separately to the two parties. Both management and the union are more likely to open up and state their true feelings when they are talking to a neutral party.

The mediator uses a large amount of factual and statistical information based on a great many contract settlements across the nation. This broad, informative approach tends to win the respect of both sides and permits the mediator to add professional advice to his or her efforts at reconciliation. In carrying out his or her duties the mediator can, at times, persuade either side to move from a totally unreasonable position, can improve access to channels to higher officials, and can in other ways facilitate smooth negotiations and prompt settlements.

Although many cities, both large and small, carry out labor negotiations routinely without the aid of a mediator and may never have felt the need for one, they should examine their labor negotiations for any potential improvement that might be obtained with a mediator. Since a decision on a mere twenty-five cents in labor negotiations can cost a city thousands of dollars, the price of a mediator could be an extremely prudent investment.

Once a particular mediator has been helpful and has gained rapport with the negotiating teams, that person should be used in succeeding negotiating sessions. Past knowledge and experience are cumulative, and a well-qualified mediator will tend to become even more effective with each succeeding negotiation.

Arbitration The term *arbitration* refers to a decision-making process by a neutral party. Usually this decision is final and binding. When management and union leaders have tried unsuccessfully to reach agreement on some contract issue, grievance case, or disciplinary action, they are said to be *at an impasse*. At this point the climate is ripe for arbitration.

Most arbitration is carried out with either a single arbitrator or a panel of three. An arbitrator (or arbitrators) can be obtained through the American Arbitration Association, a national organization, that maintains lists of arbitrators, from which a selection can be made. An arbitrator can also be chosen locally by joint agreement of management and labor. A common method of finding an arbitrator—or group of arbitrators—who will be agreeable to both parties is the strike-off procedure: a list of potential arbitrators is prepared and each side alternately strikes a name until the resulting selection remains by default. Regardless of the selection method it is extremely important that both management and the union are content with the choice and willing to be bound by the arbitrator's decision.

Compulsory binding arbitration is often considered an alternative to the strike. Since the strike has particularly undesirable consequences in fire departments, this alternative is receiving more attention. The reason for the lingering unpopularity of binding arbitration seems to be that final decisions are taken out of the hands of both the union and management. The growing support for binding arbitration is coming from those fire departments that wish to avoid the grave dangers of a firefighter strike with its inevitable loss of public trust. These departments look to binding arbitration as perhaps their best bargaining tool.

Although it can be argued by management that even binding arbitration will not stop a strike by determined, militant workers, the IAFF has produced a report claiming that, where a state has passed a law granting compulsory/binding arbitration, there has not been a recorded strike of firefighters since that law was passed.[58] While this may be true, it should also be noted that binding arbitration can severely weaken the power of both management and union leaders.

One special type of binding arbitration which is gaining in popularity is final offer arbitration. This requires the opposing sides to make what they feel are their most generous offers. The arbitrator must then choose either one or the other—without compromise. This technique forces both parties to be realistic and tends to draw the final offers closer together. Since an issue put before final offer arbitration faces certain and swift resolution, such arbitration can be effective in preventing a strike. James L. Stern and others, in their treatise *Final-Offer Arbitration,* say that "the support for final-offer arbitration has come from labor-management neutrals and other observers of labor relations *in the public sector* [emphasis added], who see the procedure as a substitute for a work stoppage with its own pressures to resolve impasses.[59]

If the arbitration process (either conventional or final offer) is selected to resolve an impasse it may speed negotiations so that settlement is actually reached *before arbitration moves to fruition.*

Stern and others point up this particular effect of arbitration proceedings. Table 13–2 is adapted from a table in *Final-Offer Arbitration.* It summarizes

Table 13–2 Negotiations and method of resolving negotiations between Pennsylvania municipalities and fire department organizations: 1969–74.

	Negotiations for the labor agreement effective in year						
	1969	1970	1971	1972	1973	1974	Total
Negotiations without resort to arbitration	3	1	4	6	4	2	20
Arbitration award	4	2	3	4	1	5	19
Negotiations, but method of resolution not reported	1	2	1	1	1	1	7
Total	8	5	8	11	6	8	46

Source: Reprinted, by permission of the publisher, from: James L. Stern, Charles M. Rehmus, J. Joseph Loewenberg, Hirschel Kasper, and Barbara Dennis, *Final-Offer Arbitration: The Effects on Public Safety Employee Bargaining,* Lexington, Mass.: Lexington Books, D. C. Heath & Company, 1975, p. 13, Table 2–1 (bottom half). Copyright 1975, D. C. Heath & Company.

cases recorded by the American Arbitration Association in Pennsylvania, and shows a breakdown of negotiation settlements. The text indicates that the proportion of agreements in which arbitration was initiated before the settlement to the total number of negotiated settlements is probably similar in larger statistical populations.[60]

Since both management and union leaders prefer to settle their own affairs rather than bring in an outsider, there is strong internal incentive to reserve arbitration for true impasse issues.

Fact-finding One method that has proved extremely helpful in the public sector in resolving an impasse is fact-finding. This method uses arbitrators but lacks the binding quality of arbitration. It does point the parties in a similar direction and it returns them to the bargaining table for further negotiations.

Fact-finding as a system has both advantages and disadvantages. An important advantage is the willingness of both union and management to be involved in a process which is neutral and is designed to explore differences and yet will not bind either party by its findings.

A fact finder or a fact-finding panel can also turn to outside groups, such as city councils, to point out the necessity for additional funding or other requirements needed for an effective labor settlement.

Where strikes and binding arbitration are both out of the question owing to legislation or tradition, fact-finding offers an alternative that can often work. One authority in Wisconsin, James Belasco, claims that fact-finding by arbitrators has promoted collective bargaining.[61]

Fact-finding does, however, have its weaknesses. There is a general apathy toward fact-finding on the part of both management and labor when the final and binding arbitration step is available. Both groups have a tendency not to supply their strongest evidence or exhibits during this phase, and there is a strong feeling among professionals and public employee relations boards that this step is an exercise in frustration.

The greatest disadvantage of fact-finding is that it does not actually resolve a dispute, and yet another disadvantage is a tendency for arbitrators to recommend compromise solutions which do not really satisfy either party in a dispute.

City administrators can keep this method in mind; having weighed its advantages and disadvantages, they might find it to be an acceptable alternative.

The strike Strikes are by no means an inevitable conclusion to a collective bargaining process, particularly if both sides adopt the professional approach recommended above. Yet strikes do occur, and it is a well-known fact of life that both management and the union suffer. When a fire department goes on strike the public also suffers. Nobody can win. Yet from September 1966 to September 1977 strikes had occurred in some eighty-six locals of the IAFF, and all but four had occurred since the IAFF removed its time-honored prohibition against strikes.

In the Foreword to the Public Personnel Association's 1970 guide for public officials on dealing with strikes, Kenneth O. Warner, executive director of the association, stated that "a public official subjected for the first time—or even for the tenth time—to the frenetic pressures and turmoil of a strike would be quick, no doubt, to echo Shakespeare's plaint that troubles '. . . come not as single spies, but in battalions.'" He went on to point out that the decade of the 1970s gave signs of becoming a "decade of militancy," just as the 1960s had been a "decade of change." He added that every day and a half in the first three months of 1970 some public service in the United States had a strike. Such strikes occur in cities from the very small to the very large, cover the full spectrum of public employee agencies, and have no respect for existing high pay scales and excellent working conditions. Warner also pointed out that "any public official so far gone in wishful thinking or utopian speculation as to consider his agency immune from a strike need only scan his morning paper."[62]

Every public administrator needs to face the fact that strikes really do happen. Any mayor or city manager in the country could, at some unforeseen time, find pickets in front of his or her fire stations. It is vitally important to understand strikes and to be prepared to deal with them.

A typical attitude of management tends to be, "We'll worry about a strike when it happens." While this approach involves the least time and effort, it is potentially the most disastrous. A methodical plan is a necessity. Carmen Saso sums the matter up as follows:

The author believes that most of the quantitative stresses of a potential crisis whose general characteristics are already known can be identified well in advance of the emergency's occurrence. It thus becomes possible, and highly practicable, to make those calculations and estimates, together with related decisions and preparations, that will lessen the emergency's impact when it does occur. Having gone this far, a logical added step would be to encompass these preparatory measures within a comprehensive plan, ready for instant implementation when the need arises.[63]

Saso goes on to point out that management's strike planning should not be construed as a battle plan by public employees or their union representatives. Rather, it should be made clear that it is a plan to protect the fire department in which both parties have a significant interest.[64]

Saso provides a list of considerations that the fire department manager should have planned for *before* employees walk off their jobs; the following items are adapted from some of his suggestions:

1. The ability to provide fire protection without striking members or their equipment (i.e., What are the limits to which the city can practically go?)
2. The ability to maintain communications with the public, the striking members, and the union leaders
3. An analysis of the rights of employees who choose to work during the strike—and the consequences of letting them work
4. The liabilities of the city
5. The legal actions possible
6. The potential effects on labor relations after the strike.[65]

At the very least, management must have an organizational plan for higher echelon personnel and a contingency plan for continuing services. When a strike seems imminent the chief legal official of the city, the chief of police, and the insurance officials should all be notified. Plans should be made for an information central command post for maintaining and distributing key information to employees, union leaders, the press, and the public.

Other actions are required as soon as a strike actually occurs. When that happens the difference between a crisis management approach with no prior planning and a methodical approach based on detailed plans will become crucial. Where a well-made contingency plan exists it needs only to be activated.

Communication among all key personnel concerned with or affected by the strike is important. Such persons include legislators, state and local officials, news media personnel, and employees. A carefully selected tactful spokesman for management can often make the difference between public support and public opposition.

City administrators should be well aware of the fact that strikes are invariably a matter of last resort and are only reluctantly agreed to by organized fire-fighters. Much opposition to a fire department strike occurs from within the organization. Dennis Smith has argued that firefighters are a special type of employee and should not strike:

Because of his special expertise, the fire fighter is irreplaceable. Therefore, his responsibility to continue in his service is an ethical not a legal one. Without him there is devastation. All other civil servants should have the right to strike, for they do not share in this unique ethical consideration.[66]

The fact that a strike by public employees is illegal can, however, work in their favor. Albert Shanker, president of the United Federation of Teachers, spoke before a commission of inquiry on public employees, stating:

Right now, the greatest power we have is the very illegality of the strike. It's the illegality that puts us on the front page, holds the troops together, and actually strengthens the bargaining power of the employees. Much of our public support is based on this fact, even if the people don't know the specific issues: "If those civil servants are willing to break that law," they say, "somebody must have done something terrible to them." A good 25% of the public is not aware of the issues involved, but nevertheless has that kind of sympathy.[67]

The legal options which are available to counter illegal strikes are broader and more powerful than those in the private sector. Injunctions, criminal prosecutions, invocations of state statutes prohibiting strikes, and other tactics are possible but should only be considered after extremely careful deliberation—and only with the advice and consent of the chief legal official in the city. Often injunctions are ignored by strikers and final amnesty yields a net minus for management.

As a strike continues, the degree of tension and turmoil faced by management will be diminished by any planning and professional foresight which preceded the strike. For the duration, a levelheaded approach, extensive internal communications, an absence of vindictiveness, and a sincere attempt to resolve conflict will all speed the end of the strike.

When the strike is over all parties should be able to enjoy a quick return to normal conditions. The process requires effort, however, and management should be prepared to facilitate a smooth transition to harmony and efficiency in the department. A joint public statement with the union is necessary. Attention to high priority issues most affected by the work stoppage is required; and an assurance that both sides are willing to subordinate their emotions is important. It is necessary to show that management will not harbor ill feelings against strikers and that the union will not harbor ill will against nonstrikers. Any unfinished issues (e.g., damaged property, terminated benefits, missed wages) should be shifted immediately into normal channels, and all parties should move ahead with the work to be done.

The strike is by far the most challenging area of labor relations. It demands the keenest management skills and calls for the most delicate balance of firmness and fairness. Since each strike has a unique personality, much of the ability of management to cope with a strike is dependent on a custom-tailoring of the approach to the local issues. Undoubtedly, the best approach is prevention of strikes by establishing (and maintaining) a favorable labor relations environment.

After the contract is signed

Because the process of negotiating an agreement is complex and results in obligations on the part of both management and the union, the agreement invariably takes the form of a written agreement. This document then becomes the Bible of labor relations for the ensuing contract period. Both union and management officials will be involved with administration and servicing of the contract during that period.

Contract administration Interpretations of specific clauses in the contract can become extremely troublesome to both parties. This, unfortunately, is worsened if too little attention was paid initially to the specific contractual language.

According to Heisel the union business agents feel that they will best serve their membership by handling the following three types of recurring activities:

1. *Grievance handling.* [The agent] will represent members with grievances, at least above a certain level of appeal.
2. *Discipline.* [The agent] will represent members involved in disciplinary actions.

3. *Consultation.* [The agent] will be the point of contact between management and the union in a wide variety of communications and consultations.[68]

Management should have a labor relations director to deal directly with the union representative. Usually a personnel department, a civil service commission, or an independent department of labor relations is ideally suited for this purpose. Heisel points out that there should be some buffer between the union and the chief executive and, therefore, there must be a clearly designated official in charge of labor relations.[69]

Figure 13–7   Collective bargaining agreements represent the outcome of a negotiating process demanding the best in professionalism on the part of both management and labor representatives. The contract signing ceremony is thus of considerable symbolic importance. In this representative ceremony (1976), President Ted Blakemore of Norman, Oklahoma's, Local 2067 and City Manager James Crosby (seated) sign a contract agreement while local members Warren McKinnsey, Perry Brown, and Dale Holzenbeck look on. (Source: International Association of Fire Fighters—AFL–CIO, CLC.)

Earlier in this chapter contract clauses were shown to cover the following five areas: (1) routine clauses, (2) union security, (3) the rights of management, (4) grievance procedure, and (5) conditions of employment.[70] Each of these is subject to difficulty in interpretation and should have professional legal input when developed. Heisel stresses the importance of this legal input:

Particularly when the agreement is a binding contract, the importance of professional legal service cannot be overemphasized. It is difficult to write precisely what you mean. Lawyers are trained in this art. Their legal experience teaches them the traps that await careless draftsmanship. Most public agencies have legal departments with full-time staffs available to serve other departments. When such services are not available, a labor lawyer can be retained as a consultant to assist in preparing the labor agreement. . . . It is extremely helpful to the lawyer if he can participate as a member of management's negotiating team prior to preparing the agreement, so that he will have a full understanding of the desired content.[71]

The employee is the individual around whom the contract is framed. It is for the protection of the employee that both management and the union honor the agreement. The enforcement of the contract, however, can become a difficult problem since the employee is subject to regulations from, and owes allegiance to, several groups simultaneously. These groups, which are all a part of the personnel process, are depicted in Figure 13–8.

Figure 13–8 Internal organizational groups involved in the personnel process.

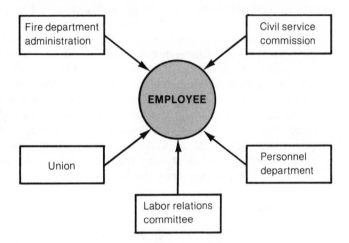

Since each city will have its own combination of several of these groups, and some unique set of interrelationships among them, each city administration will have to adopt its own approach to union contract administration. It must determine how to interface optimally with the various groups. The key overriding consideration should be the adoption of an unambiguous, detailed document that specifies all procedures in writing. Also, formalized training in contract administration will ensure that all groups are aware of their respective roles.

Grievance procedure Throughout the duration of a contract, employees will at times feel that they are being treated in violation of some clause in the agreement. When an employee (or a group of employees) publicly alleges a violation, a grievance is born. Grievances can cover wages, fringes, working conditions, and disciplinary actions. In cities with a working civil service system the grievance procedure may be handled by this agency in the absence of meaningful collective bargaining laws, or where local ordinances mandate its use. In others, the fire department administration, the personnel department, or a special committee may handle grievances.

The grievance procedure is the established systematic means of handling alleged or real contract violations which are formally registered. This should be spelled out in the written contract or, if detailed elsewhere, should be sanctioned in the contract. There will be a specified number of steps in the grievance procedure and a time limit on each step.

The first step is talking to the immediate supervisor—often the person who made a decision leading to the grievance. Many issues can be resolved at this point.

If the employee is not satisfied, he or she then goes to higher levels in the fire department chain of command, usually as specified in the agreement.

If the grievance is not settled by fire administrators it moves to the personnel department, to civil service channels (rarely), or to some other city organization. The final step is an appeal to a neutral outsider, such as an arbitrator. The employee is bound by this ultimate decision.

The time requirement specified for each step in the grievance procedure is an element necessary to make the system workable. An employee who feels he or she has a grievance should be required to state his or her case promptly, usually within several working days. By the same token the employee deserves a response which is equally prompt. Time requirements should be specified for each additional step and should be progressively longer as higher levels of appeal are exhausted. An effective grievance procedure will include the provision that if the employee does not respond within required time limits the grievance is considered settled in favor of management, and if management does not respond within required time limits, the grievance is considered settled in favor of the employee.

Fire departments have been a "silent service" according to Assistant Chief Norman Wells, personnel director within the Cincinnati fire department. He explains that firefighters have traditionally been dedicated public servants quite willing to accept a certain degree of inequity in their conditions of employment. The picture is changing, according to Chief Wells, into one in which firefighters are becoming more vocal and are more aware of the rights they can demand; hence fire administrators can expect an increasing number of demands and grievances.[72] The implication is clear. Management must have a workable grievance procedure and must have qualified professional personnel handling the procedure at each step along the way.

The outlook

The task of handling labor relations in a modern fire department is not easy. The current period of militancy presents a real challenge. Employee awareness is increasing, demands are accelerating, and personnel policies are becoming more complex. Progressive city administrators have to adopt a flexible attitude and use their full talents to deal with modern labor relations.

Ralph Flynn has used Tacoma, Washington, as an example of the type of progressive thinking that is effective in labor relations. When Tacoma's firefighters wanted a fifty hour workweek cut to forty-eight hours (an expensive proposal requiring sixteen new firefighters), management adopted an agreement with the union to reduce the workweek and/or increase salaries through a redeployment of manpower. In evaluating the project, Tacoma's then city manager, William V. Donaldson, was quoted by Flynn as making the following statement:

The fire fighters got their 48-hour week, the citizens got better fire protection and the City held the line on costs. The City's experience in this area has been so satisfactory that we asked the union to participate with us in appointing two new deputy chiefs and made it clear to the appointees that their appointment was a result of this joint activity.[73]

This is only one example of participatory management, an increasingly popular method of capitalizing on union sophistication. Another example applauded by Flynn was the manager's participatory management in equal opportunity hiring. In this case he asked the fire department how to enlist minority members. The firefighters' union took the initiative in recruiting qualified minorities and providing preemployment training. As a result, the firefighters' union accepted the minorities willingly since they were hired without a compromise of recruitment standards. Flynn made the following comment on the then city manager:

Donaldson may lose his membership in the public administration Bund for this kind of heretical activity and sophisticated good sense. But I'll bet I'm not the only one reading his words who would like to meet him or, better yet, live in his city. It would be reassuring to know that men like those in Tacoma Fire Fighters' Union were on call when I needed them.[74]

While managers are developing new professional attitudes and applying the latest techniques in management theory, they are also feeling changes in external parameters, all of which changes the nature of their job in labor relations.

For years, new theories and techniques in management have provided valuable assistance to industrial leaders and private sector managers. In recent years these tools have been gradually incorporated into the public arena and are proving to be just as valuable to public administrators. For example, while marketing managers have for years used quantitative tools for optimal location of warehouses and retail outlets, fire departments now use similar techniques for optimal firehouse location.

The new technique of management by objectives (MBO) is an example of a system using employee participation and goal setting to increase organizational effectiveness. Since it is based on communication and cooperation at all levels in a fire department, it has received joint support by IAFF locals and fire administrators.[75]

Professional attitudes toward labor relations in the fire service on the part of both management and labor (whether unionized or not) will be helped by general progressiveness in the organization and will be hindered by conservative and inflexible thinking.

In Kramer's national survey of fire departments, referred to earlier, the nation's fire chiefs rated four factors on the degree to which each had inhibited progressiveness in six areas of the fire service. The four factors were budget limitations, lack of management expertise, labor unions, and civil service. Table 13–3 summarizes the data collected.

Table 13–3 Seriousness of factors contributing to management lags (0 = no effect; 1 = some effect; 2 = serious effect).

		Budget limits	Lack management expertise	Labor unions	Civil service
A.	Technology and equipment	1.61	.88	.65	.53
B.	Apparatus and tactics	1.42	.80	.49	.42
C.	Training and personnel	1.43	.79	.72	.68
D.	Productivity and efficiency	.83	1.08	1.19	.73
E.	Planning and administration	1.04	1.15	.72	1.65
F.	Computer and data processing	1.57	1.03	.20	.35
	Overall average	1.31	.96	.67	.61

Source: Taken, with minor adaptations, from William H. Kramer, *A Managerial Analysis of Municipal Fire De-* *partments* (Cincinnati: University of Cincinnati Press, 1977), p. 106.

The findings in Table 13–3, based on 121 out of the nation's 145 largest fire departments, show that, in the opinion of fire chiefs surveyed, labor unions have hindered progressiveness less than has a lack of management expertise among fire administrators.[76] If conclusions can be drawn from this study, one would certainly be that fire administrators and union leaders must cooperate for mutual advancement and a progressive future. Since the labor relations field is a changing one and since new demands are continually being placed on firefighters and fire administrators, the only successful path for both to follow is one of cooperation, communication, and professional mutual respect. A labor relations climate which is characterized by strife and turmoil hinders an organization significantly. A climate which is healthy and progressive, on the other hand, can greatly increase organizational effectiveness.

1 For detailed coverage of personnel management, see the following book in the Municipal Management Series: Winston W. Crouch, ed., *Local Government Personnel Administration* (Washington, D.C.: International City Management Association, 1976).

2 A very useful publication for following items of current interest in the personnel field is *Personnel Literature*, a monthly prepared by the U.S. Office of Personnel Management Library, available from the Government Printing Office (Washington, D.C.) The International Personnel Management Association (Washington, D.C.) publishes books and monographs, a current list of which is available on request. Its Public Employee Relations Library (PERL) series includes monographs on a variety of personnel subjects. Prentice-Hall, Inc. (Englewood Cliffs, N.J.), publishes *Personnel Management: Policies and Practices*. The Bureau of National Affairs, Inc. (Washington, D.C.), publishes several series in looseleaf editions. *The Municipal Year Book*, annual, International City Management Association (Washington, D.C.), provides police and fire personnel data among other information on municipal management. In some editions data on unionism, employer–employee relations, and other personnel subjects are given. *Public Personnel Management*, bimonthly, International Personnel Management Association, is the major publication in the public personnel field. It is written and edited primarily for those specializing in personnel administration. A book and pamphlet notes section serves as a useful guide to current literature. *Fire and Police Personnel Reporter*, published monthly by the Public Safety Personnel Research Institute, Inc. (Evanston, Ill.), describes current court cases and key legislative developments concerning fire and police personnel issues.

3 Peter F. Drucker, *Management: Tasks, Responsibilities, Practices* (New York: Harper & Row, Publishers, 1974), p. 308.

4 Ibid., p. 30.

5 National Civil Service League, *A Model Public Personnel Administration Law* (Washington, D.C.: National Civil Service League, 1970), pp. 8–12. The proposed model law has generated considerable and continuing debate; see, for example: Jean J. Couturier and Harold E. Forbes. "The Model Public Personnel Administration Law: Two Views—Pro and Con," *Public Personnel Review* 32 (October 1971): 202–14. See also: International Personnel Management Association, *Guidelines for Drafting a Public Personnel Administration Law* (Chicago: International Personnel Management Association, 1973).

6 For details and evidence, see: Jean J. Couturier, "The Quiet Revolution in Public Personnel Laws,"*Public Personnel Management* 5 (May–June 1976): 150–67.

7 Chester A. Newland, "Public Personnel Administration: Legalistic Reforms vs. Effectiveness, Effi-

ciency, and Economy," *Public Administration Review* 36 (September/October 1976): 536. In addition to this article, see the various federal and state actions cited annually in *The Municipal Year Book* (Washington, D.C.: International City Management Association). The 1977 edition, for example, commented on a number of wide-ranging legal decisions that are profoundly applicable to personnel management.

8 Douglas I. McIntyre, "Merit Principles and Collective Bargaining: A Marriage or Divorce," *Public Administration Review* 37 (March/April 1977): 186–87.

9 Garry M. Whalen and Richard S. Rubin, "Labor Relations and Affirmative Action: A Tug-of-War," *Public Personnel Management* 6 (May–June 1977): 149. While seniority systems have been under attack, a bona fide seniority system has been upheld by the U.S. Supreme Court. See: *International Brotherhood of Teamsters* v. *United States* (Case no. 75–636); and *United Airlines* v. *Evans* (Case no. 76–333).

10 William M. Mooney and Gerald W. Shanahan, "Personnel Management," in *Local Government Police Administration*, ed. Bernard L. Garmire (Washington, D.C.: International City Management Association, 1977), p. 285.

11 Winston W. Crouch, "Local Government Personnel Administration: The Setting," in *Local Government Personnel Administration*, ed. Crouch, p. 18.

12 W. Donald Heisel, "Administering the Personnel Function," in ibid., p. 28.

13 Mooney and Shanahan, "Personnel Management," p. 286.

14 Ibid., pp. 286–87.

15 This list of recommendations is excerpted, with some cuts and with appropriate modifications, from W. Donald Heisel and Patrick V. Murphy, "Organization for Police Personnel Management," in *Police Personnel Administration*, ed. O. Glenn Stahl and Richard A. Staufenberger (Washington, D.C.: Police Foundation, 1974), pp. 8–11.

16 George E. Wetherington, Jr., Laurie S. Frankel, Harry E. Diezel, and Joseph D. Russell, Jr., *Personnel Practices in the Municipal Fire Service: 1976*, Urban Data Service Reports, vol. 9 no. 2 (Washington, D.C.: International City Management Association, February 1977), p. 1.

17 Frederick W. Zuerchner, "Manpower Planning," in *Local Government Personnel Management*, ed. Crouch, p. 61. The author goes on to present a comprehensive review of the alternative locations of the manpower planning function. The arguments parallel those given in the present text dealing with the central and departmental personnel units.

18 In October 1971 the International Association of Fire Fighters implemented its Labor Recruitment Program through contracts with the U.S. Department of Labor. The purpose of this national outreach program is to help raise the minority representation in the fire service.

19 Mooney and Shanahan. "Personnel Management," p. 290.

20 Ibid.

21 There is a rapidly growing body of literature on women and the public service. See, for example: Dorothy Jongeward and Dru Scott, *Affirmative Action for Women: A Practical Guide* (Reading, Mass.: Addison-Wesley Publishing Co., 1974); Rosalind Loring and Theodora Wells, *Breakthrough: Women into Management* (New York: Van Nostrand Reinhold Company, 1972); Donald O. Jewell, ed., *Women and Management: An Expanding Role* (Atlanta, Ga.: Publishing Services Division, School of Business Administration, Georgia State University, 1977); and Bette Ann Stead, *Women in Management* (Englewood Cliffs, N.J.: Prentice-Hall, Inc., 1978).

22 Mooney and Shanahan, "Personnel Management," pp. 291–92.

23 "What Rights for Whites?" *Time,* 24 October 1977, p. 98. An excellent and comprehensive discussion of affirmative action is provided by Carl F. Goodman, "Equal Employment Opportunity: Preferential Quotas and Unrepresented Third Parties," *Public Personnel Management* 6 (November–December 1977): 371–97.

24 Two examples of carefully and scientifically designed research studies pertaining to test validation can be found in: W. Considine et al., "Developing a Physical Performance Test Battery for Screening Chicago Fire Fighter Applicants," *Public Personnel Management* 5 (January–February 1976): 7–14; and W. W. Ronan, Charles L. Anderson, and Terry L. Talbert, "A Psychometric Approach to Job Performance: Fire Fighters," *Public Personnel Management* 5 (November–December 1976): 409–22.

25 See: Considine et al., "Developing a Physical Performance Test Battery," for a successful application of construct test validation.

26 Stephen Wollack, "Content Validity: Its Legal and Psychometric Basis," *Public Personnel Management* 5 (November–December 1976): 406.

27 For a complete explanation of job analysis, see: U.S., Civil Service Commission, *Job Analysis for Improved Job-Related Selection* (Washington, D.C.: Government Printing Office, 1975).

28 For a systematic approach to getting the best results from an affirmative action program, see: Robert H. Flast, "Taking the Guesswork out of Affirmative Action Planning," *Personnel Journal* 56 (February 1977): 68–71.

29 For details, guidelines, and examples pertaining to this subsection, see: J. David Palmer, "Recruitment and Staffing," in *Local Government Personnel Administration,* ed. Crouch, pp. 86–97.

30 For details, guidelines, and examples, see ibid.

31 An excellent series of articles, along with a comprehensive bibliography on assessment centers, can be found in *Public Personnel Management* 3 (September–October 1974).

32 Don Driggs and Paul M. Whisenand, "Assessment Centers: Situational Evaluation," *Journal of California Law Enforcement* 10 (April 1976): 132.

33 Ibid.: 135.

34 The National Fire Protection Association authors and publishes several standards on personnel qualifications for various fire department positions including fire apparatus driver/operator, fire inspector, fire prevention education officer, and fire service instructor. See, especially: *Fire Fighter Professional Qualifications,* NFPA no. 1001 (Boston: National Fire Protection Association, 1974), which identifies the professional levels of competence required of fire department members and covers the entrance requirements and the first three levels of progression thereafter.

35 Chester A. Newland, "Motivation, Productivity, and Performance Appraisal," in *Local Government Personnel Administration,* ed. Crouch, pp. 264–65.

36 Ibid., pp. 265, 277.

37 Among useful resources available in the area of public employee labor relations are: the publications in the Public Employee Relations Library (the PERL series) of the International Personnel Management Association (IPMA), 1850 K Street N.W., Washington, D.C. 20036; and the publications and *LMRS Newsletter* of the Labor–Management Relations Service (of the National League of Cities/U.S. Conference of Mayors/National Association of Counties), 1620 Eye Street, N.W., Washington, D.C. 20006. For a broad perspective and coverage of federal and state legislation affecting municipalities in many areas, including fire services, see: the various editions of *The Municipal Year Book,* published annually by the International City Management Association (ICMA), 1140 Connecticut Avenue, N.W., Washington, D.C. 20036. For a wider perspective on labor relations, see: Harold S. Roberts, *Roberts' Dictionary of Industrial Relations,* rev. ed. (Washington, D.C.: Bureau of National Affairs, 1971). Two selections from the Municipal Management Series that contain applicable information are: John Matzer, Jr., "Labor–Management Relations," in *Local Government Police Management,* ed. Garmire, pp. 310–33; and Cabot Dow, "Labor Relations," in *Local Government Personnel Administration,* ed. Crouch, pp. 212–33. Other useful works are: Jack Stieber, *Public Employee Unionism: Structure, Growth, Policy* (Washington, D.C.: Brookings Institution, 1973); and U.S. Department of Labor, Bureau of Labor Statistics, *Brief History of the American Labor Movement* (Washington, D.C.: Government Printing Office, 1976).

38 Benjamin J. Taylor and Fred Witney, *Labor Relations Law,* 2nd ed. (Englewood Cliffs, N.J.: Prentice-Hall, Inc., 1975), p. 98.

39 *NLRB* v. *Jones and Laughlin Steel Company,* 301 U.S. 1 (1937); Archibald Cox and Derek Curtis Bok, *Labor Law* (Mineola, N.Y.: The Foundation Press, Inc., 1969), pp. 98–101.

40 Taylor and Witney, *Labor Relations Law,* p. 197.

41 Ralph J. Flynn, *Public Work, Public Workers* (Washington, D.C.: The New Republic Book Company, 1975), p. xi.

42 Ibid., p. 82.

43 Didactic Systems, Inc., *Management in the Fire Service* (Boston: National Fire Protection Association, 1977), pp. 331–32.

44 William M. Kramer, *A Managerial Analysis of Municipal Fire Departments* (Cincinnati: University of Cincinnati Press, 1977), p. 11.

45 Didactic Systems, *Management in the Fire Service,* p. 336.

46 William F. Glueck, *Management* (Hinsdale, Ill.: The Dryden Press, 1977), pp. 483–508.

47 Kramer, *A Managerial Analysis of Municipal Fire Departments,* pp. 76–77.

48 Ibid.

49 "1976 Annual Death and Injury Survey," *International Fire Fighter*, November 1977, pp. 9–16.
50 Didactic Systems, *Management in the Fire Service*, p. 336
51 Ibid., pp. 330–46.
52 Donald F. Favreau, *Fire Service Management* (New York: The Reuben H. Donnelley Corporation, 1969), p. 123.
53 Ibid., p. 127.
54 Ibid., pp. 127–28.
55 W. D. Heisel, *On Public Employee Negotiation* (Chicago: International Personnel Management Association, 1973), p. 72.
56 Ibid., pp. 77–87.
57 Ibid., p. 98.
58 Walter Lambert, "Compulsory/Binding Arbitration Kit," report distributed by the International Association of Fire Fighters to its locals, Washington, D.C., 1976.
59 James L. Stern et al., *Final-Offer Arbitration: The Effects on Public Safety Employee Bargaining* (Lexington, Mass.: Lexington Books, D. C. Heath & Company, 1975), p. 143.
60 Ibid., p. 13.
61 James A. Belasco, "Public Employee Dispute Settlement: The Wisconsin Experience," in *Government Labor Relations in Transition*, ed. Keith Ocheltree (Chicago: Public Personnel Association, 1966), pp. 10–11.
62 Kenneth O. Warner, Foreword to *Coping with Public Employee Strikes*, by Carmen D. Saso (Chicago: Public Personnel Association, 1970), p. iii.
63 Saso, *Coping with Public Employee Strikes*, p. 3.
64 Ibid., pp. 5–6.
65 Ibid., pp. 11–12.
66 Dennis Smith, ". . . But Not Fire Fighters," *The Washington Star*, 14 August 1977.
67 "Albert Shanker," in *Should We Jail Public Employees?* ed. David C. Ford (New York: Workers Defense League, 1973), p. 49.
68 Heisel, *On Public Employee Negotiation*, p. 135.
69 Ibid.
70 Didactic Systems, *Management in the Fire Service*, p. 336.
71 Heisel, *On Public Employee Negotiation*, pp. 113–14.
72 From an interview with the authors.
73 Flynn, *Public Work, Public Workers*, p. 49.
74 Ibid., p. 57.
75 Desmond D. Martin and William M. Kramer, "MBO Pays Dividends in Cincinnati with Improvements in Three Areas," *Fire Engineering* 44 (June 1977): 16–18.
76 Kramer, *A Managerial Analysis of Municipal Fire Departments*, p. 106.

14 Measuring and evaluating productivity

The word *productivity* ultimately derives from the Latin words *pro* (forward) and *ducere* (to lead). The entire thrust of this book is, in fact, intended to lead forward those responsible for the management of fire services in a local government context. Each individual chapter, in one way or another and in one area or another, represents the view of one or more specialists as to how management principles and practices can be strengthened. In this sense every case study cited, and every example given, is designed to enhance productivity in the broad sense. The task of the present chapter is to bring these specialized applications together in a systematic way; to sharpen the analytical focus; and to discuss in some detail the following questions: What is productivity? Why is it important to measure it? How is it to be measured? How can comparative data be utilized? And what are some of the optimal theoretical principles involved?

Four general points should be made at this point for the benefit of local government practitioners.

The first point is that the chapter begins with a straightforward discussion of some of the elementary concepts involved regarding productivity. It is hoped that this early section will be of particular use to those approaching the subject for the first time or with little prior experience.

The second point is that the approach set out in the remainder of the chapter is a systematic one. As has been indicated, there are many illustrations of specific uses of productivity procedures in other chapters in this book. The purpose of the present discussion is to set these in an overall context. It is recognized, however, that many fire service managers will wish to adapt these general principles to specific uses—to the particular political, socioeconomic, and even geographical circumstances of their particular communities, and also to particular applications within the fire service in those communities. Managers will therefore want to supplement the coverage in this chapter by referring to the specialized coverage elsewhere in the book and to their own experience and organizational needs.

The third general point to be made is that the central portion of this chapter makes an attempt to apply the principles involved in productivity studies to the specifics of individual fire departments and communities by drawing on a study and workbook developed for just this purpose in the later 1970s. Readers are encouraged to use the worksheets in the above-mentioned workbook[1] in order to take an active part in the measurement of productivity in their own communities and fire departments. The format used and the statistics cited will of course be refined and otherwise subject to evolution over the years ahead: readers can incorporate their own changes and interpolations as necessary. The *principle* of applying measurements of productivity on a systematic basis will, however, remain valid for the forseeable future, and the exercise presented in this chapter is intended to give that principle a broader dissemination.

The fourth and final point to be made by way of introduction is that the coverage in the latter portion of the chapter, unlike that at the beginning, is given over to a more technical discussion of productivity for those readers interested in exploring some of the principles—including the mathematical principles—involved. Readers new to the subject may wish defer studying these portions of the chapter until they have familiarized themselves with some of the works cited in the endnotes and in the bibliography to this chapter.

The chapter is organized into six sections. The first section, in answering the question "What is productivity?" emphasizes the importance of a systems approach, examines the concepts of efficiency and effectiveness as well as productivity, and also introduces the idea of total system costs. The second section answers the question "Why measure productivity?" in terms of overall allocation strategies and internal management aspects. The third section explores methods of measuring productivity by looking at some total systems measures, at intercommunity comparisons, at methods of using data, and at some additional measures. The fourth section examines the use of comparative data to achieve greater productivity. The fifth section is more theoretical, examining optimal specifications involved in operations research activities, including queuing theory and mathematical programming models, while emphasizing the need for close cooperation on the part of all involved. The chapter ends with a brief evaluative conclusion.

What is productivity?

What impact does the opening of a new firehouse have on productivity? What is the effect of a gradually aging firefighter work force on productivity? Does the use of Rapid Water, walkie-talkies, rear mounted aerial ladders, or a new computerized dispatching system enhance or degrade productivity? Is it more or less productive to double the building inspection program? To answer such questions—and many others like them—fire managers and other local government managers should start with a basic question: What is productivity?

Productivity is a difficult concept to define. In the manufacturing industry, for example, productivity appears to be synonymous with efficiency—it is the relationship between the cost of making some product and the price obtained upon the sale of that product. Unlike the manufacturing industry, the fire protection service does not produce goods, and so defining productivity relies instead on specification of output measures. This leads into a systems view of the fire protection service.

A systems view

The local government fire protection service, many experts have held, is a system.[2] What, then, is a system? A system is a collection of entities or objects, with a set of well-defined relationships among them, which is characterized by a clear purpose or goal. The entities or objects for the fire service include personnel, vehicles, organization structure, policies, and plans. The purposes or goals are the enhancement of human living conditions by the prevention of fire and the minimization of the spread and hence damage of those fires which occur. Like other systems, the fire service is a subsystem of larger systems. For example, it is a component of the city or county government and is also a part of the overall community fire suppression and prevention system. This latter larger system includes citizens who install their own fire alarms and extinguishers, private fire alarm companies, insurance companies, and water supply services including hydrants. Like other systems, the fire protection service also has many subsystems within it. These include various organizational units such as suppression activities, fire prevention, and the maintenance of equipment. Like other systems, the fire protection system operates in an environment which contains factors that affect the operation of the fire service but are largely *not* under the control of the fire service. This environment includes the weather, housing and construction practices, the socioeconomic makeup of the community and its surrounding area, density, street and traffic patterns, and many other factors.

The two key concepts bringing order to this diversity are goals and controllability. Determining what is in the system and what is outside is in fact the process of defining system boundaries. This, in turn, follows from the establishment of the goals of the system and an analysis as to whether the components are controllable for purposes of meeting the goals. Those items which are controllable are called *decision variables* (to use the technical systems vocabulary), while those that are not are either located in the larger system of which the fire service is a subsystem or located in the environment. This can be illustrated by an example. Present construction practices may be part of the fire protection service set of decision variables if the fire service can secure changes in the building code. However, the current inventory of housing and commercial stock is largely a result of previous and obsolete codes and hence is uncontrollable from the standpoint of the fire service. This stock therefore belongs to the environment.

Systems can be further characterized as having inputs and outputs. The inputs are the resources supplied to the system, while the outputs are the final product resulting from the methods of *transforming* these resources to meet needs (economists would say *demands*) from the environment. To be specific, the *inputs* into the fire protection service are the short term (that is, annual) dollar amounts that are then transformed into salaries, debt service, materials and tools, vehicle maintenance, and other items. Other inputs are of a longer term or capital nature, including vehicle purchase expenditures and money spent for firehouse construction or rehabilitation. The methods of transformation or allocation of these resources include response patterns, deployment of fire companies, firefighting strategies, organizational arrangements such as supervision and training practices, and other items. The *outputs* are represented by the confinement of damage and fire spread, the performance of rescues and "saves," and the prevention of fire. These are issues which relate directly to achievement of the goals of the fire service.

Efficiency, effectiveness, and productivity

Efficiency, effectiveness, and productivity are all concepts used in this technical context to assess the performance of an organization. The term *efficiency* pertains to the relationship between inputs and transformations. One might say that a building inspector is more efficient than other building inspectors if he or she can inspect more of the same types of buildings in a single day than other inspectors with the same background and qualifications. Similarly, volunteer firefighters are always (in this technical context) more efficient than paid firefighters because they provide coverage at a far lower cost. Efficiency measures, however, are not generally very useful in the fire protection service because they do not relate to the outputs or final products of the system. Measures which relate inputs to outputs are denoted as *effectiveness* measures, and, therefore, some policy or procedure is said to be more effective if it enhances the organization's achievement of its goals. Paid living-in firefighters, for example, might bring about lower response times to fire alarms and thus (again, in this technical context) would be more effective in achieving the goals of limiting damage and spread of fire. The building inspector who prevents more fires is more effective regardless of the number of buildings that he or she inspects in a single day. It often occurs that what is efficient is not effective and what is effective does not appear to be efficient.

How does *productivity* fit into this context? Productivity, as understood in this discussion, is concerned only with effectiveness. It measures the relationship between inputs and outputs (achievement of goals). Productivity is not necessarily linked to efficiency.

One of the reasons why efficiency has been a more popular concept than productivity is that outputs in the public sector are often poorly defined and as a result difficult to measure.³ This is not true as a rule for the simple transformation of resources that constitutes inputs. It is not difficult to record the number of inspections or the number of alarms that constitute the work load for a given period. Such measures do not, however, contain the sense of quality or goal achievement that relate to effectiveness and productivity. In addition, productivity measures typically include total system costs such as dollars lost owing to fires, insurance premiums paid, and money spent for private fire alarm services —costs which are not among the data items collected by a typical fire protection service in a community. Furthermore, the important measures include fires prevented, rescues and saves made, and fires confined in terms of spread. These quantities are difficult if not impossible to define, and the information must often be inferred from actual data rather than directly measured. In spite of such obstacles, an increasing number of local government managers are in agreement that it is worthwhile to undertake the measurement of outputs and thus of productivity. It is also a fact that several promising starts in this process had been made by the later 1970s. This research is discussed later in this chapter.

Total system costs

In keeping with a systems perspective of the fire protection service, it is important to elaborate on the concept of total system costs. These include not only the operating cost of the governmental unit charged with fire suppression and prevention activities but also all other costs paid as a result of the need to prevent and suppress fire, regardless of who pays such costs. It is not easy to determine which costs belong in the total system cost and which do not but a simple test may help. For example, we might assume that a chemical is developed which could make every substance nonflammable. Furthermore, this chemical is very inexpensive and can be applied to every possible hazard including pipes, housing, trees, automobiles, and materials which are later discarded as rubbish. In this nonflammable world there would be no need for fire suppression, prevention, insurance or any other cost connected with the fire service. The items which would be saved would constitute the total system cost.

Unfortunately, in reality we still have a flammable world—and this is the key point: the total system costs are ultimately paid by the citizens of the community. These costs are paid in property, income and sales taxes, payments to insurance companies, uninsured losses, costs resulting from depletion and destruction of the community's physical plant, and other items. Losses of human life and injuries are also important, although they are unquantifiable (in dollar terms) aspects of these costs. It should be emphasized that the annual fire department budget (discussed in Chapter 12) is only a part of such costs.

In the framework of total system costs, we are then able to redefine the idea of productivity. Any allocation of resources into the total fire protection function that results in reducing the total system costs is *productive*, no matter who pays directly and who benefits. If the fire service were to increase its annual expenditures by adding fire companies, and such an increase were more than offset by lower fire insurance payments in the community, such a change would increase productivity as defined here. Ultimately, as has been noted, the citizens of the community bear the cost of the total fire protection system. They should be indifferent as to what they are paying (insurance premiums or taxes) as long as the total cost decreases. (One qualification, however, is in order. The preceding statement is not quite accurate because it omits the important consideration of the incidence or burden of payment which may not be equal throughout the community. This is a matter of extreme complexity and is beyond the scope of this chapter.)

The total system cost framework is depicted in Figure 14–1. Three cost curves are shown. The curve that begins in the bottom left is costs related to

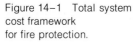

Figure 14–1 Total system cost framework for fire protection.

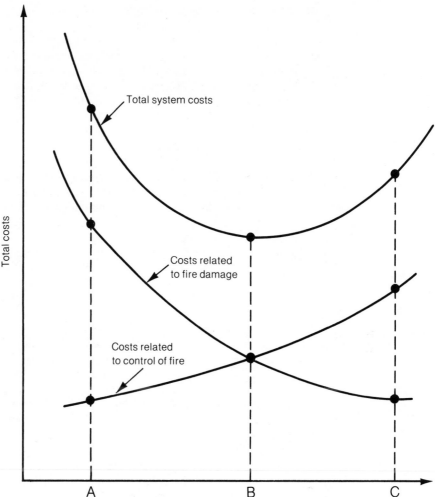

Total system costs

Total costs

Costs related to fire damage

Costs related to control of fire

A   B   C

Amount of money spent by a community fire protection service

control of fire and represents that amount of money the community spends on the governmental fire protection service. This curve begins at some low value which represents a small department. As more money is invested in the fire service, the curve moves upward. At the broken line B this curve intersects costs related to fire damage and then continues upward. Costs related to fire damage are all expenses that result from fire beyond the cost of maintaining the fire service. When the cost of the fire service is kept at an unreasonably low level there may not be a sufficient number of prevention activities or fire companies to limit spread and damage, so that the costs related to fire damage are high. This is the situation at A. At C the community has a large fire service so that the costs of fire are at a minimum. However, the expense of maintaining this service is now very high. The total system cost is shown as the top curve and represents the addition of the lower two curves. It is lowest at line B, which is also the intersection of the other two curves. Productivity can then be illustrated graphically as movement toward line B.

Figure 14–1 is hypothetical. Therefore, it is not correct to assume from line B that the optimum amount of money to invest in the fire service is equal to the annual loss and damage due to fire, because this latter amount omits many other costs. The purpose of this figure is merely to depict total system costs as related to some of the components.

Why measure productivity?

Although there are significant obstacles in the way of developing an accurate measure of productivity, the process of trying to measure productivity is likely to result in some significant benefits. The two major benefits are: (1) as an aid in developing the best governmental allocation strategies in terms of total system costs; and (2) as an aid in improving the management and control of the fire protection service.

Overall resource allocation strategies

The best resource allocation strategies are those which minimize total system costs. This process may involve increasing the fire protection service's share of the community budget. In most communities which rely on property taxation to support the municipal government, an agency's request for more money is not a popular step. It therefore becomes important for such an agency to show that total system costs are likely to decrease as a result of its receiving additional funding. While this type of justification is generally not made, it is often implicit at the heart of major resource allocation decisions.

For example, during the 1950s many fire departments received new appropriations to install mobile radios. Prior to this, there had been only two locations where the fire company could be contacted—the firehouse and the fire alarm (telegraph) box. Communication at the box was difficult because headquarters could transmit or receive from the fire company only when the company was present at the box. This would, typically, occur at points when (1) the company required additional assistance and would transmit a second alarm or (2) when it had finished operations and "tapped out." At this latter point, the company could be directed to respond to another fire. The dispatcher, however, would not know in advance when tapping out would occur so that he or she would often dispatch a more remotely located company to a new incident. The advent of radio profoundly improved communications. Multiple alarms could be transmitted by radio, and, in addition, companies returning to quarters could be contacted en route and redirected to a new incident. In addition, some cities now required companies to undertake building inspections with their apparatus because the company could also be directed to respond to a fire. What two-way radio accomplished was to extend the communication network beyond the firehouse, which resulted in more rapid response time and, in some cases, better fire prevention (through more inspections). Such changes lowered the total system cost of fire, although it increased the costs for the fire service. While the improvements in response time could have been achieved without radio by adding fire companies, this would have cost far more than radio service.

With increasing pressure on the tax base for most communities, it becomes very important to be able to show that increases in spending can be offset by decreases elsewhere in the total system. Contemporary budgeting systems which include planning-programming-budgeting (PPBS) and zero-based budgeting (ZBB) emphasize these aspects.

In addition, it sometimes happens that the total system costs can be reduced by actions taken by other governmental units. In such a case it becomes important for the fire service to advocate increasing the resources of these other units. For example, in large cities fires in vacant buildings are a major load on the fire service. Vacant buildings are serious hazards not only because a single building can be ignited many times before its ultimate demolition but also because increasing dilapidation makes a building increasingly more hazardous for firefighters. Injuries that firefighters sustain in vacant building fires increase the days lost to injury, and also increase disability retirements which exert an enormous impact on the pension funds. There is no question that firefighting is among the most dangerous occupations but it seems foolish to extinguish a fire and risk firefighters' lives for a building which will be demolished and where there are rarely citizens in need of rescues. Consequently, in such cities, fire chiefs have argued for more rapid demolition of such structures. When this requires that additional resources be devoted to other government agencies, chiefs have advocated that these other agencies' budgets be increased.

Recently the term *productivity bargaining* has become popular. This describes a situation in which pay raises in a union contract are given in return for changes in work rules or some other concession which then allows management to meet its goals at lower costs. The examples just given suggest that the fire protection service engage in productivity bargaining with the municipality. For each additional increase in resources, the fire protection service would then obligate itself to deliver some decrease in total system costs.

Internal management aspects

Measuring productivity is also useful for the internal management of the fire protection service. The community fire protection service contains many subsystems, and top management is responsible for resource allocation among these subsystems. Such subsystems usually include suppression, prevention, planning, and administration and may also include maintenance of vehicles, communications networks, and firehouses. The same types of issues that face the mayor or city manager responsible for overall governmental fiscal performance are faced by the top management of the fire service in internal resource allocation decisions among subsystems. The criterion of minimizing total system costs can also be used practically in this context. This criterion is especially useful for evaluating new programs and for establishing management by objectives (MBO).

The Rapid Water (or slippery water) project launched by the New York City–Rand Institute is an example of how total system costs can be lowered by better allocation of resources within a community fire protection service.

This project involved the injection of a water soluble polymer into the pump at the engine. Slippery water is a chemical which reduces the turbulence or friction of water in the hose stream and thereby allows delivery of a larger volume of water at a higher than normal pressure from an existing line. The potential advantage of this chemical was that firefighters would be able to use a smaller diameter hose which would be much lighter and therefore easier to carry up a flight of stairs. During the project, it was demonstrated that firefighters could reach the third story of a tenement three minutes faster carrying $1\frac{1}{2}$ inch hose rather than the typical $2\frac{1}{2}$ inch line. In addition, this meant that firefighters could stretch two lines into the fire building at the same time from the same pumper instead of waiting for the second pumper to arrive. The fire department estimated that the use of slippery water was equivalent to placing an additional man on each of its existing pumpers. The annual cost of the chemical was estimated to be $100,000 as compared with an expenditure of $20 million to add an additional firefighter to each pumper. Such a saving meets any criterion for productivity improvement.[4]

Every new tool, technique, or procedure should be regarded as an experiment in which the outcome should be considered in total system terms. This will enhance management and control of the fire service. However, as experienced managers will recognize, this process involves the exercise of caution.

The following is an example of a situation that effective managers have learned to avoid. In another large city the fire department was responsible for maintenance of the communications network, which included underground telegraph cable and aerial lines. Prior to the annual budget, the director of the communications bureau assembled all his foremen and lectured them on the need for increased productivity—by which he meant getting more work out of the journeymen electricians. One of the foremen went back to his office and thought of a better method of replacing aerial lines and then recommended it to the director. The method used at the time involved two crews, each of which contained a journeyman electrician and a helper and each of which had its own truck. During the replacement operation each crew was assigned to an adjacent telegraph pole where the journeyman would ascend the ladder and stretch and splice the wire, while the helper would bring tools and materials up to him and would also steady the ladder. The foreman suggested using bucket trucks (also known as cherry pickers) instead, with controls in the bucket so that the journeyman could move it up or down as needed. Under such an arrangement the helper would not be needed and one man crews could do the work of the present two man crew. In addition, the occasional disabling injury resulting from a fall from the ladder would be averted.

The foreman's report and the accompanying requisition for the new types of trucks unfortunately lay on the director's desk. As far as is known, they were never purchased. The effect on morale was shattering.

By this example we do not mean to suggest that in focusing on total system costs the manager should ignore constraints imposed by the budget. However, in this case the manager issued a call for higher productivity and as a result received a suggestion which would have increased the number of jobs performed by a factor of two. This is far more than could have been realized by exhorting the men to work harder.

To summarize, the measurement of productivity is important to the overall governmental resource allocation process and the resource allocation process within the fire service. Also, it is important to emphasize that, if a productivity program is properly managed, it can do much to raise morale in the fire service.

How to measure productivity

Three methods

Three ways to use measures of productivity are as follows:

1. To compare productivity measures among many communities
2. To compare these measures within a single community over time
3. To develop optimal performance specifications and then to measure current performance against these optimal measures.

Comparing a community to others is undertaken to find out whether a community performs better, equally well, or worse than similar communities. There are some major limitations in this approach which may lead to the erroneous conclusion that one community has a more productive fire protection service than a second. The differences between communities may come from other causes. First, differences between communities may be a result of using noncomparable data. Each community may have different definitions of what constitutes a structural fire, to say nothing of such items as saves and rescues. Second, each community may have unique conditions which affect suppression and prevention, such as the presence of hospitals and airports which might generate the need for extra fire protection. Also, the effects of weather, street and traffic patterns, and other unusual community characteristics may make two apparently similar cities actually very different in their needs for fire protection services. Possibly, also, in some cities fire protection functions may be performed by other city or county agencies and thus may not be reflected in overall fire protection costs. Such functions could include building inspection, maintenance of fire vehicles and buildings, and maintenance of the alarm system. A third problem with interjurisdictional comparisons is that even if one city's measures place it high among cities in its class, it is only ranking itself against the average performance in that class. All the cities in that class may have low performance. However, in spite of these limitations, it can be helpful (but, of course, not conclusive) to compare performance against similar classes of communities.

The second type of comparison involves comparing a community's productivity measurements against measurements made at earlier times in the same community. Generally this type of comparison avoids the problems of unique data definitions and different community characteristics that appear in the interjurisdictional comparisons. There are, however, still some limitations. Long term comparisons of performance, for example over a five year period, raise difficulties in interpreting measures as a result of changing community characteristics. In a five year period residential patterns can change, new shopping centers may be constructed, and new traffic patterns may emerge. In addition, vacant buildings are burned out, demolished, and often rehabilitated. Short term year-to-year comparisons do not present such a problem and can give a better picture of whether or not the fire protection service is improving its productivity. But these short term comparisons do not address the question of whether such improvement is all that could be expected or is minimal. (For example, productivity in manufacturing industries increases about 2 percent per year. No one is sure whether a 5 percent increase is attainable, in which case the 2 percent change is a positive but insignificant part of the potential gains, or whether the 2 percent represents the maximum improvement that is reasonable to expect.) Whether the increase or decrease in the productivity of the fire protection service is significant or insignificant requires the interpretation of informed fire service managers. Nevertheless, it is important to be able to assess year-to-year changes.

The third type of comparison is the most challenging and the most difficult to undertake. It begins with a specification of optimal (that is, the very best) performance and then compares prevailing practices against that optimum. In order to develop a specification of optimal performance, it is necessary to first develop a model (usually a mathematical model or a simulation model) of the physical phenomena and their relationships for the fire service. This would include, for example, an estimate of the demand for service (number of fires) and of how the department would respond to such a demand. One can use the model to predict the best way to respond to that demand or as informed hindsight as to what the response should have been.

The work done in this area has focused on fire station location, deployment of fire vehicles, manning patterns and work schedules, and the effectiveness of fire prevention inspections. For example, a community fire protection service could use some of the computerized fire station location models developed by Public Technology, Inc. (PTI), to determine if the same average response time to fire alarms (the time between dispatch to a fire and arrival) could be attained with fewer firehouses and fewer fire companies (see Chapter 19 for a discussion of fire station location). The measure of productivity loss from existing fire station configurations would be the difference in expenditures between the present costs and the projected costs under a new configuration. The new configuration would constitute an optimum.

This type of work is often of considerable mathematical complexity and, typically, is beyond the capability of a community fire protection service to undertake on its own. It is usually done by specialists in statistics or operations research who serve as consultants. In addition to PTI, this work has been done by the New York City–Rand Institute, Johns Hopkins University, the University of Denver, and others. A rather interesting aspect of this work, which separates it from other measures of productivity, is that it is *constructive*—that is, it points the way to increasing productivity. The other comparative approaches merely indicate where a community stands with respect to similar communities.

These three methods will be discussed and illustrated later in this chapter, after further discussion of total system costs.

Total system measures

There is a simple (if somewhat fanciful) test that may be used to determine whether an item should be included in the fire protection service system. It was suggested earlier in this chapter that a nonflammable world should be considered, and it was stated that the costs that would be saved in that kind of world would constitute the total system costs. A list of these costs is given as Figure 14–2.

This list is by no means complete, and still its length and complexity are dismaying. Trying to list all of these costs would be a major research project in itself. For example, consider item 1*f*, the water supply. It would clearly not be

1. **Fire suppression: direct to government**
   a) Dollar expenses for firefighters, including direct salary and fringe benefits (purchase of group health insurance, life insurance, FICA, pensions)
   b) Debt service payments on fire vehicles, communications equipment, and firehouse construction
   c) Annual operation and maintenance expenditures on vehicles, firehouses, and communication equipment, including heat, electricity, gasoline, and labor
   d) Replacement of firefighting tools and equipment, including hose, axes, etc.
   e) Maintenance of fire clothing and uniforms
   f) Expenditures for construction, operation, and maintenance of the water supply allocated to fire protection
   g) Salaries and materials used in the fire services for housekeeping functions such as accounting, purchasing, payroll preparation, and planning, or salaries for people in other agencies who perform those functions for the fire protection service
   h) Expenses for police services at fires, ambulance services, hospital emergency room charges, etc.
   i) Demolition of buildings destroyed by fire

2. **Fire prevention: direct to government**
   a) Salaries and indirect expenses for building inspectors, tank truck inspectors, etc. (regardless of which agency pays them), vehicles, and other operating expenses
   b) Arson investigation expenses (may include percentage of state fire marshal's services, also police expenses for arrests, county attorneys, judges, prisons, and parole)
   c) Community and public relations expenses
   d) Housekeeping functions as in 1, *g*, above

3. **Costs borne directly by citizens (excluding taxes which are contained in 1 and 2, above)**
   a) Losses due to fire (uninsured property losses from fire, smoke, or water damages)
   b) Insurance payments
   c) Relocation expenses
   d) Salaries for days lost through injuries and medical costs
   e) Fire prevention costs including code compliance, smoke detector installation and maintenance, standpipe and siamese fixtures, hoses, and extinguishers
   f) Payments to private fire alarm companies

4. **Nonmonetary losses borne by everyone**
   a) Pain, suffering, loss of functions as a result of being injured in fire
   b) Deaths

Figure 14–2   Total system costs of fire protection.

appropriate to charge the entire water supply expense to suppression as (quite apart from industrial use) some is used for drinking, washing, cooking, sanitation, and swimming. However, in the absence of the need to use water for extinguishment, smaller mains could have been used. Thus some proportion of the construction, maintenance, and operating costs of the water services agency should be charged to the fire protection system. But it is not possible to determine what the proper figure should be.

Instead, analysts usually try to first specify the entire range of total system costs (as we have done) and then concentrate on those which (1) are measurable and (2) capture a large part of the total system costs. In the *Municipal Fire Service Workbook* the authors suggest six measures which can be used to represent total systems costs. These include number of fires, dollar value of property loss, fire department expenditures broken down by prevention and suppression, fire-related civilian deaths and injuries, firefighter deaths and injuries and, finally, what the authors define as total costs, which is the sum of total fire department expenditures and dollar value of property losses. It is relatively easy to collect data on these items which seem to capture a large part of total system costs. The authors then discuss the development of measures that can be compared between communities. In addition, the authors present data for 1974 from a large sample of cities so that departments can compare their measures against those of other communities. The arithmetic is simple, the data collection seems reasonably painless, the principles involved are important, and the results of the comparisons should be worthwhile. To perform these measurements, the reader is referred to the discussion below and to the *Municipal Fire Service Workbook*.[5]

Principal categories of productivity measurements given by the *Municipal Fire Service Workbook* are as follows:

1. Measures of effectiveness (outputs)
    a) Prevention
        (1) Number of fires per 1,000 population
    b) Suppression and prevention
        (1) Property loss per fire
        (2) Civilian casualties per 100 fires
        (3) Firefighter casualties per 100 fires
        (4) Property loss per capita
        (5) Property loss per $1,000 market value
        (6) Civilian casualties per 100,000 population
2. Inputs
    a) City type
    b) Fire department type
    c) Fire department expenses
        (1) Total operating budget of the fire department per capita
        (2) Total operating expenses less fire department expenditures for both emergency medical services (EMS) and salaries for building inspectors
        (3) Building inspectors' salaries
3. Measures of total system costs
    a) Average property loss plus total operating budget
        (1) Per capita
        (2) Per $1,000 market value
        (3) Per fire
    b) Plus total building inspectors' salaries per capita.[6]

The relationships among these various measures are shown in Figure 14–3. As mentioned previously, the characteristics of the community impose con-

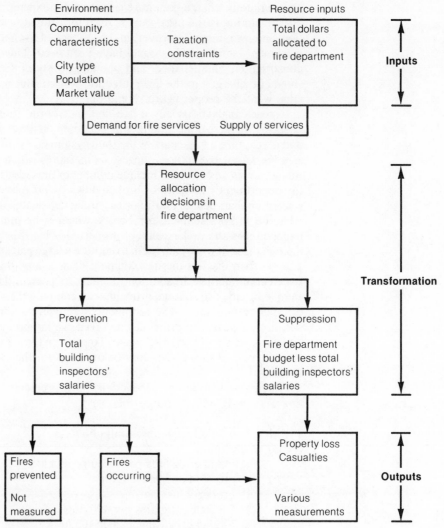

Figure 14–3   Relationships among categories of measurements.
(The arrows show the flow of decisions, and, to some degree,
the direction of causation.)

straints on the fire protection service. First, the community characteristics create the supply of services by limiting the amount of money available to the overall governmental unit which funds the fire protection service and therefore affects the size of the fire protection service's budget. Simultaneously, the community contains citizens who want their lives and property protected in case of fire, and thus they demand a fire protection service. With the amount of money available, the department then allocates funds to the two functions of prevention and suppression. Funding for prevention is found by using the total salaries allocated for building inspectors regardless of whether such costs appear in the fire department budget or the budget of some other agency. Suppression expenditures are found in the remainder of the fire department budget after expenses for emergency medical services, if any, are subtracted. (In a case where a department includes both EMS and building inspection in its budget, expenditures from both categories should be subtracted to arrive at the cost for suppression.) The allocation of funds between these two units is a key managerial decision and represents a major transformation of resources made by the department. The funds allocated to building inspection service are then transformed again into fire prevention inspections, for the purpose of delaying or inhibiting the onset of fire. A critical output measure (of performance) is the number of fires prevented, which unfortunately cannot be collected directly (indirect methods are described later in the text). For those fires which occur, the suppression component of the department then attempts to minimize casualties and damage. The measures shown above such as property losses and civilian casualties (per 100,000 population, per 100 fires, and per $1,000 market value) are *joint* measures of suppression and prevention. Effective firefighting can reduce casualties and property damage but this is also a primary purpose of inspections which, for example, require unblocked exits, fire walls, stairs and escapes, and sprinklers and standpipes.

The bottom line for the citizen is how much fire costs. This quantity is contained in the total cost measures which represent the amount of money spent on the fire service plus the amount lost in property damage. Like the other figures, these numbers are corrected for population, market values, and number of fires to make them comparable among jurisdictions or within a community over time. Such comparisons are the primary purpose of the *Municipal Fire Service Workbook*. Their results are presented and explained below.

Intercommunity comparisons

As mentioned earlier, differences in the values of the productivity measures among cities can emerge from many factors other than differences in productivity alone. Communities will have different water supplies, land use, traffic patterns, populations, and geographic factors or may have different methods of collecting and interpreting data. Therefore, if your community appears to spend more on fire protection and to receive less, it is not necessarily a cause for alarm. Nor can it be interpreted from these measures that, if your performance is equal to similar communities, yours is effective. As with any statistical data, considerable judgment is needed in interpreting the data.

The *Municipal Fire Service Workbook* presents a model for using and interpreting these data.[7] This model (Figure 14–4) is a good systems view of the fire protection service. The differences between your performance and that of others can be attributed to controllable and uncontrollable factors. To the degree that those can be identified, the department has the beginnings of a program to improve productivity. However, the relationship between controllable factors such as response time and code enforcement, and performance measures such as number of casualties, has not been established. In other words, if your department's average response time is four minutes (time between the dispatch and arrival of the first due pumper), it is not clear how many casualties would be averted by reducing the average response time to three minutes. Some research has been done on these relationships, which will be discussed later in this chapter. This research plus professional knowledge of the particular firefighting problem in your community should point to where productivity improvement can begin.

How to use the data

The data discussed in this section[8] were collected by the authors of the above-mentioned workbook from a survey of 1974 data from 1,413 departments. Each department that responded was classified according to (1) size of the population served and (2) type of city and composition of the fire department. Cities were

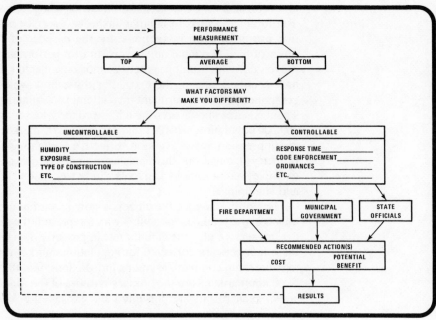

Figure 14–4   Steps to the improvement of the fire protection system.
(Source: Research Triangle Institute (RTI), International City
Management Association (ICMA), and National Fire
Protection Association (NFPA), *Municipal Fire Service Workbook,*
Washington, D.C.: Government Printing Office, 1977, p. 62.)

classified as *center cities,* defined as urban areas with populations greater than
50,000, *ring cities,* defined as communities in urban areas which border central
cities, and *fringe cities,* defined as cities in a metropolitan county but outside
an urbanized area.

The complete classification scheme, together with the number of departments
in each class, is shown below:

1. *Under 5,000 population*
   Ring: fully volunteer   61
   Ring: mostly volunteer   27
   Fringe: fully volunteer   361
   Fringe: mostly volunteer   43
2. *5,000 to 25,000 population*
   Ring: fully volunteer   111
   Ring: mostly volunteer   62
   Ring: mostly paid   32
   Ring: fully paid   32
   Fringe: fully volunteer   85
   Fringe: mostly volunteer   50
   Fringe: mostly paid   25
3. *25,001 to 100,000 population*
   Ring: mostly volunteer   21
   Ring: mostly paid   13
   Ring: fully paid   46
   Center: fully paid   20
4. *Over 100,000 population*
   Center: fully paid   38
      Total   1,027

The logic involved in the classification of departments is that each class represents different (and, therefore, incomparable) types of fire protection problems. For example, cities with predominantly volunteer forces would spend less money on firefighting than cities with paid departments, but the cities with volunteer forces might experience more fire damage because, in theory, it would take volunteers longer to respond to a fire than it would take paid forces. The classification according to city type deals with length of runs and traffic patterns. Ring departments would have longer runs than fringe or central cities, while fringe and central cities would be likely to have more traffic congestion; thus, the classification of departments into comparable units is intended to control for various differing community characteristics.

The data are organized into first quartile or lower 25 percent, median, and third quartile or upper 25 percent ranges. The first quartile means that 25 percent of the cities (of a given type) had values that were below the specified value and 75 percent had values above. The upper 25 percent range means that 75 percent had values below the specified value and 25 percent had values above. The median means that half the cities had values below the one recorded and half had values above. These values are shown in Figure 14–5.

Assuming that your city has a population of 42,000, is located in a ring area, and has a fully paid department, the numbers of interest to you will be in the third column from the right in Figure 14–4, as your city fits into the 25,001 to 100,000 population, ring, fully paid category. Next to the heading "Prevention, No. of fires per 1,000 population protected," three numbers are shown. The top 25 percent of cities experienced 7.97 fires (or fewer) per 1,000 population. The median had 10.25 fires per 1,000, and the lower 25 percent had 13 fires (or more) per 1,000 population. The number in parentheses below these entries is the number of cities in the sample, which in this case is 36.

The method of finding the quartiles is as follows. We might assume that the following seven cities are reporting the number of fires per 1,000 population: (1) Paris, 3.2; (2) London, 3.3; (3) Athens, 4.2; (4) Moscow, 5.7; (5) Brussels, 6.1; (6) Rome, 7.2; and (7) Bonn, 8.4. First, the cities are put in rank order from lowest to highest, as here. The median is city 4, Moscow, and the appropriate number of fires is 5.7. Half the cities have ratings below Moscow (Paris, London, and Athens) and half have ratings above (Brussels, Rome, and Bonn). The general formula for finding the median in a sample that is ranked is to choose the $(n + 1)12$ city if n is odd. When n is even, then you take the value for the $n/2$ city and the $(n + 2)/2$ and average them. Thus, if we had 8 cities we would find the average between the city 4 and the city 5's values.

To find the first and third quartiles, the sample should be split into two parts. When the sample size is odd, both parts include the city with the median value. In the sample seven cities, the first split would include Paris, London, Athens, and Moscow (the median) and the second would include Moscow, Brussels, Rome, and Bonn. Each split is then treated independently and we find the medians as the first and third quartiles, respectively. Hence, both the splits are even and so the even rule for the median is applied so that the values are averaged for the $n/2$ city (2, or London) and $(n + 2)/2$ city (3, or Athens) to give a lower quartile value of $1/2(3.3 + 4.2) = 3.75$. We do the same for our upper split, averaging the values of Brussels and Rome to obtain 6.65 as the upper quartile.

Thus, one can conclude that approximately 25 percent of the cities have values lower than quartiles, half the cities have values lower than the median and half higher, and approximately 25 percent of the cities have values higher than the upper quartile.

The rules for finding the lower and upper quartiles are somewhat more complex for samples of even size but in principle they operate in the same way as for the odd size samples.

Under suppression, there are a variety of measures. The full range is not shown in Figure 14–4. Details can be found in the *Municipal Fire Service Workbook*.[9] Inputs are treated in the same way as effectiveness measures. For this treatment and for total organizational performance measures, again the reader is referred to the above workbook.[10]

The above discussion has shown the reader how to use the appropriate categories to place the reader's department. All that is required then is to compute the data on worksheets and then match such data against the tables in the *Municipal Fire Service Workbook*. Readers are cautioned that the difference between their scores and those reported in the tables do not necessarily indicate that their city is a poor performer (or is highly productive). The differences may be due to different community characteristics not to the performance of the department. Careful judgment is needed in interpreting these differences.

CHART 1 – EFFECTIVENESS MEASURES

PERFORMANCE MEASURES	UNDER 5,000 POPULATION				5,000 - 25,000 POPULATION							25,001 - 100,000 POPULATION				OVER 100,000
	RING		FRINGE		RING				FRINGE			RING			CENTER	CENTER
	Fully Vol.	Mostly Vol.	Fully Vol.	Mostly Vol.	Fully Vol.	Mostly Vol.	Mostly Paid	Fully Paid	Fully Vol.	Mostly Vol.	Mostly Paid	Mostly Vol.	Mostly Paid	Fully Paid	Fully Paid	Fully Paid
PREVENTION																
No. of fires per 1,000 population protected																
RATINGS:																
More effective	6.08	5.21	5.87	17.84	2.69	6.63	4.91	3.28	1.57	4.66	4.23	4.01	6.58	7.97	7.24	9.69
Median	9.20	9.49	10.77	25.61	5.94	9.43	9.75	10.37	3.90	10.87	9.19	7.44	9.32	10.25	12.78	11.80
Less effective	22.98	23.26	14.31	49.56	9.48	15.95	22.94	16.99	12.56	18.10	20.19	12.99	12.42	13.00	19.23	17.89
(N)[†]	(23)	(16)	(109)	(20)	(40)	(38)	(19)	(20)	(29)	(33)	(9)	(12)	(13)	(36)	(13)	(31)
SUPPRESSION																
Dollar property loss per capita																
RATINGS:																
More effective	3.19	3.94	5.53	8.70	5.63	5.10	3.67	3.65	2.51	4.76	7.95	3.98	4.94	5.52	5.39	7.11
Median	7.62	13.03	13.80	30.18	8.06	7.69	7.85	6.68	4.17	9.72	11.40	10.35	7.05	7.28	10.40	12.29
Less effective	20.38	81.32	30.22	42.61	16.04	11.98	10.72	10.26	9.64	19.70	12.39	19.15	11.35	13.82	14.96	14.65
(N)[†]	(32)	(13)	(141)	(22)	(39)	(46)	(18)	(22)	(28)	(35)	(13)	(10)	(12)	(34)	(14)	(31)
Dollar property loss per $1,000 market value																
RATINGS:																
More effective	*	*	.64	.62	.58	.34	.10	.15	*	.54	*	*	.52	.33	.31	.64
Median	*	*	1.34	.97	1.02	.50	.58	.34	*	1.17	*	*	.68	.52	.54	1.05
Less effective	*	*	4.30	1.46	1.60	.75	.73	.60	*	1.29	*	*	.94	.74	2.10	1.80
(N)[†]	(7)	(7)	(49)	(14)	(15)	(26)	(12)	(13)	(8)	(19)	(7)	(8)	(9)	(28)	(13)	(30)

[†] Number of Fire Departments in Sample

* Insufficient Number of Cases in Sample

Figure 14–5 Effectiveness measures. (Source: RTI, ICMA, and NFPA, *Municipal Fire Service Workbook*, p. 31.)

As an additional caution it is suggested that the reader *does not* compare data across categories. Not only is the sample size too small, but, as has been mentioned, departments will differ in other respects. Indeed, intercategory comparisons is beyond the scope of the workbook's analysis.

Some additional measures

In a 1977 report,[11] some additional measures of effectiveness of fire protection service have been developed. The authors begin with a criticism of certain effectiveness measures, some of which were presented earlier in this chapter. For example, they cite property loss figures (the adjusted property loss used in the workbook study) as more related to the wealth of the community than the effectiveness that fire suppression shows at the fire scene. Similarly, fire-related deaths and injuries statistics often result from events that are uncontrollable by the fire department (such deaths and injuries may have occurred before the fire department arrived on the scene or even before the department received an alarm). Also, using the number of fires that occur as a measure of prevention effectiveness obscures the fact that some fires may be preventable (perhaps by a more intensive inspection program) whereas some are not (they may have been caused by lightning, arson, or events beyond the scope of even the most intensive prevention program). The report continues by stating that direct rather than indirect measures of the phenomenon of interest can be made (Figure 14–6). These measures would then be more useful in assessing changes in productivity.

Program	Objective	Specific new measures
Mainly suppression but also prevention	Minimize civilian casualties	Number of saves; percentage of fires involving at least one save; average number of persons saved per fire incident saves
	Minimize fire damage	Fire spread at arrival; fire spread at control; time between arrival and control
	Minimize property loss	Square footage of damage multiplied by costs of new construction per square foot of the building type
Only prevention	Minimize the onset of "preventable" fires	Rate and percentage of fires that are "relatively" preventable by inspection; comparison of these rates between inspected and uninspected buildings; measurement of changes in rates increase in time from last inspection

Figure 14–6   Specific new measures for assessing productivity. (Source: Adapted from Philip S. Schaenman et al., *Procedures for Improving the Measurement of Local Fire Protection Effectiveness,* Boston: National Fire Protection Association, 1977, pp. xx–xxii.)

Three objectives are shown in Figure 14–6 which relate primarily to fire suppression but also in a secondary manner to prevention. These are: to minimize civilian casualties; to minimize fire damage; and to minimize property loss. As has been discussed in this chapter, prevention can have an impact on these objectives even if they are measured in "per fire" terms (for example, property loss per fire), as a large component of the inspection effort involves making sure that exit doors are clearly labeled and means of egress are not blocked, that sprinklers and standpipes are installed where they should be and are in working condition, and that similar items which do not in themselves prevent the onset of fire but make firefighting more effective are in working order. Measures of the effectiveness of the civilian casualty objective are based on the number of saves, or rescues, and are shown as the percentage of fires involving at least one save, the average number of persons saved in fires requiring at least one save, and the average number of persons saved per fire incident requiring saves. Measures associated with minimizing fire damage include the difference between fire spread at arrival and at control and the time interval between arrival and control. Property loss measures relate to the square footage of damage evaluated at its replacement cost. Finally, measures associated with prevention are those directly concerned with preventable fires.

What is gained by using these measures is that the quantity of interest is measured directly rather than being inferred. What is lost is the ability to use currently available statistics and the possibility that these new measures may be difficult to define. For example, suppose the quality of "total fires per capita" (as used in the workbook study as a measure of prevention activities) is compared between two cities. What one really wants to compare is the number of *preventable* fires per capita in the two cities. If the ratio of preventable to unpreventable is the same in both cities, the total number of fires may be compared. If it is not the same, a comparison is meaningless. If London had 1.2 fires per capita of which 0.7 were preventable and Brussels had 1.1 fires per capita, 0.9 of which were preventable, comparing total numbers of fires would produce the erroneous results that London's prevention effort was inferior to that of Brussels, whereas the opposite conclusion was actually the case.

The key difficulty is making such measures operational and collecting data. There seems to be no single commonly accepted standard as to which fires are preventable and which are not. Definitions of what constitutes a save are also not commonly established. The danger is that within a single city different observers will use different definitions which may be inconsistent.

It was this problem that led the authors of the 1977 report to undertake field research in nine fire departments.[12] The first stage of the research involved classifications of fires so that preventability could be assessed. In order of least preventable to most, they were as follows:

1. Incendiary, suspicious origin, and natural cause fires
2. Careless action fires, primarily related to smoking and thus considered relatively preventable by education but less so by inspection
3. Fires caused by mechanical or electrical failure, considered somewhat preventable by inspection
4. Fires due to storage practices.[13]

The other difficult category, that of saves, was disaggregated into smaller categories by the events involved in the save and the characteristics of both the victim and the fire. These included such issues as: (1) why the rescue was conducted (occupant asleep, trapped, etc.); (2) how the rescue was conducted; (3) the physical condition of those rescued and other characteristics of the fire (in same room as the victim, victim on fire floor, etc.).[14] The second stage of the research involved the question of whether two trained observers (for example, a battalion chief and an engine company officer) at the scene would produce consistent reports of the events. They concluded that, while there might be some disagreement between such observers about some aspects of the operation, in general fire spread and rescue information was assessed consistently. This naturally required some training in the interpretation and application of these measures.[15]

Thus, these newer measures contain more information than the *Municipal Fire Service Workbook* measures for assessing productivity. However, there are some problems in making them operational.

Using comparative data
to become more productive

Figure 14–4 presented steps to be used in improving the productivity of the fire protection service. From a comparative analysis of a community's data with either itself (over time) or with similar communities it is possible then to determine where improvements can most profitably be made. Thus it becomes necessary to identify the controllable variables which would have the greatest impact on total systems cost. Unfortunately, none of the comparative information can be used to identify these variables. This is why such analyses are not constructive. (Constructive methods for assessing productivity are discussed later in this chapter.)

There is, fortunately, a middle ground. In a technical supplement to the *Municipal Fire Service Workbook* the authors address a useful question: namely, what characteristics of a municipal fire protection service would contribute to good scores on the various measures of effectiveness, inputs, and measures of total system costs discussed in the previous section.[16] This section describes their study methodology and the results, and closes with some discussion of the limitations of the analysis.

As has been noted, the demand for fire protection services is generated by the local community. The department then allocates resources to meet this demand. Therefore, it is important to focus on (1) the amount of resources devoted to each activity performed by the department (for example, prevention and suppression) and (2) how effectively these resources are used. Components of total system costs affected by these two factors are: (1) the total number of structural and outside fires, (2) the average dollar loss (property loss) due to fire, and (3) the Insurance Services Office (ISO) rating of the local community. The annual number of fires can be useful as a measure of the prevention effort. Property loss statistics also are a measure of prevention (to a small degree) but primarily are connected with suppression. The ISO rating affects the amount of money property owners must pay for fire insurance and is therefore a component of the total system costs, but one specifically not included in the fire service organization budget. These variables are also related to two other major items in the study: (1) the size of the fire department budget and (2) the total salaries paid for building inspections, which measure the intensity of effort in the municipal fire service as a whole and the prevention effort, although they do not measure how well such services are being carried out.

These five variables are likely to have a causal relationship among each other. This relationship is seen in Figure 14–7, where + denotes that both variables are likely to increase or decrease together (are positively correlated), while − indicates that they move in opposite directions (are negatively correlated). Thus, in communities with a large number of fires, a large fire department budget would be expected because the community's demand for fire protection services is large. Similarly, the total investment in building inspection would be likely to be large in communities with a large number of fires where there is an attempt to reduce fires by prevention. In communities with a good ISO rating (a low number), investment in inspection would tend to be high so as to reduce fire incidence, thus the negative sign is used for that relationship. Similarly, a good ISO rating and a large fire department budget would also be likely to be found together. As the ISO rating decreases numerically (improves), property losses would probably decrease, thus a positive sign is warranted. The relationship between property losses in fire and the size of the budget would probably change over time; consequently, whether it is positive or negative would depend on when this relationship is measured. If property losses are high the department might raise its expenditures (a positive relationship), which over time might result in lower property losses. At a single point in time, a department might be found with a large budget which is intended to control high property losses or a large budget *which is already* controlling property losses. Thus the $+/-$ notation on property losses.

Figure 14–7   Relations among five major variables.

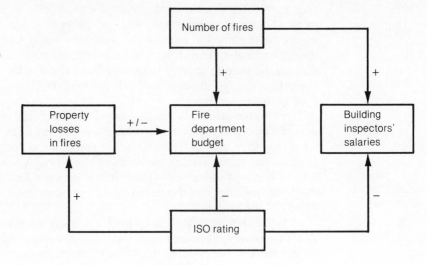

Figure 14–7   Relations among five major variables.

The simultaneous equation analysis

These five variables contain the results of a number of decisions made by the fire protection service, that is, they are usually related to other variables and also to each other. The technical name for such variables is *endogenous variables,* which is a generalization of the notion of *dependent variables* (those which result from action taken on controllable variables and from the environment). The methodology used is simultaneous equation analysis, also known as two stage or three stage least squares.[17] The major issue in this type of methodology is to determine how large the relationship is between variables and of what sign it is. Thus, this type of analysis can address, for example, whether a 10 percent increase in the number of fires produces an increase or decrease in the amount of money spent on building inspectors' salaries. Simultaneous equation models have become more popular in recent years and will continue to be used in public sector analyses. The results of a simultaneous equation analysis made of each of the five variables is given immediately below.

The results of the analysis are seen in Figure 14–8. Variables are coded as follows: D means endogenous variable; $+$ means that a significant positive relationship was found between the dependent variables; $-$ denotes a significant negative relationship. A zero (0) means that the variable was included in the equation but the relationship was insignificant, that is it might have been due to chance. This type of result occurs when no clear-cut association is found between the variables in question, and it is customarily interpreted (in the literature) that such variables are unrelated to each other. The important issue in this type of study is the relationship between controllable variables and those endogenous variables which go into total system costs.

The study universe from which these results were drawn was confined to approximately 120 municipalities with populations of at least 25,000. The relatively small size of the sample and also some missing data raise questions about how well such results may be generalized. However, this study is nevertheless presented because of its methodological importance and the intriguing nature of its results.

As seen in Figure 14–8, equation 1 relates the total number of fires to: (1)

Variables and definitions	Equation number				
	1 (No. of fires)	2 (Property loss)	3 (ISO rating)	4 (Building inspectors' salaries)	5 (Fire department budget)
Endogenous variables					
Total structural and outside fires, 1973–74	D			+	+
Average property loss, 1970–74, in constant 1974 $		D			
ISO rating, 1974		0	D	0	–
Total building inspectors' salaries, 1973–74				D	
Total fire department budget, 1973–74					D
Exogenous (controllable) variables					
Number of fires per person, 1974			0		
Average dollar loss per fire			0	0	0
Building inspectors' salaries per capita, 1973–74	0	0	+		–
Average salary per building inspector				+	
Total fire department prevention functions, 1974				+	+
Total municipal prevention functions, 1974	–	0	–		
Average building inspections per house, 1973–74	0			0	
Average longest response time, 1974		+			
Mixed fire department (1 if volunteer and paid, 0 if one type)					0
Percent paid, 1974		0	–		+
Average firefighter salary, 1974					0
Strength of union influence, 1974					
Number of hours of training per new recruit		0			+
Fire department budget per capita		0	–		
Total population served, 1970	+	+	0		
Area in square miles				0	+
Per capita income, 1970		0			
Percent of population with white collar jobs, 1970	0				
Percent of population on welfare, 1970	+				
Percent of population under 6 years old, 1970	0				
Percent of population over 65 years old, 1970	0			0	
Number of houses per square mile, 1970		–			
Percentage of houses built before 1939	0	0	–	0	
Percent of houses owner occupied, 1970	0				
Percent of buildings over 13 stories, 1970					+
Percent of buildings in manufacturing, 1970	0	0	–	0	0
Annual precipitation, 1970			+		
Mean wind speed, 1970	0				
Total days with temperature below 32°F, 1970	+		–		
Government type (1 if city manager, 0 otherwise), 1974				0	0
Per capita tax collected, 1970				0	+

Figure 14–8   Results of the simultaneous equation analysis (see text discussion).

building inspectors' salaries per capita; (2) total municipal prevention services; (3) average number of building inspections per house; (4) number of people served by the department; and (5) a series of variables representing socioeconomic type variables, housing construction, and temperature. Of this set of variables, prevention services is the only one which has a negative relationship, that is, the larger the prevention effort (so measured) the smaller the number of fires. (The elasticity is -0.93, indicating that a 10 percent increase in prevention services would result in a 9.3 percent decrease in fires.) Other measures of prevention, such as number of inspections per house and per capita building inspectors' salaries (that is, total salaries of building inspectors divided by the population served), however, do not seem to affect fire incidence. The socioeconomic variables also do not affect fire incidence except for population and the percentage of people on welfare, both of which are positively associated with fire incidence. Temperature also affects fire incidence which is shown to be positively related to the number of days below freezing.

The second equation attempts to find the variables causally related to property loss. The major findings are the positive relationship with response time and the negative relationship with houses per square mile. Thus, as distances increase (that is, as density measured by house per square mile decreases) and response time increases, property loss due to fire also increases. Population served also is positively associated with increases in property loss. The ISO rating, per capita building inspectors' salaries, training hours, fire department budget per capita, income, and the two building measures seem to have no effect on property loss. This seems strange, as some of those variables affected the number of fires (in equation 1) and would be expected to have some impact on property loss. But such effects may wash out. For example, one would expect per capita income to positively affect property loss because higher income means that there is more valuable property that can be destroyed by fire. However, the higher the income, the greater the demand may be for fire department services which would be felt in a larger number of companies and therefore a lower response time. This may or may not be the case, and the analysis does not indicate whether this linkage exists.

Equation 3 probes into variables associated with the ISO rating. It should be remembered that a numerically lower ISO rating means a lower fire insurance premium; thus, negatively associated variables indicate policies to pursue. The results contain some surprises. One would expect the ISO rating to worsen with increased number of fires per person and increased average loss per fire, but neither seems to affect the rating. Prevention functions, such as the percent paid and the per capita budget, have the expected negative sign, as does the percentage of buildings in manufacturing and the percentage of houses built prior to 1939. Climate variables should be expected to have a positive impact on ISO rating, that is the rating should worsen with adverse weather. This, however, seems to be the case only for precipitation, and not for temperature.

The fourth equation focuses on the total expenditures for building inspection personnel, which is a measure of prevention. An increase in fires is associated with an increase in this dependent variable, as is the variable related to prevention. The other variables do not seem to be related.

Finally, the fifth equation deals with the factors related to the size of the fire department budget. The total number of fires, the total fire department prevention services, the percent paid, training hours, area in square miles, percent of tall buildings, and per capita tax are all associated with increases in the budget, while the ISO rating and per capita building inspectors' salaries tend to decrease the budget.

Conclusions based on the analyses

These findings are clearly tentative and require further research before they can be directly useful as policy recommendations. One intriguing conclusion seems to be the role of fire prevention (through building inspectors' salaries per capita) in equation 5 in decreasing the overall fire department budget, and also with prevention (through total municipal prevention) in equation 1 in decreasing the number of fires. Whether prevention activities are cost-effective is a matter for future studies. This is a rather critical area for resource allocation strategies in the fire protection service.

The results of this type of study are highly sensitive to the choice of variables to be included in each equation. This choice should be made on theoretical grounds, but in some cases it is not clear whether a variable should be included or excluded. The authors of this study have generally been careful in their choice of the variables to include or to omit from each equation. There are some other analyses in this study which select different variables and emerge with somewhat different results. Furthermore, in the future there are likely to be additional analyses of this type which will use different variables and as a result may produce different conclusions.

It should also be borne in mind that an analysis such as this cannot hope to cover all the special cases of each particular community and generally represents a sort of "average" community behavior. Thus, the main conclusion about the usefulness of fire prevention in reducing costs may hold on the average, but not for certain communities. The effect that this study found may, for example, be due to prevention activities in commercial and industrial facilities and not in residential buildings. Thus, in some cities increased fire prevention activities may not be productive. The conclusions from the above analysis must, therefore, be regarded as tentative and suggestive, and not as definite as of this date.

Optimal specifications:
operations research approaches

The simultaneous equation model presented in the previous section can be thought of as a mathematical representation of the operations of the fire protection service (see Figure 14–8). The various input variables in the model can be classified into ten types, as follows:

1. *Effectiveness,* which includes fire incident rate and average loss per fire
2. *Prevention effort,* containing building inspectors' salaries per capita through inspections per house
3. *Suppression effort,* with variables representing response time through fire department budget per capita
4. *Size,* with variables of population served and area
5. *Socioeconomic factors,* including variables such as per capita income through percent of the population over sixty-five years old
6. *Construction,* with houses per mile through the percent of buildings over thirteen stories
7. *Industrial,* with the percent of buildings used in manufacturing
8. *Climate,* represented by annual precipitation, mean wind speed, and total days with temperature below thirty-two degrees Fahrenheit
9. *Government types*
10. *Per capita tax collections.*

The purpose of such a model is to find variables closely associated with the key output variables of ISO rating, number of fires, property loss, total budget, and prevention expenditures. This type of analysis then points to such relationships, suggesting ways to change departmental resource allocations for the various activities so that the output variables may be improved. As an illustration of this point, it should be noted that the analysis showed that shortened response times could be associated with decreases in property damage. However, the analysis does not discuss how to decrease response time. Each of the many possible ways of decreasing response time, which include adding new fire companies, changing fire company locations, improving communications strategies, and changing alarm assignments, would perhaps meet this goal. However, each would also have different budgetary consequences and therefore each would have a different impact on total system costs. Which strategy is best?

The above analysis can only answer such a question after the fact, that is after an experiment has been run. But in general it is undesirable to run experiments on this scale, that is, one does not want to build an alternative set of firehouses to test new deployment patterns. Fortunately, there is a method of running experiments through using a more detailed mathematical model of the fire department's operations, that is, by running a simulated experiment. This type of experiment uses operations research techniques. Not only do such techniques have the potential to address the specific area in which performance may be improved, but they can also compare present operations (and productivity) with the performance that would occur if proposed changes were made. In this way differences in productivity can be assessed without any changes actually being made in the real world.

The limitation of this type of analysis is that it is generally microscopic, that is, it is limited to a single phase of departmental operations. Consequently, it is possible to develop results which may improve performance in a single area but may worsen performance in a second area. For example, by reducing the number of personnel in fire companies in an analysis it is possible to create new fire companies, each with fewer personnel at minimal cost. While this type of strategy might reduce average response time, property damage might increase because the smaller fire companies might not be able to handle damage as well as the former larger companies. If the only measure from this type of analysis is response time, what might be in reality an overall decrease in service would appear to be an improvement. Usually these analyses are limited to a single variable of interest, so that fire service managers need to use their systematic views of fire service operations to ensure that model results are properly evaluated. To put it another way, analytic model results are not a substitute for informed judgment; rather, they need to be consistent with informed judgment.

The major contributions of operations research models lie in two areas, which are discussed below. The first is the study of congestion, called *queuing*, in which the delays that occur while individuals are waiting for service are related to the number and types of servers. Such models are naturally important in the fire protection service because it is important to the overall mission to reduce delays between the time that a fire alarm is received and the time that the first-in company arrives. Queuing studies are useful for determining the number of fire companies to have, the number and location of alarm boxes they should cover, the best patterns for redeploying fire companies after a large fire depletes coverage in an area, and similar issues. The second area is called mathematical programming and is primarily oriented to resource allocation decisions in the absence of congestion. These models have been employed for locating fire stations in smaller communities and for determining the best work schedules for firefighters.

Queuing

A typical time profile for a fire vehicle is shown in Figure 14–9. At t_1 an incident occurs and at t_2 the incident has been reported to the fire alarm dispatcher by alarm box or telephone. Then the dispatcher checks to find an available fire company (in a firehouse, or in-service on the radio) and directs the company to respond to the incident. Upon receipt of the alarm at t_3, the company travels to the fire. Extinguishment operations begin at t_4 and are over by t_5, at which point the company is now available to respond to the next incident. The time from t_2 to t_4 is clearly a very important interval, because during this time a fire may be spreading and the fire vehicle has not yet arrived on the scene. The interval from t_1 to t_2 is similarly important, although there is little that the fire service can do to reduce it. The interval from t_4 to t_5 is also important, although in a different sense because during this interval the company is unavailable to respond to other incidents. If another incident should occur the next nearest vehicle would have to respond, perhaps with a more lengthy travel time.

To illustrate the nature of queuing models, it might be well to consider a city with a single fire company and to assume (for the sake of simplicity) that if the fire company is busy any subsequent fire calls must wait until the company is free. We might assume, as well, that the travel time is negligible (that is, $t_1 - t_3 = 0$). These assumptions are, naturally, unrealistic for a fire company but they fit dispatching (when there is a single dispatcher) quite well. This model is shown in Figure 14–10.

We might assume that calls for service arrive exactly once per half hour and each call lasts exactly fifteen minutes. Under these assumptions, which are called *deterministic*, we have sketched a time history of the process. At 6:00 the first call arrives; it lasts for fifteen minutes. Then the company returns to quarters to await the second call, which arrives at 6:30. No one has to wait for service and it can be seen that, in general, the firefighters are idle half the time. (To put it another way, they are used half the time, thus the utilization rate is $\frac{1}{2}$.) We could conclude that the service is not provided productively; thus, if the community had two such firehouses next to each other one should be shut down.

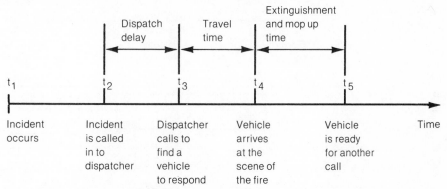

Figure 14–9 Typical time profile for a fire vehicle.
(Source: Adapted from Edward J. Beltrami,
Models for Public Systems Analysis,
New York: Academic Press, 1977, p. 77.)

Congestion in systems occurs typically because of the unpredictable nature of the arrival system and because the length of time that the extinguishment process takes is generally unknown. We might return to the model in Figure 14–10 and now assume that the average (or mean) arrival rate is two alarms per hour and the mean service (extinguishment) time is $\frac{1}{4}$ hour, but now both the exact time between alarm arrivals and the exact time for service are both random, although the averages are known. Therefore, on the average the company still remains idle half the time. However, now the following type of situation could occur (see Figure 14–10). The company could receive a call at 6:15 and a second one at 6:20. This second call might have to wait until 6:35 before the company was able to respond.

The mathematics of this situation are elementary. Denote by λ the mean arrival rate and by μ the mean service rate (= 1/mean service time). Then the average time a fire would wait for service is given as $\lambda/[\mu(\mu - \lambda)]$. In this situation, where $\lambda = 2$ and $\mu = 4$, the average waiting time would be a quarter of an hour. This is in spite of the fact that half the time the fire unit is in quarters.

To extend this simple method somewhat further, we might suppose that instead of an average of two calls per hour there is an average of three calls per hour. This would appear to still leave a comfortable margin, as the fire company would now be idle an average of fifteen minutes out of every hour. However, inserting 3 for λ into the equation shows that the average waiting time would now be three-quarters of an hour. Thus, while the number of calls has increased by only one per hour on the average, the delay has tripled. These results seem

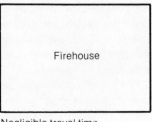

Negligible travel time

Deterministic model

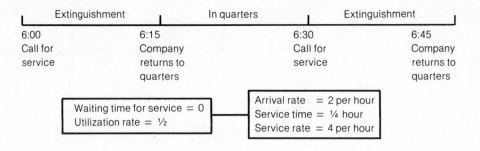

Probabilistic model

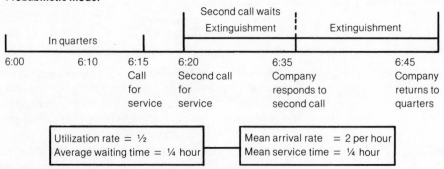

Figure 14–10   Simple queuing model for a city
with a single fire company.

incredible to people who hear them for the first time, but experience with congestion situations usually verifies such results.

We might now assume that this hypothetical city is considering three plans (Plans A, B, and C) to improve the delivery of fire service. In Plans A and B a new company is added to the firehouse. In Plan A the old company and the new company divide the work load, with the old company responding to all the even numbered boxes and the new company to all the odd numbered boxes. When two even numbered boxes arrive in succession, they both belong to the old company even if the new company is idle. The second box then waits until the old company is available. In Plan B the companies share the entire city but alternate responses, thus the first company will respond on the first alarm while the second company takes the next one. In this case a fire waits for service only if both companies are busy at the same time. Finally, Plan C does not add a new company but doubles the number of people who work in the original company. We shall assume that this will halve the average service time.[18] Using λ (arrival rate) = 3 and μ (service rate) = 4, we can now compute the effects of these changes on the average waiting time as follows:

Plan A: arrival rate halved, thus
  average waiting time = 1.5/4(4 − 1.5) = 0.15 hours or 9 minutes

Plan B: average waiting time = 0.016 hours or slightly less than 1 minute[19]

Plan C: service time halved, thus
  average waiting time = 3/8(8 − 3) = 0.075 hours or 4 minutes 30 seconds.

These results are also somewhat startling. Plan B is better than 4.5 times more effective than Plan C and 9 times more than Plan A, although each requires roughly the same level of expenditure.

This model is really more illustrative of the dispatching procedure than of fire vehicle response patterns because, so far, the effects of distance and, therefore, of travel time have been ignored. To extend the analysis to handle distance and also the second-in and third-in vehicles, it is generally necessary to construct a computer simulation model of fire department operations.[20]

A schematic description of a simulation model which would allow experimentation with various policies is seen in Figure 14–11. In such a model the user

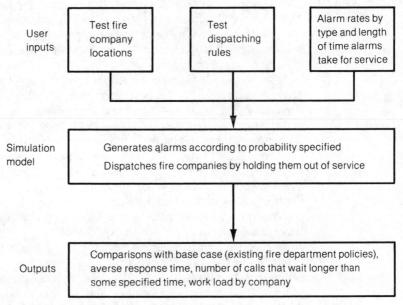

Figure 14–11 Simulation model of fire department operations.

would provide test values for *new locations of fire companies* (possibly additional companies as well); *dispatching results,* such as the geographic locations for which each company is to be first-in, second-in, etc., and the number of vehicles to respond to each call; and also *alarm rates,* which would include the number of alarms per hour broken down by type of alarm (structural fire, outside fire, false alarm, etc.). The user need not always provide all the values but could use the prevailing values already stored in the computer. Thus the user could assess the impact of a 20 percent increase in alarms on existing operations. Similarly, the user might want to test changes in response patterns with the same number of companies as at present. The computer simulation model would generate alarms by location and type of fire, would assign companies to each alarm, and would hold them out of service for a length of time equal to the sum of the travel time plus the amount of time for operation. In some implementations of this type of simulation, the computer model may also allow the time for operations to increase as travel time increases, which would simulate the effect of fire conditions worsening with increasing response delays. The simulation would then report various statistics back to the user, including the average response time, the number of alarms serviced by each company (work load), and the number of alarms that were estimated as waiting longer than some specified interval before the first-in company arrived. Comparisons between these measures and the base case measures consisting of the present strategies can be produced as part of the output from simulation models. These comparisons can be used not only to assess current productivity levels but also to assess potential levels under different resource allocation decisions.

Mathematical programming

A simulation model allows testing of various alternatives but is generally not helpful in deciding what alternatives exist. It can easily occur that specification and testing of the best decisions (for example, in terms of some measure of response time) simply elude the user. For this reason simulations are usually used together with analytical models which can create a large number of alternatives and then find the optimum. The optimum is usually defined in terms of a single output measure such as minimizing the average response time. Multiple output measures are the feature of simulations but add a significant amount of additional complexity to mathematical programming optimization models. As a result the simulation models are often used to test a range of solutions produced by mathematical programming.

Analytic models have been used for the location of firehouses, the design of response districts, and the best redeployment of companies when coverage is depleted owing to second or higher alarms. For example, a study of the fire department in Denver, Colorado, was oriented toward finding the best location of firehouses in order to find the smallest number of fire companies and their locations so that the average response time and the maximum response time did not exceed certain specified levels.[21] This model was developed in a close relationship between the analysts and the department and as a result was sensitive to the needs of the fire protection service. Although these types of models do not usually do so, this one carefully considered any new firehouse construction and was biased toward using existing facilities in order to avoid excessive capital costs. The department also indentified major hazards in the city by specifying maximum possible response times to such hazards. A range of solutions from twenty-two to thirty-six firehouses (the current level was then twenty-seven) was produced by the model and ranked in terms of response times. The model demonstrated that a configuration of twenty-five firehouses could produce response times at least as good as the existing twenty-seven firehouses. As a result the city adopted a plan calling for an eventual elimination of two pumper companies and three ladder companies with no resulting deterioration of response time. It was estimated this recommendation would save about $2.8 million over a staged six year elimination period, with an annual saving of $1.2 million thereafter. This was an improvement in productivity, as better services were delivered at a lower cost.

The need for close cooperation

The Denver research and the work of the New York City–Rand Institute is mathematically complex and typically beyond the capabilities of a community fire protection service to initiate on its own. The success of these two studies and others like them is attributable to a close working relationship between the fire service managers and the consultants. It cannot be emphasized strongly enough how important this exchange is. Mathematical models are only approximations of reality, not reality in themselves. Thus, the role of fire service managers in this relationship is to ensure that the models contain enough reality to be appropriate for their needs. Managers should insist that the mathematics be explained to them on a level that they can understand, so that they can contribute to the conceptual development of the models.

Conclusion

The first major section of this chapter began by asking: What impact does the opening of a new firehouse have on productivity? It then asked a number of questions about whether other improvements are productive. Finally, it asked: What is productivity?

Conceptually, productivity is the ratio of output measures to input measures. Output measures and input measures are difficult items to define so that it becomes almost impossible to collect data. Thus, while property damage averted and lives saved are important outputs of the fire service, these can only be measured indirectly. Furthermore, there is no agreement on how to measure them. For the measurable items, such as response time, the important causal linkage between these items and property damage has yet to be established. How much is it worth to reduce average response time from three to two minutes?

A systems view of fire department operations provides a partial solution to this problem. We define total system costs as the total of expenditures for fire protection *plus* losses due to fire. Such a measure omits human casualties and therefore certainly understates total system costs. *But it is better to work with an underestimate than with no estimate at all.* The measures presented in this chapter for total system costs are an even lower underestimate, as they omit other costs.

From the viewpoint of total system costs we can define any policy, program, or improvement as *productive* if it reduces total costs. This is certainly a valid beginning.

With this total system costs framework, a community can compare itself with other communities or it can assess its own performance over time. These comparisons need to be made with considerable care to ensure that the data are comparable in manner of data collection and in reasonable similarity of communities compared. A community cannot conclude from such an analysis that it has a productive fire protection service; it can only find that its department appears to be the same, better, or worse than others. Better measurements and new data available in the future will make these comparisons more meaningful.

Once such a comparison is made, the next important issue is the strategy used to improve productivity. Again, the research seems to fall very short of the needs of the practitioners. This chapter included an analysis of a sample of cities which examined the factors most highly associated with some output measures. The research was based on too small a sample and too limited a model to be ready for immediate generalization to all communities. Nonetheless, the results are intriguing and the analysis is competent. It is likely that additional research of this type will be performed and disseminated in the future.

Another set of useful tools for the fire service manager are those used by operations research analysts. These have been successfully implemented with important cost savings in several communities. An important contributing factor to this success was the close working relationship between the analysts and the fire service managers.

Thus, it would seem that research into productivity assessment and improvement in the fire protection service is just beginning. In the near future, at least, it will remain a significant challenge. The reward will be the delivery of superior services to the community.

1 Research Triangle Institute (RTI), International City Management Association (ICMA), and National Fire Protection Association (NFPA), *Municipal Fire Service Workbook,* prepared for the National Science Foundation, Research Applied to National Needs (Washington, D.C.: Government Printing Office, 1977).

2 Harry E. Hickey, *Public Fire Safety Organization: A Systems Approach* (Boston: National Fire Protection Association, 1973). The author develops a systems perspective on the fire protection service and then applies this perspective to its organization.

3 For further discussion of the theoretical issues involved, see: James M. Buchanan and Marilyn R. Flowers, "Local Government Expenditures: An Overview," in *Management Policies in Local Government Finance,* ed. J. Richard Aronson and Eli Schwartz (Washington, D.C.: International City Management Association, 1975), pp. 25–41.

4 This project is discussed in greater detail in: The Urban Institute, *The Struggle to Bring Technology to Cities* (Washington, D.C.: The Urban Institute, 1971), pp. 31–40.

5 RTI, ICMA, and NFPA, *Municipal Fire Service Workbook,* pp. 17–49.

6 Ibid, pp. 17–21.

7 Ibid, pp. 53–62.

8 For the discussion in this section, see: ibid., pp. 25–35. Some of this information also appears in Research Triangle Institute (RTI), International City Management Association (ICMA), and National Fire Protection Association (NFPA), *Evaluating the Organization of Service Delivery: Fire,* prepared for the National Science Foundation, Research Applied to National Needs (Research Triangle Park, N.C.: Research Triangle Institute, Center for Population and Urban–Rural Studies [1977; no longer available]).

9 RTI, ICMA, and NFPA, *Municipal Fire Service Workbook,* pp. 31–32.

10 Ibid., pp. 39–49.

11 Philip S. Schaenman et al., *Procedures for Improving the Measurement of Local Fire Protection Effectiveness* (Boston: National Fire Protection Association, 1977); this study was a joint effort of The Urban Institute (Washington, D.C.) and the National Fire Protection Association.

12 The nine participating communities were: Charlotte, North Carolina; Dallas, Texas; Fairfax County, Virginia; Lynn, Massachusetts; Newark, New Jersey; Portland, Maine; St. Petersburg, Florida; San Diego, California; and Seattle, Washington.

13 Schaenman et al., *Improving the Measurement of Local Fire Protection Effectiveness,* p. 74.

14 Ibid., p. 41.

15 Ibid., pp. 12–26.

16 RTI, ICMA, and NFPA, *Evaluating the Organization of Service Delivery: Fire,* pp. 10:1–41.

17 A good technical treatment of simultaneous equation models is found in: J. Johnston, *Econometric Methods,* 2nd ed. (New York: McGraw-Hill Book Company, 1972). See, especially: Chapters 12 and 13.

18 A similar example is provided by: Edward J. Beltrami, *Models for Public Systems Analysis* (New York: Academic Press, 1977), p. 73.

19 This analysis requires slightly more complex mathematics. The results are for a M/M/2 queue. See: Beltrami, *Models for Public Systems Analysis,* p. 75.

20 G. Carter, E. Ignall, and W. Walker, *A Simulation Model of the New York City Fire Department: Its Use in Deployment Analysis,* New York City–Rand Institute Report P–5110–1 (Santa Monica, Calif.: Rand Corporation, 1975).

21 Donald R. Plane and Thomas E. Hendrick, "Mathematical Programming and the Location of Fire Companies for the Denver Fire Department," *Operations Research* 25 (July–August 1977): 563–78.

15 Training and education

In the not too distant past the image of a firefighter held by both the general public and governmental officials was that of someone whose sole requirement for employment was physical strength. Even fire service administrators (chief officers) saw themselves as overseers of a manipulative skills occupation. Most administrative types of functions were fulfilled by personnel in other areas of the government. A typical remark by a mayor, city manager, or county administrator was, ''Chief, you just worry about putting out the fires and we'll worry about everything else.''

This type of remark was repeated so often by so many people that this concept of the firefighter was considered an unquestioned truth. It was further reinforced by the fact that the generally poorly paid low status job attracted dedicated individuals who simply performed their required tasks.

Then, several years ago, a quiet revolution began.

Personnel both inside and outside the fire service began to recognize that there were many varied skills required to perform satisfactorily. Not only were the manipulative skills of the back step firefighter involved, but there was a range of complex tasks, from that of the pumper operator to the budgetary controls of the chief officers.

In addition, the fire service began to experience a growing interest on the part of private industry in its search for new outlets for scientific developments. Also, the federal government, through its many agencies, began to make funds available for basic research.

Thus, in recent years some changes in the organizational structure of the fire service have begun to take place in recognition of this new emphasis. Today managers both inside and outside the fire department recognize that there is a need to upgrade those personnel already within the system as well as to equip new firefighters with the information required to cope with the changing environment. The key to accomplishing these new goals falls to those involved in the field of fire service training and education.

For this reason, those individuals responsible for training and educating firefighters are among the most important members of the team. This chapter is intended to outline their role and to place it within a general managerial perspective.[1]

The chapter, which is divided into seven major sections, approaches its subject by discussing the basic framework for training and education in the fire service, including types of training, the importance of management support, the placement of the training function within the organization, and the responsibilities of training personnel.

The second major section presents a detailed discussion of the development of a training program; planning, course determination, curriculum development, the delivery system, and measurement techniques and evaluation are all dealt with in this section. Development of an educational program is the subject of the third major section. The remainder of the chapter covers the scheduling of training, training record systems, qualifications for training personnel, and physical facilities for the training program. The chapter closes with a brief summary.

The basic framework

Three definitions

Fire service personnel receive their training and education in many ways and from many sources. The basic transfer of skills as well as the maintenance of these skills occurs at drills. A drill can be defined as a planned, organized practice session, conducted by the local officer, covering a single, specific topic. It usually takes place in or near the individual fire station and involves small groups from the station or battalion. Some examples of drills would include practice of hose layouts, ladder raises, advancing of attack lines, knot tying, and placement of salvage covers.

Drills can be contrasted with formal training sessions, which are structured, planned classes conducted by an individual skilled in the educational process. Training classes are usually conducted at a central location and cover an entire subject area. Subjects which are covered under the heading of training sessions would include recruit firefighting, an emergency medical technician class, pump operation, and aerial ladder operation.

Finally, there are formal educational classes, conducted by either a two year or four year college. Classes conducted under their auspices involve academic subject areas which fire service personnel need to understand to perform their job in the modern technological society. A class in fire service administration, for example, provides an understanding of administrative theory and the principles of personnel administration rather than presenting the specific procedures of an individual department. In the technical area, for example, chemistry provides an understanding of the combustion process and of the fundamental principles for the recognition of hazardous and flammable materials.

There are basic differences in drills, training, and education. Drills reinforce training which has already occurred; training provides the specific skills level needed on the job; while education gives the basic knowledge and understanding of both the technical and managerial requisites for administering the fire service.

Management support

Anthony Granito makes the following statement:

A good training program is undoubtedly the single most important factor in producing and maintaining a high level of proficiency in any fire department. It not only produces high efficiency initially, but also affects future efficiency when we consider that the rawest recruit now being trained may be chief of department or at least a senior officer in 20 or 30 years.[2]

Obviously, one of the most important keys to a successful fire service is the level and type of training given. To gain an understanding of what is needed for a successful training program, the manager will need to look at the personnel aspect of the fire service. Herein lies the ingredient that is basic to the success of the program.

Fire service training is an extremely specialized subject. There is a need not only for knowledge of the firefighter skills, but also for knowledge of the techniques of educating adults. Not every officer can become involved in the training function. It takes an individual with the technical and educational skills required—as well as dedication, enthusiasm, and drive—to make the program viable. This is where management support becomes an important factor.

If positions in the training group are looked upon solely from the viewpoint of a vacant officer's opening and filled without consideration for interest, the results could be disastrous. High turnover in training positions might indicate that individuals are taking the promotion solely for the new rank and are attempting to transfer as soon as it is practical. Apart from the loss to the training group of continuity and educational skills, such individuals lack credibility with the students. Thus, the training program degenerates to a boring, repetitive manual skills course lacking imagination. The entire fire department suffers from this promotional decision.

Management will have to arrive at alternative methods of selecting and promoting individuals in the training area. Suggestions for accomplishing this are provided later in the chapter.

The organization chart

Management has several options for placing the training function within the organization. The placement will depend on the size of the department and the importance placed on training by the administration.

In a small department it is possible to use a senior level officer (chief's rank) as a training officer as part of the normal collateral duties. However, this is not usually satisfactory, because training requires the training officer's attention.

Consequently, even small departments will need an individual whose specific job is training. This person's rank will vary with the relative importance placed on the tasks.

The most sensible arrangement is for the supervision of the training program to be at the chief officer or senior officer level. Since this individual will be directing and training personnel of all ranks, the high level is needed so that there is authority over the students. Creating the position at too low a level creates credibility problems as well as supervisory difficulties.

The decision as to whether to establish training as a separate division, to make it a part of an operating division, or to place it in a services division is dependent upon the needs of the individual department. One of the ingredients, however, remains the relative level of the senior training official.

One final option is open to administrators. The supervisor of the training function can be classified as a civilian. In this way an individual with an educational background but not necessarily a fire service background could be brought into the department. Before this alternative is implemented, however, administrators must be aware of the following drawbacks:

1. Possible morale problems
2. Possible lack of credibility because of lack of technical knowledge
3. Possible insensitivity on the part of the civilian to fire service needs and personnel.

The advantages of this organizational structure should also be considered. A civilian employee would be:

1. Motivated to work in the educational field
2. Interested in remaining in the position
3. Knowledgeable in the training field.

The responsibilities of the training personnel

The primary job of any training section is to survey the need, develop programs, and conduct the training classes. The work involves developing questionnaires, performing a needs analysis, establishing curricula, creating visual aids, preparing lesson plans, preparing course examinations, scheduling classes, and keeping training records.

But, as encompassing as the responsibilities are, training personnel have the knowledge and experience to handle a variety of other assignments.

Promotional examinations should be developed for all positions within the fire service. Whether at the entry level or at the chief officer level, the training staff is in the best position to provide the technical input. Even if the responsibility for conducting the examinations rests with the personnel department or civil service group, the technical information that can be supplied by the training staff is critical to the credibility of the examination.

At large fires or unusual calls, line personnel, particularly supervisors, are quite involved in handling the incident; coordination becomes difficult, with few individuals having an overall view of the incident. Training personnel should be dispatched on all multiple alarm fires or unusual calls to review the techniques used to carry out the operations. This review will serve the following purposes:

1. To advise the chief on problem areas and provide staff support on the scene
2. To form the basis of a critique with personnel and supervisors
3. To provide indications of subject material which needs to be covered through in-service training
4. To provide indications of subject material which should be added to the training program.

Many technical manufacturers have discovered in recent years that the fire service is a fertile area to tap. Because only basic level effort was expended in the past, the new technology can be applied to many aspects of fire service. Administrators are faced with a variety of claims for the new products, ranging from total safety protection to reduction of manpower. As budgets become more strained, the pressure to cope with reduced funds becomes greater. However, administrators must exercise care before purchasing new devices. The training staff can help by undertaking the following:

1. Conducting evaluations of the new equipment under simulated conditions, or supervising field use of some prototype models
2. Conducting surveys of fire departments already using the equipment
3. Reviewing existing literature on the success of other departments in solving similar problems.

Developing a training program

Developing a training program is a complex operation. Variables such as size of the department, use of career and/or volunteer personnel, and amount of the budget all affect the type of program. In addition, each department develops its training program to a different level.

To give comprehensive coverage, this section discusses the development of the training program from the planning stage, to course determination, to curriculum development, to course delivery and measurement and evaluation. Administrators and training personnel can bypass those areas which have already been incorporated and accomplished within their own program and can use those which will add to it. Figure 15–1 summarizes the required steps.

Planning the training program

The planning process for a training program cannot take place in a vacuum. Input from the field personnel is necessary, and their comments should be solicited. In addition to providing the planners with needed information, this will help produce a supportive attitude on their part toward the program.

Review of the organization   The first step in planning the training program is to look at the organization itself. The objectives and resources of the fire service as

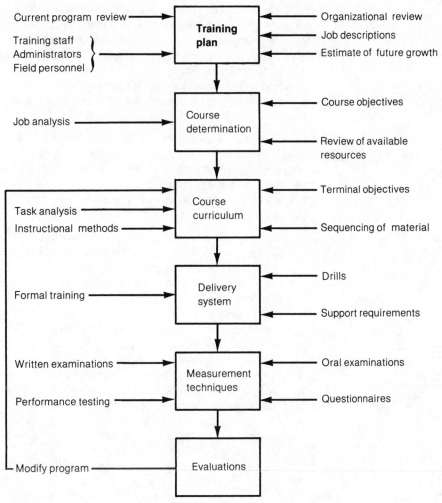

Current program review → **Training plan** ← Organizational review
Organizational review, Job descriptions, Estimate of future growth
Training staff, Administrators, Field personnel → Training plan

Job analysis → Course determination ← Course objectives, Review of available resources

Task analysis, Instructional methods → Course curriculum ← Terminal objectives, Sequencing of material

Formal training → Delivery system ← Drills, Support requirements

Written examinations, Performance testing → Measurement techniques ← Oral examinations, Questionnaires

Modify program → Evaluations

Figure 15–1 Steps in developing a training program.

well as the environment of the local government (budget, type of management, and long- and short-range goals) will all have an impact on the planning process.

At the outset there must be a clear understanding of the short- and long-range goals of both the political jurisdiction and the fire department. These should be stated in very broad terms.

From overall goals, the specific objectives of each of the divisions of the department should be established. The techniques for accomplishing the broad objectives should be prepared with all levels of staff taken into account, from division chief to the apparatus company level.

Objectives established in this manner will tend to be more dynamic and to change as needs and conditions vary, while long-term goals, if they are well thought out, will serve to keep the training program on track.

Next, the planning process should consider the resources available. A determination should be made in the following two areas:

1. The personnel resources needed to meet the goals
2. The equipment and facilities resources needed to meet the goals.

The political background and requirements of the local jurisdiction should be considered when the objectives are being written for personnel and equipment and facilities resources.

There should also be a commitment from management to support the meeting of goals and objectives through a training program. Bass and Vaughan report that "numerous studies show that lack of management support for the objectives of a particular training program reduces or eliminates its potential for serving the [organization]."[3]

Without this support the training program will be looked upon as a process to be endured but not followed. As a result, little change will take place.

Review of the job description Each position within the fire department should have a detailed job description prepared for it. By analyzing these detailed descriptions, training personnel can determine the course necessary for meeting the needs of the department.

For example, the job description of a firefighter might include the following as examples of duties:

1. Responds to fire alarms and other emergency or service calls on an assigned shift; lifts, carries, drags, lays, and connects hose lines and appliances; holds nozzles and directs fog or water streams; operates a water pressure pump; uses chemical lines, extinguishers, bars, hooks, rope lines, and other emergency equipment as necessary
2. Helps raise and climb ladders and makes forcible entry into burning buildings when necessary; makes openings in buildings and other structures for ventilation to dissipate smoke and gases and to facilitate effective firefighting
3. Performs first aid and other emergency medical services
4. Attends training sessions and participates in demonstrations as required
5. Periodically drives and/or operates emergency vehicles
6. Cleans, maintains, and assists in repairing fire and rescue equipment and apparatus and performs a variety of tasks in connection with the routine maintenance and repair of facilities
7. May assume the duties and responsibilities of officers in their absence
8. Maintains accurate records, forms, and incident reports as directed
9. Helps lift, carry, and run with cutting torches, hydraulic jacks, air compressors, stretchers, and other emergency equipment; performs rescues from hazardous sites employing ropes, ladders, and stairways
10. Performs salvage operations at the scene of the fire, such as covering furniture with salvage covers and using sawdust, brooms, mops, shovels, and other similar equipment
11. Performs overhauling operations to ensure that the fire is completely extinguished and that no walls or other structures that are in danger of falling remain at the scene of the fire
12. Replaces broken or ruptured sprinkler heads to prevent unnecessary water damage
13. Performs rescues from burning buildings and other hazardous sites, extricating and carrying victims, using ropes, ladders, and stairways
14. May serve a scheduled desk watch
15. Provides efficient and immediate emergency care to the ill or injured at the scene of an incident and during transport
16. Reports vital patient information regarding care and condition to the medical personnel receiving the patient transfer
17. Operates emergency care equipment
18. Receives radio, telephone, and telegraphic fire, emergency medical, and related calls
19. Obtains information on the nature and specific location of an emergency
20. Determines how calls should be answered in accordance with defined guidelines

21. Relays calls for assistance by radio, telephone, or other alarm devices to the appropriate fire department, rescue squad, or other agencies
22. Dispatches equipment with a degree of independent judgment and responsibility in emergency situations
23. Implements established mutual aid plans
24. Receives and relays to appropriate agencies general problems received
25. Maintains a record of the movement and location of all fire and rescue units
26. Records all communications received and transmitted, as well as the subsequent action taken.

On the basis of this list training personnel can review the need for training versus the training plan. Are the classes covering the operation of emergency care equipment? Are the field people being taught how to complete the proper reports? Are the mutual aid plans adequately covered? As each job skill is studied and the questions answered, the planning of the training program progresses.

Review of the current program Every fire department has some sort of training program. No matter how informal this program is, it should be carefully studied. During the study, the administrator should look at the following:

1. Subjects covered
2. Written material
3. Visual material
4. Equipment
5. Records
6. Budget
7. Tests and examinations.

Comparison of the current program with the needs developed by studying the overall goals and the job descriptions provides the basis for developing the training plan.

Future growth projection Finally a "best guess" estimate of the future of the department must be made. Using the short- and long-term objectives of the community, training planners must project the need for the following:

1. New stations and manpower allocations
2. New services (paramedics, hazardous materials response teams)
3. New equipment (automated pumpers).

Planners should study alternatives and other ways of accomplishing the goals and should evaluate each alternative in terms of training needs.

While this information is only a small part of the overall master fire defense plan (discussed in Chapter 6) it should be carefully studied to determine its impact on training.

Course determination

With the basics of planning completed, fire service administrators should determine the actual courses to be taught.

Job analysis Through use of the job descriptions prepared during the planning process, a detailed analysis of what is required to perform the job should be completed. This job analysis is a detailed breakdown of all the tasks performed and skills needed by an individual working at a particular level.

For the lower levels within the fire service, preparing a job analysis is relatively easy because most of the tasks are skill level and easily defined. However, as one moves up the scale to the supervisory levels, job analyses become increasingly complex.

A job analysis can be prepared by undertaking the following:

1. Watching the individual perform the task and noting each activity
2. Reviewing requests for training from field personnel and upper management
3. Interviewing the field personnel on their perceptions of what the job entails
4. Reviewing the fire service literature for job analyses performed by other fire departments
5. Conducting a survey using a questionnaire to determine the individual's perception of the job
6. Having the training personnel actually perform each task and noting the required steps.

While it is easy to list the components necessary to prepare a job analysis, actually accomplishing it is a lengthy process. Training personnel assigned to prepare the analysis should be given sufficient time to accomplish the job.

The setting of objectives   The key to a successful training program lies in establishing clear, concise objectives and in training the trainer. Mager points out the following:

When clearly defined goals are lacking, it is impossible to evaluate a course or program efficiently, and there is no sound basis for selecting appropriate materials, content, or instructional methods. . . . I cannot emphasize too strongly the point that an instructor will function in a fog of his own making until he knows just what he wants his students to be able to do at the end of the instruction.[4]

The basic reason for establishing objectives is to state the desired outcome of the course in specific terms. This outcome should be carefully stated and written, so that the desired intent is clear to all readers and means the same thing to each one.

Trainers should also exercise care in distinguishing between course content and specific objectives. For example, the statement, "Practice with ladders will be conducted," is a description of one of the activities of the course. Contrast that with the objective which might say, "The student shall demonstrate how to raise and place a thirty-five foot ladder in thirty seconds as part of a two person team."

The three steps to preparing an objective are as follows:

1. Determining the specific behavior that the student will actually exhibit as evidence of having learned the skill. In the example above, the specific behavior is to demonstrate the action. Other key words which could be used include *write, recite, compare, list, identify,* and *construct.*
2. Determining the conditions under which the student will exhibit the learned skills. Again, using our example, the conditions require that the student raise the thirty-five foot ladder, place the ladder, and be part of a two person team. If a department had both wooden and aluminum ladders the objective would specify the requirement that both kinds must be raised and placed.
3. Determining the parameters for measuring the student's performance. The example used a time limit of thirty seconds. Other parameters could include answering written or oral questions or making comparisons against a standard performance list.

It is important to remember that most objectives will have all three elements. In some cases it will not be possible to include them all. The test of whether there is a clear objective is if the answer to the following questions is yes:

1. If a fire training supervisor were given the objective and a student to perform it, would the supervisor and the objective writer both agree on a competent performance by the student?
2. If a student performed the objective more than once in exactly the same manner, would the evaluation be consistent?

Finally, it is not necessary to include the entire objective in a single sentence. As the skills get more complex, it will take additional sentences to describe the objective desired. The final criterion for the acceptability of an objective is its clarity.

Course selection   Now that course objectives have been written, they can be combined to create a group of programs which will answer the identified needs. If one of the objectives is: "To require all new firefighters to complete all of the objectives of the Firefighter II program identified in NFPA 1001[5] within six months of being hired," then the training staff knows what level of courses is necessary.

A typical fire department that also provides an emergency medical services delivery system might determine the need for the following courses:

1. Recruit level firefighting
2. Advanced skills for firefighters
3. Firefighter refresher training
4. Emergency vehicle driving
5. Pump operation and hydraulics
6. Aerial ladder operation
7. First level supervision training
8. Mid-management training
9. Hazardous materials incidents
10. Emergency medical technician
11. Cardiopulmonary resuscitation
12. Paramedic
13. Instructor training.

Each of these has been included because the goals of the community and fire department when translated into specific objectives have identified them. There may be a great community desire to teach cardiopulmonary resuscitation to civilians, and the fire department will incorporate this desire into one of its objectives. It will then fall to the training staff to develop, schedule, arrange for instructors and space, advertise, teach, and certify the course.

A careful analysis of each of the goals and objectives must be made to ensure that they are all covered by appropriate programs.

Available resources   It would be very difficult for the training staff to design, implement, and teach all of the courses noted above. The work load and the required expertise are beyond the capability of many training staffs. For this reason other sources must be investigated.

In recent years an increasing number of two year colleges have offered advanced work in fire science subjects. Funding exists, and specialized instructors are available for some of the advanced educational classes. At this point it is important to remember the distinction between education and training.

Four year colleges offering degrees in engineering, public administration, and urban studies are another source of information. These institutions should be surveyed to determine what courses are open to fire service personnel. Many classes are offered off-campus; therefore, research should not be restricted to local schools. Training personnel might approach schools in other areas and should find out how many students would be required for specialized classes to be conducted in their jurisdictions.

Graduate study is another available resource. While the number of fire service personnel pursuing advanced degrees is small, the next few years will see a greatly increasing amount. As with the undergraduate courses, there are many off-campus facilities available.

In many areas vocational or trade schools will provide courses for fire service personnel. The particular classes vary, but in many states there is a highly developed delivery system to bring firefighter training into the field.

Almost every state has a statewide fire training program. While their location in the organization chart varies, these programs all provide training classes at the local jurisdiction and at a central campus. Some state programs emphasize skills level training, while others cover such advanced subjects as staff and command, instructor training, management techniques, and handling hazardous materials incidents.

Several governmental agencies and national associations conduct regional training programs. The National Fire Academy of the U.S. Fire Administration develops training programs which are taught throughout the country. Students from these classes can then go out and teach in their local jurisdictions. Classes covering a wide diversity of subjects such as pesticide incidents, instructor training, and arson investigation are being taught.

The U.S. Department of Transportation and the U.S. Environmental Protection Agency also conduct training courses in specialized areas. Training personnel need to keep abreast of these offerings.

Many of the national fire service organizations conduct yearly conferences as well as professional development programs. The International Association of Fire Chiefs, the International Society of Fire Service Instructors, and the National Fire Protection Association (NFPA) hold one or two conferences a year. In addition, they sponsor training programs on such subjects as hazardous materials, understanding the fire safety codes, and management techniques.

Within a fire department's immediate area, other local jurisdictions conduct training classes. The areas of specialized knowledge of the officers of these other departments varies greatly. Training personnel should explore the possibility of running joint training classes utilizing these special skills. Expenses for such classes could be distributed over several jurisdictions. (Further discussion of training and educational resources can be found in Chapter 4.)

Curriculum development for local programs

In the previous section the answers to the questions of who is to be taught and what courses will be taught were developed. The next question is what to include as the contents of the courses.

The objectives and goals of a particular fire service course have been established. With this as a basis the curriculum can be established. The steps of the process are: task analysis, terminal objectives, sequencing of the material, and selection of the instructional technique.

Task analysis The job description given earlier provided an overview of the types of tasks an individual would have to perform. That description is, by its very nature, broad in scope. At this point, however, it is necessary for training staff to get down to the specific. The preparation of a task analysis is therefore the next step.

A task can be defined as "a logically related set of actions required for the completion of a job objective. Stated another way, a task is a complete job element.''[6]

Each task to be performed should be listed. While much of this can be done from memory, the individual doing the analysis should actually watch the job being performed to complete the list.

For each task listed, an estimate of how frequently it is performed as well as its relative importance should be made. This will enable the trainer to make judgments on how much time should be spent learning each task.

Another factor which will influence learning time is the degree of difficulty of the task. The harder it is to master the skill, the more time it takes to teach it.

To collect this data in a systematic way a standard form should be utilized. A sample form is shown in Figure 15–2.

Job title

Task description	Performance frequency	Relative importance[1]	Degree of learning difficulty[2]

1 Use a scale of 1 to 3 to indicate relative importance, with 1 very important to 3 fairly unimportant.
2 Use a scale of 1 to 5 to estimate learning difficulty, with 1 very easy to 5 very difficult.

Figure 15–2 Sample task analysis record sheet.

As the curriculum is prepared, the trainer must apportion the time so that important items are stressed, difficult items are allotted enough teaching and practice times, and items that are performed frequently are stressed.

Finally, merely listing a task may not be enough to ensure that the subject is covered in depth. With some complex tasks it may be necessary to break down the task into its component parts. Thus, the trainer is assured that all the necessary parts of the task will be taught.

To illustrate this procedure we might consider the following example:

Task description: place and raise a thirty-five foot ladder
Performance frequency: twice a week
Relative importance: 1
Degree of learning difficulty: 2.

To ensure that the necessary information will be given to the student on how to perform this task, a detailed breakdown should be prepared, for example:

1. Removal of ladder from storage rack
2. Types of carries (two person flat or beam)
3. Placement of ladder
4. Calculation of distance from wall to base of ladder
5. Raising of ladder
6. Lowering of ladder.

If such a detailed study is not completed, the instructor may inadvertently omit a key portion of the process. Several detailed task analyses have been performed by research organizations and are available for use by trainers.

Terminal objectives   Earlier in this discussion, to determine what courses were necessary, course objectives were prepared. In the same way terminal objectives for the student upon completion of the class also need to be developed. The procedure is the same as that described in the course determination discussion.

The major difference between the task analysis and the preparation of the terminal objectives is that the task analysis covers all the steps necessary to accomplish the job; this includes information which has been learned previously either on the job or earlier in the course. On the other hand, the terminal objectives do not cover what has already been learned. As Mager says, the objectives "represent a clear statement of instructional intent, and are written in any form necessary to clarify that intent."[7]

Sequencing of material   The material for each course must be taught in a logical sequence. The trainer should prepare the outline so that foundation material is taught first, before proceeding to the more complex subject areas. Mager describes five techniques to use when determining the sequencing of material:

1. General to specific: cover the overall view first, gradually working down to specific procedures.
2. By interest: the first item to be taught is the one the student is most interested in. From here work to the areas of least interest but of required knowledge.
3. By logic: cover the material which needs to be used as the foundation first, and build upon this information.
4. By skill: teach the material by skill so that groups of subject areas are mastered separately.
5. By frequency: cover the skills which are needed most frequently first, working down to those least used.[8]

Instructional techniques   As the course curriculum is developed, a variety of instructional techniques can be used to present the material. Some material can be presented only in one way, while some can be approached from a variety of angles. The instructor should select a technique that will do the job and will also maintain interest in the subject. Several techniques are described below.

Lectures   The lecture method is the technique used most frequently. Here, the instructor merely stands in front of the students and speaks. For the most part it is a one way conversation, and the only interruptions are questions.

The most serious drawback to the lecture technique is its inability to take into account the different levels of students. Their capabilities, attitudes, and interests can vary so widely that the lecture may not reach them all. This can mean that a student's mind will wander from the subject. The best thing that can be said for the lecture is that it is inexpensive and is easy to prepare.

Demonstrations   The demonstration technique is an excellent one for teaching manipulative skills. This is a three step process entailing the following:

1. Demonstration of the skill by the instructor
2. Student practicing of the skill under the supervision of the instructor
3. Testing of the student to determine that the skill has been learned.

Discussion The discussion method is used when interaction between students is necessary. There is not usually an instructor as such, but a leader who guides the discussion and keeps it on track. This method is an effective way of getting conceptual data across as well as creating a change in attitudes.

Since there is a great deal of interaction, material which is unclear can be amplified and explained. This is the greatest advantage of the discussion over the lecture method. The students are led to ask questions, discover possible answers, and evaluate such answers as solutions. This leads to greater understanding and retention of material.

The key to successful use of the discussion technique is the leader. This individual must be able to keep the interest up, promote a learning atmosphere, and keep the conversation going. Care must be exercised to ensure that the leader does not turn the discussion into a lecture by assuming control of the conversation. There is a great deal of preparation for the leader if the discussion is to accomplish its goal.

Case studies The trainer can prepare in writing either an actual or a fictitious case history problem in the subject area to be studied. Through this case study method the student can develop an understanding of the principles being taught. Instead of a single, simple answer, the student learns that there are several ways to attack a problem, each with advantages and disadvantages. These must be weighed before a course of action is selected. Since each student will look at the problem in a different way, a number of alternative solutions can be explored by the group.

Role playing One of the best ways to learn how to deal with an issue is to observe the event actually occurring and then to decide on a course of action. In this method, the drama is brought to the classroom. Role playing involves preparing a script and using the trainees to play out the roles.

Usually the students chosen as participants are given sketchy information about the overall problem and the types of personalities involved. From this they improvise the script to produce play. The remaining students then discuss the outcome.

As with other teaching techniques there are major advantages and disadvantages. This method is not suitable for all types of subject material. In addition, the skill of the students in spontaneously developing the script is important. They should not overact, make facetious comments, or ridicule other personnel outside the context of the problem. Specific advantages are that the students participate; the technique simulates the real world; it teaches attitude importance; it gives practice in interpersonal skills; and students receive immediate feedback.

Simulation Training officers in fire ground command is a difficult process. A large scale fire is difficult to reproduce in the classroom. As a result, simulation techniques have become increasingly popular. There are basically two kinds of simulation: visual techniques and live techniques.

With a combination of slide and overhead projectors and special equipment it is possible to visually produce a simulated fire. The fire actually appears to be burning the building and can visually be increased or decreased in size. To add to the realism, communications equipment is added along with a dispatching system. Some departments project different views of the same incident in which the personnel coordinating the incident are unable to see the other views. This forces the officers to utilize the communications system.

A simulated exercise can be an excellent means of training individuals to handle a large scale incident. A staged hazardous materials accident with victims made up to simulate various injuries can provide training for firefighting as well as for emergency medical services. And officers can learn the problems of command as well as the need for a central operating post.

The success of each of these two techniques, however, lies in the realism with which the exercise is conducted. As the students become involved, the pace picks up and the tension builds. The instructors and evaluators need to prepare the problems very carefully to maintain the realism.

Figure 15–3 Simulator training room. (Source: Huntington Beach, California, Fire Department.)

Games Many games have been designed to illustrate the desired subject to be learned. These games can vary in length from an hour to as long as a week. They can be as simple as putting information on a sheet of paper, or they can be complex and can involve interaction with a computer. Subjects range from management styles, to personnel management, to teamwork.

The major advantage of this technique is the involvement of the student in the problem solving and the conclusions. Games can also illustrate the use of various management tools under active conditions.

One of the best uses of games in training fire service supervisors is the in-basket exercise. Each student is given an in basket of written materials such as incoming letters, memoranda, procedures, grievances, and meeting notices. The student then must make the decisions dealing with all of these pieces of paper. Some of these matters will be delegated to subordinates. Others will require preparation of a reply, while others may be answered directly by the student.

Again, the instructors will need to review many possible alternatives and establish some expected, standardized responses. The students can then discuss their solutions and the reasons they were chosen.

Programmed instruction Programmed instruction is a written presentation that provides step-by-step procedures and immediate feedback to the student concerning the understanding of the material.

The text is so written that, after providing some information, students must respond to questions. On the basis of the answers to the questions, the students are directed to other parts of the text. Where students give the wrong answer, further explanation is provided. If they answer correctly they move on to more complex material.

Many programmed texts have been prepared, and a variation of this procedure using computer terminals has been developed. In this latter method the information is displayed on a screen. After the text is read and understood, questions are presented. Using a keyboard, the student answers the questions. As with the written material, wrong answers cause a repeat of the descriptive material, while correct answers lead to the next step.

The delivery system

There are a number of different ways of delivering the training program to the field personnel. Each has its advantages and its disadvantages. Training personnel need to be familiar with the alternatives so as to select the method which will best meet the objectives. Two methods are discussed below.

Formal training Formal training is planned and conducted by training personnel. Specific courses with a standard curriculum are offered on a regular schedule.

Recruit training is given when a new group is hired; pump operation is given so that personnel can advance to this rank; and first level officer training is given so that personnel can complete the course before promotional examinations are conducted.

Formal training is conducted in a classroom setting (and through drill ground evolutions); the students are usually relieved of any responsibility for responding to emergency calls.

A standardized lesson plan, visual aids, and tests are used in the program to ensure that consistency is maintained between classes. Records are kept of the student's progress and final grade.

Drills Formal training can be contrasted with drills. Drills are conducted in-station, by the officer on duty. Personnel are usually available for emergency response during a drill.

The subject areas covered by drills are generally those at a skill level and need constant repetition for maintenance of a high level of readiness. Subjects such as hose lays, ladder raises, and salvage cover throwing are all in the category of drills. Such subjects as street, hydrant, and fire protection device locations can also be included in the drills.

One of the major responsibilities of a training staff is to ensure that the various shifts in the different stations perform their jobs in the same manner and to the same level of competency. This requires that a standard set of lesson plans be prepared. The officers who do the training must be taught the correct operational procedures so that they can use the lesson plans correctly. This type of standardization is critical to success at the scene of an incident.

Support requirements The support of both the full-time instructors and the field personnel requires that some material be prepared in advance. This material includes lesson plans, visual aids and equipment, and examinations.

Lesson plans for the formal training and for drills should be prepared and should provide in detail the material to be covered, the time necessary, and the objectives to be achieved.

Visual aids supplement the training program. They should not be the major part of the program, and they are not included to beautify the program or to provide entertainment to the students. Each visual should support the program and be an integral part of it. Students quickly recognize when a visual is used as a time filler and soon lose interest.

Granito states that visual aids are fairly easy to evaluate because they are intended to:

1. Focus attention on elements of an operation or system to make it more simple. An example of this is the use of slides to illustrate the many valves and special piping necessary in a dry pipe sprinkler system. Picking out parts of a system at one time isolates but also clarifies operations.
2. Stimulate the senses. For example a motion picture that attracts visual and audio attention to the working of an extinguishing agent such as Light Water.[9]

A specific type of equipment is required to display each type of visual aid. Training personnel should carefully consider the department needs and should select only a few types of visual aids. This will help reduce capital costs for expensive equipment that may be used infrequently. Consideration should also be given to sharing equipment with neighboring departments.

Examinations are useful for both the student and the instructional staff. They provide feedback on the program and on the level of understanding which has been achieved. Preparing a meaningful examination requires a certain skill and this skill should be provided to the instructor. A discussion of measurement techniques follows.

Measurement techniques

Measurement techniques vary with the accuracy required. For example, if you were asked to supply *approximately* fifty feet of rope your measurement technique would be different from what it would be if you were asked to supply *exactly* fifty feet of rope. This is also the case when tests are being used to measure what a student has learned in a particular class. The instructor must learn to select the correct measuring instrument for the technique selected. Micheels and Karnes make the following statement:

Test results can be useful in evaluating the accomplishment of individual students and classes, in comparing different methods of teaching, in helping to provide for individual differences, and in finding out where the supervisory program needs adjustment or change.[10]

There are basically four means of measuring achievement. These are: oral examinations, skills testing, questionnaires, and written examinations.

Oral examinations An instructor obtains feedback from the students as a class progresses by questioning the students many times during the session. This serves to indicate how well the subject matter is understood. Instructors should prepare oral questions for key learning points and should insert them directly in the lesson plan to ensure that they are covered during the class.

Skills testing Much of fire service training involves manipulative skills. It is necessary to demonstrate that a skill has actually been learned. Thus, the instructor needs to prepare a test which will require the use of a specific skill, will be repeatable, and will also be measurable.

One way of accomplishing this is to prepare a skills sheet detailing, step by step, the actual technique to be followed. Point values should be assigned for each step. If the skill requires a joint effort, then the value of each contributor needs to be established in advance. Finally, a time limit for the performance of the skill should be set.

Questionnaires When carefully prepared, questionnaires can determine the current knowledge of the personnel and can point to areas in which training is needed.

There are basically two types of questionnaires. The first asks for an opinion of what areas need improvement, while the other asks factual questions which indicate what levels of knowledge the field personnel have.

Training staff should be sure that their questions are clear, concise, and understandable. The analysis technique should also be determined in advance.

Written examinations Written examinations are the most commonly used measurement technique. A variety of questions can be asked. Each has its own advantages and disadvantages. The types of questions should be selected so that the objectives of the test are met. The test should be constructed according to the following steps:

1. List the behavioral objectives of the course
2. Review the curriculum for additional objectives (checking step)
3. Identify the expected student outcomes from each behavioral objective (inventorying step)
4. Prepare an outline of the number of test questions to cover each area of the subject (blueprint step)
5. Prepare test questions for each subject area in accordance with the blueprint
6. Prepare instructions for taking the test so that the students can complete it without asking questions
7. Review the test for clarity and grammar (and to ensure that the correct answer is not given away by the phrasing of the question)
8. Prepare the answer key (if an essay test is used, prepare the major points which must be included in the answer and assign a point value for each)
9. Analyze the test after it has been given and improve the questions.

Evaluations

Evaluation of the training program is critical. After investing a great deal of staff time and funds, fire service administrators need to have a way of determining whether the program is accomplishing its objectives.

To carry out the evaluation, training supervisors can use opinion surveys, observation of performance, or analysis of documentation.

Opinion surveys An opinion survey asks the trainee for reactions to the program. The specific good and bad points are enumerated. For best results the forms should be anonymous.

The instructor should first prepare a written comment sheet and distribute it to the students as soon as the class is finished. The form should be easy to read and to record so the results can be analyzed easily. The instructor should leave room for the students to make general comments. It is important to allow enough time for the form to be completed.

Once the results have been analyzed the instructor should revise the program as necessary. This kind of feedback is essential if training is to make an impact on field operations.

Observation of performance Training personnel can objectively observe the operations at the scene of an incident without getting intimately involved. For this reason, they make excellent evaluators of the procedures being used and of the areas which need training, from skills level to command level.

Analysis of documentation By reviewing such documentation as performance appraisal reports, injury reports, vehicle accident forms, and absenteeism reports, training personnel can get an indication of areas where training is needed.

Performance appraisals done by field supervisors very often point out skills with which the individual is having difficulty. If these same shortcomings are repeated in other personnel, remedial training may be necessary.

Injury and vehicle accident reports point up particular acts which are not being performed safely. Perhaps a defensive driving class with emphasis on approaching an intersection is necessary. Are there injuries from using an axe incorrectly? Are there smoke inhalation injuries because personnel are not wearing their breathing apparatus? All of these provide information on needed training.

Finally, absenteeism can be looked at for long-term or progressive injuries, as well as retirement costs. Classes in, for example, the correct way to lift heavy objects may be necessary.

It should be emphasized again that evaluation should lead to such corrective action as is necessary. Only then will a training program be meaningful.

Developing an educational program

As was stated early in this chapter, there is a difference between training and education: training provides the information required to perform on-the-job skills, while education gives the background and foundation for supervising and administering the fire service. Therefore, while much of the information given earlier in this chapter on developing a training program applies also to education, there is a modified procedure for developing an educational program. The major steps in the latter, as discussed below, are: planning the program, course determination, curriculum development, course delivery, and measurement and evaluation. The steps are the same as those for a training program, but the input to each varies. This can be seen in Figure 15–4.

Planning the educational program

Educational programs for the fire service usually involve regions rather than just the local department. Few departments are large enough to warrant a program exclusively for their own use. Therefore, input from all concerned parties should be sought. Personnel to include are: fire service administrators, training personnel, field personnel, educators, and budgetary officials. Each can provide information and expertise on the needs of the program that will help make it a success.

Approval authorities Whenever a college level program is to be used there are usually several local and state organizations that will have to approve the program. Individuals who are going to implement such a course will need to learn exactly who must approve the course so that the plan and the schedule can be established.

Review of the organizational objectives The organizational objectives were developed for the training program. These must now be analyzed in light of which goals will require training and which will require education.

Review of the current program The needs of the fire service personnel should be analyzed to see if they are being met by the training program. Areas which are not could be handled at the educational level.

Future growth projection College level programs for the fire service have had a dramatic increase in the last few years. This is particularly true of the two year

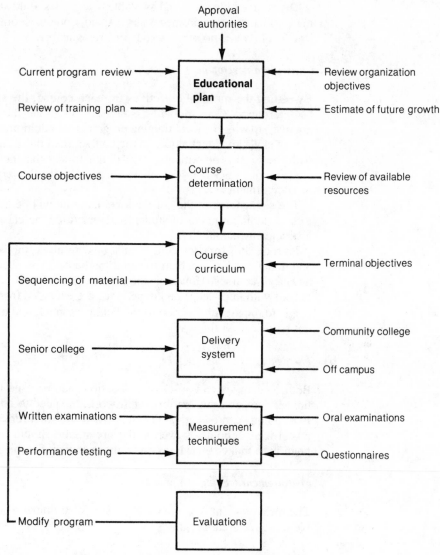

Figure 15–4   Steps in developing an educational program.

programs. However, as the number of fire service personnel who receive degrees increases there will be fewer individuals available for the program. The major infusion of personnel will then come from recent high school graduates without field experience. This will affect the programs because many of these students will want to attend on a full-time basis in preference to the part-time requirements of working firefighters.

The future should be evaluated carefully before the new program is initiated. How many current fire service personnel will attend? What will the enrollment be of recent high school graduates? What funding will be available? For how long a period will this pool of students be available? When all these questions have been answered, a decision can be made as to whether to proceed with the development of a program.

Course determination

During the planning of the training program, a determination of necessary courses was completed. The job analysis given for training programs also applies to educational needs.

The course objectives and available resources should all be looked at to determine which courses are necessary. Again, courses should be taught at the college level only if no other resources are available.

Curriculum development

By setting the terminal objectives for each course, the specific curriculum can be determined. Care should be exercised to see that the material covered does not overlap with the local training programs. In addition, if there is some discussion of skills level techniques in the course, then these should be in accordance with the local requirements. This is not to say that new ideas should be excluded, but rather that they should conform with the requirements of the local fire departments.

The sequencing of the college level material will be influenced by many factors, including number of students, demand for the class, funds available, and instructor availability.

Prerequisites for each course must be carefully established. Some knowledge and understanding of chemistry and mathematics is necessary for some of the advanced courses. However, the prerequisites should not be so rigid that individuals with knowledge and experience are excluded from the class. The objective is to impart information to the field personnel, and artificial barriers should not be placed in the way.

The delivery system

Both on-campus and off-campus locations can be used for the program. Since fire service personnel perform shift work, the need to commute a long distance to a campus can be a great obstacle. Arrangements for college classes off-campus at local schools or even in the fire station should be considered. The key point is to make the classes convenient enough for the students to attend.

Measurement techniques

The measurement techniques discussed for training programs are also applicable to educational programs.

Evaluations

Evaluations of college programs are usually made on a formal basis by the accrediting authority. The courses and curricula are carefully evaluated to see if the needs of the students are being met. Random questionnaires are sent to students and former students to see what areas of improvement are necessary.

Fire service administrators should also prepare periodic questionnaires on the college program for their personnel who are a part of the student population. Some of the techniques used for measuring training programs can be used for educational programs.

Feedback on the evaluation should be provided to the college administrators so that programs may be improved. Another suggestion is to implement an advisory board which will bring together the various interests to discuss the objectives of the program. Membership on this board could include: fire department personnel from each jurisdiction; emergency medical personnel; college program coordinators; high school counselors; and also vocational education representatives.

Educational programs are important to the success of a fire department. It takes good planning and a knowledgeable staff to make a program meaningful. Care should be taken to see that the steps are followed and that suggestions are implemented.

The scheduling of training

It is the task of the training staff to prepare a training schedule for in-service drills and formal training classes. In addition, in departments with career personnel, the training staff should ensure that firefighters on each shift receive the same classes and have an opportunity to attend the formal classes.

In-service drills

The training staff should prepare a schedule of topics to be covered by in-service drills. The instructors for these classes would be the field officers, who would use lesson plans prepared by the training division. The classes would be conducted in the field or at the training facility. These drills should also be scheduled at night so that practice can be obtained under conditions which more closely simulate an incident. However, safety precautions should not be jeopardized for a drill and alternative topics should be scheduled in case inclement weather causes outside work to be cancelled.

It is important to remember that each firefighter must be familiar with a vast array of information. Without continuous reinforcement in the form of drills the skill level will drop. This is what fire service administrators need to guard against.

Formal training classes

Classes conducted at the central training facility by the training staff are formal training classes. They are offered at regular intervals and follow the same curriculum each time a class is conducted.

Schedules for these classes should be planned so that firefighters can either be detailed to a class or can attend on their own time. For career personnel this would mean offering a course in the daytime and repeating it again in the evening. For volunteer personnel classes should be offered in the evenings and on weekends.

Administrators with both career and volunteer personnel should keep the schedule as flexible as possible. Classes should not be restricted just to one or the other. A volunteer who works nights should be able to attend daytime classes, even if the majority of the people in the class are career employees. This will ensure that the same training is offered to each group and will also promote good relations.

Training records systems

Every fire department, no matter how small, requires a system for recording information on the training completed. Whether the system is a simple index card file for 25 individuals in the department or a computer printout for 5,000 employees, the need is the same. These records should provide basic information on in-service drills, formal training, education, and special courses completed by all personnel. It is important that these records be kept up-to-date, as they can form the basis of management decisions.

The American Insurance Association makes the following recommendation on such records:

Tests, examinations and grading contribute very little toward department or personnel evaluation unless the results of such tests are recorded and filed for future reference and use. Training records should reveal the status of training and accomplishments of each individual, company, platoon or department; they should be complete enough to tell a true story, but need not be complicated. Again it must be emphasized that the training officer should devise a record system that meets the needs of his own department.

The training officer's records should consist of:

1. Daily training record.
2. Company training record.
3. Individual training record.
4. An inventory of equipment assigned to the training officer or school.
5. A complete reference library.[11]

There are basically two types of records to be kept. Each fire department member should have a permanent record of the courses taken, as well as any which the individual may have taught. In addition, records of the training conducted daily should be kept.

Individual training records

An individual's training records become the permanent source of information for that person as long as he or she is associated with the fire department. Items which should appear in this record include: person's name, social security number, date of appointment, ranks held, courses taken (with class hours and dates completed), grade (if applicable), name of instructor, and also instructor's comments.

Daily training records

From an analysis of daily training records administrators can determine which areas are being practiced and which are being neglected. These daily records provide a measure of a department's efficiency and also indicate the areas where changes are needed.

However, administrators should guard against the development of a paper program wherein field officers merely fill in the training forms without actually conducting the classes. The fire department then looks good on paper but probably does not perform well in actual practice. This can be avoided if the training staff monitors in-service classes on a random basis and if each company performs a series of evolutions against an established department standard.

The information on the daily training records should include: subject taught; date; time of start and finish of the class; company and, if applicable, shift; instructor; equipment used; and personnel attending the drill.

Data processing of records

In the larger departments, both career and volunteer, maintaining up-to-date training records can be quite a chore. With all on-duty personnel drilling daily or, in a volunteer department, at least weekly, the volume of paperwork is enormous.

One way of overcoming this problem is to have all of the record keeping automated through a data processing system. Almost all jurisdictions have at least a small computer for handling payroll and accounting requirements. The fire department should be able to utilize this equipment, as training records use only a small amount of the storage capability. Certainly, it could be worth the effort for fire service administrators to explore this possibility.

If records are to be automated the data collection can be very simple. All that is needed is to assign a number for each course or drill that will be taught. A three digit number should be sufficient for almost all departments. A fourth digit can be added to indicate which agency conducted the course. Other facts which should be included on the data form are: name, social security number, assigned station, shift, indication of whether the individual is career or volunteer, grade, man-hours of training, and name of instructor.

Once the data have been stored in the computer, fire service administrators will want to determine the type of output desired. (The subject of data collection, processing, and analysis is treated in detail in Chapter 18.)

Qualifications for training personnel

As has been stated earlier, a good training program is the key to an efficient fire department. It therefore follows that personnel selected for the training division should be of very high caliber.

Unfortunately, in many departments, when a promotional vacancy exists in training, the next person on the eligibility list is given the job. In many cases this person wants the promotion but is not really interested in training. Consequently, as soon as the promotion becomes final this person asks for a transfer back to the field.

This lack of experience and interest on the part of training personnel results in lowered morale and problems with the program. Very little training is accomplished and the efficiency of the department drops.

Fire service administrators should consider establishing a separate career ladder for training personnel. While this would involve a specific promotional examination for each level in the training staff, the resultant efficiency created would outweigh the added burden of preparing the examinations. (The approach, however, is suitable only for very large organizations.)

Physical facilities

However good the training instructors are, the physical facilities will still play an important role in the success of a program. These facilities include such items as classrooms, offices, storage space, training and drill facilities, test facilities, and an air recharging facility.

Classrooms

Classrooms should be designed so that a variety of seating arrangements is possible. For example, for a lecture the seats should be arranged in rows. For the discussion method a horseshoe arrangement is preferable. Therefore, the seats should not be fixed in place.

Seating should be comfortable with an ample writing surface. This could be provided by separate tables for each student or by chairs with a built-in writing surface.

There should be at least one chalkboard or blackboard in the classroom. Several boards would be more advantageous. If size and funds permit, consideration should also be given to providing a hook and loop board, a white board for use with special markers, a movie screen, a cork board, and hangers and clips for posters.

A special area for simulation is also a desirable feature at a training facility. Here all levels of officers can be trained under nearly real conditions to react to all kinds of incidents. Specialized projection equipment is needed, as well as public address equipment to simulate the radio system. Making the classroom and simulation room suitable for dual use would be of great assistance to the training staff.

A locker room and shower facility for students is also necessary. Duplicate facilities for men and women should be provided.

Offices

There is a great need for the training staff to have an area in which to prepare their lesson plans, visual aids, promotional examinations, and reports. In addition, they will need clerical support to maintain the training records. Areas for meetings with students for counseling purposes are also essential.

Administrators will need to avoid the temptation of locating the training staff in a small, makeshift area. It is important to remember that the attitudes of officials toward training will directly reflect on the program. The need for adequate working space is critical to the success of the program.

Storage space

When a training facility is designed, one item that is frequently overlooked is sufficient storage space. The fire training academy needs to keep a great deal of equipment on hand, including such items as different sizes and styles of nozzles, smoke ejectors, generators, axes, ladders, pike poles, power tools, pry bars, breathing apparatus, protective equipment, rope, salvage covers, portable lights, electric cord reels, and hose.

If the fire department is also responsible for emergency medical services, then storage space for this specialized equipment is also necessary. Splints, bandages, collars, and dressings are all needed for training.

Visual aid projection equipment is also a necessary ingredient of the training school. Sufficent projectors must be kept on hand for simultaneous classroom use as well as for placement in the field. Along with the storage requirement for these units comes the support equipment such as spare bulbs, screens, power cords, and remote control cords.

Equipment mock-ups and parts which have broken down will be collected by the training staff. Worn out pump impellers, a broken alarm box, or a damaged propane cylinder all can be used in the classroom. Storage space for these is also necessary.

Training and drill facilities

The best way to teach personnel how to fight fires is to have them do it under live conditions. Since fires in structures cannot be produced on demand, a facility for doing this must be constructed. The key requirements are that the facility simulate as many occurrences as possible as safely as possible.

The major criteria for a training building would include the following:

1. Live firefighting in a single dwelling
2. Live firefighting in garden type apartments
3. Live firefighting in a high rise facility
4. Live firefighting in a basement
5. A place to practice entry through various doors and windows
6. A place to practice ventilation on flat and pitched roofs
7. A place to practice rescue from ladders
8. A place to practice lowers by rope
9. A place to practice elevator rescue
10. A sufficient water supply to allow a flow of 5,000 GPM
11. A drafting basin
12. Flammable liquid pits
13. Flammable gas props
14. A electrical service mock-up
15. A driver training course.

The products used for the exterior of the building should be of such nature that repeated heating and cooling will not damage them. Interior walls should be able to withstand the same stresses from repeated fires. Care must be taken to ensure that these are not bearing walls. Floors and ceilings must be protected from the high heat conditions developed by the training fires.

A wide variety of door and window styles should be installed so that practice for entry can be gained. Sufficient funds for repair will need to be included in the training budget. Actually breaking glass and climbing through a window is better for instruction purposes than is simulating the operation in the name of economy. The latter is false economy in the truest sense of the word.

Figure 15–5 Flammable liquid fires present an increasing firefighting challenge and are an integral part of training programs today. (Source: Anne Arundel County, Maryland, Fire Department. Bill Schneck photograph.)

Some sort of a vantage point for the training supervisor is also necessary. From here the supervisor can view the overall operation, ensure that all safety standards are met, and control the training session. Some sort of communication, either by radio or loudspeaker, with those on the drill ground is necessary.

Test facilities

One of the major responsibilities of the training staff is to provide periodic testing of equipment. The Insurance Services Office requires that certain tests be performed and that accurate records be kept. At a minimum, the training facility should be set up to provide tests of fire department pumpers, tests of fire department aerial ladders and telescoping and articulating buckets, and tests of ground ladders.

For these purposes special drafting pits with instrumented test stands are necessary. Also needed is test equipment for the ladder testing.

If the local department is responsible for fire extinguisher recharging, then testing facilities for the shells is necessary.

Figure 15–6   Training buildings are constructed to simulate live conditions. (Source: Dayton, Ohio, Fire Department.)

Air recharging facility

Whenever live firefighting is conducted, a great many self-contained breathing apparatus bottles will be used. The size of the class and the duration of the fire will determine how much air is used. In a six-hour class with twenty students there may be forty to fifty bottles of air used. Since the expense of keeping so many spare bottles on hand is prohibitive, some way of filling the bottles on the scene is needed.

A bottle recharging facility should be installed at the training grounds. If a simple cascade system is used, then these large bottles must be carried to a central compressor station for recharging. If a compressor is also installed at the training ground, then the cascade system can be kept fully charged.

When purchasing a breathing air recharging system for the training facility, it is important to ensure that the following conditions are met:

1. The compressor is large enough to quickly recharge the system and also reach the pressures required by the systems being used
2. The air is filtered between the compressor and the storage bottles so that it meets minimum standards of purity
3. The recharging station is safe, convenient, and quick to use
4. The valves are easy to operate and the gauges conveniently located for reading
5. The excess moisture can be dumped easily
6. The intake is situated so that clean outside air is taken

7. The system has incorporated within it the necessary safety features, including overpressurization protection.

A word on design

Fire department administrators contemplating either building a new facility or modifying their existing one should visit several existing facilities before the design work begins. It is important to learn the good and bad features of current facilities before committing funds.

Summary

This chapter has emphasized the importance of good management of the fire department training and education program. Starting with the framework of fire service training and education, the chapter next discussed, in considerable detail, the development of the training program. The next major section of the chapter dealt with the development of the educational program, which follows similar lines to that of the training program. The latter part of the chapter dealt with scheduling of training, training records, qualifications for training personnel, and, finally, training facilities. Throughout, the importance to management of a well-run program has been stressed.

1   The subject of training in a general local government context, also oriented toward a managerial perspective, is dealt with in the following book in the Municipal Management Series: Neely D. Gardner, "Employee Development and Training," in *Local Government Personnel Administration,* ed. Winston W. Crouch (Washington, D.C.: International City Management Association, 1976), pp. 143–64.

2   Anthony R. Granito, *Fire Instructor's Training Guide* (New York: Dun·Donnelley Publishing Corporation, 1972), p. 1.

3   Bernard M. Bass and James A. Vaughan, *Training in Industry: The Management of Learning* (Belmont, Calif.: Wadsworth Publishing Company, Inc., 1969), p. 78.

4   Robert F. Mager, *Preparing Instructional Objectives* (Belmont, Calif.: Fearon Publishers, 1964), p. 3.

5   National Fire Protection Association, *Fire Fighter Professional Qualifications,* NFPA no. 1001 (Boston: National Fire Protection Association, 1974).

6   Robert F. Mager and Kenneth M. Beach, Jr., *Developing Vocational Instruction* (Belmont, Calif.: Fearon Publishers, 1967), p. 10.

7   Ibid., p. 29.

8   Ibid., pp. 59–61.

9   Granito, *Fire Instructor's Training Guide,* p. 110.

10 William J. Micheels and M. Ray Karnes, *Measuring Educational Achievement* (New York: McGraw-Hill Book Company, 1950), p. 82.

11 American Insurance Association, *Fire Department Records,* Special Interest Bulletin no. 152 (New York: American Insurance Association, 1975), p. 1.

Part four: Technology, communications, and data

16 Managing innovation: an overview

Fire officials often fail to take advantage of available innovations (whether technical or nontechnical) because of their unfamiliarity with (or, at times, resistance to) the change process. Since change is commonplace in our socioeconomic system and since its impact on our working environment is increasing, it is essential that every command officer within the fire service become familiar with the process of managing innovation. This chapter, therefore, defines innovation, explores some of the factors that precipitate innovation, investigates the organizational and personal incentives related to innovation, surveys barriers to the innovation process with which management might be confronted, and explains the innovation process itself. Finally, the chapter discusses in detail the leadership role that the fire administrator needs to fulfill to carry out the change process.

This chapter, then, marks a break with the foregoing chapters, which have dealt with specific functional areas of fire service management. It shifts perspective and takes a look at a broad theme—one that spans the various functions—before returning to specific areas. A knowledge of, and, what is more pertinent, an ability to effectively manage, the process of innovation is important to all fire service managers, who, throughout their careers, will be continually confronted with change. It should be pointed out, however, that this chapter offers only an overview of its subject—but, it is hoped, an overview that will enable managers to approach the details of management in various functional areas with greater insight. It should be borne in mind that innovation is an ongoing process; examples of innovations appearing in this text are not necessarily permanent solutions to a problem. In this rapidly changing field they may be replaced by newer, more effective solutions.

What is innovation?

The term *innovation* as used in this chapter denotes an individual or a group perception of something as being new, regardless of its objective newness. Innovation can include new ideas, new concepts, and new methods and procedures, as well as new products. Innovation implies the capacity to change or to adapt.[1]

While some innovations have been adopted by individual fire departments, it has been recognized (as is constantly emphasized in this book) that fire loss in the United States is a problem that has not been approached with the full range of fire protection ideas, methods, concepts, procedures, and hardware available.[2]

As a result of this recognition of the need for further research and study, conferences have been organized, studies have been authorized, and committees have been formed. The U.S. Congress responded by approving the Fire Research and Safety Act of 1968. This act created the National Commission on Fire Prevention and Control. In 1974 the National Fire Prevention and Control Administration (NFPCA), an agency of the U.S. Department of Commerce, was authorized. In October 1978 the NFPCA became the U.S. Fire Administration (USFA).

These developments reflect an increased interest on the part of public and private organizations in the overall effectiveness of the nation's fire protection system. Inquiries are being made by research groups into fire prevention, fire protection, and fire suppression methods currently used. Surveys and questionnaires are being formulated and circulated, and the results are being analyzed. In addition, long-term national goals for the fire service are being discussed. These activities signal forthcoming changes for the fire service, and they provide further reasons why the matter of managing innovation should be of special interest and importance to fire officials who have managerial responsibility.

Incentives for innovation

The fire protection system established by a governmental policy-setting body usually reflects the fire protection standards of the community or the fire district. Each fire official, having the responsibility for directing an operation of the fire protection delivery system, also has the obligation to maintain locally established and accepted fire protection standards. And each fire official has the added responsibility of providing the designated services in the most economical way possible; at the same time the service furnished must be the most effective possible. Finally, the capability must exist to deliver the service not only efficiently but also in a timely way.

Unfortunately the fire service is finding it increasingly difficult to maintain an effective and timely delivery system because of financial constraints which affect the capabilities of a labor-intensive operation. This factor, along with the rising expectations of the public for better fire protection and for additional services, contributes to the difficulties encountered by the fire service. Yet it is also true that these conditions can encourage innovation.

New technologies themselves force innovation. A change in the organizational structure, added services, the installation of a computer, or the acquisition of new apparatus or equipment all mandate that certain procedures be modified. Also, innovation is often brought about by any change which affects the bureaucracy or by a shift in the nature of the clientele.[3]

The rapid acceptance by the public of smoke detectors is an example in which an innovation has produced a greater awareness on the part of the public of the dangers of fire. The acceptance of this technological innovation could also alter the public's expectations about the level of fire service furnished to a community. Any shift in the expectations of the public concerning the standard of fire service offered to a residentially zoned area could have an impact on the level of service furnished to commercial and industrial zones of the same community.

Pressure emanating from another level of government can provide the incentive to a local government to undertake an innovation. Often, federal and state agencies have programs which reward innovators and penalize those who maintain outmoded methods of operation. The reward is often in the form of monetary grants which can be used to hire additional personnel, purchase much needed apparatus and equipment, or qualify departmental personnel for certain training programs.

Pressure tactics originating from the citizens who are served often result in the adoption of an innovation. This pressure may originate with a special interest group that feels the service being provided is inadequate, or the service is inferior to that being provided to other segments of the community. If this situation is ignored the issue often accelerates in importance and can become one of the reasons for a political upheaval that could have an impact on the fire delivery service.[4]

A citizen movement has an extraordinary ability to encourage innovation or to permit potential innovations to emerge and operate. And client movement can often provide resources and support for individuals who want to innovate.[5]

As Chapter 13 has indicated, unionization has been recognized as yet another social force that has brought about changes in an organization.

Most often, changes can be attributed to the abilities of single individuals who, when successful, will be emulated by others.[6] These changes (designed to solve a particular problem) may affect the organizational structure, the operations, or the procedures of a fire department. Sometimes these changes have a secondary effect of improving the climate for introducing additional innovations. For example, a program to develop standard performance and design specifications for a fire pumper would have as primary goals cost savings and improved operational capabilities; secondary effects of such a program would result in the reexamination of firefighting strategy and tactics, manning requirements, and a range of equipment associated with the pumper.[7]

Another opportunity for innovation is present when strain and stress exist within the organization and dissatisfaction with the status quo is evident; these negative symptoms can become motivating factors. A change brought about under these circumstances is likely to have a very positive impact on the individuals involved and can promote a climate which further facilitates change. Change of this type has a specific target audience where the majority often is supportive of change programs.[8]

Whether forces outside the organization advocate change or whether the situation within the organization favors an innovative climate, innovation will not occur without leadership that provides encouragement, positive reinforcement, direction, and timely follow-through.[9]

Barriers to innovation

Factors involved

Just as leadership can be a facilitator for change, so lack of leadership can be a barrier to change. Often the leadership of an organization becomes complacent and self-satisfied regarding the organization's level of performance and does not react to indicators that call for a revision in the routine of the department. Many chief executive officers, having been confronted with some change management opportunities in the past and having successfully implemented them, have decided that the last change was the final change. Since their ideal fire protection delivery system has been achieved, they have decided to maintain the status quo. Accompanying this abdication of the leadership role is a failure to comprehend the accelerating rate of change with which society generally—and the fire service in particular—is faced. Ignoring the inevitability of change can be classified as a barrier to innovation.

Lack of leadership within an organization is by no means the only barrier to needed change. There are many others, and, while they are often recognized, they are just as often ignored. The fire official who learns to recognize these barriers and to avoid them, or who can perhaps turn them to his or her advantage, will be the more successful in managing change.

Since most fire departments are an integral part of the bureaucratic structure, the conservatism associated with the bureaucracy becomes another factor inhibiting change. Novel solutions using resources in a new way are likely to appear threatening to the incumbents. This threat most often affects those members of the organization having a bureaucratic orientation who are more concerned with the internal distribution of power and status than with organizational goal accomplishment.[10]

The modern fire department is traditionally organized in a quasi-military form. This results in greater inequality of social standing and abilities, and in a corresponding inequality in contribution and awards.[11] Also, since promotion within the system is often predicated by a person's ability to conform, the more success an individual attains, the more vague and subjective becomes the standard by which that individual is judged. Eventually the only safe posture is conformity. Innovation is not likely to occur under those conditions.[12]

The fire service is exempt from the sanction of economic failure faced by private businesses that neglect to alter their operation in order to furnish the most economical service available, or whose leadership refuses to seize new opportunities.[13] In addition, innovations hold few personal rewards for the participants, and there are few penalties for failure to adapt to a changing environment.[14]

In a bureaucratic organization people are punished for mistakes as well as for wrongdoing. People are punished for failures within their jurisdictions whether these failures are due to their activities or not. Thus, an individual may hesitate to advise an organization about a new procedure or process even though the probabilities of a satisfactory outcome for an innovative undertaking are good. Should the project fail, the individual may be judged as a personal failure.[15]

This attitude can result in few, if any, risks being taken by the leadership within an organization: thus the fear of risking failure, which could result in termination, peer ridicule, or loss of influence, becomes another barrier to change. When an individual with these feelings occupies a top leadership role there are few others within the hierarchy who are going to risk exposure. And in most cases there will be few people in the bureaucratic hierarchy with sufficient power to bring about change if the chief fire officer is opposed to, apathetic toward, or disinterested in an innovative program.[16]

As an added inhibitor to change, most government employees have a semi-guaranteed tenure: promotion is based on capability to score well in an examination process, on seniority, or on the possession of certain credentials. Consequently, there is little incentive for risk taking.

One of the most frequently heard generalizations about resistance to change is that "resistance occurs when those affected by a change perceive it as threatening." The fear of loss of status, prestige, or power is often cited as a major reason for such resistance. An innovation which threatens the value of the knowledge or skills now utilized by an employee also produces resistance. Unions may well participate in opposing change believed to be detrimental to the membership, or believed to be a threat to the survival of the union movement.

Any change that challenges currently held beliefs is almost certain to bring about resistance.[17] If an individual feels that a contemplated change will result in a loss of self-esteem, or that it will threaten his or her sense of competency, expose a weakness, affect his or her status role in a negative manner, or affect his or her influence with the peer group, a high level of resistance can be expected.

People resist changes when they do not understand them or when the reasons for change are not clearly defined. Many organizations are resistant to any change which can be categorized as "not invented here." And a fundamental principle of resistance is that people resist being forced to change.

As an example of resistance to change in a specific area of fire service, the results of a study dealing with innovation regarding the purchase of equipment are described immediately below.

An example: the purchase of equipment

A comprehensive research effort undertaken by Pugh-Roberts Associates, Inc., titled *Factors Affecting Innovation in the Fire Services,* analyzes innovation in the fire service from the standpoint of the market for firefighting equipment, the industry which produces the equipment, and the purchasing environment.[18]

Although the authors of the above-mentioned report estimate the fire services market to be a rather large one, they suggest that it is relatively unattractive because its profit potential is small and uncertain and it is slow to accept new products. The study notes five barriers to innovation resulting from the nature of the market.

The first barrier is the highly structured nature of the firefighter's job, which is designed to maintain organizational cohesiveness. Innovative products must be evaluated in terms of the effect they would have on firefighters' morale. The result is often that innovations that meet with resistance from the firefighters are rejected regardless of potential benefits accruing to the organization. Seldom do persons in leadership roles question the validity of such resistance.

Second, fire department personnel policies are often a barrier to innovation. Leaders are often promoted on the basis of seniority and test scores rather than on managerial capability. This may lead to the inability to cope with problems encountered in introducing innovations, which may, in turn, lead to the rejection of innovative products or programs. The fact that leaders of most fire agencies normally spend their entire careers in one department limits interdepartmental communication and results in a rather narrow interpretation of perceived needs. This parochial attitude further limits the market for innovation.

Third, limited funds for purchasing equipment act to limit the sales potential of innovative equipment. Manpower is by far the largest expenditure in a fire department's budget, usually exceeding 90 percent of the total. Moreover, when local government capital expenditures for water supply systems and fire stations are added to fire protection costs, the proportion spent for firefighting equipment recedes even further.

Fourth, the lack of objective equipment evaluation reports to assist fire officials, combined with the officials' limited technical expertise, may cause uncertainty as to whether the equipment will be evaluated properly. This could contribute to lengthy field tests and to reliance on fire equipment distributors as sources of technical advice.

Finally, market fragmentation and a lack of standards to assess equipment needs make it difficult for fire officials to justify deviations from past purchasing policies.

From the perspective of equipment production, the nature of the fire equipment industry is a barrier to innovation. It is generally characterized by older, established firms with small profit margins. Such firms are often on the verge of financial difficulties because of market fragmentation. Each jurisdiction purchases independently, and customized equipment is frequently required. The market situation discourages larger, diversified firms from entering the picture. Evidence compiled by the authors suggests that most firms in the fire equipment industry are not prepared to produce significant innovations. Firms that are capable of innovating develop new products for markets other than the fire service.

According to the authors of the research study the purchasing environment includes a number of outside influences that affect fire department purchasing decisions and decisions of manufacturers. Since these influences are not related to cost and performance, they inhibit the introduction of innovation. Five such outside influences are listed below.

First, the report notes that there is no dissemination mechanism which would bring manufacturers and fire departments together. New techniques and equipment are not brought to the attention of fire departments, and potential markets are not made known to developers of technology.

Second, National Fire Protection Association (NFPA) specifications for fire equipment have assumed quasi-legal status in state courts in civil actions. Because of possible damage claims involving equipment-related injuries where the equipment does not meet NFPA specifications, fire departments may be wary of otherwise superior equipment.

Third, the insurance industry's rating schedule is based on six requirements for fire protection equipment and apparatus. Potential equipment and apparatus purchases are to be examined for their potential effect on local insurance rates as much as for their effect on fire protection. The purchase of innovative equipment to replace traditional equipment may increase insurance rates, which would reduce the incentive to buy it.

Fourth, there is often a lack of understanding between purchasing departments and fire departments. City buyers may not understand fire department requirements and recent technological developments and thus may resist the purchase of innovative equipment.

Finally, equipment purchasing decisions may be influenced by the close relations that often develop between fire officials and distributors of firefighting equipment. Distributors may have a vested interest in the products they presently sell, to the detriment of new products.

The innovation process

With a knowledge of the possible advantages accruing to an organization from the adoption of an innovation, and with an awareness on the part of the leadership of the pitfalls facing an organization interested in adopting an innovation, management should explore the process itself. A thorough understanding of the process will help fire protection agency officials maximize the advantages of adopting an innovation, and at the same time a familiarity with the process to be pursued will bring an awareness of how to minimize the effects of those factors which detract from the successful implementation of an innovation.

Recognition and exploration

The innovation process can be translated into a series of events starting with the recognition, by someone in the fire department, of a need to alter a method now in use or to overcome a shortcoming in a procedure currently in use. This initial perception might result in the formulation of an idea which could serve to fulfill the perceived need.

Most often, a series of ideas is explored. The ideas could be generated by fire personnel within the organization in search of a solution; through a search conducted by fire personnel on an assigned or voluntary basis into how other fire departments have resolved a similar problem; or through information and data discovered in trade journals, texts, or other reference materials. Personal contacts are a resource for ideas. It has been said that in the public sector individual relationships constitute one of the best communication networks. It follows that many of the ideas adopted by fire officials originate through this informal and haphazard network among fire chiefs, fire training officers, personnel of fire prevention bureaus, and members of affiliated unions.

Professional organizations serving members of the fire service also serve as repositories of ideas. Individuals associated with a state university, a regional fire academy, a community college, a local industry, or a state municipal organization might also be sources of ideas that could be of benefit to the fire chiefs or members of their staffs who are seeking a solution to a vexing need.

Evaluation

Out of an idea an invention may come. The invention may be nothing more than a combination of several ideas, or an idea that is the result of modifying another idea through the addition or deletion of subcritical elements.[19] The "not invented here" syndrome has been mentioned. While this has not been an affliction of all fire departments, the reluctance to undertake a program or to install a process successful in another community is all too prevalent. The fact that most local fire agencies insist on designing original specifications for new apparatus, and on continually redesigning those same specifications, illustrates the individualistic approach that has come to be identified with the fire service. To maximize the use of the limited resources available to the fire service, greater sharing of ideas is essential. Modification of any idea which results in the process or procedure being made more useful should nevertheless be encouraged. This phase of the innovation process is called research and development, and it is during this stage that the invention is improved upon so as to provide greater potential utility for the user.[20]

The innovation will undergo close scrutiny by those on whom it will have an impact. Each party will be concerned with determining how threatening the innovation is to the individual and to the group, ascertaining the advantages to be accrued from its use, and, subsequently, accepting or rejecting it.

Some innovations are tried on a pilot basis by an organization. This approach to implementation gives the user an opportunity to test the acceptability of the innovation and also reveals to the user the consequences of fully adopting the

---

Technology innovation sources
Recognizing that local government officials require a more formal system for depositing, storing, and retrieving ideas, the Council of State Governments, the International City Management Association, the National Association of Counties, the National Governors' Association, the National League of Cities, and the U.S. Conference of Mayors organized Public Technology, Inc., in 1971 to help fill this information void. From this initial action several other programs have evolved which offer fire officials opportunities to avail themselves of the latest information and data concerning new developments. Many of these programs have been made possible

through the National Science Foundation in an effort to accelerate the use of new technology within local government.

As a result of these exploratory efforts, several state and regional innovation groups, formally organized to service local government, now operate in many areas of the country. Cities and counties of all sizes have science advisers or technology agents who are available to assist fire operation personnel in the generation of ideas to bridge a recognized performance gap. In addition, the federal laboratories will provide local officials with the results of research conducted within their facilities on fire-related matters.

---

innovation. The possibility of trying out an innovation on a small scale is of interest in minimizing possible unanticipated consequences—noneconomic as well as economic.[21]

Acceptance and implementation

The final step in the innovation process is the acceptance of the innovation and its implementation into the ongoing operational procedures of the fire service. The true test of the successful implementation of an innovation is its institutionalization.

There are other factors which, while not an integral part of an innovation process, do contribute to whether the innovation will be accepted or rejected by the fire service. Visibility is one that has to be considered. How visible is the innovation to others? The easier it is to see the results of an innovation, the more likely it is that it will be adopted. An innovation is also more likely to be accepted by fire officials if one of the early adopters is recognized as a leader within the fire profession. Complexity of the innovation, as perceived by fire personnel, will have an impact on whether it will be adopted throughout the fire service, and, if so, how rapidly. Some innovations are less easily understood by potential users than are others, and, consequently, will be adopted more slowly. In general those ideas requiring little learning investment on the part of the implementer will be accepted earlier.[22]

An examination of firefighter acceptance of innovation verified that some innovations seemed to catch on more quickly than others.[23] They tended to be those that would not affect the organization of fire attack but only the efficiency of the individual (e.g., newer, lighter breathing apparatus; power saws to replace hatchets). The items least likely to be adopted would have required the entire restructuring of firefighting procedures.

Managing the change process

The difference between a successful innovation and an unsuccessful attempt to innovate quite often lies in the capabilities (or lack of them) exhibited by management personnel within the particular fire department.

Pressures for change

Fire administrators of the future will have to live with change. The pressures forcing change will be constant; these pressures will be directed toward these administrators by their superiors, by their peer group, and by their subordinates. And the requested changes will often be conflicting—having been proposed by groups with differing interests. Finally, the fire administrators of tomorrow, though fully trained and competent in their management skills, will find themselves in the midst of change that has not gone so well.

The diversification of services delivered to the public by fire personnel will precipitate change in the delivery system. As Chapter 10 has indicated, we are now witnessing an expansion of the role of the firefighter to that of paramedic. Many departments are seeing the number of fire calls being equaled and even surpassed by requests for emergency medical services. This diversification has brought about changes in training, manning of apparatus, and allocation of manpower.

The importance of emergency medical service has been pointed up to the fire service by the enthusiastic support of the citizens of a community for this service. In fact, this has been one of the few innovations accepted by the fire service in recent years that has resulted in an alteration in the traditional value system of the fire service. More change can be expected in this area because of the increasing awareness on the part of the public about its availability, and also because provision of emergency medical services is rapidly becoming a prerogative of the fire department and is being added to the repertoire of the deliverable services of a progressive fire system.

New technologies will also cause the fire administrator to advocate change. Procedures will have to be revised, manning standards may be affected, and strange-looking equipment will replace the more familiar tools. Computers will replace the need for manpower to carry out repetitive and boring tasks. Closed circuit television, combined with microdata processing units, will alter the curricula and formats of fire training, will affect staff meetings, and will be instrumental in improving tactical fire operations. Each of these changes will give rise to additional change within the fire delivery system. Each of these new technologies can also help the fire administrator establish within the organization a climate in which change will more readily be accepted. This can be accomplished through involving others in the change process, through requiring the fire management team to organize and plan for change, and through knowing how to implement change while minimizing the risks of change. All of the above tasks will require that the fire chief or the command officer within the fire department provide the leadership necessary to effectuate change in a successful manner.[24]

The role of the chief fire executive

In a change-oriented environment the chief fire executive will devote more time, and will direct a substantial part of the efforts of the organization, toward adjusting to rapidly evolving technologies. Therefore, fire agency officials will need to make a commitment to long-range planning. Without this commitment on the part of the fire official, the day-to-day routine will take more time than he or she can spare for all of the assigned responsibilities.

The attitude of top officials, while essential to foster change, is only one necessary element in creating and cultivating a suitable climate for change. Another requirement is to recruit staff who are involved in and committed to the program.

Top fire department officials also have the responsibility of interesting their subordinates in improving the operations of the organization through planned change. A fire chief cannot delegate responsibility to others for communicating the particulars of the proposed plan to members of the task force that is carrying out that plan. Chief executives will need to be personally committed to the program. It is the task of chief executives to define in understandable language the objectives of the program.

In many respects chief executives will need to undertake the "marketing" of the change program and, for example, to remind other chief officers that they bear the responsibility of providing leadership to show others the advantages of future changes. In other words, the leadership style of the chief executive should include a sales component.

While the chief fire officer will ultimately delegate considerable authority for implementing change to others, the chief officer should maintain a coordinating role in the total change effort to assure maximum improvement, to determine that the original objective is intact, and to assure that those in charge of the program are both responsive and responsible—and that, in addition to performing well, they are expanding their capacity to carry out change.

In this context, the fire chief, when making appointments to top administrative posts, should consider carefully an individual's capability to support change. (It is important, too, that the individuals who are going to bring about change have the opportunity to find out what new technologies are available.)

The role of middle management

While it remains the chief executive's responsibility to motivate top management, the assistant deputy or battalion chiefs should, in turn, influence middle management personnel by providing them with an environment in which they can achieve greater influence, both upwards and downwards, and in which they can become key implementers and communicators.[25]

Middle management personnel, in turn, have the responsibility of enlarging the participatory opportunities in the change process for nonmanagerial employees. Nonmanagerial employees should be fully advised as to the details of the contemplated change, the reasons for the change, the expected alterations in the work program, and the anticipated advantages to be gained by the organization as a result of implementation of the innovation.

Planning for change

The management of change is not simple; it cannot be isolated or tucked away on a shelf to be utilized only when needed. The management of change is a con-

Pitfalls in the change process

Preparing for change versus changing . . . Managers often find themselves confronted by a whole series of preliminary steps which apparently must precede progress toward the main goal. For example, to achieve the ultimate result, it may be necessary to have more sophisticated supervision. Therefore, they begin by working on supervisory training. Employees may not understand or sympathize with the need for change. So programs are undertaken to analyze and cope with employee attitudes.

The organization structure may not be appropriate for the changed circumstances in which the company will be operating. Thus it would seem that a new organization structure must be created to permit progress. Perhaps new controls, new performance measures, and new managerial tools ultimately will be required. As the list grows, the manager becomes increasingly awed by the number of preliminary steps he must take before he can start moving toward his major change goals. He invests increasing amounts of energy and money in these preparatory steps. . . . Often this turns into endless and time-consuming preparation for progress which remains always just around the corner.

Delegating to staff or consultants Some managers decide that current demands will continue to take all the time and energy they have. Gearing up for change is going to have to be done by staff people or consultants. These experts can, of course, be useful in creating the tools and designing programs which are supposed to lead to change. They can produce useful and insightful reports and recommendations. The one thing they cannot produce is change itself. . . .

Focusing on one element of change— with fingers crossed . . . The impor-

tance of the major objective on the one hand and the inertia of the enterprise on the other may impel a top manager to try a desperate lunge. For example, a conference is called. . . . The managers are told to put aside all distractions and concentrate on the major objective. Unrealistic demands are made. The managers return to their jobs, sometimes steamed up, sometimes cynical. Either way, within a short time the old work patterns reassert themselves.

Deferring action for a more propitious day . . . There is nothing about ill-defined change goals, no matter how important they may ultimately be, that impels action *today*. The manager . . . can be uneasy about the lack of progress today. Nevertheless, there are so many ways he can convince himself that action may be put off until tomorrow. . . .

Major surgery The forces for change have a way of catching up. Thus an enterprise may find it has been preparing and delaying too long. Suddenly the top managers have no choice. Drastic surgery is required. Departments are merged and reorganized; managers are replaced; money is poured into the company. Unfortunately, even though the enterprise pays a big price for it, surgery doesn't always produce the desired results. . . . Moreover, in taking drastic action, the baby may be thrown out with the bath water, and the enterprise may wind up weaker than before. . . .

Thus the enterprise remains trapped in its present, or it inches toward its future too slowly.

Source: Excerpted from Richard A. Bobbe and Robert H. Schaffer, *Mastering Change: Breakthrough Projects and Beyond,* American Management Association Bulletin no. 120 (New York: American Management Association, Inc., 1968), pp. 4–6.

tinuous process that calls for meticulous planning. The planning for change must be considered as a part of almost every decision that the chief makes.

Choosing the change group   No change program should be initiated that does not allow for the participation of several people. One of the responsibilities of the fire chief in implementing the change process is to evaluate the strengths and weaknesses of key personnel whose talents will be necessary to successfully carry out the program. From these separate evaluations should come the framework of a management team.

Team members should be selected on the basis of their knowledge of the situation to be explored. They should represent special functions such as personnel, accounting, or fire prevention—those activities which may affect or be affected by the contemplated change.[26] Those organizations (both inside and outside the

---

Elements of success   The main elements of success in the adoption of slippery water technology for the use in urban fire service . . . appear to have been the following:

The systems approach was crucial in analyzing the fire department for potential areas of applying technology and producing savings.

A knowledgeable person was in a position to see how technology could be mated with a particular problem.

The cooperation and commitment of industry, even though it was withheld until pressed and persuaded, was essential to the final development.

A close working relationship between outside experts and department heads and employees was important for two reasons—first, to gain acceptance of the notion of innovation, and second, to help assure success through the

contribution of their operational expertise.

There were innovative chiefs and managers in the department who, under appropriate conditions, were willing to engage in a novel development program.

A demonstrable benefit was presented to citizens—in this case, improved efficiency of a vital service—and the story was carefully presented and not oversold.

Without attention to all these factors, it is doubtful that New York City would now be implementing this new approach to putting fires out much more quickly and economically.

Source: Excerpted from The Urban Institute, *The Struggle To Bring Technology to Cities* (Washington, D.C.: The Urban Institute, 1971), p. 40.

---

government) whose support and cooperation would be useful in the achieving of optimum value and advantage from the change should also be represented. Finally, representatives of groups who will have their work habits changed or whose procedures will be altered should be included. The inclusion of someone who is considered representative of a certain work group helps to prevent the feeling that all of the details of the change have not been disclosed, that there exists a "hidden agenda" that will reveal itself when it is least expected.

Selecting the first step   The members of the task force, change group, or committee should be given the opportunity during the selection of the first step objective to express their opinions on programs or projects which would prove, in their opinion, to be most useful to the organization. The project that will serve as the pilot undertaking should be selected at as early a date as possible, to generate enthusiasm. The project selected should directly affect the organization by causing a change that has been thoroughly discussed but has not been acted upon in any way. The change objective should be capable of achievement through the use of resources presently available from various staff functions connected with the fire department, and through the use of outside help that is currently provided through ongoing appropriations. The project, when possible, should also be a part of a larger undertaking.

The initial project should be selected not only because of need but also because it can be achieved. The first change program is probably one of the most important. If the first venture is successful, each member of the group who participated in the program will have increased confidence in his or her own capabilities. Group members will also be enthusiastic about undertaking a new, different, and more difficult program. Other members of the organization, though not directly participating in the project, will share in the feeling of accomplishment.

It is essential to the success of the program that the chairperson of the change group be change-oriented, be a good listener, and be able to organize the individuals involved into a team. If this is not the case, the pilot undertaking will be short-lived, and this will discredit the total endeavor.

It should always be borne in mind that there are two objectives to the undertaking—a short-range objective and a long-range one. The former is to achieve the defined goals which represent the end product of the particular pilot program; the latter is to develop the managerial capabilities of the participants.

Committing the plan to writing One of the first responsibilities of the task force should be to commit all plans connected with the project to writing. A program seldom proceeds as anticipated; also, people often have differing perceptions of the same point. In addition, too many participants have short memories concerning commitments made. For these and other reasons it is prudent to have the details of a program transcribed and distributed to all task force members.

The written plan should include information concerning individual responsibilities for each task, anticipated date of completion of each individual's assignment, and ways in which the individual can measure accomplishment toward his or her specific objective. To ensure that these tasks are being completed in a timely manner, a review process should be incorporated into the procedure. This step also serves to coordinate the work of the different participants and to avert diverse approaches on the part of individuals working with the same subject.

Providing direction While the term *change* has connotations of adventure, excitement, and exploration, the change process is in truth tedious and exacting. Yet it is the rigor of the process which brings each detail into focus and thereby avoids the unplanned results. The more often the change process is implemented and the more closely it is followed, the greater is the chance of success for each undertaking.

Appointing a task force does not diminish the responsibility of the chief to provide the ongoing direction necessary to a successful completion of the mission. Periodically, meetings should be called by the chief officer at which each participant has the opportunity to make a progress report outlining his or her activities since the last meeting. These gatherings will communicate the continuing efforts on the part of each individual to the chief executive and, in turn, will demonstrate the enthusiasm and support of top management.

Generating enthusiasm If the top official of the department lacks enthusiasm or fails to demonstrate strong support for the pilot project, it is probably doomed to failure. Pessimism is contagious, and certain individuals often seem to gain satisfaction from hawking the reasons why a project or program will not or cannot succeed. This development is likely to occur when a dissident member discerns only superficial support from top department officials for a project.

While enthusiasm for change is more difficult to generate throughout an organization, it is certainly a feasible goal. And enthusiasm, too, can be contagious. People tend to perform better in an optimistic environment, and they strive to accomplish tasks that are seldom contemplated in an atmosphere lacking in this optimism. Since both enthusiasm and pessimism are often products of the manner in which communication is phrased, it is important to consider an individual's attitude when considering him or her for the task force.

On the other hand, if the proposed change is found to be disadvantageous to the mission of the organization, or if it adversely affects its service capabilities, the task force should be disengaged from pursuing it. If the chief officer is confident that the contemplated innovation will truly be detrimental to the organization, the efforts of the task force should be redirected to another program. This situation most certainly can arise, especially during one of the early undertakings. A negative conclusion concerning a contemplated change should not be tagged as a failure. Instead, the basic elements which caused the selection of the project should be reevaluated. Such a conclusion in itself cannot be construed as a failure but must be viewed as a part of the learning pattern of how to manage change.

Communicating successfully It is important that people be kept informed of the project's progress. This can generate enthusiasm and excitement among those who might otherwise become suspicious and nonreceptive. As questions on the part of those not directly involved in the project arise, they should be handled expeditiously and answered thoroughly and honestly. A procedure of directing questions should be designed to provide for two way communication, if one does not already exist within the department. Not only questions, but ideas, are often generated—ideas which may help the task force avoid certain pitfalls that might otherwise have gone unnoticed.

Once two way communication has been established, it should be used faithfully to provide rapid feedback to an employee's recommendation. If suggestions have been favorably received and are being considered for incorporation into the plan, or for implementation, the individual should be told so and given an approximate date as to when to expect to see some results of the suggestion. If a recommendation offered by an individual or a group is to be rejected for any reason, it is just as important—perhaps more so—to communicate the reasons why. The more thorough and complete the reasons cited for the rejection of offered suggestions are, the more those who made the recommendations will understand why they were not applicable—and the more confident they will feel about making additional suggestions (suggestions that might prove more usable because of the knowledge they have gained).

Those employees who have taken the time and made the effort to communicate with the task force, and whose suggestions have been accepted, should be rewarded for their contribution. These rewards might consist of a letter of commendation or recognition and might graduate to a cash award or to time off.

An award should not be made until a suggestion has been implemented and has proven worthwhile. If an award is made only to stimulate interest in the project, and not to reward a genuine contribution, then employees will lose faith in the total award plan. Such an attitude can result in a complete failure of the pilot project and can also have an adverse impact on the entire change program.

Activating and evaluating The fire chief and other fire command officials, along with members of the task force, may find that they are unable to choose a project that meets the established criteria, and only then do they realize that the selection of a first phase assignment is more difficult than anticipated. Some departments faced with such a situation have gone through a needs assessment procedure which identifies the most important steps that should be undertaken in each division of the agency. Many projects have been identified through this procedure. The results can be put in priority order by a task force and decisions can then be made about which issues to address.

Once an initial project undertaking has been completed, the participants should critique the selection of the task, the procedure used, the detailed assignments and the schedule, for the purposes of improving the process and providing greater satisfaction for future participants. The first project should be looked upon as a learning experience by each participant. Trying to produce an error-free process on the initial endeavor will prove discouraging to the project team, if not disastrous to the continuation of the project itself. Several projects will have to be initiated and completed before project members will come to realize that the process is becoming easier, that obscurities are being brought into focus, and that the participants are developing an ability to see the total problem in much more detail.

As the tasks become more complex, additional time will be required to develop a suitable work plan. As the projects are expanded in scope the impact on various work groups will tend to increase. Relationships between work groups (for example, the fire prevention bureau and the fire suppression bureau) will have to be evaluated, and relationships between the fire department and other departments (for example, the building inspection department) may possibly be affected.

Dealing with obstacles   As the project becomes more complex and involves more people from various divisions, and as it affects a larger number of bureaus or departments, the greater is the number of obstacles that may be encountered. Sometimes information and data essential to the project are unavailable because of lack of power on the part of the task force members to secure this data, or because key people will not provide the data necessary or the authority to obtain that data. This type of development often brings about self-doubts on the part of task force members regarding their ability to accomplish the goals. And data on an operation that might be adversely affected by the anticipated change can sometimes be difficult to secure. This situation often occurs when it is believed that the employees identified with the affected operation will suffer adversely from the change.

Overcoming these obstacles sometimes requires negotiating for the required information. In any event, eliminating or overcoming the roadblock usually results in lost momentum on the part of the task force. It is important that these obstacles, whether natural or contrived, are not allowed to obscure the reasons for the project. The uncovered obstacle may be the very reason why progress has been lacking within the organization.

Learning from the process   Managing the change process is part of change itself. Most certainly it is a learning experience for anyone who has undertaken its management. Through incorporating this process into the department, the chief officer begins to realize the undeveloped potential that exists within the organization. The change process becomes a tool to develop managers: the better the job they do, the better managers they become. Thus, the change process has short-term and long-term benefits for the individual members of the group implementing the change, for the chief officer responsible for the change process, for members of the fire delivery organization, and, most important, for the citizens they have the responsibility of serving.

Summary

While the management of change is a complex undertaking, it is a critical element that fire officials must practice as well as understand if they are to meet the increasing demands that will be placed upon them in the future by elected and appointed officials, professionally-oriented fire groups, special interest groups, and individual citizens. Fire officials will increasingly receive requests from various individuals associated with these groups who are critical of the quality, the timeliness, and the adequacy of the service rendered to them. Representatives of a number of the same groups will also inquire about the possibility of new or expanded services. At the same time, others will be complaining about the cost associated with the current service capability.

As these conflicting demands increase in frequency, fire officials will become more familiar with such areas as the availability and applicability of modeling techniques for locating fire response facilities. Electronic data processing and work processing devices will become important adjuncts to chief fire officers in providing up-to-date analyses on the performance of the fire agency, and in projecting their manpower, apparatus, and equipment requirements for tomorrow and for the next ten years. The apparatus and equipment will tend increasingly to be self-contained, requiring minimal attention during operation. Scarce, valuable, and expensive manpower will be employed to supervise the automated and semiautomated tools which, to a great degree, will handle many routine situations.

This situation sets the stage for the fire officials of tomorrow. These officials may find that confidence in their own capability to manage change will be the critical element in helping them to understand and control the future.

1   Victor A. Thompson, "Bureaucracy and Innovation," *Administrative Science Quarterly* 10 (June 1965): 1.

2   John W. Lawton, *A National Agenda for Programs To Increase the Introduction of Innovations in the Fire Services* (Washington, D.C.: Public Technology, Inc., 1973), p. 1. Innovations in the fire service, as well as other successfully implemented new techniques in local government management, are presented as case studies in the Municipal Management Innovation Series, a series of reports published by the International City Management Association, Washington, D.C. Among these reports, see especially: Fred S. Knight, *The Mini-Pumper: New Applications and New Potential,* Municipal Management Innovation Series no. 1 (January 1975); and Fred S. Knight, *Fire Service Productivity: The Scottsdale Approach,* Municipal Management Innovation Series no. 16 (March 1977). A number of the Municipal Management Innovation reports, including the two mentioned above, have been collected in the following publication: Fred S. Knight and Michael D. Rancer, eds., *Tried and Tested: Case Studies in Municipal Innovation* (Washington, D.C.: International City Management Association, 1978).

3   Norman I. Fainstein and Susan S. Fainstein, "Innovation in Urban Bureaucracies: Clients and Change," *American Behavioral Scientist* 15 (March–April 1972): 514.

4   Ibid.: 519.

5   Ibid.: 528.

6   Ibid.: 530.

7   Lawton, *Programs To Increase the Introduction of Innovations in the Fire Services,* p. 9.

8   Human Interaction Research Institute, *Putting Knowledge to Use: A Distillation of the Literature regarding Knowledge Transfer and Change,* prepared for the U.S. Department of Health, Education, and Welfare, National Institute of Mental Health, Mental Health Services Development Branch (Rockville, Md.: National Institute of Mental Health, 1976), p. 38.

9   Edward M. Glaser, "Knowledge Transfer and Institutional Change," *Professional Psychology* 4 (November 1973): 439.

10   Thompson, "Bureaucracy and Innovation": 7.

11   Ibid.: 3.

12   Ibid.: 6.

13   Fainstein and Fainstein, "Innovation in Urban Bureaucracies": 516.

14   Ibid.

15   Thompson, "Bureaucracy and Innovation": 10.

16   Fainstein and Fainstein, "Innovation in Urban Bureaucracies": 517.

17   Human Interaction Research Institute, *Putting Knowledge to Use,* p. 40.

18   Alan Frohman and Edward Roberts, *Factors Affecting Innovation in the Fire Services* (Cambridge, Mass.: Pugh-Roberts Associates, Inc., 1972). The following summary, which has been excerpted, with minor changes, from Lawton, *Programs To Increase the Introduction of Innovations in the Fire Services,* pp. 5–8, was itself taken from the Pugh-Roberts report, cited here, generally, and from pp. 117–23, specifically.

19   E. M. Rogers and John D. Eveland, "Diffusion of Innovations Perspectives on National R & D Assessment: Communication and Innovation in Organizations," paper prepared for the National Sci-

ence Foundation National R & D Assessment Program, n.p., n.d., p. 41.

20 Ibid.

21 Public Affairs Counseling, *Factors Involved in the Transfer of Innovations: A Summary and Organization of the Literature,* prepared for the U.S. Department of Housing and Urban Development, Office of Policy Development and Research, (Washington, D.C.: U.S. Department of Housing and Urban Development, January 1976), p. 49.

22 Ibid.

23 Malcolm Getz, "The Economics of Fire Departments," in *Research Report from the M.I.T.— Harvard Joint Center for Urban Studies* (Cambridge, Mass.: Joint Center for Urban Studies, 1978), p. 5.

24 Patrick H. Irwin and Frank W. Langham, Jr., "The Change Seekers," *Harvard Business Review* 44 (January–February 1966): 81.

25 Ibid.: 84.

26 Ibid.: 82.

17 Managing communications systems

Each fire control manager is charged with the responsibility of receiving requests for assistance and of notifying those personnel responsible for handling the reported emergency. The means by which this is accomplished is part of fire communications. Fire communications also includes the method by which various units are monitored and the means by which these units issue and receive instructions.

Historically, fire departments generally did not keep up with the technology available to help them accomplish their fire control mission. This is changing rapidly, and many fire chiefs are becoming aware of the potential of electronics in fire protection. It is now possible for fire departments to take advantage of new radio capabilities as well as improved alarm systems. Communications systems incorporating electronic computers enhance the fire chief's capability to control fire. Computers can also provide the fire chief with an evaluation of fire department activities.

In recent years fire communications has advanced from basic radio and telegraph to the more sophisticated systems incorporating telephone, television, and computers. These new methods are being tested and are found to be fast, efficient, and reliable.

This chapter is not intended to be a manual for designing a communications system. Rather, it is an overview of the options available to a fire department. The design of any fire communications system will vary from department to department. It is important that existing systems be evaluated on past performances, and that each department evaluate its own communications needs.

Proper research and planning are essential aspects of managing a fire department today. A major part of this effort should include a master plan for communications. This plan will include long-range planning requirements for periodic evaluation of needs and capabilities. This will alert the fire control manager to new requirements as may be dictated by changing trends in population and development. Evaluation and planning are discussed in a number of contexts throughout this book (see Chapter 6 for a discussion of planning for fire protection in general). This chapter should be considered in its context with certain closely related subjects in this volume (for example, emergency medical services [EMS], dealt with in Chapter 10).

An overview

The following discussion appears under nine major headings. The first section, an overview, provides a brief historical background and then discusses the various organizations involved in communications. The second section is concerned with the management of communications operations centers, while the third section covers emergency medical services communications. Various alarm systems are the subject of the fourth major section. The next two sections cover, respectively, the radio system and the telephone system. A brief section on educating the public follows. The eighth section covers computer-aided dispatch, and the ninth provides a brief summary and a look at the future.

Historical background

The basic requirements for fire department communications have not changed over the years. The means of reporting a fire and the ability to maintain contact with fire units are still the most important parts of communications. There are, however, additional requirements such as the ability to contact other fire departments for mutual aid, and the recall of off-duty personnel.

Our history shows that various means have been employed to accomplish this. Church bells, messengers, coded steam whistles, and many other devices have been employed to warn citizens of a danger from fire. In the nineteenth century the introduction of hand wire communications brought with it a more rapid and reliable means of reporting fire. Additionally, alarm box systems brought the fire reporting capability to the individual occupancy.

The tremendous advances in electronics brought about by World War II and the space program have resulted in expansion of the use of radio in the fire service. Many fire departments now include in their planning a radio capability for all personnel on or off duty. In sum, never before has the fire service been offered such a variety of communication equipment and communication capabilities.

Organizations

In recognition of the need for cooperation in the growing area of public safety communications, several organizations were formed to meet a variety of needs. These organizations tend to have a broad influence across the public communications spectrum. An awareness on the part of fire managers of the specific interests and services of these organizations will save time and energy when the fire manager is developing a communications program.

The Associated Public-Safety Communications Officers, Incorporated (APCO), began as a nonprofit police communications group in 1935, with the intent of bringing together that portion of the public safety element involved in communications. As the number of users increased, so did the areas of membership, extending to administrators and communications personnel of police, fire, highway maintenance, civil defense, forestry and conservation, emergency medical, and local government radio services around the world. APCO seeks to promote an understanding among its members of developments in, and state-of-the-art of, public safety communications as regards all areas of the communications community—from towns, cities, counties, and states to federal agencies. Developments are concerned with the components associated with methods, systems, frequencies, and similar elements that pertain to public safety communications.

APCO's monthly publication, *The Bulletin,* informs the membership of ongoing projects of the organization, items that are before the Federal Communications Commission (FCC), and highlights of local chapter meetings. Local chapters exist across the country and handle on the local level the promotion of active discussion and participation in seminars and lectures dealing with the various aspects of public safety communications. Each year regional conferences, as well as a national conference, are held to bring together the top leaders and product manufacturers to inform the membership on the state-of-the-art.

APCO is considered the largest frequency coordination body for police and local government radio services in the United States. It retains an attorney in Washington, D.C., who is licensed to appear before the Federal Communications Commission regarding matters of concern to its members.

Over the years APCO has issued a number of publications that have been beneficial to the communications community. Among these are: *The Public*

Safety Communications Standard Operating Procedure Manual; The Police Telecommunications System, providing criteria for effective systems and future planning and/or modification; and *The Public Safety Standard Frequency Coordination Manual.*[1]

The International Municipal Signal Association (IMSA) was formed to represent the signaling element of the public safety community. Its broad membership extends to fire and police alarm centers, as well as to traffic control maintenance, civil defense, streetlighting, emergency medical services, and local government radio communications. Through its local chapters, the viewpoints and problems of the membership are discussed and noted for the information of all members. IMSA maintains an office in Washington, D.C., which keeps members informed of activity on the federal government level that may have an impact on any of the areas represented.

IMSA, which acts as the frequency coordination group for the fire service, also appears before the Federal Communications Commission on matters that relate to the areas of communications associated with its members. (It should be noted that, as of the end of 1978, neither IMSA nor APCO had been recognized by the FCC as the representative group for the new emergency medical services communications element.)

IMSA features a number of training sessions at its annual conference and also (at the local level) at its business conferences.[2]

In addition to APCO and IMSA there are other organizations that maintain smaller committees which are concerned with communications. Among these organizations are the International Association of Fire Chiefs, the International Association of Chiefs of Police, and the Law Enforcement Assistance Administration of the U.S. Department of Justice (LEAA).

Many fire departments maintain membership in these organizations. It can be of benefit to the department for the fire manager to assign fire department personnel who have a communications responsibility to join such organizations. Those individuals selected should report on a regular basis to the fire chief on information that might affect fire department operations.

Communications operations centers

The local government entity has the responsibility for providing its citizens with a means of access to the fire safety delivery service. It is also a local government responsibility to provide for clear, efficient communications links between a dispatch center and field units. The methods and equipment employed should encompass all components of the fire delivery service as described elsewhere in this book.

The size of the communications center, and the type of center (such as local, county, or state), will govern the varieties of equipment and manning elements used. This chapter will cover those elements that are considered a part of the total systems concept of communications. Each responsible agency should address its plans to these elements and to the degree of operation required.[3]

Most jurisdictions submit requests for proposals (RFPs) which are sent to manufacturers for their response. These RFPs are the plan for a desired system. The manufacturers will respond to the degree that they are able to construct that system. Several opinions have been offered concerning a total system package versus an individual element package. Most jurisdictions have found that it is better to contract with one firm to handle the responsibility for the total system and then to permit that firm to subcontract for the various components. In this way the government entity receives the completed system with all interlocking components functioning according to specifications.

Facility requirements

The agency charged with providing the fire safety delivery service may not be the agency that provides communications for that service; however, the total systems concept should be planned so that there is a cohesive link between all elements. While, of course, facility elements will vary from community to community according to individual needs, the following general guidelines are offered for planners and operators of such systems.

The communications center should have an alternative source of power, capable of handling operations up to seventy-two hours under emergency conditions. This alternative method should be self-sustaining and should be tested on a monthly basis under load. Many local administrators have found that an on-site generator offers a better form of alternative power than the method of having different feeder lines from the local power company.

To facilitate dispatch the center should be so designed that requests for assistance can be handled within thirty-five to fifty seconds of receipt of call from a citizen. Studies have shown that all elements of the dispatch weigh heavily on the total response time (see Chapter 2). Master planning techniques (see Chapter 6) concern themselves with the location of fire stations (see Chapter 19) in relation to demand zones and area of population to be served, while employing the response time of approximately four and one half minutes as a criterion. If a communications center is improperly designed, this can add significantly to that response time. It is essential that the time required for processing calls for assistance be considered a major factor in the design of any emergency communications system. Proper placement of consoles, the correct type of equipment at each position, and sound procedures for the operational flow of incidents will help accomplish the efficient handling of requests from the community for a service.

Geographic files covering the area of response of a given center should be readily accessible to dispatch personnel. During the mid-1970s various jurisdictions began placing this type of material on automatic access microfiche units.[4] In addition to geographic files, these units could also store hazards files, pre-plan layouts of major structures, utility cutoff information of large complexes, city water distribution plans, and special indexes of additional resources. The use of microfiche affords storage of a bulk of data in a minimum of space, capable of being retrieved in a matter of seconds.

Communications centers should be so situated as to afford security for the facility. Consideration should be given to limited access doors, combination locks, and closed circuit video monitoring of entrances and exists. Doors should be sized for normal personnel access and also for passage of equipment housed within the center. It seems somewhat inconsistent to put the heart of a communications control center in a location that is not protected from both the elements and people.

Equipment installed in the center should be provided with fail-safe circuits to ensure performance reliability. In addition, easily located and labeled panels need to be installed so that any malfunctions can be immediately located and reported.

Detector systems or automatic alarms terminating in the communications center should be so configured that they can be easily identified. They may be either manually operated or automatic, and should be linked to coding schemes that result in efficient responses. National Fire Protection Association (NFPA) standard 73 explains the requirements for these systems and the various methods of termination.[5]

Any type of external signaling device (such as tone alerting) used for notifying stations and personnel should be equipped with fail-safe circuits for continuity. If station alerting is done by tone signaling, a backup method or procedure should be maintained for those uncalculated down times of the equipment. For systems with the necessary backup units it should be an established practice to test these components under actual conditions periodically, to maintain competency of personnel as well as reliability of equipment.

The communications center should have a means of communicating with adjacent communities and should maintain formal mutual aid agreements covering responses across jurisdictional boundaries. Past history has shown that no community can be certain that it will not have to rely on the assistance of another community in time of disaster or conflagration. Many large cities found this out during the civil disturbances of the 1960s. A large number of jurisdictions have adopted 154.280 MHz as the mutual aid frequency for their locale. This frequency was approved by the FCC for just such a use. In the later 1970s in the Washington–Baltimore corridor this frequency covered some twenty-five jurisdictions in an area covering 7,832 square miles and having 519 stations. Such mutual aid arrangements are on the increase today.

The communications center should be so equipped as to be self-sustaining for a minimum of five days (there should be a kitchen, rest areas, restrooms, etc.). Many centers operate on a twenty-four hour basis and need facilities for the off hours (4:00 P.M. to 8:00 A.M.) when most of the normally available facilities are closed.

The communications center should exhibit emergency operations plans for increased activity, covering increased manning, variation in operations, and changes in dispatching. Formal plans should be available for handling requests from other jurisdictions for disasters or for normal operating conditions. These plans should be tested on an annual basis to ensure that personnel are familiar with the policies and to keep current with the conditions of the time.[6] Unfortunately, it is often only after a major incident that the value of planning ahead is appreciated.

Personnel requirements

Personnel selection for dispatch positions should be carried out in accordance with documented testing procedures that include functional job related skills, qualification appraisals, and performance assessment. (Selection of personnel for the fire service generally is discussed in detail in Chapter 13.)

Several communities have developed tests for dispatcher candidates. These are administered to applicants to help establish those who would be able to function under the actual conditions present in today's centers.[7]

Personnel assigned to the communications center should possess the relevant skills from Firefighter I under NFPA standard 1001.[8] As a starting point for discussions, this standard provides a base from which to work in developing the needs of a particular community and the service it wishes to provide. This standard covers both the physical and job function standards. Standard 1001 and the APCO publication *The Public Safety Communications Standard Operating Procedure Manual,* mentioned earlier, will assist a community in the development of its own standard for its personnel.

The communications staff should exhibit an ongoing training program for all personnel assigned to the center and involved in field operations. The time constraints of dispatch mandate that personnel remain constantly aware of operational procedures and modes of operation and that they be able to execute them within acceptable time periods.

The communications staff should develop and establish a set of published procedures governing all aspects of operations within the center. These procedures would form the basis for training and would serve to clarify the standards set for the center.

There should be a minimum of one Fire Officer II (as per NFPA standard

1021)[9] on duty per shift. This requirement should apply to those centers which are specifically fire and rescue. For the combination type of center (police, local government, fire, EMS, etc.), a Fire Officer II should be available to the center for decisions that would require such an officer's expertise. Communities would do well to maintain on-duty expertise to handle the judgment situations that arise and to allow their personnel to make independent decisions when they feel conditions warrant such decisions.

For centers that handle emergency medical services, there should be a minimum requirement for one emergency medical technician (EMT) on duty per shift. An EMT provides the center with an individual who has been trained to understand the terminology of emergency medical services and who is capable of assisting the field units that would be operating through the center. The EMT provides a great advantage in helping the citizen who may telephone and be in need of immediate assistance; such a citizen might very well be instructed on how to take necessary action to save a life. A program in Phoenix, Arizona, allows for the medically trained dispatcher to offer assistance on the telephone until one of the emergency units arrives on the scene. And at least one fire department has trained all its dispatchers as emergency medical technicians.

The communications staff should maintain a close liaison with other community activities and agencies to ensure coordination in both day-to-day and emergency operations. When a disaster or other multiple alarm situation occurs there is no time to begin negotiations over responsibilities or where the lines of authority begin and end.

The communications staff should participate in meetings to establish coordinated mutual aid policies with adjacent jurisdictions. They should also meet with the local telephone company to formulate plans covering the use of backup equipment should system failure occur. Several centers have been built over the years with redundant radio equipment yet have lacked the proper backup for telephone lines. Building alternative telephone trunks can be costly; therefore, it is important to view alternatives and develop cost-effective methods of handling short-term losses of telephone communications.

Emergency medical services communications

As Chapter 10 has indicated, the early 1970s saw the emergence of a new service that would eventually become a large part of the fire service delivery system. This service became known as *emergency medical services* (EMS). The Federal Communications Commission allocated ten channels, two call channels and eight "med" channels, in the 460 MHz frequency range, for the operation of medically-oriented transmissions. To the numerous areas of the country where the services of a physician are great distances from many citizens, this new emergency medical element was a boon. Departments adding the medical services element to their delivery system found that it soon came to occupy over half of their activity and that it encompassed numerous hours of training, both initially and for maintenance of skills.

The emergence of EMS introduced a new phase of communications—the transmission of EKG (electrocardiograph) information from patient to hospital. The med channels were assigned specifically for the communications between physician and paramedic. These channels were duplex in nature, meaning that it was possible to transmit and receive simultaneously. Console units for the base station were set up in the emergency rooms for close proximity. Early operations indicated that the operation of base stations was best handled by specially trained dispatchers, which led to the assignment of dispatchers to the hospital base stations or the relocation of the base station equipment to the central communications center.

In certain metropolitan areas the base station equipment is located in one central point where all channels are assigned to the jurisdictions using the service on an as-needed basis. In the metropolitan Baltimore–Washington, D.C., area, for example, there are approximately twelve jurisdictions, including Washington, D.C., and Baltimore, sharing eight med channels. The communications center for each of the jurisdictions contacts an adjacent jurisdiction when a med channel is needed above the single channel assigned. (As an example, the city of Alexandria is assigned to med 5.) When an additional channel is needed the center contacts adjacent jurisdictions to determine what channels are in use or what channels could be used. Each jurisdiction is assigned a tone code for its particular main channel and for any time that it accesses its system.

An important backup to emergency medical service radio communications is the use of telephone patching. (Patching involves the capability of connecting mobile units, through their radio, to telephone lines, and vice versa.) This serves to link the paramedics with additional medical resources and to bridge those areas where radio communications are obstructed by terrain or buildings, or where frequencies are overloaded.

In Orange County, California, the county communications department provides a full-time coordinated program for EMS channel control. Paramedics are dispatched by their own communications center, but en route to a call the paramedic unit is assigned a frequency and a base hospital by the county EMS dispatcher. This procedure ensures that frequencies are being used efficiently with less crowding and little confusion. The work load on base hospitals has been reduced, which allows a higher level of service to the EMS recipient.

The addition of EMS operators and equipment to the fire communications system brings with it increases in costs and responsibilities. Current trends, however, indicate that fire departments will continue to be involved in EMS. The fire control manager needs to integrate the fire and EMS communications in a manner that least affects the fire control mission and, at the same time, allows for an efficient EMS program.

The nature of EMS and fire communications is that they both serve to control emergencies. The expansion of a fire system by the addition of an EMS system is not an unfavorable situation, but it is important that clear and concise procedures and thorough training programs be implemented.

While this form of emergency service has become expensive to the department operating it, the service is one that the community supports and regards as a benefit.

Receipt of alarms

There are several means by which a fire department related incident may be reported to an alarm receiving center. Included in the following sections are discussions of some of the special systems of street boxes and circuits which transmit alarms from the public, and of the fire department equipment that is needed to handle these calls.

It is important that the fire manager keep in mind the primary objective of receiving alarms: that of dispatching the necessary number of fire units to the scene of an emergency in the least amount of time possible. Dispatchers should be provided with alarm information forms and clear instructions for filling them out. Use of a predetermined format will ensure that dispatchers obtain pertinent information about each incident. Duplication can be reduced if the alarm information includes the address or the location of the incident, the type of emergency, the date and time the alarm was received, and the informant's telephone number or the means by which the alarm was received.

The responsibility for receiving alarms brings with it the need to evaluate each alarm to determine if an emergency really exists. Fire alarm operators should be trained to efficiently interrogate persons reporting an emergency, not only to gain additional information regarding the incident but also to help reduce the number of false alarms.

Nonautomatic fire alarm systems

A municipal or other fire protection district usually has the option of buying and maintaining its own fire alarm system or subscribing to a service provided by the telephone company. In deciding between a privately owned system and one that is leased, consideration should be given to which system provides the most suitable and financially feasible equipment for the area to be serviced.

While it is not the purpose of this text to recommend one system over another, some of the advantages and disadvantages of each system may be pointed out for comparison purposes.

Telegraphic systems A telegraphic fire alarm system is generally purchased by the agency providing fire protection, which is then responsible for all operations and systems maintenance. Therefore, the costs of salaries and equipment, repair facilities, and additions to the system should be included in the considerations. The system owner must provide any independent power source and a backup power source, which helps to maintain reliability since it guards against interruption of service.

The connection between the telegraphic alarm box and the alarm receiving center is provided by an electrical circuit carried over open aerial wires or through underground or supported cables. In the most basic circuit, one wire runs from the alarm center to the box and whenever possible returns back to the alarm center following a different route. It is also possible to have a pair of wires running between the two locations following a single route. Some circuits are backed up with a "ground" connection which provides the receiving of an activated box alarm even though the circuit may be broken. Several alarm boxes can be maintained on one circuit, and where automatic grounding is provided it is possible to carry twice as many boxes on the same circuit.

Telegraph boxes are relatively simple to operate; this is usually done by pulling a lever. When the alarm is activated, an inner mechanism transmits a coded telegraphic signal to the alarm receiving center at least three, and sometimes four, times. The coding identifies the location of the box (which is not necessarily the location of the emergency). Once activated, an alarm box must be rewound before it can be used again.

Telephone systems A telephonic fire alarm is usually leased from the telephone company, which maintains and services the equipment. Telephonic alarm boxes are connected individually to the alarm receiving center by a pair of wires that run from the box through the telephone company cables into a central telephone office and continue from there to the fire department switchboard.

Like the telegraphic system, the telephone box alarm is easy to use. Merely lifting the receiver off the hook transmits a signal to the alarm receiving center. The location of the box should be identified at the alarm receiving console so that once voice communication is established the dispatcher need only verify the existence of an emergency at that location. The dispatcher also has the capability of determining the nature of the emergency and other pertinent information.

Because more exact information is obtainable, the fire dispatcher is able to be more selective in the equipment dispatched, sending only the number of units required to deal with the emergency.

Radio boxes A third, less frequently used, alarm system is the radio box system, which depends on batteries instead of electrical current as a power source and uses a radio frequency to transmit signals. Radio alarm boxes may be preferred in large sparsely populated areas where telephone or telegraph systems are not financially feasible or not readily accessible. It is possible that transmission of radio alarms may be interrupted by radio interference, but otherwise the system is no more vulnerable to interruption of service than the other types of alarm systems.

Equipment specifications and definitions of functions for all types of alarm systems are available in NFPA standard 73, mentioned earlier. These standards are based on equipment requirements and do not reflect a comparison, or competing services; rather, they are safety guidelines established for maximum efficiency and performance.

Automatic alarm systems

In the simplest terms, an automatic alarm system would be defined as one that does not need people in order to function. In practice, this is not true, nor is it desirable. A human element is needed to prevent the dispatch of fire units by false or accidental alarms. No matter how simple or reliable a system is, there will be malfunctions. Supervision of these devices by trained personnel will prevent needless misuse of firefighters and equipment.

There are several ways in which fires may automatically be reported to a fire department. These include direct line heat or smoke detectors as well as water pressure drop and water flow indicator devices on sprinkler systems. Depending on design, these devices may transmit a signal to the local fire department, provided a communications link exists. Most electronic systems may be adapted to provide this link to the fire alarm center.

The ability to report emergencies has now been made available to the homeowner. Many devices in use in small businesses and homes may be adapted to report emergencies directly to the local agency. There are several companies that have developed or are developing emergency reporting systems utilizing telephones, cable television, and portable radios. Apart from these new devices, the long proven electronic detection systems can be used on a large scale. This is best exemplified by Disney World, Florida, an amusement park and residential area in which all structures have an automatic fire detection and reporting system tied to a central alarm center.

Public officials should consider a total automatic reporting capability in their community master plan. Master planning provides the opportunity of delivering an automatic fire reporting capability to every person. Planning should allow for expansion of the central alarm receiving center as may be necessary.

It is anticipated that fire departments will be required to provide facilities for the receipt of alarms on an unprecedented scale. The introduction of home computer terminals, automatic telephone dialing, and other equipment offer the homeowner a direct link to the fire alarm center.

Careful evaluation of these new capabilities is necessary. New standards will have to be developed and enforced. Recent observations have already identified some problems. Automatic dialing, prerecorded message machines are difficult to locate. Strong winds, malfunctions, and minor earthquakes may set off several devices at one time, needlessly tying up primary telephone emergency lines. A public information effort is needed to correct this. One fire department instructs those citizens with automatic telephone dialing machines to program a number other than the primary emergency line.

The radio system

The elements that comprise a communications system are illustrated in Figure 17–1. These represent the basic elements and can be found in varying quanti-

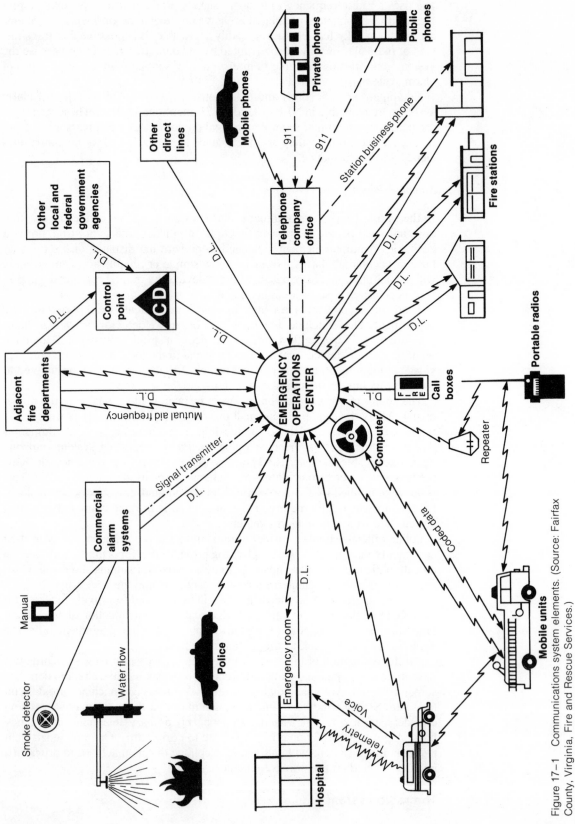

Figure 17–1   Communications system elements. (Source: Fairfax County, Virginia, Fire and Rescue Services.)

ties, depending on the size of the center. Those elements that apply to telephone systems are explained in the telephone system section, later in this chapter. The present section examines the radio system elements and their relationship to the total system.

Frequency assignments

Frequency allocations are controlled by the Federal Communications Commission, under the rules outlined in Title XLVII, Part 89, of the *Code of Federal Regulations*. Frequency allocations for the fire service have been assigned in the low band, 30–50 MHz; VHF band, 150–172 MHz; UHF band, 460 MHz range; and the 800 MHz range. Localities follow formal filing procedures defined by the FCC. In the area of fire frequencies, the IMSA acts as the clearinghouse to review and advise the FCC on any new applications for license. The IMSA maintains a frequency coordinator in each of its chapters throughout the United States. The various bands generally correspond to the type of area being served—for example, 30–50 MHz low band to rural areas, VHF band to urban areas and cities, 460 MHz to urban areas and larger cities, and 800 MHz to large metropolitan areas. The Chicago fire department was the only fire department licensed in the 800 MHz as of January 1979. The MHz ranges selected depend mainly on the characteristics of the geography and terrain in which the signals are going to be transmitted, along with power restrictions, antennae heights, and application.

The assignment of frequencies also began as an availability of channels. The fire service generally began communications operations on the low band, 30–50 MHz. As that band became saturated, localities making application were forced to apply for the VHF band. As the VHF band became saturated in an area, applicants were directed to the 460 MHz range. Now that the 460 MHz range is becoming saturated with licensed stations, applicants in certain areas are forced to apply for the 800 MHz range. The scarcity of available frequencies is usually the paramount reason for changing to the higher frequencies, although in some cases it is the operational characteristics of the system that necessitate the higher bands. As an example, tall buildings, lower power, shorter distances from towers, are characteristics that generally favor the 460 MHz range for operations.

Base stations

Considerable variety is available in the selection of base station equipment, ranging from a small desk top unit to the larger console designs. Along with the variety of design configurations available, there exists a large selection of options to the planner. The human engineering design of base station equipment was addressed in the British journal *Applied Ergonomics,* in an article by Walter R. Harper.[10] The author discusses a case study done on the command and control functions for the Los Angeles fire department. Among the topics discussed are seating, lighting, noise, wall colors, temperature controls, console design, and control center layout. Of interest to all concerned with the design and placement of base station consoles is his approach to the matching of operational requirements, operator tasks, and computer-aided capabilities to produce the optimum configuration. This configuration is also intended to utilize basic frames and panels that were considered off the shelf items. For the novice in the area of console design and layout of communication centers this article is highly recommended.

Mobile units

Mobile units are now produced in a variety of sizes and with varying power and channel capacities. Manufacturers have been able to miniaturize the main control head so that it can be accommodated in the following small surface areas: under dash, between seat consoles, behind the front seat for fire apparatus, and in some cases on the dash itself. Development has also progressed to the point where it is now possible to have a mobile unit that transmits both voice and digital signals. Various manufacturers offer units that also transmit identification codes, and signals for automatic vehicle location systems. New designs have also addressed the problems associated with engine noise and the background sounds from sirens and air horns. Today's units also use the modular concept of construction. This type of design affords more efficient maintenance, less down time, and greater product reliability. Agencies are able to stockpile spare components to expedite repair, at an overall cost that is less than the cost formerly expended for mobile radio maintenance.

Portable radio units

One of the most valuable results of today's technological advances has been in the area of portable radio units. These units cover all of the bands except the 800 MHz range. Power ranges are from one to five watts. Small hand held units have been designed to handle several channels, with options for various antennae styles, remote microphones, and various battery sizes and switch control styles. These units have also been designed to withstand high temperatures and other adverse conditions that are usually found on the fire ground. Portable units have also been coupled with helmet controls that seek to offer a hands-free method of transmitting and receiving. Public Technology, Inc., has been working to develop smaller size units for the fire service that would offer all of the functions needed in a more manageable form. It has been stated that with today's technology it would be possible to manufacture a portable unit that would be no larger than a pack of cigarettes, and at a cost that would allow every firefighter to be equipped with an individual unit. These units would be mounted in specially designed pockets on the individual's protective clothing and would also be designed so that all engine company personnel would be on one frequency, truck personnel would be on another, etc. Portable units have also been designed to allow the use of vehicle repeaters in the transmission link to the central communications center. This gives the senior officer on the fire ground the flexibility of moving from a mobile unit while still maintaining contact with the communications center or with the units on the scene.

In the late 1970s it became possible to equip portable radio units with a scanning capability. This scanning function is the same as that previously available for mobile units and the popular monitor receivers. It should be noted that this increased capability did not significantly increase the size of the radio unit.

Teleprinters

The teleprinter, introduced to the military in the early 1950s, has become a reliable communications tool. Operating on a digital radio frequency, the teleprinter receives short-burst data signals and then prints the message on paper. Currently, several police and fire departments have incorporated mobile teleprinters. Several fire departments now use teleprinters to disseminate general information, instructions, and weather conditions to their stations. One department sends dispatch as well as occupancy data while teleprinter-equipped emergency vehicles are en route to the fire scene. Teleprinters can utilize ordinary household current as well as mobile power sources.

Mobile terminals

Using a typewriter type keyboard and a television type cathode-ray tube (CRT), mobile terminals provide a two way data link. The operator uses the keyboard to enter data such as name, address, and vehicle license plate number. A computer switches the data to the appropriate memory or agency. The data available on the name, address, or license number is then sent to the mobile terminal and displayed on the CRT. Usually this requires a radio frequency other than a voice channel. The direct access of occupancy data is a valuable firefighting tool for the fire ground commander.

The telephone system

The commercial telephone system is the most readily available and commonly used means of reporting emergencies to the fire department. Regardless of its availability and widespread use, however, the telephone system should be considered a secondary rather than primary means of fire alarm service because of its vulnerability to disruption of service. An earthquake, tornado, or other natural disaster may disable telephone service, as may such "manmade" interruptions as accidents, sabotage, or even a strike of telephone company employees.

While it is possible to obtain specific information from a telephone informant, it is also likely that the calling party may be too excited to give accurate information, which would delay the fire department response. There may also be unintelligible calls from residents who cannot speak English, or confused calls from passersby who are unfamiliar with the area and cannot give the correct location of the existing emergency. Fire department dispatchers should be equipped with street and address index files which allow them to verify the existence of a given street and identify its location. The address file may also contain information on the correct fire department response to a given address, as well as other pertinent information such as an identifying map or district number and the closest cross street. If desired, these files may be expanded to include special notations on public and commercial building addresses, including (but not limited to) references on target hazard assignments, storage of flammable or hazardous materials, information on building construction, and names and phone numbers of persons to contact in case of emergency at that address.

In the event that an informant hangs up after giving information too rapidly or incoherently for it to be copied correctly, the dispatcher should be provided with equipment that will play back or automatically recall the most recent incoming calls. Playback devices should not interfere with the continuous recording of other incoming calls, radio transmissions, and other important voice communications.

The fire department should have at least one telephone line reserved for incoming emergency calls; in areas of larger populations, two or more emergency lines may be necessary. These lines should be separate from those used for routine business calls. Where two or more emergency lines exist, the telephone company should provide automatic switching so that if one line is in use other incoming calls will be transferred to the other available lines.

Universal emergency telephone number

Since the introduction by the Bell System of the 911 concept in the 1960s, this emergency device has come to serve close to one-fourth of the nation's population. Since its introduction many factors have slowed its progress; however, an ever increasing number of jurisdictions have taken to legislating its implementation. Those faced with this task may find several hurdles to overcome before operation is in fact a reality. Questions will need to be answered regarding differences between political boundaries and telephone exchanges, common agreement on the processing of calls between the various public safety agencies, and type of employee to staff the answering positions. These questions apply equally to small rural areas, cities, urban areas, and counties, and at the state level.

Two new Bell System features associated with 911 should be considered by all who plan to implement citizen access by this method. Automatic number identification (ANI) and automatic location identification (ALI) offer benefits not previously available through the 911 system. Agencies would have the capability of instantly knowing a calling party's telephone number and location. In the fire and rescue service this capability would be especially useful in combating the large numbers of false alarms each year. In addition, coupled to computer-aided dispatching, this capability has a potential of reducing dispatch time to fifteen seconds or less. Such a time saving in the area of EMS could increase the number of saves, those who leave the hospital after treatment (assuming that service should be delivered within four minutes, in critical cases, to be effective). It is important to note that any reduction in response time will have a positive effect on a department's service to its community.

Other available features include exchange trunk identification, line hold, and ring back capability. While these features have their worth, it is necessary to plan ahead to consider the alternatives and cost–benefits of each. Many jurisdictions that have opted for all of the above features now note that they lose a certain amount of "busy" routing if their exchanges are of the new electronic type. This usually means that there is a set number of dedicated trunks from an exchange routed to the 911 center. If all of these trunks should become busy, calls would not be forwarded to another exchange and then to the 911 center. In such a case the calling party would receive a busy signal. When planning a 911 center one of the key questions to resolve is: Under what circumstances will a calling party receive a busy signal?

Automatic number identification and automatic location identification, although technically feasible, may not be available in all communities owing to local constraints and to the tariffs which govern the offerings of the Bell System in the local areas. Scientific Technical Laboratories has developed a transponder readout unit to be marketed to telephone companies. This unit, in inaudible tones, questions the calling party's telephone, also equipped with a transponder, and displays the number on a small unit next to the owner's own telephone. The Chicago 911 system has automatic number identification and automatic location identification.

Portable telephones

The introduction of portable telephones is considered by many to be extremely beneficial to the fire service. Several experimental projects are under way in various areas of the country (New York, Chicago, and the Washington, D.C., area) to study the impact and practicality of this technology. Once these units begin to be offered by the local telephone companies, it should be anticipated that the public safety entity will add them to its communications system. With the crowding of the airwaves and the restrictions of radio operation, portable telephone units will begin to emerge as a viable link in the overall fire communications system. Many of the functions that are (or should be) done by radio today could be done more efficiently by a telephone unit of the future. The basic fire ground report by the fire ground commander could be transmitted by telephone with more information, and the fire ground commander could, in turn, receive more information from the communications center. The elements of the fire service engaged in prevention and inspection would have a more efficient means of keeping in touch with their agency and those with whom they deal on a daily basis. For situations which require a security link for transmission of information, the telephone would be a better method than the radio, even though there are now scramblers available for radio units.

Public information

Even the most advanced alarm receiving system cannot ensure a prompt fire department response if the public is not well educated on how to use the system and on the proper procedures for reporting emergencies. Public education should be considered an important function of the fire department. While in many areas the size of the population prohibits actual person to person contact, there are nevertheless opportunities available for instructing a large number of people at one time, such as in schools, in hospitals, and in factories and other commercial buildings. Information can also be made available through radio, television, and the newspapers. Education may include instruction on the correct operation of fire alarm boxes; on the information to impart when reporting an emergency; and on preventive fire safety for homes, offices, and public assemblies.

In addition to fast and accurate reporting of emergencies, public education can serve to make the citizens of a community aware of the services provided by their fire department and may also prove to be an important factor in reducing the number of false alarms.

Computer-aided dispatch

In the 1970s the fire service witnessed a growth of interest in computer technology. Taking their cue from the private sector, fire chiefs began to see that computers could greatly improve fire department operations. Several police and fire departments took the first step. They introduced computer technology into their record keeping procedure. This, as it turned out, was only the beginning.

While computers do not work miracles, they do have some outstanding capabilities. Computers can receive, collate, and interpret data in a matter of seconds. They can provide for monitoring of water systems and fire protection equipment. They are capable of monitoring fire apparatus location and can dispatch the closest units to the scene of an emergency. Because of the computer speed and storage capabilities, fire chiefs have at their fingertips most of the information needed to make sound management decisions.

The fire alarm center has long been considered the "heart of a fire department." It is there that information about an emergency is first received and it is there that most major decisions are made during emergencies. While the public has come to rely on the fast response to an emergency request, the alarm center can suddenly experience an overloading owing, for example, to a major fire or to simultaneous accidents. The lack of depth in most alarm centers poses a serious problem. It results in a delay of service due to lack of knowledge, failure to monitor field units, and an insufficient number of personnel. For this reason many centers purposely overstaff.

The introduction of computer-aided dispatch (CAD) to the fire service constitutes, in itself, a new era. The brief history of CAD clearly indicates that it is a most efficient and reliable addition. Experience has shown that, with proper planning, a CAD system is well worth the investment.

Several fire departments using CAD have experienced savings in personnel costs. All have reduced dispatcher work load. One fire department now has fire and rescue activity automatically evaluated and available in written and/or map form every twenty-four hours.

In its early phases of development computers were both bulky and expensive. Furthermore, specialists were required to program and operate them. This is no longer the case. It is now possible to purchase a computer not much bigger (and usually smaller) than a radio console. Since a basic program can be installed at the time of manufacture, fire department data can be administered by the fire dispatcher. The most common configuration for a CAD is one that has a keyboard-type terminal, a CRT display, and a central processor. Many companies offer several options to the user. Before deciding on these options, a potential user needs to analyze the system's capabilities.

Uses and capabilities

The most common use of a CAD is that of response data retrieval. This is similar to a run card. The operator, using the keyboard, enters an address and transmits it to the central processor. The address is matched against the computer records (normally kept in core or magnetic tape). After making a match, the computer displays on the CRT the predetermined response to the emergency. The operator then verifies the availability of the recommended units and dispatches them in a conventional way.

If the CAD is given proper programming and has an expanded memory it is possible to add occupancy data. In Huntington Beach, California, the fire and police departments keep up to twelve different types of data for each occupancy. These data are automatically printed out, on a thermal printer in the alarm office, at the time of dispatch. They can also be retreived in a nonemergency situation, but then only by key personnel.

The status of units is important to the dispatcher. Using the keyboard, an operator can update a unit's status. This status can also be displayed on a CRT or display board. The San Francisco fire department uses the keyboard to change status of units on a large lighted display. The board displays a unit identification and uses colored lights to indicate its availability.

The introduction of mobile digital status entry units, coupled to the mobile radios, eliminates the manual status change: a fire officer need only depress a button to change his or her status through the computer. This function requires a base logic unit that acts as an interface between the conventional radio and the computer status files. Digital status changes can also be printed out on printers which are located in the alarm center.

An extremely beneficial capability is that of teleprinting. Through the addition of a printer control terminal to the computer, response data, occupancy information, and status of units may be transmitted to the field units. (At least two CADs, at the time of writing, transmitted dispatch and general information by teletype to the fire station.) Teleprinting differs from this in that data are transmitted by the computer to the vehicle over a digital radio frequency.

All routine and emergency activity can be logged on hard copy (paper printers) as well as on magnetic tape. This provides the fire department with an automatic radio and dispatch log. The data collected can be stored on magnetic tape and returned to storage after they have been used for data processing.

A dispatch computer can also be used as a message switch device. This is extremely useful in that it saves time. Data may be switched to their appropriate destination as soon as they are received. The interface of emergency reporting and emergency dispatch systems creates the need for rapid and correct switching. Through proper programming it is now possible for an alarm center to receive a fire alarm and transmit to the correct units the occupancy information and dispatch data in as short a time as three seconds.

There are several types of automatic vehicle monitoring systems available. In most cases a computer is needed to interpret the electrical impulses or signals received by the system. These signals are usually coded, and represent geographic coordinates. The computer can rapidly interpret the signals and then display the vehicle location on a graphic display. It is also possible to log a vehicle's mileage and route of travel during a given period.

Not all fire departments will want to take advantage of these capabilities. It is recommended, however, that due consideration be given to each option available. All fire departments will experience obsolescence and deterioration of equipment. Thorough research and evaluation should take place prior to replacing equipment with devices that fail to improve or expand an alarm center capability.

Examples of CAD use

Current use of CAD varies from the simple run card retrieval to a complete fire department monitoring and evaluation system. The Oklahoma City fire department has a CAD that retrieves response data and uses digital status entry units. Plans call for a complete system that will incorporate all facets of fire department activity.

The Los Angeles fire department uses a CAD which has enabled it to consolidate several alarm centers into one central facility. Several departments are using various capabilities. One department has planned its CAD around the community's emergency operating plans; it has included the head office of emergency preparedness and the police department in its CAD program.

Figure 17–2   Fire operations room of a computer-aided dispatch center. (Source: Huntington Beach, California, Fire Department.)

The Huntington Beach, California, fire department has one of the most extensive CADs in service. Utilizing a minicomputer as a message switch, and a storage unit, this department has made excellent use of the computer. The computer, which is shared with the police, receives burglar alarms and fire alarms automatically. The computer checks the units to be assigned against the status files. It then alerts and teleprints the dispatch and occupancy data to the units selected into a teleprinter. The incident is monitored to its conclusion by the computer. The incident activity is logged on hard copy and interpreted with previously collected data. This gives the alarm center a continuous monitoring capability and gives the fire chief an up-to-date evaluation of emergency activity. Huntington Beach is also developing an automatic vehicle monitoring system.

Several departments have taken advantage of the message switch capability to alert fire stations, turn on lights, and open fire apparatus bay doors. This requires a linking of the computer to signal relay systems. To avoid overloading, the computer is carefully programmed to accomplish these tasks one at a time. The tasks appear to occur simultaneously owing to the speed at which a computer works.

Control of the CAD

The best approach to CAD is a stand alone system, that is, one that both resides in and is administered by the fire department. This will result in a system designed specifically for fire and rescue operations. Where a stand alone system is not possible because of shared facilities or funds, fire departments may join with other public safety agencies. In this case clear standard operating procedures are imperative. It is important to establish priorities and lines of authority to avoid misunderstanding or conflict. Some agencies will find that, for political or financial reasons, a data processing division of a city or county will want control of a CAD. If this is the case, an authority higher than the fire chief or the electronic data processing manager should make policy with emergency service as the priority.

Since dispatching is a twenty-four hour function, no system should be considered that relies on a computer which operates only during normal business hours. This would be most likely to occur where a time-shared computer is available. Because of the emergency nature of its use, CAD should at all times be under the physical control of the agency using it.

Purchase versus leasing

The decision on whether to buy or lease a CAD depends on the funding position of the fire department. There are, of course, advantages to both. Purchasing a CAD at the beginning of its use involves a one time expenditure. There will, of course, be costs for repair, maintenance, and upgrading. Leasing offers smaller expenditures over a period of time. Leasing usually includes repair and maintenance but seldom includes upgrading as new technology becomes available.

Agencies considering a CAD should consider a lease-purchase plan. Lease-purchase plans are favorable to the user. The supplier will usually repair, maintain, and upgrade a system as necessary. Leasing a system will give the user an opportunity to evaluate its reliability and performance. If the system is found to be defective or unreliable, the user will not have made a large capital outlay for it.

Standards

To date no standards have been fully developed for computer-aided dispatch. However, as CAD is in fact performing functions previously carried out on a smaller or slower scale, the following guidelines should suffice:

1. NFPA standard 73 (mentioned earlier) should be used where applicable
2. NFPA standard 75 should be used for the protection of the computer[11]
3. Volume 7 of the *National Fire Codes* should be reviewed in connection with protecting the entire alarm reporting system[12]
4. The manufacturer's recommendations for CAD installation, protection, and use should be followed
5. A standard operating procedure should be developed

6. A training program should be introduced that includes extensive orientation and periodic review and testing.

A word of caution is in order. Computers are not as complex or mysterious as they seem. If a department is contemplating an upgrading of communications, the computer should not be excluded outright. Most colleges and universities offer opportunities to learn computer technology. With a fire service background and some basic orientation in computer science, the fire protection manager can evaluate what role, if any, a CAD may play in community fire protection. The money spent to send a departmental team to review existing CADs is nothing compared to the money spent on a system that does not meet a department's needs.

Summary and outlook: the new technology

The discussion in this chapter opened with an overview of fire department communications, including a brief description of organizations that can serve as sources of information. Sections on communications operations centers and EMS communications followed. Next, a discussion of receipt of alarms included descriptions of alarm systems. Following this, the radio system, the telephone system, and computer-aided dispatch were covered at some length. It is now in order to sum up the present and to take a look into the future.

As a by-product of the space program, the technology of communications has made giant steps from the days of tubes and transistors up to the latest microprocessors. These microprocessors offer large capacity, high reliability, and low cost. A microprocessor using complementary metal oxide semiconductor circuits (CMOs) has been designed on a chip of less than a quarter of an inch on a side. It was designed as a communications control element containing 8,000 transistors, capable of executing 434 different instructions, and operating at speeds of up to 2 MHz yet consuming less than 0.1 watt of power.

The technology of microprocessors has enabled the industry to begin addressing the latest needs of the fire and rescue service. Portable hand held units can now be manufactured that are the size of a cigarette pack, and that can be voice-actuated from a small ear receiver/transmitter. Residential smoke detectors and heat detectors can be equipped to transmit their signals to receiving stations, thus facilitating a faster response by the public safety delivery system. A pilot study in a suburb of Dallas is utilizing a similar form of technology, the computer, to receive signals from residential properties when police, fire, or emergency medical services are needed. The individual property owner simply depresses the button on his or her unit for the service needed; this signal is decoded by the computer and services are dispatched. Paramedic personnel can now receive specific medical file information about their patient from computer files while they are on the scene of the incident.

With the new technology reducing size and costs, it is possible to conceive of a time when every person in a community will have a direct link to the fire and rescue service. The expansion of 911 and radio alarm boxes, and the availability of alarm options through telephone, cable television, and computer terminals, suggest that fire alarm centers will take on a new look. The modern alarm center should be able to receive a request for service from any of the new methods. The increase in population will result in an increase in fire and rescue calls.

Those responsible for the receipt of alarms need to begin planning now for the alarm center of the future. It will be larger and more expensive. It will develop a sophistication requiring new skills and knowledge. It will include the upgrading of existing systems as well as the incorporation of new capabilities.

Its objectives will remain the same. It will receive requests for assistance and it will identify, alert, and dispatch the field units responsible for emergency control. As units arrive at the scene, it will provide technical as well as logistical support as requested. Finally, it will collate the data and make them available to the fire chief.

The fire communications system of the future is available today. Many fire departments are now incorporating the new technology into the existing system. It is important that consideration be given to a total system, so that service to the community will keep pace with the demands of society.

1   Current editions of these and other publications, as well as other information on APCO's services, are available from: APCO, P.O. Box 669, New Smyrna Beach, Florida 32069.

2   Further information on IMSA's services can be obtained from: International Municipal Signal Association, 1511 K Street, N.W., Washington, D.C. 20005.

3   Information concerning planning documents can be found in the information exchange library of APCO (see note 1), or by contacting jurisdictions that have completed a system.

4   Typical of these were the Bruning Model 95 and the Image Systems Model 201 microfiche units.

5   National Fire Protection Association, *Public Fire Service Communications,* NFPA no. 73 (Boston: National Fire Protection Association, 1975).

6   The U.S. Department of Defense, Defense Civil Preparedness Agency, Washington, D.C. 20301, has guidelines in this area for those who need them.

7   APCO has available a number of entrance tests and procedures through its information exchange library. These are tests that are being or have been utilized by jurisdictions around the country. A nominal fee is charged for this service. (See note 1.)

8   National Fire Protection Association, *Fire Fighter Professional Qualifications,* NFPA no. 1001 (Boston: National Fire Protection Association, 1974). As of the late 1970s the NFPA had work under way on a specific standard for communications personnel.

9   National Fire Protection Association, *Fire Officer Professional Qualifications,* NFPA no. 1021 (Boston: National Fire Protection Association, 1976).

10   Walter R. Harper, "Human Factors in Command and Control for the Los Angeles Fire Department," *Applied Ergonomics* 5 (March 1974): 26–35.

11   National Fire Protection Association, *Protection of Electronic Computer/Data Processing Equipment,* NFPA no. 75 (Boston: National Fire Protection Association, 1976).

12   National Fire Protection Association, *National Fire Codes,* vol. 7, NFPA no. FC-7 (Boston: National Fire Protection Association, 1977).

Data collection, processing, and analysis

Good data are essential to managing a modern fire department of any size. Today, when management science is used more and more by police and other public services, and when tight budgets sometimes dictate layoffs and the outright closing of fire stations, adequate data to explain the fire department's needs and successes are essential if a fair share of attention and resources is to be obtained for fire protection.

Good data are also needed if managers are to use fire department resources efficiently. It is vital to know at all times what tasks are at hand, what resources are available, and how these resources are deployed. It is important to know when apparatus is due for preventive maintenance. It is important to know what mixes of equipment and company sizes have been needed in the past and on what types of fires, so that decisions such as when to (and when not to) purchase mini pumpers or aerial apparatus can be made correctly. And it is necessary to know what problems are causing injuries to firefighters, to reduce both suffering and lost time.

But it is not just to run an efficient department and to make the case for budgets that fire department managers need good fire data: the data can help save lives and property. It is a rare department indeed that has the resources to carry out all types of fire protection programs as well as it would like to. Good data can help fire department managers understand the details of their local fire problems and thus do a better job of targeting their limited resources in prevention and suppression.

This use of data can be clarified by an analogy. In military jargon, G–1 is operations and G–2 is intelligence. Not only are these functions next to each other numerically, but they are intimately connected in the field—that is, if the military commander is to be successful. The leaders of the fire command have the same responsibility. They need both tactical and strategic intelligence on the enemy—fire. The fire "intelligence units" should have a similar intimate relationship with their leaders, knowing what their leaders' information needs are and feeding them tactical and strategic information as needed. Fire department managers can still fight without intelligence data, but many of them would agree that experience shows that they can do a much better job if they know exactly where the enemy is and what it is like.

An understanding of the need for good data, then, is growing in the fire community. Although few people join the fire service because of an interest in or skills in data collection and analysis, the data competency of large numbers of junior and middle level fire officers is increasing. A growing number of departments are obtaining the services of skilled analysts, and large numbers of chiefs have been motivated to upgrade their data systems. Even the smaller community can join this process by using minicomputers and other technological innovations.

A fire chief with good information at hand is likely to get recognition for it from both city management and the local media. If chiefs happen to come to the job directly from heading a data analysis or research unit, or should they have such experience in their fire service background, then they have the facts to back up their judgment and have demonstrated certain skills increasingly in demand in modern fire management.

This chapter is intended to enhance such management skills by discussing the key management issues and options in developing fire data collection, processing, and analysis functions in a local fire department. The discussion applies both to starting and to improving a fire data system. It applies to communities of every size and type, rural or urban, paid or volunteer. The decisions made will differ from department to department, but every department needs to have these data functions if it is to be successful, whether the data processing is done solely with paper and pencil for one hour a week, or whether the department has its own computer system and a full-time analysis staff.

The scope of this chapter includes data for day-to-day operations and data for policymaking, with emphasis on the latter because it is more neglected and is less amenable to "top-of-the-head" ideas. The fire service manager is probably more accustomed to managing personnel and equipment on a day-to-day basis than to planning prevention strategies for the department, by reason of both training and experience. It should be added that fire protection, rather than emergency medical services (EMS) or other fire department duties, will be emphasized in this chapter, although the data systems discussed can apply to all types of incidents.

An overview

This chapter is organized as follows: it begins with an introductory survey of some examples of the information to be sought and of the terms commonly used. The second section focuses on data analysis and use by indicating how managers can identify their fire problem and by discussing how information can be displayed. The third section takes a practical look at how managers can get started in this area. The next three sections cover, respectively: staffing and organization; sources of data; and computer processing. The seventh section identifies certain key challenges that managers will have to face, and the eighth section provides a summary and a managerial checklist for action.

Examples of information to be sought

What types of information would we like to get from a good fire data system? An example might be seen in Figure 18–1, which shows a map of the fire incident rates per 100,000 population by census tract for a hypothetical city (Community X). The darker areas are those with the higher rates. The data have been averaged for a three year period to reduce the effects of chance, which might cause individual tracts to be uncharacteristically high in any one year. The figure shows that the incident rates are highest in two areas of the city: one a cluster of tracts in the old part of the city, the other a single tract in the east. The rates are generally medium in tracts adjacent to the high ones and relatively low elsewhere, with a few interesting exceptions. (Why are they different from their neighbors? one might ask.) The rates indicate which areas are suffering disproportionately relative to their numbers in the population and suggest which areas are most in need of help in preventing fires.

Figure 18–2 shows the census tracts with the largest average number of fires per year. That information, coupled with more details on the severity of fires and their time of day, can help in deciding where suppression forces should be located (see Chapter 19). It also indicates where the bulk of the fire problem is. Note that the two figures have different types of information. To reduce the number of fires in the city by half, for example, it is not enough to know which groups have the highest rates per capita (Figure 18–1) because they may comprise only a small fraction of the city population. The most dilapidated and fire prone area of the city may have 20 percent of the population and its fire rate may be twice that of the rest of the city. But the majority of fires may occur in the rest of the city.

Figure 18–3 shows the causes of fires (and of civilian injuries) in the city areas with the highest fire rates compared to the causes in the rest of the city. Note that in the high incidence areas fires caused by arson (incendiary/suspicious) and by children playing are more of a factor than in the rest of the city. These cause profiles can help guide citywide prevention efforts and can also suggest what special programs are needed in each area. Similar profiles can be developed for each census tract for more detailed guidance. Similar profiles can also be developed for larger areas, such as counties, where fire incidence of individual towns is too low to provide statistically significant breakdowns.

Another example of information useful for fire prevention is a file of hazardous materials located by address. (Such information can be used to alert firefighters en route to a fire of hazards they may encounter on the scene.) The information could be stored in a computer and made available instantaneously to dispatchers, or even transmitted to a teleprinter or other readout device in the fire apparatus itself.

The types of information in the above examples can be useful to departments of all sizes. The data on which they are based can be stored, and can be analyzed manually or by computer, depending on the size of the department and the resources available.

Definitions of terms

The terms in the title of this chapter and the term *data system* as used in this chapter have the following definitions.

Data collection   This is the process of gathering data into the fire department from such primary sources as incident reports or from such secondary sources as United States census tapes.

Data processing   This is the process of converting the raw data collected into useful files, formats, and numbers, either by hand or by computer, and maintaining a data base for easy reference.

Data analysis   This involves doing computations on the data collected in the data base and interpreting the results for policymaking, operational, and other decisions.

Data system   This is the set of people, equipment, and procedures used to collect, process, and analyze fire-related data to produce information in a useful form. This terminology is somewhat more elegant than such an expression as record keeping, but the concept of a *system* is useful to keep in mind. A system has inputs, processing of the inputs by people or machines, and outputs. This corresponds roughly to the terms collection, processing, and analysis. The pitfall to be avoided is that of a system that only "keeps records" and does not produce anything from those records.

Data analysis and use

The main purpose of a fire data system is to better describe and track the local fire problem through the use of numbers. The use of the system will be discussed first, and the mechanics involved will be covered later in the chapter.

Many of the important ways of using fire-related data are discussed in other chapters. Here we will focus on two topics: (1) describing the fire problem in a

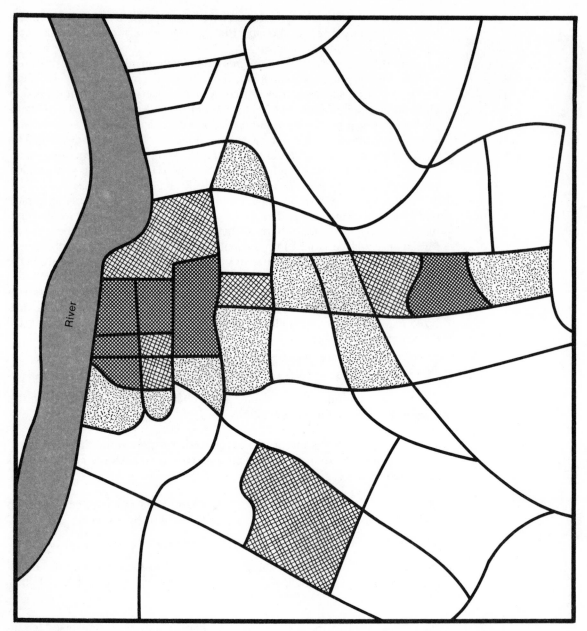

Residential fires
per 100,000 residents

 600 and over

400 to 600

200 to 400

Less than 200

Figure 18–1   Fire incident rates by census tract:
three year average, 1975–77 (Community X).

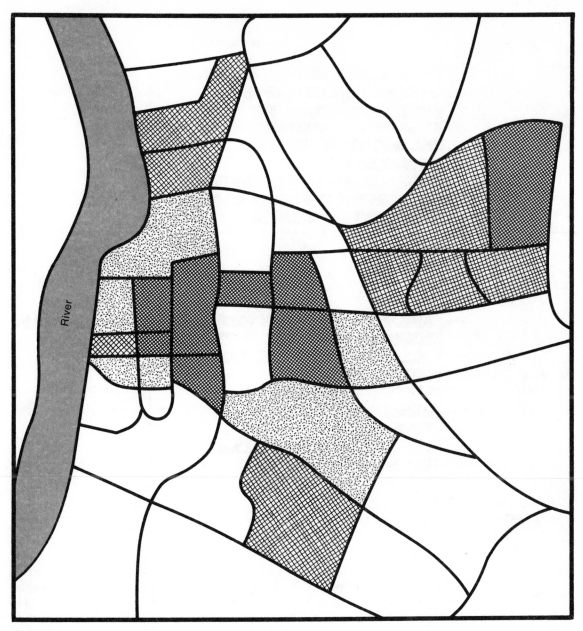

Residential fires
per tract

Over 100

50 to 100

25 to 50

Less than 25

Figure 18–2   Number of fires per census tract:
three year average, 1975–77 (Community X).

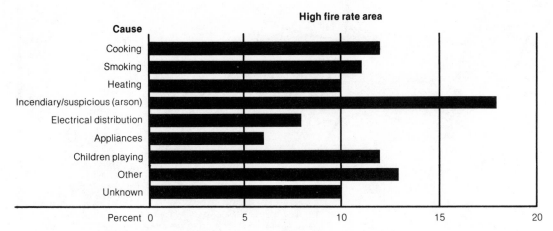

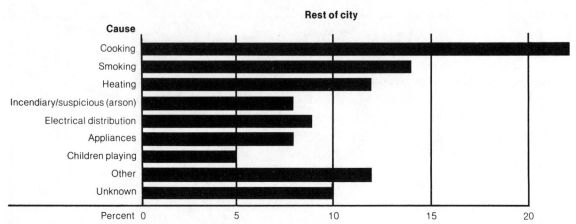

Figure 18–3 Fire incidence and civilian injuries
by type of fire compared for high fire rate area
and rest of (hypothetical) city.

community and drawing implications for policy of various types; and (2) presenting the results of analysis. Chapter 6 describes how to approach the overall planning of fire protection. The analysis discussed here concentrates on only one part of the master planning process described in that chapter—the characterization of the existing fire problem in terms of the kinds of fires that are occurring and the nature of the losses. This information is at the heart of many aspects of prevention and suppression policy.

Identifying the fire problem

The key analysis that every fire department should consider is answering the what, where, who, why, and when questions about the fires, casualties, and losses in the community. Some of these basic questions, and the elements needed to answer these questions, are outlined below (with some possible breakdowns):

1. What burned?
    a) Type of property
        (1) Structures (by type of construction, height, etc.)
        (2) Vehicles (e.g., cars, trucks, trains, planes)

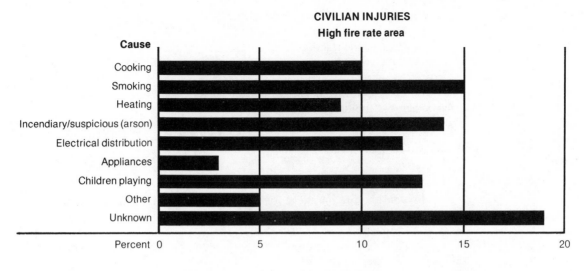

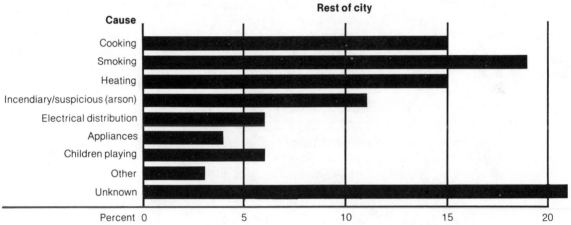

Figure 18–3   (continued).

(3) Outdoors (e.g., forest, crops, trash)
(4) Other
b) Type of occupancy
(1) Residential
(2) Stores and offices
(3) Institutions
(4) Schools
(5) Public assembly
(6) Basic industry
(7) Manufacturing
(8) Storage
(9) Vacant
(10) Under construction
(11) Other
2. Who suffered losses?
a) Owners or occupants (by household income, household race, or ethnic group)
b) Casualties (by age, sex, race, ethnic group, role [firefighter, civilian, other])

3. Where did the fire occur?
    a) Geographical area
        (1) Census tracts or areas
        (2) Central business district versus residential and other business areas
        (3) "Natural" neighborhood divisions
4. When did the fire occur?
    a) Time of day
    b) Day of week
    c) Month
    d) Season
    e) Year
5. How did the fire, casualty, or loss occur (including ignition and spread factors)?
    a) Cause of fire
        (1) "General" cause (e.g., arson, children playing, carelessness with smoking materials)
        (2) Ignition factor (e.g., incendiary, child playing, short circuit, discarded material)
        (3) Equipment involved in ignition (e.g., electric motor, television, blowtorch, stove)
        (4) Form of heat of ignition (e.g., spark, matches, cigarette)
        (5) Type of material first ignited (e.g., wood, cotton, plastic, gasoline)
        (6) Form of material first ignited (e.g., mattress, chair, cabinet, insulation)
    b) Automatic detection or suppression effects
        (1) Sprinkler performance
        (2) Fire or smoke detector performance
    c) Prevention factors
        (1) Inspection history
        (2) Relevant hazards outstanding
        (3) Types of codes in effect
        (4) Other
    d) Reasons for spread
        (1) Material contributing most to flame
        (2) Material contributing most to smoke
        (3) Avenue of flame spread
        (4) Avenue of smoke spread
        (5) Other
    e) Suppression factors
        (1) Response time of first unit
        (2) Special problems encountered (e.g., equipment failure, blocked access, manpower shortage, water shortage, weather)
    f) Casualty circumstances
        (1) Immediate cause of casualty (e.g., exposed to fire products; fell; struck)
        (2) Activity at time of injury
        (3) Condition before injury (e.g., asleep, drunk)
        (4) Other
6. What was the extent of the losses?
    a) Casualties
        (1) Number, severity, and nature of injuries
        (2) Number of deaths
    b) Direct property loss
        (1) Total dollar loss (structure, contents)

        (2) Insurance payout

        (3) Extent of smoke, heat, water, fire control damage (e.g., confined to object of origin, confined to room)

        (4) Number of buildings destroyed

    c) ''Indirect'' losses

        (1) Dollars (for fire-related medical, temporary lodging, food, and other expenses)

        (2) Person-days displaced from home

        (3) Person-days lost from work

        (4) Number of people displaced from neighborhood by fire

        (5) Number of households with serious psychological problems resulting from fire

        (6) Number of households with significant irreplaceable objects lost

        (7) Number of pets killed.

To better understand the fire problem it is necessary to view groups of the above data elements together. There are many, many combinations that might be considered, and it is not possible to view them all here. Analytical judgment and an understanding of the community are needed in deciding how to break out the data most meaningfully. Some suggested cross-tabulations were shown in Figures 18–1 to 18–3. Somewhat more complete sequences are shown in Tables 18–1 to 18–7. Often, once a few tables such as those shown are prepared, questions will immediately arise as to why certain numbers are large or small; that is, the initial findings will themselves be highly suggestive of further questions.

Much of the analysis of fire data consists simply of arranging the right data in tables and then looking for the large numbers; these indicate the big parts of the problem. There are all sorts of fancy statistical techniques that one can apply to data, but many of the most important types of analysis require a much simpler approach and the use of common sense. Some fire service managers may have a fear of analysis, especially when tables appear as computer printouts. Most of the important analysis nevertheless consists of finding the big number in a table and asking why it is big. This might require the use of other tables to break it down further, as illustrated in Tables 18–1 to 18–7.

Because of space limitations only a few types of questions, from the first high level summary down to a low level of detail, are followed here. The same approach can be applied to other problems.

Absolute numbers, rates, and percentages

Before taking up the discussion of tables it is important to understand the three types of statistics that can be used in each table. The basic types are: the *number* or *count* of fires (or incidents, or casualties, or the amount of dollar loss); the *rate* of these events or losses per capita (or per building unit or per some other unit); and the *percent* of the problem falling in each subcategory.

The *absolute number* is the raw count showing how big the problem is. It indicates the work load in the department, and the raw absolute losses to the citizens. Total dollar loss from fire may be compared to total dollar loss from crime, or traffic accidents, or natural disasters. A similar procedure can be followed with the absolute number of casualties.

But the absolute number does not indicate how severe the problem is relative to the population at risk. That is the role of the *rates*. The per capita rates are derived simply by dividing the absolute number of incidents (or losses) by the number of people in the population being served. (In connection with per capita rates, the reader should also see the discussions, in the latter part of this chapter, on matching numerators and denominators and on scaling.)

Per capita rates are needed to compare one part of a community to another, or one group to another, or one community to another, in a fair way. The more people a community has, the more fires and losses one expects, other things being equal. As a community increases or decreases in population over time, it is the rates per capita which should be considered—and not just the absolute number of fires—to see if the problem is getting better or worse. Another way to do this is to plot the change in the number of fires or losses against the change in population and see whether the problem is increasing more slowly or faster than the population is undergoing change.

Most "per capita rates" are actually per capita per year. But sometimes the term *rate* is used to refer to the number of fires per year and not the number of fires per capita per year. The two types of rates are often confused.

In addition to computing rates on a per capita basis, there are other types of useful rates that can be computed. For example, the rate of fires can be computed per household or per dwelling unit. Dollar loss from business fires can be computed per million dollars of sales. Dollar loss from structural fires can be computed per million dollars of assessed value.

The third type of statistic is the *percentage*. This can be used to express the relative proportion of the problem due to different causes, or the relative proportion of the problem falling on each victim group.

To show how the three different statistics might be used, suppose that a fire chief is asked, "How severe is the fire problem associated with smoking in this community?" He might respond that there were 200 injuries and three fatalities associated with such fires last year, indicating that the problem is indeed significant. He might also indicate that the number of casualties per million population (the rate) was 25 percent lower than the average rate for communities of his size, probably as a result of an intensive public education campaign he conducted. That is, relative to other places, his community was doing fairly well, though the problem was still significant. He might also note that fires related to smoking accounted for 50 percent of all fire casualties in his community and that, therefore, smoking was still the number one cause of fires.

The absolute number of casualties alone would not indicate how well the community did in relation to others. For example, New York City during the 1970s had more fire deaths than any other city in the United States. But on a per capita basis, New York City had one of the lowest fire death rates of the top ten cities.

On the other hand, the number of fires per capita can be misleading by itself. Alaska had a fire death rate per capita that was twice as high as that of the next highest state in the mid-1970s, but the total number of deaths per year was about fifty, which was only one-tenth that of New York State or California.

In the same way, knowing the percentage of fires caused by, for example, smoking as opposed to those caused by heating systems reveals their importance in relation to each other but does not indicate whether they are large or small compared to other problems, or to other communities, or to previous years. Since percentages always add up to 100 percent, they do not indicate the severity of the problem but only which parts of it are greater than others.

Thus, all three types of statistics—absolute numbers, rates, and percentages —are needed to adequately describe the fire problem.

Top down analysis

Tables 18–1 to 18–7 illustrate how a "top down" analysis of the fire problem may be started. Only one table has been broken out by all three principal types of statistics—absolute numbers, rates, and percentages (Table 18–2)—but each of the other tables could be given similar treatment. The data shown for each table are hypothetical but are more or less realistic.

The analysis starts in Table 18–1 with the examination of the total number of calls received in one year by the fire department of Community X, by time of day. These calls are broken down into emergency and nonemergency calls; the emergency calls are further broken down into fires versus other calls. This shows the total work load of the department and the relative frequency of fires compared to other calls. Most calls in Community X are not fires but are calls for emergency medical services (EMS). The fire department, though formed to fight fires, performs many other functions. The number of calls of different types, broken out by time of day and weekday/weekend, is useful for scheduling both personnel and departmental activities. For example, inspections, training, and equipment maintenance may be scheduled for low periods of activity.

Table 18–1 Total fire department calls (Community X, 1978).

Calls	Weekday			Weekend (Sat./Sun.)			Total
	7 A.M.– 2 P.M.	3 P.M.– 10 P.M.	11 P.M.– 6 A.M.	7 A.M.– 2 P.M.	3 P.M.– 10 P.M.	11 P.M.– 6 P.M.	
Emergency calls							
Fires	1,040	1,310	700	460	490	300	4,300
EMS	4,130	3,500	2,370	1,200	2,890	910	15,000
False alarms	105	1,400	195	220	180	100	2,200
Good intent/scares	500	900	300	200	350	150	2,400
Other emergencies	25	125	50	50	50	100	400
Nonemergency	120	150	50	60	80	40	500
Annual total	5,920	7,385	3,665	2,190	4,040	1,600	24,800

Only the fire problem will be analyzed from Table 18–2 onward. This discussion will not deal further with the nonfire analysis.

The number of fires and their losses in terms of deaths, injuries, and dollars are shown in Table 18–2 for the four major occupancy types: residential; nonresidential structure; mobile; and outside. Residential is further broken down into one and two family units; apartments; and other (for example, hotels and boardinghouses). This table gives a brief overview of the severity of the fire problem and the types of property where the problem is concentrated. All five types of measures (number of fires, civilian deaths, civilian injuries, firefighter injuries, dollar loss) are important to consider. Firefighter deaths should also be considered when they occur.

According to Table 18–2, the greatest number of fires in Community X occur in outside properties, but these fires are minor trash or grass fires for the most part, and cause little loss. The greatest number of deaths and injuries occur in residential fires. The number of deaths is usually a small number (less than ten) for most communities, but may be high in any one year because of a single large fire. Therefore, a misleading picture may be formed if only one year is considered. While a high year may also occur by chance for injuries, these tend to be based on a larger number of incidents.

Dollar loss is highest for nonresidential structural fires in Community X, with over 10 percent of the total loss from fire coming from one large industrial fire. While this fire should be counted in the loss, it is useful to note the fraction of the loss from the one fire alone, especially if such a fire was a relatively rare occurrence.

Table 18–2 Fire overview showing losses by
occupancy type (Community X, 1978).

Occupancy type	Fires	Civilian deaths	Civilian injuries	Firefighter injuries	Dollar loss ($000)
Absolute number					
Residential	1,024	9	83	69	2,400
One/two family	752	6	54	45	1,700
Apartments	219	3	27	20	500
Other	53	0	2	4	200
Nonresidential structures	655	1	7	25	2,630[1]
Mobile	673	0	5	0	300
Outside	1,966	0	2	5	20
Total	4,318	10	97	99	5,350
Rate (per 100,000 population)					
Residential	271	2.4	22	18	636
One/two family	256	2.1	19	N.A.	586
Apartments	288	3.9	36	N.A.	658
Other	N.A.	N.A.	N.A.	N.A.	N.A.
Nonresidential structures	174	3	2	7	697
Mobile	178	0	1	0	79
Outside	521	0	1	1	5
Total	1,111	2.7	26	26	1,418
Percentage					
Residential	24	90	86	70	45
One/two family	17	60	57	45	32
Apartments	5	30	28	20	9
Other	1	0	2	4	4
Nonresidential structures	15	10	7	25	49
Mobile	16	0	5	0	6
Outside	45	0	2	5	0
Total	101	100	100	100	100

Note: Here, and in subsequent tables, totals are rounded.
1 Includes one industrial fire with a $540,000 loss.

Table 18–2 also shows that most fires in Community X are not in structures, but most losses are, and casualties are concentrated in residences. The majority of casualties in residences are in one and two family dwellings. However, the rate of fires is higher for apartment dwellers than for those living in one and two family dwellings. That is, the bulk of the life safety problem is in homes, especially in one and two family dwellings; but it may be more cost-effective or more equitable to target prevention programs on apartments first, because they have a higher rate, with their residents suffering disproportionately higher losses.

In addition to the current year's figures many departments show the previous year's figures and/or the change from the previous year for each item. This can indicate improvement, or the reverse, from one year to the next. But this year-to-year comparison may be misleading because of a small number of incidents or because of the peculiarity of either one of the years. Another and perhaps better method is to compare the current year to the average number of fires or losses per year over a period of several years. Alternatively, the current year data can be put in tables and the longer term trends can be shown in graphs as in Figure 18–4, where trends for similar communities are also shown. The figure shows that in Community X injuries and deaths have had an upward trend over the decade. The death rate is more irregular than the injury rate because of the small numbers involved: one or two fires can significantly influence the rate in a given year. According to Figure 18–4, Community X shows a somewhat worse record than its peer group as regards deaths and injuries. Dollar losses in Community X also have an upward trend, even when computed in constant dollars; that is, the increase is not just from inflation. However, in terms of dollar losses Community X had a somewhat better record than its peer group.

Table 18–3 carries the analysis of life safety in residences further by showing

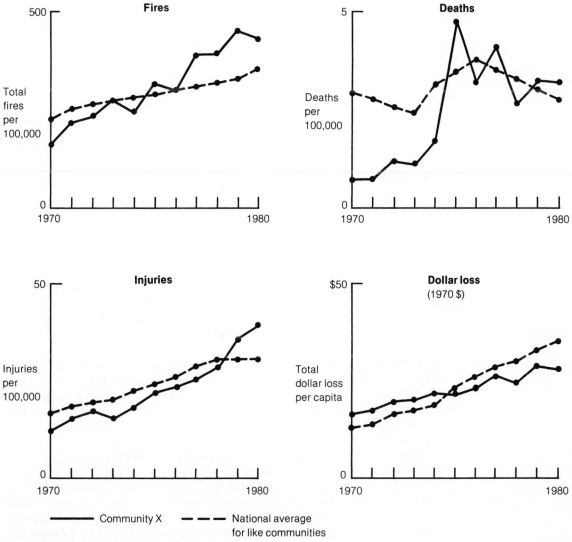

Figure 18–4   Trends in fire losses (Community X, 1970–80).

the general cause distributions for the different types of losses. The leading cause of deaths and injuries in residences in Community X is seen to be fires related to smoking. In terms of dollar loss, however, the leading causes are incendiary/suspicious fires and fires related to heating. And cooking is the leading cause in terms of the number of fires. (It should be noted that the same type of information is presented graphically in Figure 18–3; managers may wish to consider which method of presentation they find more effective.)

More details on the leading cause of deaths and injuries in Community X— fires related to smoking—are shown in Table 18–4. From the table it is apparent that the problem centers on cigarettes dropping on bedding or mattresses, or on upholstered furniture, with the ignition factor being the person who accidentally dropped or discarded the cigarette.

Table 18–3   Causes of residential fires and losses (Community X, 1978).

Cause	Fires	Civilian deaths	Civilian injuries	Dollar loss
Cooking	16%	10%	12%	8%
Smoking	15	20	14	8
Heating	12	10	11	14
Incendiary/suspicious	13	10	12	14
Electrical distribution	8	10	8	13
Appliances	8	0	5	4
Children playing	8	10	9	5
Open flame, spark	9	10	3	3
Other	2	0	11	10
Unknown	11	20	15	20
Total	100%	100%	100%	100%

For further insight into how and why the casualties occurred, it is useful to consider the condition of the victims at the time of the fire. Table 18–4 shows that for fires related to smoking in Community X a large percentage of the victims were intoxicated or asleep.

After analyzing one of the major problems, such as smoking, in detail, one can pursue another leading problem, that of heating. Table 18–5 shows the beginning of the detailed analysis for fires related to heating. The table indicates that for fires in Community X involving central heating systems, the most frequent problem was mechanical failure, and the second most serious class of problem was misuse of combustibles or storage of combustibles too close to the heating system. For fires related to fireplaces the major problem was faulty installation.

Heating system problems could be further defined in terms of whether the systems are powered by gas, electricity, or oil, as well as the brands and models most frequently involved. More popular brands would be expected to show up more frequently, all other things being equal. But sometimes a particular product will appear much more frequently than its numbers in the community would lead one to expect.

What can fire managers do with the above types of information? As this information shows the types of residences having the most severe problem and types of fires they are having, the information can be used to prepare public education programs for the particular groups with these problems. The same type of data broken out by area of the city can show where home-to-home inspections can have the greatest payoffs, or where the homeowners' or tenants' associations ought to be contacted. The data also indicate the types of information that should be provided. The fires related to smoking, for example, point to the use of smoke detectors and to warning people of the dangers of smoking while intoxicated. People might be advised to get "approved" fire resistant mattresses and upholstered furniture, or high quality polyester mattress pads (these pads retard ignition). The heating system problems suggest recommendations for proper maintenance of central heating systems, care in storing combustibles, and proper installation of fireplaces. While these suggestions are not new, the data can show which prevention practices to emphasize in a given area and occupancy type. A focused message may have greater impact than one with a great deal of assorted information which may cover too many relatively minor suggestions.

Table 18–6 illustrates types of analysis possible for nonresidential structures by showing the cause distribution of fires for each of the major nonresidential occupancy types in Community X. The largest numbers in the table suggest which types of causes might be considered first in targeting inspections (for each occupancy type). An analogous table for dollar loss and casualties should also be considered before making decisions in this area. Tables showing the absolute amounts of casualties and losses for each occupancy type would show the relative size of the problem among occupancy types, to help indicate which types of occupancies should be the chief targets of a program.

Table 18–4 Details of fires in residences, related to smoking (Community X, 1978).

	Most common scenarios: deaths and injuries[1]			
Percent of cases	Type of smoking material involved in ignition	Form of material ignited	Type of material ignited	Ignition factor
25	Cigarette	Bedding	Cotton	Misuse of heat (discarded or dropped)
16	Cigarette	Mattress	Cotton	Same
15	Cigarette	Upholstered furniture	Various	Same
44	Other or unknown			

1 Condition of victims at time of injury:

		Comments on victims (from written descriptions on incident reports):
Intoxicated	45%	Often the smoker who caused the fire
Asleep (not intoxicated)	29%	Includes the smoker who caused the fire and others in household
Drugged	4%	
Awake	16%	Usually the smoker
Other	6%	Often other members of household such as dependent children in other than room of origin.

In addition to providing information on where to concentrate inspections and public education programs, a series of increasingly detailed tables of causes of fires can be used to evaluate the success of a community's fire protection programs. For example, a program aimed at reducing the number of fireplace fires in single family dwellings should be measured by its impact on that type of fire rather than on the total number of fires. It might be impossible to determine whether a program aimed at a particular problem was beneficial by looking only at the total number of fires. On the other hand, that program may have caused an increased fire awareness in general, and the rates of many types of fires may go down as a result. (But observing a downward trend in the total rate after such a program is started does not necessarily mean that the program caused the drop. Fires might be experiencing a downward trend in general, for unidentified reasons; separating out the effectiveness of a particular program might require also examining the fire experience of control groups of occupancies that were not exposed to the program.)

Another type of analysis crucial to the fire problem is determining the reasons for firefighter injuries, which make up a large portion of the total injuries from fire. Table 18–2 showed that firefighters had about the same number of injuries as civilians for fires reported to the fire service. Table 18–7 shows that 25 percent of firefighter injuries were due to smoke inhalation. The rest of firefighter injuries were relatively evenly distributed across various parts of the body, indicating that the firefighter outfit needs improving all over and not just in a single weak link.

Many other types of analyses can be done; those cited above are intended merely to suggest some of the important areas.

Table 18–5   Details of heating-related fires in residences (Community X).

Ignition factor	Central heating	Fixed local heating	Portable heaters	Chimney	Fire-places	Water heaters	Other and unknown	Total fires
Mechanical failure	58%	35%	23%	30%	10%	23%	36%	33%
Short circuit	11	4	11	0	0	2	9	5
Automatic control failure	12	7	3	0	0	3	7	5
Lack of maintenance, worn out	8	4	1	16	5	3	2	7
Part failure, leak, break	7	9	2	10	3	8	9	6
Other malfunction	19	11	6	4	2	6	9	9
Misuse or operation deficiency	28	38	63	25	25	71	42	37
Fuel spilled	2	2	1	0	0	9	4	3
Combustible too close to heat	3	3	8	1	1	9	0	4
Improper container or improper storage of flammable material	10	11	22	7	6	33	13	13
Other misuse of material ignited	4	4	1	4	9	4	7	4
Other operational deficiency	9	18	31	13	9	16	18	13
Design, construction, installation deficiency	8	19	8	40	56	4	18	23
Construction deficiency	1	6	0	10	25	1	0	8
Installed too close to combustible	4	7	6	15	11	2	13	7
Other	3	6	2	15	20	1	5	8
Other	2	2	1	2	2	1	2	2
Unknown	5	6	4	3	3	2	2	5
Percent of fires	101%	100%	100%	100%	100%	100%	100%	100%

Displaying information

Busy fire service managers and city officials tend to have neither the time nor the inclination to pore over detailed tables of numbers, however important that may be. Those who do have the patience and skill are still faced with the problem of conveying the information to their colleagues, their superiors, their staffs, and the public. Thus, it is extremely important that the fire service manager see not only that necessary information is produced but that it is presented in a way that enables the key results to be understood quickly and the most important points to be made as clearly as possible. This is doubly true when the results are to be presented in a speech or briefing rather than in a written document, but it is important no matter what the medium is. Magazines, newspapers, television news, and even television commercials point to the fact that simple tables are used to get information across quickly. Good display may not only make the difference of whether a point is understood, but also of whether the information is even considered. Ideally, the analysts employed by the department should have access to a city graphics staff to help prepare displays of important information for reports and presentations, and they should be encouraged to use it.

Good practice on displays includes having short, accurate titles, clear lettering, accurately labeled information, and identification of the source of the data presented. Displays should be designed to be as self-standing as possible; that is, they should not depend on the text or on the speaker's words to be understood, at least at a first level of comprehension.

Table 18–6 Causes of nonresidential fires by occupancy type (Community X).

Cause	Public assembly	Education	Insti-tutions	Stores, offices	Basic industry	Manufac-turing	Storage	Vacant, construc-tion	Other	Total fires
Incendiary/suspicious	23%	55%	24%	19%	17%	7%	28%	71%	29%	29%
Electrical distribution	13	6	5	15	19	7	7	0.5	5	8
Open flame, spark	3	1	9	4	11	9	7	5	11	6
Smoking	8	13	33	9	3	6	5	2	3	8
Exposure	2	0.7	0.2	5	1	3	7	2	8	4
Cooking	24	2	4	2	1	2	0.6	0.3	0.9	4
Appliances	3	2	9	8	5	6	1	0	0.5	3
Heating	6	4	3	8	15	7	6	1	11	6
Flammable liquids	0.6	0.7	0.2	3	4	8	4	0.2	0.5	3
Children playing	1	3	1	2	0	0.6	10	6	11	5
Natural	2	2	1	1	3	8	4	0.3	2	3
Air conditioning, refrigeration	3	1	2	2	2	0.6	0	0.1	0.5	0.9
Gas	0.1	0	0.2	1	2	3	0.6	0	0	0.8
Explosives, fireworks	0.4	0	0	0	0	0	0.4	0	0.5	0.2
Other equipment	1	3	2	4	9	20	2	0.5	0.5	4
Other heat	3	2	1	4	3	5	4	3	2	4
Unknown	7	6	4	12	4	8	16	7	15	11
Total fires	100%	101%	99%	101%	99%	100%	103%	99%	100%	100%

Some of the most basic and useful types of displays are illustrated in this chapter. Figure 18–3 is an example of a basic bar chart, in this case showing the proportion of fires that are due to different causes. The bar chart is very good for showing at a glance which parts of the problem are large and which are small, and relatively how large and small they are.

Figure 18–4 illustrates simple trend plots of fires and losses over time. The inclusion of the line showing the death rate for "like" communities (of similar size, region, etc.) serves as a benchmark for comparison.

Figures 18–1 and 18–2 illustrate how the fire problem varies from one part of the community to another. The darker the shading is, the worse the problem is. This type of plot can be done in terms of the absolute number of deaths (or fires or dollar losses) or the relative number per capita. There is a great variety of possibilities for imaginative displays.

Getting started

How does a manager develop a fire data system that can provide the type of information discussed in the previous section? The development should start with setting goals for the system and then defining objectives.

Goals and objectives

Every department needs to formulate its own goals, but for many the goals might be something like the following: to see that *accurate, timely, understandable* information is *available* with necessary *detail* and *comprehensiveness* for:

1. Setting priorities between fire and other local problems
2. Setting priorities among local fire prevention and suppression programs
3. Targeting programs to the groups most in need
4. Identifying alternative solutions to fire protection problems
5. Assessing progress over time
6. Allocating resources
7. Supporting suppression and prevention operations
8. Carrying out day-to-day department administration.

Table 18–7   Nature of firefighter injuries (Community X).

Type of injury	No.	Per-cent	Part of body injured	No.	Per-cent
Smoke inhalation	25	25%	Head, neck	12	12%
Smoke and burns	4	4	Arm	9	9
Burns only	11	11	Body, trunk, back	11	11
Wound, cut, bleeding	17	17	Leg	10	10
Dislocation, fracture	3	3	Hand	11	11
Complaint of pain	6	6	Foot	4	4
Shock	1	1	Internal	31	31
Strain, sprain	17	17	Multiple parts	4	4
Other	13	13	Other	4	4
Undetermined	2	2	Undetermined	3	3
Total	99	100%	Total	99	100%

Another goal might be: to provide data needed by state and federal agencies and private organizations for assessing the fire problem and guiding research, codes and standards, public education, and other programs.

Setting objectives to meet these goals requires addressing the following questions:

1. What are the intended uses of the information in the system?
2. Who are the intended users (both the immediate ones and those at the end of what may be a chain of users)?
3. What compatibility is needed between your data system and others?
4. How often are output reports needed from the system, and how current must the data be?
5. How accurate must the data be?
6. How much can you spend for different levels of quality and convenience?

For example, the system might be required to produce manning reports daily for the chief of suppression operations that are accurate to the employee. The system might also be required to produce summaries of the causes of fires by occupancy type, once a month, for the chief and the fire marshal, accurate to within 2 percent.

All too often, data systems start with a definition of what the inputs to them will be (that is, what types of records will be kept about fires, inspections, buildings, etc.) or what types of computer hardware will be used to produce them, instead of what information is needed to make decisions and answer questions likely to arise. As a result, one often finishes having collected a large amount of data that is never used, and not having, or not being able to find, the data that are critically needed.

Once decisions are made about the types of data to collect, and the types of manual or computer systems that will be used to process the data, it is often difficult to change these decisions for several years. This is true not only because of physical or economic constraints, but also because of psychological constraints. The average person tends to dislike filling out forms. Once you train employees to fill out forms a certain way, there is much inertia to overcome in making changes.

Flexibility can be built into a system to some extent by thoughtful design of input reports and by obtaining general purpose computer software that allows various types of output reports to be generated. But it is important for fire managers to think through some of the key uses of the data before designing input forms and processing systems, and not merely to assume that if they collect all the types of data that they can think of and buy a computer, then they will be able to produce the reports needed in a timely and affordable manner. Experience emphatically indicates otherwise.

What are the uses for the data system?

There is a wide variety of uses that might be considered in planning a data system. Some have been discussed in the preceding section. A broader set, consisting of twelve items, is given immediately below.

Policy planning   The data system can provide information for planning both prevention and suppression policies. For example, it can tell whether under existing prevention policies the fire rate in the community is going up or down and, if it is changing, whether this is being caused by the fire rates for apartments, single family dwellings, or businesses, or by some combination of occupancies. For those occupancies with the greatest problems, either in absolute terms or in change over time, the causes of fires can be ascertained. For example, it might be found that the fire rate and losses in the community are rising almost entirely because of an increase in residential fires in four census tracts, with three factors leading: children intentionally setting fires; increased use of space heaters owing to recent severe winters; and lack of attention to cooking left on stoves. These findings can suggest the need for starting a juvenile fire setters' counseling program and a public fire education program focusing on proper use of space heaters and on hazards of cooking. If a community-wide program is not feasible, the program could focus first in the most severely affected areas.

For suppression, the data system can show how well the loss per fire is being held down. The data system also can provide information on response times to emergency calls in various areas of the community; frequency of fires; manning levels used at various types of fires; times of day, week, and year of most fires; and similar areas. This information can help guide policies on whether more stations are needed or whether existing ones should be relocated; the desirability of variable versus constant manning levels; and the need for new types of apparatus (such as might be the case if high rise fires were on the increase).

Decisions regarding the best mix of volunteer and paid firefighters can be assisted by such information as the number and types of fires, the number of paid and volunteer firefighters who typically work on the scene, the times of day when most fires occur, and changes in the success in combating fires.

Day-to-day department management   The minimum data system in any fire department will need to provide information on who are the personnel in the department, what units they are assigned to, and whether they are on duty. Similarly, the system will need to keep track of what apparatus is available, which apparatus is in maintenance, what the backup is, what is deployed, etc. This is the basic information needed to know what is available for various missions and what is being used for calls in progress. This information is needed whether the system is all manual or whether it uses computer-aided dispatch.

The data system may be required to indicate not only what the current status of personnel and equipment is, but also to schedule resources, identify substitutes, and warn of resource scheduling problems.

In addition to helping with day-to-day management of the total force, the data system may be required to provide information for managing prevention activities: for example, information on the various types of buildings in the community, whether they have had fires, when they have last been inspected, and when their next inspections are due. The data may be kept in a way that makes it easy to match the causes of fires with the conditions discovered during inspections, so that the effectiveness of inspections can be assessed.

There are, of course, also requirements for keeping financial records as part of the budgetary process discussed in Chapter 12.

Day-to-day operational decisions   The data system can furnish information that can aid suppression operations while they are under way. It can provide information from pre-fire plans on the following: how to fight fires in particular places, special hazards that may exist, numbers of invalids, types of built-in suppression, etc. The data system can also furnish information useful for filling out the incident report on a fire, such as time of alarm, building value, building ownership, and construction. The data system can help prevention operations in real time with information on violations outstanding and past suspicious fires associated with a property being inspected.

Budget requests   The data system can support budget requests by providing information on work loads, for example, numbers of calls by type of call, and if they are showing an upward or a downward trend. For example, many departments are experiencing sharp increases in EMS calls and may need additional rescue units, and some departments are experiencing more multiple alarm calls than before and may require additional units or additional manning per unit.

The data system may also show that new types of hazards are appearing that require new equipment, for example, an increased number of high rise fires requiring new aerial apparatus or special high rise firefighting packages. On the other hand, information may be needed to estimate effects of potential budget reductions. Information on the frequency of multiple simultaneous calls and on the relationship of losses to response time can be used to estimate how severely increased the problem may become after various types of cutbacks.

Budget requests for new services can be tied to information on the detailed characteristics of the fires being experienced by the community. For example, the knowledge that space heaters placed too close to combustibles is a major problem in the community, and that this problem caused twenty fires and a $500,000 loss in the previous year, might be useful in arguing for the production costs of public service spots on radio or television to warn the local population of this particular hazard. Budget requests can also be supported by general profiles of the fire problem which show that the fire department is "on top of things," and by program evaluations as discussed below.

Program evaluation   The data system can aid in assessing the effectiveness of both newly instituted and long-standing fire protection programs. For example, it might provide data on firefighter on-duty heart attacks after institution of a physical fitness program, or firefighter head injuries after a change in helmet design, or firefighter smoke inhalation injuries after purchase of demand-breathing apparatus. It also might provide data showing whether serious fires have decreased after home inspection has been instituted in one part of the community, and, if so, whether the reduction was in types of fires that the program was aimed at or in all types of fires (indicating that the existence of the program rather than the particular content might be more significant).

Bargaining agreements   The data system might be required to provide information on whether productivity is going up or down, in support of wage or manning level agreements. For example, the data system might indicate that an increasing number of calls was being handled by the same size force, which would imply that personnel were doing more work and therefore might be justified in seeking higher wages. On the other hand, a reduction in the number of fires after a period in which the force was used to increase prevention efforts might also be a reason for supporting a pay increase.

Demonstration of achievements   Effectiveness and productivity measures, and information on the nature of the local fire problem, can be used to show both local decision makers and the public that the fire department is successfully handling the public trust and doing its job.

Fire code development   The data system can provide information about structural configurations associated with the greatest fire spread and can identify problems requiring stronger codes or stronger code enforcement.

Consumer product regulations   The data system can help identify consumer products repeatedly involved in fires; or, conversely, it may provide information showing that certain products being considered for regulation rarely are involved in fires.

Setting of research priorities   Identification of the fire scenarios accounting for the greatest amount of fire deaths, injuries, and dollar losses can provide input into local fire department, local university, or national fire research efforts.

Use at state, regional, and national levels   Data for the above purposes also are of interest at higher levels of government. Data aggregated at state or national levels can provide base lines against which local governments can compare themselves. The data can help identify problems that may not be visible at the local level because of the relatively small number of incidents that may occur in any one jurisdiction. The data may help decision makers at all levels of government set priorities between fire protection and other problems and also within fire protection, target programs, and measure progress over time. The most effective way to achieve these higher level goals is to include the necessary data elements in local data systems in a form compatible with state and national fire incident reporting systems.

Response to outside requests   Most fire data systems are frequently used to answer requests for fire information from industry, researchers, regulatory agencies, local officials, and others. Some of the requests may be to support local decisions on particular items of legislation.

A final word   Although the above long list of proposed uses may seem somewhat intimidating, many of the uses can be satisfied with the same basic core of data, and not all of the uses have to be included at the start.

Who will use the data system?

There are many potential users of a local fire data system, including the fire chief, the mid-level chiefs, and almost every officer in the department; the city manager and his or her staff; the city council; the local media; various city departments; budget personnel; industry; and the public. Some of these users are likely to use the system much more frequently than others. Some will be "primary" users who will actually put their hands on the system to obtain the outputs or directly access the files (for example, the fire department's analysts), while other, "secondary," users will use the data only after it is analyzed by others (for example, the city manager or the local media).

It is important to identify the users and the different ways in which they may interact with the system in order to choose the best language and output formats for the system and also to decide on whether to spend the effort making the system easy to use for those with little data training. For example, if the fire chief is expected to look at computer printouts, their formats and column headings should be as clear as possible. Even if the chief can read complex printouts, the time it takes to do so and the problems in showing them to anyone else may dictate a need for greater clarity than if the computer reports are to be used only by analysts. If departmental officers are to be able to request information directly from computer terminals, the system might be designed to work in a high level computer language that is close to plain English. The system also might be designed to inform the user on what choices he or she has, much as is done by automatic teller stations in banks.

The price paid for simplicity of outputs and system operation is both in dollars (it costs more to develop) and in efficiency for the frequent user. A good deal of information can be packed on a page of computer printout, which reduces the volume of paper to be handled and may speed analysis. But the cost-effectiveness of a data system can be ridiculously poor if its information is not given much use. Investing in clear output formats and ease of operation may increase the costs of setting up the data system but may significantly improve the efficiency and effectiveness of the whole department in the long run.

How often are the data needed?

Timeliness of the data is important, but a price is paid for producing reports too often, as it is for missing data when they are needed. The frequency with which data should be generated depends partly on how fast the data are likely to change, partly on how fast remedial actions can be taken, and partly on the tastes of the user. Fairly complete statistical reports are needed perhaps only once a year, as part of the budget process or of annual departmental policy planning. At the other extreme, information on availability of personnel and equipment needs to be displayable continuously to identify the forces available to fight emergencies.

In general, information will be required from the data system at one of the following frequencies: real time (that is, instantaneously); daily; weekly; monthly; quarterly; annually; or upon request, but not instantaneously.

It is important to be realistic in setting requirements for the system and to avoid getting much more computer equipment and software than is needed, generating reports that never get used, and actually reducing usage by inundating users with too frequent reporting.

The frequency of generating various types of information may be influenced by the needs of those outside the city. For example, the state or federal government may require information on a monthly or quarterly basis that a local government needs only annually because of the small number of incidents it has and the difficulty in observing patterns over short intervals of time. But when the data are aggregated by the state for many small communities, patterns can be determined without waiting as long.

How accurate must the data be?

There is no simple way to specify accuracy requirements, that is, how "good" the data need to be. Accuracy needs to be good enough to answer with reasonable confidence the question being asked. It varies from question to question. For example, fire chiefs need to know exactly how many and which engine companies are available for dispatching at any instant. But they can probably afford to miscount the number of fire calls each company has in a year by 2 or 3 out of 500; though they would not want to be off by 50, because then they would not know if a 10 percent change in fire calls was due to successful prevention or to miscounting.

Fire chiefs not only have to have accurate data; they also have to be able to demonstrate publicly that they do. Local officials need to believe the data are credible if they are to use them in making decisions. It is not enough to say that records are "as accurate as possible," or that data provided by the chief are to be believed because the chief is a reputable officer. Consideration should be given to regular monitoring of accuracy and to routine use of quality control procedures.

On the other hand, too much precision can also be costly. For example, dollar loss usually cannot be estimated down to the last dollar and certainly not down to the last cent. It is unnecessary and may even be counterproductive to ask firefighters to be overly precise in estimating dollar loss. It makes little sense to spend more money on appraising minor damage than the value of the damage itself.

What aspects of "accuracy," then, should be considered in designing a fire data system? The first is the *accuracy and completeness of the individual fire incident reports, inspection records, or other records in the system.* Accuracy of information starts with the ability of the data collectors (probably fire officers or fire investigators for most records) to determine the facts about what happened at the scene of the fire or other incident. For example, they must be able to determine the cause of the fire with a reasonable degree of confidence for most incidents. Therefore, the data system requirements generate a training requirement.

After determining the facts about an incident, the next step toward accuracy is entering the information properly on the forms and giving the data items numerical codes, if that is called for. If the facts are known but miscoded, for all purposes thereafter it is the same as if the investigation was incorrectly carried out in the first place. Fire officers therefore need training in filling out the paperwork correctly. The data system design can itself influence the ability of the firefighter to correctly enter and code data by the simplicity of the system, by the clarity of training and instruction materials, and by the clarity of the forms to be filled out. Providing feedback to the data collectors on common errors and on their own errors also is important. Error detection might be built into the system in several ways: through checking by supervisors of the reports made by their subordinates; through centralized checking by clerks of all information input to the system; through computer screening of all inputs, including checks on the "reasonableness" of the entries; and through feedback from those who actually use the system and who find suspicious or questionable results when data are analyzed.

Completeness in filling out all entries called for on each form and completeness in filling out forms for each incident also should be encouraged. Otherwise, if, for example, the number of firefighter injuries is filled out only on 80 percent of the fires attended, might it not be assumed that the remaining 20 percent of fires had no injuries? Or that they had injuries in proportion to those on the 80 percent filled out? If there had been 100 injuries during the previous year, for example, the chief would want to know whether this year there were, again, 100, or 80, especially if the chief had instituted a special firefighter safety program or a physical fitness program. In the same way, if departments send in some unknown percentage of their incidents to their state reporting system, the state does not know whether the real fire situation has improved or worsened, or whether observed changes are due to changes in completeness of reporting. *It is important to stress completeness of reporting* with an accurate record for every single call made. The amount of data provided for different types of calls may vary, but there must be some record for every call so that fire managers can account for the work load of the department, can have records should legal questions arise, and can understand the magnitude of the problem faced by the fire department and how it changes over time.

The next kind of accuracy consideration is the *accuracy of data processing*. It is important to avoid a situation in which data are properly reported only to be scrambled when they are entered into a computer. This may imply the need for such controls as verification keying in addition to the initial keying, and the need for designing input forms with an eye to making it easier for keypunchers to enter data. It also suggests a need to consider giving the clerks who do the keying some information on the intent of the system so that they can catch errors. (It is amazing how proficient a good keypuncher can be in doing this.) The computer programs that process the data can also check to see whether the numerical entries on the forms are allowable codes and whether the data are reasonable. These checks can catch some keypunch errors but will not catch errors in which one legal code is incorrectly used in place of another legal code.

The third major type of accuracy consideration is the *accuracy of the analysis* made with the data. Poor analysis can distort information based on accurate data. For example, many cities have only a small number of fire deaths each year. Year-to-year changes might be caused simply by random fluctuations as opposed to real changes in the underlying nature of the problem. A 10 percent reduction in the number of fires from 10 a year to 9 a year is more likely to be due to chance than is a 10 percent reduction from 1,000 fires to 900 fires. Fire service managers should be aware of the statistical significance of changes in their data so that they do not mistakenly change their policy because of random fluctuations in the data from year to year. The more unreliable the input data are in the data system, the more important it is to have a competent analyst to interpret the data and try to cope with the errors in them.

Fire officers of captain rank or higher should, if possible, be trained in analysis sufficiently to be able at least to describe the fire problem in their own area. This is a third type of training needed to improve fire data systems, in addition to training in investigation and reporting.

More accuracy is usually needed for estimates of year-to-year differences than for absolute totals, because it is the changes that will be used to evaluate whether the local fire problem is improving or worsening, and whether programs are working. The estimate of the total amount of dollar loss (or fire deaths or injuries) may be off somewhat, but a knowledge even of the scale of the losses can be useful for setting priorities of fire versus other municipal problems, and for receiving a rough indication of how well the city is performing in relation to other cities. Overall accuracy requirements, therefore, may be paced by the accuracy needed to assess year-to-year changes.

Iterating the design

It is difficult to spell out all of the above requirements at the first attempt. Generally it is necessary to make some assessment of the data system's requirements.

In most departments there will be some sort of existing data system—even if it is merely composed of manual records and rudimentary annual reports. These departments may find it useful to go through the following steps:

1. Describe the existing data system in the above terms (uses, users, information furnished, accuracy, reporting intervals, etc.)
2. Describe the ideal system and one or more alternatives midway between the existing system and the ideal
3. Develop tentative designs for each set of requirements
4. Cost out each design, including money for computer time, printing, data analysts, and other specialists versus what can be achieved with in-house resources
5. Revise the designs until a satisfactory, cost-effective approach is defined.

Staffing and organization

The fate of the fire department can often be determined by whether the chief and the city management have good information on its needs and performance, and whether they can answer questions raised by the city council, the general public, and others. The organization and staffing of the data function largely determine whether the data function will be the major asset that it can be.

Organization

Many medium-sized and large departments have established a research and planning unit or an analysis unit—under a variety of names. Typically, this unit has responsibility for producing annual reports, providing data during the year on questions the chief or others may have, helping develop master plans for the department, and assisting in special studies such as evaluating the cost-effectiveness of new equipment or determining the most frequent types of injuries occurring to firefighters. Sometimes part or all of the analysis function is undertaken by the fire prevention bureau.

Staff skills

The research unit needs to have four basic skills either within it or available to it on short notice. Three of these skills are: an understanding of the fire problem; the ability to analyze and evaluate data accurately; and computer programming skills where there is access to a computer. The fourth skill is the ability to write clearly and to translate statistics into words and figures that can be quickly understood by the chief, the city council, and others.

Staff size

The analysis role may be filled by personnel ranging from one person giving part of his or her time in a small volunteer department to a separate four or five person unit for analysis with perhaps another unit of several persons for data processing in larger departments. A typical mix for a medium-sized department might consist of a fire officer of captain or battalion chief rank heading the unit, with one or two "analysts" and a secretary who might double as a research assistant.

Organization placement and trust

The physical positioning of the unit and the influence of its head can significantly affect whether the data are used. The head of the analysis unit should preferably be physically close to the chief and trusted. This helps keep the anal-

ysis unit tuned in to department priorities and helps ensure that its products will
be tailored to the needs of the main users.

It also is important that the users have confidence in the source of their information. In one large city a data analysis section with a first rate analyst heading
it was relatively wasted because it was physically remote from the department's
chiefs, and a good working relationship had not been developed between the
section head and the chiefs to overcome this distance barrier. In another large
city a one man analysis and computer programming operation made a major
contribution to department decisions by literally being on the other side of a
private door to the department head's office, and having his trust.

Civilians or firefighters?

The ideal member of an analysis unit is a fire officer with academic training in
analysis techniques or a flair for working with numbers. As the general educational level of the fire service rises, an increasing number of paid departments
have such personnel available. Some departments have found latent skills in
computer programming or data analysis among their firefighters. In volunteer
departments there often are engineers, computer programmers, doctors, lawyers, and others with analytical backgrounds who might be used for the fire data
analysis function.

Firefighter personnel assigned to light duty are another potential resource for
data tabulations and limited analysis; but unless they are given adequate training
they should not be counted on for producing accurate analyses or interpretations of the data any more than they could be expected to be proficient EMTs
without training.

Hiring civilian analysts and programmers is another option that should be
considered. There are many success stories in which a civilian analyst knowing
little or nothing about fire departments has, in a period of weeks, acquired
enough insight from working with a fire chief or a head of an analysis unit to
begin making a useful contribution to the department.

There are also many success stories in which departmental secretaries have
been able to enrich their jobs by undertaking simple data analysis tasks such as
tallying fires by various causes or checking incident reports for completeness.
Often, after a period of on-the-job training, they are able to detect and correct
errors in the data and to prepare reports.

Departments might also consider using volunteer analysts who are not firefighters but who might be "fire buffs" or might be willing to contribute their
services to the community. Sometimes this can be done in connection with a
local college, with benefits to students and fire departments alike. Students also
can be used as relatively inexpensive statistical aides on a part-time basis, especially for helping with seasonal crises such as budgets.

Future chiefs of departments?

Heading the analysis section might be considered as one of the important rota-
tional assignments for future chiefs of the department. As the fire service competes with other city departments for increasingly scarce municipal dollars, it is
one of the prime responsibilities of a chief to understand the fire problem in the
community and to use quantitative information to argue persuasively.

Sources of data

The task of specifying the data to be collected for a local fire data system can be
approached from two directions: defining what information is wanted and then
identifying the means of collecting it; or considering the readily available

sources and the most that can reasonably be obtained from them. In practice the two approaches tend to converge. There are a few common sources that provide much of the data needed for most of the uses described in the previous section.

It is useful to consider data sources in two groups: those which come from fire department collection and those which come from sources outside the fire department. The fire department sources include incident reports, investigation reports, inspection records, lists of department resources and their status, pre-fire plans, and special studies. Sources from outside the department include building and occupancy data from city planning and tax records; socioeconomic and demographic data from the U.S. Bureau of the Census or from local planning departments; and data on the performance of other fire departments, states, regions, and the nation.

Incident reports and logs

Perhaps the most basic building block of a fire data system is the incident report filled out for each call the fire department goes out on. In most departments the incident report is filled out by the officer in charge of the first due company at the scene or by a higher rank officer in charge of the scene. Incident reports are also filled out by companies from other departments providing mutual aid.

In the past, every fire department devised its own report with its own choice of data elements and definitions. The incident report varied from a simple one-line record in a log to a detailed form with over ninety data elements. The result was that data from different departments could not be compared or added with confidence "apples to apples."

To help remedy this situation, the National Fire Protection Association (NFPA) organized a fire reporting committee which is made up of representatives of the fire service, industry, fire professional organizations, and federal agencies. The committee developed the fire incident reporting system known as the 901 system. It includes model incident and casualty reports applicable to all types of calls.

Figure 18–5 is a sample of an NFPA 901 system incident report. These reports contain a rich array of data elements, including the type of incident (whether a fire, false alarm, gasoline spill, rescue run, etc.); the number of personnel and types of equipment used at the scene; the times of arrival at the scene and of going back into service; the number of civilian and firefighter casualties; the extent of damage and estimated loss; the cause of the fire in terms of the source and form of the heat of ignition, the type and form of the material first ignited, and the ignition factor that brought the heat in contact with the material ignited; the type of construction; the existence of fire detectors or sprinklers and whether they worked; the particular brand and model of equipment involved in the ignition; and related details.

The incident report requires only a few items to be filled out in the case of an incident other than a fire; a few more items are needed for an outside or vehicle fire; and the greatest amount of detail is needed for a structural fire involving casualties. The progressively increasing detail is meant to correspond roughly to the importance of the fire and the usefulness of the additional information.

In addition to the incident report a separate casualty report is filled out for each civilian or firefighter casualty, giving details of the reasons for the injury, the severity of the injury, where it was treated, and other information on the circumstances. A typical casualty report is shown in Figure 18–6; it corresponds to the fire described in the incident report in Figure 18–5.

Corresponding to the data elements on the incident and casualty reports is a dictionary of terms and the numerical codes for each term.[1] Firefighters write in a description of each item appropriate to a given incident, and either they or a

Figure 18–5 Sample fire incident report for a residential fire (used in NFIRS and based on NFPA 901).

Avery, Del. Fire Department — 902F 6/77 LAYOUT 2

Fill In This Report In Your Own Words

(ANY STATE) INCIDENT REPORT

1 ☐ Delete 2 ☐ Change

A — 1 | FDID: 17634 | Incident No.: 000471 | Exp. No.: 00 | Mo.: 05 | Day: 16 | Year: 72 | Day of the Week: Thurs | Alarm Time: 5/021 | Time—"In Service": 1116

B — CORRECT ADDRESS | No.: 133 | Dir.: NW | Name: Pleasant Apt. #6 | Type: St | Zip Code: 19701 | Census Tract: 1066.00

C — Occupant Name: Lawrence P. Ford | Telephone: 302-752-0327 | Room or Apt.: 6

D — Owner Name: James E. Caldwell | Address: 14 Delmar Dr., Avery | Telephone: 302-799-4241

E — Method of Alarm from Public: Box alarm 2883 | 2 | Type of Situation Found: Bedroom fire | 11

F — Type of Action Taken: Extinguishment | 1 | Co. Inspection District: E2 | Shift: 3 | No. Alarms: 1 | Mutual Aid: 1 ☐ Rec'd 2 ☐ Given

G — No. Fire Service Personnel Used at Scene: 016 | No. Engines Used at Scene: 002 | No. Aerial Apparatus Used at Scene: 001 | No. Other Vehicles Used at Scene: 001

COMPLETE ON ALL INCIDENTS

H — 2 | No. Incident-related Injuries^ Fire Service: 001 Others: 002 | No. Incident-related Fatalities^ Fire Service: 000 Others: 000 | Complex: APT. 42

I — Fixed Property Use: Apartment House 422 | Mobile Property Type^^: N/A 08

COMPLETE IF CASUALTY OR FIRE

J — Area of Fire Origin: Bedroom 21 | Level of Fire Origin: Twenty feet 3 | Termination Stage: Flame 3

K — Equipment Involved in Ignition (if any)^^: Hot Plate 25 | Form of Heat of Ignition: Short Circuit 23

L — Type of Material Ignited: Cotton 72 | Form of Material Ignited: Curtain 36 | Ignition Factor: Short Circuit 54

ALL IGNITIONS

M — Structure Type: Multiple Use Building 2 | Construction Type: Brick and Wood 5 | Construction Method: Site-built 1

N — Extent of Flame Damage: Confined to room 3 | Extent of Smoke Damage: Confined to Bldg. 6 | Extent of Water Damage: Confined to bldg. 6

O — Extent of Fire Control Damage: Confined to room 3 | Detector Performance: No detectors 8 | Sprinkler Performance: No sprinklers 8

P — IF FLAME SPREAD BEYOND ROOM OF ORIGIN | Type of Material Generating Most Flame: N/A 98 | Avenue of Flame Travel: N/A 98

Q — IF SMOKE SPREAD BEYOND ROOM OF ORIGIN | Type of Material Generating Most Smoke: Blanket 72 | Avenue of Smoke Travel: Corridors 2

FOR STRUCTURE FIRE ONLY — COMPLETE IF FIRE

R — Method of Extinguishment: Pre-connect lines 1

S — Estimated Total Dollar Loss: 000002700 | Property Damage Classification: $2700 3 | Time from Alarm to Agent Application: Four minutes 3

ALL FIRES INCIDENTS

T — Officer in Charge (Name, Position, Assignment): Robert E. Barrett, Capt. Eng. 2 | Date: 5-16-72

Member Making Report (If Different from Above): Louis R. Jones, F. F. Eng. 2 | Date: 5-16-72

COMPLETE ON ALL INCIDENTS

^ List name, age, sex, and description of injury for each casualty on form 902G

^^ Complete Below

☐ Check box if remarks are made on reverse side.

U — 3 | If Mobile Property | Year | Make | Model | Serial No. | License No. (if any)

V — 4 | If Equipment Involved In Ignition: Hot Plate | Year: 1950 | Make: Colony | Model: X-Y-2 | Serial No.: 106-N78 | Voltage (if any): 110-V-AC

central office codes each item using the standard code provided. For example, one item on the form is the "fixed property use" of the place having the fire. If the fire was in a year-round, single family residence, it would be coded as 411. If the fire was in an apartment in a six unit building, it would be coded 422. If the fire was in a hotel, it would be 441. This system makes it easy to count the number of single family dwelling fires in a community (by adding all the fires where the first two digits of fixed property use are 41), or the total number of residential fires (all fires in which the first digit is a 4). Fires in one community then can be added or compared to those in another.

Since the NFPA 901 incident report has been put into use by the fire service, many suggestions for improving the codes have been made. These are collected by the NFPA Fire Reporting Committee and proposed to the field; revisions to the 901 system are made approximately once every five years (not more frequently, to avoid having to retrain firefighters in the coding too often).

In any type of report to be filled out routinely, there is always a compromise between the level of detail to collect on each incident and the data burden placed on the firefighter. Almost anyone who thinks about what should be collected will come up with a slightly different idea. It is, however, extremely important that fire departments collect a common core of data; even though it will

Figure 18–6 Sample casualty report accompanying incident in Figure 18–5 (used in NFIRS and based on NFPA 901).

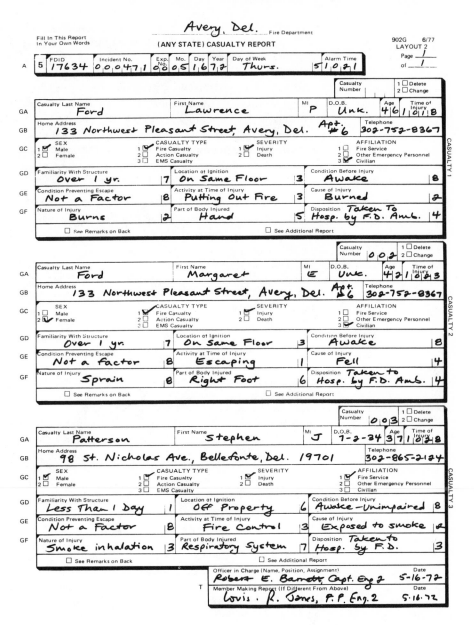

never be perfect for all, it should be the best consensus possible. Individual communities may wish to add additional items of interest to themselves that are not collected nationally. They may also wish to break out some of the elements in more detail than is done by the existing coding system.

Examples of data elements which some state or local governments have added to the form are: severity of nonfatal injuries; number of stories in the building of origin (in addition to the level where the fire started); and more details of the types of equipment used to handle an incident, such as the number of hose lines and their diameter, and the number and types of ladders.

Some local departments use a checklist format for their incident report. Standard items are listed under headings that encompass the kinds of information ordinarily needed. These items can be checked off, as applicable; written out entries are reserved for unusual cases. There are many pros and cons to using checkoff forms. The main issues are the simplicity of these forms, and the limited need to consult manuals to fill them out, versus the possibility that they may encourage firefighters to mark one of the check boxes instead of expending the effort to fill out the "other" box when the checkoff list does not fit the situation. The checkoff forms also require larger forms and/or smaller print to fit all items in.

Another major decision is whether to have the field officer who filled out the form also provide the numerical code for each entry or to have coding done centrally at the municipal or state level. The main advantages of central coding are the consistency of the coding and the fact that less training is needed by each line officer. The person who fills out the form need only know the definition and intent of each entry and can then enter what happened in his or her own words.

National Fire Incident Reporting System (NFIRS) The National Fire Incident Reporting System is a way of collecting comparable data on fires and other incidents for use at local, state, and national levels. The system is coordinated by the National Fire Data Center, which is one of the major program areas of the U.S. Fire Administration.

The basic idea in the system is to collect a core of reliable data—that recommended in the NFPA 901 Fire Reporting System—on a large enough sample of fires so that the local fire problem can be adequately assessed and fair and accurate information provided to the entire fire community.

The local departments send either incident and casualty forms or computer tapes containing the equivalent information to their state office responsible for statewide fire statistics; usually this is the state fire marshal's office. The state office uses the information in developing statewide fire reports, fire codes, inspection practices, and public education programs, and for answering questions raised by local fire departments, industry,

elected officials, and other interested parties.

Most states provide each fire department participating in the system with a feedback report anywhere from once a month to once a year, and upon request. The states also send quarterly tapes to the National Fire Data Center, where they are used along with data from other sources to prepare estimates of the magnitude and characteristics of the United States fire problem. The information is also used to support legislation, to provide guidance to industry, to help set priorities in fire research, and to provide base line information to local governments against which they can compare their own performance and help assess their own needs.

Participation by states in NFIRS is voluntary, though the goal is to get as close to 100 percent participation as possible by the early 1980s. Within most states, participation of local governments in the state system is also voluntary, although most states have laws requiring the transmittal of at least some key information to the state on certain classes of fires.

On the other hand, the field officer filling out the form may not provide enough detail to distinguish between two categories of codes, and the central coder must either guess at the additional detail, or lose it, or spend time contacting the officer who filled out the form. Both systems work, each has its backers, and data at present are not adequate to indicate the superiority of one over the other.

Fire investigation reports

Another major source of fire data in addition to incident reports is fire investigators' reports. Most communities investigate incendiary or suspicious fires and fires involving deaths. Some communities investigate all building fires, all fires with severe injuries, and fires of special interest.

The fire investigation reports form an especially important pool of data because they describe the most significant fires in the community and are conducted by personnel who are highly trained in investigation. The investigations also provide more details than are available from routine incident reports. They can be invaluable for understanding exactly what types of remedial actions are necessary.

Although traditionally used for special types of fires, as noted above, in-depth investigations can also be used to obtain more understanding of common types of fires that do not result in large losses but that collectively are important to life safety or property loss.

The format of the in-depth investigation report should parallel that of the incident report to the extent possible so that data on the basic incident file can be easily improved.

Building inspection records

Most fire departments inspect at least some classes of institutional and commercial occupancies. Some inspect much broader classes of occupancies, including residences (see Chapter 8). Each inspection is usually documented, and the record includes the following: date, inspector, hazards found, hazards removed, and warnings or citations issued. Many departments keep a file, organized by occupancy type and address, on each building in the community. The file often includes records of inspections prior to the occupation of the building, permits issued, routine inspections, and correspondence in connection with hazards and with reinspections to see that hazards were removed. Sometimes information on fires that took place in each building is also included in the file, so that the building's fire history can be compared to its inspection history. More often, the fire information is stored in a separate file which can be correlated with the inspection file. Some communities, such as Charlotte, North Carolina, have taken pains to record hazards in terms similar to those used to describe causes of fires, so that inspection practice can be linked to its results. For example, a change in the number of fires of electrical origin can be compared to a change in the number of inspections in which electrical problems were found.

Dispatch records

Much valuable information is obtained in the process of receiving an emergency call and dispatching equipment to it. Dispatch records may be in the form of voice tapes, printed forms, informal notes, or computer files. Information associated with a dispatch often includes the nature of the call, the time of receipt of the call in the department, their time of arrival at the scene, the time the fire was knocked down, and the time the equipment was back in service. Of course the address and often the type of occupancy and the name of the person reporting the fire also are recorded. This information can serve as a valuable source for completing incident reports. The number of dispatches made can be used to check that incident reports are filled out for each call. The dispatcher also is usually the one who assigns an incident number to a call; that number becomes the key to coordinating various records on a particular incident.

In computer-aided dispatch systems (see Chapter 17) much of the dispatch information is entered during the course of an emergency call or other call by the dispatcher directly into a computer. This information can be matched to other information on the fire provided separately by the officer at the scene, which reduces the officer's paperwork and improves the reliability of the data.

Equipment and personnel status

Perhaps the most essential information in the fire department is where its equipment and personnel are located at any moment and whether they are available for service. This information must be available for dispatchers and may actually be built into the dispatch system itself (see Chapter 17).

Equipment maintenance records

Data on each piece of apparatus as to when it is serviced and the nature of the servicing, when it is improved (for example, with new pumps), and its equipment complement are also needed to help keep inventories, prepare budget requests, determine maintenance schedules, and plan for new purchases. The length of time out of service is also important, for assessing the efficiency of the department in keeping its equipment available and for evaluating different types of equipment (see Chapter 20).

Personnel records

As in any other organization, files are needed on each employee with information such as attendance record; pay record; special skills; injury and sickness history; and personal characteristics such as age, sex, height, and weight. This information is needed in order to deal fairly with each employee and to maintain a profile of the department for developing training programs, planning pension programs, etc. (see Chapter 13).

Budget and financial records

As such records are discussed in detail in a number of books and articles,[2] they will not be discussed in this chapter. (The reader is, however, referred to Chapter 12.)

Pre-fire plans and hazard files

Many departments work out in detail what equipment will be needed and how a fire should be fought for at least the larger buildings they protect and those with the greatest potential life loss, as well as those which are of most value to the community. These pre-fire plans may include information on where hydrants are located and where built-in fire suppression systems exist (especially sprinklers and standpipes), as well as special hazards or situations that firefighters should be aware of. These plans may also include a list of additional units that may be needed. This pre-planned information may be transmitted by radio and may even appear on remote teleprinters or video displays in the apparatus on the way to the fire, depending on the sophistication of the technology available.

In addition to pre-fire plans, several types of special files with information useful to suppression operations are maintained by various communities. These files include the following information:

1. Location of invalids: the number, age, likely room, and type of disability of invalids
2. Hazardous materials storage: the type of material and its approximate quantity and location
3. Dangerous animals file: the existence of large dogs, lions, poisonous snakes, or other animals which can pose a hazard to firefighters (Kansas City, Missouri, maintains such a file).

Special fire department studies

Many fire departments conduct "one shot" or occasional studies that provide useful information. Examples include estimates of indirect losses from fires, surveys of the attitudes of residents or businesses about fire department effectiveness, and detailed supplementary incident reports on certain types of fires.

Structure and occupancy files

Many fire departments keep track of fire-related information about buildings and occupancies in the community. As has been discussed above, they often keep information on buildings that receive inspections, that have fires, or that have unusual hazards.

Going beyond this, some departments keep records identifying every structure in the community. This building census is valuable for planning inspection policies, for computing risk by occupancy type, and for assessing hazards and needs as part of fire protection master planning. Sometimes these files are developed by the building department; sometimes they are developed by "walk around" surveys by the fire department itself. For some communities, maps can be purchased of every structure in the community from commercial firms, but these are not always kept up-to-date.

It is useful to keep some record of the number of occupancies of different types, as well as the number of buildings. A large office building may have many businesses within it, and for some planning purposes it is important to know both the number and types of businesses as well as the fact that they are in the building.

City records, such as building and construction permits, land use maps, and property tax records can all help furnish information on the number of structures and the types of occupancies in each unit. Property tax records can also be used as a starting point for estimating loss and for assessing property value at risk. But many types of property are not included on the tax records, or are not described in sufficient detail. The "walk around" surveys are generally the most thorough source.

Vacant building files

Some communities maintain files of vacant or abandoned property. The information in these files may include the type of structure, whether it is secured or not (that is, boarded up and locked), whether it is located next to occupied property, and whether it is scheduled for demolition. This information is useful in providing other city agencies with information on the number and location of abandoned properties, and in persuading them to get rid of vacant buildings as soon as possible to prevent arson and vandalism and to reduce their likelihood of spreading fires to occupied structures. (Newark, New Jersey, maintains such a file.)

Socioeconomic/demographic data

Much information on the characteristics of the people and property of a community is available from the U.S. Bureau of the Census, although the information may be almost ten years out of date at certain times during each decade. To supplement the census data, planning department data with information on population estimates, number of housing units by types, amount and location of substandard housing, amount of business, etc., is often available. Much of the data will be tied to census tracts, which is one reason why it is important for fire departments to record the census tract of each incident on their incident reports.

As was mentioned earlier, the various types of input records may be stored in manual or computer files. The next section discusses some of the issues involved in deciding whether to automate the data system and some of the choices in obtaining computer-based systems.

Computer processing

The computer has been described by some fire officers as the fourth major technological change to improve fire departments, the other three being the internal combustion engine, the centrifugal pump, and the radio. The first change improved mobility and response time. The second improved the reliability and efficiency of providing water at high pressure. The third improved communications. The fourth major change—the computer—can sharply improve the amount of information available to the fire officer and make it more timely and more accurate.

As computer processing costs go down, and as computer hardware becomes smaller, cheaper, and a more familiar tool everywhere from the grocery store to the laboratory, the use of computers in fire departments of all sizes is likely to rise.

To use a computer or not?

The fire service manager must decide whether to get the department involved in computer processing. One computer expert, looking at the fire service, stated: "It is no longer a question of can and should fire departments of all sizes utilize modern computer and telecommunication technologies; the only question is when."[3]

The use of computers today   In the last half of the 1970s one could summarize the use of computers in the fire service as follows:

1. Most of the large municipal fire departments have acquired, or will acquire within the next few years, a computer capability.
2. While the majority of municipal fire departments do not yet use computers, growth curves indicate that *within the next decade* in all probability this situation will reverse itself—*it will be an exception to find a municipal fire department without a computer application.*
3. Computer use in county fire departments follows the same trend as that in municipal fire organizations.

4. Even in municipal fire departments where computers have been utilized, computer use is limited; the most popular applications are uniform fire reporting or vehicle maintenance record keeping.
5. As yet, significant inroads have not been made in fire department computer use in the primary operational and management concerns of municipal fire departments: fire prevention, fire suppression, fire resource management.

Source: Myron Weiner, "Low-Cost Computer Technology for Fire Data Systems," draft report to the U.S. Fire Administration, Washington, D.C., September 1978.

If the department has less than 100 calls per year and expects to use only information easily derived from hand tallies, such as the number of fires occurring each year, then it may not be necessary. On the other hand, a fire service manager often needs information processed in many different ways during the year, and it becomes quite time-consuming and perhaps impossible to get the necessary information quickly if a computer is not used. For example, at one time a manager might want to know the number of fires by time of day and type of occupancy, and at another time the number of firefighters and pieces of apparatus that went to calls of different types. And, after getting this information, the manager may decide to look at it by company. The manager might also want to look at equipment used by day of the week. As one starts to use information, it inevitably leads to additional questions that require more work. When the information is not in a computer the follow-up question can take as long (or longer) to answer as the original question if the full set of questions was not known in advance. This is one of the great advantages of having access to a computer. The user can get the information developed in many different ways in a relatively short time once the investment has been made in setting up the data files, computer programs, and administrative procedures that make it possible to generate different types of reports.

Choosing a computer and computer services

Computer service is a highly technical field that is rapidly changing, with computer hardware and software capabilities improving and costs decreasing. It takes someone in the computer field to keep abreast of these developments. Most departments should consider hiring a computer consultant to help in deciding whether to acquire or to improve computer services and in selecting the most appropriate equipment and computer software for their needs and budget. Some of the issues to consider in starting or improving computer capabilities are discussed below.

Purchase or rent? Among the basic hardware decisions that must be made is whether to buy or rent a computer for the fire department, or whether to rent access to a computer from a vendor or other city department. City computer sections are not always set up to deal with fast turnaround requests, and the advantage of the computer over analysis by hand is lessened when the fire department does not have direct control over its use.

Sometimes it is cheaper for the fire department to rent its own service rather than use that of the city because of the peculiarities of local practices in billing and setting priorities, or because of personnel skills available, or for other reasons. Sometimes it is wise for a fire department to buy its own computer; small computers that are adequate for many departments are continuing to go down in price. The widely held belief in the economy of scale of centralized large computers no longer holds true for many situations. But having its own computer often brings new headaches to the fire department. Just as owning a car requires providing for its maintenance, so does owning a computer. It is often more convenient and more economical overall to leave the technological computer operations problem to a hired hand and use the departmental technical expertise to work the fire problem. On the other hand, kits for building one's own computer can be obtained fairly inexpensively, and improvements will no doubt continue to be made in the amount of computer power available from kits and the ease in setting up the computer.

As we enter a time for which it is projected that householders will use computers as utilities for all sorts of everyday functions, from balancing checkbooks, to keeping food inventories, to controlling energy consumption, it is likely that computers will appear less exotic to even small fire departments. Electronic calculators already are used in computing many kinds of costs around fire departments. Some departments (Chicago, for example) already have portable minicomputers complete with keyboard and video screen and cassette for memory storage that are used to store and analyze fire incident data. Other departments have started using multiple terminals hooked to central computers.

Number and type of terminals Once a decision to use a computer is made, the number and location of computer terminals will need to be decided upon. Computer terminals have keyboards for entering data into the computer, and a video screen or printout device, or both, for getting data out and checking inputs. Computer terminals might be located either centrally, or in a few key locations such as the fire protection bureau, central records, and the office of the chief. Or the computer terminals might be more widely distributed to battalion chiefs or even companies.

Requirements study for obtaining a computer system The fire department should prepare a statement which should include:

1. Purpose or goals of the ADP system
2. Problems to be resolved
3. Functions to be performed
4. Benefits to be derived
5. Projected life of system
6. System requirements which must be satisfied (should include input/output frequency, media for communicating with the system, volume of transactions, and turn-around time requirements)
7. Output report requirements, and who will be the recipients of reports
8. Constraints on available resources (describe the requirements that will be levied on the organization and identify any outside assistance needed, such as data keying personnel)
9. Costs of present way of operating
10. Implementation plan.

Feasibility study by the supplier The ADP vendor or city ADP group should prepare a study which should describe:

1. Problems to be solved and how the mission will be supported
2. Proposed solution
3. Alternative solutions
4. Present and future impacts on the mission
5. Benefits for management: cost savings; manpower savings; other tangible and intangible savings
6. Objectives and steps to develop system
7. Resource requirements: additional personnel; training; space; site preparation; maintenance
8. Cost summary: development costs; operating costs; maintenance costs
9. Telecommunications requirements and costs estimates
10. Proposed installation schedule.

As the price of terminals drops, or in situations where it is more difficult to get funds for personnel than for capital expenditures, the remote terminals can be used to save firefighters time and paperwork and also to provide a check at the source of the information being fed into the computer. This use of remote "smart" terminals is not a widespread practice yet, but it may become so in the future. A great deal of time is consumed by officers on paperwork (which encompasses everything from maintaining rosters, to filling out incident reports, to preparing monthly reports, to filling special information requests). Having input forms "built into" the terminal, where the operator is prompted as to what to fill in and reasonableness checks are applied to what he or she enters, can speed up the data entry and also improve data quality.

The decisions on terminals depend on the flexibility and convenience needed in data manipulation, the importance of having access to the data when it is wanted as opposed to waiting a day or several days, whether the city or someone else sets priorities on use of a shared machine, and the need for confidentiality. As has been noted, the department should seek expert assistance in making these decisions.

Software packages In addition to the hardware decisions, there are software decisions to make. Should the department use the National Fire Incident Reporting System software, or the Uniform Fire Incident Reporting System of NFPA, or other software packages? Should the community purchase a standard statistical software package that permits various types of manipulations of data and various report formats? Should the community develop its own software tailored to its own needs? Or some combination of the above? The answers depend on how comprehensive a data system is desired, what computer programming expertise the department has available, and how useful the department finds the existing software packages.

Turnkey system As an alternative to making the technical decisions about the computer system or working with an expert consultant to make them, a department can hire a private company to develop a "turnkey system." The company assembles the computer hardware needed, writes and tests the computer programs, and "turns the key" for the system over to the user, who needs only a minimum of instructions on its use.

Steps toward automation Once the department decides to start or to improve a computer system it generally needs to go through the following steps:

1. *Statement of requirements:* what the department needs, and what its constraints are, stated in plain English
2. *Feasibility study:* what computer companies or city computer departments need to tell the fire department in response to the requirements statement
3. *System design:* detailed specification of computer system components (hardware and software) and how they will work together
4. *Implementation plan:* steps and timetable proposed to get the computer systems operational
5. *Budget approval:* final agreement to spend the money on the specifics in the design and implementation plans
6. *Computer program specifications:* the technical requirements for the computer programs that are to process the data that is put into the system into a data base and useful output reports
7. *Program development:* the design and actual writing of the computer programs
8. *Program documentation:* the written description of the computer programs; this should be kept up-to-date as programs are changed, to facilitate testing and to allow new programmers to pick up where former ones left off (this is a crucial management responsibility sometimes omitted in the haste to get a system working)
9. *Testing:* seeing whether the computer programs work
10. *Implementation:* the final step, going operational.

Some problem areas to consider

Three major problem areas that a fire manager should be aware of in developing a good data system are quality control, analysis blunders (misuse of data), and "data disuse."

Controlling the quality of the data base

"Garbage in, garbage out" is now a classic saying in data processing. If you put erroneous data into your fire data system, then it is difficult to get meaningful information out. It is not impossible: clever data processing and a good understanding of the major sources of errors often can produce useful information from data with a great deal of error in them. But it is not prudent to count on this, and the fire service manager should build quality control steps into the data system, starting from the initial determination of the details about a fire before an incident report is even filled out. (See the earlier discussion on design of the data system.)

Motivating for better data Firefighters, like most other people, do not like to fill out forms. Improving a fire data system often involves increasing the amount of paperwork on individual incidents, and that is likely to be resisted. Since even with the most sophisticated computer system the old adage, "garbage in, garbage out," still applies, it is the obligation of fire service managers to motivate their forces to collect the best data possible. One approach for doing this is to explain to every person in the department how the information will be used by the community, state, and nation.

Fire service managers should also consider "making a deal" with the firefighters whenever part of the writing work load is reduced through automation. A common example is when a department goes to computer-aided dispatching and some of the routine information concerning the incident can be obtained automatically from the dispatch operation. When the writing burden can be reduced in this way there is an opportunity to consider expanding the detail and improving the quality of the rest of the data that the firefighter collects, especially information on the causes of fires and their associated losses. A similar kind of "deal" can be considered when the amount of data to be collected for minor incidents or nonfire incidents is reduced in order to obtain better information on the more serious incidents.

The first step in improving the quality of data is to train fire officers and investigators to be able to determine cause and other information about a fire as well as they can be established. Instruction on fire investigation and on filling out incident reports and other reports should be considered as part of the basic training of fire officers, and perhaps all firefighters. Those filling out reports should understand the definitions of the various elements to be filled out and the numerical codes to be applied to each. Even such basic expressions as, "What is a fire?" and, "What is a building?" need to be carefully defined. For example, if a fire sweeps through twelve units of garden apartments in which every three units are separated by a fire wall and all units are under one roof, was it one, four, or twelve buildings that were destroyed? (For fire protection studies the answer is four: fire walls delineate buildings.)

Supervisors can periodically monitor their officers' capabilities for investigating fires by occasional on-the-scene checking. Simulated field tests can also be used to train and rate officers in investigation and reporting.

The entry of data on the incident report or other forms can be reviewed by a supervisor before it is submitted. For example, in Columbus, Ohio, company officers fill out the incident reports in draft and the battalion chiefs prepare the final copies; this requires the latter to review each form. Some communities also have a clerk in the central records office check each incident report or other record for completeness and reasonableness before it is keypunched.

When data are entered directly by fire officers into computer terminals instead of on paper, the computer can be used to check for valid codes and to cross check different elements to see that all necessary elements have been filled out and that values inserted are reasonable. This immediate check gives fire officers feedback on any suspected problems with the data while the data are still fresh in their minds.

The operation of keying data from incident forms onto cards or tapes, or directly into computer memory, can also introduce errors, of course. These can be reduced somewhat by having each entry verified by a second keypuncher. Another approach is to use on-line entry, where the person entering the data sits at a computer terminal with a display of the incident form in front of him or her. He or she copies data from written forms directly onto the screen, where it can be visually verified and also checked by the computer for valid codes and reasonableness. The state of Alaska, for example, uses this on-line keying procedure for entering data from its incident reports into the computer; in this way it was able to reduce the error rate of the keypunching operation in 1978 from 40 percent to 10 percent merely by switching to on-line entry, and then down to 1 percent by having error detection checks done by the computer before an incident was permitted to be added to the master file. With this procedure, any problems noted by the computer can be reviewed by the keypuncher to see whether the information was not entered at all on the original form or was entered incorrectly, or was keyed incorrectly. If the fault was not in keying but in the original incident report, that report can be sent back for correction.

Once data are entered into a data base, they still may have errors, even after passing a certain number of computer checks and human checks. Sometimes these errors are discovered in the process of using the data, where the reasonableness of the information for a particular incident report or a number of incident reports can be examined. Unlikely results found in the course of analyses can provide clues to data collection problems and should be relayed back to the training and retraining process.

In addition to accuracy problems with individual records, another type of accuracy problem is that of missing records. For incident reports a check can be made against dispatch records to see if there is an incident report for every dispatch made.

Common analysis errors

There are many analytical pitfalls that can destroy the validity of information based on good raw data. A few pitfalls are described below. Managers should ensure that people experienced in analysis either do the analysis or check it.

Accuracy of results Accuracy means how closely it is possible to estimate, for example, the risk of a resident of the community having a fire. Accuracy is a combination of how much it is possible to remove bias from an estimate and the precision of the estimate: how little variation there is in making repeated estimates. The smaller is the number of incidents in the data base from which the estimates are made, the less precise the estimate can be. For example, if the community had four deaths last year, then the expected number of deaths this year would be 4 ± 2. Table 18–8 shows the precision[4] associated with different numbers of deaths (or incidents). Even in a large community, precision can be a problem, as, for example, when death rates are to be estimated by census tract or population subgroup.

When precision is low it is difficult to say whether year-to-year changes are statistically significant: that is, whether they occurred from true changes in the underlying situation and not just by chance. The more accurate the data are, the better one can determine whether year-to-year changes are statistically significant.

The problem in dealing with small numbers can be partially compensated for by using multiyear averages instead of a single year's data. Another approach is to look at larger areas or larger population groups. For example, it is usually difficult for a small town department to determine trends in the causes of fires for itself alone, but by looking at the data for a group of towns like itself it may get a better picture in a shorter period of time.

One of the important pitfalls to avoid as a fire manager is to attribute—or allow others to attribute—small changes in performance based on small numbers of events to doing a better or worse job. If there were four deaths in the community last year and this year there were five, that "25 percent increase" may be due entirely to chance and should not be used as a dramatic statistic by itself. Again, it should be pointed out that there is a danger in using percentage changes without also declaring the change in the number of incidents or sample size on which the statistic is based. Reporters often like to report such dramatic changes and often fail to mention that the changes were not statistically significant. That is a responsibility for management.

Table 18–8   The precision of estimates.

Count	Relative precision
4	50%
9	33%
16	25%
25	20%
44	15%
100	10%
400	5%

Note: One way in which this table can be interpreted is as follows: if a city has 25 deaths per year over some period, the chances are about 2:1 that there will be 25 ± 20%, or 25 ± 5, or 20 to 30 deaths in the next year. For chances of 19:1, the interval would be doubled, giving 25 ± 10 deaths.

Bias   An estimate may be biased by fire officers' consistently using an incorrect definition, for example, including overheat conditions, scares, or mutual aid runs in the count of fires. Bias might also be introduced intentionally if there is widespread concern for reporting too much (or too little) fire dollar loss, with the result that most dollar loss estimates might be low (or high). Another situation in which bias may occur is when a "short" form (or no form) is used for fires with "low loss" (for example, below $200—in which case fires actually estimated at $300 to $400 might be labeled as being below $200 to avoid paperwork).

In some situations it is possible to adjust statistics for bias when the bias can be estimated quantitatively. But if the bias is unknown, or if bias changes from year to year, it is difficult to undertake comparisons over time or between communities, or to estimate the magnitude of the problem.

Bias can be partially prevented by emphasizing the importance of using consistent definitions and by emphasizing the importance of making estimates as accurate as possible, without shading statistics upward or downward. If individual fire officers take it upon themselves to "adjust" statistics to emphasize one aspect of the problem or another, it can only lead to chaos in viewing department-wide information.

Rates versus absolute numbers   As has been mentioned, the rate of events per capita is often confused with the absolute number of events. For example, in the 1970s blacks had a higher fire death rate than whites in terms of number of deaths per million population, but more whites died in fires than blacks. That is, although the risk was much higher for a black than a white, there were many more whites in the population and the net effect was that a larger number of whites died in fires.

Matching numerators and denominators   When quoting a statistic such as the number of deaths per capita it is common to use all fire deaths in the community as the numerator but only the number of residents in the community as the denominator. While it is true that residents may be killed in fires either while working or while at home, there could be a distortion in the impression left about risk if a significant number of fire deaths occurred to visitors or commuters. The most comparable statistics are those in which the numerator and denominator pertain to the same group: for example, the number of deaths to apartment dwellers per 100,000 apartment dwellers, or the number of fire deaths in mobile homes per 100,000 mobile home dwellers (see Table 18–2).

Rates may be computed with numbers of buildings, numbers of certain types of equipment, or any of a wide range of factors in the denominator, depending on whether one wishes to view risks relative to the number of "potential targets," or relative to the "population (people or things) at risk," or the "population (people or things) to be served." For example, a community might observe that two-thirds of the fires related to cooking were associated with electric stoves. But that would not indicate whether electric stoves were a greater relative hazard than gas stoves. The larger number observed for electric stoves might simply mean that there were more electric stoves in the community than gas stoves. To find out, the rate of electric stove fires per 10,000 electric stoves in the community would have to be compared to the number of gas stove fires per 10,000 gas stoves.

Scaling   A common denominator is used in making comparisons over time or from one community to another so that relative risk can be determined. A risk can be computed "per 1,000,000 population," "per 100,000 population," or "per capita (person)": these are merely different forms of the same statistic. Three deaths per 100,000 is exactly equivalent to thirty deaths per 1,000,000 population (see Table 18–2). It does not matter if your community has 50,000 or 5,000,000 population; you can compute rates per 10,000 or per 1,000,000 or per anything else. You have a .300 batting average whether you hit safely 3 out of 10 times or 300 out of 1,000 times. The principle is the same for determining risks.

It is often helpful when quoting rates to use a form of statistic so that the numerator comes out greater than one. For example, it is easier for most people to grasp the idea of 35 deaths per 1,000,000 population than of .035 deaths per 1,000 population.

Treating "unknowns" in statistics   Many data elements are left blank or reported as "unknown" on incident reports and other types of records. When it comes time to report summary statistics, there arises the question of how to treat these unknowns and blanks. For example, typical statistics on the causes of fire deaths for a typical community might appear as follows:

Causes	% of problem
Smoking	30%
Cooking	8
Incendiary/suspicious	8
Heating	7
Electrical distribution	5
Children playing	5
Other	12
Unknown	25
Total	100%

When a fire manager is asked what percentage of deaths over a particular period of time were due to smoking, is the answer "30 percent," or "at least 30 percent," or "40 percent" (30 divided by 75, the sum of the known causes)? The last computation assumes that the unknowns are distributed in the same way as the knowns, which may or may not be true. In quoting arson statistics, for example, some assume that fully half of the unknowns are arson.

Once again, the suggested approach is simply to say which form of statistic is being presented—whether it does or does not include unknowns. A better but more complex solution is to research a sample of fires for which unknowns were reported (to the extent that they can be) to see if the causes really were known but not recorded for any of a variety of reasons, or whether these fires were so large and intense or complex that it was not possible to determine the cause, even with expert investigators.

Legal responsibility for information on incident reports and other reports
Many fire officers are concerned that information they provide may be used in court, and that they may get themselves or others in trouble if it is not exactly right. This leads to concerns about recording any dollar loss figures for fear of becoming involved in insurance suits or to concerns about reporting arson for fear of libel.

The legal facts (and proper legal advice should always be sought) are that in most, if not all, cases a fire officer's estimate of dollar loss is not taken as that of an authority unless the fire officer has credentials as an appraiser or has other special skills. The fire chief may be responsible for describing what happened at the fire, and what was damaged, but the chief is not personally liable nor is the chief the authority on what the loss was. To emphasize this, wording on incident reports can stress *estimated loss* and *probable cause,* rather than *actual loss* or *cause.*

Some officers fear recording information because they are afraid it will hurt others —not in a legal way, but emotionally or otherwise. An example is when parents are responsible for the fire death of their child by some careless action. These officers should be made aware that when they do not accurately report the cause of a fire they may be contributing to misinformation that might lead to unnecessary deaths in the future. In every case, fire officers should be encouraged to record the best information they can.

Another approach is to train for better fire investigations and to encourage firefighters to record the known information, even if it is not accurate beyond the shadow of a doubt.

Problems in aggregating data   To make data more understandable and meaningful it is often necessary to aggregate detailed data into more general categories. For example, in starting an analysis of the fire problem in the community, it is important to know how many deaths and injuries, and how much dollar loss, occurred in residential and nonresidential properties. But depending on how we aggregate small categories into large ones, we can change the way the fire picture looks. For example, deaths in hotels and motels are often lumped with deaths in permanent residences in the category labeled "residential." This will work as long as the hotel/motel type of fire is not predominant. But what about a year in which there are twenty deaths from a hotel fire and ten from all other residences? Noting that there were thirty residential fire deaths without any further explanation would give a misleading impression.

A similar situation arises in describing the leading causes for fire: for example, the six leading causes of fire in Ohio in 1976 were cooking, smoking, heating, incendiary/suspicious, electrical distribution, and appliance related fires, in that order. But if electrical appliances and electrical distribution had been lumped together into a single electrical category, that combined category would have appeared higher than all of the others except cooking. And the combined category would have been the highest one if it had included fires involving electrical space heaters from the heating category and electrical stoves and ovens from the cooking category. Depending on the question to be answered, any of these groupings could be the best.

From the fire service perspective, it may be a good starting point to choose aggregated categories in a way that groups together types of fires that lead to similar types of prevention or suppression policy. For example, if the main problem with electrical stoves and ovens is not so much electrical faults but rather that people cook improperly on them, such fires may be more usefully combined with cooking fires from gas stoves in presenting an overview of the fire problem.

An even better safeguard is not to stop at the highly aggregated categories but to try to find the big parts of the problem and to express them as scenarios rather than as simplistic causes. For example, instead of simply reporting the top three causes of residential fires as cooking, smoking, and heating, it is more useful to describe the leading causes in terms such as "unattended cooking during early evening," "smoking by intoxicated persons who drop cigarettes on upholstered furniture or bedding at night," and "central heating systems that either malfunction from not having been cleaned or that cause fires from combustibles being placed too close to them." This expanded information gives more insight into how to combat the problem and also may make the image of the problem more vivid in the public's mind.

The fire problem may be considered from different perspectives for different purposes. For example, one might want to know how frequently plastics are involved in a fire regardless of the cause, because they may give off highly toxic fumes. One might want to know how often wood products are involved, to contrast them with plastics and to see if codes pertaining to wood construction would affect fire ignitions or spread. If one were looking from a consumer product safety point of view, one might want to know the ten products most often involved in fire ignitions. Safeguards might be built into products such as electric stoves and ovens even if they are not "at fault" for many fires. Sprinkler systems, smoke hoods, or smoke or heat detectors also could be built into them or into the surrounding room to help reduce fire incidents. Again, common sense in devising categories and in pursuing more detailed causes may provide the best answers.

Not using data at all

One of the cardinal sins of setting up a data system is to spend a great deal of time and energy in collecting and processing the data and then not to use the data in decision making. The data may be used in annual reports and to answer questions on how many of certain types of fires occurred, but the impact of the data system on fire protection may be much less than it could be.

Like a muscle, a fire data system will atrophy if it is not used. As soon as the basic data collectors—the line officers—get the impression that the information is not being used, they may take the process of filling out incident reports and other forms less seriously. It is important that the line officers see how the information they collect is being used. They can also be told about problems with the data, which will give them another indication of the serious intent of those using the information, in addition to providing particulars on how to improve the information.

Summary and recommendations

This chapter opened with a discussion of information to be sought and of terms in common use in data collection, processing, and analysis. The analysis and use of data were discussed next, followed by a detailed coverage on starting a data system. The next subjects treated were the staffing and organization of the data system, sources of data, computer processing, and some challenges involved in using data. A summing up, given below in the form of recommendations, closes the chapter.

Use of data

The fire manager should ensure that the data collected are analyzed and interpreted, and that key points are appropriately displayed. Too much information winds up in drawers, unused. Especially important is knowledge of the number and per capita rate of fires by occupancy and by cause. The data should be further broken down to detail the profiles and circumstances for injuries, deaths, and dollar loss. The key analysis technique is simply arraying data in tables and looking for the large numbers which indicate the large parts of the problem. Upon finding the large numbers, the next step is to ask what caused the fire (or casualty) in successively deeper levels of detail to the limit of the data system. "One shot" special studies should be used to fill gaps in information or to get detail beyond that possible from routine reports.

Motivation

The fire manager should be sure that the fire officers who collect the data understand its purpose and hear about its uses. If they are not properly motivated, quality will suffer.

Training and retraining

All personnel who actually collect or analyze fire-related data should be trained in how to collect the data, including the definitions to use and the intended uses. The same personnel should be periodically retrained in common errors that are occurring and on any changes to the data system. The training periods also offer a good opportunity to discuss the use of the system.

Controlling quality

The fire manager should set up quality control procedures for the department's data regardless of community size. These procedures may include supervisory review of the incident reports of officers, community-wide reviews by a fire coding clerk, and computer screening of data as they are fed into the machine. Checks by hand or by computer can screen for valid codes, logical consistency between data elements, completeness of filling out forms, possession of all necessary forms for an incident, and consistency with information available from other sources.

Processing by computer

As computers and terminals become cheaper, more convenient, and easier to use, it will be practical for smaller communities to use computers. Computers small enough for use in the home and car will be suitable for the smallest firehouse.

Computer processing may be available from the department's own machine, either purchased or leased, or through a department's own terminals accessing the local government's computer or that of a private vendor. Expert help is needed to choose the best arrangement for a particular community.

Keeping compatible with state and national systems

Fire managers should try to keep a core of data compatible with the format and coding used by state and national fire data systems, so that their department may contribute to the creation of the larger picture used for developing laws, standards, and research that ultimately affect their own community. The common core of data also will allow fire managers to accurately compare their community to others. Collecting data with standard definitions is especially important for smaller communities, where aggregation of data among like communities offers a chance to see patterns that an individual community cannot produce.

Staffing and organizing carefully

The person or group charged with data analysis for the fire department should be readily accessible by the senior managers in the fire department and should be closely tied to the decision making in the department so that appropriate data can be provided when needed.

1 See: National Fire Protection Association, *Uniform Coding for Fire Protection,* NFPA no. 901, and *Fire Reporting Field Incident Manual,* NFPA no. 902M (both, Boston: National Fire Protection Association, 1976).
2 For example, see: J. Richard Aronson and Eli Schwartz, eds., *Management Policies in Local Government Finance* (Washington, D.C.: International City Management Association, 1975); and Lennox L. Moak and Albert M. Hillhouse, *Concepts and Practices in Local Government Finance* (Chicago: Municipal Finance Officers Association, 1975).
3 Myron Weiner, "Low-Cost Computer Technology for Fire Data Systems," draft report to the U.S. Fire Administration, Washington, D.C., September 1978.
4 For a more complete discussion, see: U.S., Fire Administration, National Fire Data Center, *Fire in the United States* (Washington, D.C.: Government Printing Office, 1978), Appendix 4, pp. 167–76.

Fire station location, design, and management

For the average citizen, the first image that comes to mind when the fire service is mentioned may well be the doors to a fire station opening and one or more vehicles emerging to speed off dramatically to the scene of a fire. This popular image is not without merit, for the location and physical design of fire stations, and their successful ongoing management, are prime determinants of a community's ability to respond to fires. Having the right type and number of fire stations, located in the right places, enables the policymakers and appointed managers of a jurisdiction to house firefighters, apparatus, and equipment in a rational way for maximum use of resources. Doing this successfully may be a key test of managerial ability (both inside and outside the fire department) in a local government setting increasingly more marked by competition for scarce resources.

Conversely, the penalties are high—and extremely visible—for poor location or design of facilities, or for poor management of facilities; and these penalties are felt by the fire department itself, by the local government, and, indeed, by the local taxpayers. With poor location and design of facilities, response time becomes excessive and if a tragedy occurs that incident may be well publicized. Firefighter morale may suffer. (It should be remembered that the fire station and its status as an environment for both working and living are of concern to employees in a special way; no other local government department has a parallel situation.) When location and design of facilities—and morale—are poor, fire station related injuries increase, as do costs for maintenance, energy consumption, and operations.

Initial costs for a new fire station may seem high, especially at first glance. Half a million to a million dollars was not unusual as an estimated cost for a new station in the late 1970s and the question for the 1980s was how much this figure would go up.

A comparison of the actual design and construction costs for a new station with the long-term costs of operating the facility over its lifetime, however, makes a striking fact evident: compared to expenditures for salaries and benefits for firefighters and compared to the costs of firefighting equipment and apparatus and building operations, the price of the station itself is small. Actual costs for building the station are only a fraction of the total operational costs for the fire station over its lifetime.

If this argument is turned around, then it clearly makes a great deal of managerial sense to pay close attention to fire station location and design. Without great additional construction expense, response time can be improved and fire stations can be designed to function more efficiently; to be more easily maintained; to consume less energy; to be better protected against damage from potential natural hazards and from vandalism; and to adjust more readily to changes in apparatus design, staff levels, and department operation. Skimping on initial costs for a new fire station can prove to be a very costly mistake a few years later. An increasing number of decision makers in local government are recognizing these facts. But this was not always the case, as the discussion immediately below will indicate.

Recent trends

In the late 1960s fire station design and location were considered cut and dried matters. The Insurance Services Office (ISO) guidelines for station location were followed. The biggest issue in station design seemed to be the safety and advisability of poles from upper floors as a means for firemen to reach the trucks.

Some striking changes have occurred since. There are new analytic approaches to determining fire station location which can have a major impact on the number and placement of stations. In 1974 the ISO guidelines were revised. In the mid-1970s, in thirty-nine states filing plans, fire stations came under regulations of state departments of occupational safety and health. "Firemen" gave way to "firefighters"; women entered the fire service in increasing numbers. Security and vandalism became problems in fire stations; no longer did all jurisdictions want all-glass garage doors to show off the apparatus. Stations need protection, too, especially if not always occupied. Energy became a national problem and conservation of energy in fire stations became a real concern. Delivery of emergency medical services (EMS) became a common fire department activity. Environmental protection was seen as a problem, and fire departments had yet more difficulty in locating their training sites. Finally, some jurisdictions changed work shifts for firefighters and brought into question the need for dormitory bed space. Jurisdictions had to consider closing stations for various reasons, and the concept of portable or relocatable fire stations came into practice. Taken all together, these and other factors (including inflation and the effects of Proposition 13-type taxpayer sentiments) have had a significant impact, all of which centers around the topic of this chapter—the fire station.

Overview

This chapter is intended to provide an overall guide to managers both inside and outside of the fire department on major issues in the location and design of fire stations. Therefore, the management perspective is emphasized throughout. It should be noted at the outset that the chapter discusses location and design factors not as ends in themselves but rather as the foundations on which successful ongoing management operations must be based. The alternative, as noted above, is both inefficient and costly.

The chapter is divided into four sections. The first examines the issues involved in facility location. The second analyzes capital budgeting for fire stations, covering cost estimating, life cycle costing, the use of relocatable temporary stations, leased fire stations and their adjunct facilities, developer assistance, alternative uses for fire stations, and standardized designs. It should be read with the general budgetary framework presented in Chapter 12 in mind. The third section takes a look at facility design. It discusses station functions, disaster and emergency considerations, security factors, energy conserving building systems, and a number of special design impacts, ranging from the use of air rights structures to proper training facilities. The fourth section presents a brief summary and a look at future trends.

Facility location

Location of fire stations is an issue of considerable importance, both to management of fire services directly involved in the delivery of fire protection and to general management, planners, and budget officers. As a result, new management approaches have been considered and new tools developed. The objective of this new interest has been to reduce the reliance on subjective judgment or prescriptive rules of thumb as the only basis on which to make location decisions. Fire facility location has historically been a subject of considerable citizen interest. New approaches and new tools are therefore aimed at providing a rational basis for definition of protection requirements and site selection that can be explained to the public and could serve as a common reference point for discussing and evaluating alternative sites.

Criteria for site selection

Normally, the starting points for site selection would include consideration of the following factors:

1. Location of existing facilities
2. Location of city owned land
3. Age, condition, and serviceability of current facilities, evaluated against changing development patterns, street networks, traffic patterns, and areas of demand for fire protection
4. Projected growth or change in fire protection needs
5. New firefighting technology, which may change the requirements for station location (and design)
6. Changes in the nature of the firefighting work force.

The existing stock of current facilities represents a sunk cost to the community, and every review of facility location generally considers the location of these current assets as a baseline. Analysis of the other factors noted above, however, is much more complex, and reliance has been placed on available rules of thumb such as the basic calculations of fire flow (measured in gallons per minute [GPM]), and distance from the companies which would respond in order: first due, first alarm, and maximum multiple alarm.

A combination of these flow requirements and distance factors has provided the basis for fire station location and has been widely promulgated by the American Insurance Association (see Special Interest Bulletin no. 176).[1] Those same tables have formed part of the basis for grading cities into fire protection classes, under guidelines provided by the Insurance Services Office.[2]

Because of the apparent economic implication of basing location decisions on requirements which are also used for insurance class grading, the fire flow and distance relationships provided a mechanism for making station location decisions. Recently, however, a series of changes have begun to take place which should allow the consideration of other important factors in location decisions. These changes include the following:

1. A more detailed understanding of ISO recommendations (and their real economic implications) on the part of fire department management and other local government officials
2. Grouping of traditional insurance grading classes into clusters whereby the rate difference between particular classes is minimized
3. Differing treatment of highly urbanized areas in insurance grading
4. The role of state insurance commissioners who regulate insurance carriers in calling into question the actual significance of grading classes and, therefore, grading guidelines.

New analytic tools

The above changes have created the opportunity for fire service and other local government managers to use new tools, and such analytic tools have now begun to emerge from a variety of sources. Two efforts in this direction are in significant use now, and other efforts are expected to develop.

Fire protection master planning The first of these developments is fire protection master planning, a community-wide approach to analyzing and understanding fire protection needs (discussed in detail in Chapter 6). This approach is being promulgated by the U.S. Fire Administration (formerly the National Fire Prevention and Control Administration). Fire protection master planning emphasizes

the development of a Master Plan to provide an organized approach to defining, obtaining, and maintaining the level of fire protection and the fire prevention and control system desired by the community. The Plan:

- defines the current and future fire protection environment by establishing and maintaining a comprehensive data base;
- defines accepted life and property risk levels by setting goals and objectives;
- defines the fire protection system which provides the level of service commensurate with the level of accepted risk;
- identifies and justifies the resources necessary to develop and operate the fire protection system;
- provides a detailed program of action to implement and maintain the system.[3]

As the master planning approach is tested and implemented in communities across the country, the community-wide participation called for in its fundamental approach to resource allocation can lead to many innovative developments, including new approaches to facility location.

Fire Station Location Package (FSLP) A second development is the creation of a new management tool, based to a greater degree on response time (rather than distance), which allows the rapid consideration (through simulation techniques) of alternative locations and location strategies. The U.S. Department of Housing and Urban Development (HUD) funded a two year program to develop such a tool and the cities of Wichita, Kansas, Newark, New Jersey, and Dallas, Texas, assisted Public Technology, Inc. (PTI), in developing this tool in their own local environments. This tool, called the Fire Station Location Package (FSLP), is now in use in more than 100 local governments.[4]

The basic approach used by FSLP is to evaluate fire station locations on the basis of predicted response times to potential fires. Because of the lack of national data at this time, each local government must create its individual trade-offs between the value of the reduction effect (or increase) in response time capabilities and the concurrent dollar costs of building and operating additional fire stations to achieve such capabilties.

Using a computer to facilitate the identification and analysis of many pieces of information, a jurisdiction can promptly display the advantages and disadvantages of a particular locational plan for fire stations, and can show clearly and objectively a picture of response time effectiveness among the various locations that may be candidates for inclusion in a fire deployment plan. In this process the most important input is not, in fact, the "scientific" use of numerical data, but rather the extensive interactions between the various decision makers (such as a city manager, a fire chief, and a budget director), each of whom may have different viewpoints and approaches to the same problem. It is this intensive and aggressive interchange of viewpoints among the major decision makers, assisted by a wealth of well-formulated and defensible data, that makes FSLP extremely helpful in the attempts of many local governments to improve productivity in their fire services.

As an example, consider the city of San Bernardino, California, with a population of approximately 110,000. In 1972 the city was providing service from eleven fire stations, and their average response time (which is one of the indicators that can be used to measure the effectiveness and efficiency of a given plan) was roughly 4 minutes. After using FSLP they were able to close down four fire station sites, build three new stations in different locations, and finish up with an improved response time of approximately 3.2 minutes. What this means in local government productivity terms is evident: San Bernardino was able to improve its overall service to the public by over 20 percent while at the same time saving roughly $150,000 a year in operating costs.

The city of Phoenix, Arizona, used FSLP to improve its future planning capabilities. Its original capital improvements program had included plans for the addition of fourteen stations to the current thirty which the Phoenix fire department operated. However, through the use of FSLP the city was able to come up with an alternate plan which allowed the fire department to improve the projected average travel time by over 30 percent, while at the same time adding only eleven stations. The operational savings of approximately $1.2 million annually are, thus, cost savings that are not immediately felt but that will be felt in the future operations budget for the Phoenix fire department.

The final results of any implementation depend on the local environment of an implementing jurisdiction as well as on the aggressiveness and imagination of the executives who use FSLP. Experience with this tool, however, has shown that a careful implementation plan coupled with strong management input will result in an objective and justifiable plan which can help a local administrator achieve productivity gains in the fire services area.

The emergence of the U.S. Fire Administration, which is empowered to sponsor and perform research in areas which can lead to reduced fire loss, and the development of new analytic tools such as FSLP, appear to be leading elements in rethinking the role of fire stations in fire protection planning. This revision process is only beginning to take place, and new considerations, tools, and approaches are almost certain to emerge.[5]

Capital budgeting for fire stations

Once a jurisdiction has determined that it should relocate fire service facilities, retire certain existing stations, or build new stations, the capital budgeting phase begins. In general outline the capital budgeting process is straightforward. Each municipal agency, including the fire service, prepares a budget request for new capital projects such as construction and major equipment purchases. Each budget line will have a description and will be covered by a written justification. Generally, capital budgets are prepared for a multiyear period and are annually revised. Capital budget requests for each department are assembled and then reviewed. The review, by city management, checks priorities for all capital projects, checks the availability of funds from bonds, grants, tax revenues, and other sources, and may result in the need to change the individual department requests. Frequently it may be necessary to eliminate low priority requests, extend schedules for other projects, and, in some cases, expedite schedules for top priority projects. Comprehensive capital authorization budgets assembled by the administration then go before the jurisdiction's council or commission for approval. Actual appropriation of funds follows but may be contingent on many possible factors, including voter approval of bond referenda and availability of necessary state or federal grants.

Timing is the single most important factor in the capital budgeting process, for several reasons. Most important, the amount of funds available to a jurisdiction for capital projects is less easily changed than are project completion schedules. Bond limits, outside grants, and tax rates change over time, but generally they are outside the immediate control of the jurisdiction. Project timing and phasing, on the other hand, can be controlled directly.

Other timing concerns need to be dealt with as well in preparing capital budgets. Fire station budget priorities need to be developed in terms of the impact each station can make on fire department response capabilities. Those stations providing the greatest impact generally will be budgeted first. Similarly, jurisdictions may want to consider use of lower cost relocatable stations to be installed in high priority sites until sufficient funds are available for construction of permanent stations. When permanent stations are built, the relocatable facility can be moved to the next most important site.

Community growth, as described in the location section of this chapter, shows up again in the budget process as an important timing element, determining when stations really must become operational.

Inflation is another timing factor to be considered. Generally, in recent years increases in construction costs have outpaced inflation in other sectors of the economy. As a result, budget estimates which are realistic in one year may become quite insufficient in later years. The inflationary factor puts a premium on near term completion of projects and requires that cost escalations be considered when station construction schedules are extended or delayed. It should also be continuously monitored when long-range facilities planning goals are being developed and revised.

Cost estimating

Costs for the design and construction of a fire station are extremely variable because of differences in interest rates; land acquisition costs; differences in station design and required site improvements; labor rates and material cost variations; and site-specific features including exposure to natural hazards such as earthquakes. Because of these variables it is generally appropriate to use conservative cost estimating, especially during feasibility and programming studies.

Jurisdictions involved in recent or continuing fire station development programs can use cost records from recent stations as a basis for estimating costs for new stations. Other jurisdictions, however, will need to collect data from outside sources—especially from nearby jurisdictions with recent experience in fire station construction. In many cases it will be worthwhile to have an independent cost estimate prepared to substantiate the cost estimates made by the station's architect. The importance of reliability in cost estimates merits significant emphasis.

Life cycle costing

Public construction has increasingly been criticized for a shortsighted emphasis on minimizing initial costs for new construction projects including fire stations. The criticism focuses on jurisdictions that pass up long-term or life cycle savings that can be gained through high standards of quality in favor of short-term but smaller savings in initial design or construction cost. Provision for station expansion, long-term energy savings, and design for low maintenance are the three most important areas of concern in terms of life cycle costs.

The argument against skimping on initial costs holds especially true in providing low maintenance interior and exterior finishes for the station and in providing amenities for firefighters which make the fire station a more livable place. Low maintenance interior and exterior finishes are important to reduce the amount of required routine cleaning and to avoid situations in the future where maintenance of finishes (e.g., painting) is put off indefinitely because of tight operating budgets. For firefighters, the station may be their home much of the week. Morale is likely to be much higher if the station finishes remain in good repair. Additional station amenities such as recreational equipment and comfortable lounge space can also help maintain firefighters' enthusiasm for their work. Physical fitness equipment can help maintain physical conditioning. Initial costs for such items are insignificant compared to costs which can occur if firefighters become dissatisfied with their work—or out of condition physically.

If expenditures for such amenities reduce absenteeism and show the firefighter that the jurisdiction takes pride in its fire service, such initial costs will prove to have been a good investment.

Relocatable temporary fire stations

Several jurisdictions have begun using relocatable or temporary fire stations to ease the immediate capital budget impact of a facility expansion program. The basic desirable features of these stations is that they can be put in place quickly, they cost far less than a permanent station, and they can be relocated to other sites. Relocatable stations are discussed later under special facility design impacts.

Leased fire stations and adjunct facilities

Local fire departments have begun to consider using leased buildings to house their operations when special conditions exist.

The city of Dayton, Ohio, has experienced a period of rapid growth, partly owing to an annexation program. That growth prevented selection of a permanent site for one of its needed new fire stations. (Fire facilities are sited for a fifty year service life). Dayton decided to have a temporary station built to its design specifications by a private developer/contractor. The city leased the new building for five years. Under the renewable lease for this two bay fire station the city pays annual lease payments to use the building and pays additional costs for maintenance, utilities, and property taxes. Building defects which occurred during the first year were covered by a building warranty.

The station was constructed within 120 days of project approval by the city. In the third year of the lease (1978) the fire department was still satisfied.

The Dayton fire department later leased an existing building to serve as a repair facility for its apparatus until final plans were developed to provide a permanent repair garage at its fire training ground. At the time of this writing, the city was considering the lease of an existing building as another interim fire station if growth and change again preclude an expenditure for a new permanent station.

Leasing can be a viable alternative to premature establishment of permanent facilities where patterns of community change do not allow determinations of permanent sites or facility needs, but where some service is necessary immediately. Leasing may also solve problems of meeting service needs in lean budget years when an expenditure of several hundred thousand dollars for construction of a new station is not possible. One important consideration for leased or developer owned facilities is that site selection must be very carefully thought out, since the developer–owner of a designed-for-lease building will often need to find a commercial use for it after the fire department has moved out. Such a need may eliminate certain residential sites from consideration.

Developer assistance

Another capital budget aid is used in some jurisdictions to hold down the cost of new stations. In these jurisdictions, developers of major commercial or residential projects are required to also provide land for new fire stations or to construct station facilities which can provide protection for their projects. Agreement by the developers is required prior to approval of the project by the jurisdiction. Land requirements and facility specifications are set by the jurisdiction and regularly inspected to assure compliance by the developer. The rationale for requiring developers to provide land and/or fire facilities is that the general citizen should not be taxed to cover the indirect capital construction costs (schools, roads, fire stations, etc.) directly related to the new development.

Alternative uses for fire stations

Many jurisdictions have found it necessary or appropriate to close fire stations, sometimes even while they are constructing stations in new locations. These jurisdictions are then faced with the problem of what to do with the decommissioned stations. Several jurisdictions have taken innovative approaches to this problem—for example, converting fire stations to use solely as rescue squad stations, or to use as repair or maintenance garages, or offering them for sale to private owners.

Standardized designs

Another approach that can be used to hold down new station costs by jurisdictions planning construction of several stations over a span of years involves developing one or more basic fire station designs which can be used repetitively (or with minor modification) in more than one site. Through the use of standardized designs, the objective is to reduce design and engineering needs, and therefore the fees for the same, for stations built to the same basic designs. It should be noted, however, that this does not eliminate the need for some additional architectural and engineering services on these projects. Plans are almost certain to require modification by the original design professional for a number of reasons. These include site differences, such as unique site layout and soil conditions, and modifications and improvements to the original plans based on experience with earlier stations, as well as modifications of external or internal appearance.

Even with these modifications, however, enough of the basic station design can remain intact to provide significant savings in design fees. Fairfax County, Virginia, has used three basic designs in its fire station development program and believes strongly in the approach. Los Angeles, California, uses standard design plans for cost economy and control of design quality.

Facility design issues

Fire stations provide the primary support for local fire defense planning, which also includes building code provisions, zoning controls, public ordinances, water supply, and programs to educate the general public regarding fire safety. Together these form the backbone of local fire protection. Development of community plans for fire suppression and fire prevention are covered elsewhere in this book (notably in Chapter 6).

One key to successful fire department operations is the functioning of the fire station. Well planned, flexibly designed fire station buildings can provide adequate service for many years to the constantly changing communities in which they are situated. Some modifications, however, may be required during their service lifetime.

The typical fire station houses firefighters, vehicles, and equipment. The space requirements for a given station are tailored to the specific needs of the service area to be protected. Primarily, a fire station must provide the fastest possible response to fires. Therefore, floor plans and building egress routes must be designed to efficiently move firefighters and equipment through the station and out to the street without delays.

Communities are frequently in a state of flux in that people and businesses are constantly moving into and out of them, zoning regulations are being changed, and building codes and other construction controls are being improved. Population densities change as residential, commercial, and industrial growth or decline occur. All of these factors, and others as well, may affect the burdens placed upon fire services to provide facilities, equipment, and personnel. Fire stations can also change. New services, delivery techniques such as emergency

Fairfax County, Virginia, Fire Station No. 24.

Fairfax County, Virginia, Fire Station No. 25.

Fairfax County, Virginia, Fire Station No. 26.

Figure 19–1   Six typical fire stations.
(Source: Fairfax County stations,
courtesy Fairfax County Fire and Rescue
Services, Fairfax, Virginia;
District of Columbia stations,
courtesy District of Columbia
Fire Department, Washington, D.C.)

Fairfax County, Virginia, Fire Station No. 28.

Washington, D.C., Fire Station No. 4.

Washington, D.C., Fire Station No. 2.
Note: five additional floors of city office space
are designed to be built above this
two story fire station.

Figure 19–1 (continued).

medical services and community use of facilities, and altered manpower requirements may affect fire station functions. A fire station must therefore be designed to be flexible enough to serve both present and future fire service needs with a minimum of costly renovation and down time. Continuing increases in construction costs place added demands that fire stations be functionally adequate as long as possible.

At the end of its term of usefulness, a fire station may be recycled for another public function. Foresight during the design process can increase the range of possibilities for alternative use of retired fire station buildings as warehouses, maintenance shops, or other facilities by allowing for additions to and alterations of the existing building space with a minimum of difficulty.

Basic station functions[6]

The basic tactical unit of the fire department, the fire company, is a group of firefighters assigned to a station and operating one or more pieces of apparatus. Larger jurisdictions may operate many stations with multiple companies using various types of specialized apparatus and equipment. Each company may contain up to thirty or more firefighters. However, small fire departments with just one station comprise about 70 percent of the firefighting forces in this country.

Fire departments carry on four basic kinds of activities in day-to-day operations; these are:

1. Administrative or management activities, which include planning, record keeping, and supervision
2. Fire prevention activities, such as provision of information services, fire safety inspections, and investigations into the causes of disastrous fires
3. Operations, including fire suppression, search and rescue, and provision of emergency medical services—a growing trend in many areas
4. Support activities of maintenance and training which ensure adequate response in all functional activity areas.

Fire department facilities to support those functions may consist of fire stations, communications centers, administrative offices, repair facilities, and training grounds. Any of these may be combined into a single facility. Particularly in smaller jurisdictions, costs and service needs may dictate that multiple functions be housed in one facility.

Detailed station functions[7]

As has been stated above, activities in fire stations can be categorized in four primary areas. The actual functional areas in which these activities are carried out are listed in Figure 19–2. Because each fire department and station may have unique characteristics, this list cannot be considered complete, but it does include the primary functional areas generally associated with basic and many optional operations and can serve as an aid in initial considerations of spaces required in a new facility.

Not all fire stations will contain every space listed in Figure 19–2, but each will contain the basic categories of functional areas. Some stations will have additional facilities which are not related to actual firefighting services. Among these are, for example, a gym or game room, an auditorium, or a meeting hall; these may be community-oriented and can be revenue producing, especially in volunteer departments. Administrative space requirements will vary with the fire department organization and the distribution of battalion chiefs and other officers throughout the jurisdiction.

A primary concern for an efficient fire station is the circulation system within the building. During an alarm situation firefighters must move quickly from

Administrative
Lobby or reception area
Staff offices
Clerical area
Conference room

Fire prevention
Fire prevention/inspection office
Training room

Operations
Apparatus room
Communications room
Watch room

Support function areas
Hose care area (hose tower
  or dryer area)
Equipment storage
Dormitory
Locker area
Day room
Food preparation/dining
Training room
Exercise room

Mechanical equipment areas
Mechanical room
Emergency power generator area
  (may be remote from building)

Vehicle related
Maintenance/repair area
Motor court (protected
  outdoor work area)

Exitways/circulation
Halls/stairs/pole area
Exits

Figure 19–2   Typical functional areas of fire stations.
(Source: Adapted from AIA Research Corporation,
Seismic Design for Police and Fire Stations,
Washington, D.C.: AIA Research Corporation,
1978, p. 77.)

other areas to the apparatus room. Circulation must be designed to facilitate this emergency movement. Some guidelines are listed below:

1. Primary employee activity areas should have direct access to the apparatus room
2. Exit doors from employee activity areas should swing in the direction of travel to the apparatus room
3. There should be view panels in doors to prevent accidents
4. Doors into corridors and into the apparatus room should be released to prevent accidents
5. Circulation to the apparatus room should not cross sleeping areas
6. There should be one way access to fire pole shafts to prevent reverse circulation and congestion
7. Circulation paths to the apparatus room should not cross
8. Long corridors should be avoided
9. Corridor lighting should be bright
10. Corridors should be acoustically treated
11. Corridors should be securable from public access
12. Automatic controls for station lights should be alarm-activated at night.

Certain design considerations for station functional areas can improve overall efficiency and facilitate maintenance of stations. The following guidelines would apply to dormitories:

1. The dormitory should always be separated from noise producing areas of the station
2. Lockers, shower areas, and restrooms should be buffered from sleeping areas
3. A separate sleeping area and exit should be provided for emergency

medical services personnel if an EMS vehicle operates from the fire
station
4. Accommodations for female personnel should be considered
5. Private sleeping areas should be provided for officers
6. There should be one locker for each person housed in the station.

The guidelines below are applicable to the apparatus room:

1. Adequate circulation space should be provided around vehicles
2. Special firefighter equipment stored near trucks (turnout coats, boots, etc.) should be easily accessible
3. Protected electrical outlets should be mounted well above the floor to permit hosing down of the apparatus room
4. Automatic HVAC (heating, ventilating, air conditioning system) shutoff when apparatus doors are open can be provided to reduce energy waste
5. Apparatus room exit doors (usually providing a fourteen foot clear height opening) should be sized to accommodate all apparatus (with future needs considered)
6. Apparatus lanes and exits should allow all vehicles to exit independently of others
7. Ventilation of the apparatus room should be provided to remove fumes from vehicle testing and warmup
8. In cold climates, filler outlets for apparatus water tanks should be provided in the apparatus room
9. Apparatus doors, normally electrically operated, should be manually operable if power fails.

The following guidelines apply to public areas:

1. Public areas should be secured from the apparatus room and the private areas of the station
2. Public restrooms should be provided if public use of meeting rooms is planned
3. Handicapped needs should be addressed in all public areas.

Disaster/emergency considerations

Fire stations, as part of every jurisdiction's disaster/emergency response network, should be designed with consideration given to specific contingencies.
The potential impact of local hazards (e.g., earthquakes, hurricanes, floods) on
both the building and its source of supply for power, water, and sewer should be
assessed and appropriate design and planning measures implemented. These
measures may include the following:

1. Provision of emergency power generating equipment and batteries for essential station functions (communications, fuel pumping, etc.)
2. Manually operable apparatus doors
3. Operable station windows for ventilation
4. An emergency sanitary system
5. A potable water storage capacity
6. Specific structural protection for stations located in flood areas, seismic risk zones, tornado prone areas, and other areas subject to natural disasters.

Security considerations

Apart from a functional need to separate public and private fire station functions, crime and violence toward public institutions in some urban areas has

prompted fire departments to provide additional security in stations and on apparatus. Effective security measures which can be taken include the following:

1. Limiting of windows on perimeter walls and apparatus doors
2. Use of offset entrance doors (inner/outer) to prevent direct hurling of missiles or firing of gunshots into the station
3. Automatic closing of apparatus doors after trucks leave—especially if the station is left empty of personnel
4. Use of centralized electronic monitoring of the station perimeter condition when it is vacant.

Energy conserving building systems

Rising costs of energy have had a heavy impact on public construction in recent years, and the outlook is for more of the same. Although initial steps to reduce energy consumption in existing stations (e.g., turning down thermostats, reducing lighting, tuning up boilers, sealing building perimeter openings) are important, energy conservation will best be achieved by rethinking the design of buildings and energy consuming systems. Some of the recent steps which have been taken in fire stations including the following:

1. Addition of more insulation to improve insulating values of walls, roofs, and floors
2. In design plans, better building orientation to sunlight and shade and use of adjustable controls for admitting or rejecting natural light
3. Reduction of northern exposure window areas and use of double glazing throughout
4. Use of heat exchangers to reduce loss of exhaust heat
5. Insulation of air circulation ducts to reduce transmission loss in HVAC systems
6. Use of automated apparatus room heater shutdown when doors are opened
7. Use of hose towers to enable low cost drying of large amounts of hose with natural ventilation (hose towers also effectively drain hose and can be used to dry tarps, salvage covers, and other large items as well as doubling as training towers when so designed)
8. Use of heat pumps for reduced HVAC costs
9. Application of solar-augmented heating, cooling, and domestic hot water supply equipment.

An energy conservation study should be part of the preliminary design phase of fire station projects, to achieve the closest integration possible of the building and its energy system requirements.

Special design impacts

Combined facilities When fire stations are combined with other public services in a single building, care must be taken to assure proper separation of fire and nonfire activities. Separate entrances to the fire station and other activity areas should be provided, and unrestricted exits for fire apparatus are a necessity. If interior spaces for fire and nonfire activities interconnect, then a method of securing the fire station area from the rest of the building is required for times when nonfire services are inactive. If other building activities are not essential during emergencies, perhaps separate mechanical, plumbing, and electrical systems should be provided. Adequate, secure on-site parking for fire service personnel should be provided.

In the interest of holding down construction costs, combined facilities can be economical. When other essential twenty-four hour operations can be combined with fire operations the need for separation of building systems and provision of special security can be reduced.

Flexible fire station design   Because the fire protection needs of jurisdictions are always changing, a fire station which is adequate today may require extensive expansion or modification in just a few years. It is necessary for local fire stations to be designed and constructed to accommodate, at very least, anticipated changes to their staff, equipment, and services. Only when they have been designed for flexibility and adaptability to change can these essential facilities expand and adjust to meet new demands with cost-effective alterations.

The following design measures, among others, can increase building adaptability and alterability:

1. Load bearing masonry perimeter structure or load bearing interior partitions should not be used
2. Modular hung ceilings and removable interior partitions which can be relocated can be included in the design
3. Electrical wiring can be run down from ceiling to wall outlets and switches or floor troughs may be used in areas not subject to wetting
4. The HVAC system should be designed for expansion
5. A one story building can be designed to carry another future floor above
6. The facility can be designed for anticipated expansion, to be staged as required.
7. The total site impact from building expansion should be considered before an expandable building is planned.

Air rights structures   Washington, D.C., designed its Engine Company No. 2 as an air rights structure. Built in an initial phase as a two story structure this reinforced concrete building is designed to accommodate five additional stories of District of Columbia government offices above as part of a full block development. The station is an example of a local government approach to intensive and cost-effective use of an expensive downtown site. Underground parking for the complete building was provided in Phase 1 construction. An additional significant fact about this station is that its design intentionally emulates that of an award winning eight story office building across the street, a feature which is desirable when neighborhood character should be maintained. (This station is shown in Figure 19–1.)

Demountable temporary fire stations   Local needs for permanent fire stations cannot always be met immediately, owing to capital budget constraints. Montgomery County, Maryland, for example, is experimenting with demountable lightweight fire stations for use as interim facilities until money for permanent stations becomes available. Two demountable stations for county use—including state work—were estimated to cost much less than two permanent stations and can be erected in about thirty days. Once permanent stations are built the demountable stations can be stored or reerected elsewhere.

Washington, D.C., uses an inexpensive design for its demountable fire stations, to be used when providing them as interim stations during renovation of existing stations. A trailer is used to house administrative functions; a wood-framed shed to house the apparatus is placed between the wall of the building being renovated and the trailer. As the walls of the trailer and the existing building serve as shed side walls, only two short end walls—one a roll-up door—are needed to fully enclose the apparatus space. The District of Columbia plans two future uses of the demountables in its overall cost cutting activities which include renovating rather than replacing as many stations as is practical.

Another benefit of this use of demountable temporary stations is that personnel can be hired and trained and equipment purchased immediately for eventual use at the permanent stations; this spreads the annual budgetary impact of providing new facilities.

Emergency medical services   The fire service has gone well beyond first aid with the recent trend toward providing prehospital care at the scene of emergencies. Many fire departments provide ambulance service or on-the-scene first aid. Because of a trend toward more specialized emergency care, some departments have chosen to train additional personnel or their ambulance crews in EMS techniques, which can involve the use of sophisticated equipment for monitoring and stabilizing patient condition and for communicating such data to a medical center prior to patient arrival. A federal voluntary design standard for vehicles used for EMS transport has been developed. Because of the dimensions of the vehicle, local jurisdictions which are planning to institute EMS and utilize the vehicle standard should plan their fire stations to house such vehicles. Where separated ambulance bays are used, their exit doors should be sized to accommodate such vehicles.

Ambulance and EMS crews housed in fire stations respond on a twenty-four hour basis to calls which may not require fire apparatus. Therefore, quarters for ambulance crews should be separated from the general sleeping area and provided a separate exit. Ambulances should have direct access to the exit doors without movement of firefighting apparatus. (A detailed discussion of EMS is contained in Chapter 10.)

Typical station configurations[8]   There are several basic types of building configurations which have been consistently used for independent fire stations. They correspond to methods of connecting the apparatus room with the rest of the building. The internal organization of a station is determined in part by the manner in which other functional areas of the station are arranged with respect to the apparatus room on the basis of design and site factors.

Six typical configurations are shown in Figure 19–3. They are described below.

Sandwich   This plan places the apparatus room between two perimeter segments which can separately house administrative/public and dormitory/private functions. It also simplifies circulation to the apparatus room and allows front and rear egress from the station for apparatus. This plan, however, restricts expansion of the apparatus room as future needs might require.

Side-by-side: two story   The two story side-by-side plan has most of the benefits of the sandwich, with a somewhat more complex circulation system because of its two levels. Such a plan with dormitory facilities on an upper level may require use of poles for circulation to the apparatus room. Apparatus room expansion is facilitated with this plan arrangement, site permitting. Also, this plan requires less extensive use of HVAC duct work and can potentially be more economically conditioned.

Side-by-side: one story   This type of plan permits expansion of the apparatus room and retains the front/rear exits for apparatus. Circulation in the dormitory and operational areas may become more complex.

Over and under   With an over and under plan, the operations and/or dormitory functions all take place above the apparatus room. This type of plan requires special consideration for public and handicapped access, and for the location of the watch room to give full view of the apparatus room and exit doors. Such a

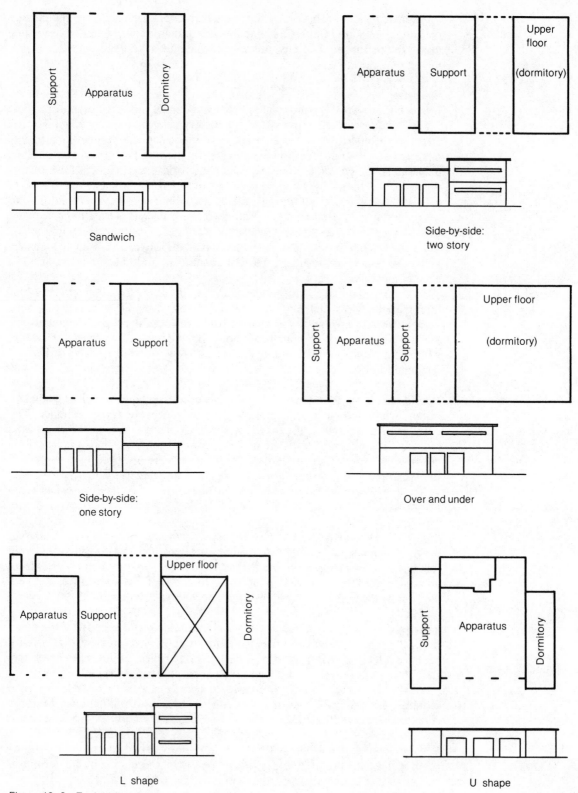

Figure 19–3 Typical fire station configurations.

plan may require use of poles for access to apparatus. The apparatus room and the operational and dormitory spaces can be expanded easily. Ventilation of apparatus exhaust fumes must be carefully considered.

L *shape* The L-shaped plan allows front exiting only for apparatus by wrapping operational and dormitory facilities around the rear of the station. Such a plan may be necessary when narrow, deep sites must be used. Circulation to the apparatus room can be simplified with this type of plan.

U *shape* The U-shaped plan arrangement allows easiest access from all activity areas to the apparatus room but precludes any expansion of apparatus space. If central HVAC is used, duct work runs will be extensive.

Station site The development of a fire station site should satisfy two primary goals. First, the exitways will need to be designed to allow vehicles to move directly to the street; this design should preferably include an alternative exit route. Second, an adequate exterior motor court for vehicle maintenance and for employee and guest parking should be maintained. Another factor is that in some urban neighborhoods a properly landscaped buffer to the community may be needed and should be provided.

Fire station exit ramps should allow the apparatus to move directly from the station to the road without having to back up or maneuver excessively in the process. Curved ramps should be avoided for several reasons, including the following:

1. As apparatus may increase in size with changing needs, curved ramps may become inadequate
2. It is more difficult for returning apparatus to back into a station from a curved ramp than from a straight one.

An alternative exit route from the rear of the station should be provided in the event of a blocked primary exitway. Such a rear exit may allow apparatus to be pulled rather than backed into the station after a call.

The motor court may be located in the front or rear of a station if the site is adequate. It should contain parking for two work shifts as well as space for extra vehicles that may be stored or temporarily parked at the station. It should be securable from public access.

Public access to fire stations requires at least limited provision of public parking. Such parking should be visible at the front of the station and should be clearly marked. Public parking on apparatus exit ramps and in front of apparatus doors should not be permitted. Stations which contain community facilities such as auditoriums or public classroom programs should provide additional off-street public parking on lighted lots. Parking spaces (twelve feet wide) and curb cuts for handicapped persons should be provided at all public parking areas.

Training facilities Fire department training as the basis for firefighter efficiency at the fire ground will be conducted at properly equipped facilities. Training facilities may be located at a principal local fire station or at a separate local site, or may be set up on a county, state, or regional basis, so as to train individuals from many jurisdictions.

Local training facilities may consist of dual purpose hose/training towers at fire stations which provide only limited simulation activities or may be comprehensive centers with several types of training buildings and other simulation equipment. General repair and storage facilities may also be located here.

A training center should be capable of simulating all types of fire and fire rescue situations that a jurisdiction expects to encounter. Its facilities may consist of classrooms, a simulated fire ground with buildings designed to simulate different types of fire situations, simulated hazardous types of outdoor fires, and test and simulation equipment. It should be developed on a site which is large enough to provide full maneuverability to apparatus and personnel and should have hydrants located appropriately. Because of the need for security and firefighter concentration during training, as well as the smoke, heat, and noise generated, residential sites are not recommended for training centers.

Some normal training center equipment includes the following:

1. A hydrant system which can supply the entire training area.
2. A draft basin with a recirculation system for used water for testing pumpers.
3. A drill structure of some type to train firefighters to work in burning and smoke-filled buildings. Such structures may contain different types of standard window frames, entrances, exits, and hazards. Roof entry may be simulated.
4. A system of roads for circulation around the fire ground and each simulated fire station.
5. Open pits for simulating burning spills and vehicles.
6. Storage facilities for tools, equipment, etc.

Buildings housing classrooms, assembly space, and administrative functions should be located apart from the fire ground simulation area.

Summary and outlook

The theme of this chapter has been the proper managerial approach to the location of fire station facilities, the capital budgeting process involved, and facility design issues. Key aspects for decision makers have been emphasized throughout, and it is recognized that appropriate modification of the principles and practices discussed should be made in the light of the unique characteristics of each community, which will vary according to size, geographical location, economic health, and socioeconomic and political environment.

What of the future? Looking forward to the 1980s and perhaps beyond, a jurisdiction considering new fire station locations and construction should plan on a continuation of present trends but should also anticipate the fact that some surprises are likely to lie ahead. Managers inside and outside the fire department (and, indeed, elected officials and the community at large) would probably be wise to pay serious attention to the following considerations:

1. *Energy conservation.* These problems are likely to get worse before they get better.
2. *Natural hazard protection.* Municipal insurance ratings and federal programs will place more emphasis on prevention and protection. New criteria and standards are to be developed.
3. *Facility provisions for women in fire and emergency medical services.* With the events of the last few years, the growing role of women in these services is a reality, not a possibility.
4. *Occupational safety.* Whether or not existing building occupant safety regulations are legally binding for jurisdictions, Occupational Safety and Health Act provisions related to safety in fire stations should be followed.
5. *Tighter municipal budgets.* Because of the unpredictable nature of municipal revenues, several years of tight budgets should be anticipated during the lifetime of a fire station. At the least, it is wise to design stations of durable materials with low maintenance requirements. Preventive maintenance is usually one of the first things cut from an

operating budget. If preventive maintenance is overlooked during tight budget years the result could be a shortened service life for a fire station as well as higher maintenance costs and lower station effectiveness in later years.

6. *Changes in resource requirements, equipment, and urban development.* It is hard to predict the future, but some "blue sky" thinking may be worthwhile. Smoke detectors came into widespread use in the late 1970s. Will automatic home fire extinguisher systems develop in the 1980s? Or will increased insulation in buildings for energy conservation have the negative side effect of making serious fires develop more rapidly? Major changes in a jurisdiction's needs for fire protection and the ways in which protection is delivered deserve serious consideration. What seems to be distant today might quickly become a reality.

1 American Insurance Association, *Fire Department Stations and Companies: Location, Distribution and Response,* Special Interest Bulletin no. 176 (New York: American Insurance Association, 1975).

2 Insurance Services Office, *Grading Schedule for Municipal Fire Protection* (New York: Insurance Services Office, 1974.)

3 National Fire Prevention and Control Administration, National Fire Safety and Research Office, *Urban Guide for Fire Prevention and Control Master Planning,* (Washington, D.C., National Fire Prevention and Control Administration, [1977]), p. 2:3.

4 Public Technology, Inc. *Fire Station Location Package* (Washington, D.C.: Public Technology, Inc., 1976).

5 The PTI developed Fire Station Location Package is one of several such tools which are currently in use to improve the overall effectiveness of fire services. New York RANN (Research Applied to National Needs), which is now disbanded, developed a fire station locator for the city of New York which used an approach similar to that of PTI's FSLP. Babbitt and Wilcox Consultants using existing response/distance criteria developed and are currently marketing a fire station location methodology. Certainly there are other methodologies which have achieved local or regional acceptance.

6 The material appearing in this section, on fire station functions and functional areas, is adapted from: AIA Research Corporation, *Seismic Design for Police and Fire Stations* (Washington, D.C.: AIA Research Corporation, 1978), pp. 71–83, 214–17. This design manual was developed within a research program that involved the authors of this chapter as participants. The National Science Foundation/Research Applied to National Needs financially supported this research.

7 Ibid.

8 The material appearing in this section is adapted from: ibid., p. 275.

Fire apparatus and equipment management

People are the most costly factor in fire department management. In some paid fire departments they account for upwards of 90 to 95 percent of the total budget (this subject has been explored in Chapters 12 and 13). Buildings and facilities (discussed in Chapter 19) account for a portion of the remainder; consumable supplies from gasoline to toilet paper account for some of the rest. Since few American fire departments allocate funds for research and development, most of what is left is spent for apparatus and equipment—the often expensive tools of the firefighter's trade.

Seen as a percentage of the total budget, apparatus and equipment do not appear impressive. It should be borne in mind, however, that many fire department costs are fixed (there is, in fact, not much an elected council member can do about personnel costs apart from making retrenchments in the areas of pay raises or fringes); therefore, those items of expenditure for mobile fire apparatus and equipment such as hose, nozzles, protective clothing, and breathing apparatus (items which are only too visible in the budget document) can be fair game for the economic axe. Fire department and other managers will ask, or will be asked, whether they can justify that $75,000 for a pumper which may not be used to its full capacity more than once or twice each year—or whether they can justify twice that amount for an aerial ladder which is not useful for fire-fighting or rescue incidents higher than the seventh or eighth floor of a new high rise. If the old nozzles still work, why should they buy new ones? And just how many ways are there to squirt water?

Excellent texts addressing these and similar questions are available at the skill training level[1] and at the detailed consensus standard level of the National Fire Protection Association series that grew out of the original Pamphlet no. 19.[2] This chapter addresses these questions from a management perspective and, on the various issues discussed, raises such management questions as: Why? What are our objectives? Is there a more cost-effective way of accomplishing the same objectives? Can we incorporate available technologies to make fire ground operations less labor-intensive, thereby gaining more per dollar and per worker hour?

As the discussion throughout this book has indicated, such management considerations face unique challenges with respect to the fire service. On the one hand, what private industry would regard as a market is extremely fragmented because of the large number of fire departments found in communities of differing sizes throughout this country. Furthermore, many fire departments are volunteer departments with their own special needs and approaches. On the other hand the psychology of the fire service is also unique, and the shared experience of facing danger helps shape the group attitudes of firefighters and of departments as a whole. These factors are mentioned because they help to shape many of the decisions made regarding apparatus and equipment, for example, a decision to buy customized rather than standard equipment (a matter discussed in this chapter) or a decision regarding innovations in apparatus (see also Chapter 16 for a discussion of the management of innovation).

To place the present chapter in full context it should also be understood that sound management of apparatus and equipment necessitates full attention to such matters as purchasing and bidding procedures, the status of warranties, the keeping of records, and the acquisition of accurate and up-to-date information generally.[3] This chapter is divided into eight major sections. The first introduces the basic concepts involved—the evolution of the triple combination pumper and the distinction between engine work and truck work. The second section discusses pump capacities and mountings, and the third examines the role of the water tank, while the fourth takes a closer look at truck work and the role of ladders. Several issues affecting costs are the subject of the fifth section; these are the issues of custom versus commercial, ego versus innovation, and repair versus replace. The sixth section examines the growing role of specialty equipment, the seventh details the important role of hose—a key traditional element—and the eighth shifts the focus toward the future by examining the significance of some innovations of the 1970s (including the mini pumper, also discussed in the sixth section of the chapter). The chapter ends with a brief conclusion and summary.

Basic concepts

In Chapter 3 the ''complex simultaneity'' of fire ground operations was summarized and a review was given of the basic types of fire apparatus needed to transport people and equipment to fire scenes and to other integral parts of a fire suppression operation.

Since water is the basic extinguishing agent for structural and nonstructural fires for ordinary combustibles, and under certain circumstances for some flammable liquid fires, proper water application is critical. In the United States the piece of fire apparatus which, with its crew, carries out water application is called the triple combination pumper, or triple combination engine, depending

Figure 20–1   A typical triple combination pumper, including a water tank and associated booster hose, a volume pump, and a load of hose. (Source: Maxin Motor Company.)

on local traditions. The *triple combination* had its origins in the nineteenth century, when the three elements of the triple combination—a pump, a water or chemical tank, and fire hose—were carried by three different vehicles. The steam pumper, belching fire and smoke, remains a familiar and nostalgic picture. The hand drawn or horse drawn hose reel responded with the steam pumper. (Its descendants live on primarily in industrial fire brigades, where water is supplied at high pressures to hydrants by fixed fire pumps, and hose lines are simply stretched from the hydrants, with no need for a mobile pumper.) The chemical engine, which was the ancestor of our modern booster tanks and perhaps of mini pumpers as well, was simply a closed tank filled with a solution of baking soda dissolved in water. A bottle of sulfuric acid was suspended inside the tank with a break or spill device; when the operator desired to discharge the contents of the tank the acid was mixed with the soda solution, and carbon dioxide gas was generated rapidly and in sufficient volume to force a useful stream through small diameter hose and onto the flames in question. (The operating procedures were in fact identical to those used in the soda and acid portable fire extinguisher.)

The triple combination pumper of today takes water from its own tank, from a hydrant, or from a static water source such as a river or cistern and pumps it through connected lengths of fire hose and out of a nozzle at appropriate pressure to reach the seat of the flames or to cool the heated area involved. The apparatus and the fire crew in this operation are termed an *engine company* or *pumper company,* and the work itself, in fire departments which tend to rigid specializations of tasks, is known as *engine work.*

Fire departments that make a specialization of *engine work* invariably define most of the nonapplication of water tasks at a fire scene as *truck work.* Truck work involves a great many diverse tasks, including the following: raising necessary ladders; forcing entry into buildings; opening up the fire building to ventilate smoke and fire gasses (to stop the spread of fire throughout the structure and to make entry and attack easier for engine company firefighters) and to search for hidden fire; rescuing trapped or endangered building occupants; and protecting the building and its contents from excessive smoke and water damage. Using power operated ladders or elevating platform apparatus (if it is available) is also a part of truck work, but it should be made clear that engine work and truck work *both* must be performed at a working fire, even if only engine companies are present.

The next two sections of this discussion cover two of the chief components of the triple combination engine or pumper—the pump and the tank. The third component—fire hose—is discussed later in this chapter, immediately preceding the section on innovations, to which, in fact, it is linked.

Pumps: capacity and mounting

Capacity

Though early mobile fire apparatus mounted pumps of various capacities, the combined influences of the National Fire Protection Association (NFPA), the International Association of Fire Chiefs (IAFC), and the National Board of Fire Underwriters (ancestor of the current Insurance Services Office [ISO]) brought about a standardization of components. Pumps for mobile fire apparatus are usually rated in increments of 250 gallons per minute (GPM), starting with the minimum standard size of 500 GPM and running up through 2,000 GPM. This *rated capacity* must be deliverable when suction is taken from a static water source ten feet below the pump intake and the discharge pressure at the pump is 150 pounds per square inch (psi). A piece of fire apparatus mounting a pump with a capacity below 250 GPM is considered to be mounting only a booster pump, and such a vehicle would not be given credit in the ISO grading schedule for pumping capacity.

Until the late 1940s pumping apparatus might carry positive displacement pumps of the rotary gear or piston types, but since 1950 the centrifugal pump has been essentially universal on modern mobile pumping apparatus.

In the past, situations arose on the fire ground which demanded occasional discharge pressures higher than the standard 150 psi. In addition, early gasoline engines lacked the horse power to deliver such pressures through a single centrifugal impeller. Thus, 500 GPM capacity, multi-stage centrifugal pumps were developed which utilized two or more impellers on a single shaft with lower individual capacities, which were valved and plumbed to deliver the rated capacity at 150 psi when set in the *volume* or *parallel* valve position. The pump would also deliver a proportionally reduced volume at a proportionally higher pressure when the valves were set in the *series* or *pressure* positions. Most commonly, this pump was a two-stage pump which on the pressure setting for a 500 GPM pump might deliver 250 GPM at 250 psi discharge pressure measured at the pump.

Although modern gasoline and diesel engines are fully capable of delivering the horse power for such elevated discharge pressures through a single (or single-stage) impeller, the two-stage pump, even with its increased maintenance problems and needless complexities of design and operation, remains a most popular design. Some less tradition-bound fire departments have gone to single-stage pumps even for their massive 2,000 GPM units.

Perhaps it is only the American cultural notion that "bigger is better," and perhaps not, but (although statistics are shaky at best) the most popular size pump capacity is reported to be increasing.[4] Through the early 1960s the 500 GPM size seemed most popular. As of the later 1970s, pumps of 750 to 1,000 GPM were popular in rural and suburban departments, with municipalities tending to 1,000 GPM, 1,250 GPM, and, occasionally, larger capacity units. The NFPA notes that the 500 GPM capacity pump is seldom specified any more (this situation is discussed later in this chapter under the heading Specialty Apparatus).

When considering pump capacities for mobile fire apparatus, managers should consider certain sound management questions. What are the objectives? What are the alternatives? What types of structural and nonstructural fire situations are likely to be encountered in the jurisdiction? What volumes of water at what pressures are necessary to control the maximum feasible fire in these situations? How much water can available suppression personnel effectively apply? How much water is the community water supply capable of delivering? What is the difference in cost between a 500 GPM and a 750 GPM? Between a 750 GPM and a 1,000 GPM? Between a 1,000 GPM and a 1,250 GPM?

Such questioning can lead to some interesting discoveries. One chief was under considerable pressure from his firefighters to buy a 1,250 GPM or a 1,500 GPM pumper for use in his city's warehouse district because the firefighters felt that the increased pumping capacity was justified, and because the larger fires often experienced there made it desirable to be able to run more than four standard hose streams off the pumper. (Traditionally, because a standard hose stream is considered to be one flowing 250 GPM at appropriate pressures, a 500 GPM pumper has two $2\frac{1}{2}$ inch outlets, a 750 GPM pumper has three $2\frac{1}{2}$ inch outlets, a 1,000 GPM pumper has four $2\frac{1}{2}$ inch outlets, etc.)[5]

This chief's community was well hydranted, with superior water supply volumes available at relatively high residual pressures at the hydrants. He therefore determined that he would purchase a 1,000 GPM pump but would specify that it be plumbed with six $2\frac{1}{2}$ inch outlets plus the usual $1\frac{1}{2}$ inch outlets for preconnected attack lines. The pumper was delivered and put through its acceptance tests and then was hooked up to a fire hydrant, where it pumped in excess of 1,650 GPM at 150 psi. Since major fires in this community were seldom fought with pumpers taking water by suction from static sources (the conditions for pump rating and acceptance testing), the city gained increased pumping capability at moderate prices.

It may be significant that, whether by weight of sheer tradition or because of sophisticated analysis, the Washington, D.C., fire department has stayed with the 750 GPM pumper as its basic unit well into the late 1970s. In fairness, it should be noted, however, that the department uses a special method. Each of its engine companies is actually made up of two 750 GPM triple combination pumpers: one of these hooks up to a hydrant and pumps water to the second which is at the fire scene and from which attack hose lines are stretched.[6] (The cost-effectiveness of this concept has in fact been questioned.)

Mounting

Fire pumps are most commonly located in two positions—midships (just to the rear of the vehicle cab) or front mount (forward of the vehicle cab). Thousands of relatively inexpensive and simple to operate fire engines were manufactured with the traditional reliable 500 GPM front mount pump for civilian and military fire departments across this country and throughout the world. Some front mounts of 750 and even 1,000 GPM were also manufactured, but weight and balance became problems with the larger sizes. Perhaps, perversely, because of the front mount's simplicity and low cost, a gradual shift away from its use occurred.

It is an interesting fact that, after the shift from the simple front mount to the midships mounted pump, fire chiefs discovered that their pump operators had lost two important capabilities—a speedy hookup, and the ability to "pump and roll"—which had been routine with the front mount. Formerly, a driver/pump operator desiring to hook up his front mount to a fire hydrant had only to nose his vehicle towards the hydrant, aiming it and stopping when his eye determined that the pump was close enough for a length of supply hose to reach from the hydrant outlet to the pump inlet. In addition to this capability and because the drive for a front mount pump came off the front of the vehicle's engine and not from a complex of gears located behind the vehicle's transmission (as with the midships), a unit with a front mount pump had the capacity to pump water while being driven (a decided advantage when fighting brush fires or highway accident fires).

To regain the ability to aim the nose of a pumper at a hydrant for simple, speedy hookup, fire chiefs began to specify a third pump intake, piped through to poke out of the front of the apparatus where the entire pump had been. To regain the ability to "pump and roll," fire chiefs began to specify a separate power takeoff unit to drive a separate booster pump, which was added at an additional cost. Of course the booster pump, by definition, delivers less water than a standard pump. A general management challenge is worth noting at this point. Unlike their counterparts in private industry, fire department managers have rarely, under such circumstances, taken time from the day-to-day pressures of their work to ask, Why? What is the objective here? Are there alternative, cost-effective means to the same end?

With the growth in popularity of the midships mounted pump, there came a gradual increase in the complexity of the pump operator's control panel. While there are no statistics on this matter it seems reasonable to assume that firefighter/pump operators want respect for their ability to deal effectively with complex tasks. Perhaps, then, the more complex the pump panel looks, the more impressively respectable is the ability of the person who knows how to operate it. At any rate, it seems evident that very little "human factor" engineering has gone into pump panel design.[7]

Individual pressure gauges linked to individual discharge gates allow the pump operator to calculate, using one of several fire ground hydraulics rules of thumb, how many gallons per minute are flowing through the hose line attached to that outlet and, from that calculation, to know within certain limits whether the nozzle pressure is appropriate for developing a good fire stream. It is interesting to note that, for some time, flow meters have been available which indicate how much water is actually flowing in the line (a pressure gauge will register whatever pump pressure is being developed, even if *no water* is moving through the hose), but, once again, these are not in widespread use in the fire service.

The water tank

The next element to be considered in a triple combination pumper is the water tank. Current editions of NFPA no. 1901[8] specify a minimum water tank capacity of 300 gallons. This booster tank, once it left the horse drawn chemical engine for a remount on motorized apparatus was initially conceived of as a water source for fighting inconsequential fires in automobiles and trash containers. It was the rural and small town fire departments, which often had no water mains and fire hydrants, that taught the American fire service that apparatus with pumps and larger tanks of water could effectively control a wide range of building fires as well. These smaller fire departments demonstrated that, by preconnecting 1½ inch and even 2½ inch fire hoses to pump outlets and providing a separate hose bed for the preconnects, a firefighting team could start pumping water much more quickly than a team equipped in a more traditional manner. Once again, the at that time innovative concept of larger water tanks and preconnected 1½ inch attack lines, though introduced to the fire service by Lloyd Layman in two NFPA publications in the early 1950s,[9] was slow to catch on.

The NFPA reports that, even though the minimum recommended tank size for pumpers is 300 gallons, most new pumpers have larger tanks.[10] Some effective attack pumpers mount 1,000 gallon tanks, although this, of course, requires a vehicle designed for such heavy operating loads. Pumpers with these larger tanks in some jurisdictions do not lay out a supply hose from a hydrant on the way into a fire but commence the attack with preconnected lines and tank water, relying on second arriving units to provide a continuing supply. For fire departments operating in areas with little or no hydrant distribution, mobile water tanker vehicles (with or without standard fire pumps) operating to supplement attack pumpers are recommended, but the NFPA suggests that serious thought be given to the matter before such a vehicle with a tank larger than 1,000 gallons is ordered. While some fire departments do operate semitrailer tanker units with nearly 5,000 gallon capacities, such heavy units have limited mobility, especially on rural roads or in areas with bridges incapable of bearing such loads.[11]

The truck company

Single unit versus double unit

Recommended good practice for response to a building fire is two engines and a truck company or unit capable of performing truck work.[12] This traditional response has proved a remarkably effective one given appropriate personnel. Research on Alexandria, Virginia, has indicated that 97 percent of all the *working* fires in that city of some 120,000 people—a city which has both extensive closely built (sometimes frame construction) historical districts and also extensive modern high rise residential and commercial construction—were controlled by the manpower and apparatus of only the basic two engine companies and one truck company response.[13] At the time of the study, Alexandria engines and trucks had nominal four person crews on duty.

An analogy has occasionally been made that compares engine companies to the Army infantry and truck companies to the Army engineers.[14] Older, more traditional communities tend to rigidly specialize firefighters according to their company assignments. It is not unusual to find young firefighters assigned to busy New York City truck companies who have responded to thousands of alarms but who cannot remember the last time they handled a fire hose—which is, after all, engine work. There have been serious discussions in such fire departments as to whether truck companies should be dispatched with engines to calls for automobiles or piles of trash on fire in the street (for, after all, engine companies apply water and truck companies "merely" use tools—although these tools may be used to stir up the trash or to cut open the car seats to ferret out hidden fire). The situation became of sufficient concern to New York City's fire department that an article essentially urging commonsense flexibility was published in that department's magazine in 1970.[15]

Ladders

In the 1950s one could still find ladder truck companies operating in American cities which were indeed just ladder trucks (they were called *city service ladder trucks*). They had a complement of ground or hand ladders (depending on local terminology) but did not have the power operated aerial ladder (or the elevating platform that came in in the 1960s) common today. These city service ladder trucks were allowed a larger complement of firefighters than were aerial ladder companies, because the people aboard the city service units were the way the ladders got up.

NFPA consensus standards address tests for working strength for both ground and power operated ladders; total number of feet of ground ladders that should be carried on a ladder truck (the consensus changes from time to time and had dropped from some 208 feet in the 1960s to approximately 163 in the late 1970s); and the various tools which make up a sound complement.[16] Lengths of fire department ground ladders are usually measured in terms of working lengths, and these ground ladders customarily allow access to third or fourth story windows or roofs. Power operated aerials usually come in 65 foot, 75 foot, 85 foot, and 100 foot lengths,[17] though longer ones may be purchased, usually from European suppliers. Similarly, elevating platforms are available in comparable lengths, with the longest running about 90 feet, but with at least one manufacturer offering a platform in the 125 to 150 foot range (Tucson, Arizona, Anchorage, Alaska, and Philadelphia, Pennsylvania, for example, all operate one of these units).

Rating bureau engineers applying the ISO grading schedule tend to give full credit to aerial ladders and elevating platforms (when otherwise appropriately equipped with ground ladders and tools, salvage covers, etc.) within this range of lengths. Some manufacturers offer modular "junior" aerials and elevating platforms of 50 to 55 foot lengths which may be mounted on otherwise standard pumper apparatus capable of carrying the extra weight. These units are often given half credit as aerials and full credit as pumpers by these rating bureau engineers.[18]

One Illinois department operating six engine companies and one aerial ladder found itself facing a change in insurance classification by the ISO unless it purchased and staffed an additional standard aerial ladder. Instead, that community's fire chief chose to equip five of his six engines with 55 foot modular junior aerials (the sixth, had it been so equipped, would no longer have fit into its firehouse). Thus, each such engine company was able to gain rapid power aerial ladder access to fourth or fifth story heights without the necessity of using firefighters to set ground ladders. The ISO gave the community half aerial ladder credit for each such unit, and the community came out with more aerial ladder credit than it would have had had it followed ISO recommendations. No additional personnel were required by this innovative approach, and all five pumpers were so equipped at *less* than the dollar cost of purchasing a standard aerial (with no additional personnel costs).[19]

Figure 20–2 The
articulated boom—
the early concept
of the elevating
platform.
(Source: Ward LaFrance.)

Figure 20–2 The articulated boom—the early concept of the elevating platform. (Source: Ward LaFrance.)

A British device long traditional in that country's fire service is of some interest at this point. The pump escape is a wheeled extension ladder, probably
somewhat longer than the longest ground ladder customary in this country,
which is mounted on a pumper with the wheels at the rear of the pumper and the
ladder laid along the top of the vehicle. A single firefighter can apparently de-
mount the escape and wheel it into position to rescue building occupants or to
provide an exterior access to a fire building for other firefighters. Though mentioned occasionally by American firefighters who have visited the United Kingdom and seen it in service, the device has never caught on here, although it
permits one firefighter to raise a ground ladder which in America would require
approximately five or six firefighters. A modification of the pump escape idea
might be possible should an American manufacturer be able to adapt some very
similar self-powered devices routinely in use in the construction industry.

Once again, managers should ask themselves: What are our objectives? What
are we trying to accomplish? Are there reasonable alternatives?

On the face of it, the objectives seem clear: access to floors above ground
level for purposes of rescuing occupants endangered by fire; access to these

same floors for firefighting crews more rapidly than would be the case if they climbed interior stairs; and utilization of large calibre nozzles (usually termed *ladder pipes*) mounted on the aerial ladder or platform for combating large fires on these same floors.

In fact, around the turn of the century the length of the power operated aerials in New York City (then traditionally 85 foot units) was the controlling factor in determining the allowable height for "new law" tenements in that city.[20] Today, faced with high rise construction and faced with the fact that most aerials cannot reach effectively much beyond the seventh or eighth story, managers must ask themselves some painful questions, the principal one being that of how much money it is worth to fire jurisdictions to be able to reach those floors between the fourth floor (attainable over the modular 50 to 55 foot units) and the seventh or eighth floor (attainable over the 100 foot standard aerials which cost far more than the engine mounted modulars). From the examples of Tucson, Philadelphia, Anchorage, and others with aerials and platforms beyond 125 feet, it would seem that it is definitely worth the cost to some.[21]

Other questions arise, concerning aerial ladders versus elevating platforms. When Chicago pioneered the elevating platform concept it realized that there were operations that the platform mounted on an articulating boom could perform which the aerial could not, and, similarly, there were operations that the aerial ladder could perform which the platform could not. Chicago wisely settled on a mix of apparatus types. Because some fire chiefs wanted the continuous path to the ground provided by an aerial as well as the increased safety and comfort of the platform, some manufacturers developed a compromise unit called an aerial platform.

Figure 20–3 The Sutphen Aerial Tower, incorporating a telescopic aerial with ladder and an operator's compartment or basket. It incorporates features of both the aerial ladder and the elevating platform. (Source: Sutphen Corporation.)

Fort Wayne, Indiana, purchased such a telescoping aerial platform and mounted twin turret ladder pipes in the basket, each ladder pipe capable of delivering a 750 GPM stream. This "two gun" approach has proved successful in that city for attacking fires involving wide areas of floors within reach of the apparatus and for attacking fires which involved more than one story within its reach.[22]

Combination vehicles

If a triple combination pumper is equipped with a standard truck company complement of ground ladders, tools, and equipment, it is usually called a *quad*. If it is equipped with such ground ladders, tools, and equipment, and a power operated standard length aerial or elevating platform, it is often referred to as a *quint*. Such combination pieces of apparatus are sometimes purchased by cities that hope to avoid the expense of two separate vehicles. Quads are now as scarce as city service ladder trucks, but quints continue to be popular.

However, unless the fire department operates several such combination pieces awkward tactical situations can arise. The military fire department at West Point operated such a quint several years ago, but occasionally situations arose in which a pumper was needed at a hydrant and the only pumper available was the quint, with the result that the aerial, tools, and equipment were at the hydrant instead of at the fire.

The two principal problems of such combination vehicles are: failure to adequately specify performance objectives and make sure such performance capabilities exist before accepting delivery; and failure to staff such a combination piece adequately enough to cover both engine and truck work functions.

Also, failure to engineer the rig properly can result, for example, in quints that cannot pump water if the aerial is in use and cannot use the aerial if the pump is in use. The modular units used in Rock Island, Illinois and on the Syracuse maxi pumpers (discussed later) are equipped with telescoping waterways alongside the square cross section telescoping beam which supports the aerial, and these permanent waterways supply a 1,000 GPM automatic nozzle (discussed later) permanently mounted as a ladder pipe. The operator can quickly raise the modular aerial and fire a high volume blast of water into a fire-involved space, even using tank water.

Issues affecting costs

Custom versus commercial

Before moving on to specialized apparatus and to certain innovations which may lead to more cost-effective fire department operations, we should take a brief look at three special issues affecting costs. The first of these is a long-lasting fire apparatus issue: the virtue of custom-made fire apparatus versus commercial apparatus. Perhaps if the fire service had kept more usable, accurate records, the issue or argument would be over. In any case, many firefighters and chiefs have strong feelings about the virtues of custom versus commercial apparatus and equally strong feelings about the respective merits of one or another so-called custom manufacturer.

When we use the word *commercial* in relation to fire apparatus, we do not mean it in the conventional sense, as when we apply it to standard models of automobiles, mass manufactured and available with various stock options. Although the situation may have begun to change in the late 1970s, in the face of the sheer realities of cost, mass produced fire apparatus has not been a successful enterprise for apparatus manufacturers and marketers in the United States.[23]

Commercial fire apparatus means that instead of using mass produced vehicles fire departments use apparatus constructed according to the purchaser's specifications on a vehicle chassis which could just as well have gone under a fuel oil tanker or a freight hauler. (Custom fire apparatus advocates do not often pause long enough to realize that one of the most popular "custom" manufacturers, the manufacturer of Mack trucks, is also a major manufacturer of over-the-road rigs. A look into the factories of other "custom" manufacturers might show artisans also at work on mass produced orders for a commercial or governmental trucking enterprise.)

The argument traditionally runs that commercial apparatus, while cheaper than custom, does not last as long. (Indeed, some commercial rigs built to less than precise specifications were produced which, for example, relied for cooling partly on the rush of air natural to over-the-road driving. Fire pumpers, however, sit in one place and pump, often for hours, and a cooling system not designed for such service has often failed.)

The custom versus commercial argument has also been applied to the purchase of aerial ladders. If a fire department has been less than careful in its specification writing or its acceptance testing, it has sometimes found itself with a low bid from a manufacturer more at home building power operated ladders for utility companies than building the same for rugged use on the fire ground.

"Lemons" of course, have never been the sole province of either commercial or custom manufacturers. Far more important to fire chiefs than the commercial/custom question is the need to keep careful, usable, and accurate records. There should be carefully kept records of operation and maintenance costs of apparatus *by manufacturer* (and of engine and pump components by manufacturer), records of service quality, records of the manner in which salesmen and manufacturers have lived up to promises and warranties, records of the way fire apparatus has held up under fire ground operating conditions. Through such records, the fire chief can often exercise some control over which manufacturers are permitted to submit bids—and, therefore, some control over quality.

Ego versus innovation

Given the helpful guides incorporated in NFPA no. 1901, perhaps the single factor most responsible for driving up the costs of both custom and commercial fire apparatus is the belief that individual communities have unique requirements or, rather—to put it bluntly—it is at times the fierce independence and ego of some fire chiefs (and at times of their elected and appointed superiors). Certainly innovations and progressive modifications which lead to cost savings in the long run are worth the financial outlay, but excessive outlays on chrome and brass are another matter.

On the other hand, fire managers who have put money into innovations that have ultimately led to economies have often been derided by their peers. We have made some progress, but chiefs who ask management questions can make more. The late R. J. Douglas, who founded Oklahoma State University's School of Fire Protection, was the first fire chief in West Virginia to specify a windshield for a piece of motorized fire apparatus. For his revolutionary trouble he was derided by other fire chiefs who wondered if his men were so soft that "they couldn't take it."[24] A generation later his spiritual descendants specified enclosed cabs for fire apparatus—and were also asked if another generation of firefighters "couldn't take it."

Once the cabs began to be enclosed, however, progressive fire chiefs began to move their crews off the dangerously exposed riding positions on the running boards and tailboards of engines and trucks and into more protected jump seats (though occasionally firefighters were still killed in these seats in traffic accidents, or in falls from semi-open positions). While Detroit had provided completely enclosed crew cabs in the 1930s, only Memphis and a few other cities had begun to provide completely enclosed crew cabs in the 1950s (in earlier years Memphis fire crews were so large that not all the firefighters assigned to a rig could fit inside and some still rode the back step).

With the pressures on managers to achieve greater productivity from on-duty paid fire crews, many departments began sending fire crews aboard their apparatus on building familiarization tours, pre-fire planning inspections, and even on code enforcement inspections. Radio kept these crews in touch with fire alarm headquarters and they were able to respond to alarms from inspection sites.

However, firefighters inspecting in uniform called to an alarm often had to change into helmets, coats, boots, and breathing apparatus while hanging onto exposed back steps or while balancing precariously in jump seats. Furthermore, American fire apparatus bodies are generally not built enclosed so as to afford protection from the weather to hose, tools, and other equipment. For these reasons, in-service inspection activities have generally been confined to fair weather. It would seem, therefore, that innovation in the form of enclosed crew cabs and fire apparatus bodies might be worth the outlay in terms of returns in increased productivity.

Repair versus replace

The last of these three special issues affecting costs is the issue of whether to repair or to replace.

One city public safety director, a retired naval aviator, remembered how the Navy had rebuilt and furbished the ancient but venerable DC–3s, significantly extending the useful service life of these workhorse airplanes; he embarked on what he believes was and is a successful program of similar rebuilding and refitting of overage city fire apparatus. Managers may want to carefully evaluate the repair or replace concept for their own communities.[25] For example, many older chassis were never designed to carry of today's larger water tanks and other equipment; however, these units may be convertible to rescue squads or fast attack rigs.

Specialty apparatus

Many kinds of specialty fire apparatus are in use today. Americans have grown accustomed over the years to calling their fire departments to assist them in many kinds of emergencies—fire-related or otherwise. Although truck companies routinely carry a wide variety of tools and equipment, many cities have developed rescue squads which carry more specialized tools and equipment. While these units may or may not carry small pumps and hose, most are equipped with booms and winches, jacks, cutting tools and power equipment for extricating the trapped and injured from all manner of emergency situations, from building collapses to auto accidents or mass transit accidents.

Once again, it is important to emphasize the need for managers to analyze their own municipal situations and determine their needs and objectives. One city may decide to equip, staff, and run a separate rescue squad. Another may choose to put light duty rescue equipment on each neighborhood engine company while equipping each truck company with the heavier and more specialized tools and equipment. Still others, who have found multiple uses for the mini pumper have discovered that, when equipped for heavy rescue, with booms, winches, etc., the minis also make excellent rescue vehicles.

CFR apparatus

Crash fire rescue (CFR) apparatus is specially designed for the special hazards of airport protection. The Federal Aviation Administration (FAA) sets standards for designing, staffing, and equipping CFR vehicles on the basis of an airport's FAA classification.[26] The NFPA has also developed a set of consensus standards for aviation-related fire/rescue services.[27]

CFR apparatus is usually designed with all-wheel drive to enable it to perform effectively on or off paved surfaces, and it is usually engineered for even more rapid acceleration than structural apparatus. Ordinarily, CFR vehicles do not stand in place and pump as do structural units; rather, being almost completely self-contained, they roll up to a downed aircraft and provide an evacuation path through the flaming fuel spill with foam solutions (aqueous film forming foam, fluoro-protein, or protein) spewed from turrets operated from inside the vehicle.

Then rescue crews in special protective clothing move down the evacuation path, effect rescues, and move themselves and their rescuees back down the safe path, which is being maintained by the turret operators and other CFR fire-fighters using hand lines.

Structural pumping apparatus should also be equipped to control relatively large-scale spill fires, off base crashes of aircraft, highway vehicular accidents, and other types of spills and fires. Modular units suitable for mounting on structural apparatus exist, such as high, medium, and low expansion foam proportioners, and twin agent units capable of discharging potassium bicarbonate for quick knockdown and aqueous film forming foam for quick cover-up of flammable liquid fires. Of course, fire crews assigned to structural apparatus should be given basic cross training enabling them to deal effectively with such nonstructural incidents.[28]

The mini pumper

For many years fire departments with extensive brush, grass, or forest lands in their jurisdictions have used small pickup truck types of units, with small capacity pumps, small water tanks, and hose and tool assortments appropriate to this type of firefighting. These units often were equipped with all-wheel drive to facilitate off-the-road mobility. Use of such brush trucks kept larger, standard pumpers available for structural alarms and also spared the more expensive units the battering attendant to off-the-road operations.

In the late 1960s and early 1970s, faced with the necessity of a fire department reorganization, Syracuse, New York, pioneered a concept which came to be known as the *mini pumper*. The mini, as originally conceived, was more than a brush truck. Rather more like a scaled down standard pumper, minis were initially built on a 10,000 pound gross vehicle weight chassis, with perhaps a 250 gallon water tank and a 250 GPM booster pump, a couple of preconnected hose lines (initially 1½ inches and later 1¾ inches—see the next section of this chapter), and some 700 or 800 feet of 3¾ inch supply hose (standard size, large diameter supply hose in Syracuse), and costing usually less than half of what a standard pumper cost.[29]

In Syracuse, a mini pumper is paired with a maxi pumper (a more nearly standard pumper, usually of approximately 1,500 GPM capacity and equipped with a 55 foot modular aerial). A five person crew is assigned to each such two piece company; the mini responds to single unit calls for grass, trash, cars in the street, etc., with a two person crew, leaving the maxi station-bound with the three remaining members so that the response district is not left unprotected during such nuisance alarms. A building fire alarm draws two or more of these two piece companies, plus appropriate ladder trucks.[30]

Research in Alexandria, Virginia, has indicated that, for three years of actual fires studied in that community, between 65 and 85 percent of all alarms could have been handled by mini pumpers. Harry Hickey suggests a modification of the two man mini/three man maxi, by reversing the manning levels, as has been provided in Philadelphia.[31]

One other suggestion may prove to be something close to a management breakthrough. The ISO grading schedule evaluates a community's ability to deliver its required fire flow, and thus "requires" a certain number of pumpers as well as a total pumping capacity necessary to deliver the water. A mini pumper equipped with a 250 GPM booster pump counts only as one adds its 250 GPM capacity to the rest of the capacity of the community's pumps. However, if the mini is in fact a 500 GPM minimum basic NFPA no. 1901 pumper (still very inexpensive to purchase, in fact by the late 1970s becoming almost a standard stock item with some manufacturers) the grading schedule will give the city *full pumper credit.* The cost difference between the booster pump equipment and the 500 GPM pump-equipped minis is not significant, but the grading schedule payoffs may make the 500 GPM mini worth its cost.

All-wheel drive

The virtues of all-wheel drive for fire apparatus should not be overlooked by managers, at least as far as minis or other attack structural pumpers are concerned. All-wheel drive for CFR apparatus has long been accepted for the on-and-off runway performance.

Even in urban settings, all-wheel drive can give important flexibilities. In such situations as fire hydrants located too far from the pavement, fires in buildings rendered nearly inaccessible by snow or mud or because a driveway is clogged with cars or other fire apparatus, or fire/rescue incidents in the rubble-strewn areas of natural disasters or civil disturbances, all-wheel drive may prove practicable, whereas these situations may prove insurmountable for two-wheel drive vehicles.

Hose

The third component of the triple combination engine or pumper (discussed earlier) deserves some separate consideration.

Traditionally, American fire hose other than small diameter booster line has come in two sizes, in terms of inside diameter, though the origins of these sizes are lost. Two and a half inch fire hose was the basic size. The so-called standard hose stream of 250 GPM is very nearly the amount of water delivered through a $1\frac{1}{8}$ inch solid stream nozzle at a fifty pound nozzle pressure attached to a $2\frac{1}{2}$ inch hose.

Yet, although John Freeman advocated the use of 3 inch hose for supplying water to pumpers and to heavy stream appliances when he did the famous studies which are still our guides for friction loss calculations,[32] it took the American fire service more than fifty years to generally accept the idea of using hose with an inside diameter larger than $2\frac{1}{2}$ inches.

For whatever reasons, American fire departments until very recently remained partial to screw thread couplings for their fire hose, with a male thread on one end and a female swiveled coupling on the other. Even after the Europeans demonstrated the clear advantages of the so-called Stortz couplings which had no male or female aspects but could couple either end to either end, most Americans stayed with the screw thread couplings. Toward the end of the 1970s European fire hose manufacturers began to make increasing inroads into the American market, and with this came an increase in the use of the Stortz on fire hose, even though this use required adapter fittings for pumper intake and discharge gates, hydrant valves, and similar applications.

Today many departments routinely lay out hose of 3 inches inside diameter or larger from hydrants or pumpers at the water source to a pumper at the fire scene. The larger diameter hoses usually come in inside diameters of 3, $3\frac{1}{2}$, 4, 5, and 6 inches; the virtue of such larger diameter hoses may be indicated when it is realized that, for example, approximately ten psi can push *approximately* 200 GPM through 100 feet of $2\frac{1}{2}$ inch hose, 350 GPM through 3 inch, 500 GPM through $3\frac{1}{2}$ inch, almost 800 GPM through 4 inch, 1,200 GPM through 5 inch, and almost 2,000 GPM through 6 inch hose.

Ten to 20 foot lengths of both rigid and flexible fire hose of 4, 5, and 6 inch diameters have always been used on modern pumpers as hard and soft suctions, and these tended to be manufactured with screw thread couplings. However, for departments desiring to carry several hundred feet of larger diameter hose, screw thread couplings tended to be manufactured only up through the $3\frac{1}{2}$ inch hoses—also usually the largest size hose to be manufactured with a fabric jacket covering an extruded tube.

Of perhaps greater interest is what has been happening with hand line fire hose of less than $2\frac{1}{2}$ inches in diameter.

Innovations of the 1970s

Developments affecting fire hose

Three developments of the early 1970s will continue to grow in popularity, making it possible for fewer firefighters to deliver more water more rapidly in fire combat. Two of these developments grew out of the Rand Corporation's work with New York City's fire department, when Union Carbide developed a long chain polymer which was environmentally safe and which, when added to the water being discharged from a pumper through hose streams, smoothed the normally churning turbulance into laminar flows of relatively high capacity with relatively low friction loss. This development made it possible to push nearly 200 GPM through $1\frac{1}{2}$ inch fire hose. The development then of fire hose with an inside diameter of $1\frac{3}{4}$ inches instead of $1\frac{1}{2}$ inches (both sizes use $1\frac{1}{2}$ inch couplings) made it possible for 250 gallons of treated water to be delivered per minute through hose of essentially the same weight and flexibility as the traditional $1\frac{1}{2}$ inch attack lines. Previous to the long chain polymer (which has the brand name of Rapid Water) and the $1\frac{3}{4}$ inch hose, such volumes could only be applied through the heavier, less flexible standard $2\frac{1}{2}$ inch hose. Of course, fewer firefighters are needed to move the smaller line into position and operate it.

Independent of these developments, but wonderfully coincident, was a water spray nozzle invented by a steel company engineer and volunteer fire chief which was capable of creating a fire stream with appropriate pressure, shape, and reach within an incredible range of flows—from 50 to 350 GPM—without manual adjustment. With normal spray nozzles, if a pump operator failed to supply 100 gallons per minute at 100 psi nozzle pressure to a spray nozzle designed to function at that pressure and capacity, a decent fire stream would not develop. The so-called automatic nozzle would take whatever water comes to it and adjust the discharge opening until the necessary 100 psi was developed and the stream thrown. The automatic nozzle made it possible to use Rapid Water with spray nozzles, because its design allowed it to take advantage of the increased flow with no manual adjustments whatsoever.

Many fire departments have adopted automatic nozzles and $1\frac{3}{4}$ inch hose without the rather expensive Rapid Water proportioners and are enjoying modestly increased fire flows. But, once again, technology conscious Syracuse has made a more complete commitment to innovation—in this case to automatics, Rapid Water, and $1\frac{3}{4}$ inch hose—than has any other city. Traditional $2\frac{1}{2}$ inch hose has disappeared from Syracuse rigs now that $3\frac{1}{2}$ inch hose is used for hydrant to pumper supply lines and for pumper to heavy stream appliance discharge lines, while the innovative $1\frac{3}{4}$ inch hose with traditional $1\frac{1}{2}$ inch couplings makes up all hand held hose lines. Rapid Water and automatic nozzles make possible the hand line delivery of fairly large volumes of water with smaller size fire crews.

Mini pumper technology

The previously discussed mini pumper technology could actually advance the cause of year-round code enforcement inspections by firefighters. Traditional fire apparatus is not designed to endure long periods of standing in cold weather without running the engine, pumping water, etc. If mini pumpers were designed and built: (1) completely enclosed and winterized to protect pumps, water tanks, and gauges from freezing; and (2) in modules so that, when a chassis wears out from the increased over-the-road activity that goes with year-round, day in and day out scheduled code enforcement inspection, the module could be lifted off and mounted on a fresh vehicle chassis, a new productivity might be realized. And, of course, in terms of purchase, operation, and maintenance mini pumpers are cheaper than traditional, usually custom-made, apparatus and if equipped with a 500 GPM pump will usually qualify for ISO grading schedule credit as a pumper.

Public Technology, Inc.[33]

Public Technology, Inc. (PTI), is a not-for-profit corporation in Washington, D.C., dedicated to applying existing technologies to problems of the cities. Several PTI projects relate directly to fire department problems. PTI, working with the U.S. National Aeronautics and Space Administration (NASA) and the Scott Aviation Corporation, developed in the middle 1970s significantly improved, lightweight, self-contained breathing apparatus for firefighters. The National Aeronautics and Space Administration, perhaps the most knowledgeable agency in the United States on designing life support systems for hostile environments, is now also working with PTI on firefighter protective clothing, and on a number of other projects.

Working with Hughes Aircraft Company, another PTI project team developed an infrared device, known as Probeye, which enables a firefighter, scanning a smoke-obscured room, to discern any objects in the room with temperatures varying significantly from the ambient temperature of the room. This device and others designed on the same principle are said to assist rescuers in locating bodies in vision-obscured areas and to assist overhauling crews in detecting hidden fire behind walls, floors, and ceilings. The device has also been used successfully to quickly discover which fluorescent light fixture ballast is burning out, saving fire crews time that is otherwise needed to search large lighted areas, and saving the business occupants needless disturbances.

The Grumman Aerospace Corporation worked with a PTI team to develop a radio transmitter which attaches to a hand line nozzle and makes it possible for the nozzle operator to increase or decrease the flows to or pressures at the nozzle. Syracuse, New York, which helped pioneer a number of other innovations, is now equipping its mini and maxi pumpers with this device—a move which will free some of the driver/pump operators for other fireground duties. Now nozzle operators can control their pumps from the fire zone, and one driver/pump operator can safely monitor several pumping units.

Some strong advocates of the automatic nozzle believe that its advantages make the radio control attachment unnecessary, even though the radio control device has only been used with automatics of the 50 to 350 GPM variety. If a pump operator knew by previous experimentation with his or her engine tachometer and flow meters that a certain engine speed flowed the maximum gallons per minute available from his or her engine, the operator could simply set the engine at that speed (once hose lines were attached to the pump's various discharge outlets and were charged with water) and the nozzle operators could control the flow at their individual automatic nozzles by adjusting the nozzle's ball valve.

As long as pumpers were located reasonably close to each other, a single pump operator might oversee two or three units by constantly moving among them. Of course, the radio control device has an additional provision not possible with the above "makeshift," and that is that when a malfunction occurs at a pump a signal is sounded to bring a pump operator to the pumper, and the radio control valve also signals to the nozzle operators that their water supply is in danger of becoming unreliable.

When an engine company rolling in on a fire alarm intended to lay a long supply line from a fire hydrant to a location farther on toward the fire, it was necessary to leave a firefighter at the hydrant to attach the hose to a hydrant outlet, wait for the engine to lay out more hose on its way to the fire, wait for the crew to uncouple the hose from the hose bed and recouple it to the water intake on the pump, and wait for an appropriate signal from the pump operator at the scene before turning on the hydrant. Only after so doing could the hydrant firefighter rejoin the other members of the crew and assist in firefighting. In the late 1970s Syracuse began experimenting with a radio controlled hydrant valve which allows the firefighter to dismount from the engine, couple the radio controlled valve on the supply hose to the hydrant, open the hydrant (the radio controlled valve remains shut), remount the engine, and proceed to the fire ground. When the pump operator has the supply line hooked up, a radio signal opens the control valve automatically and water is supplied to the pump. Of course, if the nozzles are also linked by radio to the pump throttle, the pump operator, too, can rejoin the crew.

Innovations and productivity

Many jurisdictions, faced with the fixed costs of personnel, are sorely tempted to save what few dollars they can by ignoring some of the technological labor-saving, manpower-multiplying devices and systems discussed in this chapter. In the late 1960s, when power saws which would cut wood, concrete, and steel were introduced for the fire service market, many cities were slow to adopt them. One Chicago truck company captain bought one of the then new power saws with his own money for use by his crew on his shift and found that one man with the saw could open a roof much more rapidly than three or four firefighters with axes. But it was a long while before such incidents made an impression on officials wrestling with the budget.

In the middle 1970s a Rapid Water proportioner cost approximately $25,000 per installation, an amount calculated to raise the blood pressure and lower the enthusiasm of many municipal managers. Many fire chiefs found it nearly impossible to convince their superiors that a Rapid Water proportioner was a one-time investment while a paid firefighter with salary and benefits would cost as much as the innovation in one year—and more in subsequent years; yet that one firefighter added to this total force would not make much of a marginal difference, whereas the Rapid Water proportioner would make it possible for two firefighters to deliver the water on a fire where formerly at least three firefighters were required. Indeed, as a result of this situation, the municipal policy-makers suddenly and surprisingly found themselves on the side of their firefighters' union—opposing the Rapid Water system.

Summary and conclusion

The example just cited of resistance to a technological innovation highlights a theme that has been evident throughout this chapter and, indeed, throughout much of this book. In a time of scarce local government resources and increasing competition for those resources among the main areas of local government activity, it behooves those responsible for fire department management (from the point of view of self-interest, at very least) to take a close look at ways of improving the management of their departmental resources. Fire apparatus and equipment management is a key area in which improvement has been and can be made. But it is still fair to state that many fire chiefs and their elected and appointed superiors need to begin to think about technology in terms of manpower multiplication and productivity—an attitude already found in most of modern industry.

This need has been emphasized throughout the discussion in this chapter, starting with the section on the basic concepts relating to fire apparatus and equipment, and continuing through the succeeding sections on: the capacity and mounting of pumps; the role of the water tank; the equipment needs of the truck company; the question of custom versus commercial and other considerations affecting overall cost; and the roles of specialty equipment and of hose. The final section, which takes a look at some of the innovations of the 1970s (innovations whose use is becoming more widespread and which will, in turn, be supplanted by the discoveries and applications of the 1980s and beyond), places particular emphasis on the importance to fire service of the managerial recognition of the place of technology in this area of local government.

1   See: International Fire Service Training Association, *Fire Apparatus Practices*, no. 106 (Stillwater: Oklahoma State University, International Fire Service Training Association, current edition); and also the following publications of the National Fire Protection Association (NFPA), both published in Boston by the National Fire Protection Association: *Operating Fire Department Pumpers* (current edition); and *Operating Fire Department Aerial Ladders* (current edition).

2   See the following NFPA standards, all published in Boston by the National Fire Protection Association: *Screw Threads and Gaskets for Fire Hose Connections*, NFPA no. 194 (1974); *Fire Hose*, NFPA no. 196 (1974); *Care of Fire Hose*, NFPA no. 198 (1972); *Automotive Fire Apparatus*, NFPA no. 1901 (1975) (Formerly no. 19, *Specifications for Motor Apparatus*); *Recommended Practice for the Maintenance, Care, Testing and Use of Fire Department Aerial Ladders and Elevating Platforms*, NFPA no. 1904 (1975); *Standard for Fire Department Portable Pumping Units*, NFPA no. 1921 (1975); *Standard on Fire Department Ground Ladders*, NFPA no. 1931 (1975).

3   These matters are explored in detail, with respect to local governments generally, in the following book in the Municipal Management Series: William E. Korbitz, ed., *Urban Public Works Administration* (Washington, D.C.: International City Management Association, 1976); see the following chapters in this book: Shimon Awerbuch, Robert J. Hoffman, and William A. Wallace, "Computer Applications in Public Works," pp. 53–85; Richard R. Herbert, "Public Works Finance," pp. 86–109; George A. Cumming and Ronald W. Jensen, "The Purchasing Function in Public Works," pp. 190–208; John Howley and Robert S. Stewart, "Equipment Management," pp. 209–29.

4   National Fire Protection Association, *Fire Protection Handbook*, 14th ed. (Boston: National Fire Protection Association, 1976), p. 9:47.

5   Ibid., p. 9:65.

6   From a 1978 interview with a Washington, D.C., fire department chief officer. Some fire departments may retain the two piece company concept described here at least in part because, during civil disturbances or other unusual fire department situations, off-duty firefighters are brought back to duty and the two piece companies split into heavily manned single piece companies, which effectively doubles available firefighting forces.

7   A. K. Rosenhan and Ray Johnson, "Engineering

8   National Fire Protection Association, *Automotive Fire Apparatus*, NFPA no. 1901.

9   Lloyd Layman, *Attacking and Extinguishing Interior Fires* (1952), and *Fire Fighting Tactics* (1953), both published in Boston by the National Fire Protection Association.

10 National Fire Protection Association, *Fire Protection Handbook*, p. 9:48.

11 Ibid., p. 9:49.

12 Warren Y. Kimball, *Fire Attack 1* (Boston: National Fire Protection Association, 1966), p. 5.

13 Harry E. Hickey, *A Comparative Analysis of Resource Allocation Plans for Urban Fire Safety* (Laurel, Md.: The Johns Hopkins University Applied Physics Laboratory, 1977), p. 223.

14 Kimball, *Fire Attack 1*, p. 2.

15 Martin F. Henry, "Single Unit Operations," *WNYF*, Issue no. 4, 1970, pp. 12, 13.

16 See the following NFPA standards: *Automotive Fire Apparatus*, NFPA no. 1901; *Maintenance, Care, Testing and Use of Fire Department Aerial Ladders and Elevating Platforms*, NFPA no. 1904; *Fire Department Ground Ladders*, NFPA no. 1931.

17 National Fire Protection Association, *Fire Protection Handbook*, p. 9:49.

18 Richard L. Ulrich, "Management Analysis and Innovative Technology Pay Off," *Fire Chief*, February 1976, p. 29.

19 Ibid.

20 Francis L. Brannigan, *Building Construction for the Fire Service* (Boston: National Fire Protection Association, 1971), p. 149.

21 Robert H. Ely, "Is Our Equipment Obsolete?" *Fire Command*, November 1970, p. 23.

22 Richard L. Ulrich, "High-Rise Learning by Burning Drill," *Fire Chief*, February 1975, pp. 28–31.

23 J. F. Finnegan, Jr., "The Case for Standardized Fire Apparatus," *Fire Chief*, February 1976, pp. 36–37.

24 From a personal conversation with Professor Douglas.

25 A. K. Rosenhan and Ray Johnson, "Repair or Replace?" *Fire Chief*, May 1975, pp. 33–35.

26 U.S., Department of Transportation, Federal Aviation Administration, *Regulations*, part 139: *Certification and Operations: Land Airports Serving CAB-Certified Air Carriers* (Washington, D.C.: Government Printing Office, December 1974).

27 See the following NFPA standards: *Standard*

Students Study Fire Pump Apparatus Panels," *Fire Chief*, August 1975, pp. 54–56.

538 *Managing Fire Services*

Operating Procedures, Aircraft Rescue and Fire Fighting, NFPA no. 402 (1973); *Aircraft Rescue and Fire Fighting Services at Airports and Heliports,* NFPA no. 403 (1975); *Aircraft Rescue and Fire Fighting Techniques for Using Structural Fire Apparatus,* NFPA no. 406M (1975); *Evaluating Foam Fire Fighting Equipment on Aircraft Rescue and Fire Fighting Vehicles,* NFPA no. 412 (1974); *Aircraft Rescue and Fire Fighting Vehicles,* NFPA no. 414 (1975).

28 International Fire Service Training Association, *Aircraft Fire Protection and Rescue Procedures,* no. 206 (Stillwater: Oklahoma State University, International Fire Service Training Association, current edition).

29 From a personal letter from Assistant Chief Frank Burke, Training Officer, Syracuse, New York, Fire Department.

30 Ibid.

31 From a conversation with Harry E. Hickey regarding the study cited in note 13.

32 National Fire Protection Association, *Fire Protection Handbook,* p. 9:3.

33 Information on the innovations discussed here, and on many others, is available from Public Technology, Inc., 1140 Connecticut Avenue, N.W., Washington, D.C. 20036.

Part five:
The outlook

21 The outlook

The major fire service problem areas which have emerged during the 1960s and 1970s have been analyzed in the various chapters of this book. Chapter authors have presented their concepts, described emerging trends, and assessed the needs of the fire service for the decade of the 1980s and beyond. An attempt to summarize and predict the outlook for managing fire services requires an understanding of evolving changes, not only in the fire service but also within the total structure of local government and our society.

It would appear that the recent period of sustained and continuing economic, population, and tax-base growth in most areas of the United States is ending. Thus, local government is confronted with the need to continue governmental services at a constant or rising level while financial resources are static or declining. This need, coupled with continuing inflation, realignment of financial resources, and continuing increase in energy costs, means local government no longer possesses the financial flexibility of previous years.

The fire service in the 1970s, through adaptation and innovation, met the challenge of increased demand for a newer fire service function—effective emergency medical delivery systems. The fire service role in these systems has generated new personnel recruitment, training, and education needs. The fire department role in emergency medical services requires personnel who can interact effectively with well-educated and well-respected persons in other parts of the local community's medical system. This fire service involvement mandates continuing education and training and has provided the impetus for additional education at institutions of higher learning. The role of the local fire department in both design and delivery of emergency medical services will be expanded because of community demand. The fire department in many communities has already evolved into a total emergency aid organization, with the time and effort devoted to the rescue and emergency medical service far exceeding the time and effort expended on fire prevention and suppression.

The composition of the fire service is changing dramatically as younger and better educated men and women enter the service. This trend of the 1960s and 1970s will continue. In addition, the work of the fire department in fire prevention and public education will increase. The acceptance of women in the fire service has been accelerated by the changing nature of the local fire department. In many areas of fire department and fire service innovation, it would appear the volunteer fire services have been more perceptive and innovative in adapting to changing roles and, thus, facilitating the entry of women into the fire service.

The fire service executive and other fire management personnel in local government seem to be aware of the changing nature of the fire department primarily because of the ever-escalating demand for emergency medical services and the less dramatic but significant increase in fire-related responses. There do not appear to have been many significant or innovative changes, however, in the organizational and management structure of the local fire department. No dramatic increase is evident in new personnel concepts, including the use of part-time personnel, with the exception of use of more civilian employees in many of the support and service areas. Thus, organization for delivery of fire and emergency medical services still is predominantly either/or—that is, organized on either a total volunteer or a fully paid personnel basis. The many useful variations and combinations of paid, part-paid, and volunteer personnel have yet to be implemented to meet the demand, response, and resource needs of most local fire departments.

Community reaction to local government in the late 1970s, evidenced by the citizen frustration and resultant attempts to deal with the escalating costs of government, resulted in property tax limitation referenda and other measures. These citizen reactions are likely to continue in the 1980s. Thus, the forthcoming and continuing challenge to the fire service manager is to maintain a publicly mandated level of service with static or declining resources. In addition to traditional fire suppression and prevention activities, fire service managers will be faced with the rising demands for emergency medical services (mentioned earlier), better methods of fire suppression for deteriorating urban areas, and the economic conditions which have facilitated incendiary fire setting. Fire service managers of the 1980s will strive to answer the following questions: How do you meet increasing fire service demands? How do you provide fire service more effectively? How do you provide fire service more efficiently?

Managing Fire Services has been written to help the fire service manager provide more effective and efficient operations in the 1980s. Principles of problem solving, methods, practices, and examples have been presented by authors for adaptation and use in local fire departments and other agencies. Procedures for increased productivity, improved personnel management, adaptation of technology, and organization of personnel, equipment, and resources into a fire service delivery system have been examined in this volume. The greatest value of this book will be the creation of additional concepts and procedures for the solution of fire service problems by fire service personnel. Therefore, this book is envisioned as a catalyst—a means for the communication of ideas, concepts, and procedures—and as a source of encouragement for fire service and government managers.

The fire service is not just an agency or an organization; the local governmental unit which is the focus of both the problem and the solution is the local fire department. The local fire department is only one element of the fire protection system and must compete for its resources with other equally essential units of local government. The most effective means of competition for resources by fire department personnel and managers must be the efficiency and effectiveness of their services to the local community. Thus, the eventual solution to immediate as well as future problems is the fire department's most valuable resource: competent, efficient, and dedicated personnel.

The most important responsibility of the fire service manager is the way he or she works with fire service personnel. The interaction of fire service personnel, fire service management, and local government management will determine the adequacy of fire and rescue services delivered to citizens both today and in the future.

Bibliography and resource guide

This bibliography is highly selective and represents informed judgments about basic materials of managerial interest in the proliferating area of fire services. It is intended to supplement the material cited in the endnotes to individual chapters in this book with a selection of basic books and research reports on the many specific subjects within fire services management. This bibliography and resource guide is arranged by chapter for the convenience of the reader, although some items will of course cover several of the many functional divisions of the text. Such references will, therefore, be shown in each applicable chapter.

To help readers supplement the materials set out in the chapter listings of this bibliography, the following synopsis identifies some of the standard reference sources and information available in journals, yearbooks, and association publications with application generally to the fire services management field.

A fundamental reference source for statistics of concern to fire service managers is the *Statistical Abstract of the United States,* published annually by the U.S. Bureau of the Census and obtainable from the U.S. Government Printing Office, Washington, D.C. 20402, or through any U.S. Department of Commerce district office. The annual appendix entitled *Guide to Sources of Statistics* is an invaluable guide to the many specialist statistical reference sources applicable to the fire services. *The Municipal Year Book* (published annually by the International City Management Association, Washington, D.C.) is an authoritative reference source, containing detailed guides to further sources of information—organizations as well as bibliographic materials—in local government management, including fire services. The *Fire Protection Handbook* (published by the National Fire Protection Association, Boston, Massachusetts, revised about every five years) contains data on loss of life and property from fire, information on the behavior of materials under fire conditions, and many other facts on

changes in fire protection techniques, systems, and equipment.

Many specialist fire service organizations have been described (and their addresses provided) in Chapter 4 of this book. The major organizations presented immediately below are sources for a large variety of useful information about fire services management in general.

The National Fire Protection Association (470 Atlantic Avenue, Boston, Massachusetts 02210) publishes numerous codes, standards, recommended practices, and manuals in all areas of fire protection; the *Fire Protection Handbook; Fire Journal* (the bimonthly membership magazine); *Fire Command* (a monthly magazine for fire service leadership); *Fire Technology* (a quarterly journal); and various books, as well as educational and audiovisual materials.

The United States Fire Administration (formerly the National Fire Prevention and Control Administration; USFA, P.O. Box 19518, Washington, D.C. 20236) publishes numerous reports, many brochures on public education, and the monthly newsletter *Resource Exchange Bulletin*. It also sponsors the fire reference service *Fire Technology Abstracts* (bimonthly).

The International Association of Fire Fighters (1750 New York Avenue, N.W., Washington, D.C. 20006) publishes the monthly magazine *International Fire Fighter*. The "Annual Casualty Report," published in the November issue, attracts national interest.

The International Association of Fire Chiefs (1329 18th Street, N.W., Washington, D.C. 20036) publishes a variety of informational and educational materials about fire protection, including its monthly magazine, *The International Fire Chief*.

The Insurance Services Office (160 Water Street, New York, New York 10038) publishes the *Grading Schedule for Municipal Fire Protection, The Commentary on the*

Grading Schedule for Municipal Fire Protection, and other materials on fire protection insurance ratings.

The International City Management Association (1140 Connecticut Avenue, N.W., Washington, D.C. 20036) publishes *The Municipal Year Book,* and the quarterly newsletter *Fire Management Review;* fire service management topics are covered frequently in many other ICMA reports.

In addition to the association journals, fire service periodicals on general topics include: *Fire Chief* (monthly magazine, published by the H. Marvin Ginn Corporation, Publications Division, 625 N. Michigan Avenue, Chicago, Illinois 60611), *Firehouse* (monthly magazine, published by Firehouse Magazine Associates, 515 Madison Avenue, New York, New York 10022), and *Fire Engineering* (published by Dun·Donnelley Publishing Corporation, 666 Fifth Avenue, New York, New York 10019). There are many different periodicals on special subjects, for example arson investigation, communications, and labor relations; some of these are cited in the endnotes to the appropriate chapters. Those cited, and other special periodicals, can be obtained from the appropriate organizations.

1 The Evolution of Fire Services

Bare, William K. *Introduction to Fire Science and Fire Protection.* New York: John Wiley & Sons, Inc., 1978.

Bond, Horatio, ed. *Fire and the Air War.* Manhattan, Kan.: Kansas State University, Military Affairs/Aerospace Historian, 1974.

Bush, Loren S., and McLaughlin, James. *Introduction to Fire Science.* Beverly Hills, Calif.: Glencoe Press, 1970.

Cannon, Donald J., ed. *Heritage of Flames: The Illustrated History of Early American Firefighting.* New York: Doubleday & Company, Inc., 1977.

Ditzel, Paul C. *Fire Engines, Firefighters.* New York: Crown Publishers, Inc., 1976.

Dunshee, Kenneth Holcomb. *As You Pass By.* New York: Hastings House, 1952.

Lyons, Paul R. *Fire in America!* Boston: National Fire Protection Association, 1976.

Smith, Dennis. *Dennis Smith's History of Firefighting in America.* New York: The Dial Press, 1978.

2 Management Options in Fire Protection

Adrian, Charles R. *Governing Urban America.* 5th ed. New York: McGraw-Hill Book Company, 1977.

Banovetz, James M., ed. *Managing the Modern City.* Washington, D.C.: International City Management Association, 1971, Chapters 1, 2, 3, 5, and 6.

Bollens, John C., and Schmandt, Henry J. *The Metropolis: Its People, Politics, and Economic Life.* 3rd ed. New York: Harper & Row, Publishers, 1975.

Hickey, Harry E. *A Comparative Analysis of Resource Allocation Plans for Urban Fire Safety.* Laurel, Md.: The Johns Hopkins University Applied Physics Laboratory, 1977.

———. *Public Fire Safety Organization: A Systems Approach.* Boston: National Fire Protection Association, 1973.

Institute for Local Self Government. *Civilians in Public Safety Services.* Alternatives to Traditional Public Safety Delivery Systems, no. 5. Berkeley, Calif.: Institute for Local Self Government, 1977.

———. *A Public Safety Employees Contractual System.* Alternatives to Traditional Public Safety Delivery Systems, no. 1. Berkeley, Calif.: Institute for Local Self Government, 1977.

———. *A Tale of Two Cities: Master Planning—An Alternative to the Common Practice of Incremental Decision-Making.* Alternatives to Traditional Public Safety Delivery Systems, no. 4. Berkeley, Calif.: Institute for Local Self Government, 1977.

More, Henry W. *The New Era of Public Safety.* Springfield, Ill.: Charles C Thomas, 1970.

Swersey, Arthur J.; Ignall, Edward J.; Corman, Hope; Armstrong, Philip; and Weindling, Joachim. *Fire Protection and Local Government: An Evaluation of Policy-Related Research.* New York City–Rand Institute Report R–1813–NSF. Santa Monica, Calif.: Rand Corporation, 1975.

3 The Fire Department: Management Approaches

Didactic Systems, *Management in the Fire Service.* Boston: National Fire Protection Association, 1977.

Favreau, Donald F. *Fire Service Management.* New York: Reuben H. Donnelley Corporation, 1969.

Fyffe, David E., and Rardin, Ronald L. *An Evaluation of Policy Related Research in Fire Protection Service Management.* Atlanta: Georgia Institute of Technology, School of Industrial and Systems Engineering, 1974.

Gratz, David B. *Fire Department Management: Scope and Method.* Beverly Hills, Calif.: Glencoe Press, 1972.

International City Management Association. "Public Safety: The Firefighting Function." In *Small Cities Management Training Program,* booklet 7. Washington, D.C.: International City Management Association, 1975.

Powers, Stanley Piazza; Brown, F. Gerald; and Arnold, David S., eds. *Developing the Municipal Organization.* Washington, D.C.: International City Management Association, 1974.

Research Triangle Institute; International City Management Association; and National Fire Protection Association. *Municipal Fire Service Workbook.* Prepared for the National Science Foundation, Research Applied to National Needs. Washington, D.C.: Government Printing Office, 1977.

"What Now for the Fire Service?" *Public Management,* November 1970, entire issue.

4 Other Organizations and the Fire Service

Bugbee, Percy. *Principles of Fire Protection.* Boston: National Fire Protection Association, 1978.

Fire Marshals Association of North America. *State Fire Marshals' Conference Report: Recommendations on Federal and State Roles in the Fight against Fire.* Conference report, NFPCA Grant 7706. Boston: Fire Marshals Association of North America, 1977.

Insurance Services Office. *Commentary on the Grading Schedule for Municipal Fire Protection.* New York: Insurance Services Office, 1977.

————. *Grading Schedule for Municipal Fire Protection.* New York: Insurance Services Office, 1974.

O'Brien, Donald M. *A Centennial History of the International Association of Fire Chiefs.* Washington, D.C.: International Association of Fire Chiefs, 1973.

Richardson, George J. *Symbol of Action.* Washington, D.C.: International Association of Fire Fighters, 1974.

Todd, A. L. *A Spark Lighted in Portland: The Record of the National Board of Fire Underwriters.* New York: McGraw-Hill Book Company, 1966.

5 Productivity, Technology, and Data Collection

Boise Center for Urban Research. *Enhancing Productivity in Local Government: A Primer for Citizen Interest Groups.* Boise, Idaho: Boise Center for Urban Research, 1975.

Gordon, B. B.; Drozda, W.; and Stacey, G. S. *Cost Effectiveness in Fire Protection.* Columbus, Ohio: Battelle Memorial Institute, 1969.

Hatry, Harry P.; Blair, Louis H.; Fisk, Donald M.; Greiner, John M.; Hall, John R., Jr.; and Schaenman, Philip S. *How Effective Are Your Community Services? Procedures for Monitoring the Effectiveness of Municipal Services.* Washington, D.C.: The Urban Institute and International City Management Association, 1977.

Lawton, John W. *A National Agenda for Programs To Increase the Introduction of Innovations in the Fire Services.* Washington, D.C.: Public Technology, Inc., 1973.

National League of Cities. *Municipal Fire Service Trends.* Washington, D.C.: National League of Cities, 1972.

New York City–Rand Institute. *Final Report: 1969–1976.* Santa Monica, Calif.: Rand Corporation, 1977.

Schaenman, Philip S., and Swartz, Joe. *Measuring Fire Protection Productivity in Local Government.* Boston: National Fire Protection Association, 1974.

6 Management and Planning for Fire Protection

Clark, William E. *Wingspread II: Statements of National Significance to the Fire Problem in the United States.* Racine, Wis.: The Johnson Foundation, 1976.

Humble, John W. *How To Manage by Objectives.* New York: AMACOM, 1973.

International City Management Association. *An Assessment of the Transferability of the Community Fire Master Planning Program* [with *An Executive Summary*]. Report prepared for the National Fire Prevention and Control Administration. Washington, D.C.: International City Management Association, 1977.

Mission Research Corporation. *A Conceptual Description of Statewide Fire Protection Master Planning.* Santa Barbara, Calif.: Mission Research Corporation, 1976.

National Fire Prevention and Control Administration, National Fire Safety and Research Office, *A Basic Guide for Fire Prevention and Control Master Planning.* Washington, D.C.: National Fire Prevention and Control Administration, [1977].

————. *Urban Guide for Fire Prevention and Control Master Planning.* Washington, D.C: National Fire Prevention and Control Administration, [1977].

7 Managing Fire Prevention

Clet, Vince H. *Fire-Related Codes, Laws and Ordinances.* Encino, Calif.: Glencoe Press, 1978.

Fyffe, David E., and Rardin, Ronald L. *Fire Protection Service Management.* Prepared for the National Science Foundation, Research Applied to National Needs. Atlanta: Georgia Institute of Technology, 1974.

National Commission on Fire Prevention and Control. *America Burning.* Washington, D.C.: Government Printing Office, 1973.

National Fire Protection Association. *Fire Prevention Code.* NFPA no. 1. Boston: National Fire Protection Association, 1975.

Research Triangle Institute; International City Management Association; and National Fire Protection Association. *Municipal Fire Service Workbook.* Prepared for the National Science Foundation, Research Applied to National Needs. Washington, D.C.: Government Printing Office, 1977.

Robertson, James C. *Introduction to Fire Prevention.* Beverly Hills, Calif.: Glencoe Press, 1975.

Whitewood Stamps, Inc. *Public Fire Education Planning.* Washington, D.C.: National Fire Prevention and Control Administration, 1977.

8 Managing Inspection Services

Hatry, Harry P.; Blair, Louis H.; Fisk, Donald M.; Greiner, John M.; Hall, John R., Jr.; and Schaenman, Philip S. *How Effective Are Your Community Services? Procedures for Monitoring the Effectiveness of Municipal Services.* Washington, D.C.: The Urban Institute and International City Management Association, 1977.

Institute for Local Self Government. *Public Safety Inspection Consolidation: An Alternative to Divided Responsibility for Total Fire Protection.* Alternatives to Traditional Public Safety Delivery Systems, no. 3. Berkeley, Calif.: Institute for Local Self Government, 1977.

Schaenman, Philip S.; Hall, John R., Jr.; Schainblatt, Alfred H.; Swartz Joseph A.; and Carter, Michael J. *Procedures for Improving the Measurement of Local Fire Protection Effectiveness.* Boston: National Fire Protection Association, 1977.

Tuck, Charles, A., Jr., ed. *NFPA Inspection Manual.* Boston: National Fire Protection Association, 1976.

Urban Institute and International City Management Association. *Measuring the Effectiveness of Basic Municipal Services: Initial Report.* Washington, D.C.: The Urban Institute and International City Management Association, 1974.

9 Managing Fire Control

Bennis, Warren G. *Organization Development: Its Nature, Origins, and Prospects.* Reading, Mass.: Addison-Wesley Publishing Co., 1969.

Caplow, R. *How To Run Any Organization.* New York: Holt, Rinehart, & Winston, 1976.

Gratz, David B. *Fire Department Management: Scope and Method.* Beverly Hills, Calif.: Glencoe Press, 1972.

Lippitt, Gordon L. *Organizational Renewal: Achieving Viability in a Changing World.* Englewood Cliffs, N.J.: Prentice-Hall, Inc., 1969.

Newman, William H. *Process of Management: The Concepts, Behavior, and Practice.* 4th ed. Englewood Cliffs, N.J.: Prentice-Hall, Inc., 1977.

Page, James O. *Effective Company Command for Company Officers in the Professional Fire Service.* Alhambra, Calif.: Borden Publishing Company, 1973.

10 Managing Emergency Medical and Rescue Services

Erven, Lawrence W. *Handbook of Emergency Care and Rescue.* Encino, Calif.: Glencoe Press, 1976.

National Academy of Science, National Research Council. *Accidental Death and Disability: The Neglected Disease of Modern Society.* Washington, D.C.: National Academy of Sciences, 1966.

Page, James O. *Emergency Medical Services.* 2nd ed. Boston: National Fire Protection Association, 1978.

————. "The Graying of Paramedics." *Paramedics international* 2 (Summer 1977): 14–17.

U.S. Department of Transportation, National Traffic Safety Administration. *National Training Course for the Emergency Medical Technician-Paramedic.* 15 booklets. Washington, D.C.: Government Printing Office, 1977.

Willemain, Thomas R., and Larson, Richard C. *Emergency Medical Systems Analysis.* Urban Public Safety Systems, vol. 4. Lexington, Mass.: Lexington Books, D. C. Heath & Company, 1977.

11 Managing Fire and Arson Investigation

Aerospace Corporation. *Survey and Assessment of Arson and Arson Investigation.* Prepared for the National Institute of Law Enforcement and Criminal Justice. El Segundo, Calif.: The Aerospace Corporation, 1976.

Battelle Columbus Laboratories. *Arson: America's Malignant Crime.* Final Report from the Leadership Seminars for Developing a Coordinated Attack on Arson. Prepared for the National Fire Prevention and Control Administration. Washington, D.C.: National Fire Prevention and Control Administration, 1976.

————. *Final Report on Resource Assessment for Arson Education and Public Awareness.* Prepared for Ohio FAIR Plan Underwriting Association, Blue Ribbon Arson Committee. Columbus, Ohio: Battelle Columbus Laboratories, 1975.

Carter, Robert E. *Arson Investigation.* Encino, Calif.: Glencoe Publishing Company, 1978.

International Association of Arson Investigators. *Selected Articles for Fire and Arson Investigators.* Marlboro, Mass.: International Association of Arson Investigators, 1975. Available to members only.

National Fire Protection Association. *Arson: Some Problems and Solutions.* NFPA SSP–38. Boston: National Fire Protection Association, 1976.

12 The Budgetary Process

Aronson, J. Richard, and Schwartz, Eli, eds. *Management Policies in Local Government Finance.* Washington, D.C.: International City Management Association, 1975.

Ayres, Douglas W. *Integrative Budgeting System: A New Approach from Old Failures.* San Juan Capistrano, Calif.: By the Author, 25572 Purple Sage, 1977.

Czamanski, Daniel Z. *The Cost of Preventive Services: The Case of Fire Departments.* Lexington, Mass.: D. C. Heath & Company, 1975.

Jernberg, James E. "Financial Administration." In *Managing the Modern City,* pp. 347–76. Edited by James M. Banovetz. Washington, D.C.: International City Management Association, 1971.

Lee, Robert D., Jr., and Johnson, Ronald W. *Public Budgeting Systems* 2nd ed. Baltimore, Md.: University Park Press, 1977.

Moak, Lennox, and Hillhouse, Albert. *Concepts and Practices in Local Government Finance.* Chicago: Municipal Finance Officers Association, 1975.

Pyhrr, Peter A. *Zero-Base Budgeting: A Practical Management Tool for Evaluating Expenses.* New York: John Wiley & Sons, Inc., 1973.

13 Personnel Management and Labor Relations

Crouch, Winston W., ed. *Local Government Personnel Administration.* Washington, D.C.: International City Management Association, 1976.

Flynn, Ralph J. *Public Work, Public Workers.* Washington, D.C.: The New Republic Book Company, 1975.

Heisel, W. D. *On Public Employee Negotiation.* Chicago: International Personnel Management Association, 1973.

International City Management Association. *Effective Supervisory Practices: Better Results through Teamwork.* Washington, D.C.: International City Management Association, 1978.

Saso, Carmen D. *Coping with Public Employee Strikes.* Chicago: Public Personnel Association, 1970.

Stern, James L.; Rehmus, Charles M.; Loewenberg, J. Joseph; Kasper, Hirschel; and Dennis, Barbara D. *Final-Offer Arbitration: The Effects on Public Safety Employee Bargaining.* Lexington, Mass.: Lexington Books, D. C. Heath & Company, 1975.

U.S. Civil Service Commission. *Job Analysis for Improved Job-Related Selection.* Washington, D.C.: Government Printing Office, 1975.

14 Measuring and Evaluating Productivity

Beltrami, Edward J. *Models for Public Systems Analysis.* New York: Academic Press, 1977.

Hatry, Harry P.; Blair, Louis H.; Fisk, Donald M.; Greiner, John M.; Hall, John R., Jr.; and Schaenman, Philip S. *How Effective Are Your Community Services? Procedures for Monitoring the Effectiveness of Municipal Services.* Washington, D.C.: The Urban Institute and International City Management Association, 1977.

Hickey, Harry E. *Public Fire Safety Organization: A Systems Approach.* Boston: National Fire Protection Association, 1973.

Research Triangle Institute; International City Management Association; and National Fire Protection Association. *Municipal Fire Service Workbook.* Prepared for the National Science Foundation, Research Applied to National Needs. Washington, D.C.: Government Printing Office, 1977.

Schaenman, Philip S., and Swartz, Joe. *Measuring Fire Protection Productivity in Local Government.* Boston: National Fire Protection Association, 1974.

Schaenman, Philip S.; Hall, John R., Jr.; Schainblatt, Alfred H.; Swartz, Joseph A.; and Carter, Michael J. *Procedures for Improving the Measurement of Local Fire Protection Effectiveness.* Boston: National Fire Protection Association, 1977.

Urban Institute. *The Struggle to Bring Technology to Cities.* Washington, D.C.: The Urban Institute, 1971.

15 Training and Education

Allen, David; Bodner, William S.; Lano, Richard I.; and Meyer, John M. *A Study of the Firemen's Occupation.* Sacramento, Calif.: University of California, Division of Vocational Education, and California State Department of Education, Bureau of Industrial Education, 1968.

Boeing Aerospace Company and Washington State Commission for Vocational Education, Fire Service Training. *Firefighter Skills Study: Preliminary Investigation of Degradation of Firefighter Skills.* Olympia, Wash.: Washington State Commission for Vocational Education, Fire Service Training, 1974.

Granito, Anthony R. *Fire Instructor's Training Guide.* New York: Dun-Donnelly Publishing Corporation, 1972.

International Fire Service Training Association. *Fire Service Training Programs.* 2nd. ed. Stillwater: Oklahoma State University, 1971.

————. *Instructor Training.* 3rd. ed. Stillwater: Oklahoma State University, 1973.

Rose, Homer C. *The Development and Supervision of Training Programs.* Chicago: American Technical Society, 1964.

Van Rijn, Paul. *Job Analysis of Entry Level Fire Fighting in the District of Columbia Fire Department: A Duty/Task Approach.* Washington, D.C.: U.S. Civil Service Commission, Personnel Research and Development Center, 1977.

16 Managing Innovation: An Overview

Frohman, Alan, and Roberts, Edward. *Factors Affecting Innovation in the Fire Services.* Cambridge, Mass.: Pugh-Roberts Associates, Inc., 1972.

Heins, Conrad F., *Fire Safety: A Case Study of Technology Transfer.* Report CR 2594. Washington, D.C.: National Aeronautics and Space Administration, 1975.

Knight, Fred S., and Rancer, Michael D., eds. *Tried and Tested: Case Studies in Municipal Innovation.* Management Information Service Special Report no. 3. Washington,

D.C.: International City Management Association, 1978.

Lawton, John W. *A National Agenda for Programs To Increase the Introduction of Innovations in the Fire Services.* Washington, D.C.: Public Technology, Inc., 1973.

Russell, John R. "Fire House Location in East Lansing." In *New Tools for Urban Management.* Edited by Richard S. Rosenbloom and John R. Russell. Boston: Harvard University, Graduate School of Business Administration, 1971.

Urban Institute. *The Struggle to Bring Technology to Cities.* Washington, D.C.: The Urban Institute, 1971.

17 Managing Communications Systems

Associated Public-Safety Communications Officers. *APCO Public Safety Communications Standard Operating Procedure Manual.* 15th ed. New Smyrna Beach, Fla.: Associated Public-Safety Communications Officers, 1978.

Institute for Local Self Government. *Alarm Systems Management.* Alternatives to Traditional Public Safety Delivery Systems, no. 6. Berkeley, Calif.: Institute for Local Self Government, 1977.

————. *Civilians in Public Safety Services.* Alternatives to Traditional Public Safety Delivery Systems, no. 5. Berkeley, Calif.: Institute for Local Self Government, 1977.

National Fire Protection Association. *Public Fire Service Communications.* NFPA no. 73. Boston: National Fire Protection Association, 1975.

U.S. Government. *Code of Federal Regulations: Title 47 (Telecommunications).* Washington, D.C.: Government Printing Office, 1977.

18 Data Collection, Processing, and Analysis

Anochie, O. Martin. *Using Minicomputers in Local Government.* Management Information Service Reports, vol. 10 no. 8. Washington, D.C.: International City Management Association, August 1978.

Brice, Herman W. "Transition to Computerized Fire Reporting." In *Proceedings Forty-fifth Annual Fire Department Instructors Conference.* Kansas City, Mo., 30 March—3 April 1973.

DeGaeta, Paul F. "The Computer in the Fire Service." *Firehouse,* November 1978, pp. 24–51.

Kraemer, Kenneth L., and King, John L. *Computers, Power, and Urban Manage-*

ment: What Every Local Executive Should Know. Professional Papers in Administrative and Policy Studies, vol. 3. Beverly Hills, Calif.: Sage Publications, 1976.

Kraemer, Kenneth L.; Mitchel, William H.; Weiner, Myron E.; and Dial, O. E. *The Integrated Municipal Information System: The Use of the Computer in Local Government.* New York: Praeger Publishers, 1974.

National Fire Protection Association. *Uniform Coding for Fire Protection.* NFPA no. 901. Boston: National Fire Protection Association, 1976.

Schaenman, Philip S.; Hall, John R., Jr.; Schainblatt, Alfred H.; Swartz, Joseph A.; and Carter, Michael J. *Procedures for Improving the Measurement of Local Fire Protection Effectiveness.* Boston: National Fire Protection Association, 1977.

19 Fire Station Location, Design, and Management

AIA Research Corporation. *Seismic Design for Police and Fire Stations.* Washington, D.C.: AIA Research Corporation, 1978.

Chaiken, Jan M.; Ignall, Edward J.; and Walker, Warren E. *Deployment Methodology for Fire Departments.* New York City–Rand Institute, HUDR–1853. Santa Monica, Calif.: Rand Corporation, 1975.

Hemmeter, Paul A. "Leased Fire Station Serves Growth Area." *Fire Chief,* August 1976.

Hudiberg, Everett, ed. *Fire Department Facilities, Planning, and Procedures.* Stillwater, Okla.: International Fire Service Training Association, 1970.

Kimball, Warren Y. *How To Judge Your Fire Department.* Boston: National Fire Protection Association, 1972.

Moldenhour, L. E., and Vogel, Joshua H., eds. *Design of Fire Stations.* Seattle, Wash.: Association of Washington Cities and University of Washington, Bureau of Government Research and Services, 1965.

Public Technology, Inc. *Fire Station Location Package.* Washington, D.C.: Public Technology, Inc., 1976.

Walker, Warren E. *The Deployment of Emergency Services: A Guide to Selected Methods and Models.* New York City–Rand Institute, HUDR–1867. Santa Monica, Calif.: Rand Corporation, 1975.

20 Fire Apparatus and Equipment Management

Ely, Robert, *Fire Officer's Guide to Fire Apparatus Maintenance.* Boston: National Fire Protection Association, 1975.

Erven, Lawrence W. *Fire Company Apparatus and Procedure.* Beverly Hills, Calif.: Glencoe Press, 1974.

Hudiburg, Everett, ed. *Fire Apparatus Practices.* Stillwater, Okla.: International Fire Service Training Association, 1970.

Kimball, Warren Y. *Fire Attack 1: Command Decisions and Company Operations.* Boston: National Fire Protection Association, 1966.

———. *Fire Attack 2: Planning, Assigning, Operating.* Boston: National Fire Protection Association, 1968.

List of contributors

Persons who have contributed to this book are listed below with the editors first and the chapter authors following in alphabetical order. A brief review of experience and training is presented for each author. Since many of the contributors have published extensively, books, monographs, articles, and other publications are omitted.

John L. Bryan (Editor, and Chapters 4 [Parts B and C] and 21) is Professor and Chairman of the Department of Fire Protection Engineering at the University of Maryland. He has bachelor's and master's degrees from Oklahoma State University and a doctorate from The American University. He has consulted with federal, state, and local governments. He has twenty-seven years of both paid and volunteer fire department service.

Raymond C. Picard (Editor, and Chapters 9 and 21) is Fire Chief, Huntington Beach, California. He entered the fire service in 1950 and was with the city of Pasadena Fire Department for sixteen years. He joined the Huntington Beach Fire Department in 1966 as Assistant Fire Chief and succeeded to Fire Chief in 1968. He is a graduate of Pasadena City College and the University of Southern California and has done extensive teaching throughout the state of California. He has served on the California State Board of Fire Services, and on professional committees of the National Fire Protection Association, the California Fire Chief's Association, the International Association of Fire Chiefs, the National League of Cities, and the U.S. Fire Administration.

David S. Arnold (Chapter 4, Part F) is Director, Publications Center, International City Management Association. He has been with ICMA since 1949 with a variety of responsibilities in research, editing, writing, and publications production. From 1943 to 1949 he was on the field staff of Public Administration Service, Chicago. He holds a bachelor's degree from Lafayette College and a master's in public administration from the Maxwell Graduate School, Syracuse University.

Douglas W. Ayres (Chapter 12) is Adjunct Professor in the School of Public Administration at the University of Southern California. He has served as Professor at California State University at Long Beach; City Manager of Inglewood, California, Salem, Oregon, and Melbourne, Florida; and staff consultant with Public Administration Service, Chicago. He holds a bachelor's degree in political science from the University of North Carolina and a master's in public administration from Syracuse University. He currently is General Manager of Leisure World–Laguna Hills, California, and a major stockholder of its parent company, Professional Community Management, Inc., of Newport Beach, California.

Joseph N. Baker (Chapter 16) is City Manager, Orange, California. He was previously a Vice President of Public Technology, Inc., with responsibility for PTI's West Coast operation. He has a bachelor's degree from the University of Missouri—Kansas City, and an M.P.A. from the University of Kansas. Mr. Baker's twenty-five years in local government include positions as City Manager of Gladstone, Missouri; Assistant City Manager of Boulder, Colorado; and, most recently, ten years as City Manager of Burbank, California. While Manager of Burbank, he also chaired Public Technology, Inc.'s, National Fire Innovation Group. The City of Burbank received a number of awards for energy innovations during this time, and Mr. Baker was the recipient of the Management Innovation Award of the International City Management Association in 1974.

Harry C. Bigglestone (Chapter 4, Part A) is Supervisor, Public Protection, Insurance Services Office of California. He has served as the 1977–79 President of the Society of Fire Protection Engineers, a multinational organization. He holds a bachelor's degree in mechanical engineering from the University of Arizona, saw service in the U.S. Navy during World War II, and has been active in the American Water Works Association and the voluntary standards committee efforts of the National Fire Protection Association.

Joseph M. Carlson (Chapter 19) is Assistant Director, Technology Commercialization Division, Solar Energy Research Institute, Golden, Colorado. He was previously a Vice President of Public Technology, Inc. Before that, he was Chief, Dissemination and Program Evaluation Division, of the National Aeronautics and Space Administration's Technology Utilization Office. He holds a bachelor's degree in economics and an M.A. in economics from Kansas State University.

Robert E. Carter (Chapter 11) is Chief Fire and Arson Investigation Specialist, Public Fire Protection, National Fire Protection Association. He holds a bachelor's degree from Davidson College, North Carolina. He was previously State Supervisor for Fire Service Training for the Virginia Department of Education, and before that was Chief Deputy Fire Marshal in charge of arson investigation in Virginia. He is past President of the International Association of Arson Investigators, and has lectured at arson seminars throughout the United States and in Puerto Rico. He was Chairman of the Joint Council of National Fire Service Organizations in 1976.

Harry Diezel (Chapter 8) is Chief of the Virginia Beach, Virginia, Fire Department, where he has served since 1974. He was formerly with the Fairfax County, Virginia, Fire and Rescue Service.

William V. Donaldson (Chapter 13, Part B) is City Manager of Cincinnati, Ohio. He has a B.A. from the University of Denver. He has held a variety of positions in local government since 1955, and has served as City Manager in Montclair, California; Scottsdale, Arizona; and Tacoma, Washington. Mr. Donaldson was the winner in 1970 of the International City Management Association's Management Innovation Award. He has served as President of the Arizona City Manager's Association, and as lecturer or consultant to groups such as the National Science Foundation, the state of Alaska, and The Urban Institute.

Michael A. Greene (Chapter 14) is Assistant Professor of Management Science at The American University, where he holds a joint appointment with the Center for Technology and Administration and the School of Government and Public Administration. He received a bachelor's degree from Columbia University and a doctorate from Carnegie–Mellon University. Dr. Greene was a Senior Program Analyst with the New York City Fire Department.

Marie V. Hayman (Chapter 4, Part D) is Deputy Director of the Management Research Center, International City Management Association. She also directs several public safety programs within the center including law enforcement, disaster, and fire. She holds a bachelor's degree from George Washington University and has done graduate work in both criminal justice and public administration.

Harry E. Hickey (Chapter 2) is Assistant Professor, Fire Protection Curriculum, College of Engineering, University of Maryland, where he has taught since 1960. He serves as a consultant to groups such as the U.S. Fire Administration, the National Fire Protection Association, and the Fire Problems Group of the Johns Hopkins University Applied Physics Laboratory. He has also been a volunteer firefighter for many years. Professor Hickey holds a Ph.D. in public administration from The American University, and is the author of many articles and books on fire protection topics.

Warren E. Isman (Chapter 15) is Chief and Director of the Montgomery County (Maryland) Department of Fire and Rescue Services. He has served as a consultant for the International Association of Fire Chiefs; Public Technology, Inc.; and the U.S. Fire Administration. He has participated in programs and workshops and on committees for various fire service organizations, working especially in the area of hazardous materials. Chief Isman holds a bachelor's degree in physics from the City College of New York and has completed all the course work for an M.A. in education.

James L. Kolb (Chapter 9) is Battalion Chief, Los Angeles City Fire Department. He also serves as an adviser/consultant to private business; city, state, and federal governments; the U.S. Air Force; the National Aeronautics and Space Administration; and the United Nations. He contributed to the development of the U.S. Fire Administration, and was a major contributor of original thought for, and served as the Chief Program Manager for, the Long Range Master Planning for the Fire Service project of the National Bureau of Standards–USFA. Prior to entering the fire service and management fields, he worked in the insurance industry. Mr. Kolb is currently enrolled at the Graduate School of Business Administration, University of California at Los Angeles.

William M. Kramer (Chapter 13, Part B) is Associate Professor of Management at Xavier University in Cincinnati, Ohio, and Lecturer at the University of Cincinnati. He received bachelor's and master's degrees, and a doctorate, from the University of Cincinnati, as well as an M.B.A. from Xavier University. Dr. Kramer is also a professional firefighter with the Cincinnati Fire Department and serves as Chairman of its Management Task Force. He does consulting and conducts seminars for public administrators.

Léonard G. Marks (Chapter 12) is Instructor in the Fire Science Department of Santa Ana College, California. He has served as Assistant Professor at the University of Maryland and at California State University at San Jose, and as Deputy Fire Chief for the city of San Jose, California. He holds a bachelor's degree in accounting from San Jose State University and a master's degree and doctorate in public administration from the University of Southern California.

Raymond L. Mulhall (Chapter 17) is a Lieutenant with the Montgomery County (Maryland) Department of Fire and Rescue Sevices, assigned to the Communications Section of the Operation Services Division. He is completing work on his bachelor's degree at the University of Maryland. He served as Chairman of the Communications Committee of the Metropolitan Washington Council of Governments' Fire Chiefs Subcommittee. Prior to entering the fire service Mr. Mulhall worked for the Sperry Rand Corporation as an Associate Engineer at the Goddard Space Flight Center.

James O. Page (Chapter 10) is Executive Director of the ACT Foundation, a nonprofit organization dedicated to the improvement of emergency medical services (EMS). He has served as Director of a regional EMS system in New York State, as Chief of the statewide EMS program in North Carolina, and as a Chief Officer with the Los Angeles County Fire Department. He holds a juris doctorate from Southwestern University and is a member of the California bar. He is a consultant to numerous organizations and serves as Contributing Editor to *Fire Chief* and *Paramedics* magazines.

James C. Robertson (Chapter 7) is State Fire Marshal of Maryland. He holds an associate degree in fire technology from Oklahoma State University and a bachelor's degree from the University of Southern California. He has served as Assistant State Fire Marshal and in several other fire service positions.

Charles H. Rule (Chapter 8) is Fire Chief, Alexandria, Virginia, where he has served for three years. He is a graduate of Oklahoma State University's School of Fire Protection and spent four years in the fire service of the U.S. Navy. Chief Rule served as Fire Chief in Greenfield, Wisconsin, for thirteen years, then in the same position in Fairborn, Ohio, for two years, before coming to Alexandria. He was a participant in the Wingspread II Conference. He is presently working toward a degree in urban planning at Northern Virginia Community College.

Philip S. Schaenman (Chapter 18) is Associate Administrator for the National Fire Data Center of the U.S. Fire Administration, a position he has held since October 1976. Prior to that, he was Director of the Analysis and Evaluation Division in the U.S. Fire Administration Data Center. Mr. Schaenman was a Senior Research Associate at The Urban Institute in Washington, D.C., from 1972 to 1976. While there, he was Project Manager for studies of ways to assess the impacts of land development, and also for a variety of studies relating to performance measurement of state and local government services, including fire, police, and transportation services. Mr. Schaenman has an M.S. in electrical engineering from Stanford University, a B.S. from Columbia University's School of Engineering, and a B.S. from Queens College, New York.

Edward F. Seits (Chapter 4, Part E) is the Executive Assistant to the California State Fire Marshal and Editor of that office's publications. He directs the California Fire Incident Reporting System, Fire Service Training Program, and Public Information and Education Programs, and is Executive Secretary to the State Board of Fire Services. He has served as project director and consultant on statewide development programs in the areas of master planning for fire education and training, and information resource exchange systems. He holds a bachelor's degree from the University of Southern California.

Robert N. Sockwell (Chapter 19) is Research Associate for the AIA Research Corporation in Washington, D.C. He was previously a Project Architect for various building technology and energy projects at Public Technology, Inc. He holds a bachelor's degree in architecture from Howard University and is a registered architect.

John E. Steen (Chapter 6) is a private consultant in Santa Barbara, California. He holds a bachelor's degree from the Newark College of Engineering. Previously he worked as a staff member of the Mission Research Corporation in Santa Barbara. His work is in the research and development of management and planning systems.

Victor D. Subia (Chapter 17) is a Fire Captain with the Huntington Beach, California, Fire Department. He was Project Manager for that department's Computer Aided Dispatch System. He has been an Instructor in Fire Communications at Johns Hopkins University Applied Physics Laboratory and the University of Maryland. He is an Instructor at Santa Ana College and is a consultant on fire communications and computerized fire protection systems.

B. J. Thompson (Chapter 1) is Fire Chief, Santa Ana, California. He holds bachelor's and master's degrees from California State University at Long Beach and a doctorate from Union Graduate School, Antioch, Ohio. He has worked in various positions in the fire service since 1955, including nineteen years with the Santa Fe Springs, California, Fire Department. Chief Thompson has served on numerous committees for state and federal fire service organizations.

Thomas V. Tiedeman (Chapter 19) is Vice President and General Manager of the Research and Management Foundation of the American Consulting Engineers Council. He worked previously as Program Director for Energy and Building Technology Programs at Public Technology, Inc. He holds a B.S. from the University of Michigan and a master of architecture degree from the State University of New York at Buffalo.

Costis Toregas (Chapter 5) is Vice President for Fire Services, International Pro-

grams, and Decision Support Systems, at Public Technology, Inc. He has been directly involved with the development, demonstration, and on-site technical assistance phases of a variety of innovative tools for fire service management, and has worked extensively with local government officials on the application of technology to local problems. He holds a bachelor's degree in electrical engineering and master's and doctoral degrees in environmental systems engineering from Cornell University.

Richard L. Ulrich (Chapters 3 and 20) is Assistant Professor of Political Science and Coordinator of Fire Science at Montgomery College, Rockville, Maryland. An alumnus of Oklahoma State University's School of Fire Protection, he holds a bachelor's degree in English education from Arizona State University and a master's in public administration from the University of Illinois, and has done doctoral work in adult and continuing education at Northern Illinois University. A third generation firefighter, he has been both a paid and a volunteer firefighter; he has also served as an English teacher, adult educator, and political organizer, and as Chief Administrator of the Fire Department and the Code Administration and Enforcement Department of DeKalb, Illinois.

Paul M. Whisenand (Chapter 13, Part A) is the President of Management Assessment Centers (MAC), Costa Mesa, California, a firm specializing in public personnel recruitment, selection, and management development training. He has authored or co-authored fourteen textbooks. In addition, he is a Professor at California State University, Long Beach. Dr. Whisenand earned his doctorate in public administration from the University of Southern California.

Index

Glueck, William F., on organization characteristics, 340–42, *340*
Grading Schedule for Municipal Fire Protection (Insurance Services Office). *See* Insurance Services Office grading schedule
Great Fire of London, 1666, 13, 14, 93
Greenleaf, Abner, and water tower, 30
Greenleaf, Albert, and water tower, 30
Griggs v. *Duke Power Company*, 323

Haines, Reuben, and hose wagon, 27
Hale, George C., and hose tower, 30
Hamilton, Alexander, and volunteer fire companies, 34
Hammurabi, code on building construction, 10
Hand-in-Hand Insurance Company, founded by Benjamin Franklin, 14, 35
Hanson, Frank R., and Seattle, Washington, arson strike force, 285–86
Hartford Insurance Group, Junior Fire Marshal program, 185
Hatry, Harry P., productivity studies, 136
Hayes, Daniel D., and early aerial ladder trucks, 29
Hazardous materials
federal regulations on, 124, 188
storage, 174
Health Systems Agencies (HSAs), 239, 241, 262
Hickey, Harry E.
resource allocation model, 88
study of ISO grading schedule in Alexandria, Virginia, 61–63
Highway Safety Act of 1966, and emergency medical services, 231
Hillandale, Maryland, computer use in pre-fire planning, 86–87
History of civilization and influence of fire, 3, 4–9
Hoboken, New Jersey, fire on waterfront, 1900, 17
Hook and ladder companies, history, 25, 28–29
Horses. *See* Fire horses
Hose
description, 533–34
development, 27–28, 30, 533
Hot Springs, Arkansas, fire, 1913, 19–20
HSAs. *See* Health Systems Agencies
Hubbs, David J., and hose carts, 28
Huntington Beach, California, computer-aided dispatch system, 450, 451–52, *451*

Hydrant valve (radio controlled), 86, 535
Hydrants
development of, 27
standards for, 105

IAFC. *See* International Association of Fire Chiefs
IAFF. *See* International Association of Fire Fighters
ICMA. *See* International City Management Association
Ignall, Edward J.
on privately operated fire departments, 51
on regional consolidation of fire departments, 52, 53
on response time, 42–43, *43*
Ignition sources
history, 4–7
matches, 6–7
IMSA. *See* International Municipal Signal Association
Information systems. *See* Data collection, processing, and analysis
Informational organizations and the fire service, 92, 108–12, 131
Innovation
apparatus and equipment, 33, 86, 138–39, 140, 530–31, 532–38, *139*
barriers to, 138–39, 419, 421–24
in communications systems, 435, 436, 443, 446–54, *451*
definition, 419
future trends, 433
incentives for, 420–21
and labor unions, 421, 422
management of, 419–34
process, 424–26
Public Technology, Inc., 86, 120, 140, 425, 503–4, 519 n., 535–36
see also Technology; individual technological innovations
Inspection services, 215
consolidation of fire and inspection services, 204–7, 211–12
coordination of fire and inspection services, 207–9
educational programs, 195
historical perspective, 196
management, 195–213, *198, 200, 202, 203, 204, 205, 210, 211*
management cycle, 195, 197–212, *198, 200, 202, 203, 204, 205, 210, 211*
organizational structure, 202–4, *202, 203, 204, 205*

Municipal Management Series

**Managing
Fire
Services**

Text type
Times Roman, Helvetica

Composition
Progressive Typographers, Inc.
York, Pennsylvania

Printing and binding
Publication Press, Inc.
Baltimore, Maryland

Paper
Pub Brite offset

Design
Herbert Slobin

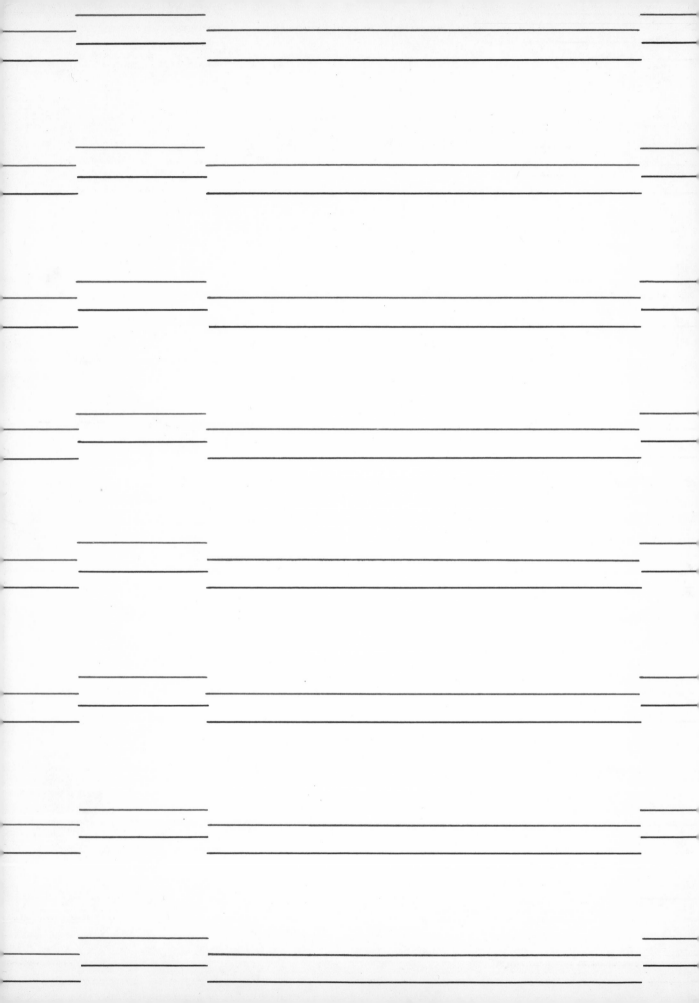